# WEST ACADEMIC PUB EMERITUS ADVISOR



---

# PRINCIPLES OF BUSINESS TORTS & UNFAIR COMPETITION

**Colin P. Marks**
*Rubey M. Hulen Professor of Law*
*University of Missouri—Kansas City School of Law*

**Douglas K. Moll**
*A.A. White Professor of Law*
*University of Houston Law Center*

CONCISE HORNBOOK SERIES™

WEST ACADEMIC

860 Blue Gentian Road, Suite 350
Eagan, MN 55121
1-877-888-1330

Published in the United States of America

ISBN: 978-1-64708-492-9

*To Stefanie, Asher, Samara, Daisy, and TJ,*
*who make it all fun.*

*—DKM*

*To my mother and father, who have always*
*supported me in all my endeavors, and to*
*my children Savy-Jo and George,*
*who make me happy every day.*

*—CPM*

# Acknowledgments

We would like to thank several people for their assistance in the preparation of this book: Professor Marks' research assistants including James Beiter, Avery Garret, Caitlin Harrington, Jasmine Kang, Falak Momin, Layne Mustain, Carolina Pena, and Cason Shipp; and the wonderful folks at West Academic Publishing.

Colin P. Marks
Douglas K. Moll

# Summary of Contents

# Table of Contents

# PRINCIPLES OF BUSINESS TORTS & UNFAIR COMPETITION

# Introduction

*What are business torts?* The typical first-year Torts class focuses on torts that cause personal injury and property damage. While there is usually some discussion of economic losses (e.g., an accident victim's lost wages or medical expenses), the discussion of such losses is generally incidental to the primary focus on the physical harm sustained by the victim. Business torts have a different focus. Such torts often cause "pure economic loss"—i.e., economic harm without any accompanying personal injury or property damage. For example, in a fraudulent investment scheme, the victim loses money, but rarely suffers bodily harm or property damage. Think of a business tort, therefore, as tortious conduct that primarily harms a plaintiff's wallet rather than his person or things.[1]

*What is unfair competition?* Unfair competition is an umbrella term used to describe "an array of legal actions addressing methods of competition that improperly interfere with the legitimate commercial interests of other sellers in the marketplace."[2] Examples of unfair competition actions include claims for deceptive marketing, trademark infringement, and theft of trade secrets. Each of these claims seeks a remedy for conduct that allegedly constitutes an inappropriate method of competing in the marketplace. Although unfair competition is used in this book primarily as a generic term to describe the various causes of action discussed in Chapters 6–10, many states retain unfair competition as a "catch-all" cause of action of its own. In other words, if a defendant inappropriately competes in a manner that has not yet been recognized by existing causes of action, a catch-all unfair competition claim could be used to challenge the conduct.[3]

*Why study business torts and unfair competition together?* Business torts and unfair competition are similar in a number of ways. First, like business torts, unfair competition practices generally result in pure economic loss. Thus, both areas provide a

---

[1] There are, of course, exceptions. For example, if a landlord fraudulently misrepresents that an apartment complex is safe to a prospective tenant, the misrepresentation may result in personal injury if the tenant is assaulted. The misrepresentation may also result in property damage if the tenant's personal property is stolen or otherwise harmed.

[2] RESTATEMENT (THIRD) OF UNFAIR COMPETITION (1995) (foreword).

[3] *See id.* § 1(a) (allowing a plaintiff to recover for deceptive marketing, trademark infringement, appropriation of trade secrets, and for "other acts or practices . . . determined to be actionable as an unfair method of competition, taking into account the nature of the conduct and its likely effect on both the person seeking relief and the public").

nice counterpoint to the personal injury and property damage coverage of a standard introductory Torts course. Second, both areas form the core of a typical non-personal injury civil litigation practice. A commercial (i.e., business) litigator, in other words, frequently handles lawsuits involving business torts and unfair competition. As a result, knowledge of these topics is essential for any litigator wishing to have a practice broader than personal injury disputes.[4] Third, business torts and unfair competition are thematically related in that both areas reflect the type of conduct that society considers permissible (and impermissible) in a business context. Their collective law regulates the conduct of business transactions and seeks to promote fairness and competition.

Because of these similarities, the line between what is considered a business tort and what is considered unfair competition is not entirely clear. Do not let this trouble you. The terms have substantial overlap[5] and, for our purposes, the distinction is not important. In this book, we organize the material on business torts (Chapters 1–5) and unfair competition (Chapters 6–10) around two general criteria. First, business torts are largely governed by common law, while unfair competition practices are mostly regulated by statute. In general, therefore, Chapters 1–5 of the book focus on causes of action whose governing principles are provided by the common law, while Chapters 6–10 of the book focus on causes of action whose governing principles are provided (at least partially) by statute.[6] Second, much of the business torts material in Chapters 1–5 of the book is the subject of the Third Restatement of Torts, while much of the unfair competition material in Chapters 6–10 of the book

---

[4] *Cf.* Jay M. Feinman, *Teaching Economic Torts*, 95 KY. L.J. 893, 893–94 (2006–07) ("In practice, disputes involving economic torts are expanding as a mainstay of civil litigation practice, both because of the apparently infinite capacity of businesses to engage in questionable and dispute-generating behavior and because of the entrepreneurship of lawyers as the profitability of personal injury litigation declines due to the success of the tort reform movement in contracting the rights of victims of personal injuries.").

[5] *See, e.g.*, DAN B. DOBBS, THE LAW OF TORTS § 457, at 1300 (2000) (stating that "[u]nfair competition is a general term that includes deceptive trade practices, acts such as trademark infringement, and appropriation of trade values," and noting that "[a]ll of these are torts under common law rules"). The fact that unfair competition practices were once included in the Restatement of Torts is further evidence of the overlap between business torts and unfair competition. *See* RESTATEMENT (THIRD) OF UNFAIR COMPETITION (1995) (foreword) ("The subject of unfair competition was to have been addressed in the Restatement, Second, of Torts, as it had been in the original Restatement of Torts. However, it was eventually decided that the law of unfair competition had evolved to the point that it was no longer appropriate to treat it as a subcategory of the law of Torts.").

[6] Once again, this is true "in general" and not as an absolute matter. For example, as you will learn, many state unfair competition actions are governed by common law principles and not by statute. Nevertheless, we discuss these actions in the latter chapters of the book.

is the subject of the Third Restatement of Unfair Competition.[7] Thus, the subject matter of these Restatements has guided, to some extent, the division of topics in this book.

As mentioned, Chapters 1–5 of the book cover business torts. These chapters address the economic loss rule between non-contracting parties (Chapter 1); misrepresentation, including fraud, negligent misrepresentation, and innocent misrepresentation (Chapter 2); tortious interference with economic relations, including intentional interference with existing contract and prospective contract (Chapter 3); breach of fiduciary duty (Chapter 4); and the economic loss rule between contracting parties (Chapter 5). The material focuses primarily on principles articulated by the Second and Third Restatements of Torts.[8] The American Law Institute—an association of lawyers, academics, and judges—author the Restatements and, like all Restatements, their text and comments represent an effort to capture the law as developed by the courts. Keep in mind that the Restatements are influential and are persuasive to many courts, but they are not binding.

A major theme in this portion of the book involves the boundary between the law of tort and the law of contract. Tort claims are often more attractive to plaintiffs than contract claims because of the potential for punitive and mental anguish damages in tort. Contract law generally prohibits such recoveries.[9] Tort claims between contracting parties, however, can undermine the bargain that the parties struck. As you will learn, therefore, the law has developed limitations on when contracting parties are permitted to assert tort claims against one another.

Chapters 6–10 of the book cover unfair competition. These chapters address deceptive marketing (Chapter 6); commercial disparagement, including injurious falsehood (Chapter 7); misappropriation (Chapter 8); trade secrets (Chapter 9); and trademark infringement (Chapter 10). The material focuses on common law and statutory principles articulated by various sources, including (among others) the Third Restatement of Unfair Competition, the Lanham Act, and the Uniform Trade Secrets Act.[10]

The major themes in this portion of the book are the virtues of competition and the role of the law in regulating competitive

---

[7] *See* RESTATEMENT (THIRD) OF TORTS: LIABILITY FOR ECONOMIC HARM (2020); RESTATEMENT (THIRD) OF UNFAIR COMPETITION (1995).

[8] *See* RESTATEMENT (SECOND) OF TORTS (1977); RESTATEMENT (THIRD) OF TORTS: LIABILITY FOR ECONOMIC HARM (2020).

[9] *See* RESTATEMENT (SECOND) OF CONTRACTS §§ 353, 355 (1981).

[10] *See* RESTATEMENT (THIRD) OF UNFAIR COMPETITION (1995); Lanham Act, 15 U.S.C. §§ 1051–1141n; UNIF. TRADE SECRETS ACT §§ 1–12 (1985).

behavior. If competition is valued, why not encourage competition to any extent? What considerations might justify limiting the types of conduct that count as permissible competition?[11]

As this discussion has revealed, business torts and unfair competition actions play an important role in our civil litigation system. The information in this book should help you to appreciate and understand that role.

[11] *See generally* RESTATEMENT (THIRD) OF UNFAIR COMPETITION § 1 cmt. a (1995) ("The freedom to engage in business and to compete for the patronage of prospective customers is a fundamental premise of the free enterprise system. . . . The freedom to compete necessarily contemplates the probability of harm to the commercial relations of other participants in the market. . . . Liability is imposed under this Section, and under this Restatement generally, only in connection with harm resulting from particular methods of competition determined to be unfair.").

# Chapter 1

# THE ECONOMIC LOSS RULE (I)

Business torts often cause "pure economic loss"—i.e., economic harm without any accompanying personal injury or property damage.[1] The policy considerations surrounding pure economic loss and whether (and when) it should be legally compensable are different from those surrounding injuries to person and property. The decision of *State of Louisiana v. M/V Testbank*[2] highlights such considerations. The M/V Sea Daniel and the M/V Testbank collided in the Mississippi River Gulf outlet. Approximately twelve tons of pentachlorophenol spilled overboard. The U.S. Coast Guard closed the outlet to navigation for approximately three weeks and "all fishing, shrimping, and related activity was temporarily suspended in the outlet and four hundred square miles of surrounding marsh and waterways."

Forty-one lawsuits were brought asserting claims by "shipping interests, marina and boat rental operators, wholesale and retail seafood enterprises not actually engaged in fishing, seafood restaurants, tackle and bait shops, and recreational fishermen." Defendants (the owners of the M/V Testbank as well as related parties) moved for summary judgment as to all claims for pure economic loss—i.e., economic loss "unaccompanied by physical damage to a proprietary interest." The district court granted summary judgment as to all claims except those asserted by commercial fishermen.[3] A panel of the Fifth Circuit affirmed.

---

1 Stand-alone emotional or reputational harm is not considered to be "pure economic loss." As a consequence, torts causing only emotional or reputational harm are characterized as personal torts rather than business or economic torts. *See, e.g.*, 3 DAN B. DOBBS ET AL., THE LAW OF TORTS § 605, at 461 (2d ed. 2011) ("In contrast, economic torts inflict pecuniary or financial costs upon the plaintiff that do not result from injury to person or property or even from stand-alone emotional distress. Stated more broadly, torts to the person and torts to tangible property are not economic torts and come under none of the strictures applied to economic tort claims. Thus neither reputational harm encompassed by the defamation rules nor stand-alone emotional harm results in a stand-alone economic tort even if financial damage is inflicted; both are personal torts.").

2 752 F.2d 1019 (5th Cir. 1985).

3 *See id.* at 1027 n.10 ("A substantial argument can be made that commercial fishermen possess a proprietary interest in fish in waters they normally harvest sufficient to allow recovery for their loss. Whether the claims of commercial fishermen ought to be analyzed in this manner or simply carved from the rule today announced . . . or allowed at all, we leave for later. That is, today's decision does not foreclose free consideration by a court panel of the claims of commercial fishermen."); *see also*

On reexamination en banc, the Fifth Circuit retained the rule that physical damage to a proprietary interest is required to recover economic losses in unintentional tort actions. As part of its holding, the *Testbank* majority sparred with the dissent over the meaning of an earlier U.S. Supreme Court precedent, *Robins Dry Dock v. Flint*.[4] In *Robins*, the time charterer[5] of a steamship sued for lost profits when the defendant dry dock negligently damaged the ship's propeller. The propeller had to be replaced, which took the ship out of operation for another two weeks. The charterer sued the dry dock company for loss of the use of the ship during the two-week period.

Although the dry dock company was unaware of the charter party when it damaged the propeller, the *Testbank* majority noted that "delay losses by users of the ship were certainly foreseeable." Nevertheless, the U.S. Supreme Court denied recovery and held that "a tort to the person or property of one man [the owner of the steamship] does not make the tortfeasor [the dry dock company] liable to another [the time charterer] merely because the injured person [the owner of the steamship] was under a contract with that other [the time charterer] unknown to the doer of the wrong [the dry dock company]."[6] The *Testbank* majority referred to this holding as a "pragmatic limitation imposed by the Court upon the tort doctrine of foreseeability."[7] Significantly, the *Testbank* majority interpreted this holding to also apply to plaintiffs who have no contractual connection to the entity whose person or property was damaged: "If a time charterer's relationship to its negligently injured vessel is too remote,

---

RESTATEMENT (THIRD) OF TORTS: LIABILITY FOR ECONOMIC HARM §§ 7 cmt. e, 8 cmt. d (2020) (discussing the claims of commercial fishermen as public nuisance actions).

4 275 U.S. 303 (1927).

5 A time charterer is similar to a lessee, but the charterer is not viewed as having a proprietary interest in the vessel. As Professors Dobbs and Bublick explain:

> Holmes notes that there was "no demise," archaic language that students may or may not get. "No demise" here means not a full "lease" but a time charter—the owner provides the personnel to operate the boat and the "lessee" merely establishes ports of call[.] The difference for Holmes is that you cannot conceive of the plaintiff as the owner of the vessel for the term—the plaintiff merely has the right to receive the owner's services, including use of the boat. That means the plaintiff's right is a contract right, not a property right.
>
> . . . .
>
> [*Robins*] involved a *time* charterer, with the ship still in the possession of the owner and actually operated by the owner's employees, so that it was not a "demise" and the charterer had no property interest in it.

DAN B. DOBBS & ELLEN M. BUBLICK, TEACHER'S MANUAL TO ACCOMPANY CASES AND MATERIALS ON ADVANCED TORTS: ECONOMIC AND DIGNITARY TORTS 392, 395 (2006).

6 *Testbank*, 752 F.2d at 1022 (quoting *Robins*, 275 U.S. at 309).

7 *See also* 3 DAN B. DOBBS ET AL., THE LAW OF TORTS § 610, at 470 (2d ed. 2011) ("Under the *Robins* rule, liability for the plaintiff's pure economic loss is rejected even if the defendant could foresee economic harm to the plaintiff, which is to say the rule is a bright-line, no-duty rule. The rule is thus not merely an application of the *Palsgraf* foreseeability rule.").

other claimants without even the connection of a contract are even more remote." Stated differently, "[i]f a plaintiff connected to the damaged chattels by contract cannot recover, others more remotely situated are foreclosed *a fortiori*."[8]

*Testbank* sets forth the general rule that in actions for unintentional torts, a plaintiff cannot recover for economic loss in the absence of personal injury to the plaintiff or damage to the plaintiff's property.[9] This principle is the clear majority rule in this country, and a number of courts refer to it as the "economic loss rule."[10] In effect, as between noncontracting parties, the rule bars negligence and strict liability claims that seek recovery for pure economic loss. The rule has no application, however, to unintentional tort claims

---

[8] Under the dissent's view, *Robins* simply barred a plaintiff from bringing a negligent interference with contract claim. As the dissent observed: "*Robins* held only that if a defendant's negligence injures party *A*, and the plaintiff suffers loss of expected income or profits because it had a contract with *A*, then the plaintiff has no cause of action based on the defendant's negligence." According to the dissent, the holding should not be understood as a limit on the recovery of foreseeable economic losses in negligence, as the facts of *Robins* (in the dissent's view) did not involve foreseeable injury. *See Testbank*, 752 F.2d at 1039 (Wisdom, J., dissenting) ("*Robins* prevented plaintiffs who were *neither proximately nor foreseeably injured* by a tortious act or product from recovering solely by claiming a contract with the injured party." (emphasis added)). Thus, the dissent seemed to argue that *Robins* did not preclude a negligence action if a plaintiff could establish foreseeable economic loss. *See id.* at 1045 (Wisdom, J., dissenting) (noting "[t]he inapplicability of *Robins* to plaintiffs who have been proximately and foreseeably injured").

[9] *See* RESTATEMENT (THIRD) OF TORTS: LIABILITY FOR ECONOMIC HARM §§ 1(1), 2 (2020) (stating that "[a]n actor has no general duty to avoid the unintentional infliction of economic loss on another," and defining "economic loss" as "pecuniary damage not arising from injury to the plaintiff's person or from physical harm to the plaintiff's property").

[10] *See, e.g.*, Southern California Gas Leak Cases, 441 P.3d 881, 883 (Cal. 2019) ("[T]he extent of consensus across other jurisdictions confirms . . . that claims for purely economic losses suffered from mere proximity to an industrial accident create intractable line-drawing problems for courts. So the claims before us are best not treated as compensable in negligence."); Coastal Conduit & Ditching, Inc. v. Noram Energy Corp., 29 S.W.3d 282, 287–88 (Tex. App. 2000) ("This issue has been addressed in non-admiralty contexts by other jurisdictions, a majority of which hold that, in the absence of privity of contract and accompanying personal injury or property damage, a plaintiff cannot recover for purely economic losses resulting from another's negligence."); *see also* LAN/STV & STV, Inc. v. Martin K. Eby Constr. Co., 435 S.W.3d 234, 235 (Tex. 2014) ("In actions for unintentional torts, the common law has long restricted recovery of purely economic damages unaccompanied by injury to the plaintiff or his property—a doctrine we have referred to as the economic loss rule.").

A few courts seem to have rejected the *Testbank* rule, at least in limited circumstances. *See, e.g.*, Union Oil Co. v. Oppen, 501 F.2d 558, 570 (9th Cir. 1974) (allowing commercial fisherman to recover for lost profits following an oil spill); People Express Airlines, Inc. v. Consolidated Rail Corp., 495 A.2d 107, 118 (N.J. 1985) (permitting an airline to recover lost profits when the defendant's negligent chemical spill prevented the airline from using its facilities); *see also* J'Aire Corp. v. Gregory, 598 P.2d 60, 61–64 (Cal. 1979) (allowing a contractor who undertook construction work pursuant to a contract with the owner of the premises to be liable in tort for business losses suffered by a lessee when the contractor negligently failed to complete the project with due diligence).

that seek recovery for personal injury or property damage, with or without accompanying economic harm.[11]

The *Testbank* court raised a number of policy arguments in support of retaining the economic loss rule:

*Indeterminate liability*: Economic losses can easily spread, while physical injuries are more limited. Quoting from a law review article by Professor James, the majority noted that "the physical consequences of negligence usually have been limited, but the indirect economic repercussions of negligence may be far wider, indeed virtually open-ended." The majority later referred to the "wave upon wave of successive economic consequences" caused by the Testbank's collision, such as when "[t]he vessel delayed in St. Louis may be unable to fulfill its obligation to haul from Memphis, to the injury of the shipper, to the injury of the buyers, to the injury of their customers." Because these consequences are often foreseeable to the negligent defendant, the defendant would be liable for them under ordinary proximate cause principles.

Comment c to § 1 of the Third Restatement makes the same point:

> Economic losses proliferate more easily than losses of other kinds. Physical forces that cause injury ordinarily spend themselves in predictable ways; their exact courses may be hard to predict, but their lifespan and power to harm are limited. A badly driven car threatens physical harm only to others nearby. Economic harm is not self-limiting in this way. A single negligent utterance can cause economic loss to thousands of people who rely on it, those losses may produce additional losses to those who were relying on the first round of victims, and so on. Consequences of this sort may be at least generally foreseeable to the person who commits the negligent act.

The comment also provides a reason why this indeterminate liability matters—negligent defendants could face tremendous liability that

[11] *See, e.g.*, RESTATEMENT (THIRD) OF TORTS: PHYSICAL AND EMOTIONAL HARM § 7 (2010) ("An actor ordinarily has a duty to exercise reasonable care when the actor's conduct creates a risk of physical harm."); *id.* § 4 (" 'Physical harm' means the physical impairment of the human body ('bodily harm') or of real property or tangible personal property ('property damage'). Bodily harm includes physical injury, illness, disease, impairment of bodily function, and death."); *see also* W. PAGE KEETON ET AL., PROSSER AND KEETON ON TORTS § 92, at 658–59 (5th ed. 1984) ("There is a general rule of tort law to the effect that one who acts is under a duty to exercise reasonable care to avoid physical harm to persons and tangible property of others . . . . But in general there is no duty or obligation imposed by law and apart from promises or guarantees made in bargaining transactions to use reasonable care to prevent economic loss by interfering with contractual and business relations.").

is out of proportion to their culpability. By definition, negligent conduct is unintentional (accidental), and that lesser level of culpability does not warrant such significant liability. According to the comment, "[t]hose liabilities may in turn create an exaggerated pressure to avoid an activity altogether."

*Protection through contract*: Who is in the better position to use contract to mitigate the risks of economic loss? The *Testbank* majority argued that the tortfeasor may not be able to procure third-party (liability) insurance for open-ended economic losses because the indeterminate nature of the liability makes it difficult for an insurer to calculate an appropriate premium. Put differently, an insurer needs to have some idea of the magnitude of the risk to set a premium that will provide funds for expected claims while still allowing the insurer to earn a profit. The indeterminate nature of economic harm makes this difficult, if not impossible.[12] The inability to obtain insurance, one might argue, will drive many ventures out of business, as the risk of open-ended liability is too great. Setting an arbitrary policy limit does not solve the problem, as an insured would still be subject to potentially catastrophic damages that exceed the limit.

On the other hand, the *Testbank* majority argued that victims of economic harm are in a better position to obtain first-party insurance for their losses. A business interruption policy, for example, can be priced by an insurer based on the operational data of any particular insured. As the majority noted, any particular victim's potential losses are "finite and readily discernible."[13] Comment c to § 1 of the Third Restatement makes these same points more generally:

> Risks of economic loss tend to be especially well suited to allocation by contract. First, economic injuries caused by negligence often result from a decision by the victim to rely on a defendant's words or acts when entering some sort of transaction—an investment in a company, for example, or the purchase of a house. A potential plaintiff making such a decision has a full chance to consider how to manage the risks involved, whether by inspecting the item or investment, obtaining insurance against the risk of

12 *See Testbank*, 752 F.2d at 1029 ("As Professor James has noted, '[s]erious practical problems face insurers in handling insurance against potentially wide, open-ended liability. From an insurer's point of view it is not practical to cover, without limit, a liability that may reach catastrophic proportions, or to fix a reasonable premium on a risk that does not lend itself to actuarial measurement.' ").

13 *See id.* ("By contrast, first party insurance is feasible for many of the economic losses claimed here. Each businessman who might be affected by a disruption of river traffic or by a halt in fishing activities can protect against that eventuality at a relatively low cost since his own potential losses are finite and readily discernible. Thus, to the extent that economic analysis informs our decision here, we think that it favors retention of the present rule.").

disappointment, or making a contract that assigns the risk of loss to someone else.

*Predictability*: The economic loss rule provides a predictable, bright-line rule. The majority argued that a traditional foreseeability approach was too uncertain in its determination of whether a claim may proceed. According to the majority, a court's ability to adjudicate requires a "determinable rule of law," and a foreseeability approach is less effective in that sense than a bright-line economic loss rule.

The dissent advocated for a public nuisance approach, which was rejected by the majority on the same "lack of predictability" basis. A public nuisance characterization requires a court to decide that a plaintiff has sustained "particular damages"—damages which are substantially greater than the damages suffered by the general public. According to the majority, such an inquiry lacks sufficient predictability:

> The problem in public nuisance theory of determining when private damages are sufficiently distinct from those suffered by the general public so as to justify recovery is as difficult, if not more so, as determining which foreseeable damages are too remote to justify recovery in negligence. In each case it is a matter of degree, and in each case lines must be drawn. With economic losses such as the ones claimed here the problem is to determine who among an entire community that has been commercially affected by an accident has sustained a pecuniary loss so great as to justify distinguishing his losses from similar losses suffered by others. Given the difficulty of this task, we see no jurisprudential advantage in permitting the use of nuisance theory to skirt the *Robins* rule.

The dissent in *Testbank* raised a number of policy arguments as well:

*Compensation for victims*: The dissent pointed out that the cost of the majority's rule is that innocent plaintiffs with foreseeable injuries will be unable to recover. According to the dissent, the usual tort doctrines of foreseeability and proximate cause, "as refined in the law of public nuisance," provide a better approach: "The limitation imposed by 'particular' damages, together with refined notions of proximate cause and foreseeability, provides a workable scheme of liability that is in step with the rest of tort law, compensates innocent plaintiffs, and imposes the costs of harm on those who caused it."

*Foreseeability*: Although the dissent acknowledged the majority's criticism that foreseeability lacks predictability (in that it requires a case-by-case determination of liability), the dissent observed that foreseeability is well-established as the inquiry in physical injury disputes: "Certainly such an inquiry would be no different from our daily task of weighing such claims in other tort cases."

*Deterrence*: The dissent argued that liability helps to deter negligent conduct from occurring. While the dissent agreed that "incentives to avoid accidents do not increase once potential losses pass a certain measure of enormity," the dissent recognized that this limit was difficult to identify.

Is the dissent's rule necessary to deter negligent conduct from occurring? Because tortfeasors face liability for negligent conduct that causes personal injury or property damage (and because a tortfeasor cannot always be certain that it will cause only economic loss), the law already provides some deterrent effect. Indeed, if the collision was caused by the negligence of the M/V Testbank, its owners would presumably be liable for the property damage caused to the M/V Sea Daniel. Moreover, the law is not the only deterrent of negligent conduct. Market pressure to be a safe and reliable shipper, for example, would encourage potential tortfeasors to act carefully to earn future business.

On the other hand, when an accident causes no personal injury or property damage (other than damage to a natural resource), perhaps the economic loss rule does not provide a sufficient deterrent to negligent conduct. In such situations, legislative action may be necessary to incentivize precautionary measures. For example, the Oil Pollution Liability and Compensation Act of 1990, which was passed in the aftermath of the Exxon Valdez spill, imposes "[d]amages equal to the loss of profits or impairment of earning capacity due to the injury, destruction, or loss of real property, personal property, or natural resources, which shall be recoverable by any claimant."[14]

*Availability of insurance*: The dissent disagreed with the majority's assertion that victims are better able to obtain insurance:

> It is true that denial of recovery may effectively spread the loss over the victims. It is not certain, however, that victims are generally better insurers against the risk of loss caused by tortious acts having widespread consequences. Although the victims do possess greater knowledge of their circumstances and their potential damages, we do not know

[14] 33 U.S.C. § 2702(b)(2)(E). Stated more generally, statutes can alter the *Testbank* rule (as they can alter any common-law doctrine) and provide a recovery.

whether insurance against these types of losses is readily available to the businesses that may be affected.

An important point should be made here. In the business torts area, courts frequently differ over the policy implications of a particular decision. The *Testbank* majority believed that first-party insurance will be readily available; the dissent disagreed. Who is right? In the opinion, neither side provided any empirical or other evidence to back up its position. The claims were simply unsupported assertions. This is not uncommon in judicial policy disputes—judges make arguments based on what they think will occur as a result of a particular decision, but the arguments on both sides are often driven more by differing viewpoints on how the world works rather than by any hard evidence.

Despite the implication from *Testbank*, the economic loss rule is neither limited to the maritime setting nor is it restricted to large-scale accidents.[15] Although the Second Restatement has no provision addressing the rule, the Third Restatement makes clear that the *Testbank* rule is broader than the factual setting of *Testbank* itself. Section 1 of the Third Restatement generically asserts that "[a]n actor has no general duty to avoid the unintentional infliction of economic loss on another," and several illustrations apply the rule to bar a plaintiff's recovery in situations not involving large-scale accidents. Similarly, § 7 of the Third Restatement broadly states that "a claimant cannot recover for economic loss caused by: (a) unintentional injury to another person; or (b) unintentional injury to property in which the claimant has no proprietary interest."

Why shouldn't the economic loss rule be restricted to the large-scale accident context? After all, when the prospect of unending, indeterminate liability is absent, applying the rule may seem unnecessary. According to the Third Restatement, the two main policy rationales behind the rule are (1) an aversion to indeterminate and disproportionate liability, and (2) a preference for deferring to contractual protection. If either policy basis is implicated, a plaintiff's recovery is typically denied. As comment e to § 1 explains:

> Courts consider, first, whether recognizing a duty of care would expose the defendant to indeterminate or disproportionate liability. They consider as well whether parties in the plaintiff's position can reasonably be expected

[15] *See, e.g.*, Coastal Conduit & Ditching, Inc. v. Noram Energy Corp., 29 S.W.3d 282, 283–84, 287–88 (Tex. App. 2000) (noting that the rule has been adopted "in non-admiralty contexts by other jurisdictions," and applying the rule to prevent a plaintiff excavation company from recovering in negligence for its economic losses (increased overhead and other expenses) caused by the defendant failing to mark or mismarking its underground gas lines).

> to protect themselves against the loss by contract. An affirmative answer to either question results in no liability, which is the typical result when a plaintiff seeks to recover for economic loss in tort outside the recognized headings of this Chapter.

Thus, under the Third Restatement, a party's ability to protect itself by contract may still warrant application of the rule, even in the absence of indeterminate or disproportionate liability. When both policy rationales are absent, however, application of the economic loss rule may not make sense. As the comment continues:

> In some such cases, however, the scope of a defendant's liability for economic loss is no more troubling than it would be in cases of physical harm: the set of potential plaintiffs is compact, and the size of the potential liability to them is clear and proportionate to the defendant's culpability. In some cases, too, the plaintiff is in a poor position to allocate the risk of economic loss by contract, whether directly or indirectly. Where those conditions hold, a duty of care may reasonably be found. A court should not labor under a presumption against liability when the rationales for restricting it are absent.

Business torts usually avoid the application of the economic loss rule set forth in *Testbank*. Although business torts typically involve pure economic loss, many of the torts are intentional in nature (e.g., fraud, interference with existing contract, interference with prospective contract), which places them outside the scope of the rule. Moreover, many jurisdictions (as well as the Third Restatement) allow certain negligence-related torts to proceed, such as professional malpractice and negligent misrepresentation, even when the plaintiff has only incurred economic harm.[16] Thus, the *Testbank* rule tends to preclude only general negligence and strict liability actions that seek recovery for pure economic loss. This observation reveals the inaccuracy of judicial statements describing the economic loss rule as a principle that "there is generally no liability in tort for causing pure economic loss to another." As mentioned, intentional torts, professional malpractice, and negligent misrepresentation are all

---

16 *See, e.g.*, William Powers, Jr. & Margaret Niver, *Negligence, Breach of Contract, and the "Economic Loss" Rule*, 23 TEX. TECH L. REV. 477, 480 n.13 (1992) ("Moreover, the 'economic loss' rule is applicable, if at all, only in negligence and strict products liability. It does not preclude recovery for pure economic loss in cases involving fraud, negligent misrepresentation, or intentional interference with contract."); *see also* RESTATEMENT (THIRD) OF TORTS: LIABILITY FOR ECONOMIC HARM § 1(2) & cmt. d (2020) (noting that "[d]uties to avoid the unintentional infliction of economic loss are recognized principally on the terms stated in §§ 2–8 of this Chapter," which include professional negligence and negligent misrepresentation).

permitted tort causes of action that allow recovery for pure economic loss.

The economic loss rule is one of the most confusing doctrines in all of tort law. Most of the confusion stems from the fact that there is not one rule that applies in all contexts; instead, the "rule" has multiple strands with different policy rationales. Indeed, the rule of *Testbank* reflects only one strand of the economic loss rule. Consider the following observations:

> Two quite different types of cases implicate the economic loss rule. In the first type, represented by *Testbank* . . . , the plaintiff and defendant are strangers (that is, they do not have a contractual relationship). One rationale for precluding recovery of pure economic loss in these cases is a fear that the purely economic consequences of a defendant's negligence are not limited by the normal tort limit on the scope of a negligent defendant's liability, foreseeability on a case-by-case basis. Another rationale is that plaintiffs are in a better position than defendants to evaluate their own susceptibility to pure economic loss and protect against the economic loss through first-party insurance. . . .
>
> . . . .
>
> In the second type of case, the plaintiff and the defendant are not strangers. They either have a contractual relationship, or if they are not in technical privity of contract, they are at least indirect parties to a market transaction. A rationale for precluding recovery of pure economic damages in these cases is that the bargaining process, and therefore contract law, is a better method of assigning economic risks than are the socially imposed norms of tort law. This does not mean that we should give the parties unlimited power to assign risks of economic loss. Rather, it merely means that we should decide such questions using the tools of contract law, including the appropriate rules about privity of contract, third-party beneficiaries and unconscionability.
>
> Many of the cases of this second type have involved strict products liability claims, where an additional reason exists for precluding recovery of pure economic loss. If courts permitted plaintiffs to recover under strict products liability for pure economic loss caused by poor performance of the product, they could be accused of impinging on the domain of the warranty provisions of the Uniform

> Commercial Code (the "Code"). Strict products liability and warranty are similar in that they require proof of a defect but, at least nominally, they do not require proof of the defendant's fault. It would be problematic to have a tort theory similar to warranty that is not bound by the other requirements of the Code, such as privity, notice, disclaimers, and remedy limitations. . . . Thus, courts seemingly have been compelled to carve out a core of "economic" disputes to keep strict products liability from displacing the Code entirely.[17]

As the above passage indicates, the *Testbank* holding involves the "stranger" strand of the economic loss rule—i.e., when the plaintiff and the defendant do not have a contractual relationship. Business torts, as mentioned, usually avoid the application of this strand of the rule. The relationship between business torts and the "nonstranger" strand of the rule, however, involves different considerations—a topic which will be discussed in Chapter 5.[18]

---

17 William Powers, Jr. & Margaret Niver, *Negligence, Breach of Contract, and the "Economic Loss" Rule*, 23 TEX. TECH L. REV. 477, 481–83 (1992).

18 The Third Restatement does not refer to the principle articulated in § 1 as the "economic loss rule." Instead, that term is reserved for the principle that there is no liability in tort for negligently caused economic loss between contracting parties. *See* RESTATEMENT (THIRD) OF TORTS: LIABILITY FOR ECONOMIC HARM §§ 1 cmt. b, 3 (2020). As mentioned, this "between contracting parties" (or "nonstranger") strand of the economic loss rule is discussed in Chapter 5. *See also* 3 DAN B. DOBBS ET AL., THE LAW OF TORTS § 611, at 475 (2d ed. 2011) ("As a matter of terminology, some courts think of the economic loss rule as including the stranger cases; others think of the economic loss rule only in connection with claims by a plaintiff who has a contractual, or at least near-privity relationship with the defendant.").

# Chapter 2

# MISREPRESENTATION

Misrepresentation refers to a collection of related torts that all address liability for economic harm caused by a plaintiff's justifiable reliance upon a defendant's material misstatements. Most often, such misstatements cause the plaintiff to enter into a bargain or other transaction that does not turn out how the plaintiff expected. Liability may be based on the defendant's intent to deceive (the tort of "fraud" or "deceit"), its negligence (the tort of "negligent misrepresentation"), or upon a policy requiring the defendant to be strictly liable for its inaccurate statements (the tort of "innocent misrepresentation"). Each of these misrepresentation torts will be discussed in the materials below.

## A. INTENTIONAL MISREPRESENTATION (FRAUD)

The tort of fraud (also known as "deceit," or referred to imprecisely as "misrepresentation") has existed for hundreds of years. In *Neurosurgery and Spine Surgery, S.C. v. Goldman,*[1] the court described the historical origins of the tort and the modern context in which it typically arises:

> We begin our discussion by noting that the tort of fraudulent misrepresentation is often surrounded by unnecessary confusion, because misrepresentations themselves often play large roles in a variety of other torts. For instance, an untrue assertion may be at the heart of an action for false imprisonment, conversion, or trespass to land. A misrepresentation is the essence of torts such as defamation, interference with contractual relations, and malicious prosecution. A malicious, outrageous lie may even give rise to a cause of action for intentional infliction of emotional distress. In summary, a great number of causes of action stem from misrepresentations.
>
> However, not every misrepresentation gives rise to a cause of action for fraudulent misrepresentation. The origin of fraudulent misrepresentation lies in the common law action of deceit, which was a very narrow tort. See *Pasley v. Freeman,* 100 Eng. Rep. 450 (K.B.1789); *Derry v. Peek,* 14 A.C. 337 (H.L.1888). Prior to the eighteenth century,

1 790 N.E.2d 925 (Ill. App. Ct. 2003).

recovery on the action of deceit was not available unless the misrepresentation was part of some contractual dealing between the parties. Then, in 1789, in *Pasley*, it was held that one who fraudulently induced a third party to extend credit to a person known to be untrustworthy was liable to the defrauded party. Deceit, as a distinct tort, thus came into being, independent of any contractual relationship.

In 1889, in *Peek*, deceit became the tort we today refer to as fraudulent misrepresentation. In *Peek*, the directors of a tramway company issued a prospectus to induce the public to subscribe for stock; the prospectus contained the following unqualified statement: "[T]he company has the right to use steam or mechanical motive power instead of horses * * *." In fact, however, the company had no such right inasmuch as the government permitted the use of steam as a motive power only if the company first obtained governmental consent and the company had never obtained such consent. Peek, a stockholder who had purchased shares on the faith of the prospectus, brought an action for deceit. The court concluded that the defendants had honestly believed the statement to be true, although they had no reasonable grounds for any such belief. It was held that the action could not be maintained, since nothing more than negligence was shown.

Historically, the torts of deceit and fraudulent misrepresentation have been limited to cases involving business or financial transactions between parties, right down to the first recorded cases, *Pasley* and *Peek*. See W. Prosser, Torts § 105 (4th ed.1971); see also *Johnson v. State,* 447 P.2d 352, 365 (1968) (holding that the tort of fraudulent misrepresentation applies only to interferences with financial or commercial interests). The United States Supreme Court has similarly observed:

> "[M]any familiar forms of * * * conduct may be said to involve an element of 'misrepresentation,' in the generic sense of that word, but '[s]o far as misrepresentation has been treated as giving rise in and of itself to a distinct cause of action in tort, it has been identified with the common law action of deceit,' and has been confined 'very largely to the invasion of interests of a financial or commercial character, in the course of business dealings.'" *United States v. Neustadt,* 366 U.S. 696, 711 n. 26 (1961), quoting W. Prosser, Torts § 85, at 702–03 (1941).

The tort of fraudulent misrepresentation has also historically been limited to cases where a plaintiff has suffered a pecuniary harm. See W. Prosser, Torts, § 105 (4th ed.1971); see also Restatement (Second) of Torts § 531 (1976) (defining damages only in terms of pecuniary loss). Where a plaintiff has sustained physical harm, recovery will lie in one of the above other tortious actions. See E. Kionka, Torts 268 (2d ed.1993). Indeed, fraudulent misrepresentation is purely an economic tort under which one may recover only monetary damages. *McConkey v. AON Corp.,* 354 N.J.Super. 25, 59, 804 A.2d 572, 593 (2002) (holding that damages in a fraudulent misrepresentation action are limited to those that are pecuniary); *Jourdain v. Dineen,* 527 A.2d 1304, 1307 (Me.1987) (holding that pecuniary damages are essential to a fraudulent misrepresentation cause of action).

> "Although the invasion of an economic interest by tort or by contract breach will often cause the plaintiff personal distress, the interest ordinarily protected in such cases is purely an economic interest.... Accordingly the usual rule is that the plaintiff must show pecuniary loss in misrepresentation cases and the damages are limited to such pecuniary loss, with no recovery for emotional distress." D. Dobbs, Remedies § 9.2(4), at 559–60 (2d ed.1993).

While no court has yet specifically declined to extend fraudulent misrepresentation to noncommercial situations or to damages for physical harm, there is little occasion to depart from the historical trend that our predecessor courts have created because other nominate tort actions have provided adequate remedies. See W. Keeton, Prosser & Keeton on Torts §§ 105 through 110 (5th ed.1984). Simply put, fraudulent misrepresentation has emerged as a tort distinct from the general milieu of negligent and intentional wrongs and applies only to interferences with financial or commercial interests where a party suffers some pecuniary loss.

As *Goldman* indicates, the tort of fraud is typically concerned only with pecuniary loss in business or commercial settings—i.e., misrepresentations in commercial transactions that result in financial harm without causing injury to person or property. While some of the statements in *Goldman* suggest that the tort of fraud is *never* associated with physical harm, that assertion is too strong, as there is authority indicating that a fraud action may be maintained when misrepresentations result in bodily injury or property damage.[2] Similarly, there is authority allowing a fraud action to be maintained in a non-commercial setting.[3] Nevertheless, *Goldman* accurately captures the typical scope of the fraud action—pecuniary loss in the business or commercial setting—and it is this typical scope that is the focus of the materials in this section.

While the elements of the common-law fraud action may differ slightly among jurisdictions, the courts generally agree that the plaintiff must establish the following: (1) a false, material representation was made; (2) when made, the speaker knew or believed that the representation was false, or recklessly asserted it without any knowledge of its truth (the "scienter" requirement); (3) the speaker made the representation with the intent to induce the plaintiff to act or to refrain from acting; (4) the plaintiff justifiably relied upon the representation; and (5) the plaintiff suffered injury resulting from such reliance.[4]

The cause of action for fraud often has a heightened pleading requirement. For example, Rule 9(b) of the Federal Rules of Civil Procedure requires a complaint alleging fraud to state "the circumstances constituting fraud . . . with particularity." Many states have a similar requirement.[5] Some jurisdictions also elevate the

---

[2] *See, e.g.*, O'Hara v. Western Seven Trees Corp., 142 Cal. Rptr. 487, 489, 492 (Ct. App. 1977) (allowing a plaintiff who was raped to bring a fraud cause of action against the owners of an apartment complex alleged to have "knowingly misrepresented the safety and security of the complex with the intent to induce appellant to rent an apartment"); *id.* at 491 ("An action [of fraud] may be maintained to recover for physical harm proximately caused by a defendant's deceit."); B.N. v. K.K., 538 A.2d 1175, 1176, 1182–84 (Md. 1988) (allowing a fraud claim by a plaintiff who alleged that the defendant concealed the existence of his genital herpes and transmitted the disease to her via sexual intercourse); RESTATEMENT (SECOND) OF TORTS § 557A & cmt. a (1977) ("The rule here stated permits a tort action of deceit to be maintained, when there is physical harm to person, land or chattels of a person who justifiably relies on [a fraudulent misrepresentation].").

[3] *See, e.g.*, *B.N.*, 538 A.2d at 1182 ("It is true that this tort [fraud] is usually applied in a business setting, or to one in which some pecuniary loss is claimed. Obviously, this [sexual transmission of herpes dispute] is not that kind of case. But a business setting and pecuniary loss are not necessarily required."); W. PAGE KEETON ET AL., PROSSER AND KEETON ON TORTS § 105, at 726 (5th ed. 1984) (citing cases where a fraud action was allowed "for tricking the plaintiff into an invalid marriage or marriage with one who is physically unfit, or for inducing the plaintiff to leave a husband, or to incur criminal penalties").

[4] *See, e.g.*, *Goldman*, 790 N.E.2d at 933; Trenholm v. Ratliff, 646 S.W.2d 927, 930 (Tex. 1983); *see also* RESTATEMENT (SECOND) OF TORTS § 525 (1977) (stating similar elements); RESTATEMENT (THIRD) OF TORTS: LIABILITY FOR ECONOMIC HARM § 9 (2020) (same).

[5] *See, e.g.*, John Doe 1 v. Archdiocese of Milwaukee, 734 N.W.2d 827, 839–40 (Wis. 2007) (noting that a Wisconsin statute "pertaining to pleadings for fraud . . . states [that] 'the circumstances constituting fraud or mistake shall be stated with particularity,'" and further observing that "[w]e have interpreted this statute to require that 'allegations of fraud must specify the particular individuals involved,

evidentiary standard that a plaintiff must satisfy in a fraud action. Rather than the usual civil standard of "more likely than not" or "preponderance of the evidence," some jurisdictions require the plaintiff to satisfy a higher standard of "clear and convincing evidence."[6] The Third Restatement of Torts discusses this standard of proof issue in comment e to § 9:

> The elements of a tort claim ordinarily must be proven by a preponderance of the evidence, but most courts have required clear and convincing evidence to establish some or all of the elements of fraud. They reason that a claim of fraud is easy to allege and often has damaging side effects; it may injure the reputation of the defendant and entitle the plaintiff to seek punitive damages. Those points may be accurate, but in themselves they do not fully explain the higher standard of proof because they are true of many other intentional torts as well. The special treatment of fraud is better understood as a protection against encroachment into the law of contract by the law of tort. An allegation of fraud often arises from an exchange between the parties. The claim may allow the plaintiff to obtain more aggressive remedies in tort than contract law would provide. The law generally prefers that disputed transactions be resolved by the law of contract, and so makes escape from that body of law somewhat more difficult than the assertion of a tort claim that has no other legal home. Granted, some claims of fraud arise outside contractual settings; those patterns are less common, however, and the rules about the standard of proof have been devised for the typical case.
>
> A majority of courts apply the clear-and-convincing standard of proof to all elements of a claim for fraud. A minority apply it to scienter and perhaps to certain other elements of the tort, but not to damages. This Restatement favors application of the heightened standard of proof only as far as the rationale for it will carry. The rationale is convincing when applied to an assertion that the defendant made a false statement knowingly, because that element of the tort—scienter—distinguishes a fraud claim from a

---

where and when misrepresentations occurred, and to whom misrepresentations were made' ").

[6] *See, e.g.*, *In re* Marriage of Cutler, 588 N.W.2d 425, 430 (Iowa 1999) ("Proving fraud is a difficult task. A plaintiff must prove several factors by clear and convincing evidence, including (1) misrepresentation or failure to disclose when under a legal duty to do so, (2) materiality, (3) scienter, (4) intent to deceive, (5) justifiable reliance, and (6) resulting injury or damage.").

claim of negligence that would be extinguished by a contract between the parties. See § 3. Once a defendant's culpable state of mind has been proven, however, it is difficult to see why the plaintiff should be put to a harder task in proving causation than would be necessary if the defendant were merely negligent. Applying a more demanding standard to the proof of damages is still harder to support. The best justification is that a jury might be confused by different standards of proof for different elements of a fraud claim, but juries are assigned more demanding tasks often enough. Because these issues have yet received only occasional judicial attention, this Restatement leaves to developing case law the details of when clear and convincing proof ought to be required. It recommends, however, that the heightened standard be applied sparingly and be justified by good and specific reasons whenever it is used.

## 1. Misrepresentations and Omissions

A misrepresentation can, of course, take the form of oral or written words. Importantly, however, a misrepresentation can also be based on conduct that asserts the existence of a fact.[7] The decision of *Lindberg Cadillac Co. v. Aron*[8] provides a nice illustration. The defendant bought a car from the plaintiff. As part of the purchase, the defendant traded in a 1957 Imperial. The Imperial's motor block was cracked, but the cracks had been painted over and concealed by a filling station operator, allegedly on the instruction of the defendant.[9] The defendant did not mention the cracks upon trading in the car to the plaintiff (Lindberg). Lindberg resold the car to a third party who brought it back complaining that it was overheating. The cracks were discovered, and Lindberg refunded the third party's money. Lindberg then sued the defendant for fraud.

Although there were no verbal or written representations by the defendant, the court concluded that there was a "positive fraudulent concealment," which sufficed as a misrepresentation. As the court concluded: "The acts of the defendant as stated above were designed to, and did, defraud the plaintiff, and there is no merit to the contention that a case in fraud was not made."

---

7 In the evidence context, this is called "assertive conduct"—non-verbal conduct intended as an assertion.

8 371 S.W.2d 651 (Mo. Ct. App. 1963).

9 The defendant claimed that the filling station operator said nothing about cracks in the motor block, and that the defendant was therefore unaware of any problems. The trial court found for the plaintiff, which suggests that it did not credit the defendant's version of events.

As *Lindberg* teaches, oral or written words are not necessary for a misrepresentation. An action can suffice. The substance of the misrepresentation made by the defendant was that the motor block was not cracked, and the misrepresentation was made by allowing the filling station operator to paint over the cracks. One might say that the defendant's action (instructing the filling station operator to paint over the cracks) was the conduct-equivalent of saying or writing "the motor block is not cracked."

Consistent with *Lindberg*, comment b to § 525 of the Second Restatement of Torts makes clear that a misrepresentation can be established by "words spoken or written" or "any other conduct that amounts to an assertion not in accordance with the truth." In short, as comment b observes, "words or conduct asserting the existence of a fact constitute a misrepresentation if the fact does not exist." Section 550 makes the same point by explicitly noting that "concealment or other action" designed to prevent a person from acquiring material information suffices as a misrepresentation. The Third Restatement similarly notes in comment c to § 9 that "a misrepresentation need not take the form of a statement" and that "[i]t may arise from conduct rather than words."[10]

A misrepresentation can also be established by a half-truth. Section 529 of the Second Restatement defines a half-truth as "[a] representation stating the truth so far as it goes but which the maker knows or believes to be materially misleading because of his failure to state additional or qualifying matter." The Third Restatement (in § 9 cmt. c) similarly states that "[l]iability may likewise be found if a speaker believes a statement is true as far as it goes but knows that it is misleading because it is incomplete or not duly qualified." In layman's terms, one might define a half-truth as follows: the speaker says something that is true, but not everything that the speaker knows, and what the speaker didn't say, makes what the speaker did say, misleading.[11]

In addition to affirmative misrepresentations (i.e., words or conduct), silence can also serve as the basis for a fraud claim, but only if there is a duty to speak between the parties. Consider the decision

---

10 *See also* 3 DAN B. DOBBS ET AL., THE LAW OF TORTS § 682, at 701 (2d ed. 2011) ("Responsibility for this kind of misrepresentation is not limited to cases of concealed defects in tangible property. Concealment of assets, losses, profits or other material financial information from a buyer or partner may also subject the defendant to liability for misrepresentation. Concealment of a conflict of interest can operate in the same way.").

11 *See also* Kannavos v. Annino, 247 N.E.2d 708, 711 (Mass. 1969) ("Although there may be 'no duty imposed upon one party to a transaction to speak for the information of the other . . . if he does speak with reference to a given point of information, voluntarily or at the other's request, he is bound to speak honestly and to divulge all the material facts bearing upon the point that lie within his knowledge.' ").

of *Swinton v. Whitinsville Savings Bank*.[12] In September 1938, the defendant sold a house to the plaintiff in Massachusetts. The home was apparently infested with termites. The plaintiff sued for fraud and alleged that the defendant was aware of the termite infestation but said nothing about it. The plaintiff further alleged that he incurred significant expenses for repairs. The defendant moved to dismiss on the grounds that the facts pled, even if true, did not state a claim for relief. The court agreed with the defendant and affirmed the lower court's dismissal of the claim. The court referenced "[t]he rule of nonliability for bare nondisclosure" and stated that there "was nothing to show any peculiar duty to speak" in the facts pled. Instead, there was simply "a business deal at arm's length" where there is no general duty to speak.

*Swinton* reflects the traditional common-law rule that silence is not fraudulent unless there is a duty to disclose, and there is no duty to disclose merely because the other party would find the information to be beneficial.[13] As a matter of policy, is this rule a sensible one? The purpose of the rule would appear to be the encouragement of self-protection. We want people to actively protect their own interests and not stand idly by waiting for others to inform them of everything they need to know. The general "no duty to disclose" rule supports this idea—the person who fails to investigate and gather relevant facts before making a decision bears the risk that the decision will turn out badly ("let the buyer beware").[14]

The problem with such a rule is that "no one could think of all possible questions that would reveal some material defects in a house [and] [t]hat is even more so when it comes to more complex business deals in which the material facts are not about physical defects." As a result, "the nondisclosure rule may pose a substantial risk or burden."[15] Indeed, in *Swinton*, the court pointed out that termites were not a common problem in Massachusetts, which suggests that buyers might not know to investigate the issue. The rule makes sense

---

[12] 42 N.E.2d 808 (Mass. 1942).

[13] *See, e.g.*, RESTATEMENT (SECOND) OF TORTS § 551 & cmt. a (1977); RESTATEMENT (THIRD) OF TORTS: LIABILITY FOR ECONOMIC HARM § 13 (2020).

[14] *See also* DAN B. DOBBS, THE LAW OF TORTS § 481, at 1375 (2000) ("[T]he traditional rule treats mere nondisclosure differently, holding that the bargainer is not ordinarily obliged to make affirmative revelations of known material facts. The seller could not hide the termite infestation, for that would be concealment, but he was not obliged to mention termites if the buyer did not ask. Under the traditional rule, the buyer can avoid the problem by asking the right question; if the seller denies the termite damage he knows to exist, he has made a knowingly false representation and is liable. Regulations or customs of real estate brokers may avoid the problem by inspections and formal disclosure statements. Sophisticated buyers now know to inspect for hazardous waste, lest they become liable for its cleanup, and many buyers will be protected in the termite case by asking a question or seeking inspection.").

[15] *Id.*

when the defect (or the potential for the defect) is obvious to all parties, or when the plaintiff can easily discover the information.[16] But when the defendant knows of a defect that is not obvious and that can only be discovered with great expense or difficulty, the rule seems particularly harsh.

When considered from the buyer's standpoint, another rationale for the general "no duty to disclose" rule is that it provides an incentive for parties to produce new information. To illustrate, assume a different rule where sellers and buyers must disclose all information about material defects and virtues related to the subject matter of the transaction. The buyer of Farmer Brown's property has spent considerable time and energy producing and examining geological data that reveals a great store of oil/natural gas/valuable minerals underneath Farmer Brown's land. If the buyer must reveal that information, Farmer Brown will surely charge more for the land (or refuse to sell it at all), which reduces if not eliminates the buyer's ability to profit from the new information that the buyer generated. If the legal rule does not allow the party who produces new information to benefit from that production, there may be no incentive to generate the information in the first place. If we consider information to be valuable, this is not an ideal result. Such an argument might push one towards a rule that says that sellers always have to disclose material defects (because they usually discover the defects by happenstance and without a great expenditure of resources), but buyers do not have to disclose material virtues (because they usually discover the virtues through a costly investigation, and because we want to encourage buyers to incur those costs to generate new and valuable information).

Given the harshness of the general "no duty to disclose" rule,[17] it is not surprising that a host of exceptions have developed. According to § 551 of the Second Restatement, there is a duty to speak before the transaction is consummated when (a) the parties are in a fiduciary or similar relationship of trust and confidence; (b) the speaker has uttered a misleading half-truth; (c) the speaker has learned that a previous statement is untrue or misleading, even though the statement was true or believed to be true when made; or (d) the speaker has made a statement with no expectation that it will

---

[16] *Cf.* W. PAGE KEETON ET AL., PROSSER AND KEETON ON TORTS § 106, at 737 (5th ed. 1984) ("[The rule] finds proper application in cases where the fact undisclosed is patent, or the plaintiff has equal opportunities for obtaining information which he may be expected to utilize, or the defendant has no reason to think that he is acting under any misapprehension.").

[17] It is important to note that this general "no duty to disclose" principle is a common-law rule. In many jurisdictions, statutes have changed the rule in the real estate context. Indeed, many states have property statutes requiring the seller of residential real estate to affirmatively disclose all sorts of defects about a listed home.

be acted upon, but has subsequently learned that another is about to act in reliance on the statement.[18] Do these exceptions seem sensible?

*Fiduciary or confidential relationship*: A fiduciary relationship is the highest duty imposed by law.[19] A true fiduciary relationship requires the fiduciary to put the beneficiary's interests ahead of its own. In such a relationship, there is no room for deceptive silence. If the fiduciary is obligated to put the beneficiary's interests first, the fiduciary is not allowed to benefit from informational advantages that the fiduciary possesses (again, any self-interest must be subordinated). As a consequence, the fiduciary would have to disclose all known material information to the beneficiary. Indeed, a duty to disclose is an important aspect of any fiduciary relationship. This is in contrast to an arm's length relationship where each party is expected to look out only for its own interests, informational advantages can be exploited, and a duty to disclose is not typically present.[20]

*Half-truths*: Half-truths are fraudulent because they present a misleading picture of the truth. Because a half-truth is half affirmative statement and half silence, the Second Restatement seems to cover them in two places. Section 529 indicates that a half-truth, due to the affirmative statement aspect, can be fraudulent, while § 551(2)(b) effectively completes the analysis by making clear that a half-truth, due to the silence aspect, can be fraudulent. Indeed, comment g to § 551 states that "there may be recovery either on the basis of the original misleading statement or of the nondisclosure of the additional facts."

*Learning that a previous statement was untrue was made*: In comment h to § 551, the Second Restatement explains the rationale as follows: "One who, having made a representation which when made was true or believed to be so, remains silent after he has learned that it is untrue and that the person to whom it is made is relying upon it in a transaction with him, is morally and legally in

---

18 *See, e.g.*, RESTATEMENT (SECOND) OF TORTS § 551(2)(a)–(d) (1977); *see also* RESTATEMENT (THIRD) OF TORTS: LIABILITY FOR ECONOMIC HARM § 13(a)–(b) (2020) (describing situations where an actor has a duty to speak).

19 *See generally* Chapter 4 (discussing fiduciary duty).

20 For examples of fiduciary or confidential relationships, see RESTATEMENT (SECOND) OF TORTS § 551 cmts. e–f (1977). *See also* W. PAGE KEETON ET AL., PROSSER AND KEETON ON TORTS § 106, at 738 (5th ed. 1984) ("Another exception is found where the parties stand in some confidential or fiduciary relation to one another, such as that of principal and agent, executor and beneficiary of an estate, bank and investing depositor, majority and minority stockholders, old friends, or numerous others where special trust and confidence is reposed. In addition, certain types of contracts, such as those of suretyship or guaranty, insurance, partnership and joint adventure, are recognized as creating something in the nature of a confidential relation, and hence as requiring the utmost good faith, and full and fair disclosure of all material facts.").

the same position as if he knew that his statement was false when made." This seems sensible. The law does not require you to speak in the first place, but if you do speak, you should not be able to leave a misleading impression, even if you did not realize that you were leaving a misleading impression when you first made the statement. Once you have made an affirmative statement, you have an obligation to update the accuracy of that statement until the transaction is complete.

Significantly, this duty to update presumably ends as soon as the transaction is entered into. Once the parties are contractually bound to one another, surely there is no duty to continue to update the accuracy of pre-contract statements. Otherwise, it would seem that any party who decides to breach a contract would be liable for fraud if he did not convey that intention immediately to the other party. That is not the law. Indeed, § 551(2) indicates that any duty to disclose is "before the transaction is consummated."[21]

*Learning that a statement is being relied upon*: Once again, the rationale appears to be that a person has no general obligation to speak, but if he chooses to speak, he has a duty to make sure that his statement is not misleading. If he discovers that someone is relying upon his misleading statement, he needs to correct it, even if he did not initially make the statement thinking that someone would rely. This seems sensible as well; if you speak, you need to make sure that your statement does not knowingly mislead anyone, even if you did not think that it was false in the first place (§ 551(2)(c)) or that anyone would rely on it (§ 551(2)(d)). Once you come into the knowledge that your statement is false, or that someone is relying on it, you need to correct the misleading nature of your statement.

The Third Restatement collapses the four subsections of § 551(2)(a)–(d) into two subsections (§ 13(a)–(b)). It does not appear that any significant change in substance was intended. Section 13(a) seems to cover the same ground that was covered by § 551(2)(c)–(d). Section 13(b) is substantially the same as § 551(2)(a). Section 551(2)(b) on half-truths has been omitted from § 13—presumably on the ground that a half-truth subjects a speaker to liability as an

---

21 *See also* DAN B. DOBBS, THE LAW OF TORTS § 481, at 1375 (2000) (noting that "[a]ffirmative duties of disclosure are imposed when . . . the defendant has made a representation that is true at the time it was made but that becomes untrue or misleading *before the bargain is consummated*." (emphasis added)). *But see* RESTATEMENT (SECOND) OF TORTS § 535 & cmt. a (1977) (providing liability for a "continuing misrepresentation": "The rule stated in this Section applies only when the plaintiff is known by the defendant to be relying upon a fraudulent misrepresentation made by him in respect to a previous transaction that has been either consummated or abandoned and when the defendant enters into a second transaction without disclosing the falsity of the original misstatement.").

affirmative misrepresentation. Inclusion in the "silence as fraud" section, therefore, is unnecessary.[22]

The Second Restatement also provides in § 551(2)(e) that a party to a business transaction has a duty to disclose "facts basic to the transaction, if he knows that the other is about to enter into [the transaction] under a mistake as to them, and that the other, because of the relationship between them, the customs of the trade or other objective circumstances, would reasonably expect a disclosure of those facts." (As discussed below, the Third Restatement has comparable language in § 13(c).)

What constitutes a basic fact, and when would it be reasonable to expect disclosure of such a fact? These questions are hard to answer. According to comment j to § 551, a basic fact "is a fact that is assumed by the parties as a basis for the transaction itself," and "it is a fact that goes to the basis, or essence, of the transaction, and is an important part of the substance of what is bargained for or dealt with." Significantly, a basic fact is not simply a material fact: "Other facts may serve as important and persuasive inducements to enter into the transaction, but not go to its essence. These facts may be material, but they are not basic." Comment j also refers to comment c to § 16 of the Restatement of Restitution. That comment in the Restatement of Restitution suggests that a basic fact is "a fact assumed by [the parties] as a basis on which they entered into the transaction."

Although this guidance is not particularly clear, a basic fact appears to be one that significantly affects the subject matter of the transaction itself. By asking (1) what is the subject matter of the transaction, and (2) does the undisclosed fact reveal a significant defect in the subject matter, some sense of a basic fact might be obtained.

Even if it is a basic fact, § 551(2)(e) does not require its disclosure in all instances. It must be (1) a basic fact; (2) that one side knows the other is mistaken about; and (3) that the other would reasonably expect to be disclosed given "the relationship between them, the customs of the trade or other objective circumstances." This third prong is also difficult. When would it be reasonable to expect disclosure of a basic fact? It is difficult to give any definitive guidance here. In comment l to § 551, the following is stated:

---

22 *See* RESTATEMENT (THIRD) OF TORTS: LIABILITY FOR ECONOMIC HARM § 13 cmt. a (2020) ("A statement that is misleading if not properly qualified may support liability under § 9 without reference to the principles stated here. This Section, rather, recognizes liability at common law for nondisclosure as such—that is, for a failure to disclose unaccompanied by any statement that would support liability by itself.").

> It is extremely difficult to be specific as to the factors that give rise to this known, and reasonable, expectation of disclosure. In general, the cases in which the rule stated in Clause (e) has been applied have been those in which the advantage taken of the plaintiff's ignorance is so shocking to the ethical sense of the community, and is so extreme and unfair, as to amount to a form of swindling, in which the plaintiff is led by appearances into a bargain that is a trap, of whose essence and substance he is unaware. In such a case, even in a tort action for deceit, the plaintiff is entitled to be compensated for the loss that he has sustained. Thus a seller who knows that his cattle are infected with tick fever or contagious abortion is not free to unload them on the buyer and take his money, when he knows that the buyer is unaware of the fact, could not easily discover it, would not dream of entering into the bargain if he knew and is relying upon the seller's good faith and common honesty to disclose any such fact if it is true.

This passage is filled with generalities and few specifics.[23] The fact pattern that seems the strongest for triggering § 551(2)(e) involves latent defects that the plaintiff cannot discover through a reasonable investigation. After all, if the general "no duty to disclose" rule is animated by the idea that parties should self-protect by discovering defects through their own investigations, the rule should arguably be

---

[23] The passage below attempts to provide a bit more specificity by stating that courts have considered a wide variety of factors in trying to determine when a duty to disclose is warranted, but it too lacks any definitive guidance:

> [T]here has been a rather amorphous tendency on the part of most courts in recent years to find a duty of disclosure when the circumstances are such that the failure to disclose something would violate a standard requiring conformity to what the ordinary ethical person would have disclosed. . . . Some factors of importance are as follows: (1) The difference in the degree of intelligence of the parties to the transaction. This is simply because the community sense of justice demands it; (2) The relation that the parties bear to each other; (3) The manner in which the information is acquired. Information which affects the value of the subject matter of a contract may have been acquired by chance, by effort, or by an illegal act. It makes a difference on the ethical equality of non-disclosure; (4) The nature of the fact not disclosed. In contracts of sale of real property, if the vendor conceals an intrinsic defect not discoverable by reasonable care, there is a much greater likelihood of the existence of a duty to disclose the non-discoverable and intrinsic defect than there would be to disclose something extrinsic likely to affect market value; (5) The general class to which the person who is concealing the information belongs. It is much more likely that a seller will be required to disclose information than a purchaser; (6) The nature of the contract itself. In releases, and contracts of insurance, practically all material facts must be disclosed; (7) The importance of the fact not disclosed; (8) Any conduct of the person not disclosing something to prevent discovery.

W. PAGE KEETON ET AL., PROSSER AND KEETON ON TORTS § 106, at 739 (5th ed. 1984).

different when self-protection is not reasonably practicable—i.e., when even a thorough investigation would not discover the defect.[24]

Ultimately, the obligation to disclose basic facts may be more of a standard than a rule. Put differently, the obligation simply represents a fuzzy principle of business ethics that courts use when they believe that one party has taken advantage of another party's ignorance in a way that goes beyond typical informational advantages.[25]

The Third Restatement has comparable language in § 13(c), although it refers to a "basic assumption" behind the transaction rather than "facts basic" to the transaction. The change in language seems designed to align the section more closely with Restatement (Second) of Contracts § 152, which involves a mutual mistake between the parties "as to a basic assumption on which the contract was made." Comment b to § 152 states the following:

> A mistake of both parties does not make the contract voidable unless it is one as to a basic assumption on which both parties made the contract. The term "basic assumption" has the same meaning here as it does in Chapter 11 in connection with impracticability (§§ 261, 266(1)) and frustration (§§ 265, 266(2)). See Uniform Commercial Code § 2–615(a). For example, market conditions and the financial situation of the parties are ordinarily not such assumptions, and, generally, just as shifts in market conditions or financial ability do not effect discharge under the rules governing impracticability, mistakes as to market conditions or financial ability do not justify avoidance under the rules governing mistake. The parties may have had such a "basic assumption," even though they were not conscious of alternatives. Where, for

[24] *Cf.* Stambovsky v. Ackley, 572 N.Y.S.2d 672, 676 (App. Div. 1991) ("Where a condition which has been created by the seller materially impairs the value of the contract and is peculiarly within the knowledge of the seller or unlikely to be discovered by a prudent purchaser exercising due care with respect to the subject transaction, nondisclosure constitutes a basis for rescission as a matter of equity. Any other outcome places upon the buyer not merely the obligation to exercise care in his purchase but rather to be omniscient with respect to any fact which may affect the bargain. No practical purpose is served by imposing such a burden upon a purchaser. To the contrary, it encourages predatory business practice and offends the principle that equity will suffer no wrong . . . without a remedy.").

[25] *See* RESTATEMENT (SECOND) OF TORTS § 551 cmt. l (1977). When a failure to disclose can result in physical harm, a number of courts seem willing to find that a duty to disclose is triggered. *See, e.g.*, B.N. v. K.K., 538 A.2d 1175, 1179 (Md. 1988) ("One who knows he or she has a highly infectious disease can readily foresee the danger that the disease may be communicated to others with whom the infected person comes into contact. As a consequence, the infected person has a duty to take reasonable precautions—*whether by warning others* or by avoiding contact with them—to avoid transmitting the disease." (emphasis added)).

example, a party purchases an annuity on the life of another person, it can be said that it was a basic assumption that the other person was alive at the time, even though the parties never consciously addressed themselves to the possibility that he was dead.

The Third Restatement also drops the term "objective" and simply states that "other" circumstances (rather than "other objective circumstances") would warrant disclosure. Comment d to § 13 of the Third Restatement emphasizes superior knowledge and access to information as important factors behind disclosure of a "basic assumption":

> One party often knows more than the other about the subject of an exchange between them. That difference, without more, creates no obligation of disclosure. Better information is a legitimate advantage at the bargaining table, and the law encourages its acquisition. In some cases, however, an imbalance of knowledge creates a duty in the better-informed party to disclose it. Liability on this theory requires, first, a showing that the fact at issue was basic to the transaction. Second, the plaintiff must have a legitimate reason to rely on an adversary to supply the information. Part of that reason usually is a difference in each side's access to the facts. If one party knows something that the other cannot find out, letting the other suffer for its ignorance may not usefully encourage the discovery of knowledge and may offend ordinary standards of fairness. Even when two parties have different access to basic facts, however, rules to govern the defendant's obligations are hard to state. Liability on this basis typically arises from conduct that represents a clear violation of business ethics. Such conclusions depend in significant part on commercial customs, which vary in different settings.

An illustration of a basic facts dispute is provided by *Griffith v. Byers Construction Company*.[26] The plaintiffs were purchasers of new homes in Wichita, Kansas. They sued the developer, Byers Construction Company, for fraud. They alleged that Byers developed the home sites and graded them to make it impossible for the plaintiffs to discover the high saline content of the soil. They further alleged that Byers did not otherwise disclose the saline levels. After the plaintiffs purchased houses, landscaping failed (grass, shrubs, and trees all died) because of the soil's salinity.

---

26 510 P.2d 198 (Kan. 1973).

The trial court granted summary judgment for Byers. It held as a matter of law that the fraud claim failed because of the lack of privity between Byers and the homeowner plaintiffs. (The residential lots were sold by Byers to builders, who in turn constructed the houses and sold them to the plaintiffs. Thus, the only contracts were between Byers and the builders, and between the builders and the homeowners. There was no contract between Byers and the homeowners.)

The Supreme Court of Kansas reversed the summary judgment in favor of Byers and remanded. It concluded that the failure of Byers to disclose the high saline content of the soil fit within the holding of *Jenkins v. McCormick*[27]—a decision holding that "[w]here a vendor has knowledge of a defect in property which is not within the fair and reasonable reach of the vendee and which he could not discover by the exercise of reasonable diligence, the silence and failure of the vendor to disclose the defect in the property constitutes actionable fraudulent concealment." The court also concluded that the *Jenkins* rule was similar to the basic facts exception of § 551(2)(e).[28]

Can *Griffith* be explained as a decision that turned on the basic facts exception? It would seem so. First, the fertility of the soil would appear to be a basic fact. The subject matter of the transaction is a house and accompanying lot, and the undisclosed fact (i.e., the yard will not support grass or plant life) reveals a significant defect in that subject matter. Second, Byers (the developer) knew that the homeowners were unaware of the high saline content of the soil. Third, the homeowners would reasonably expect disclosure because

---

27 339 P.2d 8 (Kan. 1959).

28 With respect to privity, the court concluded that privity between the plaintiff and the defendant was not required in a fraud action. Citing § 531 of the Second Restatement, the court indicated that "the doctrine of privity provides no defense to appellee Byers if appellants were within a class of persons appellee intended to reach," and it noted that "[l]iability for misrepresentation is not necessarily limited to the person with whom the misrepresenter deals." The court concluded that the plaintiff homeowners "were in that class of persons desiring building lots in a choice residential area whom appellee intended and had reason to expect would purchase and build their homes." *See also* RESTATEMENT (THIRD) OF TORTS: LIABILITY FOR ECONOMIC HARM § 12 cmt. b (2020) ("The plaintiff need not have dealt directly with the defendant. It is enough if the defendant had reason to expect that the plaintiff would receive the statement and rely on it. Nor need the defendant know the specific identities of those who were likely to rely; awareness of a class of potential victims is sufficient.").

Through its grading and development of the property, Byers effectively represented (allegedly) that the soil was suitable for residential landscaping. Did Byers intend for the homeowners to rely on that representation, or at least have reason to expect that they would? Of course. It knew that the lots were ultimately for homeowners, it knew that homeowners would not be interested in the lots without "soil fertility," and it knew that builders would not be interested in building houses that homeowners would not want. Simply put, Byers allegedly hoped that builders and homeowners would believe its representation; otherwise, Byers would not have been able to sell the lots for residential development. *See also* Section A(3) (discussing intent to induce reliance).

the high saline content of the soil was not apparent, and Byers allegedly graded and developed the lots in such a way that "it became impossible for a purchaser to discover the presence of these salt areas." Once again, where self-protection is not reasonably practicable, the general "no duty to disclose" rule seems inapposite.

How does this third point fit within the language of § 551(2)(e)? Is there something in the relationship between a developer and a homeowner that makes disclosure reasonably expected? Perhaps if the undisclosed fact affects the normal use and enjoyment of one's home, as the inability to landscape would, disclosure would be expected. Is there something in the customs of the trade that would make disclosure reasonably expected? We would need to know more about what developers typically disclose to builders and homeowners to assess this possibility. What about the "other objective circumstances" category? That seems broad enough to encompass a "self-protection is not practicable" argument, but it has no obvious stopping point. Would anything that seems "fair" fall within the "other objective circumstances" language?

Instead of a silence claim, could one understand *Griffith* as a *Lindberg*-like fraudulent-misrepresentation-through-action claim (often called a "fraudulent concealment" claim)? Just like the motor block cracks were painted over to conceal them, Byers allegedly developed and graded the land so that the saline content could not be discovered. Its action was the conduct-equivalent of saying or writing "this soil is suitable for residential landscaping." Thus, § 550 of the Second Restatement would seem to be directly applicable. The Third Restatement similarly notes in comment c to § 9 that "a misrepresentation need not take the form of a statement" and that "[i]t may arise from conduct rather than words."

Notice that this is a superior basis for the fraud action. When fraud is premised on silence, the plaintiff has an additional hurdle to overcome as part of the prima facie case—the plaintiff must establish a duty to disclose.[29] This can be difficult, especially between arm's length parties, and particularly because of the vagaries of the basic facts exception in § 551(2)(e) and § 13(c). When fraud is premised on an affirmative misrepresentation (words or conduct), however, there is no need to establish a duty to disclose. After all, the plaintiff's claim is not based on silence—it rests instead on an affirmative act of fraud. Not having to establish a duty to disclose makes it easier for the plaintiff to prevail on the claim.

[29] *See* RESTATEMENT (SECOND) OF TORTS § 551 (1977); RESTATEMENT (THIRD) OF TORTS: LIABILITY FOR ECONOMIC HARM § 13 (2020).

Compare *Griffith* to the decision of *Blaine v. J.E. Jones Construction Co.*[30] In *Blaine*, the plaintiffs purchased homes from J.E. Jones Construction Company ("Jones")—the company that developed the subdivision and built their houses. The plaintiffs claimed that Jones failed to disclose its intent to build a nearby apartment complex in the subdivision, and that such failure constituted fraud. The court disagreed:

> For the purpose of our discussion, we have assumed, without deciding, that the Jones Company did intend to build apartments when plaintiffs purchased their homes; therefore, it did have superior knowledge of this fact. Nonetheless, we still find it had no duty to disclose that fact.
>
> First, there is no indication that any party's intelligence was superior to another. Plaintiffs were college educated. Second, the parties did not bear any special relation to each other beyond their status as buyer and seller. There was no evidence that a confidential relationship of any sort developed between the parties or that the parties were in a fiduciary relationship, such as executor and beneficiary of an estate, or attorney and client. The existence of such a relationship makes it more likely that a duty to disclose would be found. However, here the transactions at issue were the normal arm's length sales of homes.
>
> Third, the nature of the fact not disclosed is an extrinsic fact, not an intrinsic defect. In sales contracts, if the vendor conceals an intrinsic defect not discoverable by reasonable care, there is a greater likelihood that a duty to disclose will be found than if the fact is something extrinsic to the property likely to affect market value. The intent to build apartments in the future is not a defect in plaintiffs' houses which is not discoverable by reasonable care; rather, the intent is a fact that normally can be ascertained by reasonable inquiry. . . .
>
> Fourth, the contract is an arm's length sales contract for property, it is not a release or contract of insurance where arguably, all material facts must be disclosed. Fifth, the concealer in this case is a seller. A seller is more likely to have a duty to disclose than a buyer.
>
> The sixth factor is the importance or materiality of the fact not disclosed. Admittedly, a developer's intent to build apartments on nearby property could have an effect on a

30 841 S.W.2d 703 (Mo. Ct. App. 1992).

reasonable buyer's decision to buy a house, and, thus, intent is an important fact. However, the significance of this fact is lessened by its extrinsic nature. The fact may affect the market value of the house, but is not a defect in the house itself. Moreover, the Jones Company's intent to build apartments was a decision about the use of land zoned multi-family which could have changed at any time. The actual layout of the multi-family buildings in fact did change from the time of the original [filing with the county] to the actual constructed buildings. Furthermore, a developer could reasonably expect that a potential buyer would inquire about the zoning of his and nearby undeveloped property, as well as potential uses for the undeveloped property.

. . . .

Finally, the seventh factor is the respective knowledge of the parties of the fact and their means of acquiring this knowledge. There is no question in this case that the existence of multi-family zoning and a proposed layout of the multi-family buildings were a part of the public record. Plaintiffs and potential buyers had access to the information, and indeed plaintiff Ronck did get zoning information from St. Louis County. Admittedly, the multi-family buildings were not designated as any particular type of multi-family building. Such a designation was not required by St. Louis County.

Here, again, however, the public disclosure of zoning for multi-family units puts a reasonable purchaser of a house in close proximity on notice to inquire about the type of multi-family units to be built. Indeed, plaintiffs here testified they made this inquiry.

The fact the Jones Company or its agent allegedly responded with false representations may be the factual basis for fraud based upon false representation. It is not, however, a factual basis for nor relevant to the imposition of a naked duty to disclose on the Jones Company. . . .

It is clear then that the respective knowledge of each party and the means of acquiring . . . this knowledge was not unbalanced or unfair. The zoning information was available and within the reasonable reach of the plaintiffs. It is true that public record of an undisclosed fact may not necessarily negate a party's duty to disclose; however,

> reasonable availability of the fact to the party claiming fraudulent disclosure still remains a factor in the analysis.
>
> Quite simply, the undisclosed fact in this case, the Jones Company's intent, should not trigger a duty to disclose. The undisclosed fact was not an intrinsic defect not discoverable by reasonable care; rather, it was, under plaintiffs' chosen theory, an extrinsic fact which was discoverable by reasonable inquiry.
>
> A developer in the marketplace should not be saddled with the duty to disclose that, as one of the available options under multi-family zoning, he intends to build apartments. The Jones Company, as any other developer, could assume, quite sensibly and rationally, that a buyer would check the public record or ask the developer or its agent to acquire information about the zoning of his and nearby property. It is not unreasonable for an innocent developer with no intent to deceive to believe that the disclosure of multi-family zoning is sufficient notice to a rational buyer of a house near a then undeveloped multi-family zone.

The result in *Blaine* seems consistent with the result in *Griffith*. The *Griffith* court, citing *Jenkins*, emphasized the inability of the plaintiffs to reasonably discover the defect. It is that inability to self-protect that arguably led the court to find a duty to disclose. By contrast, in *Blaine*, the court explained that the plaintiffs could have reasonably discovered the developer's intent by checking the public record to ascertain the multi-family zoning status.

In addition, the defect in *Griffith* was to the subject matter of the contract itself. The contract was for the purchase of a house and accompanying lot, and the lot could not be used in a way that a residential purchaser would typically expect (landscaping). In *Blaine*, the defect was not to the subject matter of the contract itself. The houses purchased were not defective at all; the plaintiffs were simply complaining about the status of nearby developments. As the *Blaine* court concluded, "[t]he undisclosed fact was not an intrinsic defect not discoverable by reasonable care; rather, it was, under plaintiffs' chosen theory, an extrinsic fact which was discoverable by reasonable inquiry."

What about the court's comment that "a developer could reasonably expect that a potential buyer would inquire about the zoning of his and nearby undeveloped property, as well as potential uses for the undeveloped property"? If a plaintiff's ability to ask questions suffices as an ability to reasonably discover a defect, most latent defect cases should be resolved against plaintiffs. After all, a plaintiff can always ask the defendant about the presence of a particular defect, and if the defendant affirmatively answers in a false manner, a fraud claim based on the affirmative misrepresentation can be brought. The problem is that the range of potential property defects is arguably limitless, and it seems unreasonable to require a plaintiff, who is relying on the good faith of the defendant, to ask all the right questions about defects that the plaintiff may not even foresee.

The court's comment is presumably based on the context of the case. The *Blaine* court thinks that it is reasonable to obligate home buyers to inquire about the zoning of their property and nearby land, particularly when the zoning status is a matter of public record. The *Griffith* court implicitly seems to think that it is unreasonable to obligate home buyers to inquire about the "soil fertility" of their property. These conclusions seem reasonable, but not free from debate.[31]

Would the basic facts exception change the result in *Swinton*? When purchasing a home, a termite infestation is a significant defect in the house itself (it damages the structural integrity of the home). Surely that is a basic fact; indeed, the Restatement says as much.[32]

Just because it is a basic fact, of course, does not mean that disclosure is required. As § 551(2)(e) indicates, the seller must know that the buyer is mistaken as to the fact, and there must be something that would lead a buyer to reasonably expect disclosure. As discussed, the strongest case for disclosure under this section involves hidden defects that the buyer cannot discover through a reasonable investigation. Are termites such a defect? At least in Texas, termites are a well-known hazard, and a termite inspection by the buyer is a standard part of any real estate transaction. Are there parts of the country where termite risks are basically nonexistent such that termite inspectors are hard to find (or prohibitively expensive)?[33] If so, perhaps an argument can be made

---

[31] *Cf.* RESTATEMENT (THIRD) OF TORTS: LIABILITY FOR ECONOMIC HARM § 13 cmt. d (2020) ("In Illustration 8 [involving foundation defects in a house that were not discoverable by the use of ordinary care; the buyer had obtained a customary and competent inspection], denying recovery would give future buyers an incentive to invest in more expensive inspections that would rarely be worth the cost. It is more efficient to require the seller to reveal what he knows in the sales contract. In Illustration 11 [involving a driveway that encroached on a neighbor's property, but buyer did not get a survey or inspect public records], by contrast, requiring each side to inform itself of the facts—or even just requiring the buyer to put direct questions to the seller—is not unduly burdensome, and is consistent with the commercial customs that govern real-estate transactions.").

[32] *See* RESTATEMENT (SECOND) OF TORTS § 551 illus. 3 (1977).

[33] *Cf.* Swinton v. Whitinsville Sav. Bank, 42 N.E.2d 808, 809 (Mass. 1942) (stating that "the infestation of buildings by termites has not been common in

that a buyer cannot discover the hazard through a "reasonable" investigation, but if termite inspectors are as plentiful and affordable as they are in Texas, this argument seems like a non-starter. The big point to see is that, although an infestation of termites may be a basic fact, the result in *Swinton* (there is no duty to disclose the infestation) may not change.

Does it make a difference that the buyer would have to retain an expert to discover the termite problem? It would seem to turn on what is considered a "reasonable" investigation. As mentioned, if the expert is prohibitively expensive, or is one that is not typically employed in the type of transaction at issue, then perhaps the use of the expert would fall outside the scope of a reasonable investigation. In such circumstances, the buyer would not be charged with knowledge that the expert could provide.

Keep in mind that there may be a statute or regulation in the jurisdiction that affirmatively requires the seller to disclose if there have been any termite problems.[34] These statutes effectively flip the general "no duty to disclose" rule. If the seller lies and indicates that there have been no termite problems, he has made an affirmative misrepresentation and may be sued for fraud on that basis (rather than on the basis of silence).

As a final note, consider the following with respect to the buyer's nondisclosure:

> . . . . A person may with perfect honesty and propriety use for his own advantage the superior knowledge of property he desires to purchase that has been acquired by skill, energy, vigilance, and other legitimate means, [a]nd in the ordinary business and commercial affairs of the world he is not under any legal obligation to disclose to the person he is trading with the reasons that influenced him to desire the property or his views as to its value, or the sources of information at his disposal. Nor need he disclose the knowledge that he has concerning the circumstances or condition that may depreciate or enhance its value. If any other rule were adopted, it would have a depressing tendency on trade and commerce by removing the incentive to speculation and profit that lies at the foundation of almost every business venture. Every purchaser of land or other property of value buys it because he believes he can make a profit on the investment, or because he needs it in

---

Massachusetts and constitutes a concealed risk against which buyers are off their guard").

[34] *See supra* note 17.

> his business or for some purpose of his own; and he is not required to explain the reasons that induce him to make the purchase, or give to the seller any information concerning the purpose to which he intends to put the property.[35]

As previously discussed, forcing buyers to disclose virtues in the property that are unknown to the seller would remove the incentive to produce new information. Thus, most courts and commentators align with the position taken in this passage—buyers generally have no duty to disclose hidden virtues.[36]

### 2. Scienter

In many ways, scienter is the heart of the fraud cause of action because it gives a false statement its fraudulent character. Broadly understood, scienter can be thought of as an "intent to deceive"—i.e., a false statement must be made with the intent to deceive the plaintiff. In general, that intent to deceive can be demonstrated by proving that the defendant represented a matter as true while (1) knowing that it was false or (2) not knowing that it was true.

The case of *Receivables Purchasing Co. v. Engineering & Professional Services, Inc.*[37] discusses the concept of scienter and its general meaning. EPS was the general contractor on a construction project. RJS was a subcontractor. Receivables bought the rights to certain invoices that RJS sent EPS for work. Before it bought each invoice, Receivables would call EPS's project manager, Richard D. Getts, Jr., to confirm that the work had been completed and that EPS had approved the invoice for payment. EPS eventually refused to pay four of the invoices that Getts represented as approved for payment.

---

[35] Hays v. Meyers, 107 S.W. 287, 288 (Ky. 1908); *see also* DAN B. DOBBS, THE LAW OF TORTS § 481, at 1376 (2000) ("It has been generally thought that buyers are under no duty to disclose material facts to sellers. The leading case on the point held that the buyer was not required to disclose market factors (that peace had been declared) [*see* Laidlaw v. Organ, 15 U.S. (2 Wheat.) 178 (1817)], but some other authority has gone on to say that the buyer need not disclose facts about the very property being purchased either. [*See* Harrell v. Powell, 106 S.E.2d 160 (N.C. 1958).] A fiduciary buyer, like a fiduciary seller, must make full disclosure of material facts.").

[36] It is important to note that misrepresentations, regardless of their form, must be material to be actionable. *See, e.g.*, RESTATEMENT (THIRD) OF TORTS: LIABILITY FOR ECONOMIC HARM § 9 cmt. d (2020) ("Liability for fraud attaches only to misrepresentations that are material."); *see also* RESTATEMENT (SECOND) OF TORTS § 538 (1977) (stating that "[r]eliance upon a fraudulent misrepresentation is not justifiable unless the matter misrepresented is material"). Why does fraud require the misrepresentation to be material? *See, e.g.*, W. PAGE KEETON ET AL., PROSSER AND KEETON ON TORTS § 108, at 753 (5th ed. 1984) ("The most cogent reason for the requirement of materiality is that of promoting stability in commercial transactions. It has been described as 'some assurance that the representee is not merely using the misrepresentation as a pretext for escaping a bargain that he is dissatisfied with on other grounds.' "). For more on materiality, see the discussion of reliance in Section A(4) below.

[37] 510 F.3d 840 (8th Cir. 2008).

Receivables filed suit against EPS claiming that Getts's representations were fraudulent.

The district court granted summary judgment for EPS, concluding that no evidence created a genuine issue of material fact regarding whether Getts knew or should have known that the invoices would not be paid. The Eighth Circuit disagreed with that standard. It concluded that, under Arkansas law, the courts would likely impose fraud liability for knowingly false representations and knowingly ignorant representations, but not for representations that the speaker "should have known" were false (because Arkansas does not recognize a negligent misrepresentation cause of action).

Receivables produced evidence that Getts had a motive to induce Receivables to purchase the invoices—he knew that RJS depended on Receivables' purchases to continue working.[38] Getts admitted that he signed the invoices as "approved" solely for the benefit of RJS so that it could continue to receive financing, and he further stated that he did not consider the distinction between the work being accomplished and the invoice being approved. According to the court, "this evidence gives rise to a reasonable inference that [Getts] was at least unaware of whether his representations that the invoices were, in fact, approved and would be paid were true or false." Finding that genuine issues of material fact existed on the fraud claim, the court reversed the judgment for EPS and remanded for further proceedings.

The *Receivables* court used the terms "knowingly false misrepresentations" and "knowingly ignorant misrepresentations." A knowingly false representation means a statement, represented as true, that the speaker knows is untrue. A knowingly ignorant misrepresentation means a statement, represented as true, that the speaker does not know is true. The two types of representations show the difference between "I know that it is false" and "I do not know that it is true." Either way, when the representation is put forth as truthful, scienter is established.[39]

---

[38] Receivables was engaged in factoring, which involves providing financing to a business by purchasing the accounts receivable of the business at a discounted price. Most likely, RJS needed cash to continue working, and it could not wait for EPS to pay the invoices (perhaps, for example, the invoices were not due for 90 days). Receivables presumably bought the invoices at a discount from RJS, which provided RJS with immediate cash and avoided the need for RJS to wait for payment from EPS. Receivables expected to profit by collecting full payment from EPS on the invoices and earning the difference between the full amount paid by EPS and the discounted amount that Receivables paid RJS for the invoices.

[39] Keep in mind that the unreasonableness of a defendant's belief that a statement is true may be strong circumstantial evidence that the defendant does not actually hold the belief. *See, e.g.*, Stromberger v. 3M Co., 990 F.2d 974, 978 (7th Cir. 1993) ("No doubt some statements are so outlandish that no one in his right mind could

Did Mr. Getts know that his "approved for payment" statements were false? He may have stated that the invoices were approved—while knowing full well that they had not yet been approved—because he wanted to ensure that Receivables continued to finance RJS. But the important point here is that even if Getts did not know that his statements were false, he can still be liable if he did not know that his statements were true. As the *Receivables* court observed: "We therefore believe that the Arkansas Supreme Court would hold that liability for fraud attaches in cases where a defendant lacked knowledge that his or her representation was false but did not know whether it was true or not."

Many courts capture the notion that scienter includes knowingly false representations and knowingly ignorant representations by stating that fraud can be found when the speaker knows that his statement is false or when he makes the statement with "reckless indifference as to its truth." As one commentator observed, "[t]he language of recklessness . . . may be misleading to contemporary Americans who might be led to think of highly irresponsible driving," but the language is "not about some extreme form of negligence, but about a lack of belief in the truth of the representation."[40] In the

---

think them true when he said them, and then intent to defraud could be inferred from the statement itself."); Derry v. Peek, 14 App. Cas. 337, 375–76 (H.L. 1889) ("I can conceive of many cases where the fact that an alleged belief was destitute of all reasonable foundation would suffice of itself to convince the Court that it was not really entertained, and that the representation was a fraudulent one."); *see also* RESTATEMENT (SECOND) OF TORTS § 526 cmt. d (1977) ("The fact that the misrepresentation is one that a man of ordinary care and intelligence in the maker's situation would have recognized as false is not enough to impose liability upon the maker for a fraudulent misrepresentation under the rule stated in this Section, but it is evidence from which his lack of honest belief may be inferred."); DAN B. DOBBS, THE LAW OF TORTS § 471, at 1347 (2000) ("Under the *scienter* test, ordinary negligence, such as the defendant's failure to ascertain facts with reasonable care or his failure to formulate misrepresentations more accurately, is not enough for liability. . . . If the defendant makes a representation that, given his other knowledge, a reasonable person *should* know to be false, the trier may at times be permitted to infer that he *did* know it to be false and hence that he had made a knowingly false statement.").

40 DAN B. DOBBS, THE LAW OF TORTS § 471, at 1346 (2000); *see also* RESTATEMENT (SECOND) OF TORTS § 526 cmt. e (1977) ("In order that a misrepresentation may be fraudulent it is not necessary that the maker know the matter is not as represented. Indeed, it is not necessary that he should even believe this to be so. It is enough that being conscious that he has neither knowledge nor belief in the existence of the matter he chooses to assert it as a fact. Indeed, since knowledge implies a firm conviction, a misrepresentation of a fact so made as to assert that the maker knows it, is fraudulent if he is conscious that he has merely a belief in its existence and recognizes that there is a chance, more or less great, that the fact may not be as it is represented. This is often expressed by saying that fraud is proved if it is shown that a false representation has been made without belief in its truth or recklessly, careless of whether it is true or false."); RESTATEMENT (THIRD) OF TORTS: LIABILITY FOR ECONOMIC HARM § 10 cmt. c (2020) ("It is sometimes said that a statement is fraudulent if its maker believes it to be false or is reckless as to its truth or falsity. This last possibility must be treated with care because 'reckless' has a range of meanings in law. The recklessness sufficient to support a claim of fraud occurs when a speaker acts in conscious disregard of a risk

leading 19th century decision of *Derry v. Peek*[41]—a decision that was highly influential upon American courts—Lord Herschell defined the scienter requirement in a similar manner:

> [F]raud is proved when it is shown that a false representation has been made (1) knowingly, or (2) without belief in its truth, or (3) recklessly, careless whether it be true or false. Although I have treated the second and third as distinct cases, I think the third is but an instance of the second, for one who makes a statement under such circumstances can have no real belief in the truth of what he states. To prevent a false statement being fraudulent, there must, I think, always be an honest belief in its truth. And this probably covers the whole ground, for one who knowingly alleges that which is false, has obviously no such honest belief.

The Restatement's articulation of scienter would also encompass knowingly false representations and knowingly ignorant representations. Section 526 of the Second Restatement states that "[a] misrepresentation is fraudulent if the maker (a) knows or believes that the matter is not as he represents it to be, (b) does not have the confidence in the accuracy of his representation that he states or implies, or (c) knows that he does not have the basis for his representation that he states or implies."[42] Knowingly false representations would clearly satisfy the scienter requirement under § 526(a). If you represent that something is true while knowing that it is not true (or simply believing that it is not true), it falls within the scope of § 526(a).[43]

Knowingly ignorant representations would satisfy § 526(b). If you represent that something is true without knowing whether it is true or not, you have misrepresented your confidence in the accuracy of your representation. You did not say that "you think" this is true, or "you believe" this is true; you simply asserted the matter as factual

---

that a statement is false, as by offering it without qualification while knowing that it may well be untrue. . . . In other legal settings, recklessness may be defined to resemble gross negligence, but a statement reckless in that sense does not subject its maker to liability under this Chapter. However negligent it may be, an utterance is not fraudulent if made in the belief that it is true and that it accurately reflects whatever confidence and basis for belief the speaker may possess.").

[41] 14 App. Cas. 337 (H.L. 1889).

[42] Section 10 of the Third Restatement is nearly identical to § 526 of the Second Restatement. The below analysis, therefore, would also apply under the Third Restatement.

[43] *See* RESTATEMENT (SECOND) OF TORTS § 526 cmt. c (1977) ("If the maker of the representation knows the matter to be otherwise than as represented, the fraudulent character of the misrepresentation is clear. However, knowledge of falsity is not essential; it is enough that he believes the representation to be false.").

without any hedging. Simply put, your representation conveyed certainty when, in reality, you were not certain. That would meet the scienter requirement of § 526(b).[44]

While § 526(b) addresses claims that the speaker has misrepresented his confidence in the accuracy of his statement, § 526(c) addresses claims that the speaker has misrepresented the basis for his statement.[45] Taken together, notice that a single statement may contain several components—(i) a representation about the truth of the matter asserted, (ii) a representation about the speaker's confidence in the accuracy of the statement, and (iii) a representation about the basis for the speaker's statement. The deceptive character of any one of these components can be enough to satisfy the scienter requirement of fraud:

> A statement often includes several components to which the rule of this Section, and the requirement of scienter, might apply: the literal truth of the matter stated (the number of square feet in a house, the financial condition of a company), but also implied claims about the speaker's confidence in the statement and basis for asserting it. These latter points are representations in their own right, even if they are not explicit. They can be true or false, just as the literal substance of the claim can be true or false. Thus a speaker may offer a statement as certain despite having doubts about it, or imply that a claim is

---

[44] *See id.* § 526 cmt. e; DAN B. DOBBS, THE LAW OF TORTS § 471, at 1348 (2000) ("But even if, as a psychological proposition, such a defendant might be in a sense honest about the fact asserted, he has dishonestly represented at least one thing, namely the extent of his knowledge. He can readily avoid liability if he avoids making a statement as one of known fact, for example, by stating his belief or by indicating the limits of his knowledge."); *see also* RESTATEMENT (SECOND) OF TORTS § 538A cmt. b (1977) ("A representation of fact is a positive assertion that the fact is true. It implies that the maker has definite knowledge or information which justifies the positive assertion."); *id.* § 538A cmt. c ("The form of the statement is important and may be controlling. 'I believe that there are ten acres here,' is a different statement, in what it conveys, from 'The area of this land is ten acres.' The one conveys an expression of some doubt while the other leaves no room for it."); *cf. id.* § 538A cmt. d ("The form of the statement is not, however, controlling in all cases. A statement that is in form one of positive assertion of a fact may be made under such circumstances that it must be understood as conveying only an expression of the maker's belief, not free from doubt. This may be true particularly when the recipient knows that the maker has no information concerning the fact asserted and therefore can only be stating his belief. . . . The question is thus not alone one of the language used but of the sense in which it is reasonably understood.").

[45] *See* RESTATEMENT (SECOND) OF TORTS § 526 cmt. f (1977) ("A representation of fact may be expressly stated to be based upon the maker's personal knowledge of the fact in question or even upon his personal investigation of the matter. So, too, though not expressly so stated, the representation may be made in a form or under such circumstances as to imply that this is the case. A misrepresentation so made is fraudulent even though the maker is honestly convinced of its truth from hearsay or other sources that he believes to be reliable.").

founded on personal observation when it is based on hearsay. In such cases, the speaker may think the substance of the claim is true, yet still commit a knowing misrepresentation with respect to the basis for the claim or the confidence it warrants. The speaker then has the necessary state of mind to support liability for fraud if the other elements of the tort are satisfied.[46]

As a final note, a motive to injure or harm is not a required element of the tort of fraud. If scienter is established, the defendant can be liable even if he meant no harm or simply intended to do the plaintiff a favor. The presence of a motive to injure or harm, however, is often relevant to the issue of punitive damages.

### 3. Intent to Induce Reliance

As mentioned, courts generally agree that a fraud action requires the speaker to make the representation with the intent to induce the plaintiff to act or refrain from acting. In general, a plaintiff in a fraud claim can be anyone whose reliance the defendant intended to induce, or anyone whose reliance the defendant had reason to expect.

The decision of *Ernst & Young, L.L.P. v. Pacific Mutual Life Insurance Co.*[47] provides a nice illustration of this "intent to induce reliance" requirement. InterFirst was in financial difficulty and it began to negotiate a merger with RepublicBank. Ernst & Young ("EY") audited RepublicBank's financial statements for the year ending 12/31/86 and gave an unqualified opinion that the statements fairly presented the bank's financial condition. RepublicBank incorporated the audit report into its 1986 annual report for shareholders and its publicly filed Form 10-K.

The merger occurred in June 1987. RepublicBank offered securities as part of the merger, and it issued several prospectuses containing EY's audit report. After reviewing public information related to the merger, including the merger prospectuses, Pacific purchased 1982 InterFirst notes because they were now backed by the merged bank. (Pacific did not buy any securities offered in the prospectuses; it merely relied on the representations in the prospectuses about the financial health of the merged entity in deciding to purchase InterFirst notes.)

The merged entity, First RepublicBank Corporation, ultimately disclosed serious financial problems with its real estate portfolio and

---

[46] RESTATEMENT (THIRD) OF TORTS: LIABILITY FOR ECONOMIC HARM § 10 cmt. b (2020).

[47] 51 S.W.3d 573 (Tex. 2001).

filed for bankruptcy. Pacific sued EY for fraud, asserting that the audit opinion contained misrepresentations about RepublicBank's financial condition as of 12/31/86. EY moved for summary judgment on the ground that it did not intend for Pacific to rely on representations made in the 1986 audit report when Pacific made the decision to buy 1982 InterFirst notes. The trial court granted the motion. The court of appeals reversed and concluded that there were fact issues related to whether EY had "reason to expect" Pacific's reliance under § 531 of the Second Restatement.

The Supreme Court of Texas rejected EY's argument that fraud required privity between the plaintiff and the defendant. Instead, the court determined that the "reason to expect" standard of § 531 was consistent with Texas law. According to the court, the reason to expect standard did not require contractual privity, but it did require a degree of certainty that went beyond mere foreseeability. Pacific submitted affidavits indicating that it is commonly known or expected in the investment community that investors in all securities backed by a merged entity would rely upon information in an audit report, but the court concluded that this evidence was insufficient to satisfy the reason to expect standard. As the court noted: "The generalized industry practice or understanding the [Pacific] affidavits describe is insufficient to show that Ernst & Young possessed information of an especial likelihood that investors like Pacific would rely on Ernst & Young's statements in the merger-related prospectuses in purchasing securities InterFirst had issued years earlier." The court reversed the judgment of the court of appeals and rendered judgment for EY.

Does the Restatement require privity between the plaintiff and the defendant in a fraud action? As the *EY* court explained, privity is a direct relationship between parties, usually established by a contractual relationship. EY agreed to perform auditing services for RepublicBank; thus, EY only had a direct contractual relationship with RepublicBank. There was no direct relationship, contractual or otherwise, between EY and Pacific.

As first mentioned in the *Griffith* discussion, however, § 531 of the Second Restatement does not require privity between the plaintiff and the defendant. Section 531 can be characterized as a "who can be a plaintiff" rule. That section, in part, makes clear that a fraud plaintiff can be any person (or class of persons) who the defendant intends or has reason to expect to act in reliance on the misrepresentation. There is nothing in § 531 requiring privity.[48] Section 533 makes it even clearer that privity is not required. Section

48 Illustration 4 to § 531, for example, concludes that the CPA is liable to C Company—a party the CPA had no contact with whatsoever.

533 is simply an application of § 531, and it generally indicates that a defendant can be liable to a plaintiff who the defendant had no contact with at all, so long as the defendant intended for the statement to reach the plaintiff or it was highly foreseeable that the statement would reach the plaintiff.

Section 531 of the Second Restatement indicates that a defendant can be liable to persons or classes of persons "whom he intends or has reason to expect" to rely upon the misrepresentation.[49] The "intends" part of the clause would seemingly cover liability to persons or classes of persons (1) whose reliance is desired by the defendant, and (2) whose reliance is believed by the defendant to be substantially certain to result, even if not desired.[50] What then does the "reason to expect" part of the clause cover? According to comment d to § 531, one has reason to expect a result "if he has information from which a reasonable man would conclude that the result will follow or would govern his conduct upon the assumption that it will do so." It is not simply a foreseeability inquiry into whether a reasonable man would conclude that reliance *may* occur; it is a narrower inquiry into whether a reasonable man would conclude that reliance *will* occur.[51] This notion is perhaps better understood as "highly foreseeable" or "expected"; indeed, the *EY* court stated that the reason to expect standard "requires a degree of certainty that goes beyond mere foreseeability."

It would seem then that § 531 would cover the following scenarios deriving from information known to the defendant: (1) reliance that *the defendant* desires to induce; (2) reliance that *the defendant* believes with substantial certainty will be induced (even though the defendant does not desire to induce it); (3) reliance that *a reasonable man* would conclude will be induced (even though the defendant neither desires to induce it nor believes with substantial

---

[49] *See also* RESTATEMENT (THIRD) OF TORTS: LIABILITY FOR ECONOMIC HARM § 12 cmt. b (2020) (discussing the same concepts).

[50] *See* RESTATEMENT (SECOND) OF TORTS § 8A & cmt. b (1977) (stating that "[t]he word 'intent' is used throughout the Restatement of this Subject to denote that the actor desires to cause consequences of his act, or that he believes that the consequences are substantially certain to result from it"); *id.* § 531 cmt. c; RESTATEMENT (THIRD) OF TORTS: LIABILITY FOR PHYSICAL AND EMOTIONAL HARM § 1 (2010) stating that "[a] person acts with the intent to produce a consequence if: (a) the person acts with the purpose of producing that consequence; or (b) the person acts knowing that the consequence is substantially certain to result").

[51] *See* RESTATEMENT (SECOND) OF TORTS § 531 cmt. d (1977) ("[I]t is not enough that he recognizes, or as a reasonable man should recognize, the risk that it may be communicated to them and they may act upon it. . . . The maker of the misrepresentation must have information that would lead a reasonable man to conclude that there is an *especial likelihood* that it will reach those persons and will influence their conduct. There must be something in the situation known to the maker that would lead a reasonable man to govern his conduct on the assumption that this *will occur.*" (emphasis added)).

certainty that it will be induced). The first two scenarios focus on what the defendant desires or believes (a subjective inquiry); the third scenario focuses on what a reasonable person would believe (an objective inquiry). Section 531 would not cover reliance that a reasonable man would conclude *may* be induced, as that is effectively a foreseeability inquiry.

Is there an argument that EY intended to induce Pacific's reliance? Intent would require proof that EY desired to induce reliance or believed with substantial certainty that reliance would result. Can it be argued that EY desired to induce the reliance of potential investors because, allegedly, several of its partners had significant outstanding RepublicBank loans, and if RepublicBank got into financial difficulties, those loans would be called? This is clearly a stretch. Even if true, the class of persons intended to be affected would seem to be those who transacted with RepublicBank in a primary offering (because that would provide money directly to RepublicBank). Pacific bought on the market in a secondary transaction.

Was there a class of persons whose reliance was believed by EY to be substantially certain to result? Arguably yes—the class of persons looking to invest in securities backed by RepublicBank. Doesn't an accounting firm like EY believe that potential investors are substantially certain to rely on its audit report? Isn't that what the Pacific affidavits were effectively saying—i.e., EY knows that investors in securities backed by RepublicBank will rely on its report?

Perhaps one could argue that accounting firms know there is a risk of reliance, but they do not know that reliance is "substantially certain." After all, some investors might choose to emphasize factors other than an audit report (e.g., past history of repayment, credit reports, the quality of the company's business model or employees, prospects for the industry, reputation of officers). To know that reliance is "substantially certain," perhaps something more than "what most investors do" is required. With public companies, however, it is hard to believe that any significant number of investors exist who do not at least partially rely on the presence of a clean audit in making a decision.

Of course, the *EY* court's opinion focused on the "reason to expect" language. Why was the "generalized industry practice or understanding" described in the Pacific affidavits insufficient to satisfy that language? According to the court, "[g]eneral industry practice or knowledge may establish a basis for foreseeability to show negligence," but it does not show that EY "possessed information of an especial likelihood" that investors like Pacific would rely on its audit report. The idea seems to be that mere knowledge of what investors typically do and how audit reports are typically used is not enough to establish the "especial likelihood" of reliance required to meet the "reason to expect" standard. The defendant apparently needs some specific information—beyond generalized industry knowledge—and that specific information must lead a reasonable person to conclude that reliance will result. Here, EY had no specific knowledge beyond what anyone in the industry knew; thus, reliance by investors may have been foreseeable, but the risk of reliance was no greater than what it would be for anyone possessing generalized industry knowledge (i.e., the risk of reliance did not rise to the level of being "especially likely").[52]

Keep in mind that § 531 also requires the plaintiff to rely "in the type of transaction" that the defendant intends or has reason to expect to influence. Thus, even if the plaintiff is a person whose reliance the defendant intends or has reason to expect to induce, the defendant will not be liable if the transaction that occurred was substantially different from the transaction contemplated by the defendant.[53]

What factors might cause a transaction to be substantially different from the transaction contemplated by the defendant? A substantial change in the economic risks of the contemplated transaction would presumably count. Comment g to § 531 suggests that a mortgage transaction in the amount of $10,000 is not substantially different from a mortgage transaction in the amount of $20,000 when secured by the same land, but it is substantially different from a bond issue in the amount of $1,000,000 secured by all of the assets of the company. This presumably means that the downside of defaulting on a $10,000 mortgage secured by a parcel of land is similar to the downside of defaulting on a $20,000 mortgage secured by the same parcel of land, but is substantially different than the (far worse) downside of defaulting on a $1,000,000 loan secured

---

[52] *Cf. In re* Enron Corp. Securities, 490 F. Supp. 2d 784, 824–25 (S.D. Tex. 2007) ("Therefore to establish fraudulent intent, Plaintiffs must allege and show more than that information was available in the investment community, pursuant to industry custom, and that it was foreseeable that it would reach them; Plaintiffs must show that Plaintiffs' 'reliance must be 'especially likely' and justifiable, and that the transaction sued upon must be the type the defendant contemplated.' ").

[53] *See* RESTATEMENT (SECOND) OF TORTS § 531 cmt. g (1977) ("This does not mean that the transaction into which the plaintiff enters must be identical with that contemplated by the defendant. It may differ in matters of detail or in extent, unless these differences are so great as to amount to a change in the essential character of the transaction."); *see also* RESTATEMENT (THIRD) OF TORTS: LIABILITY FOR ECONOMIC HARM § 12 cmt. b (2020) ("The same general principles apply to the types of decisions affected by the defendant's statements: liability extends to transactions of the kind the defendant meant to influence by the fraudulent statement, or had reason to believe would be influenced by it.").

by all of the company's assets. A defendant engaging in fraud to influence the $10,000 mortgage transaction, in other words, would still be liable if the $20,000 mortgage transaction actually occurred, but would not be liable if the $1,000,000 bond issue actually occurred. At bottom, "[n]o definite rules can be stated, and the question in each case is whether the transaction that in fact results is sufficiently similar to that which the defendant has reason to expect to hold him responsible for the loss incurred in it."

Does the approach of § 531 seem sensible? Why shouldn't those who make fraudulent misrepresentations be liable to anyone whose reliance is foreseeable? After all, fraud is an intentional tort. As a general matter, "responsibility for harmful consequences should be carried further in the case of one who does an intentionally wrongful act than in the case of one who is merely negligent or is not at fault."[54] One could argue, therefore, that a defendant engaging in fraud should be liable for any reasonably foreseeable reliance, and that the elevated "reason to expect" standard of "especial likelihood"/"highly foreseeable" is out of place.

On the other hand, when it comes to economic loss, a foreseeability standard could result in massive amounts of liability.[55] Conduct that causes physical injury tends to affect a smaller group of persons, while conduct that causes economic injury potentially affects a much larger group of persons. The accounting liability fact pattern in *EY* is illustrative—EY's audit report became part of a public filing, and it is general industry knowledge that such reports are customarily relied upon by large numbers of investors and lenders. Allowing liability for all foreseeable reliance might result in a sharp decline in the number of accounting firms who are willing to provide audit services to public companies. The narrower scope of § 531 seems designed to accommodate such concerns by protecting defendants from the amount of liability that would result from a mere foreseeability rule.[56]

Of course, the defendants protected by § 531 are, by definition, an unsympathetic lot, as they are only liable if they engaged in fraud. One might question affording them protection from catastrophic loss.

---

[54] RESTATEMENT (SECOND) OF TORTS § 435B cmt. a (1977).

[55] *Cf.* Chapter 1 (discussing economic loss and indeterminate liability).

[56] *See* RESTATEMENT (SECOND) OF TORTS § 531 cmt. d (1977) ("When only pecuniary loss results, the magnitude of the extent to which misrepresentations may be circulated and the losses that may result from reliance upon them has induced the courts to limit the liability to the narrower rule stated in this Section."); *cf.* W. PAGE KEETON ET AL., PROSSER AND KEETON ON TORTS § 107, at 743 (5th ed. 1984) ("[T]he class of persons who may conceivably learn of a misstatement and be influenced by it is so enormous that an impossible burden, likely to be out of all proportion to the fault involved, might be cast upon anyone who makes a false assertion.").

Moreover, scienter (and fraud generally) is difficult to prove, so is there really a threat to accounting firms if the law holds them liable for all foreseeable reliance? Liability is imposed only if they acted with scienter, which would seem to be adequate protection from any fear of massive liability.[57]

### 4. Reliance

Justifiable reliance is another element of the fraud cause of action.[58] Why is such a showing required? If a defendant makes a false statement with scienter and with the intent to induce reliance, isn't that conduct that we want to prohibit? Shouldn't that be enough for liability? Although there is some force to this argument, the reliance requirement seems premised on the idea that fraudulent statements causing harm are the central focus of the tort. If the plaintiff did not rely on the misrepresentation in taking some action, it cannot be argued that the statement caused any harm.

According to § 537 of the Second Restatement, a plaintiff can recover pecuniary loss resulting from a fraudulent misrepresentation only if "he relies on the misrepresentation in acting or refraining from action" and if "his reliance is justifiable." Notice, therefore, that there are two components to the reliance requirement: (1) the plaintiff must establish that he in fact relied upon the misrepresentation (subjective reliance), and (2) the plaintiff must establish that his subjective reliance was "justifiable"—i.e., his reliance was, in some sense, reasonable (objective reliance).[59]

---

[57] Note that the Third Restatement argues that the narrower scope of liability is designed to protect parties who speak often in a non-fraudulent manner. The risks of litigation require even truthful parties to "prepare for (and insure against)" such risks, and the narrower scope of liability helps such parties to "measure their potential exposure in advance." *See* RESTATEMENT (THIRD) OF TORTS: LIABILITY FOR ECONOMIC HARM § 12 cmt. b (2020).

[58] Several decisions have concluded that reliance is an element of the fraud cause of action even in a silence case. *See, e.g.*, Mirkin v. Wasserman, 858 P.2d 568, 574 (Cal. 1993) ("[I]t is not logically impossible to prove reliance on an omission. One need only prove that, had the omitted information been disclosed one would have been aware of it and behaved differently."); Schlumberger Tech. Corp. v. Swanson, 959 S.W.2d 171, 181 (Tex. 1997) ("The Swansons assert that the jury's verdict must be sustained because reliance is not an element of a claim for fraud by non-disclosure. We disagree. Reliance is an element of fraud. Fraud by non-disclosure is simply a subcategory of fraud because, where a party has a duty to disclose, the non-disclosure may be as misleading as a positive misrepresentation of facts.").

[59] *See also* RESTATEMENT (SECOND) OF TORTS § 548 (1977) (noting that "[t]he maker of a fraudulent misrepresentation is not liable to one who does not rely upon its truth").

The Third Restatement addresses reliance in § 11. It too requires reliance in fact (subjective reliance) and "justifiable" reliance (objective reliance). It also requires the misrepresentation to cause the loss, which the Second Restatement addresses in § 546.

*Williams v. Rank & Son Buick, Inc.*[60] provides a nice illustration of these points. In March of 1968 in Wisconsin, Williams went to a used car lot to buy a car. He examined a 1964 Chrysler Imperial and was permitted to test drive it for ninety minutes. He purchased the car and alleged that he later discovered that the knobs marked "AIR" were for ventilation and that the car did not have air conditioning. Williams sued for fraud, alleging that he relied on (1) a newspaper advertisement indicating that the car had factory air conditioning, and (2) the representation of a salesman that the car had air conditioning. He testified that he purchased the car mainly because it was a Chrysler Imperial and it was equipped with air conditioning. The trial court found for Williams and awarded him $150 in damages. The circuit court affirmed the judgment, and the used car lot appealed.

On appeal, the court pointed out that the advertisement allegedly relied upon appeared in the newspaper on March 21, 1968, but Williams purchased his car on March 19, 1968. Thus, the court concluded that Williams could not have relied upon the newspaper advertisement in deciding to purchase the car. With respect to the representation of the salesman, the court noted that one cannot justifiably rely upon obviously false statements—statements whose falsity could be detected through ordinary observation. The court mentioned that Williams could easily have discovered the absence of air conditioning because "a mere flip of a knob was all that was necessary." As a result, the court concluded that Williams was not justified in relying upon the salesman's representation. The judgment was reversed.

The dissent believed that "the falsity of the representation was not so obvious that it could be held as a matter of law that the respondent had no right to rely on it." It suggested that Williams' failure to test the air conditioning before purchase was excusable given that the car was purchased in March and not "in the midst of a heat wave." Moreover, because the air conditioning was represented to be factory equipment, "there would be no box-type unit under the dashboard which would be readily apparent upon entering the car."

Did the *Williams* court conclude that Williams lacked subjective reliance, objective reliance, or both? With respect to the advertisement, the court concluded that Williams lacked subjective reliance. He did not rely in fact on the advertisement in deciding to purchase the car because it was published (March 21) after his purchase (March 19).

---

60 170 N.W.2d 807 (Wis. 1969).

With respect to the representation of the salesperson, the court primarily concluded that Williams lacked objective reliance. It was unreasonable, in effect, for Williams not to "flip the [air] knob" during the ninety minutes that he test drove the car, particularly when air conditioning was, by Williams' own testimony, one of the primary reasons for his purchase.[61] The court noted that "[i]f air conditioning was, as stated by the respondent, the main reason he purchased the car, it is doubtful that he would not try the air conditioner." This might also support an argument that the court did not believe that Williams subjectively relied on the representation of the salesman. If air conditioning were that important to Williams, he would have tested it; because he did not test it, it suggests that the air conditioning was not important to him, and that the representation about air conditioning was not one that he actually relied upon in deciding to purchase the car.[62]

If the plaintiff relied in fact on the representation (subjective reliance), why isn't that enough? Why must the plaintiff also prove that his reliance is justifiable (objective reliance)? Consider the following observations:

> .... The principal argument in support of some such requirement as justifiability of reliance would seem to be that of providing some objective corroboration to plaintiff's claim that he did rely. If plaintiff can claim reliance on the basis of the kind of statement on which no reasonable person would rely for one reason or another, then it is quite likely that plaintiff did not rely and if his testimony that he did is allowed as sufficient evidence on the basis of which a finder of fact can find reliance, then it will be too easy for a party to a contract to escape the consequences of his own bad judgment in making a bargain of some kind. Therefore, the foolish nature of the plaintiff's conduct if he did rely is relevant primarily because of the likelihood that he did not rely.[63]

---

[61] As the dissent suggested, however, one wonders what flipping the knob would have done. In March in Wisconsin, presumably cold outside air would have blown into the car that would have felt indistinguishable from air-conditioned air. But perhaps the court meant that the presence of air conditioning would have resulted in some light or indicator turning on when the knob was flipped, and the absence of that indicator would have alerted Williams to a problem? Were such indicators present in a 1964 car?

[62] *Cf.* W. PAGE KEETON ET AL., PROSSER AND KEETON ON TORTS § 108, at 750 (5th ed. 1984) ("In some cases, of course, the unreasonableness of his conduct has been regarded as sufficient evidence that he did not in fact rely upon the representation—he may testify to this reliance, but the court or the jury is not compelled to believe him.").

[63] *Id.* at 749–50; *see also* DAN B. DOBBS, THE LAW OF TORTS § 474, at 1360–61 (2000) ("The justified reliance requirement, then, looks more like an indirect way of assessing two other issues. (1) Did the plaintiff rely in fact? If reliance would be foolish

Is the analysis in *Williams* consistent with §§ 540–541 of the Second Restatement? These are important provisions. Section 540 states that a recipient of a fraudulent statement may justifiably rely upon it "although he might have ascertained the falsity of the representation had he made an investigation." In other words, a fraud plaintiff does not have to make an investigation into the truth of a fraudulent statement, and this applies "not only when an investigation would involve an expenditure of effort and money out of proportion to the magnitude of the transaction, but also when it could be made without any considerable trouble or expense."[64] Thus, when it comes to fraudulent statements, even easy investigations do not have to be made.[65]

Section 541 states that one cannot justifiably rely upon a representation "if he knows that it is false or its falsity is obvious to him." According to comment a, "obvious" is "when the recipient of the misrepresentation is capable of appreciating its falsity at the time by the use of his senses."

These two sections, when read with their comments, can be confusing. Although § 540 makes clear that even easy investigations need not be made, comment a to § 541 states that one cannot recover for a misrepresentation whose falsity would be obvious "if he had a utilized his opportunity to make a *cursory examination or investigation*" (emphasis added). The next sentence suggests that recovery would be denied if "the slightest inspection would have disclosed the defect." How does one reconcile § 540 stating that even easy investigations—ones made "without any considerable trouble or expense"—need not be made, and the comments to § 541 which state that "cursory" or "slight" inspections do need to be made?

---

and unjustified, perhaps the plaintiff did not in fact rely but only claims to have done so to avoid a bad deal. (2) Did the defendant in fact make the representation and if so did he intend to induce reliance? If the plaintiff's reliance would be foolish, perhaps the defendant did not make the representation, and if he did make it, perhaps, since reliance would be so foolish as to be unjustifiable, the defendant did not intend or expect reliance. In the end, the justified reliance requirement seems less like a separate issue and more like evidence about the plaintiff's actual reliance or the defendant's culpability.").

64 RESTATEMENT (SECOND) OF TORTS § 540 cmt. a (1977). Illustration 1 makes this point as well.

65 *See also* DAN B. DOBBS, THE LAW OF TORTS § 475, at 1362 (2000) ("Commerce thrives when parties can conclude transactions without extensive investigation of representations. So the rule makes sense."); *cf.* Judd v. Walker, 114 S.W. 979, 981 (Mo. 1908) ("[G]enerally speaking, until there be written into the law some precept or rule to the effect that the heart of man is as prone to wickedness as is the smoke to go upward, and that every one must deal with his fellow man as if he was a thief and a robber, it ought not to be held that trust cannot be put in a positive assertion of a material fact, known to the speaker and unknown to the hearer, and intended to be relied on.").

The answer lies in a closer reading of the comments. As mentioned, comment a to § 541 indicates that "the rule stated in this Section applies only when the recipient of the misrepresentation is capable of appreciating its falsity at the time by the use of his senses." Thus, anything detectable by the senses would seem to be the "cursory" or "slight" investigation that plaintiffs are required to make to escape the conclusion that the falsity was "obvious."[66] Anything beyond the mere use of the senses, however, would seem to be the type of investigation that would not be required under § 540.

The analysis of the *Williams* court is clearly consistent with § 541. Indeed, the court stated that "one cannot justifiably rely upon obviously false statements." The interesting question is whether the court's analysis is consistent with § 540. Didn't the court effectively require Williams to engage in an investigation? By suggesting that he should have flipped the knob and not simply accepted the salesman's representation, the court arguably makes him do more than simply use his senses. (From his sense of sight, he saw a button that said "AIR," and might that have reasonably convinced him that the salesman was telling the truth?) One wonders if the court's suggestion is really motivated by the fact that Williams just wasn't believable, particularly after he apparently lied about his reliance on the advertisement. The court may simply have concluded that Williams was lying about everything and used the "obvious" rationale to deny him a recovery. The important point is that § 540 indicates that an investigation does not have to be performed—even if a reasonable person would have investigated because it would be simple and worthwhile in light of the magnitude of the transaction.[67]

Despite this discussion, if there are "red flags" that would put a reasonable person on notice of a statement's falsity, a court may reject a claim of justifiable reliance on the ground that it was unreasonable to proceed in the face of such warning signs without an investigation.[68] Are these "red flag" cases inconsistent with § 540?

---

[66] *See also* RESTATEMENT (SECOND) OF TORTS § 540 cmt. a (1977) (suggesting that a "mere cursory glance" would have to be made).

[67] The Third Restatement addresses these principles only in comments. In comment d to § 11, it is stated that "[t]he [justifiable reliance] requirement here does not impose a duty of active investigation on a plaintiff." The comment also states that "plaintiffs who close their eyes to a known or obvious danger that a statement is fraudulent cannot recover losses they suffer from reliance on it."

[68] *See, e.g.*, Schlaifer Nance & Co. v. Estate of Warhol, 119 F.3d 91, 98–99 (2d Cir. 1997) ("Circumstances may be so suspicious as to suggest to a reasonably prudent plaintiff that the defendants' representations may be false, and that the plaintiff cannot reasonably rely on those representations, but rather must 'make additional inquiry to determine their accuracy.' . . . The Estate's actions, the Agreement, and other circumstances should have raised more than one eyebrow, compelling SNC's officers or employees to investigate the extent of the Estate's control over Warhol's works.").

At first glance, the cases seem inconsistent because they suggest that failure to investigate can preclude a finding of justifiable reliance, while § 540 suggests just the opposite. This analysis, however, is too superficial. Section 540 is simply stating a general rule—a failure to investigate, *by itself*, cannot preclude a finding of justifiable reliance. But when there is more to the dispute, such as red flags indicating that the truth of the representation is in question, § 540 is arguably inapplicable. Put differently, § 540 addresses the significance of a failure to investigate by itself, but it does not address the significance of a failure to investigate in conjunction with warning signs. Thus, when courts conclude that reliance is unjustifiable in "red flag" scenarios without further investigation, those conclusions are not inconsistent with § 540.[69]

---

[69] *Cf.* W. PAGE KEETON ET AL., PROSSER AND KEETON ON TORTS § 108, at 752 (5th ed. 1984) ("It is now held that assertions of fact as to the quantity or quality of land or goods sold, the financial status of corporations, and similar matters inducing commercial transactions, may justifiably be relied on without investigation, not only where such investigation would be burdensome or difficult . . . but likewise where the falsity of the representation might be discovered with little effort by means easily at hand. . . . It is only where, under the circumstances, the facts should be apparent to one of his knowledge and intelligence from a cursory glance, or he has discovered something which should serve as a warning that he is being deceived, that he is required to make an investigation of his own."); DAN B. DOBBS, THE LAW OF TORTS § 475, at 1362 (2000) ("At the same time, if the plaintiff wants more detail than has been provided, or is on notice that the representation is doubtful because it is improbable or could not be stated with the precision the plaintiff demands, or because the plaintiff believes the defendant to be dishonest, the trier of fact may be permitted to find that reliance without investigation was not justified, and in some cases, courts may conclude the same as a matter of law.").

That said, some opinions contain broad language about the need for investigation that does seem to undermine § 540. *See, e.g., In re* AHT Corp., 123 Fed. Appx. 17, 18 (2d Cir. 2005) ("[I]n the context of sophisticated business transactions, where one party 'enjoy[s] access to critical information but fail[s] to take advantage of that access, New York courts are particularly disinclined to entertain claims of justifiable reliance.' Affording AHT all reasonable inferences, we agree with the district court that AHT was not entitled to rely on Moses's representations without attempting to contact Elfersy or make independent inquiries regarding his disposition toward the merger."); Nigro v. Lee, 882 N.Y.S.2d 346, 348 (App. Div. 2009) ("Here, all of the deficiencies that plaintiff has alleged could have been easily discovered by routine investigation. Plaintiff could have contacted defendants to inquire about the vehicle or its history (as defendants' advertisement specifically invited prospective purchasers to do), procured a vehicle history report (as recommended on eBay's Web site) or hired a mechanic in Nevada to inspect and/or examine the car before purchasing it. Instead, plaintiff made no attempt to ascertain the true condition or history of the vehicle prior to his purchase. Further, there can be no doubt that plaintiff could have ascertained the true facts with reasonable diligence, inasmuch as a mechanical examination of the vehicle and vehicle history report—steps which plaintiff took only *after* delivery of the vehicle—revealed exactly those conditions of which plaintiff now complains. . . . Thus, having 'unreasonably failed to investigate the truth of the alleged misrepresentation[s]' plaintiff failed to prove that his reliance on those representations was justifiable and, therefore, his causes of action sounding in fraud were properly dismissed.").

*AHT* might be explained on the grounds that AHT knew of a red flag that made its reliance unreasonable. *See AHT*, 123 Fed. Appx. at 18 ("We find AHT's contention that

If a plaintiff does investigate the truth of a fraudulent statement and chooses nevertheless to enter into the transaction, what significance should be given to the investigation? Section 547 of the Second Restatement stands for the basic proposition that if a plaintiff has relied solely on its own investigation and not the defendant's representation, then the plaintiff has not relied in fact on the defendant's statement. If there is no subjective reliance, the plaintiff loses.[70]

The mere fact that an investigation has occurred, however, does not mean that the plaintiff has relied *solely* on its own investigation. Human beings often rely on multiple pieces of information, and reliance on one piece of information does not preclude reliance on another.[71] Thus, § 547 is stating that plaintiff's investigation may be evidence of non-reliance, but it is not conclusive of non-reliance.[72]

---

its reliance was justified to be particularly unavailing where it knew that Elfersy had resigned as a BioShield officer and had reason to suspect he was at odds with the company."). Similarly, although the language of *Nigro* strongly suggests that plaintiff's fraud claim failed because he did not conduct an investigation, perhaps *Nigro* could be explained as a red flag case. Indeed, the setting of the transaction itself (the sale of a used car on eBay) might be viewed as a warning sign that made plaintiff's reliance unreasonable. Other cases, however, seem harder to explain on red flag grounds. *See, e.g.*, Lazard Freres & Co. v. Protective Life Ins. Co., 108 F.3d 1531, 1543 (2d Cir. 1997).

70 *See also* RESTATEMENT (SECOND) OF TORTS § 537(a) (1977).

71 *See, e.g.*, *id.* § 546 illus. 2.

72 *See id.* § 547 cmt. a ("It is not enough to relieve the maker of a fraudulent misrepresentation from liability that the person to whom it is made makes an investigation of its truth. It is only when he relies upon his investigation and *does not rely upon the false statement* that he cannot recover. Whether he does rely upon the one or the other or in substantial part upon both (see § 546), is a question of fact and is for the jury to determine, unless the evidence clearly indicates only one conclusion. . . . Particularly when the investigation produces results that tend to confirm the representation but are still somewhat inconclusive, it may be found that the recipient has relied upon both the investigation and the representation and that the latter has played a substantial part in inducing him to take action." (emphasis added)); *see also* DAN B. DOBBS, THE LAW OF TORTS § 475, at 1361 (2000) ("But the defendant's representation need not be the sole cause of the plaintiff's decision to act, and if the evidence shows that the plaintiff's investigation does not dispel the representation, she can appropriately rely upon both.").

It is worth noting that case law does not always follow this analysis. Some cases seem to suggest that an investigation by the plaintiff means that the plaintiff has relied upon its own investigation and not the defendant's representation. *See, e.g.*, Bartlett v. Schmidt, 33 S.W.3d 35, 38 (Tex. App. 2000) ("Many courts have held that where false and fraudulent representations are made concerning the subject-matter of a contract, but the person to whom they are made, before closing the contract inspects and examines the subject of the contract, or conducts an independent investigation into the matters covered by the representations, which is sufficient to inform him of the truth, and which is not interfered with or rendered nugatory by any act of any other party, it is presumed that he places his reliance on the information acquired by such investigation and on his own judgment based on such facts, and not on the representations made to him, and therefore he cannot have relief because his bargain proves unsatisfactory to him. The common thread of the decisions reaching this conclusion is that, regardless of the result of his investigation, the buyer's decision to undertake such an investigation indicates that he or she is not relying on the seller's

In effect, § 547 confirms that partial reliance does not defeat a plaintiff's fraud claim. But does any partial reliance count? For example, if it could be proven that the plaintiff relied 99% on its own investigation and 1% on the defendant's representation, would that suffice to establish reliance? According to § 546, reliance must simply be a "substantial factor in determining the course of conduct that results in [the] loss." As comment b indicates:

> . . . . It is not . . . necessary that his reliance upon the truth of the fraudulent misrepresentation be the sole or even the predominant or decisive factor in influencing his conduct. It is not even necessary that he would not have acted or refrained from acting as he did unless he had relied on the misrepresentation. It is enough that the representation has played a substantial part, and so has been a substantial factor, in influencing his decision. Thus it is immaterial that he is influenced by other considerations, such as similar misrepresentations from third persons, if he is also substantially influenced by the misrepresentation in question.

Would 1% reliance count as a "substantial factor"? Doubtful, but again, the defendant's representation doesn't have to be the "decisive" factor; it simply has to be, in effect, an important factor.

The Third Restatement has no direct analog to § 547. The matter would simply be handled by the requirement of § 11(a) that the plaintiff rely in fact on the misrepresentation. Section 11(c) on causation covers the same ground as § 546. The language of reliance as a "substantial factor," however, is omitted. As comment a to § 11 observes:

> The plaintiff may have been influenced by several sources, or by multiple statements—some true, some false—made by the same party. Liability is nevertheless intact if the defendant's fraud made a necessary contribution to the plaintiff's loss, typically by inducing the plaintiff to enter a damaging transaction. If the plaintiff was subject to multiple influences, each of which would have been sufficient to cause the resulting loss, the defendant whose fraud was among those influences may be held liable even though it may appear that the fraud was not a "but for" cause of the harm.

representations about the property."); *see also* DAN B. DOBBS, THE LAW OF TORTS § 475, at 1361 (2000) ("Some statements of the plaintiff-investigation rule are much broader, and would bar the plaintiff if she made any investigation at all, even if it appeared to confirm the defendant's fraudulent statements.").

Section 538(1) of the Second Restatement indicates that "[r]eliance upon a fraudulent misrepresentation is not justifiable unless the matter misrepresented is material." Section 538(2) provides that a matter is material if "(a) a reasonable man would attach importance to its existence or nonexistence in determining his choice of action in the transaction in question; or (b) the maker of the representation knows or has reason to know that its recipient regards or is likely to regard the matter as important in determining his choice of action, although a reasonable man would not so regard it." Simply put, a matter is material if a reasonable person would consider it important or if the defendant knows that the plaintiff would consider it important.

Thus, even if a reasonable man would not regard a matter as important, the matter can be material if it is something that the plaintiff considers important and the defendant is aware of it.[73] For example, assume that A knows that B is a devout believer in astrology. In an effort to persuade B to purchase stock in a corporation, A fraudulently tells B that the horoscopes of the officers of the company all indicate that the company will be successful in the next year. That misrepresentation would be considered material.[74]

Most jurisdictions indicate that a plaintiff in a fraud action must establish justifiable reliance. Is there any difference between "justifiable" reliance and "reasonable" reliance? Are there situations where we might say that a plaintiff's reliance is justifiable, but unreasonable? As discussed, the Second Restatement allows a plaintiff to prevail in a fraud action in certain situations even though the plaintiff has acted unreasonably (objectively viewed). For example, a plaintiff may act unreasonably by (1) choosing to forego an investigation into the truth of a statement when a reasonable person would investigate (§ 540), and (2) relying on statements that would be immaterial to the reasonable person (although known by the defendant to be material to the plaintiff) (§ 538(2)). Similar to (2), there may also be times when a defendant makes a representation that the reasonable person would recognize as obviously false, but the plaintiff, due to some deficiency in intelligence or other

---

[73] *See* RESTATEMENT (SECOND) OF TORTS § 538 cmt. f (1977) ("One who practices upon another's known [idiosyncrasies] cannot complain if he is held liable when he is successful in what he is endeavoring to accomplish.").

[74] *See id.* § 538 illus. 1. The Third Restatement makes the same points, although they are again buried in the comments. *See* RESTATEMENT (THIRD) OF TORTS: LIABILITY FOR ECONOMIC HARM § 9 cmt. d (2020) ("A misrepresentation is material if a reasonable person would give significant weight to it in deciding whether to enter into the relevant transaction, or if the defendant knew that the plaintiff would give it such weight (whether reasonably or not). The question, in effect, is whether the defendant knew or should have known that the misrepresentation would matter to the plaintiff.").

characteristic that the defendant knows about, is unable to recognize it as false.[75]

In other words, there are circumstances when a plaintiff's reliance is unreasonable from an objective standpoint, although the Restatement would still characterize the reliance as "justifiable."[76] The most common situations might be described as (1) the plaintiff failing to investigate and (2) the defendant preying on known idiosyncrasies of the plaintiff (which encompasses statements that are immaterial or obviously false to the reasonable man, but not to the plaintiff). With respect to these two situations, justifiable reliance and reasonable reliance are different. Outside of these circumstances, however, justifiable reliance and reasonable reliance would seem to be the same. Conduct that is unreasonable from an objective standpoint would also be unjustifiable.[77]

Contributory negligence is not a defense to fraud.[78] The plaintiff's unreasonable conduct, therefore, cannot be asserted as an affirmative defense. In general, even in comparative negligence states, the plaintiff's negligence does not reduce or preclude recovery in an action for intentional wrongdoing.[79] Keep in mind, however, that the same unreasonable conduct might be used to rebut the justifiable reliance element of the plaintiff's prima facie case. Thus, although the plaintiff's unreasonable conduct cannot be used as an affirmative defense, it may be used to defeat the plaintiff's claim by preventing a finding of justifiable reliance.

---

[75] *See, e.g.*, RESTATEMENT (SECOND) OF TORTS § 545A cmt. b (1977).

[76] *See id.* ("Although the plaintiff's reliance on the misrepresentation must be justifiable . . . this does not mean that his conduct must conform to the standard of the reasonable man. . . . Negligent reliance and action sometimes will not be justifiable, and the recovery will be barred accordingly; but this is not always the case. There will be cases in which a plaintiff may be justified in relying upon the representation, even though his conduct in doing so does not conform to the community standard of knowledge, intelligence, judgment or care.").

[77] The Third Restatement appears to reach similar conclusions. *Cf.* RESTATEMENT (THIRD) OF TORTS: LIABILITY FOR ECONOMIC HARM § 11 cmt. d (2020) ("Justifiable reliance has a personalized character. It is measured by reference to the plaintiff's capabilities and knowledge; a plaintiff's sophistication may affect a court's judgments about what dangers were fairly considered obvious. . . . The [justifiable reliance] requirement here does not impose a duty of active investigation on a plaintiff, however, and does not entitle a defendant to exploit a plaintiff's foolishness with impunity. If the defendant has deliberately preyed on the plaintiff's inattention, that inattention should not be considered an instance of unjustifiable reliance.").

[78] *See* RESTATEMENT (SECOND) OF TORTS § 545A (1977).

[79] *Cf.* RESTATEMENT (THIRD) OF TORTS: LIABILITY FOR ECONOMIC HARM § 11 cmt. d (2020) (noting that "[p]rinciples of comparative negligence do not apply to a claim of fraud").

## 5. Statements of Opinion, Law, and Intention

### *a. Opinion*

Statements of opinion present special difficulties in fraud actions. Section 538A of the Second Restatement states that an opinion is a representation that expresses only "the belief of the maker, without certainty, as to the existence of a fact," or "his judgment as to quality, value, authenticity, or other matters of judgment."[80] Many courts explicitly assert that an action for fraud must be premised on a misrepresentation of fact and not a mere statement of opinion.[81] The rationale for this assertion has been explained as follows: "[Expressions of opinion] are not fraudulent in law, because . . . they do not ordinarily deceive or mislead. Statements which are vague and indefinite in their nature and terms, or are merely loose, conjectural or exaggerated, go for nothing, though they may not be true, for a man is not justified in placing reliance upon them. An indefinite representation ought to put the person to whom it is made on inquiry."[82]

This oft-repeated assertion, however, is misleading. First, it wrongly suggests that a statement of opinion cannot be viewed as a statement of fact. At a minimum, a statement of opinion is a statement of at least one fact—the fact that it is the speaker's opinion.[83] Moreover, an opinion may be interpreted as conveying other implied facts, such as the fact that the speaker has sufficient information to justify his opinion.[84] Second, the assertion is an overstatement, as courts have allowed a misleading statement of opinion to serve as the basis of a fraud action in various circumstances when a plaintiff's reliance has been viewed as justifiable.[85] Thus, as one authority concluded: "It is more correct to say . . . that a statement of opinion is a representation of a fact, but of an immaterial fact, on which the law will not permit the opposing party to rely. When, for any reason, such reliance is regarded as

---

80 *See also id.* § 14 cmt. a ("Statements traditionally classified as opinions include judgments about the quality or value of a thing sold and views about the future likelihood of events.").

81 *See, e.g.*, Saxby v. Southern Land Co., 63 S.E. 423, 424 (Va. 1909) ("It is well settled that a misrepresentation, the falsity of which will afford ground for an action for damages, must be of an existing fact, and not the mere expression of an opinion.").

82 *Id.*

83 *See* RESTATEMENT (SECOND) OF TORTS § 525 cmts. c, d (1977); RESTATEMENT (THIRD) OF TORTS: LIABILITY FOR ECONOMIC HARM § 14 cmt. a (2020).

84 *See* RESTATEMENT (SECOND) OF TORTS § 539 (1977); RESTATEMENT (THIRD) OF TORTS: LIABILITY FOR ECONOMIC HARM § 14 cmt. a (2020).

85 *See* RESTATEMENT (SECOND) OF TORTS §§ 542–543 (1977); RESTATEMENT (THIRD) OF TORTS: LIABILITY FOR ECONOMIC HARM § 14 (2020).

reasonable and permissible, a misstatement of opinion may be a sufficient basis for relief."[86]

Consider the decision of *Hanberry v. Hearst Corporation*.[87] The appellant purchased a pair of shoes at a retail store. While walking on the vinyl floor of her kitchen, she slipped and fell and sustained severe personal injuries. She sued Hearst Corporation for negligent misrepresentation[88] because it published Good Housekeeping magazine. The magazine had given the "Good Housekeeping Consumers' Guaranty Seal" to the brand of shoes that she purchased.

The court concluded that appellant had stated a claim for negligent misrepresentation and reversed a judgment of dismissal. According to the court, a negligent misrepresentation claim was properly pled by allegations that Hearst represented that the shoes were "good ones" without satisfying itself, by testing or otherwise, that the shoes were in fact good ones. Hearst argued that its representation, as a mere statement of opinion, was non-actionable, but the court disagreed. The court noted that Hearst held itself out to the public as a disinterested third party with superior knowledge who had "examined the shoes, found them satisfactory, and [given] its endorsement."

Hearst's statement that the shoes were "good ones" is definitely an opinion. Using the language of the Second Restatement, the "good ones" assertion is Hearst's belief, without certainty, in the existence of the shoes' quality. It could also be expressed as Hearst's judgment

---

86 W. PAGE KEETON ET AL., PROSSER AND KEETON ON TORTS § 109, at 755 (5th ed. 1984); *see also* Vulcan Metals Co. v. Simmons Mfg. Co., 248 F. 853, 856 (2d Cir. 1918) ("An opinion is a fact, and it may be a very relevant fact; the expression of an opinion is the assertion of a belief, and any rule which condones the expression of a consciously false opinion condones a consciously false statement of fact. When the parties are so situated that the buyer may reasonably rely upon the expression of the seller's opinion, it is no excuse to give a false one."); RESTATEMENT (THIRD) OF TORTS: LIABILITY FOR ECONOMIC HARM § 14 cmt. a (2020) ("False statements of pure opinion ordinarily are not actionable. The reason is not that statements of opinion are incapable of being true or false; when a speaker claims to hold an opinion but does not, the claim is as contrary to the truth as any other lie. The reason for the rule, rather, is that reliance on another party's opinion is regarded in most cases as unjustifiable as a matter of law. It is better practice, and more consistent with commercial custom, for parties to rely just on statements of fact made by others and to form their own opinions on the basis of them. That rule is relaxed when there is [an] unusually good reason for the plaintiff to defer to the defendant's judgment . . . but a typical buyer is not entitled to rely on the opinions of a typical seller.").

87 81 Cal. Rptr. 519 (Ct. App. 1969).

88 Although *Hanberry* is a negligent misrepresentation case, the principles discussed regarding the actionable nature of opinions are applicable to the fraud cause of action as well. If anything, *Hanberry* is unusual in that it allowed an opinion to serve as the basis of a negligent misrepresentation claim. There is no doubt that an opinion can be the basis of a fraud claim. *See, e.g.*, RESTATEMENT (SECOND) OF TORTS §§ 525, 539, 542–543 (1977); RESTATEMENT (THIRD) OF TORTS: LIABILITY FOR ECONOMIC HARM § 14 (2020).

as to the shoes' quality.[89] Given that the "good ones" statement is an opinion, why was it actionable? The following observations reflect the heart of the court's rationale as to why the misrepresentation claim was allowed to proceed:

> . . . . Respondent was not the seller or manufacturer of the shoes; it held itself out as a disinterested third party which had examined the shoes, found them satisfactory, and gave its endorsement. By the very procedure and method it used, respondent represented to the public [that] it possessed superior knowledge and special information concerning the product it endorsed. Under such circumstance[s], respondent may be liable for negligent representations of either fact or opinion.

It is helpful to walk through the court's analysis in Second Restatement terms. Under § 539, statements of opinion can be understood to include implied factual assertions. Those implied assertions include that (1) the facts known to the maker (speaker) are not incompatible with the maker's opinion, and (2) the maker knows facts sufficient to justify the maker in forming the opinion. When Hearst represented that the shoes were "good ones" and were worthy of its seal, that opinion also conveyed the implied factual assertion that Hearst had some basis for its opinion—i.e., that it knew facts sufficient to justify it in forming the opinion. If Hearst actually had no basis for its opinion because it failed to test or otherwise examine the shoes, that implied factual assertion would be false. This, of course, is precisely what the appellant alleged.

Notice too that § 539 does not state that an opinion will *always* convey these implied factual assertions. The opinion may be interpreted by a recipient as conveying such implied assertions "if it is reasonable to do so." According to comment b, one such situation suggesting that it is reasonable to do so is "when the maker is understood to have special knowledge of facts unknown to the recipient." This "special knowledge" is what the court found that Hearst represented to the public, as the court stated that Hearst represented that it had "superior knowledge and special information" about the products that it endorsed with the Good Housekeeping seal.[90]

---

89 *See* RESTATEMENT (SECOND) OF TORTS § 538A(a)–(b) (1977).

90 *Cf.* W. PAGE KEETON ET AL., PROSSER AND KEETON ON TORTS § 109, at 761 (5th ed. 1984) ("Notwithstanding the finding of an implied assertion of fact, the true reason for these holdings appears to be that when parties do not purport to be dealing on an equal footing as to available information, the basis for the individualistic approach of the common law is destroyed.").

In addition, § 539(2) states that the recipient's belief as to whether the maker has an adverse interest is important in assessing the reasonableness of the interpretation. The idea seems to be that it is common knowledge that a speaker with an adverse interest is likely going to "exaggerate the advantages of the bargain that they are offering"—i.e., they are going to engage in "puffing."[91] In such situations, the recipient is expected to discount the claims made by the speaker and to recognize that there may be little basis for the opinion. Thus, it is less reasonable (but not impossible) to interpret an opinion as conveying implied factual assertions in the adverse-interest context.[92]

On the other hand, when the speaker does not appear to have an adverse interest (i.e., the speaker appears disinterested), the concern about puffing is not present, as "there is no apparent reason for a disinterested person to exaggerate the facts upon which it may be assumed that his opinion is based."[93] In this context, there is no need to discount the claim and it is more reasonable to interpret the opinion as conveying implied factual assertions. In *Hanberry*, the court pointed out that Hearst held itself out as a disinterested third party when it awarded its seal to a particular product. Thus, although Hearst's statement that the shoes were "good ones" was clearly an opinion, it was an opinion that could be reasonably interpreted as conveying implied factual assertions under § 539—assertions that the plaintiff had alleged were false.

Notice that the § 539 analysis is premised on the propositions that opinions can convey implied facts and that those factual assertions can be the basis of a fraud claim (just like any other factual

---

91 RESTATEMENT (SECOND) OF TORTS § 539 cmt. c (1977). Puffing is discussed further in the text below.

92 *See id.* ("The habit of vendors to exaggerate the advantages of the bargain that they are offering to make is a well recognized fact. An intending purchaser may not be justified in relying upon his vendor's statement of the value, quality or other advantages of a thing that he is intending to sell as carrying with it any assurance that the thing is such as to justify a reasonable man in praising it so highly. However, a purchaser is justified in assuming that even his vendor's opinion has some basis of fact, and therefore in believing that the vendor knows of nothing which makes his opinion fantastic."); *id.* § 539 cmt. a (providing examples of opinions conveying implied factual assertions even when made by speakers with adverse interests); *see also* Briggs v. Carol Cars, Inc., 553 N.E.2d 930, 933 (Mass. 1990) ("A statement that, in form, is one of opinion, in some circumstances may reasonably be interpreted by the recipient to imply that the maker of the statement knows facts that justify the opinion. Restatement (Second) of Torts § 539 (1977). Such circumstances were present in this case in which an uninformed person purchased a used vehicle from a dealer in such items. The defendant's representation that the vehicle was in good condition reasonably implied that it was safe and operable and that the vehicle's oil requirements would be far less than they turned out to be. Therefore, we reject the defendant's argument that its representation concerning the good condition of the Plymouth was not a statement of fact.").

93 RESTATEMENT (SECOND) OF TORTS § 539 cmt. c (1977).

assertion). Section 539, in other words, does not stand for the proposition that opinions, *as opinions*, can be the basis of a fraud claim. *Hanberry* can also be explained as a § 543 dispute, however, and § 543 (along with § 525) makes clear that opinions of apparently disinterested persons can, as mere opinions, be justifiably relied upon and made the basis of a fraud claim.

Why is it justifiable for someone to rely on the opinion of an apparently disinterested person? Simply put, we do not expect parties to have their "guard up" when they are considering the views of someone who appears to have no interest in the outcome of the transaction. As comment a to § 543 states:

> A purchaser who knows all the material facts necessary to an intelligent decision may well be required to be on his guard against attaching too much importance to the laudatory statements of his vendor as to the value or quality of the article which the latter is trying to sell. It is quite a different matter to require him to distrust the opinion of persons whom he believes to be competent and who so far as he knows have no interest in the sale.[94]

In *Hanberry*, the court found that Hearst held itself out as a disinterested third party. In addition, the fact that Hearst/Good Housekeeping held a positive opinion of the shoes was material, as a reasonable man would attach importance to the fact that a purportedly independent organization that evaluates consumer goods had given its "blessing" to a product. Thus, the facts of *Hanberry* fit nicely within the language of § 543 and can be explained on that basis as well.

The analysis under the Third Restatement would be similar. Although the Third Restatement has no direct analog to § 539 of the Second Restatement, the Third Restatement does acknowledge that opinions may convey implied facts that can serve as the basis of a fraud suit.[95] Similarly, although the Third Restatement has no direct analog to § 543 of the Second Restatement, § 14(b) of the Third

---

[94] *See also id.* ("[T]here is no apparent reason for a disinterested person to exaggerate the facts upon which it may be assumed that his opinion is based and of which the recipient knows nothing.").

[95] *See* RESTATEMENT (THIRD) OF TORTS: LIABILITY FOR ECONOMIC HARM § 14 cmt. a (2020) ("A statement of opinion may imply that its maker has knowledge of facts to support it. That factual implication, if known by the speaker to be false, can support liability for fraud under the rule of § 9 without reference to the rules stated here."); *id.* § 9 cmt. c ("Second, a misrepresentation can be implied rather than explicit. A statement of opinion may falsely imply, for example, that its holder knows of no material facts to the contrary; liability then attaches to that false implication, not to the opinion or prediction in itself.").

Restatement would appear to encompass the rationale of § 543. Comment b to § 14 states the following:

> Second, a claim of fraud may be supported by a false statement of opinion when the defendant purports to be an expert or otherwise invites deference by claiming access to knowledge that the plaintiff cannot readily duplicate. Relying on the defendant's opinion in such a case may well be reasonable and more efficient than collecting facts and forming an opinion of one's own. The law protects the plaintiff's right to so rely by imposing liability if the opinion is falsely stated and offered for the purpose of providing the plaintiff with a basis for reliance.

As another illustration of the actionability (or non-actionability) of statements of opinion, consider *Presidio Enterprises, Inc. v. Warner Bros. Distributing Corp.*[96] Warner advertised a film called "The Swarm" to potential exhibitors. Presidio owned and operated five movie theaters in Austin, Texas, and it bid $65,000 for the right to show the film, sight unseen, at two of its theaters. The film was a flop, and Presidio lost money. It asserted that statements made by Warner in promotional materials (e.g., "the most 'want-to-see' movie of the year," "your blockbuster for the summer of '78," the director Irwin Allen's "biggest and best," "one of the greatest adventure-survival movies of all time") were false, and it sued Warner for fraud and negligent misrepresentation. A jury found in favor of Presidio.

The Fifth Circuit reversed and directed the district court to dismiss Presidio's complaint. The court concluded that all of Warner's statements were opinions because they were not capable of being empirically verified. In addition, the court refused to apply a "special knowledge" exception to the general rule of non-actionability for opinions. The court reasoned, in part, that all of the representations were "sale[s]men's 'puffery,' which reasonable people do not take seriously," and that Presidio, given its sophistication, "could not reasonably have relied on Warner's puffery."[97]

What did the court mean by "puffery," also known as "puffing"? The term is used today to refer to sales talk—the common practice of vendors to exaggerate the quality of the items that they are selling. Puffing might be thought of as BS that everyone knows (or should

---

[96] 784 F.2d 674 (5th Cir. 1986).

[97] In its opinion, the court stated that "expressions of opinion are not actionable." As mentioned, this is an overstatement, as there are many cases (including *Hanberry*) permitting misrepresentation actions based on statements of opinion. *See, e.g.*, RESTATEMENT (SECOND) OF TORTS §§ 525, 539, 542–543 (1977); RESTATEMENT (THIRD) OF TORTS: LIABILITY FOR ECONOMIC HARM § 14 (2020). While it is true that, as a general rule, statements of opinion are not actionable, courts frequently state the rule misleadingly as an absolute principle.

know) is BS, and such statements are not actionable. The conventional rationale for the non-actionability of puffing is that no one can justifiably rely on such opinions because everyone recognizes them as exaggerations that are not meant to be accepted as absolute truth.[98] A more sophisticated justification posits that consumers get more information about products because puffing is allowed. Permitting lawsuits based upon sales talk might result in vendors simply ceasing to promote their wares at all, which would drastically reduce the amount of information that enters the marketplace. Of course, given that puffing is notoriously unreliable anyway, one wonders whether there is any benefit to allowing this type of information to enter the marketplace. Perhaps because puffing usually involves a grain of truth, there is still a net benefit to permitting this sort of hyperbole.

Were the statements made by Warner puffing? It can be difficult to distinguish non-actionable puffing from actionable misrepresentations. Some factors that have been mentioned by courts include: (1) the specificity of the statement (more general leans toward puffing); (2) the verifiability of the statement (not verifiable leans toward puffing because how does one prove that the statement is false); (3) the written or oral nature of the statement (oral leans toward puffing). The first two factors are obviously related in that the more general a statement is, the harder it is to prove the statement false. These two factors may simply collapse into asking whether the substance of the assertion has a single, well-accepted meaning (i.e., is there certainty as to what is being asserted). If so, the statement is likely specific and subject to being verified.[99]

---

[98] *See* RESTATEMENT (SECOND) OF TORTS § 542 cmt. e (1977) ("This is true particularly of loose general statements made by sellers in commending their wares, which are commonly known as 'puffing,' or 'sales talk.' It is common knowledge and may always be assumed that any seller will express a favorable opinion concerning what he has to sell; and when he praises it in general terms, without specific content or reference to facts, buyers are expected to and do understand that they are not entitled to rely literally upon the words."); RESTATEMENT (THIRD) OF TORTS: LIABILITY FOR ECONOMIC HARM § 9 cmt. d & illus. 6 (2020) (defining "puffery" as "a seller's broad and predictably exaggerated statements about the quality of an item, as distinct from particular claims of fact," and noting that "a buyer cannot justifiably rely on obvious 'dealer's talk' "); W. PAGE KEETON ET AL., PROSSER AND KEETON ON TORTS § 109, at 757 (5th ed. 1984) ("The 'puffing' rule amounts to a seller's privilege to lie his head off, so long as he says nothing specific, on the theory that no reasonable man would believe him, or that no reasonable man would be influenced by such talk.").

[99] *See, e.g.*, American Italian Pasta Co. v. New World Pasta Co., 371 F.3d 387, 391 (8th Cir. 2004) ("Puffery and statements of fact are mutually exclusive. If a statement is a specific, measurable claim or can be reasonably interpreted as being a factual claim, i.e., one capable of verification, the statement is one of fact. Conversely, if the statement is not specific and measurable, and cannot be reasonably interpreted as providing a benchmark by which the veracity of the statement can be ascertained, the statement constitutes puffery.").

The statements made by Warner were puffing primarily because they were general and incapable of being verified. For example, whether something is "one of the greatest adventure-survival movies of all time" is clearly a matter of taste. A great movie to one person may be a dog to another. How would this statement be proven false? By showing that it flopped at the box office? As the court pointed out, that doesn't necessarily mean that it is a bad movie from an "aesthetic evaluation" standpoint. The descriptions of "blockbuster," "giant spectacular," and "biggest and best to date" suffer from similar problems. The terms do not have precise meanings (biggest in terms of expense? biggest in terms of box office draw? biggest in terms of budget?); as a result, they are not capable of being proven false. Once again, "big" and "spectacular" to one person may be an inconsequential disaster to another.

Even if the statements were not viewed as puffing, Presidio would still be required to prove that it justifiably relied on the statements. As the court observed, there was significant evidence indicating that Presidio did not actually rely (subjectively rely) on these statements. Presidio did not submit a top-dollar bid (and a top-dollar bid would be expected if Presidio relied on the truth of the assertion that this was "one of the greatest adventure-survival movies of all time"), and it hired an expert to give it advice on whether the film was worth spending significant money on (the expert pointed out problems with the film and advised Presidio to be conservative).[100] In short, it did not appear that Presidio relied in fact upon the truth of Warner's claims.

As a general matter, a person's reliance upon the opinion of an adverse party is not viewed by the law as justifiable because a person's guard should be up when dealing with someone who has contrary interests. An adverse party is attempting to look out for its own interests, and someone dealing with an adverse party should have some degree of skepticism about the opinions being offered. The rationale here is basically the opposite of the rationale related to opinions of an apparently disinterested person. Relying on the opinions of an apparently disinterested party is more justifiable because there is no reason to be skeptical of the views of someone who has no interest in the transaction. Conversely, relying on the opinions of an adverse party is less justifiable because one should be skeptical

100 Presidio also had experience with puffing in its industry as indicated by a "bullshit" stamp that it used. *See Presidio*, 784 F.2d at 683 n.21 ("Presidio was apparently so accustomed to dealing with film promoters' hyperbole that it even had a special stamp made up with which it could imprint the word 'bullshit' on the more flagrantly offending documents.").

of the views of someone who does have a personal (and contrary) interest in the transaction.

In general, § 542 of the Second Restatement conveys that reliance upon the opinion of an adverse party is not justifiable, but it also lists circumstances where the opposite conclusion might be reached. In other words, § 542 describes situations where it may be reasonable for the plaintiff's guard to be down, even when transacting with an adverse party, such that reliance on the opinion of the adverse party may be viewed as justifiable. Such situations include when the adverse party is an expert who is providing information that the recipient does not have (§ 542(a)), when the adverse party is a fiduciary (§ 542(b)), or when there is something about the relationship with the adverse party that legitimately causes the recipient to be less wary (§ 542(c), (d)).

Section 542(a) indicates that an opinion of an adverse party can be justifiably relied upon if the speaker "purports to have special knowledge of the matter that the recipient does not have." On its face, this exception seems to apply to any situation where the speaker knows more about the subject matter of the transaction than the recipient. The comments, however, indicate that something beyond greater knowledge is required. Instead, the "special knowledge" exception seems intended to apply to transactions between relative novices and experts who are typically consulted because of their expertise about the subject matter of the transaction.[101] The typical merchant-consumer transaction involving an ordinary commodity does not appear to fall within the scope of § 542(a), as it does not involve this specialized expert situation. Once again, simply having greater knowledge than the other party about the subject matter of the transaction is not enough; instead, "special" knowledge or expertise is required.

Moreover, even when dealing with an expert who does have special experience and training, no opinion can be relied upon if it is

---

[101] *See, e.g.*, RESTATEMENT (SECOND) OF TORTS § 542 cmt. f (1977) ("The complexities and specializations of modern commercial and financial life have created many situations in which *special experience and training* are necessary to the formation of a valuable judgment. In this case if the one party has special experience or training or purports to have them, the other, *if without them*, is entitled to rely upon the honesty of the former's opinion and to attach to it the importance that is warranted by his superior competence." (emphasis added)); *see also id.* § 542 cmt. d ("The fact that one of the two parties to a bargain is less astute than the other does not justify him in relying upon the judgment of the other. This is true even though the transaction in question is one in which the one party knows that the other is somewhat more conversant with the value and quality of the things about which they are bargaining. Thus the purchaser of an ordinary commodity is not justified in relying upon the vendor's opinion of its quality or worth.").

simply puffing.[102] As the *Presidio* court noted, "[t]he 'special knowledge' exception applies typically to the opinions of specialized experts—such as jewelers, lawyers, physicians, scientists, and dealers in antiques—where their opinions are based on concrete, specific information and objective, verifiable facts."

Presidio was unable to take advantage of the special knowledge exception because the court concluded that all of Warner's statements were puffing. In addition, the court appeared to blend two other rationales. First, Presidio was not the type of novice, and Warner was not the type of expert, that § 542(a) seems intended to cover. Indeed, Presidio had experienced executives who were used to receiving promotional materials from studios about films. The mere fact that Warner may have known more about the quality of its film does not make the dispute the type of novice-expert situation that appears to be addressed by § 542(a) and the associated comments.

Second, and as previously mentioned, the court seemed to believe that Presidio did not rely in fact upon Warner's representations (Presidio did not make a high-dollar bid, it hired its own expert, and it was used to dealing with studio hyperbole). In other words, even though § 542(a) states that reliance upon an opinion of an adverse party with special knowledge can be justifiable, that language does not satisfy the requirement that the plaintiff must rely in fact upon the opinion.[103]

Section 542(b) indicates that reliance on the opinion of an adverse party may be justifiable if the adverse party "stands in a fiduciary or other similar relation of trust and confidence to the recipient." As discussed in Chapter 4, a true fiduciary relationship requires the fiduciary to put the beneficiary's interests ahead of its own. When dealing with someone who is legally required to put the recipient's interests first, it is understandable that the recipient will have its guard down and will be less wary. Put differently, it is perfectly reasonable to rely on the opinion of one who has a legal duty to look out for your interests and to treat you fairly—even if the fiduciary is on the other side of a transaction with you.[104]

---

102 *See id.* § 542 cmt. f ("The ordinary purchaser of jewelry cannot be expected to know the quality or value of the gems shown to him by a jeweler. He must rely and is therefore justified in relying upon the jeweler's statement that a diamond is of the first water; and, *after making allowance for the natural tendency of a vendor to praise his wares*, he is justified in relying upon the jeweler's statement of the value of the diamond." (emphasis added)); *see also Presidio*, 784 F.2d at 682 ("These comments [to the Restatement] indicate that the 'special knowledge' exception is inapplicable where the opinion relied on is clearly salesmen's puffery.").

103 *See* RESTATEMENT (SECOND) OF TORTS § 537(a).

104 *Cf.* RESTATEMENT (THIRD) OF TORTS: LIABILITY FOR ECONOMIC HARM § 14(a) & cmt. b (2020) ("False statements of opinion can support a claim for fraud in two general circumstances. The first arises when parties have a fiduciary or confidential

Section 542 also indicates that reliance on the opinion of an adverse party may be justifiable if the adverse party "has successfully endeavored to secure the confidence of the recipient" (§ 542(c)) or the adverse party "has some other special reason to expect that the recipient will rely on his opinion" (§ 542(d)). Comments h and i provide examples of situations that implicate these provisions. The theme of both subsections appears to be that if you take advantage of something in the recipient's character or background that you know will relax the recipient's guard, you will be responsible for the reliance that you have induced. (It sounds much like the materiality analysis of § 538(2)(b).) It is understandable that your guard was down when dealing with this adverse party because the party knowingly took advantage of something in your background that would result in you being less wary.[105]

The Third Restatement appears to collapse § 542(a), (c), and (d) into one subsection. Section 14(b) states that a false statement of opinion can result in liability if "the defendant claims to have expertise or other knowledge not accessible to the plaintiff and offers the opinion to provide the plaintiff with a basis for reliance." That general language seems broad enough to encompass the defendant inducing reliance through special knowledge, abuse of confidence, or taking advantage of known plaintiff characteristics.[106] Section 14(a) is substantially the same as § 542(b) in its coverage of fiduciary and

---

relationship. A fiduciary has a legal obligation to act for the benefit of another. The obligation arises automatically from certain formally recognized relationships, such as attorney and client or trustee and beneficiary. A confidential relationship produces similar obligations but is less formal. It arises from circumstances in which the parties are not on equal footing; one has influence over the other, and the stronger party is trusted to act for the benefit of the weaker. In a relationship of either type, it may be appropriate for the dependent party to rely on the opinions of the other.").

[105] *See, e.g.*, RESTATEMENT (SECOND) OF TORTS § 542 cmt. h (1977) ("The situation to which the rule stated in this Clause [§ 542(c)] is usually applicable occurs when the maker gains the other's confidence by stressing their common membership in a religious denomination, fraternal order or social group or the fact that they were born in the same locality."); *id.* § 542 cmt. i ("The chief application of this Clause [§ 542(d)] is to cases in which the maker of the representation knows of some special characteristic of the recipient, such as his lack of intelligence, illiteracy or unusual credulity and gullibility, which gives the maker special reason to expect that the opinion will be relied on. One who deliberately practices upon such a special characteristic, and takes advantage of it, cannot be heard to say that the reliance he sought to induce was not justified because his statement was one of opinion and therefore should have been distrusted.").

[106] *Cf.* RESTATEMENT (THIRD) OF TORTS: LIABILITY FOR ECONOMIC HARM § 14 cmt. b (2020) ("Second, a claim of fraud may be supported by a false statement of opinion when the defendant purports to be an expert or otherwise invites deference by claiming access to knowledge that the plaintiff cannot readily duplicate. Relying on the defendant's opinion in such a case may well be reasonable and more efficient than collecting facts and forming an opinion of one's own. The law protects the plaintiff's right to so rely by imposing liability if the opinion is falsely stated and offered for the purpose of providing the plaintiff with a basis for reliance.").

confidential relationships. In short, the coverage of § 14 of the Third Restatement does not seem materially different from the coverage of § 542 (and § 543) of the Second Restatement.

In *Hanberry*, Hearst opined that the shoes were "good ones." The statement was actionable. In *Presidio*, Warner opined (not precisely, but in effect) that the film was a "great one." The statement was not actionable. Are these results consistent? The key difference appears to be the status of the party that made the representation. In *Hanberry*, the opinion was given by an apparently disinterested party—a situation where the recipient's guard would be understandably down and where reliance on the statement would correspondingly be seen as more reasonable.[107] There are no concerns about puffing in this situation "since there is no apparent reason for a disinterested person to exaggerate the facts upon which it may be assumed that his opinion is based."[108] (In other words, a puffing analysis is applicable only when dealing with opinions of adverse parties.) Thus, it is understandable that such an opinion would be relied upon (§ 543), and it is more reasonable to interpret the opinion as conveying implied factual assertions (§ 539(2)). Moreover, the court found that Hearst held itself out as possessing specialized knowledge.[109]

In *Presidio*, the opinion was given by an adverse party (i.e., Presidio was the buyer and Warner was the seller). In such a situation, we do not expect the recipient's guard to be down, and the recipient is required to discount much of what the speaker says as routine sales talk or puffing. Thus, it is not understandable that such an opinion would be relied upon, and it is less reasonable to interpret the opinion as conveying implied factual assertions. In addition, the court did not find that Warner possessed specialized knowledge that would justify Presidio's reliance.

As a final note, courts often state that a fraud claim must be predicated on a statement of existing fact and not on a prediction about the future.[110] This statement is simply a variant of the often repeated (and misleading) assertion that an action for fraud must be premised on a misrepresentation of fact and not on a mere statement of opinion. After all, a prediction is merely a type of opinion—an opinion as to what will happen in the future. Thus, the rules that

107 *See* RESTATEMENT (SECOND) OF TORTS § 543 (1977).

108 *See id.* § 539 cmt. c.

109 *See id.* §§ 539 cmt. b, 542(a); *see also* RESTATEMENT (THIRD) OF TORTS: LIABILITY FOR ECONOMIC HARM § 14(b) (2020).

110 *See, e.g.*, McElrath v. Electric Inv. Co., 131 N.W. 380, 381 (Minn. 1911) ("[A]s a general rule . . . false representations, upon which fraud may be predicated, must be of existing facts, and cannot consist of mere promises or conjectures as to future acts or events.").

govern when opinions can serve as the basis of a fraud claim are applicable to predictions as well.

### b. *Law*

The traditional common-law view was that misrepresentations of law could not form the basis of a fraud claim. Thus, statements such as "this lot is zoned for commercial use" or "this house was built in compliance with local building codes" were not actionable. The justification for this view has been explained as follows:

> Statements of law likewise are commonly said to be mere assertions of opinion, which are insufficient as a basis for deceit. . . . In explanation, two reasons have been repeated, sometimes in the same decision: first, that every man is presumed to know the law, and hence the plaintiff cannot be heard to say that he reasonably believed the statement made to him; and second, that no man, at least without special training, can be expected to know the law, and so the plaintiff must have understood that the defendant was giving him nothing more than an opinion. The contradiction is sufficiently obvious. . . . The general rule seems to have arisen rather out of a deliberate policy requiring the parties to a bargain to deal at arm's length with respect to the law, and not to rely upon one another.[111]

The decision of *Nagashima v. Busck*[112] provides an illustration of the traditional view while also mentioning the more modern view represented by the Restatement. The plaintiff bought a multi-family apartment building with three units from the defendant. The defendant allegedly orally represented that the property complied with all municipal ordinances. Unfortunately, this representation was not true, as the building was zoned for a duplex and not a triplex. The buyer was required to modify the structure to comply with the applicable zoning laws, and he sued the defendant for his modification expenses and the resulting diminution in the value of the building. The trial court dismissed his fraud action on the basis that Florida precedent prevented misrepresentations of law from serving as the predicate for a fraud claim.

On appeal, the court reversed. The court cited the more modern view of § 545 of the Second Restatement but concluded that it was bound by the earlier Florida authorities. Nevertheless, the court found "nothing in [those authorities] to suggest that the supreme court intended an unscrupulous seller to profit from the fact that his

---

[111] W. PAGE KEETON ET AL., PROSSER AND KEETON ON TORTS § 109, at 758–59 (5th ed. 1984).

[112] 541 So. 2d 783 (Fla. Dist. Ct. App. 1989).

factual material misrepresentations were placed under an umbrella of protection by his material misrepresentations as to the law." The court held that defendant's misrepresentations "were primarily those of fact and as such, the . . . complaint properly stated a cause of action for fraud."

The alleged misrepresentation in *Nagashima* was that the building complied with all municipal ordinances—specifically, it was properly zoned for the three-unit building occupying the property. Under the traditional common-law view, that misrepresentation could not be the basis of a fraud claim because zoning representations were characterized as matters of law. The *Nagashima* court purported to decide the case under the traditional common-law view; nevertheless, the court found room to conclude that factual misrepresentations of matters of law were actionable. This conclusion suggests that the Florida precedents cited by the court did not strictly adhere to the traditional view or, more likely, that the *Nagashima* court was simply paying lip service to those precedents while effectively overruling them in favor of the more modern Restatement view.

Under § 545 of the Second Restatement, misrepresentations as to matters of law can be misrepresentations of fact (e.g., the statute has been repealed) or misrepresentations of opinion (e.g., the plaintiff should prevail based on the applicable precedents). If it is a misrepresentation of fact, it is governed by the normal rules covering misstatements of fact; if it is a misrepresentation of opinion, it is governed by the normal rules covering misstatements of opinion.[113]

When the defendant states, without hedging, that the property complies with municipal ordinances, that would appear to be a factual misrepresentation (indeed, the *Nagashima* court concluded

---

113 *See also* W. PAGE KEETON ET AL., PROSSER AND KEETON ON TORTS § 109, at 759–60 (5th ed. 1984):

> The present tendency is strongly in favor of eliminating the distinction between law and fact as "useless duffle of an older and more arbitrary day," and recognizing that a statement as to the law, like a statement as to anything else, may be intended and understood either as one of fact or one of opinion only, according to the circumstances of the case. Most courts still render lip service to the older rule, but they have been inclined whenever possible to find statements of fact "implied" in representations as to the law. Thus, an assertion that a company has the legal right to do business in a state carries an assurance that it has, as a matter of fact, been duly qualified; a representation that certain lands may be obtained by patent free from mineral reservations amounts to saying that the government does not classify them as mineral lands; and statements as to the title of land, the priority of a particular lien, or the validity of a note, as well as many similar legal conclusions, have been held to convey similar implications of fact. Since it is obvious that representations of law almost never are made in such a vacuum that supporting facts are not to be "implied," it would seem that very little can be left of the "general rule" in the face of a series of such decisions.

that the misrepresentations "were primarily those of fact"). It is something that one could reasonably expect to be known by the prior owner of a rental property. If the defendant was not sure, he could have stated "I think" or "I believe," or simply said nothing at all. As a factual misrepresentation, the statement is actionable under § 545(1).[114]

If the representation was viewed as an opinion, it may still be actionable. It would be an opinion of an adverse party, and none of the "exceptions" in § 542(a) would appear to be relevant. (As mentioned, the "special knowledge" exception seems intended to apply to transactions between relative novices and experts who are typically consulted because of their expertise about the subject matter of the transaction. This is simply a real estate sale between a seller and a buyer.) Perhaps § 539 could be used to argue that the opinion conveyed the implied fact that the defendant had a basis for his view or knew of nothing incompatible with his view. Such an interpretation may be unreasonable, however, as the defendant was an adverse party who did not seem to have special knowledge of facts.[115] On the other hand, the fact pattern is similar to illustration 1 of § 539. Just as the seller of the machinery stated that a room was suitable for manufacture, so too did the defendant effectively represent that the building was suitable for a triplex. The important point is that the traditional common-law view prohibited all statements of law from serving as the basis of a fraud claim. The Restatement, however, treats a statement of law like any other statement; consequently, it allows for the possibility of a fraud claim.

The Third Restatement does not contain a stand-alone section on misrepresentations of law. In comment c to § 14, however, the same idea is expressed—i.e., in certain situations, misrepresentations of law can be viewed as actionable misrepresentations of fact or actionable misrepresentations of opinion:

> .... It is sometimes said that assertions of law are matters of opinion that cannot serve as the basis for a claim of fraud. While that is often true, false legal claims sometimes have implications that are actionable or may be the subject of justifiable reliance by another party. They are best handled according to the logic of this Section: they subject their makers to liability if they imply untrue facts, or if the parties have a relationship that makes it reasonable for the plaintiff to rely on the defendant's

[114] Can a person rely on a factual misrepresentation made by an adverse party? Of course. *See* RESTATEMENT (SECOND) OF TORTS § 541A (1977).

[115] *See id.* § 539(2) & cmt. b.

opinions. They are not actionable if they amount to judgments based on facts available to both sides and on which the plaintiff can reasonably be expected to arrive at an independent view.

A statement of law can imply facts of various kinds. It may imply the existence of ordinary and nonlegal facts that justify the speaker's conclusions. Thus an assertion that one mortgage has priority over another may imply that one was made or at least recorded before the other; and a claim that a corporation has the right to do business in a state may imply that it has taken all steps necessary to be duly qualified. A statement of law also may imply the existence of legal facts: that a regulation has been passed or repealed, or that a piece of property was zoned for commercial use or not. A defendant who knowingly misleads the plaintiff with respect to any of these sorts of facts may be held liable for fraud if the other elements stated in § 9 are satisfied. . . .

On the other hand, no liability arises when one adversary in a negotiation offers another a view about the best interpretation of legal language—for example, the wording of a contract or a statute—that is equally visible to both. The defendant's statement then is a true matter of opinion, and a claim of fraud founded on it fails as a matter of law unless the rules of this Section are satisfied. They are satisfied when an attorney falsely states an opinion to a client, because an attorney and client have a fiduciary relationship. And if a party claims to have special expertise and invites reliance by the plaintiff, a plaintiff again may recover if falsely stated opinions of law follow and the other elements of liability for fraud are satisfied.

### c. *Intention*

Section 530 of the Second Restatement states that "[a] representation of the maker's own intention to do or not to do a particular thing is fraudulent if he does not have that intention."[116] An illustration of this proposition is provided by *Spoljaric v. Percival*

---

[116] *See also id.* § 530 cmt. a (1977) ("The state of a man's mind is as much a fact as the state of his digestion."); *id.* § 544 (noting that "the recipient of a fraudulent misrepresentation of intention is justified in relying upon it if the existence of the intention is material and the recipient has reason to believe that it will be carried out"); RESTATEMENT (THIRD) OF TORTS: LIABILITY FOR ECONOMIC HARM § 15 (2020) ("A statement of a speaker's intention to perform a promise may result in liability only if the intention does not exist at the time the statement is made."); *id.* § 15 cmt. a ("A false statement of the intent to do something, or not to do something, is actionable like any other misrepresentation if the elements of §§ 9–12 are satisfied.").

*Tours, Inc.*[117] Ralph Spoljaric was an executive employee of Percival. At the conclusion of his written two-year employment contract, Spoljaric initiated talks with Jessie Upchurch, president of Percival, for a new employment contract. Upchurch eventually offered Spoljaric a salary of $70,000 without a written contract. Faced with the potential departure of Spoljaric and another executive (Balestrieri), Upchurch also promised to implement a bonus plan. He instructed Spoljaric to formalize a plan in writing.

Spoljaric drafted a bonus plan and gave it to Upchurch for approval. Over an eight-month period, Spoljaric inquired about the plan repeatedly, and Upchurch responded that his New York lawyers were reviewing it. At some point, Upchurch was again shown the draft of the original bonus plan, and he responded that he had no intention of signing it.

Spoljaric sued Upchurch and Percival for breach of oral contract and fraud. The jury found for Spoljaric. More specifically, it found that Upchurch promised Spoljaric that a bonus plan would be implemented and that Upchurch had no intention of keeping the promise at the time that it was made. The court of appeals reversed and rendered, holding that there was no evidence to support the jury's finding that Upchurch did not intend to implement a bonus plan.

On appeal, the Supreme Court of Texas noted that "[a] promise to do an act in the future is actionable fraud when made with the intention, design and purpose of deceiving, and with no intention of performing the act." The court further noted that "a party's intent is determined at the time the party made the representation," and that such intent could be inferred from circumstantial evidence. The court found sufficient evidence to support the jury's findings, including the following: (1) eight months passed from the time Spoljaric gave a draft of the plan to Upchurch, and no plan was implemented; (2) Upchurch's secretary testified that Upchurch had approved an amended bonus plan shortly after receiving Spoljaric's proposed plan, but Upchurch said nothing about this when repeatedly asked about the status of the plan; (3) Upchurch insisted on an oral employment contract for Spoljaric, but demanded a written bonus plan; and (4) when Upchurch was shown the original proposed bonus plan many months later, he stated that he had no intention of signing it, and he said nothing about the amended bonus plan that he allegedly approved months earlier. As the court concluded, "[c]onsidering all of the circumstantial evidence of Upchurch's lack of intent in conjunction with Upchurch's failure to keep his promise, we hold that

117 708 S.W.2d 432 (Tex. 1986).

a fact issue of Upchurch's intent was raised sufficient to submit the issue to the jury and that there is some evidence to support the jury's answer." The court reversed the judgment of the court of appeals.

The rule of *Spoljaric* and § 530 is often implicated when parties have entered into a contract with one another. As the Second Restatement explains:

> The rule stated in this Section finds common application when the maker misrepresents his intention to perform an agreement made with the recipient. The intention to perform the agreement may be expressed but it is normally merely to be implied from the making of the agreement. Since a promise necessarily carries with it the implied assertion of an intention to perform[,] it follows that a promise made without such an intention is fraudulent. . . .[118]

Assume that a defendant enters into a contract with a plaintiff and then subsequently breaches by failing to perform. Under the rule of *Spoljaric* and § 530, are these facts alone sufficient to establish fraud? When a person enters into a contract, he implicitly (if not explicitly) represents that his intention is to perform his end of the bargain. If the person knows, at the time he enters into the contract, that he is not going to perform, then he has misrepresented his intention. That misrepresentation of intention is a factual misstatement that is actionable like any other.

The key to establishing fraud in this scenario is demonstrating scienter—i.e., demonstrating that the person knew that he was not going to perform at the time that he represented his intention to perform. As a consequence, proof of an intention not to perform is necessary *at the time the person entered into the contract*, as that is the time when an intention to perform is represented.

For this reason, a mere breach of contract is insufficient to establish fraud. A breach of contract often results because a person who did have an intention to perform at the time of entering into a contract decides, after the time of contracting, that performance cannot occur for some reason (e.g., change of heart, supply interruption, or economic changes). Such a scenario is not fraudulent

---

118 RESTATEMENT (SECOND) OF TORTS § 530 cmt. c (1977); *see also* RESTATEMENT (THIRD) OF TORTS: LIABILITY FOR ECONOMIC HARM § 15 cmt. b (2020) ("A contract itself ordinarily will suffice as a representation of the defendant's intent to perform; a party who signs a contract presumptively represents, at least by implication, an intent to do what the contract requires."); *id.* ("But that description may not apply to every case. Both parties to a contract might understand that a breach of it is likely if various contingencies arise; the purpose of the agreement may just be to make clear who pays for the resulting loss in that event. There is no liability for fraud if those facts are shown. Liability arises only when the promisor misleads the promisee.").

because, at the time of the representation, the person was telling the truth (i.e., it is my intention to perform). As the court in *Spoljaric* noted: "Failure to perform, standing alone, is no evidence of the promisor's intent not to perform when the promise was made. However, that fact is a circumstance to be considered with other facts to establish intent."[119] In theory, a person deciding to breach one second after entering into a contract is not making a misrepresentation so long as the person did have the intention to perform at the time the agreement was entered into.[120]

What evidence might suggest that a defendant did not intend to keep a promise at the time of making it? Consider the following observations:

> A plaintiff typically must use circumstantial evidence to prove that the defendant did not intend to keep a promise at the time it was made. No such inference can be drawn from a mere failure to perform the promise later. A plaintiff's case may be helped, however, by evidence of plans the defendant had at the time of the promise that were inconsistent with it; or by evidence that the promise was impossible to keep for reasons that the defendant knew (and that the plaintiff did not); or by evidence that the defendant made and broke other promises routinely, and so must have expected to break this one as well. Other facts may tend to support the innocence of the defendant's intentions: evidence that the defendant partially performed the promise, for example, or that changed circumstances make the defendant's promise costlier to honor than had originally appeared.[121]

---

[119] *See also* RESTATEMENT (SECOND) OF TORTS § 530 cmt. d (1977) ("The intention that is necessary to make the rule stated in this Section applicable is the intention of the promisor when the agreement was entered into. The intention of the promisor not to perform an enforceable or unenforceable agreement cannot be established solely by proof of its nonperformance, nor does his failure to perform the agreement throw upon him the burden of showing that his nonperformance was due to reasons which operated after the agreement was entered into."); RESTATEMENT (THIRD) OF TORTS: LIABILITY FOR ECONOMIC HARM § 15 cmt. b (2020) ("A plaintiff typically must use circumstantial evidence to prove that the defendant did not intend to keep a promise at the time it was made. No such inference can be drawn from a mere failure to perform the promise later.").

[120] *Cf.* W. PAGE KEETON ET AL., PROSSER AND KEETON ON TORTS § 109, at 764 (5th ed. 1984) ("When a promise is made in good faith, with the expectation of carrying it out, the fact that it is subsequently broken gives rise to no cause of action, either for deceit, or for equitable relief. Otherwise any breach of contract would call for such a remedy.").

[121] RESTATEMENT (THIRD) OF TORTS: LIABILITY FOR ECONOMIC HARM § 15 cmt. b (2020); *see also* W. PAGE KEETON ET AL., PROSSER AND KEETON ON TORTS § 109, at 764–65 (5th ed. 1984) ("The mere breach of a promise is never enough in itself to establish the fraudulent intent. It may, however, be inferred from the circumstances, such as

In *Spoljaric*, Upchurch failed to keep his promise to implement a bonus plan. Why was this fraudulent? What evidence suggested that this was more than a simple breach of contract claim—i.e., more than a promise made by a defendant, but not ultimately kept? Upchurch's failure to keep his promise to implement a bonus plan was fraudulent because the promise represented his intention to implement such a plan, but the jury believed that he actually had no such intention at the time of making the promise. Put differently, Upchurch orally agreed to enter into a bonus plan, but the jury found that he had no such intention at the time of the agreement.

The *Spoljaric* court did not do the best job of explaining the inferences that it made. At bottom, there was evidence suggesting the following: (1) Upchurch was faced with the prospect of losing two executive vice-presidents; (2) in response, he offered a bonus plan, but insisted that it had to be in writing, even though he was apparently comfortable with oral agreements on other employment matters; (3) he refused to approve a draft plan or to discuss it for eight months, stating instead that his lawyers were reviewing it; and (4) he explicitly stated that he had no intention of signing the original bonus plan. This evidence suggests circumstantially that Upchurch never intended to implement a bonus plan at the time that he offered it. In addition, Upchurch's credibility was surely in doubt when he allegedly approved an amended bonus plan but never mentioned it to Spoljaric, despite repeated inquiries about the status of the proposed plan. Evidence of this approved amended plan might have shown that Upchurch did intend to follow through on his promise at the time that he made it, but the strangeness of never mentioning the amended plan likely resulted in the jury believing that he was lying.

Why would a plaintiff harmed by a broken promise ever need to claim fraud? Wouldn't a breach of contract action be sufficient? A fraud action will be useful anytime there is a "defect" in the breach of contract claim that will affect the plaintiff's ability to recover in contract:

> Since a promise necessarily carries with it the implied assertion of an intention to perform it follows that a promise made without such an intention is fraudulent and

---

the defendant's insolvency or other reason to know that he cannot pay, or his repudiation of the promise soon after it is made, with no intervening change in the situation, or his failure even to attempt any performance, or his continued assurances after it is clear that he will not do so."); DAN B. DOBBS, THE LAW OF TORTS § 479, at 1370 (2000) ("Direct evidence by way of the defendant's admission by documents showing that defendant planned not to perform, or circumstantial evidence that the defendant could not have raised funds necessary for the construction, or that he had already been denied necessary permits, or even that he had demonstrated a pattern of making representations that were never performed would tend to prove that he lacked the intention he represented.").

> actionable in deceit under the rule stated in § 525. *This is true whether or not the promise is enforceable as a contract.* If it is enforceable, the person misled by the representation has a cause of action in tort as an alternative at least, and perhaps in some instances in addition to his cause of action on the contract. If the agreement is not enforceable as a contract, as when it is without consideration, the recipient still has, as his only remedy, the action in deceit under the rule stated in § 525. The same is true when the agreement is oral and made unenforceable by the statute of frauds, or when it is unprovable and so unenforceable under the parol evidence rule. The tort action may have other advantages, as when it is subject to a longer statute of limitations. In all of these cases, it is immaterial to the tort liability that the damages recoverable are identical with, or substantially the same as, those which could have been recovered in an action of contract if the promise were enforceable.[122]

In addition, and as discussed further in the next section, a fraud action can also be useful because of the potential for punitive damages.[123]

---

[122] RESTATEMENT (SECOND) OF TORTS § 530 cmt. c (1977) (emphasis added).

[123] Comments a and c to § 15 of the Third Restatement make the same points:

> .... First, a claim of fraud may permit the plaintiff to obtain an award of punitive damages that would not be available on other theories. Second, a suit for promissory fraud may allow a plaintiff to avoid doctrinal obstacles that would defeat claims for breach of contract or promissory estoppel.
>
> ....
>
> Claims under this Section are not impaired by a jurisdiction's statute of frauds. A statute of frauds extinguishes contract claims, not tort claims; it prevents the enforcement of a promise under certain circumstances if the promise is not evidenced in a writing signed by the promisor. Liability under this Section does not result in the enforcement of a promise. It results in compensation for losses suffered by a plaintiff who relied on a promise. The law of tort protects defendants against unfounded claims of deceit not by means of the statute of frauds but by the use of a heightened standard of proof with respect to the defendant's state of mind.
>
> Courts likewise state as a matter of course that the parol-evidence rule does not impede claims of fraud. The application of that principle to claims of promissory fraud may be explained in more particular terms. Two parties may sign a contract with an integration clause stating that the writing is the complete expression of their agreement; later the plaintiff might offer extrinsic evidence that the promisor never intended to perform the promise that the agreement contained. The plaintiff in such a case is not adding terms to the written contract or varying them. The plaintiff is proving, rather, that a representation implicit in the contract was false. Neither the parol-evidence rule nor an integration clause is an obstacle to such a showing.
>
> A related problem arises when the parties have a written agreement and the plaintiff claims that the defendant made a separate promise that was not reflected in the writing. The parol-evidence rule may preclude enforcement of the separate promise as a matter of contract law. The plaintiff nevertheless may assert a claim in tort that the second promise—the one outside the written

### 6. Damages

Damages for fraud are typically measured by a "benefit-of-the-bargain" (also known as "loss-of-bargain") standard or an "out-of-pocket" standard. As one commentator explained:

> The American courts are divided over two standards of measurement. One of these, the so-called "out of pocket" rule, looks to the loss which the plaintiff has suffered in the transaction, and gives him the difference between the value of what he has parted with and the value of what he has received. If what he received was worth what he paid for it, he has not been damaged, and there can be no recovery. This rule is followed in deceit actions by the English courts, and by a minority of perhaps a dozen American jurisdictions. . . . The other measurement, called the "loss-of-bargain" rule, gives the plaintiff the benefit of what he was promised, and allows recovery of the difference between the actual value of what he has received and the value that it would have had if it had been as represented. . . . It has been adopted by some two-thirds of the courts which have considered the question in actions of deceit. . . . Few courts have followed either rule with entire consistency. . . .[124]

In the more recent THE LAW OF TORTS, Professor Dobbs observes that "[m]ost courts . . . now permit the plaintiff to recover the loss of bargain, or choose the measure they deem best to fit the facts, or say with the Restatement that the plaintiff can recover under either loss of bargain or out of pocket, at her option."[125]

As mentioned, out-of-pocket damages compute the difference between the value parted with and the value received. This calculation is often referred to as a tort remedy because, like other tort remedies, it seeks to make the plaintiff whole. Benefit-of-the-bargain damages compute the difference between the value as represented and the value received. This measure is often referred to as a contract remedy because it seeks to put the plaintiff in the financial position the plaintiff would have occupied had there been no misrepresentation (just as expectation damages in contract law

---

contract—was made with no intention that it would be kept. It might seem odd that a promise the parol-evidence rule would otherwise extinguish becomes enforceable just because it was made by a promisor who never planned to keep it. Again, however, liability for fraud does not cause the promise to be enforced; rather, the plaintiff collects for damage caused by reliance on the promise.

124 W. PAGE KEETON ET AL., PROSSER AND KEETON ON TORTS § 110, at 767–68 (5th ed. 1984).

125 DAN B. DOBBS, THE LAW OF TORTS § 483, at 1380–81 (2000).

seek to put the plaintiff in the financial position the plaintiff would have occupied had there been no breach).

As Professor Dobbs observed, the Second Restatement explicitly allows the plaintiff to choose between out-of-pocket damages and benefit-of-the-bargain damages.[126] What would motivate a plaintiff to choose one measure over another? In general, a benefit-of-the-bargain award will be preferred because, unless the plaintiff entered into a bad bargain, such an award will typically result in greater damages than an out-of-pocket award.[127] That said, out-of-pocket damages may be chosen in situations where it is difficult to prove with reasonable certainty what a bargain was worth. In such circumstances, out-of-pocket losses may be a more reliable measure of damages.[128] Finally, in some cases, the victim of a

---

[126] *See* RESTATEMENT (SECOND) OF TORTS § 549 & cmt. h (1977). Interestingly, the Third Restatement includes no stand-alone provision on damages for fraud. *See* RESTATEMENT (THIRD) OF TORTS: LIABILITY FOR ECONOMIC HARM § 9 cmt. a (2020) (noting that "[t]he measurement of damages in fraud cases will be the subject of a separate Restatement"). Nevertheless, comment b to § 9 of the Third Restatement suggests a preference for out-of-pocket damages:

> Damages awarded in tort for fraud may be measured on an "out of pocket" basis: the difference between the value of what the plaintiff paid and received, along with other sums needed to restore the position the plaintiff would have occupied if the defendant had not committed the fraud. Such damages resemble a combination of reliance and consequential damages in the law of contract. Many states also let a plaintiff seek damages on a "loss of bargain" theory that resembles expectation damages in a contract case. A limitation to out-of-pocket recovery in most cases is probably more consistent with the approach of this Restatement, which seeks to distinguish clearly between contract and tort theories of recovery.

[127] For example, assume that (a) the price paid for property was $10,000; (b) the value of the property purchased was $10,000; and (c) the value of the property as represented was $12,000. The out-of-pocket measure would calculate the difference between the price paid ($10,000) and the value received ($10,000), resulting in no damages. The plaintiff received exactly what he paid for. The benefit-of-the-bargain measure would calculate the difference between the value as represented ($12,000) and the value received ($10,000), resulting in a $2,000 award. The plaintiff struck a good bargain here; thus, receiving the benefit of that good bargain is better for him.

Now assume that (a) the price paid for property was $10,000; (b) the value of the property purchased was $5,000; and (c) the value of the property as represented was $8,000. The out-of-pocket measure would calculate the difference between the price paid ($10,000) and the value received ($5,000), resulting in a $5,000 award. The benefit-of-the-bargain measure would calculate the difference between the value as represented ($8,000) and the value received ($5,000), resulting in a $3,000 award. The plaintiff struck a bad bargain here (paid $10,000 for property worth $5,000); thus, he would prefer to avoid receiving the "benefit" of that bad bargain.

[128] *See* RESTATEMENT (SECOND) OF TORTS § 549 cmt. g (1977) ("[T]here are many cases in which the value that the plaintiff would have received if the bargain made with him had been performed cannot be proved with any satisfactory degree of certainty, because it must necessarily turn upon the estimated value of something non-existent and never in fact received. In this case the benefit-of-the-bargain harm to the plaintiff becomes mere speculation, and ordinary rules of the law of damages preclude the award.").

misrepresentation never entered into a contract. In such disputes, benefit-of-the-bargain damages make little sense.

The decision of *Formosa Plastics Corp. v. Presidio Engineers & Contractors, Inc.*[129] addresses the damage measures for fraud. In 1989, Formosa began an expansion project at its facility in Point Comfort, Texas. Formosa solicited bids for the construction of 300 concrete foundations, and it included a bid package containing certain representations about the job. Presidio won the contract by submitting the lowest bid ($600,000), but it incurred significant unanticipated costs based largely on alleged misrepresentations by Formosa. After suing for fraud and other actions, the jury awarded Presidio $1.5 million in compensatory damages and $10 million in punitive damages. The trial judge suggested a remittitur reducing the compensatory damages to $700,000, which Presidio accepted.

Formosa argued that the $700,000 award in fraud damages was excessive as a matter of law. The court observed that "Texas recognizes two measures of direct damages for common-law fraud: the out-of-pocket measure and the benefit-of-the-bargain measure." Under these standards, the court agreed with Formosa that the $700,000 award was excessive. The court concluded that the evidence supported "an out-of-pocket damage award of $231,000 or a benefit-of-the-bargain damage award of $461,000."

What was Presidio's argument for a damages award of $700,000, and why did the court reject it? Bob Burnette (Presidio's President) testified that, if he had been told the truth about the project, he would have bid $1,300,000 instead of $600,000. Assuming that such a bid would still have resulted in Presidio receiving the contract, Presidio would have been entitled to $700,000 more than the $600,000 it was actually paid ($1,300,000 − $600,000).

Burnette arrived at the $1,300,000 projected bid by dividing the total amount Presidio spent on the job ($831,000) by the original expected cost of doing the job ($370,000). That suggested that the actual cost was approximately 2.25 times more than the expected cost. Burnette then effectively assumed that he would have bid 2.25 times more than he actually did, which produced $1,350,000 (2.25 x $600,000). Alternatively, he divided the 264 days that the job actually took by the 134 days that it was expected to take, resulting in a ratio of actual days to expected days of 1.97. He then assumed that he would have bid 1.97 times more than he actually did, which produced $1,182,000 (1.97 x $600,000). Most likely, he averaged the $1,350,000 and $1,182,000 figures and generously rounded up to the $1,300,000 projected bid. The court summarized these calculations by stating:

---

[129] 960 S.W.2d 41 (Tex. 1998).

"Basically, both of these methods multiplied the actual bid price of $600,000, which included a profit margin on the job, by a ratio comparing what actually occurred to what was anticipated. Thus, both of these calculations incorporated expected lost profits on a bargain that was never made."

The court rejected the $700,000 damages award because the above calculations were not consistent with the out-of-pocket or benefit-of-the-bargain measures of damages. With respect to the out-of-pocket standard, the goal is to make the plaintiff whole. The court noted that out-of-pocket damages are calculated by "the difference between the value paid and the value received." Thus, only two variables are relevant (actual value paid and actual value received), and expected lost profits are not one of those variables. Presidio parted with $831,000 (its actual expenses incurred on the job), and it received $600,000 (its winning bid and contracted-for payment). To make Presidio whole, therefore, $231,000 would need to be awarded under an out-of-pocket measure.

With respect to the benefit-of-the-bargain standard, the goal is to put the plaintiff in the financial position that he would have occupied had there been no misrepresentation. The court noted that it is calculated by "the difference between the value as represented and the value received." Once again, only two variables are relevant—what was supposed to happen (the value as represented), and what happened (the value received). Presidio's projected bid of $1.3 million does not fit either of these variables. It was a hypothetical bid that never occurred (and, as the court mentioned, probably would not have been accepted if it had been made). If Formosa had not engaged in fraud, Presidio expected to receive $600,000 and to incur $370,000 in expenses. Thus, Presidio expected a $230,000 profit had the situation been as represented. Instead, Presidio received $600,000 and incurred $831,000 in expenses, resulting in a loss of $231,000. Applying the formula, the "value as represented" is $230,000, and the "value received" is <$231,000>. The benefit-of-the-bargain award, therefore, is $461,000.

Some courts measure benefit-of-the-bargain damages by the cost of repairs. For example, in *Hinkle v. Rockville Motor Co.*,[130] the plaintiff purchased an automobile that was represented to be new, but which actually had been involved in an accident and had over 2,000 miles on it. The plaintiff failed to present evidence on the actual value of the automobile at the time of the sale. Nevertheless, he did present evidence that "the effects of the accident could be remedied and the car returned to new car condition by the expenditure of $800

---

[130] 278 A.2d 42 (Md. 1971).

for repairs." The court noted that the "evidence in regard to the cost of necessary repairs demonstrated the existence of damages and provided an adequate measure upon which they could be predicated."

Why is the cost of repairs consistent with a benefit-of-the-bargain measure of damages? Benefit-of-the-bargain damages compute the difference between the value as represented and the value received. The cost of repairs represents the financial expense required to convert an item from its present state (which the plaintiff received) to an improved state (which the plaintiff was promised). Thus, the cost of repairs approximates the financial shortfall between the value received by the plaintiff and the value the plaintiff was promised—the same shortfall that the benefit-of-the-bargain calculation is attempting to measure.

Principles of proximate causation apply to damages sought in a fraud action. Section 548A of the Second Restatement addresses proximate cause by stating that "[a] fraudulent misrepresentation is a legal cause of a pecuniary loss resulting from action or inaction in reliance upon it if, but only if, the loss might reasonably be expected to result from the reliance." Comment a to that section indicates that, "[i]n general, the misrepresentation is a legal cause only of those pecuniary losses that are within the foreseeable risk of harm that it creates." Comment b adds the following observation: "Pecuniary losses that could not reasonably be expected to result from the misrepresentation are, in general, not legally caused by it and are beyond the scope of the maker's liability. This means that the matter misrepresented must be considered in the light of its tendency to cause those losses and the likelihood that they will follow."[131]

The Third Restatement addresses proximate causation in a similar fashion in § 12: "An actor who makes a fraudulent misrepresentation is subject to liability for harm only if the risk of the harm was foreseeably increased by the fraud." Comment a to that section mentions, in relevant part, the following: "Briefly stated, a plaintiff can recover only for the types of losses that might reasonably have been expected to result from the defendant's fraud. This generally means that the fraud must have foreseeably increased the risk of the kind of harm that the plaintiff suffered."

131 *See also* Knepper v. Brown, 195 P.3d 383, 387–88 (Or. 2008) (noting that proximate cause is an element of a fraud claim, stating that proximate cause is "equivalent to the concept of 'reasonable foreseeability,'" and observing that "[a] requirement that any claimed damages be foreseeable appropriately recognizes that the scope of liability for an intentional, fraudulent misrepresentation depends on the nature of the misrepresentation, the audience to whom the misrepresentation was directed, and the nature of the action or forbearance . . . that the misrepresentation justifiably induced").

Consequential damages can also be recovered in an action for fraud.[132] As the Second Restatement explains:

> Although the most usual form of financial loss caused by participation in a financial transaction induced by a fraudulent misrepresentation is the lessened value of the subject matter due to its falsity, the loss may result from a purchaser's use of the article for a purpose for which it would be appropriate if the representation were true but for which it is in fact harmfully inappropriate. So, too, it may be the expense to which he has gone in preparation for a use of the article for which it would have been appropriate if the representation had been true.
>
> These "indirect" or "consequential" damages resulting from the misrepresentation are recoverable if the misrepresentation is a legal cause of them, as stated in § 548A. This means that they must be of a kind that might reasonably be expected to result from reliance upon the misrepresentation.[133]

In short, to be recoverable, consequential damages must be foreseeable and must be established with reasonable certainty.[134]

As in *Formosa*, courts typically allow for the possibility of punitive damages when fraud is established.[135] With respect to the recovery of mental anguish damages, however, courts have reached different results.[136]

---

[132] *See, e.g.*, RESTATEMENT (SECOND) OF TORTS § 549(1)(b) (1977).

[133] *Id.* § 549 cmt. d.

[134] *See id.* § 548A; DAN B. DOBBS, THE LAW OF TORTS § 483, at 1381 (2000) ("The [fraud] plaintiff may also recover consequential damages such as expenses incurred or profits lost in collateral affairs as a proximate result of the fraud, provided such damages are proved with reasonable certainty and do not duplicate the out of pocket or loss of bargain award.").

[135] *See, e.g.*, Rogers v. Alexander, 244 S.W.3d 370, 380, 388 (Tex. App. 2007) (concluding that "[defendants'] fraud was established by clear and convincing evidence such that an [$850,000] award of punitive damages was appropriate"); Follo v. Florindo, 970 A.2d 1230, 1245 (Vt. 2009) (noting that "our cases indicate that when defendants have been found liable for common-law fraud, it is proper to put the issue of punitive damages to the jury"); State v. Berger, 567 S.E.2d 265, 278 n.8 (W. Va. 2002) ("A plaintiff who proves common-law fraud may recover punitive damages.").

Keep in mind that the amount of punitive damages may be limited by statute. *See, e.g.*, TEX. CIV. PRAC. & REM. CODE § 41.008(b) ("Exemplary damages awarded against a defendant may not exceed an amount equal to the greater of: (1)(A) two times the amount of economic damages; plus (B) an amount equal to any noneconomic damages found by the jury, not to exceed $750,000; or (2) $200,000.").

[136] *Compare* Cornell v. Wunschel, 408 N.W.2d 369, 382 (Iowa 1987) ("One of the keys to an award of damages for fraudulent misrepresentation is that the party committing the fraud could have contemplated the claimed damage as a consequence of the fraud at the time the misrepresentation was made. Damages for mental distress are not ordinarily contemplated in a business transaction; thus, few courts have

A defrauded plaintiff may also rescind the transaction. In general, rescission "undoes" the transaction by obligating the plaintiff to return what it has received from the defendant, and by allowing the plaintiff to recover what it has transferred to the defendant. Along with rescission, fraud also gives the plaintiff a claim in restitution as necessary to avoid unjust enrichment.[137]

---

recognized their availability as an element of fraud damages."), *with* Kilduff v. Adams, Inc., 593 A.2d 478, 484 (Conn. 1991) ("Although several courts have denied recovery for mental distress in a fraud action on the ground that damages in such an action are solely intended to compensate the plaintiff for pecuniary loss . . . we concur with those jurisdictions that allow the recovery of emotional damages that are the natural and proximate result of fraud."), *and* Osbourne v. Capital City Mortg. Corp., 667 A.2d 1321, 1328 (D.C. 1995) ("We hold that, upon proof of intentional misrepresentation, a plaintiff may recover 'emotional damages that are the natural and proximate result' of the defendant's conduct. While the underlying dispute here is contractual in nature, defendants are alleged to have committed an intentional tort when they misrepresented the payoff amount of the note. Whether or not the tort was committed in a contractual context is not dispositive; mental suffering is a 'natural and proximate' consequence of intentional fraud and should be a compensable injury.").

[137] *See, e.g.*, RESTATEMENT (THIRD) OF RESTITUTION & UNJUST ENRICHMENT §§ 13(1), 51, 54 (2011).

Comment b to § 9 of the Third Restatement summarizes the differences between the remedies typically available to a defrauded plaintiff under the law of tort, contract, and restitution. With respect to rescission and restitution, the comment states the following:

> Rescission is a remedy for fraud available under the law of restitution and contract, not tort. Both sides give back whatever they received from the other, to the extent such a return is feasible. Rescission is not always available, because it requires that a reasonably complete restoration of performance be possible between both parties. These acts of restoration can be supplemented by awards of incidental damages to make up for value that cannot be fully returned, or to reflect costs that the defrauded party incurred in reliance on the transaction. Some jurisdictions allow a plaintiff to recover punitive damages in conjunction with rescission in an appropriate case. See generally Restatement Third, Restitution and Unjust Enrichment §§ 13, 54.
>
> The law of restitution may also require a defendant to disgorge consequential gains from a transaction. If fraud results in profits for the defendant that exceed the loss to the plaintiff, restitution (measured by the defendant's wrongful gain) may yield a larger recovery than tort or contract damages and may leave the plaintiff better off than if the fraud had never occurred. See Restatement Third, Restitution and Unjust Enrichment §§ 13, 51.
>
> . . . .
>
> A plaintiff may allege a right to recover under multiple theories, but cannot be compensated more than once. The pursuit of multiple remedies may also be subject to rules of election. Rescission is obviously inconsistent with an effort to enforce a contract, such as a claim for expectation damages. Less obviously, perhaps, the remedy of rescission for fraud is often held to be inconsistent with a claim for tort damages, possibly because rescission should accomplish the same restoration of position that a tort claim would. Claims for breach of contract and for tort damages are not inconsistent with one another, however, and so usually may be advanced together at trial without an election between them so long as it is clear that the plaintiff can recover under one theory or the other, but not both.

## B. NEGLIGENT MISREPRESENTATION

In general, negligent misrepresentations that cause physical injury are actionable under the same principles that govern ordinary negligence.[138] For example, gesturing that it is safe to pass on a highway when it is not, or telling someone that a ladder is strong enough to stand on when it is in poor condition, could result in negligence liability if the speaker failed to exercise reasonable care in making the representation.[139] The separate tort of negligent misrepresentation, however, focuses on negligent misrepresentations that cause pure economic loss. This separate tort, and its corresponding emphasis on economic injury, is the subject of the materials in this section.

The tort of negligent misrepresentation shares many of the same elements as the tort of fraud. There must be a false, material misrepresentation, the plaintiff must have justifiably relied, and the plaintiff must suffer injury resulting from such reliance. The primary differences between the two causes of action involve the defendant's state of mind (negligence rather than scienter) and the correspondingly narrower scope of liability for the less-culpable, negligence-based tort.

### 1. Scope of Liability

The scope of liability for negligent misrepresentation has generated a considerable amount of litigation. Who can sue, in other words, for negligent misrepresentation? Many of the judicial precedents involve accountants who are sued for negligently misrepresenting the financial health of a business in the course of an audit that they were hired to conduct. These lawsuits are typically brought not by the accountant's client, but instead by third-party investors or lenders (i.e., persons not in a contractual relationship with the accountant) who allegedly relied on misstatements in the audit report. Given that audit reports are often circulated widely in the financial community to a vast number of investors and lenders, the potential exposure for accountants is significant.

Because so many of the relevant precedents involve third-party suits against accountants, some background on the auditing process is useful:

> Although certified public accountants (CPA's) perform a variety of services for their clients, their primary function, which is the one that most frequently generates lawsuits against them by third persons, is financial auditing. An

[138] *See, e.g.*, RESTATEMENT (SECOND) OF TORTS § 311 (1977).

[139] *See id.* § 311 illus. 1–9 (providing examples).

audit is a verification of the financial statements of an entity through an examination of the underlying accounting records and supporting evidence. In an audit engagement, an accountant reviews financial statements prepared by a client and issues an opinion stating whether such statements fairly represent the financial status of the audited entity.

In a typical audit, a CPA firm may verify the existence of tangible assets, observe business activities, and confirm account balances and mathematical computations. It might also examine sample transactions or records to ascertain the accuracy of the client company's financial and accounting systems. For example, auditors often select transactions recorded in the company's books to determine whether the recorded entries are supported by underlying data (vouching). Or, approaching the problem from the opposite perspective, an auditor might choose particular items of data to trace through the client's accounting and bookkeeping process to determine whether the data have been properly recorded and accounted for (tracing).

For practical reasons of time and cost, an audit rarely, if ever, examines every accounting transaction in the records of a business. The planning and execution of an audit therefore require a high degree of professional skill and judgment. Initially, the CPA firm plans the audit by surveying the client's business operations and accounting systems and making preliminary decisions as to the scope of the audit and what methods and procedures will be used. The firm then evaluates the internal financial control systems of the client and performs compliance tests to determine whether they are functioning properly. Transactions and data are sampled, vouched for, and traced. Throughout the audit process, results are examined and procedures are reevaluated and modified to reflect discoveries made by the auditors. For example, if the auditor discovers weaknesses in the internal control system of the client, the auditor must plan additional audit procedures which will satisfy himself that the internal control weaknesses have not caused any material misrepresentations in the financial statements.

The end product of an audit is the audit report or opinion. The report is generally expressed in a letter addressed to the client. The body of the report refers to the specific client-prepared financial statements which are attached. In the case of the so-called "unqualified report" . . . two paragraphs are relatively standard.

In a scope paragraph, the CPA firm asserts that it has examined the accompanying financial statements in accordance with GAAS [Generally Accepted Auditing Standards]. . . .

. . . .

In an opinion paragraph, the audit report generally states the CPA firm's opinion that the audited financial statements, taken as a whole, are in conformity with GAAP [Generally Accepted Accounting Principles] and present fairly in all material respects the financial position, results of operations, and changes in financial position of the client in the relevant periods.

. . . . Like GAAS, GAAP include broad statements of accounting principles amounting to aspirational norms as well as more specific guidelines and illustrations.

In addition to or in place of the standardized statements in an audit report, the auditing CPA firm may also qualify its opinion, noting exceptions or matters in the financial statements not in conformity with GAAP or significant uncertainties which might affect a fair evaluation of the statements. The report may also contain a disclaimer stating the accountant's inability to express any opinion about the statements or an adverse opinion that the statements do not fairly present the financial position of the client in conformity with GAAP.

. . . [A]udits may be commissioned by clients for different purposes. Nonetheless, audits of financial statements and the resulting audit reports are very frequently (if not almost universally) used by businesses to establish the financial credibility of their enterprises in the perceptions of outside persons, e.g., existing and prospective investors, financial institutions, and others who extend credit to an enterprise or make risk-oriented decisions based on its economic viability. The unqualified audit report of a CPA firm, particularly one of the "Big Six," is often an admission ticket to venture capital markets—a necessary condition precedent to attracting the kind and level of outside funds essential to the client's financial growth and survival. As one commentator summarizes: "In the first instance, this unqualified opinion serves as an assurance to the client that its own perception of its financial health is valid and that its accounting systems are reliable. The audit, however, frequently plays a second major role: it assists the client in convincing third parties that it is safe to extend credit or invest in the client."[140]

The decision of *Credit Alliance Corp. v. Arthur Andersen & Co.*[141] introduces the first (the so-called "near-privity" approach) of three modern approaches that courts have adopted for defining the scope of liability for negligent misrepresentation. There were two appeals at issue in *Credit Alliance*. In the first appeal, the plaintiffs (Credit Alliance) were financial service companies who alleged that they provided financing to L.B. Smith, Inc. in reliance on the unqualified audit opinion of Arthur Andersen that Smith's financial statements accurately reflected its financial position. After Smith defaulted on obligations and filed for bankruptcy, the plaintiffs sued Andersen for negligent misrepresentation. In the second appeal, the plaintiff (European American Bank, or "EAB") made substantial loans to Majestic Electro Industries and some of its subsidiaries in reliance on interim and year-end financial reports prepared by Strauhs & Kaye ("S&K"). After a Majestic subsidiary defaulted and Majestic filed for bankruptcy, EAB sued S&K for negligent misrepresentation.

The Court of Appeals began by reviewing its earlier *Ultramares*, *Glanzer*, and *White* opinions. In *Ultramares*, Chief Judge Cardozo refused to allow a plaintiff to sue an accounting firm for negligent misrepresentation when the plaintiff had no contractual privity with the firm. In *Glanzer*, a plaintiff not in contractual privity with public weighers was allowed to sue for negligent misrepresentation, but only because "the plaintiff's intended reliance, on the information *directly transmitted* by the weighers, created a bond so closely approaching privity that it was, in practical effect, virtually indistinguishable therefrom." Similarly, in *White*, a limited partner not in contractual privity with accountants was allowed to sue because "the accountants knew that a limited partner would have to rely upon the audit and tax returns of the partnership, and inasmuch as this was within the specific contemplation of the accounting retainer," the relationship between the accountants and the limited partner "was clearly one approach[ing] that of privity, if not completely one with it." The court emphasized that a "relationship so close as to approach that of privity" remained the touchstone for imposing liability to noncontractual parties.[142]

---

140 Bily v. Arthur Young & Co., 834 P.2d 745, 749–51 (Cal. 1992).

141 483 N.E.2d 110 (N.Y. 1985).

142 *Id.* at 114–17 (citing Ultramares Corp. v. Touche, 174 N.E. 441 (N.Y. 1931); Glanzer v. Shepard, 135 N.E. 275 (N.Y. 1922); White v. Guarente, 372 N.E.2d 315 (N.Y. 1977)).

The court then announced a new "test" for accountant liability to noncontractual parties that purportedly derived from the pronouncements in *Ultramares*, *Glanzer*, and *White*:

> .... Before accountants may be held liable in negligence to noncontractual parties who rely to their detriment on inaccurate financial reports, certain prerequisites must be satisfied: (1) the accountants must have been aware that the financial reports were to be used for a particular purpose or purposes; (2) in the furtherance of which a known party or parties was intended to rely; and (3) there must have been some conduct on the part of the accountants linking them to that party or parties, which evinces the accountants' understanding of that party or parties' reliance.

The court noted that this test was "intended to preserve the wisdom and policy" of the three earlier precedents.

Applying the test, the court concluded that Credit Alliance did not establish "the existence of a relationship between the parties sufficiently approaching privity." Credit Alliance did not allege that Andersen was aware of the purpose for which its reports were to be used, nor did it allege any conduct linking itself to Andersen. By contrast, EAB did establish the requisite relationship by alleging that S&K knew of EAB's existence and knew that EAB was relying on S&K's reports for the purpose of making its lending decisions. Moreover, EAB alleged conduct linking itself to S&K (direct oral and written communications between the parties and meetings to discuss Majestic's financial condition and EAB's need for S&K's evaluation). The court dismissed the claim of Credit Alliance but allowed the claim of EAB to proceed.

As mentioned, in *Ultramares*, Chief Judge Cardozo refused to allow a plaintiff to sue an accounting firm for negligence based upon inaccurately prepared financial statements when the plaintiff was not in contractual privity with the firm. Cardozo's concern about permitting negligent misrepresentation claims was that any negligence would expose the accountant to liability "in an indeterminate amount for an indeterminate time to an indeterminate class."[143] That is, it is foreseeable to an accountant that its work product for a client may be relied upon by the world of banks, creditors, investors, purchasers, or sellers—anyone who makes a decision about the client that is based upon the client's financial health. Indeed, audit reports are often consulted by such parties as

[143] *Id.* at 115–16 (quoting Ultramares Corp. v. Touche, 174 N.E. 441, 444 (N.Y. 1931)).

part of their decision to enter into a transaction with the client. If ordinary negligence principles of foreseeability applied, an accountant's work would expose it to massive amounts of liability for all of the losses incurred by this huge group of parties until the information became "stale"—i.e., an indeterminate amount of liability for an indeterminate time to an indeterminate class. This massive amount of exposure would make it hazardous to continue in the business of accounting.

An audit opinion for a public company (e.g., AT&T) is a perfect example of Cardozo's concern. The audit opinion will be part of AT&T's public filings and will be accessible to the world of lenders and investors. In the aggregate, sums loaned to and invested in AT&T likely total in the billions of dollars. Because it is foreseeable that lenders and investors will rely on an audit report, an accountant governed by ordinary negligence principles would be subject to a tremendous amount of exposure.[144]

The Third Restatement echoes Cardozo's concerns about indeterminate liability: "[W]ords do not spend themselves in the way that physical forces do. They often can be circulated to one person or to thousands with little difference in cost and no reduction in their power to do economic harm when others rely on them. Liabilities that expand as easily as words travel would therefore become indeterminate and unduly widespread in many cases."[145]

Consider the new test for accountant liability to noncontractual parties announced in *Credit Alliance*. The goal of the test would appear to be two-fold: (1) establish consistency with the limiting policies set forth in *Ultramares*, *Glanzer*, and *White*; and (2) create a test that imposes liability when the defendant is made aware of the risk of the engagement and consciously chooses to assume that risk.

With respect to the first goal, it is clear that the court derived the test from its reading of the principles articulated in *Ultramares*, *Glanzer*, and *White*. In general, because of concerns over indeterminate liability, all of these precedents seek to limit the liability of a defendant for negligent misrepresentation to parties who

---

144 *But see* Bily v. Arthur Young & Co., 834 P.2d 745, 780 (Cal. 1992) (Kennard, J., dissenting) (disagreeing that accountants face unlimited liability: "Because liability has extended only to those business transactions conducted in reliance on the audited financial statements, and because audited financial statements become obsolete within a few years at most, the accountant's liability exposure has been finite and reasonably predictable in duration. Liability continues only so long as the audited financial statements reasonably influence business decisions. The amount of the potential liability is also measurable. Because it depends on the client's investment and borrowing potential, the scope of liability is necessarily proportional to the size and growth rate of the audited business.").

145 RESTATEMENT (THIRD) OF TORTS: LIABILITY FOR ECONOMIC HARM § 5 cmt. b (2020).

the defendant specifically knows will be relying on its work. A party to a contract knows that its services are designed to benefit the other party to the contract; consequently, it is fair to let the beneficiary sue for harm. When that relationship is functionally present with a non-contractual third party (i.e., a party to a contract knows that its services are designed to benefit a third party), *Ultramares*, *Glanzer*, and *White* suggest that it is similar enough to a contractual relationship to result in the same consequences.

The *Credit Alliance* test reflects these points. The elements seek to flesh out whether the accountant knows that its services are designed to benefit a third party. If the accountant does know, it is fair to let the beneficiary sue if the accountant has engaged in wrongdoing. As the elements indicate, if the accountant knows the purpose for which its work will be used, knows the person who will be using the work for that purpose, and has some sort of conduct-based relationship with that person, a court can feel comfortable that the accountant knows that its services are designed to benefit that person. It is fair, therefore, to let that person sue.

With respect to the second goal, the elements of the *Credit Alliance* test are perhaps better explained from an assumption of risk standpoint. If a defendant is aware that a third party is going to rely on the defendant's information in a particular transaction, and if the defendant nevertheless chooses to go forward with the engagement, it is fair to hold the defendant liable. After all, so long as the defendant is aware of the risk presented by an engagement, the defendant can take steps to protect itself (e.g., turn down the engagement completely, procure more insurance, or charge a higher price).

The elements of the *Credit Alliance* test reflect this assumption of risk idea. Indeed, the elements require the accountant to know the purpose for which its work will be used and the person who will be using the work for that purpose. This information apprises the accountant of the risk that it faces, and the accountant can then decide to confront, avoid, or mitigate the risk. If the accountant consciously chooses to accept the engagement with knowledge of the risk, then it is fair to hold the accountant liable for wrongdoing within the scope of that risk. (Under this rationale, the third "linking conduct" element would seem to provide objective confirmation that the accountant was, in fact, aware of the specific risk of exposure to the plaintiff.) In short, the *Credit Alliance* approach seems designed to ensure that third party liability is only imposed against a defendant when the defendant was aware of a specific risk, had the ability to protect against that risk, and consciously chose to assume it.

Does the *Credit Alliance* test satisfy Cardozo's concern? To the extent that Cardozo is concerned about indeterminate liability for accountants, the test satisfies that concern by limiting liability to a specifically known person who will be using the accountants' information for a particular purpose that the accountant is aware of. The test does not extend liability to any foreseeable user of accounting information, which is what provoked Cardozo's concern in the first place.

What is the independent function of the third element of the *Credit Alliance* test? From an assumption of risk standpoint, if the defendant knows the purpose for which its work will be used, and knows the party who will be using the work for that purpose, the defendant has been apprised of the risk that it faces (e.g., Wells Fargo Bank will be using my audit opinion to make a decision on extending a $3.5 million loan). If the defendant then makes a conscious decision to proceed with the engagement in the face of that risk, it is fair to hold the defendant liable for wrongdoing within the scope of the risk. There would not seem to be a need for the third element of the *Credit Alliance* test.[146]

As mentioned, the third element presumably serves to provide objective confirmation that the defendant was, in fact, consciously aware of the specific risk of exposure to the plaintiff. In other words, without the third "linking conduct" element, there may have been concern that courts would interpret the first two elements as a *constructive knowledge* inquiry—i.e., what the defendant should have known about the purpose for which its work would be used and the party who would be using the work for that purpose. The linking conduct element makes clear that the test is based on the defendant's *actual knowledge* because the element can only be established by showing conduct on the part of the defendant linking the defendant to the plaintiff and evidencing the defendant's understanding of that plaintiff's reliance.

What sort of conduct would satisfy this third element? The *Credit Alliance* court mentioned direct dealings with the plaintiff (through communications or meetings), agreeing with the client to prepare the report for plaintiff's use or according to plaintiff's requirements, agreeing with the client to provide the plaintiff with a copy of the report, and actually providing the plaintiff with a copy of the report. In addition, shaping an audit opinion to meet the needs of

---

146 *See, e.g.*, *Bily*, 834 P.2d at 754 ("One might question whether 'linking' conduct should be necessary if . . . the auditor knows his engagement is for the express purpose of benefiting an identifiable class of third parties. . . . In such cases, 'linkage' is arguably achieved by the auditor's conduct in undertaking and carrying out the engagement with knowledge of its specific purpose and the ultimate use to be made of the audit report.").

a particular plaintiff would surely suffice. The common thread in these examples is that the defendant has actual knowledge of a particular third party's reliance on the defendant's work, and by accepting the engagement, the defendant can be said to have assumed the risk of liability to that third party.

The *Credit Alliance* framework requires the accountant to know the purpose for which its work will be used and the person who will be using the work for that purpose. At what time should that knowledge be measured? Is it sufficient if the accountant gains this knowledge at any time before the issuance of the final audit report, or should knowledge be measured at an earlier time?

If the *Credit Alliance* framework is to be understood from an assumption of risk standpoint, the defendant's knowledge should be measured at the time of the engagement (i.e., the time when the defendant contractually agrees to provide information to another). After all, the defendant has the maximum flexibility to protect against any risk of exposure at that time. For example, it can adjust its price, contract for indemnification, or, if the potential exposure outweighs any reasonable amount of protection, simply decline the engagement. Once the engagement has been entered into, however, the defendant's ability to self-protect is greatly reduced. New exposure risks change the risk/reward calculation, but prices have already been set and contractual terms have already been negotiated. Thus, if the *Credit Alliance* approach seeks to ensure that third-party liability is only imposed against a defendant when the defendant was aware of a specific risk, had the ability to protect against that risk, and consciously chose to assume it, the time of engagement would seem to be the appropriate time for measuring the defendant's knowledge.

Why are negligent misrepresentation lawsuits against accountants typically brought by third parties and not by the accountant's client? At least part of the explanation is that the client is often the initial wrongdoer. The client usually prepares the financial statements that the accountant is auditing, and the client may intentionally misrepresent the financial position of the company. While the accountant may fail to discover the misrepresentation, the misrepresentation itself originated with the client.[147] In short, the client typically does not sue over a problem

---

147 *Cf. Bily*, 834 P.2d at 762 ("An auditor is a watchdog, not a bloodhound. As a matter of commercial reality, audits are performed in a client-controlled environment. The client typically prepares its own financial statements; it has direct control over and assumes primary responsibility for their contents. The client engages the auditor, pays for the audit, and communicates with audit personnel throughout the engagement. Because the auditor cannot in the time available become an expert in the

that it knowingly created. Moreover, the accountant's negligence may benefit the client by making the client's financial position look better. As a result, the client may not directly suffer damages in the same way that a third party might when lending or investing in reliance on an audit report. Finally, in some jurisdictions, a client's negligent misrepresentation claim against its accountant would be barred by the economic loss rule.[148]

On a related note, given that the client is often the initial wrongdoer, why isn't the client the primary target in the third party's lawsuit? As one court explained: "The client, its promoters, and its managers have generally left the scene, headed in most cases for government-supervised liquidation or the bankruptcy court. The auditor has now assumed center stage as the remaining solvent defendant and is [often] faced with a claim for all sums of money ever loaned to or invested in the client."[149]

Regardless of how a court resolves the scope of liability issue, keep in mind that a successful negligent misrepresentation claim requires proof of negligence. An accountant's failure to detect an irregularity in a client's financial information does not necessarily mean that the accountant was negligent. After all, for practical reasons of time and cost, an accountant in a typical audit reviews only a sample of the client's financial and other business transactions. Failing to examine all of the client's transactions, in other words, is not unreasonable. Moreover, a client's fraud in the preparation of financial statements may be sophisticated and very difficult to discover, even for an accountant who is conducting an audit with reasonable care.

The decision of *Citizens State Bank v. Timm, Schmidt & Co.*[150] introduces a different approach for defining the scope of liability for negligent misrepresentation. Timm was an accounting firm who prepared financial statements for Clintonville Fire Apparatus, Inc. ("CFA"). Timm also sent opinion letters to CFA indicating that the financial statements fairly presented the financial condition of CFA and that the statements were prepared in accordance with generally accepted accounting principles.

---

client's business and record keeping systems, the client necessarily furnishes the information base for the audit.").

148 *See* Chapter 5; *see also* RESTATEMENT (THIRD) OF TORTS: LIABILITY FOR ECONOMIC HARM § 5(5) (2020) ("This Section does not recognize liability for negligent misrepresentations made in the course of negotiating or performing a contract between the parties."); *id.* § 6(4) (substantially the same).

149 *Bily*, 834 P.2d at 763.

150 335 N.W.2d 361 (Wis. 1983).

Citizens State Bank made several loans to CFA allegedly in reliance on the financial statements that Timm had prepared. In 1977, Timm discovered that the 1974 and 1975 financial statements that it had prepared contained material errors. When Citizens was informed of these errors, it called the loans that it had made. CFA was ultimately liquidated and dissolved, and Citizens filed a negligent misrepresentation action against Timm for the outstanding amount due on its loans.

Timm moved for summary judgment on the grounds that it did not know that CFA intended to obtain loans from Citizens until after the loans were made, and that it similarly was not informed that its audit report would be used by Citizens or any other lender. The court concluded that third parties not in contractual privity with accountants could sue, and that "[l]iability will be imposed on these accountants for the foreseeable injuries resulting from their negligent acts unless, under the facts of this particular case, as a matter of policy to be decided by the court, recovery is denied on grounds of public policy." Because some affidavits suggested that it was foreseeable to Timm that lenders would rely on the audited statements, the court concluded that summary judgment for Timm was not warranted.

The *Citizens* court stated that "[u]nder the accepted principles of Wisconsin negligence law, Timm could be liable to Citizens if Timm's actions were the cause of Citizens' injuries and if the injuries were reasonably foreseeable unless public policy precluded recovery." This "foreseeability" approach is very much a minority position, as only a few courts have adopted it.[151]

---

[151] *See, e.g.*, Touche Ross & Co. v. Commercial Union Ins. Co., 514 So. 2d 315, 322 (Miss. 1987); H. Rosenblum, Inc. v. Adler, 461 A.2d 138, 153 (N.J. 1983). It should be noted that the *Rosenblum* decision has been effectively overruled by statute. *See* N.J. STAT. 2A:53A–25 (adopting an approach similar to *Credit Alliance*, but limited to negligent misrepresentation claims against accountants). Moreover, both precedents seem to indicate that liability only extends to those third parties who received audit reports directly from the client itself, and not simply by accessing a public filing. *See, e.g., Touche Ross*, 514 So.2d at 322 ("[T]he Court finds that an independent auditor is liable to reasonably foreseeable users of the audit, *who request and receive a financial statement from the audited entity* for a proper business purpose, and who then detrimentally rely on the financial statement, suffering a loss, proximately caused by the auditor's negligence." (emphasis added)); *H. Rosenblum*, 461 A.2d at 153 ("The principle that we have adopted applies by its terms only to those foreseeable users *who receive the audited statements from the business entity* for a proper business purpose to influence a business decision of the user, the audit having been made for that business entity. Thus, for example, an institutional investor or portfolio manager who does not obtain audited statements from the company would not come within the stated principle. Nor would stockholders who purchased the stock after a negligent audit be covered in the absence of demonstrating the necessary conditions precedent. Those and similar cases beyond the stated rule are not before us and we express no opinion with respect to such situations." (emphasis added)).

What policy arguments did the *Citizens* court make in support of its foreseeability approach? First, the court mentioned deterrence: "Unless an accountant can be held liable to a relying third party, this negligence will go undeterred." While it is true that the potential for liability can deter misbehavior, it should be noted that legal constraints are not the only possible deterrent. Accountants, after all, have reputational constraints that should help to curb misbehavior. An accounting firm who gets a reputation for sloppy work may no longer provide clients with what they need—an opinion that outside lenders and investors trust in deciding to transact with the client. Not providing the client with what it needs is bad for business, and accountants want business, so such reputational constraints may serve the same function as legal constraints in deterring negligent conduct.[152]

Of course, any deterrence gain provided by a broader liability rule may be offset by other negative consequences. Accountants may simply refuse to provide audits in fledgling industries where the risk of client failure is high. Even if they perform the audits, they may have to charge a prohibitively high fee to such clients to cover the potential risk.[153] If one believes that encouraging entrepreneurs and fledgling businesses is desirable, this inability to get an audit at a reasonable price is problematic, as it will block many of these businesses from access to capital sources that are necessary to grow and survive.[154]

---

152 On the other hand, as the Enron collapse of the early 2000s and other company scandals suggest, perhaps what the client needs (or at least wants) is a sloppy audit—one that doesn't scrutinize too much the risky financial behavior that the client is engaging in. Reputational constraints, in other words, may not discourage negligent behavior; in fact, such sloppy "I'll look the other way" behavior from the accountant may be desired by the client. If that is one's view of the world, legal constraints are necessary to deter negligent conduct.

153 *See, e.g.*, *Bily*, 834 P.2d at 766 ("Auditors may rationally respond to increased liability by simply reducing audit services in fledgling industries where the business failure rate is high, reasoning that they will inevitably be singled out and sued when their client goes into bankruptcy regardless of the care or detail of their audits."); *id.* ("Consistent with this reasoning, the economic result of unlimited negligence liability could just as easily be an increase in the cost and decrease in the availability of audits and audit reports with no compensating improvement in overall audit quality.").

154 As opposed to the typical case in this area, Timm prepared CFA's financial statements. In many cases, the client has no action against the accountant because the client prepared the financial statements and prepared them in such a way to conceal known financial shenanigans from the accountant. In this dispute, however, it appears that Timm may have been wholly at fault in negligently preparing the financial statements. If CFA borrowed more money than it should have because of Timm's inaccurate representation about CFA's financial health—a misrepresentation that CFA might not otherwise have known about itself—could CFA have an action against Timm? If so, the fear of a client lawsuit might also exist to deter accountant misbehavior, even without the broad rule of liability to third parties that the court ultimately chose.

As a second policy rationale, the *Citizens* court stated that if third party creditors are not allowed to recover, the cost of credit will increase. This is because creditors will have to charge higher interest rates or other loan fees to offset (1) the risk that they may not be able to recover if the client defaults, or (2) the cost of hiring their own independent accountants to verify the information received from the client. Conversely, if third party creditors are able to recover, the accountants can simply buy liability insurance to spread their risk.

The *Citizens* court seems to view third parties conducting their own audits or other investigations as undesirable (because it will increase the cost of credit). In contrast, other courts view such "private ordering" and "self-reliance" as a virtue (because it promotes "sound investment and credit practices and discourages the careless use of monetary resources").[155] This is an important point to notice: courts may not agree on the policy implications of a particular legal rule. What one court views as a negative consequence—third parties will have to bear their own risk—another court sees as a positive. Some courts go further and suggest that, contrary to the notion that accountants are better loss-spreaders through insurance, creditors and investors may be more effective loss-spreaders because they can diversify their loan portfolios and investments to minimize the impact of any particular loan or investment going bad.[156]

Within a particular jurisdiction, there may also be some virtue to having a consistent approach to negligence law rather than having a different negligent misrepresentation law. The *Citizens* court noted that "[t]he fundamental principle of Wisconsin negligence law is that a tortfeasor is fully liable for all foreseeable consequences of his act except as those consequences are limited by policy factors," and it concluded that "accountants' liability to third parties should be determined under the accepted principles of Wisconsin negligence law."[157]

---

155 *See, e.g.*, *Bily*, 834 P.2d at 765 ("For example, a third party might expend its own resources to verify the client's financial statements or selected portions of them that were particularly material to its transaction with the client. Or it might commission its own audit or investigation, thus establishing privity between itself and an auditor or investigator to whom it could look for protection. In addition, it might bargain with the client for special security or improved terms in a credit or investment transaction. . . . As a matter of economic and social policy, third parties should be encouraged to rely on their own prudence, diligence, and contracting power, as well as other informational tools. This kind of self-reliance promotes sound investment and credit practices and discourages the careless use of monetary resources.").

156 *See id.* at 766.

157 *See also Bily*, 834 P.2d at 755 (quoting a law review article that stated that "it is a just and rational judicial policy that the same criteria govern the imposition of negligence liability, regardless of the context in which it arises"); *cf.* Ventura County Nat'l Bank v. Macker, 57 Cal. Rptr. 2d 418, 420 (Ct. App. 1996) ("Negligent

How does the *Citizens* foreseeability approach compare to the *Credit Alliance* framework? *Citizens* creates a much broader scope of liability for defendants. That is, accountants and other defendants would prefer the narrower *Credit Alliance* approach because it exposes them to less third-party liability. The *Citizens* approach is broad and exposes defendants to any third-party injuries that were reasonably foreseeable (putting aside any public policy factors).

The affidavits submitted by Timm convey this distinction. According to the court, "[e]ach affidavit stated that the affiant [a member of the Timm firm who had worked on the CFA account] had no knowledge, until after the fact, that CFA intended to or had obtained any loans from Citizens." The affidavit of Elmer Timm, Timm's president, similarly stated that "he was never informed by any person that any audit report prepared by his firm for CFA would be used by any lender for the purpose of determining whether or not to make a loan to CFA." Significantly, however, Elmer Timm's affidavit also stated that "as a certified public accountant, I know that audited statements are used for many purposes and that it is common for them to be supplied to lenders and creditors, and other persons."

Under *Credit Alliance*, this evidence would not permit a suit by Citizens. The accountants were not aware that CFA intended to use their work to procure a loan, they were not aware that CFA was considering Citizens for that loan, and there was certainly no conduct on the part of the accountants linking them to Citizens.

Under the foreseeability approach, however, this evidence is not important. What is important is that accountants understand that their work product is commonly used by lenders, investors, and other third parties in the financial community to make decisions about dealing with the accountants' clients. Is it reasonably foreseeable to an accountant that a lender might rely on the accountant's work in deciding to make an ill-advised loan to the client? Of course. Elmer Timm's affidavit concedes this point, although even without his statement, it is common knowledge in the industry. Under the foreseeability approach, therefore, a suit by Citizens is permissible (again, putting aside any public policy factors).

As mentioned, the *Citizens* court held accountants liable for foreseeable injuries unless "recovery is denied on grounds of public policy." The court mentioned the following "public policy reasons for not imposing liability":

misrepresentation is born of the union of negligence and fraud. If negligence is the mother and misrepresentation the father, it more closely resembles its mother.").

> (1) The injury is too remote from the negligence; or (2) the injury is too wholly out of proportion to the culpability of the negligent tort-feasor; or (3) in retrospect it appears too highly extraordinary that the negligence should have brought about the harm; or (4) because allowance of recovery would place too unreasonable a burden on the negligent tort-feasor; or (5) because allowance of recovery would be too likely to open the way for fraudulent claims; or (6) allowance of recovery would enter a field that has no sensible or just stopping point.[158]

As a result of these factors, the *Citizens* foreseeability approach and the *Credit Alliance* framework may, in practice, produce similar outcomes. That is, while a foreseeability approach surely risks "liability in an indeterminate amount for an indeterminate time to an indeterminate class" (particularly when dealing with audit reports for public companies that may be relied upon by a vast number of lenders and investors), a court can always extinguish liability to foreseeable (but not "known") third parties by invoking the public policy factors. For example, liability could be extinguished on the grounds that "allowance of recovery would enter a field that has no sensible or just stopping point," "because allowance of recovery would place too unreasonable a burden on the negligent tort-feasor," or because "the injury is too wholly out of proportion to the culpability of the negligent tort-feasor." Thus, while *Citizens* is frequently cited as an example of a broad foreseeability approach—one that purportedly differs in material respects from more restrictive approaches to third-party liability—the actual scope of liability imposed by such an approach will depend on how frequently courts invoke the public policy factors to limit exposure.

The third modern approach to defining the scope of liability for negligent misrepresentation is § 552 of the Second Restatement.[159] Section 552 adopts a restrictive approach to third-party liability for negligent misrepresentation. Part of the purpose of the section is to respond to Cardozo's fear of "liability in an indeterminate amount for an indeterminate time to an indeterminate class" when dealing with negligent misrepresentations causing pure economic loss.[160] When

---

[158] Some of the factors cited by the court ((1) and (3) in particular) do not seem materially different from simply stating that the third-party's injuries were not foreseeable.

[159] *See also* RESTATEMENT (THIRD) OF TORTS: LIABILITY FOR ECONOMIC HARM §§ 5–6 (2020) (addressing negligent misrepresentation).

[160] *See, e.g.*, RESTATEMENT (SECOND) OF TORTS § 552 cmt. a (1977) ("When the harm that is caused is only pecuniary loss, the courts have found it necessary to adopt a more restricted rule of liability, because of the extent to which misinformation may be, and may be expected to be, circulated, and the magnitude of the losses which may follow from reliance upon it.").

defendants feel that they are protected from vast amounts of liability for negligent misrepresentation, they will be more willing to provide information.[161]

If the Restatement were simply trying to extinguish indeterminate liability to encourage a flow of commercial information, however, an *Ultramares*-like rule of contractual privity would have been chosen. This rationale, therefore, does not fully explain why the Restatement chose its particular approach—an approach that creates liability to a "person or one of a limited group of persons" to whom the defendant "intends to supply the information" or "knows that the recipient intends to supply it."

Like the *Credit Alliance* near-privity test, § 552 seems to reflect an assumption of risk idea. If a defendant is aware that a third party is going to rely on the information in a particular transaction, and if the defendant nevertheless chooses to go forward with the engagement, it is fair to hold the defendant liable. The Restatement approach, in other words, seems designed to ensure that third-party liability is only imposed against a defendant when the defendant is aware of the risk, has the ability to protect against the risk, and consciously chooses to assume the risk.[162]

The Third Restatement follows a similar approach to negligent misrepresentation. Comment a to § 5 suggests that the section is designed to hold a defendant liable who has "invited reliance" by the

---

[161] *See id.* ("By limiting the liability for negligence of a supplier of information to be used in commercial transactions to cases in which he manifests an intent to supply the information for the sort of use in which the plaintiff's loss occurs, the law promotes the important social policy of encouraging the flow of commercial information upon which the operation of the economy rests.").

[162] *See id.* ("A user of commercial information cannot reasonably expect its maker to have undertaken to satisfy this obligation unless the terms of the obligation were known to him. Rather, one who relies upon information in connection with a commercial transaction may reasonably expect to hold the maker to a duty of care only in circumstances in which the maker was manifestly aware of the use to which the information was to be put and intended to supply it for that purpose."); *see also* Ellis v. Grant Thornton LLP, 530 F.3d 280, 291 (4th Cir. 2008) (applying § 552 to a negligent misrepresentation clam and stating the following: "First, we examine, from the accountant's standpoint, what risks he reasonably perceived he was undertaking when he delivered the challenged report or financial statement. If the accountant is unaware of a potential risk, then liability cannot attach."); *id.* ("When Grant Thornton issued its audit report, it was not assuming the risk that third parties would rely on the report."); Bily v. Arthur Young & Co., 834 P.2d 745, 769 (Cal. 1992) ("By confining what might otherwise be unlimited liability to those persons whom the engagement is designed to benefit, the Restatement rule requires that the supplier of information receive notice of potential third party claims, thereby allowing it to ascertain the potential scope of its liability and make rational decisions regarding the undertaking. The receipt of such notice justifies imposition of auditor liability for conduct that is merely negligent."); *id.* (noting that § 552 "attempts to identify those situations in which the supplier undertakes to supply information to a third party whom he or she knows is likely to rely on it in a transaction that has sufficiently specific economic parameters to permit the supplier to assess the risk of moving forward").

plaintiff. The notion of "invited reliance" seems similar to an assumption of risk idea, as the defendant is only liable to those whose reliance he was specifically aware of at the time the defendant acted.[163]

The decision of *Ellis v. Grant Thornton LLP*[164] is a nice example of § 552 in action. First National Bank of Keystone ("Keystone") engaged in a strategy of acquiring and securitizing high-risk loans. Several of Keystone's executives concealed the failure of many of these securitizations by falsifying Keystone's books. The Office of the Comptroller of the Currency ("OCC") began to investigate Keystone, and it ultimately ordered Keystone to obtain an audit of its banking operations from a nationally recognized independent accounting firm. Keystone retained Grant Thornton.

Grant Thornton performed the audit but negligently failed to discover a $515 million discrepancy on the Keystone financial statements. Instead, Grant Thornton informed the Keystone board and shareholders that Keystone was going to get an unqualified audit opinion.

Gary Ellis was being recruited by Keystone to become its president. Ellis discussed the financial condition of Keystone with Grant Thornton representatives, and he was told that Keystone would receive a clean audit opinion. Ellis also attended a Keystone shareholders' meeting and visited the company. On both occasions, he heard Grant Thornton state that Keystone would receive a clean audit opinion. Ellis ultimately joined Keystone, allegedly in reliance on Grant Thornton's audit and its statements. When Keystone's financial problems came to light, he sued Grant Thornton for negligent misrepresentation.

The court applied § 552 of the Second Restatement to the negligent misrepresentation claim. As mentioned, a defendant under § 552 is liable only to a "person or one of a limited group of persons" to whom the defendant "intends to supply the information" or "knows

---

[163] *See* RESTATEMENT (THIRD) OF TORTS: LIABILITY FOR ECONOMIC HARM § 5 cmt. a (2020) ("A plaintiff's reliance alone, even if foreseeable, is not a sufficient basis for recovery; under either Section a defendant generally must act with the apparent purpose of providing a basis for the reliance. It may be useful to say that a defendant held liable under either Section must 'invite reliance' by the plaintiff, so long as the expression is understood to refer to the defendant's apparent purpose and not to a temptation incidentally created by the defendant's words or acts."); *see also id.* § 5 cmt. b ("This Section thus recognizes duties only in a limited set of cases where the parties have no contract on point, where the defendant nevertheless undertook to provide the plaintiff with a basis for reliance, and where holding the defendant accountable will produce a liability that is reasonably predictable and proportional to the defendant's culpability."); *cf. id.* § 5 cmt. a (noting that §§ 5–6 are "[b]oth . . . based on the logic of Restatement Second, Torts § 552, which a majority of states have adopted").

[164] 530 F.3d 280 (4th Cir. 2008).

that the recipient intends to supply it." According to the court, Grant Thornton was hired to provide information to Keystone and the OCC; thus, Grant Thornton did not intend to supply information to Ellis (a prospective employee), nor did Grant Thornton know that Keystone intended to supply the audit to Ellis. In other words, Ellis (or any other potential employee) was not a member of any limited group of persons for whose benefit the audit report was prepared. Moreover, the court concluded that Ellis could not have justifiably relied on Grant Thornton's statements because (1) Ellis was aware that the audit report explicitly stated that it was not intended for use by third parties, and (2) Ellis was sophisticated enough to understand that the audit was for the benefit of Keystone and the OCC—not for prospective employees.[165] The district court's judgment in favor of Ellis was reversed.

How would Ellis have fared under the near-privity (*Credit Alliance*) and foreseeability (*Citizens State Bank*) approaches? Under *Credit Alliance*, Ellis presumably would not have fared any better. *Credit Alliance* requires the defendant to know the party who is going to rely and the purpose for which the information will be used. Because Grant Thornton "was not aware during this [auditing] process that its audit was being performed for the benefit of potential employees of Keystone," these two requirements would not seem to be met. Further, although there was some contact between Grant Thornton and Ellis that might be characterized as "linking conduct," a court would likely conclude (as the *Ellis* court did under the § 552 approach) that such conduct came too late, as Grant Thornton "was not aware of [Ellis] until *after* Grant Thornton reached its decision to give Keystone a clean audit opinion." Finally, the *Credit Alliance* approach would surely require justifiable reliance for a negligent misrepresentation action, and Ellis would likely face the same reliance problems that the *Ellis* court mentioned.

Under the foreseeability approach, Grant Thornton would be liable if its actions were the cause of Ellis' injuries and if the injuries were reasonably foreseeable. Is it reasonably foreseeable to accountants that their audits might be relied upon by prospective employees of the client? The *Ellis* court suggested that possibility,[166] and, if so, there is a risk of liability. On the other hand, a court might

---

165 Is it really not justifiable to rely on an audit report giving a clean bill of financial health to a company that one is contemplating joining as a top executive? How else would Ellis have gotten a sense of the financial strength of Keystone?

166 *See Ellis*, 530 F.3d at 291 ("Rather, in performing its audit function, Grant Thornton was aware that its audit opinion and any statements made leading up to the issuance of the audit opinion *may* be relied upon by shareholders, investors, and perhaps potential employees such as Ellis. However, more than a tenuous awareness of this sort is required to impose liability on Grant Thornton. To hold otherwise would transform the Restatement approach into the foreseeability approach . . . .").

use the public policy factors to defeat Ellis' claim. More importantly, even the foreseeability approach would surely require justifiable reliance for a negligent misrepresentation action. Thus, Ellis would likely face the same reliance problems that the *Ellis* court mentioned.[167]

What are the differences between the *Credit Alliance*, foreseeability, and § 552 approaches? *Credit Alliance* and § 552 are similar approaches in that they both protect defendants by restricting the pool of potential plaintiffs. Both require the defendant to be aware of a particular person who will be relying on the information for a particular purpose (§ 552(2)(b) is similar to *Credit*

---

[167] The *Ellis* court emphasized the contractual disclaimer of reliance that Grant Thornton added to its audit report. Indeed, the court stated rather absolutely that "[u]nquestionably, given that the audit report stated that it was not intended for use by third parties, Ellis could not justifiably rely on the audit report in signing his employment contract with Keystone." *Id.* at 292. This analysis would seem to apply to lenders and investors as well. If contractual disclaimers can defeat the reliance requirement, it would seem prudent for accountants to include them in audit reports given that even the most plaintiff-friendly approach to negligent misrepresentation (i.e., the foreseeability approach) would still require justifiable reliance. *See also* McCamish, Martin, Brown & Loeffler v. F.E. Appling Interests, 991 S.W.2d 787, 794 (Tex. 1999) ("A lawyer may also avoid or minimize the risk of liability to a nonclient by setting forth (1) limitations as to whom the representation is directed and who should rely on it, or (2) disclaimers as to the scope and accuracy of the factual investigation or assumptions forming the basis of the representation or the representation itself.").

Similar to contractual disclaimers of reliance, the Restatement suggests that contractual agreements specifying who will receive the audit opinion will be upheld. *See* RESTATEMENT (SECOND) OF TORTS § 552 illus. 5 (1977) (allowing the accountant to specify with the client that the audit opinion will only be transmitted to a particular bank, and exonerating the accountant from liability when the client transmitted the opinion to another bank); *see also* Touche Ross & Co. v. Commercial Union Ins. Co., 514 So.2d 315, 323 (Miss. 1987) (stating, in a foreseeability jurisdiction, that "[o]f course, the auditor remains free to limit the dissemination of his opinion through a separate agreement with the audited entity"). This provides another contractual tool to help the accountant minimize its liability exposure.

Comment g to § 5 of the Third Restatement makes similar points:

> If a defendant clearly states that its guidance is supplied for the benefit of a specific recipient and no other, the defendant cannot be held liable to a similar but different recipient who relies on the information later. See Illustration 10. A defendant likewise may state that its work is meant to serve as a basis for reliance in a particular transaction and no other. If no such limiting understandings are in place, however, this Section does not require the class of parties or the transaction at issue to be the very same ones the defendant expected. See Illustration 11. In close cases, the test for substantial similarity should be kept functional: it is whether the use made of the information, if understood in advance, would likely have changed the defendant's perception of the risks taken by speaking and caused the defendant to take measures in response—such as more care, more disclaimers, higher charges, or the purchase of more insurance.

For a discussion of "no-reliance" clauses in the fraud context, see RESTATEMENT (THIRD) OF TORTS: LIABILITY FOR ECONOMIC HARM § 11 cmt. e (2020).

*Alliance*'s purpose requirement). That said, two differences are noteworthy.

First, § 552 does not require conduct linking the defendant to the third-party plaintiff. Under § 552, if the defendant intends to supply the information to a person, or knows that the recipient intends to supply the information to a person, liability to that person may arise without a further showing of linking conduct. Second, the *Ellis* court suggested that *Credit Alliance* requires the defendant to know of a *specific* person who will be relying on the information (the "precise identity of the informational consumer"),[168] while § 552 allows the defendant to be aware of a "limited group of persons" who will be relying on the information (even if the defendant is not aware of the specific person(s) within that limited group).[169]

The foreseeability approach is very different from the more restrictive approaches of *Credit Alliance* and § 552. It is the most plaintiff-friendly framework because it allows, at least in theory, a

---

168 *See Ellis*, 530 F.3d at 288 n.5 (quoting First Nat'l Bank v. Monco Agency, Inc., 911 F.2d 1053, 1059 (5th Cir. 1990)).

169 *See, e.g.*, RESTATEMENT (SECOND) OF TORTS § 552 cmt. h (1977) ("It is sufficient, in other words, insofar as the plaintiff's identity is concerned, that the maker supplies the information for repetition to a certain group or class of persons and that the plaintiff proves to be one of them, even though the maker never had heard of him by name when the information was given.").

One might question this second difference. The *Credit Alliance* opinion favorably discussed the decision of *White v. Guarente*, 372 N.E.2d 315 (N.Y. 1977). In that case, the court imposed liability on accountants to a group of limited partners, even though the accountants did not seem to know the precise identity of any of the limited partners themselves. The *White* court noted that the plaintiff "seeks redress, not as a mere member of the public, but as one of a settled and particularized class among the members of which the report would be circulated." *Id.* at 320. If the *Credit Alliance* approach would impose liability on a defendant to a known "particularized class" or "limited group," then this purported difference with § 552 is not really a difference at all. *But see* Sykes v. RFD Third Ave. 1 Assocs., LLC, 938 N.E.2d 325, 326–27 (N.Y. 2010) ("Plaintiffs' claim here fails the second branch of the *Credit Alliance* test: plaintiffs have not sufficiently alleged that they were a 'known party or parties,' as *Credit Alliance* requires. While Cosentini obviously knew in general that prospective purchasers of apartments would rely on the offering plan, there is no indication that it knew these plaintiffs would be among them, or indeed that Cosentini knew or had the means of knowing of plaintiffs' existence when it made the statements for which it is being sued. The words 'known party or parties' in the *Credit Alliance* test mean what they say."); Westpac Banking Corp. v. Deschamps, 484 N.E.2d 1351, 1352–53 (N.Y. 1985) ("Although obtaining a bridge loan may be 'a particular purpose' for which the financial statements were to be used by Turnkey—a purpose Seidman allegedly knew—the complaint does not allege that Seidman knew that Turnkey was showing the reports to Westpac. Rather, Westpac claims only that it was one of a class of 'potential bridge lenders,' to which class as a whole Seidman owed a duty, and that it should be considered a 'known party' because it was as of the date of the certification a substantial lender to Turnkey, and 'thus a prime candidate for a bridge loan.' This is not, however, the equivalent of knowledge of 'the identity of the specific nonprivy party who would be relying upon the audit reports.' "); RESTATEMENT (THIRD) OF TORTS § 5 (2020) (Reporter's Note) (stating that "New York law is notably more restrictive than this Section, and would produce different results in Illustration 11").

large pool of potential plaintiffs to sue—anyone whose injuries are reasonably foreseeable—even if the defendant is unaware of the particular plaintiff (or group that the plaintiff is in) and the particular purpose for which the plaintiff is using the information.[170]

Given these similarities and differences, which approach to third-party liability for negligent misrepresentation would a defendant prefer? A strict privity approach (e.g., *Ultramares*) is the most favorable for defendants, as liability generally extends only to parties the defendant has contracted with (and the economic loss rule might preclude a negligent misrepresentation action completely).[171] Outside of strict privity, *Credit Alliance* is probably the next most favorable approach because liability can only run (arguably) to specific persons and not limited groups, and there is the linking conduct requirement which poses a barrier for plaintiffs. Slightly less favorable for defendants is § 552 because it opens up liability to "limited groups" as well as specific persons. It also lacks the linking conduct requirement. Finally, defendants would least prefer the foreseeability approach, as it creates the broadest scope of liability to any person whose injuries could be reasonably foreseen by the defendant (putting aside the public policy factors).[172]

Section 552 implicates other issues that are worthy of discussion, including knowledge, pecuniary interests, limited groups, and various other matters. Each will be discussed below.

***Knowledge***

The defendant's knowledge is an important factor under § 552. As mentioned, § 552(2)(a) states that if a defendant "knows that the recipient intends to supply" the defendant's information to a third party, the defendant can be liable to that third party. Similarly, § 552(2)(b) indicates that such liability extends to transactions that the defendant "knows" the recipient intends to influence.[173]

At what point in time should the defendant's knowledge be measured for purposes of these standards? As explained in the *Credit Alliance* discussion, if § 552 is premised on an assumption of risk

---

170 *See, e.g.*, *Ellis*, 530 F.3d at 288 n.5 (stating that, "unlike the foreseeability approach, the Restatement approach does not extend to 'every reasonably foreseeable consumer of financial information' ").

171 *See* Chapter 5 (discussing the economic loss rule between contracting parties).

172 Of course, defendants would most prefer a jurisdiction that refuses to recognize the tort of negligent misrepresentation at all. *See* South County, Inc. v. First W. Loan Co., 871 S.W.2d 325, 326 (Ark. 1994) ("We decline to recognize the tort of negligent misrepresentation. Misrepresentation, also commonly referred to as deceit or fraud, has been an *intentional* tort in Arkansas for well over a century. . . . We see no need to recognize a new cause of action for negligent misrepresentation.").

173 *See also* RESTATEMENT (THIRD) OF TORTS: LIABILITY FOR ECONOMIC HARM § 5(2) (2020) (setting forth similar provisions).

idea, the time of engagement would seem to be the appropriate time for measuring the defendant's knowledge. At that moment, the defendant has the maximum flexibility to protect against any risk of liability. In *Ellis*, however, the court observed that " 'actual knowledge . . . should be ascertained at the time the audit report or financial statement is *issued*.' "[174]

This position seems out of step with the assumption of risk notion underlying § 552. In the accounting context, for example, assume that the terms of the engagement have been negotiated, the engagement contract has been signed, the audit has been staffed, and the audit work has been completed. Twenty-four hours before the final audit report is issued, the client informs the accountant that it will be providing several specifically named banks with the audit report for the purpose of borrowing several million dollars. Under the "time of issuance" standard, it would seem that the accountant would be bound by that knowledge and would be subject to liability to those banks for any negligent misstatements. Surely this is not the right result, as the accountant would not seem to have any ability to protect itself from this exposure, and it cannot be said that the accountant consciously chose to assume this risk.[175]

Is the knowledge required under § 552(2)(a) and (b) inquiring into the defendant's "actual knowledge" (i.e., what the defendant knew), the defendant's "constructive knowledge" (i.e., what the defendant should have known), or both? In *First National Bank v. Monco Agency Inc.*,[176] the court rejected an argument that constructive knowledge was sufficient for § 552:

> Anything less than actual knowledge, in fact, would extend liability to the bounds of "reasonable foreseeability," similar to that in New Jersey. . . . We conclude, therefore, that the Restatement requires *actual* knowledge on the part of accountants of the limited—though unnamed—group of potential lenders that will rely upon the inaccurate 1980

174 *Ellis*, 530 F.3d at 289 (emphasis added) (quoting N. Am. Specialty Ins. Co. v. Lapalme, 258 F.3d 35, 39 (1st Cir. 2001)); *see also* First Nat'l Bank v. Monco Agency Inc., 911 F.2d 1053, 1059 (5th Cir. 1990) ("Accordingly, liability is fixed by the accountants' particular knowledge at the moment the audit is published . . . .").

175 Interestingly, the analysis of the *Ellis* court reflects this timing criticism. *See, e.g.*, *Ellis*, 530 F.3d at 290 ("If the scope of the audit involved potential employees, one would expect at least some knowledge on the part of Grant Thornton *before* they formed their audit opinion."). Ellis was known before Grant Thornton issued its final audit report, but Ellis was not known at a time when Grant Thornton could have made a conscious decision to assume or reject the risk. In other words, although the court stated a time of issuance standard, it did not actually apply one. *See also Lapalme*, 258 F.3d at 41 ("[T]he rule implicitly recognizes that the risk perceived by the accountant *at the time of the engagement* cabins the extent of the duty that he owes to known third parties." (emphasis added)).

176 911 F.2d 1053 (5th Cir. 1990).

> audit, as well as actual knowledge of the particular financial transaction that such information is designed to influence.

The conclusion of the *Monco* court seems consistent with an assumption of risk idea, as liability is only imposed on defendants who are aware of particular risks and who consciously choose to assume them. Consciously assuming a particular risk suggests actual knowledge of the risk rather than imputed knowledge.

Moreover, as the *Monco* court suggests, the distinction between what a defendant "should have known" and what is "reasonably foreseeable" to a defendant is slim (if not non-existent). After all, the risks that a defendant "should have known" about are largely the risks that are reasonably foreseeable to the defendant. Thus, if the Restatement approach is going to be different from a foreseeability approach, it seems sensible to reject a "should have known" standard. Other courts have agreed with *Monco* and have concluded that § 552 requires actual knowledge.[177]

Similarly, a defendant's general knowledge of how its information is customarily used is insufficient to meet the knowledge requirement of § 552(2)(a) and (b). Illustration 10 to § 552 clearly states that "A knows that the financial statements, accompanied by an auditor's opinion, are customarily used in a wide variety of financial transactions by the corporation and that they may be relied upon by lenders, investors, shareholders, creditors, purchasers and the like, in numerous possible kinds of transactions." Nevertheless, because "A [was] not informed of any intended use of the financial statements," the illustration concludes that A is not liable. Similarly, illustration 12 to § 552 notes that A Company "knows that survey reports are customarily used in a wide variety of real estate transactions and that [they] may be relied upon by purchasers, mortgagees, investors and others." Yet because "A Company [was] not informed of any intended use of the survey report," the illustration concludes that A Company is not liable.[178]

Thus, although courts refer to § 552 as an actual knowledge rather than a constructive knowledge standard, not all actual knowledge suffices. In illustrations 10 and 12, A does have actual knowledge of who customarily uses its information, but that

---

[177] *See, e.g.*, Kohala Agriculture v. Deloitte and Touche, 949 P.2d 141, 161–62 (Haw. Ct. App. 1997); Nycal Corp. v. KPMG Peat Marwick LLP, 688 N.E.2d 1368, 1373 n.5 (Mass. 1998); Grant Thornton LLP v. Prospect High Income Fund, 314 S.W.3d 913, 930 & nn.11–12 (Tex. 2010).

[178] *See also* RESTATEMENT (SECOND) OF TORTS § 552 cmt. h (1977) ("It is not enough that the maker merely knows of the ever-present possibility of repetition to anyone, and the possibility of action in reliance upon it, on the part of anyone to whom it may be repeated.").

generalized actual knowledge is insufficient—presumably because it would expose A to "liability in an indeterminate amount for an indeterminate time to an indeterminate class." It is actual knowledge communicated by the client to the defendant that is the focus of § 552.

The Third Restatement, in illustration 12 and comment g(2) to § 5, seems to reach similar conclusions. In illustration 12, Adviser "knows that Client is in the habit of passing such recommendations on to various friends," but that generalized actual knowledge is insufficient because "Adviser does not speak for the purpose of providing those friends with a basis for reliance . . . and does nothing to suggest such an intent." Once again, the defendant's general knowledge of how its information is customarily used is insufficient. Comment g(2) explicitly indicates that generalized actual knowledge is insufficient and, like illustration 12, it explains its conclusion by referencing the absence of a purpose to induce reliance:

> A defendant's actual knowledge of a client's intentions does not, by itself, subject the defendant to liability for losses that result when the intentions are carried out. The defendant must act for the purpose of enabling the type of use the recipient makes. In Illustration 11, for example, liability is intact because the defendant's purpose is to provide information for uses such as those the client makes, though the defendant lacks knowledge of certain specific details. In Illustration 12, by contrast, the defendant may have exact knowledge of those to whom the client will pass the information, but nevertheless is not liable to them. Providing advice for distribution to the client's friends is no part of the defendant's purpose; in the absence of such a purpose, recovery would be founded on nothing more than foreseeability to the defendant that others might choose to rely on his statements. That is not a sufficient basis for liability under this Section.[179]

***Pecuniary Interest***

Section 552 is only applicable to a defendant who provides false information "in the course of his business, profession or employment,

---

[179] *See also* RESTATEMENT (THIRD) OF TORTS: LIABILITY FOR ECONOMIC HARM § 5 cmt. g (2020) ("To be held liable under this Section, a defendant must supply information for the guidance of the plaintiff. Liability is also limited to losses produced by reliance in a transaction that the defendant intended to influence. Both requirements make clear that liability is not established by evidence that the plaintiff's reliance on the defendant's information was merely foreseeable. See Illustrations 9 and 12. These elements, like those discussed in Comment f, help keep the defendant's exposure to liability clear and determinate.").

or in any other transaction in which he has a pecuniary interest."[180] A pecuniary interest is a financial or economic interest, and the most common example is when the speaker is paid for the information transmitted (e.g., paying a fee for an accountant's opinion).[181] As comment d to § 552 indicates, however, the interest can be more indirect: "Thus the officers of a corporation, although they receive no personal consideration for giving information concerning its affairs, may have a pecuniary interest in its transactions, since they stand to profit indirectly from them, and an agent who expects to receive a commission on a sale may have such an interest in it although he sells nothing." The common theme in these examples would seem to be that the speaker supplied information with the hope that the recipient's use of the information would ultimately result in an economic benefit to the speaker.

Comment c to § 5 of the Third Restatement describes the purpose behind the pecuniary interest requirement as follows:

> This requirement serves several purposes. First, it helps confine liability to cases where information is offered in a sufficiently serious spirit to make the plaintiff's reliance reasonable. Second, liability for those who speak gratuitously would tend to discourage them from speaking at all; the speech would then amount to the assumption of an economic burden (the risk of liability) without any offsetting gain that they are able to capture. Defendants who receive economic benefits for offering advice, by contrast, may well choose to speak despite the risk of liability for being wrong. They can treat that potential liability as a cost of doing business and charge accordingly or consider buying insurance against it. The "pecuniary interest" element of the tort should be interpreted flexibly to give effect to these purposes that the requirement serves.

Is it enough that the speaker gave the information in the course of his business, profession, or employment? The syntax of the first clause of § 552(1) suggests that "course of business" and "pecuniary interest" are not mere alternatives. If the clause read "one who, in the course of his business, profession or employment, or in any transaction in which he has a pecuniary interest," then giving information in the course of business OR in a pecuniary interest transaction would suffice. But the clause does not say that; instead, the word "other" is between "any" and "transaction." This suggests that the touchstone for all of § 552 is a transaction in which one has

---

[180] *See also* RESTATEMENT (THIRD) OF TORTS: LIABILITY FOR ECONOMIC HARM § 5(1) (2020) (substantially the same).

[181] *See* RESTATEMENT (SECOND) OF TORTS § 552 cmt. d (1977).

a pecuniary interest. Giving information in the course of one's business, profession, or employment is *typically* associated with a pecuniary interest, but it may not be. If it is not associated with a pecuniary interest, then it does not fall within the scope of § 552.[182]

When would giving information in the course of one's business, profession, or employment not be associated with a pecuniary interest? Perhaps pro bono work is a good example. If an attorney anonymously volunteers at a general legal assistance phone bank, for example, one might say that she is giving information in the course of her profession, but it is hard to find a pecuniary interest. If the legal assistance was not anonymous, could the prospect of future business or referrals be seen as an indirect pecuniary interest?

As another example, comment d to § 552 discusses "curbstone" opinions:

> . . . . But when one who is engaged in a business or profession steps entirely outside of it, as when an attorney gives a casual and offhand opinion on a point of law to a friend whom he meets on the street, or what is commonly called a 'curbstone opinion,' it is not to be regarded as given in the course of his business or profession; and since he has no other interest in it, it is considered purely gratuitous. The recipient of the information is not justified in expecting that his informant will exercise the care and skill that is necessary to insure a correct opinion and is only justified in expecting that the opinion will be an honest one.

Technically, this is not an example of giving information in the course of one's business without a pecuniary interest, as the comment says this is not to be regarded as given in the course of business at all. Nevertheless, this distinction seems questionable. Whenever a lawyer gives a legal opinion, isn't the lawyer acting in the course of his profession? (Is it possible to step "entirely outside of" the profession when a lawyer is giving legal advice?) It seems more sensible to say that curbstone opinions are given in the course of the speaker's business, profession, or employment, but they are not actionable because the lawyer or other speaker had no pecuniary interest in supplying the information (but again, might even offhand opinions be seen as attempts by the speaker to earn future business or referrals, which could constitute an indirect pecuniary interest),

182 *Cf. id.* ("The fact that information is given in the course of the defendant's business, profession or employment is a sufficient indication that he has a pecuniary interest in it, even though he receives no consideration for it at the time. It is not, however, conclusive.").

or because the recipient cannot justifiably rely on casual or offhand opinions.

The Third Restatement deletes the "other" between the "course of business, profession, or employment" clause and the "pecuniary interest" clause in § 5, suggesting that they are mere alternatives. (Strangely, however, § 6 retains the "other.") Read literally, liability under § 5 may be imposed upon a defendant who gives information in the course of business OR in a pecuniary interest transaction.[183] Comment c to § 5 addresses some of the issues discussed above:

> Common questions that recur concerning this element involve, first, whether defendants act in the course of their business when they supply information on occasions that are incidental to their main line of work. The requirement tends to be satisfied when the plaintiff and defendant are in a commercial relationship. Thus, employers who give information about retirement benefits to their employees have duties of care; they speak in the course of their business, even if not in performance of any particular contracts they may have with their employees. The result is the same if the plaintiff and defendant are in a joint commercial venture. The economic framework that surrounds the parties' dealings is then enough to lend a pecuniary interest to statements they make to each other that satisfy the other elements of this Section. . . .
>
> In another set of cases, the defendant makes representations to a plaintiff without any direct commercial relationship between the parties, as when a firm responds to a request for information from an outsider who does not propose to pay for it. The important question then is whether speaking will redound to the defendant's economic benefit in some reasonably clear way, perhaps because it helps another party with whom the defendant has a contract.
>
> . . . .
>
> A final difficulty involves the defendant who speaks without being paid but normally requires a fee. No rule can be stated for such cases, but liability tends not to be found

183 *Cf.* RESTATEMENT (THIRD) OF TORTS: LIABILITY FOR ECONOMIC HARM § 5 (Reporter's Note) (2020) ("The Section's reference to 'any transaction in which [the defendant] has a pecuniary interest' is meant to recognize a residual category that covers cases in which defendants do not act in the course of their 'business, profession, or employment.' Conversely, defendants who do act squarely in the course of their 'business, profession, or employment' may be held liable even if they provide advice on a pro bono or volunteer basis.").

in them; the professional who usually gets paid to speak is, when speaking without pay, typically found to have acted gratuitously. Conversely, a business that supplies information without charge on a regular basis is more likely to be held responsible for it. The regularity suggests that providing certain advice for "free" is part of the defendant's business, not an isolated favor with unconsidered implications. A lawyer who offers advice to a client in an unpaid initial consultation thus can be held liable when the advice is negligent, because consultations of that kind are a regular and necessary part of a lawyer's professional work. By contrast, an appraiser who normally charges for an opinion may be found to act outside the course of business when offering an occasional unpaid comment on the value of a painting.

***Limited Group***

What constitutes a "limited group" of persons under § 552(2)(a)? A limited group would seem to be a defined group of related persons that is distinct from the public at large. Its composition would have to be described as something other than an unlimited, indeterminate class.[184]

Are "banks" a limited group? The world of banks does not seem particularly limited, especially if it also includes related "lending" entities (e.g., credit unions, insurance companies that loan money, or wealthy individuals who loan money). On the other hand, illustration 7 to § 552 seems to indicate that banks are a limited group.

Are "investors" a limited group? Whereas banks might not be an indeterminate class (because a bank, for example, needs a state or federal charter), an investor can literally be anyone with a dollar in his pocket. The world of investors, in other words, would seem to be an unlimited, indeterminate class because the group could theoretically include anyone in the universe with money.[185]

---

184 *Cf.* Bily v. Arthur Young & Co., 834 P.2d 745, 759 (Cal. 1992) (quoting the Reporter for the Restatement as stating that "[t]he problem is to find language which will eliminate liability to the very large class of persons whom almost any negligently given information may foreseeably reach and influence, and limit the liability, not to a particular plaintiff defined in advance, but to the comparatively small group whom the defendant expects and intends to influence").

185 *See, e.g., In re* Crazy Eddie Securities Litig., 812 F. Supp. 338, 360 (E.D.N.Y. 1993) ("Plaintiffs have not cited, and the court cannot find, a single decision by any court extending an accountant's duty of care to as-yet unidentified future open-market buyers of publicly-traded securities, even when that duty is limited to the rarified class of buyers with sufficient resources to acquire control of entire companies."); Brug v. Enstar Group, Inc., 755 F. Supp. 1247, 1258 (D. Del. 1991) ("If any member of the public who might choose to invest in KCI common stock were to qualify as part of a protected class, then the 'limited group' requirement would be meaningless."); *see also*

Comment f to § 5 of the Third Restatement describes the purpose behind the "limited group" requirement as follows:

> Liability under this Section is confined to plaintiffs who may be described as a "limited group." This element of the tort helps to prevent a defendant's potential liability from becoming indeterminate and unduly widespread. Sometimes the intended audience for a statement is vast; it might include the general public or all possible investors in the stock market. Potential liability to members of such a large audience would make a speaker's exposure hard to gauge. Moreover, a speaker whose words reach a general audience will not usually be compensated by all those who benefit from hearing them. If speakers were nevertheless held liable to everyone injured by reliance on statements circulated so widely, the result would be an incentive not to speak at all. The "limited group" element of the tort corrects for these possibilities by permitting liability only to discrete classes of plaintiffs.

With respect to banks, illustrations 10 and 11 to § 5 are similar to illustrations 5–7 of § 552. Both illustrations (10 and 11) suggest that banks would be considered a limited group because Accountant is subject to liability to Second Choice Bank when nothing is said about supplying the information solely for the guidance of Lender. Interestingly, these illustrations in the Third Restatement arguably suggest that "lenders"—a group larger than simply "banks"—would be a limited group, as the illustrations are not restricted to banks (as they are in the Second Restatement). This would be an odd conclusion, as anyone with a dollar to loan might be considered a lender.

With respect to investors, illustrations 6 and 7 to § 5 suggest that all possible investors in the stock market, or the general public as a whole, are not a limited group. When a subset of the investing public is clearly defined and made known to the defendant, however, that subset can constitute a limited group (e.g., illustration 8 to § 5).

***Substantially Similar Transaction***

Under § 552(2)(b), a defendant's liability for negligent misrepresentation extends to a transaction that the defendant intends to influence or to a substantially similar transaction. It also

---

Scottish Heritable Trust, PLC v. Peat Marwick Main & Co., 81 F.3d 606, 613 (5th Cir. 1996) (following *Crazy Eddie* and stating the following: "[T]he Texas courts have intimated this same view, albeit in dicta. In *Cook Consultants,* a negligent misrepresentation case in which the defendant was a surveyor, the Texas court stated that '[u]nlike, for example, future purchasers of shares of stock attempting to hold an accountant liable, [plaintiff] Larson is not a member of an unlimited class. . . .' ").

extends to a transaction that the defendant knows the recipient intends to influence or to a substantially similar transaction. As comment j to § 552 observes:

> .... The question may be one of the extent of the departure that the maker of the representation understands is to be expected. If he is told that the information that he supplies is to be used in applying to a particular bank for a loan of $10,000, the fact that the loan is made by that bank for $15,000 will not necessarily mean that the transaction is a different one. But if the loan is for $500,000, the very difference in amount would lead the ordinary borrower or lender to regard it as a different kind of transaction. The ordinary practices and attitudes of the business world are to be taken into account, and the question becomes one of whether the departure from the contemplated transaction is so major and so significant that it cannot be regarded as essentially the same transaction.[186]

***Scope of Liability for Fraud Versus Negligent Misrepresentation***

The scope of liability for negligence torts is typically narrower than the scope of liability for intentional torts because reduced culpability on the part of the defendant justifies a lesser exposure to liability.[187] Indeed, comment h to § 552 observes:

> The rule stated in this Section subjects the negligent supplier of misinformation to liability only to those persons for whose benefit and guidance it is supplied. In this particular his liability is somewhat more narrowly restricted than that of the maker of a fraudulent representation (see § 531), which extends to any person whom the maker of the representation has reason to expect to act in reliance upon it.

The easiest way to understand how § 552 results in a lesser exposure to liability is to focus on the "reason to expect" language of § 531. As discussed in Section A(3), § 531 imposes liability on a defendant if the defendant has "reason to expect" reliance, which

---

186 For examples of substantially similar (and not substantially similar) transactions, see RESTATEMENT (SECOND) OF TORTS § 552 cmt. j & illus. 13–15; *see also* RESTATEMENT (THIRD) OF TORTS: LIABILITY FOR ECONOMIC HARM §§ 5(2)(b), 6(2)(b) (2020) (setting forth similar provisions).

187 *See, e.g.*, RESTATEMENT (SECOND) OF TORTS § 552 cmt. a (1977) ("The liability stated in this Section is likewise more restricted than that for fraudulent misrepresentation stated in § 531. When there is no intent to deceive but only good faith coupled with negligence, the fault of the maker of the misrepresentation is sufficiently less to justify a narrower responsibility for its consequences.").

means that the defendant "has information from which a reasonable man would conclude that the result would follow or would govern his conduct upon the assumption that it will do so."[188] This objective inquiry into what the reasonable man would conclude is absent from § 552, as § 552 is based solely on a subjective inquiry into what the defendant intended or knew. Thus, the scope of liability under § 531 is broader because it exposes the defendant to liability based not only on what *the defendant* intended or knew, but also on what a *reasonable person* would conclude.

In addition, while § 531 extends liability to a "class" of persons, § 552 extends liability only to a "limited group" of persons. This suggests that a permitted plaintiff under § 531 who is a member of a "class" of persons may not be a permitted plaintiff under § 552 because the class is not sufficiently "limited."[189] Once again, the scope of liability under § 531 would appear to be broader. The pecuniary interest requirement of § 552(1) also helps to limit a defendant's exposure to liability. A defendant may only be sued for negligent misrepresentation under § 552 if the defendant provided information in the course of his business, profession or employment, or in any other transaction in which he had a pecuniary interest. The fraud sections do not contain a similar restriction.

Under the Third Restatement, § 12 appears to be similar to § 531. To the extent that §§ 5–6 of the Third Restatement focus on the defendant's actual knowledge and not on what a reasonable person would have known, the analysis would seem to be similar—i.e., the scope of liability under § 12 is broader because it exposes the defendant to liability based not only on what the defendant intended or knew, but also on what a reasonable person would conclude. Other Second Restatement distinctions discussed above may similarly apply to the Third Restatement.

### *Silence Claims*

Silence can serve as the basis of a fraud claim,[190] but can silence similarly serve as the basis of a negligent misrepresentation claim?

---

[188] *Id.* § 531 cmt. d.

[189] For example, comment e to § 531 states that a "class may include a rather large group, such as potential sellers, buyers, creditors, lenders, or investors." As discussed, however, some of these groups may not be sufficiently limited (e.g., investors).

Can a similar distinction be drawn between the "type of transaction" language in § 531 and the "substantially similar transaction" language in § 552(2)(b)? In other words, for any given transaction, is the "type" of transaction a broader category than a "substantially similar" transaction? Perhaps something might be classified as the same "type" of transaction, even though it would not be characterized as a "substantially similar" transaction. If so, even this language suggests that the scope of liability under § 531 is broader.

[190] *See* Section A(1).

Under the Second Restatement, the word choice of § 552(1) would seem to preclude silence claims, as liability is imposed only on one who "supplies false information." "Supplies" suggests an affirmative act rather than nondisclosure. With respect to liability for fraud, however, § 525 also uses the affirmative-sounding language of "makes a misrepresentation," but no one doubts that § 551 brings silence within the purview of this language. In fact, § 551 effectively states that a failure to disclose a matter should be treated as equivalent to an affirmative representation of the nonexistence of the matter. One could argue that § 551 should have a similar effect on the affirmative language of § 552. After all, the text of § 551 is not limited to fraud claims, and even the placement of the section suggests that it is not limited to fraud claims (i.e., in the Second Restatement's table of contents, § 551 is not in the "Fraudulent Misrepresentation (Deceit)" topic, but is instead in the "Concealment and Nondisclosure" topic).

By contrast, comment e to § 5 of the Third Restatement explicitly indicates that "[a] failure to speak, by itself, does not support liability under this [negligent misrepresentation] Section." The comment goes on to state, however, that there is liability for half-truths.

The case law on silence-based negligent misrepresentation claims is divided.[191] Courts that refuse to recognize such a claim seem to be motivated by a reluctance to expand the tort of negligent misrepresentation.

### *Opinion Claims*

In certain circumstances, an opinion can serve as the basis of a fraud claim.[192] In the same circumstances, can an opinion serve as the basis of a negligent misrepresentation claim? On the one hand, the number of negligent misrepresentation cases allowing claims against accountants for their audit opinions suggests an affirmative answer to the question (at least with respect to opinions of persons who purport to have special knowledge of the matter). In addition,

---

[191] *Compare In re* Agrobiotech, Inc., 291 F. Supp. 2d 1186, 1192 (D. Nev. 2003) ("Pursuant to § 551, silence about material facts basic to the transaction, when combined with a duty to speak, is the functional equivalent of a misrepresentation or 'supplying false information' under Restatement § 552."), *and* Wengert v. Thomas L. Meyer, Inc., 152 S.W.3d 379, 382 (Mo. Ct. App. 2004) ("Fraudulent misrepresentation and negligent misrepresentation can arise from a person's affirmative misrepresentations or from passive nondisclosure."), *with* Eberts v. Goderstad, 569 F.3d 757, 765 (7th Cir. 2009) ("Negligent misrepresentation by nondisclosure is a claim of questionable heritage and has been soundly rejected in some jurisdictions."), *and* Martin v. Ohio State Univ. Foundation, 742 N.E.2d 1198, 1209 (Ohio Ct. App. 2000) ("A negligent misrepresentation claim does not lie for omissions: there must be an affirmative false statement.").

[192] *See* Section A(5)(a).

the comments to § 552 of the Second Restatement (and § 5 of the Third Restatement) clearly indicate that opinions are covered, and several illustrations are premised on opinions.[193]

On the other hand, the Second Restatement sections addressing opinions (§§ 539, 542–543) only discuss fraudulent misrepresentations and not negligent ones. This creates some uncertainty as to whether the sections were meant to apply to negligent misrepresentations. Moreover, some courts state unequivocally that opinions cannot serve as the basis for negligent misrepresentation claims (although courts also misleadingly make similar unequivocal statements in fraud disputes).[194]

### *Intention Claims*

Can a misrepresentation of intention serve as the basis of a negligent misrepresentation claim? From a Second Restatement standpoint, there is nothing in § 552 that would seem to prevent misrepresentations of intention from being actionable (assuming that the requirements of § 552 are otherwise satisfied). Nevertheless, the text of § 530 only applies to fraud claims, and some of the comments to § 530 suggest that a negligent misrepresentation of intent claim was not contemplated.[195] In addition, some courts have

---

[193] *See, e.g.*, RESTATEMENT (SECOND) OF TORTS § 552 cmt. b (1977) ("The rule stated in this Section applies not only to information given as to the existence of facts but also to an opinion given upon facts equally well known to both the supplier and the recipient."); *id.* § 552 cmt. e ("When the information consists of an opinion upon facts supplied by the recipient or otherwise known to him, the recipient is entitled to expect a careful consideration of the facts and competence in arriving at an intelligent judgment."); *id.* § 552 illus. 5, 10–11, 14.

Comment d to § 5 of the Third Restatement states the following:

> Liability attaches under this Section to the supply of "false information." That generally means a claim must be based on a defendant's statements of fact, not on opinions or predictions. This element of the tort might be viewed as a rule that reliance on an opinion or prediction ordinarily is unreasonable as a matter of law. An opinion or prediction may be actionable after all, however, if it falsely implies that the speaker has facts that form the basis of it, or knows of no material facts to the contrary. In addition, defendants who hold themselves out as having expertise in rendering opinions or predictions, as appraisers and auditors often do, may be held liable for negligence in forming or communicating them.

[194] *See, e.g.*, Sain v. Cedar Rapids Cmty. Sch. Dist., 626 N.W.2d 115, 127 (Iowa 2001) ("Additionally, we observe that the tort [negligent misrepresentation] applies only to false information and does not apply to personal opinions or statements of future intent."); Birt v. Wells Fargo Home Mortg., Inc., 75 P.3d 640, 657–58 (Wyo. 2003) ("The gist of the district court's reasoning, which is correct, is that negligent misrepresentation does not apply to misrepresentations of future intent or to statements of opinion. The tort of negligent misrepresentation, as defined by Restatement (Second) of Torts [§ 552], applies only to misrepresentations of facts.").

[195] *See* RESTATEMENT (SECOND) OF TORTS § 530 cmt. b (1977) ("To be actionable the statement of the maker's own intention must be fraudulent, which is to say that he must in fact not have the intention stated. . . . If the recipient wishes to have legal assurance that the intention honestly entertained will be carried out, he must see that

concluded that the tort of negligent misrepresentation does not apply to misrepresentations of intent.[196] When a rationale is given for this conclusion, it is often something along the following lines: "Indeed, the extension of negligent misrepresentation to situations involving future intentions would endow every breach of contract with a potential tort claim for negligent promise."[197]

***Defendants (Other than Accountants)***

As a final note, although much of the above material has focused on the liability of accountants, keep in mind that negligent misrepresentation claims have been recognized against many other types of defendants.[198]

## 2. Damages

Section 552B of the Second Restatement addresses damages for negligent misrepresentation. How does that section compare to § 549, which addresses damages for fraud? Section 549 allows a plaintiff in a successful fraud action to choose between out-of-pocket damages and benefit-of-the-bargain damages. The plaintiff can also recover consequential damages under § 549(1)(b). Section 552B allows a plaintiff in a successful negligent misrepresentation action to recover out-of-pocket damages, but not benefit-of-the-bargain damages. The plaintiff can also recover consequential damages under § 552B(1)(b).

Why are the damages for fraud more expansive (to the extent that benefit-of-the-bargain damages can be recovered)? Simply put, a misrepresentation made with scienter is more serious and more

---

it is expressed in the form of an enforceable contract, and his action must be on the contract.").

196 *See supra* note 194.

197 *Birt*, 75 P.3d at 658; *see also* RESTATEMENT (THIRD) OF TORTS: LIABILITY FOR ECONOMIC HARM § 5(5) (2020) (refusing to recognize liability for negligent misrepresentations "made in the course of negotiating or performing a contract between the parties").

198 *See, e.g.*, Ossining Union Free Sch. Dist. v. Anderson LaRocca Anderson, 539 N.E.2d 91, 92, 95–96 (N.Y. 1989) (architects and engineers); *id.* at 94–95 ("It is true that in many of the cases involving claims for negligent misrepresentation, the defendants are accountants. . . . But while the rule has been developed in the context of cases involving accountants, it reflects our concern for fixing an appropriate ambit of duty, and there is no reason for excepting from it defendants other than accountants who fall within the narrow circumstances we have delineated."); McCamish, Martin, Brown & Loeffler v. F.E. Appling Interests, 991 S.W.2d 787, 791 (Tex. 1999) ("We perceive no reason why section 552 should not apply to attorneys."); *id.* (noting that "[c]ourts applying Texas law have recognized a section 552 cause of action against other professionals as well," and citing cases involving an auditor, a physician, a real estate broker, a securities placement agent, a surveyor, and a title insurer); *see also* RESTATEMENT (SECOND) OF TORTS § 552 (1977) (providing illustrations involving defendants other than accountants); RESTATEMENT (THIRD) OF TORTS: LIABILITY FOR ECONOMIC HARM §§ 5–6 (2020) (same).

wrongful than a misrepresentation made with negligence. The more wrongful the conduct, the more expansive the damages.[199]

As mentioned in the discussion of fraud damages (Section A(6)), the Third Restatement includes no stand-alone provision on damages for fraud, but comment b to § 9 suggests a preference for out-of-pocket damages. With respect to negligent misrepresentation, comment l to § 5 of the Third Restatement states the following:

> Damages under this Section aim to restore the plaintiff to the financial position that the plaintiff would have occupied if the defendant had spoken carefully. This is often known as an "out of pocket" measure of recovery. Damages do not attempt to restore a plaintiff to the position that would have resulted if the false statements the defendant made had in fact been true. That would amount to an expectation or "loss of bargain" measure of recovery of the kind familiar from contract law and available in some cases of fraud. Damages here follow the usual logic of recovery for negligence. They are meant to bring home to defendants the costs of their mistakes, not to hold them to what they negligently said. . . .
>
> The distinction just drawn is most often relevant when a defendant's misstatement causes the plaintiff to enter into a transaction that is expected to be profitable but turns out badly. If the defendant's negligent advice causes the plaintiff to buy property for the sake of investment, for example, damages are not measured by the difference between the actual value of the property and the value that the defendant said it had. Damages are measured by the difference between the price the plaintiff paid for the property and the value it would have been understood to have if the defendant had used due care. The measurement is made as of the time of the transaction, not by examining how the purchase turned out later, in order to separate the harm caused by the defendant's misstatement from other influences that may affect the performance of an investment after it is made.
>
> A plaintiff also can collect for certain other losses beyond the "out of pocket" measure. These are sometimes called consequential damages, though that term can invite

[199] *Cf.* RESTATEMENT (SECOND) OF TORTS § 552B cmt. b (1977) ("The considerations of policy that have led the courts to compensate the plaintiff for the loss of his bargain in order to make the deception of a deliberate defrauder unprofitable to him, do not apply when the defendant has had honest intentions but has merely failed to exercise reasonable care in what he says or does.").

> confusion with the law of contract; "special" damages may be a better way to refer to them in tort. Either term is meant to separate the immediate losses the plaintiff took on a transaction from less direct losses also caused by reliance on what the defendant said. Whether a plaintiff can recover for the less direct losses is governed, first, by the rules on scope of liability noted in Comment i. Second, the losses must be proven to a reasonable degree of certainty. Damages under this heading may include wasted expenditures the plaintiff made in reliance on the expectations the defendant created.
>
> The principles stated in this Comment are meant as guides to decision, not as rigid categories. The notion of "out of pocket" recovery, for example, sometimes may be an awkward or unsatisfactory fit to an unusual set of facts. In that case, a court reasonably will recur to first principles and seek a measure of recovery that restores the position the plaintiff would have occupied if the tort had not been committed.

Under the Third Restatement, therefore, compensatory damages for fraud and negligent misrepresentation will often be the same, as an out-of-pocket measurement is preferred for both torts.

The decision of *Federal Land Bank Association v. Sloane*[200] discusses damages for negligent misrepresentation and provides a nice comparison with damages for fraud. The Sloanes discovered that they could get a contract from Pilgrim's Pride to raise chickens if they built new chicken houses on their farm. They applied for a $141,000 loan from the Federal Land Bank Association of Tyler to help with the construction. The loan officer at the bank informed them that the bank's board had approved the loan and that the Sloanes could proceed with site preparation work. The loan officer also communicated this information to the contractor hired by the Sloanes.

After beginning construction, the Sloanes received a letter from the bank denying their loan application. The loan was denied for valid reasons (the Sloanes had failed to include two outstanding debts on their application, and they borrowed additional money while the application was being processed), and the Sloanes were unable to obtain other financing. They sued the bank alleging that the loan officer negligently misrepresented that the loan had been approved, and they sought damages for their construction expenses, the loss of the Pilgrim's Pride contract, and the mental anguish caused by the

---

200 825 S.W.2d 439 (Tex. 1991).

bank's conduct. The jury awarded the Sloanes damages, including damages for lost profits and mental anguish. The court of appeals held that there was no evidence of lost profits and reformed the judgment.

The Supreme Court of Texas began its damages analysis by citing § 552B of the Second Restatement. The court rejected the award of mental anguish damages because § 552B provides damages only for pecuniary losses. The court also noted that § 552B does not award benefit-of-the-bargain damages, and it rejected the lost profits claim on that basis:

> The Sloanes would not have received the contract regardless of whether the misrepresentation was made. Under the legal theory of this section of the Restatement, they should not, therefore, receive the benefit of a bargain that would never have taken place. The sole reason the Sloanes did not get the Pilgrim's Pride contract is because the bank did not give them the loan money to build acceptable chicken houses. The Sloanes' claim to these damages is impermissibly predicated on giving them the benefit of the loan.

The court reversed the award of mental anguish damages and otherwise affirmed the judgment of the court of appeals.

The Sloanes ultimately received damages for "past pecuniary losses other than lost profits," which presumably included compensation for the construction expenses incurred before the loan was denied. Under § 552B of the Second Restatement, would these sums have been awarded under subsection (1)(a) or (1)(b)? Section 552B(1)(a) provides damages for "the difference between the value of what he has received in the transaction and its purchase price or other value given for it." This subsection does not fit with the facts of *Sloane*—i.e., there was no transaction between the Sloanes and the bank, no value was received by the Sloanes, and no value was given by the Sloanes. Put differently, § 552B(1)(a) typically applies when a misrepresentation about an item affects the bargain that the parties have entered into concerning that item. This does not describe the *Sloane* facts.

Section 552B(1)(b) provides damages for "pecuniary loss suffered otherwise as a consequence of the recipient's reliance upon the misrepresentation." This subsection fits the facts of *Sloane*—i.e., the Sloanes spent thousands of dollars preparing for the construction of new chicken houses because they were relying on the loan officer's misrepresentation that the loan would be approved.[201]

Why were the Sloanes unable to recover damages for the profits anticipated from the Pilgrim's Pride contract? The court's explanation as to why the Sloanes were unable to recover lost profits turns, at least in part, on the inability to recover benefit-of-the-bargain damages under § 552B(2) of the Second Restatement. That subsection makes it clear that negligent misrepresentation damages do not include "the benefit of the plaintiff's contract with the defendant." The plaintiff (Sloanes) had no contract with the defendant (Federal Land Bank), of course, so damages under that subsection were unavailable. Even if there had been a contract between the Sloanes and Federal Land Bank, however, the ability to profit on *another* contract may be viewed more as consequential damages than benefit-of-the-bargain damages, as benefit-of-the-bargain damages are usually based on the lessened value of the subject matter of the *original* contract.[202] In short, benefit-of-the-bargain damages under § 552(B)(2) may be the wrong way to characterize what the Sloanes were claiming.

Instead, couldn't the lost profits be recovered under § 552B(1)(b)? That is, if the negligent misrepresentation caused the Sloanes to miss out on financing elsewhere (e.g., it delayed the Sloanes from looking for another lender until it was too late), and if financing elsewhere would have guaranteed the award of the Pilgrim's Pride contract, the lost profits from the contract would seem to be "pecuniary loss suffered otherwise as a consequence of the plaintiff's reliance upon the misrepresentation." The court doesn't seem to address this possibility, although it does note that the Sloanes failed to obtain other financing and that "[t]he Sloanes would not have received the [Pilgrim's Pride] contract regardless of whether the misrepresentation was made." Reading between the lines, this seems to be the court's way of saying that the misrepresentation did not affect the Sloanes' ability to obtain financing—i.e., they would not have gotten a loan from anyone regardless of the misrepresentation.

---

201 *See also* RESTATEMENT (THIRD) OF TORTS: LIABILITY FOR ECONOMIC HARM § 5 cmt. l (2020) (discussing the recovery of consequential damages in negligent misrepresentation claims).

202 *See, e.g.*, RESTATEMENT (SECOND) OF TORTS § 549 illus. 2 (1977) (describing what are essentially lost profits as consequential damages rather than as benefit of the-bargain damages); *cf.* Continental Leavitt Communications, Ltd. v. Painewebber, Inc., No. 92 C 5939, 1994 WL 710745, at *8 (N.D. Ill. Dec. 20, 1994) ("The language of the Restatement, quoted above in section 552B(2), indicates that the damages recoverable do not include the benefit of a contract between the plaintiff and defendant in the negligent misrepresentation case. The Restatement does not, however, directly address the situation in this case, where the plaintiff seeks to recover from the defendant the benefit of its contract with a third party.").

Thus, any lost profits were not suffered because of the misrepresentation. If the misrepresentation did affect the Sloanes' ability to obtain financing from another lender, one wonders if the court's conclusion would have been different.

In summary, the *Sloane* opinion reads as though the Sloanes were claiming benefit-of-the-bargain damages, and § 552B(2) doesn't allow such damages to be recovered. One might question, however, whether the lost profits being claimed are accurately characterized as benefit-of-the-bargain damages. If they are not, § 552B(1)(b) would seem to be the appropriate rule rather than § 552B(2).

The court in *Sloane* denied mental anguish damages because § 552B only allows recovery for "pecuniary" losses. This refusal to allow mental anguish damages in negligent misrepresentation claims is consistent with the position of most (but not all) other courts.[203]

Given that negligent misrepresentation is a species of negligence, it is not surprising that authorities typically conclude that contributory or comparative negligence (depending upon the law of the jurisdiction) may be raised as a defense to a negligent misrepresentation claim.[204] The relationship between justifiable reliance (as indicated in § 552(1) of the Second Restatement) and contributory negligence (as indicated in § 552A) is tricky. "Justifiable" reliance (as opposed to "reasonable" reliance) suggests that a plaintiff's carelessness in relying is not necessarily fatal to a negligent misrepresentation claim.[205] Contributory negligence, however, suggests that such carelessness will always result in an inability to recover.

The Third Restatement drops the "justifiable" modifier in § 5 and simply requires the plaintiff to rely on the defendant's information. If that reliance is negligent, the plaintiff's claim is not

---

[203] *See, e.g.*, Crowley v. Global Realty, Inc., 474 A.2d 1056, 1058 (N.H. 1984) (denying recovery for mental distress); Pearson v. Simmonds Precision Prods., Inc., 624 A.2d 1134, 1137 (Vt. 1993) (same). *But see* Dousson v. S. Cent. Bell, 429 So. 2d 466, 468–69 (La. Ct. App. 1983) (allowing the recovery of mental anguish damages in a negligent misrepresentation claim).

[204] *See, e.g.*, RESTATEMENT (SECOND) OF TORTS § 552A (1977) ("The recipient of a negligent misrepresentation is barred from recovery for pecuniary loss suffered in reliance upon it if he is negligent in so relying."); RESTATEMENT (THIRD) OF TORTS: LIABILITY FOR ECONOMIC HARM § 5(4) (2020) ("A plaintiff's recovery under this [negligent misrepresentation] Section is subject to the same principles of comparative responsibility that apply to other claims of negligence."); *id.* § 6(3) (substantially the same); *see also* Florenzano v. Olson, 387 N.W.2d 168, 176 (Minn. 1986) ("We agree with these commentators and with the majority of states that have considered the issue. . . . We hold that the principles of comparative responsibility apply to negligent misrepresentation. . . .").

[205] *See* Section A(4) (discussing "justifiable" reliance versus "reasonable" reliance).

automatically barred, but principles of comparative negligence may reduce (or eliminate) the recovery. As comment j to § 5 explains:

> Restatement Second, Torts § 552 required that a plaintiff seeking to recover for negligent misrepresentation must show "justifiable reliance" on the information supplied by the defendant. This Section omits the word "justifiable" and instead adds the language of Subsection (4), treating the plaintiff's responsibility for a loss as a question of comparative fault. "Justifiable reliance" has the sound of an all-or-nothing inquiry, which is how it tends to be treated in other settings. This made sense at the time § 552 was adopted, because the Second Restatement viewed contributory negligence as a complete defense to a claim under that Section. Comparative responsibility has since become a standard principle in negligence cases, however, and courts have extended it to claims of negligent misrepresentation. Confusion has thus arisen concerning the relationship between those principles and a requirement of "justifiable" reliance; treating judgments about a plaintiff's reliance as an all-or-nothing matter, while every other type of plaintiff's negligence is a matter of degree, creates hard problems in separating those categories. The same conduct by a plaintiff can often be described as imprudent reliance or as negligence of some other kind. This Section resolves the tension in favor of comparative responsibility. Liability under this Section is a species of liability for negligence, though with restrictions on the defendant's duty and scope of liability. The plaintiff's share of blame for a loss can be analyzed as it would be in any other negligence case. "Reasonableness" best captures the relevant question about a plaintiff's reliance in a regime of comparative fault.
>
> Comparative responsibility can become an issue under this Section when a plaintiff may have relied on the defendant's statements too heavily, omitting additional precautions that ordinary prudence would have suggested. Due care does not normally require a plaintiff to duplicate precautions that the defendant should have taken before speaking. Negligence on the plaintiff's part, rather, means omitting precautions that due care would require even if the defendant had spoken carefully. But the plaintiff may have some independent obligation to investigate, even redundantly, if the stakes are high enough, or the defendant's assumption of responsibility unclear enough, to

make exclusive reliance on the defendant's statements imprudent.

Comparative responsibility also becomes important when the plaintiff had access to information that counseled against relying on what the defendant said, such as a writing that was inconsistent with the defendant's oral statements or that disclaimed their reliability. Disclaimers a defendant makes in a contract with the plaintiff are not usually important under this Section, because claims arising from a contract between the parties are matters resolved by contract law or, on occasion, by the law of professional malpractice. Between parties who have no contract, however, a disclaimer the defendant has made may bear significantly on liability under this Section. It may show that providing a basis for reliance by the plaintiff was no part of the defendant's purpose, or make the plaintiff's reliance unreasonable in other respects.

## C. INNOCENT MISREPRESENTATION

There are many legal theories of relief based upon innocent misrepresentation. For example, under contract law, if a defendant's representation can be characterized as a warranty, damages can be recovered for breach of warranty regardless of the defendant's fault.[206] The law of restitution also provides relief by allowing a plaintiff to rescind a transfer that was induced by a material misrepresentation, even if the misrepresentation was innocently made.[207] Finally, in some states, consumer protection or related statutes provide relief for innocent misrepresentation.[208]

Recovery in *tort* for innocent misrepresentation, however, is very much a minority position.[209] Although some courts purport to adopt

---

[206] *See, e.g.*, U.C.C. § 2–313 (allowing for the creation of express warranties); *id.* § 2–714 (stating the measure of damages for breach of warranty).

[207] *See, e.g.*, RESTATEMENT (THIRD) OF RESTITUTION AND UNJUST ENRICHMENT § 13(1) & cmt. c (2011) (noting that "a transfer induced by innocent misrepresentation is subject to rescission only if the misrepresentation was material").

[208] *See, e.g.*, Gennari v. Weichert Co. Realtors, 691 A.2d 350, 365 (N.J. 1997) ("Throughout its history, the [New Jersey Consumer Fraud] Act has protected consumers from deception and fraud, even when committed in good faith. . . . One who makes an affirmative misrepresentation is liable even in the absence of knowledge of the falsity of the misrepresentation, negligence, or the intent to deceive.").

[209] *See, e.g.*, Enercon v. Global Computer Supplies, Inc., 675 F. Supp. 2d 188, 194 (D. Me. 2009) (noting that "the Law Court has not adopted the Restatement's formulation of the tort of innocent misrepresentation," and rejecting the notion that "innocent or so-called 'unintentional' misrepresentation is a viable theory of tort liability in Maine"); Growall v. Maietta, 931 A.2d 667, 674 (Pa. Super. Ct. 2007) (stating that "[t]here appears to be no basis for . . . damages under a claim of innocent

such an action, the language used to describe the claim often sounds like negligent misrepresentation or fraud.[210] Further, as one commentator suggests: "Perhaps many of the cases using broad strict liability language do not entirely mean it. Some, for example, are merely rescission cases. . . . Some others have used the broad language of strict liability merely in dicta, and in still others the court may have adopted the broad rule of liability without realizing that it imposed strict liability, and certainly without giving a reason for strict liability."[211] In short, one can question whether some of the purported authorities for the tort of innocent misrepresentation actually support such a claim.

Section 552C of the Second Restatement does provide a tort cause of action for innocent misrepresentation "in a sale, rental or exchange transaction." The misrepresentation must be "of a material fact" and made "for the purpose of inducing [a person] to act or to refrain from acting in reliance upon it." Liability is imposed "for pecuniary loss caused to [the person] by [the person's] justifiable reliance upon the misrepresentation." Due to the strict liability nature of the claim, consequential and benefit-of-the-bargain damages are unavailable; instead, damages are limited to "the difference between the value of what [the person] has parted with and the value of what [the person] has received in the transaction."

Unlike in fraud and negligent misrepresentation claims, comments c and d to § 552C make clear that there is no third-party liability for innocent misrepresentation. Moreover, and as mentioned, § 552C is limited by its terms to misrepresentations of fact. According to comment e, the section "does not apply to misrepresentations of opinion, intention or law, except as they may imply misrepresentations of fact."

Although the Restatement suggests (in the caveat and comment g to § 552C) that the scope of the section is limited, the section's application to "sale, rental or exchange" transactions covers a huge amount of economic activity. As comment c explains, the section includes "any sale, rental or exchange of land, chattels, securities or

---

misrepresentation in Pennsylvania," and similarly noting that § 552C of the Restatement "has not been adopted in Pennsylvania").

210 *See, e.g.*, Richard v. A. Waldman and Sons, Inc., 232 A.2d 307, 309 (Conn. 1967) ("An innocent misrepresentation may be actionable if the declarant has the means of knowing, ought to know, or has the duty of knowing the truth."); Schurmann v. Neau, 624 N.W.2d 157, 161 (Wis. Ct. App. 2000) (stating that, for innocent misrepresentation, the representation must be made on the defendant's "personal knowledge or under circumstances in which he necessarily ought to have known the truth or untruth of the statement").

211 DAN B. DOBBS, THE LAW OF TORTS § 473, at 1354–55 (2000).

anything else of value, such as copyrights, patents and other valuable intangible rights."

Given that claims for rescission and breach of warranty are often available for innocent misrepresentation, why would a plaintiff ever desire to bring a tort action? What advantages, in other words, does a tort action for innocent misrepresentation provide? With respect to rescission, the tort action is most advantageous when the plaintiff does not wish (or is unable) to return what the plaintiff has received in the transaction (e.g., the plaintiff has made improvements to the purchased item that cannot be undone). As comment b to § 552C explains:

> .... The remedy provided in this Section is very similar to that afforded under the law of restitution. It differs, however, in a material respect. The plaintiff is permitted to retain what he has received and recover damages, rather than rescind and seek restitution, in which case he must return what he received. The tort action for damages may have a definite advantage to the plaintiff in cases in which he is unable to restore what he received in its original condition; when he has made improvements or for other reasons finds it desirable to keep what he has received rather than return it; when he is barred from rescission by delay or has so far committed himself that he has lost the remedy by an election; or when for some other reason, such as the defendant's change of position, restitution is not available to him. It may even in many cases be a better solution from the point of view of the defendant himself, since it permits the transaction to stand, rather than be upset at a later date.

With respect to breach of warranty, the tort action is advantageous because it has the potential to avoid defenses that would be applicable to a claim under contract law. As comment b observes:

> It should be added that in cases involving the sale of goods, and probably in other transactions, a somewhat similar remedy has been available in the action for breach of warranty. The latter action, despite its historic relationship to tort, has been subject to important contract defenses, notably among them the parol evidence rule. This is made explicit by the Uniform Commercial Code. (See U.C.C. § 2–202). Further, in cases involving the sale of goods, most of the innocent misrepresentations made actionable by this Section would also be actionable under the Code on the theory of breach of warranty. But it does

> not necessarily follow that actions for damages founded upon innocent misrepresentation are preempted by the Code. The measure of damages provided by this Section differs from the traditional measure of damages for breach of warranty (now embodied in the Code). Under this Section, damages are solely restitutionary in character. In contrast, the measure of damages for breach of warranty includes compensation for benefit of the bargain and for consequential losses. This difference argues for viewing the tort action under this Section as unburdened by contract (or Code) defenses. However, this issue has gone virtually unnoticed in the jurisdictions that give damages in tort for innocent misrepresentation. In a case in which, as a practical matter, the amount recoverable under this Section is substantially the same as the amount recoverable for breach of warranty, the argument against recognition of defenses traditional to the warranty action loses much of its force.

If contract defenses are not a concern, of course, a breach of warranty action is likely preferable, as the availability of benefit-of-the-bargain and consequential damages provides the potential for a greater recovery.

Under the law of products liability, an innocent misrepresentation about a product that causes personal injury or property damage is actionable.[212] Outside of the products liability context, the Third Restatement rejects a tort action for innocent misrepresentation—primarily on the ground that the economic loss rule between contracting parties would preclude such an action.[213]

---

[212] *See, e.g.*, RESTATEMENT (THIRD) OF TORTS: PRODUCTS LIABILITY § 9 (1998) ("One engaged in the business of selling or otherwise distributing products who, in connection with the sale of a product, makes a fraudulent, negligent, or innocent misrepresentation of material fact concerning the product is subject to liability for harm to persons or property caused by the misrepresentation.").

[213] *See* RESTATEMENT (THIRD) OF TORTS: LIABILITY FOR ECONOMIC HARM § 3 cmt. d (2020) (rejecting the approach of § 552C of the Second Restatement); *see also* Chapter 5 (discussing the economic loss rule between contracting parties).

# Chapter 3

# TORTIOUS INTERFERENCE WITH ECONOMIC RELATIONS

Tortious interference with economic relations is a general term that encompasses two related (but distinct) torts: (1) intentional interference with existing contract, and (2) intentional interference with a relationship that is likely to lead to a contract (often referred to as intentional interference with "prospective contract" or "prospective advantage"). Most states recognize both torts, and they are frequently asserted in commercial disputes.[1]

## A. INTENTIONAL INTERFERENCE WITH EXISTING CONTRACT

The Second Restatement of Torts distinguishes between tortious interference with the performance *owed to* the plaintiff (§ 766), and tortious interference with the performance *of* the plaintiff (§ 766A). The Third Restatement of Torts does not make the same distinction. As the Reporter's Note to § 17 observes: "The Restatement Second treated the conduct addressed by Comment h—interference with the plaintiff's own performance—as a tort distinct from interference with performance of a third party. See Restatement Second, Torts § 766A .... The two types of claim do not differ materially in operation or rationale, as courts have recognized. This Restatement therefore treats them as two aspects of the same tort: interference with contract." The discussion below follows the distinction drawn by the Second Restatement, but the analogous Third Restatement provisions are discussed as well.

### 1. Interfering with Performance Owed to the Plaintiff

The decision of *Lumley v. Gye*[2] nicely illustrates an interference with performance owed to the plaintiff and demonstrates that the act of interference may be entirely lawful. Lumley was the owner of the

---

1 Although intentional interference with existing contract (or prospective contract) is actionable, negligent interference is typically not. *See, e.g.*, RESTATEMENT (SECOND) OF TORTS § 766C (1979); RESTATEMENT (THIRD) OF TORTS: LIABILITY FOR ECONOMIC HARM § 7 (2020). This rule is consistent with the thrust of the economic loss rule between strangers—i.e., negligently-caused economic losses unaccompanied by personal injury or property damage are not compensable in tort. *See generally* Chapter 1 (discussing the economic loss rule between non-contracting parties).

2 118 Eng. Rep. 749 (Q.B. 1853).

Queen's Theater. He had contracted with the opera singer Johanna Wagner to perform for three months. Gye, the owner of a rival theater, persuaded ("enticed") Wagner to breach her agreement with Lumley (presumably Gye offered her more money to come sing at Gye's theater). Lumley sued Gye for interfering with his contract with Wagner. Gye demurred (which is effectively a motion for failure to state a claim upon which relief could be granted), but the court held that "procurement of the breach of the contract" was actionable.[3]

The facts of *Lumley* fall into a classic interference pattern—the plaintiff (Lumley) complained that he did not receive contractual performance by the other party to the contract (Wagner) because of interference by an "outsider" to the contract (Gye). *Lumley* is also significant in that the means of inducement used by Gye (persuasion and presumably an offer of more money) was not tortious in and of itself. Indeed, the case indicates that Gye "enticed and procured Miss Wagner to refuse to sing or perform." While it is not clear how Gye "enticed" Wagner, it presumably involved offering her more money to perform at Gye's theater. There is no allegation of tortious conduct, such as assault, kidnapping, or fraud—it appears that Gye simply used good old-fashioned persuasion (fueled likely with an offer of cash). This point is important because tortious interference can be caused even if the act of interference is otherwise lawful.[4]

In some circumstances, an interference tort does not seem necessary from the standpoint of compensating the plaintiff for injury. For example, Lumley clearly had a breach of contract action against Wagner for refusing to sing. Lumley's damages were presumably based on his diminished profits from lost ticket sale

---

[3] *Lumley* has been very influential. Consider the following:

> The doctrine thus announced [in *Lumley*], that intentional interference with a contract may be an actionable tort, was received at first with hesitation or disapproval, but it was reaffirmed nearly thirty years later in England, and then by degrees was extended, first to cover contracts other than those for personal services, and later to include interferences in which no ill-will was to be found on the part of the defendant. The present English law gives it full acceptance, as to all intentional interferences with any type of contract. The American courts were reluctant to accept the doctrine in the beginning, and a few of them rejected it outright as applied to interference with relations other than that of master and servant. Such decisions have for the most part been overruled, and the tort is now recognized virtually everywhere as to any contract, regardless of its character.

W. PAGE KEETON ET AL., PROSSER AND KEETON ON TORTS § 129, at 980–81 (5th ed. 1984).

[4] *Cf.* RESTATEMENT (SECOND) OF TORTS § 766 cmt. c (1979) ("In [*Lumley*], a singer under contract to sing at the plaintiff's theatre was induced by the defendant, who operated a rival theatre, to break her contract with the plaintiff in order to sing for the defendant. No violence, fraud or defamation by the defendant was alleged. . . . This case differed from earlier cases in that the means of inducement used by the defendant were not tortious toward the singer.").

revenue. Could that amount be recovered as consequential damages in a breach of contract action? Yes if (1) those damages were foreseeable at the time the contract was entered into (surely it was foreseeable to Wagner, a well-known singer, that if she did not perform, Lumley would lose ticket sales); and (2) the damages were established with "reasonable certainty"[5] (perhaps Lumley could have demonstrated, via past performances of well-known singers, that he typically sold 90% of his seats (or some similar figure), which could provide a basis for calculating damages). If recovery could be had against Wagner in a breach of contract action, there would seem to be no need for the tort.

On the other hand, there are some circumstances where a tort recovery against a third party would be useful. For example, Wagner might have been insolvent, or she might have asserted a defense that prevents a recovery in contract (e.g., if Gye had kidnapped Wagner, surely she could have raised an impossibility defense to Lumley's breach of contract claim).[6]

There may also be situations where a tort recovery is better because contract remedies are unable to fully compensate the plaintiff for its losses. For example, as a result of Wagner's breach, Lumley may very well have suffered damages to his business reputation, as he can no longer be trusted to deliver promised artists. This injury to reputation or loss of customer goodwill is likely far too speculative to satisfy the requirement that contract damages must be established with reasonable certainty. Even though there is a legitimate injury, it will likely not be recompensed. To be sure, the speculative nature of the reputation/goodwill damages may make them unrecoverable in tort as well,[7] but at least the prospect of punitive and/or mental anguish damages in tort provides the possibility of an extra source of recovery for Lumley's injuries.[8]

---

5 *See generally* 3 DAN B. DOBBS, DOBBS LAW OF REMEDIES § 12.1(3), at 69–78 (2d ed. 1993) (discussing the requirement that damages "must be proven with reasonable certainty, and must not be 'speculative' ").

6 *Cf.* RESTATEMENT (THIRD) OF TORTS: LIABILITY FOR ECONOMIC HARM § 17 cmt. d (2020) ("The plaintiff in such a case may be unable to obtain relief from the party who committed the breach, as when the breaching party has no assets or cannot be found. The rules recognized here provide, in effect, a second line of recourse for a plaintiff in that position: a right to seek relief from the party who induced the breach, if any such party exists. A plaintiff's ability to recover under this Section, however, does not require any showing that remedies under the law of contract are unavailable or defective.").

7 *See, e.g.*, RESTATEMENT (SECOND) OF TORTS §§ 774A cmt. c, 912 (1979).

8 *See id.* § 774A & cmt. a.

Although a breach of contract action and an interference action may be brought together, courts will not permit a double recovery. *See, e.g.*, *id.* § 774A cmt. e ("The fact that the plaintiff may have a cause of action against the person who has broken his contract does not prevent recovery against the defendant who has induced or otherwise

Section 766 is the Second Restatement's articulation of the tort of intentional interference with existing contract. Several points are worthy of consideration:

(a) Section 766 seems to define the tort as having four elements—intent, interference (via "induc[ement] or otherwise causing" nonperformance), impropriety, and injury. It would appear that the plaintiff has the burden of proof on these elements, but the Restatement explicitly takes no position on who has the burden of proof on impropriety.[9]

(b) The tort requires intent. Intent, as defined in comment j, encompasses (1) purpose or desire to interfere, or (2) knowledge that interference is substantially certain to result, even if the actor does not have the purpose or desire to cause the interference. As comment i indicates, to have the appropriate intent, "the actor must have knowledge of the contract with which he is interfering and of the fact that he is interfering with the performance of the contract." Obviously, one cannot have the purpose or desire to interfere with a contract if one does not know that the contract exists. Similarly, one cannot know that interference with a contract is substantially certain to result if one does not know that the contract exists.[10]

---

caused the breach, or reduce the damages recoverable from him. . . . But since the damages recoverable for breach of the contract are common to the actions against both, any payments made by the one who breaks the contract or partial satisfaction of the judgment against him must be credited in favor of the defendant who has caused the breach. Conversely . . . to the extent that there is duplication of the damages any payments made by the tortfeasor must be credited in favor of one who has broken the contract."); *id.* §§ 766 cmt. v, 774A(2); *see also* RESTATEMENT (THIRD) OF TORTS: LIABILITY FOR ECONOMIC HARM § 17 cmt. b (2020) ("A party who has committed a breach of contract, and a party who induced the breach, may both be held fully liable for the resulting injuries suffered by the plaintiff. At the same time, however, a suit under this Section and a suit for breach of contract may not be used to produce a double recovery. If the victim of a breach recovers damages from the party who committed it, for example, those damages reduce what may be due from a party who is liable for inducement of the breach under this Section.").

[9] *See* RESTATEMENT (SECOND) OF TORTS (1979) (Introductory Note to Chapter 37); *id.* § 767 cmt. k. The burden of proof and the meaning of impropriety are discussed later in Section C.

Under the Third Restatement, § 17 seems to define the tort as having four elements—intent (§ 17(1)(b), (d)), interference (§ 17(1)(e)), impropriety (§ 17(1)(c), (2)), and injury (§ 17(1)(f)). It would appear that the plaintiff has the burden of proof on these elements.

[10] *See, e.g.*, Imperial Ice Co. v. Rossier, 112 P.2d 631, 633 (Cal. 1941) ("The act of inducing the breach must be an intentional one. If the actor had no knowledge of the existence of the contract or his actions were not intended to induce a breach, he cannot be held liable though an actual breach results from his lawful and proper acts.").

The Third Restatement makes similar points. "The requirement of intent is satisfied if the defendant acted for the purpose of producing a breach of the plaintiff's contract, or with knowledge that a breach was substantially certain to result." RESTATEMENT (THIRD) OF TORTS: LIABILITY FOR ECONOMIC HARM § 17 cmt. d (2020); *see also* RESTATEMENT (THIRD) OF TORTS: LIABILITY FOR PHYSICAL & EMOTIONAL HARM

Comment p to § 766 indicates that an expression of one's general opinion that happens to induce a person to breach its contract with another should not result in liability:

> In some cases the expression of one's general opinions or advice may cause persons not to perform their contracts with another. Thus a prominent person's opinion that economic opportunities are greater in the West than in the East and his advice to young men in general that they "go West" may cause some young man to leave an existing employment in breach of his contract and seek new fortune in the West. Again a person's lecture on the perils of eating meat may cause another to break his contract and cease buying meat from his butcher; or in a public lecture or private conversation, one may persuade others not to buy foreign or union made goods. The rule stated in this Section does not afford protection against harm thus caused. Only when the actor's conduct is intended to affect a specific person is the actor subject to liability under this rule.

Even if the actor's conduct is intended to affect a specific person, some protection may be provided by First Amendment principles.[11]

(c) The interference must be by "inducing or otherwise causing" a breach. The term "inducing" refers to one party causing another party to choose not to perform. A might cause B to choose not to perform through, for example, persuasion, intimidation, threats, or a promise of benefits.[12] The phrase "otherwise causing" refers to situations where the defendant's conduct has made it impossible for

---

§ 1 (2010) (stating that "[a] person acts with the intent to produce a consequence if: (a) the person acts with the purpose of producing that consequence; or (b) the person acts knowing that the consequence is substantially certain to result"). Obviously, one cannot have the purpose to produce a breach of the plaintiff's contract if one does not know that the contract exists. Similarly, one cannot know that a breach of the plaintiff's contract was substantially certain to result if one does not know that the contract exists. *See* RESTATEMENT (THIRD) OF TORTS: LIABILITY FOR ECONOMIC HARM § 17(1)(b), (d) (2020); *see also id.* § 17 cmt. c ("Under Subsection (1)(d), liability only arises when the defendant intends to cause a breach of the plaintiff's specific contract. This does not mean that the defendant must know the details of the plaintiff's identity. It means, rather, that the defendant must intend interference with a particular contractual relationship. That is why no liability arises under this Section from ordinary advertisements.").

11 *See, e.g.*, DAN B. DOBBS, THE LAW OF TORTS § 448, at 1269 (2000) ("Under the free speech rules, he can also take a position on social and political issues, even though the position will induce others to cease all dealings with the plaintiff and even if that is the purpose of his advocacy."); *cf.* RESTATEMENT (SECOND) OF TORTS § 767(d), (e) (1979) (allowing for consideration of "the interests sought to be advanced by the [interferor]" and "the social interests in protecting the freedom of action of the [interferor] and the contractual interests of the other"); *id.* § 772 (providing a defense for interference caused by truthful statements or honest advice).

12 *See* RESTATEMENT (SECOND) OF TORTS § 766 cmts. h, k (1979).

another party to perform. Examples include "when A imprisons or commits such a battery upon B that he cannot perform his contract with C, or when A destroys the goods that B is about to deliver to C." It also includes "when performance by B of his contract with C necessarily depends upon the prior performance by A of his contract with B and A fails to perform in order to disable B from performing for C."[13]

(d) Section 766 contemplates the classic three-party interference scenario where the plaintiff is complaining that it did not receive contractual performance by the other party to the contract because of interference by an "outsider" to the contract.[14]

(e) Why are contracts to marry excluded from the scope of § 766? The literal answer, according to comment a, is because § 698 of the Second Restatement covers contracts to marry. That section states that "[o]ne who alienates the affections of a person under contract to marry or who has sexual intercourse with such a person does not thereby become liable to the other party to the contract." The policy behind such a rule is presumably because "contracts to marry" are highly personal agreements and we want friends, relatives, etc. to freely advise that the marriage is a mistake to avoid divorces and other problems down the road.[15]

Would the facts of *Lumley* satisfy the Restatement's elements of the intentional interference tort? First, did Gye act with intent? It seems as if he had the purpose to interfere with his rival's contract. Second, did Gye interfere "by inducing or otherwise causing" Wagner not to perform? It appears that he induced Wagner not to perform by using persuasion and, presumably, an offer of more money. Third, did

---

13 *Id.* § 766 cmt. h.

14 Section 17 of the Third Restatement contemplates the same three-party interference scenario. *See, e.g.*, RESTATEMENT (THIRD) OF TORTS: LIABILITY FOR ECONOMIC HARM § 17 cmt. o (2020) ("Liability arises under this Section when the defendant interferes with a contract between the plaintiff and a third party.").

15 *See, e.g.*, W. PAGE KEETON ET AL., PROSSER AND KEETON ON TORTS § 129, at 996 (5th ed. 1984) ("Friends and relatives if no others would no doubt have a privilege to give advice against marriage, so that no liability would attach to them in such cases. This, coupled with the feeling that no marriage should be encouraged if any person involved has decided it is a mistake and with a respect for personal autonomy and right of choice, suggests that the burden of litigation over issues likely to improve nothing in the parties' relationships would outweigh any limited utility that might be found in such an action."); *cf.* Hoye v. Hoye, 824 S.W.2d 422, 427 (Ky. 1992) ("We therefore . . . abolish the action known as tortious interference with the marital relation, relying on the premise that affection between spouses cannot be owned, i.e., that the underlying assumption of the tort is an anachronism.").

Unlike § 766, contracts to marry are not mentioned in the text of § 17 of the Third Restatement. The Reporter's Note to § 17 simply notes the following: "Neither this Section nor § 18 has application to contracts to marry. *See* Restatement Second, Torts §§ 766 (AM. LAW INST. 1979) and 698 (AM. LAW INST. 1977)."

the interference cause pecuniary loss to Lumley? It likely caused a loss of profits.

The only interesting wrinkle is whether Gye's interference was "improper." On the one hand, Gye's persuasion was perfectly lawful. On the other hand, perhaps an effort to purposefully interfere (via inducement or otherwise) with an existing contract should be viewed as improper in and of itself, even if the means of interference is lawful, because of the value that society places on existing contracts. In other words, if society seeks to promote the stability of contracts, one might decide that an outsider's purposeful effort to upset that stability is, in itself, improper.[16]

Under § 17 of the Third Restatement, the elements of the intentional interference tort also seem to be met: (1)(a) Lumley and Wagner had a valid contract; (1)(b) Gye knew of that contract; (1)(c), (2)(a) Gye acted for the purpose of appropriating the benefits of the Lumley-Wagner contract, as he sought to procure Wagner's services for himself; (1)(d) Gye seems to have acted with the intent to cause a breach of the Lumley-Wagner contract; (1)(e) Gye's actions did in fact cause a breach of the Lumley-Wagner contract; and (1)(f) Gye's actions likely caused a loss of profits for Lumley.

Unlike § 766, notice that § 17 of the Third Restatement defines "improper"/"wrongful conduct" within the text of the section. Assuming that Gye simply used persuasion and an offer of more money to induce Wagner to breach her contract with Lumley, and assuming that Gye actually thought that it would help his business by having Wagner perform, § 17(2)(b) and (c) would not seem to be met. Nevertheless, the facts are a textbook example of § 17(2)(a).[17]

Some authorities contend that the threat of an interference claim is beneficial because it encourages voluntary bargaining transactions between the third party and the promisee. That is, if Gye desires Wagner's services when she is under contract to Lumley, Gye will need to bargain with Lumley. If Gye approaches Wagner

---

16 *Cf.* RESTATEMENT (SECOND) OF TORTS § 767 cmt. e (1979) (discussing interference with existing contract and noting the "greater definiteness of the other's expectancy and his stronger claim to security for it"); *id.* § 767 cmt. f ("If the interest of the other has been already consolidated into the binding legal obligation of a contract, however, that interest will normally outweigh the actor's own interest in taking that established right from him."); *id.* § 767 cmt. j ("[G]reater protection is given to the interest in an existing contract than to the interest in acquiring prospective contractual relations, and as a result permissible interference is given a broader scope in the latter instance."); *id.* § 768 cmt. h (noting the "social interest in the security of transactions" when dealing with existing contracts).

17 *See* RESTATEMENT (THIRD) OF TORTS: LIABILITY FOR ECONOMIC HARM § 17 cmt. d (2020).

directly, he risks Lumley bringing an interference lawsuit against him. As one court explained:

> .... In the § 766 inducement case, the effect of tort liability is to encourage voluntary transactions. If an "inducer" wishes to receive a promisee's promised advantage, then the inducer must bargain directly with the promisee. This "bargain-forcing" aspect of inducement liability protects the security of transactions, reduces monitoring costs, encourages consensual rearrangements of contractual obligations, and avoids the negotiation and litigation costs that arise where an inducer causes a promisor to breach its contract with its promisee.[18]

Despite these apparent virtues, doesn't the tort of intentional interference with existing contract impede efficient breaches? In thinking about this question, consider the following background:

> ... [F]rom an economic perspective, a refusal to perform a particular promise may not only be defensible but desirable. If *X* and *Y* exchange promises and *X* later discovers that the future exchange to which he has agreed will be detrimental rather than beneficial to him, *X* may breach the contract so made by the exchange of promises. If *X*'s refusal to perform his promise is accompanied by sufficient compensation to *Y*, the result may be economically efficient, whereas a legal insistence that *X*'s promise be performed would be inefficient. "Efficiency" may be viewed as the utilization of economic resources in such a fashion that "value"—human satisfaction as measured by aggregate consumer willingness to pay for resources—is maximized. Normally, a refusal to perform a future exchange will result in loss to the non-breaching party that must be compensated to fulfill the expectations of that party. Thus if *X* agrees to supply 1,000 tape recorders to *Y*, a refusal by *X* to perform will require *Y* to seek an alternative supplier of the recorders. If *Y* must pay a higher price, the difference between the contract price and the higher (substitute purchase) price will make *Y* whole in terms of fulfilling *Y*'s reasonable expectations.
>
> However, assume that *X* has agreed to deliver the 1,000 recorders of a particular brand with a peculiar feature to *Y* at $200 per unit. Before the future exchange is to be performed, *Z* requires 1,000 recorders with the peculiar

18 Windsor Securities, Inc. v. Hartford Life Ins. Co., 986 F.2d 655, 661 (3d Cir. 1993).

> feature of the models *X* has promised to sell to *Y*. *X* has no more of these or any other recorders. Since *Y* has no interest in the peculiar feature, *Y* can purchase substitute recorders that will serve him at least as well as *X*'s recorders at $210 per unit. However, no substitutes would satisfy the needs of *Z*. *Z* is willing to pay *X* $220 per unit. If *X* refuses to perform his promise to *Y*, *Y* may be compensated by a $10,000 payment from *X*. Having received $220 per unit from *Z*, *X* receives a net of $10,000 more than he would have received from *Y* though *Y*, again, has been compensated. Thus *Y* is made whole, *X* receives expected value, and *Z* is satisfied. Not only are the parties better off, the society in which the parties live is also better off in terms of efficiency or value maximization. This situation is often described as one of "efficient breach" of contract. This economic analysis is consistent with the fundamental concept of contract remedies, i.e., to compensate the injured party by placing him in the position he would have occupied had the contract been performed. The protection of the injured party's expectation interest provides an incentive for the other party to breach *only* if the gain from the breach (notwithstanding compensation to the injured party) is greater than the gain from contract performance.[19]

Assuming that *Z* knows about the *X-Y* contract, won't the interference tort deter *Z* from approaching *X* (because *Z* would fear being sued by *Y* for interference)? Doesn't that diminish the likelihood that this efficient breach will occur? Consider the following observations:

(a) The interference tort undoubtedly gets in the way of efficient breach because it deters the *Z*s of the world from approaching the *X*s of the world for fear of liability. As a result, the *X*s may never know about the *Z*s, and otherwise efficient breaches may not occur.[20]

---

19 JOHN E. MURRAY, JR., MURRAY ON CONTRACTS § 6, at 14–15 (3d ed. 1990); *see also* Lillian R. BeVier, *Reconsidering Inducement*, 76 VA. L. REV. 877, 877–78 (1990) ("If Promisor regards herself as worse off performing the contract than she would be paying damages, the law of contract remedies seems to encourage her to breach and pay. The structure of that law has been convincingly interpreted to hold that a fully compensated breach of contract can be socially productive because it can, among other things, cost-effectively move resources from lower to higher valued uses.").

20 *See, e.g.*, Lillian R. BeVier, *Reconsidering Inducement*, 76 VA. L. REV. 877, 898 (1990) ("Thus, in contractual settings where there are market substitutes for Promisor's performance, the prospect of inducement liability may systematically deter efficient behavior by the contracting parties and thus impede the flow of resources to higher valuing users."); Harvey S. Perlman, *Interference with Contract and Other Economic Expectancies: A Clash of Tort and Contract Doctrine*, 49 U. CHI. L. REV. 61, 82–83 (1982) ("If allocational efficiency is the objective of contract law, legal rules

(b) The present state of the law does not seem to view this outcome negatively. Indeed, the widespread acceptance of the interference tort suggests that the law is primarily concerned with preserving the security of contractual arrangements. As mentioned, the interference tort wards off those who would otherwise interfere with existing contracts, or it requires the interferor to bargain with *Y* to change the terms of the *X-Y* transaction. Assuming that *Y* demands some compensation for modifying the terms of the transaction, this allows *Y* to share in some of the gain from the efficient breach instead of simply "breaking even" with a cover remedy. (Of course, every dollar of gain that *Y* expropriates from the efficient breach is a dollar of gain that *X* is not receiving, and at some point, the breach itself will no longer be in *X*'s financial interest.)

Notice that under this argument, efficient breaches are not prohibited by the interference tort. A value-maximizing breach can still occur, but some of the gains from the breach will have to be shared with *Y* to prevent *Y* from asserting an interference claim and deterring the interferor (*Z*) from doing the deal.[21]

(c) An efficient breach only takes place if *Y* is made whole through conventional remedies for breach of contract. Some commentators doubt that this occurs:

> The efficient breach theory contains a number of simplifying assumptions that do not hold in the real world. First, it assumes the absence of transaction costs—the costs of litigation and negotiation, which is so exceedingly high that aggrieved parties often decline to litigate. Second, the rules of contract damages often fail to compensate for all the losses of the party injured by the breach. For example, doctrines of foreseeability and certainty are barriers to the recovery of genuine losses. These barriers are justified, but in a calculation of what is Pareto superior, shouldn't these losses be calculated? Moreover, damages for mental distress

should encourage persons to search for and to take advantage of more highly valued uses for resources under their command. In efficiency terms, there is no reason why formation of one contract should bring the process to a halt or prevent third parties from inducing nonperformance of inefficient contracts. Contract rules seem designed to facilitate breach where efficiency gains result; the inducer liability rule, in contrast, seems designed to reduce the number of such breaches and thus runs counter to a plausible objective of contract doctrine.").

[21] *Cf.* 3 DAN B. DOBBS, DOBBS LAW OF REMEDIES § 12.1(2), at 17–18 (2d ed. 1993) ("[T]here is a question whether the breaching defendant should retain all the gain or 'surplus' resulting from the breach. It is possible to imagine that all the desirable efficient breaches would take place if, when the breach-opportunity is presented, the defendant renegotiated with the plaintiff to escape the contract obligation by paying damages and sharing some of the surplus. This idea in turn has created a literature concerned with the possibility that renegotiation costs will be so high that at least some efficient breaches would be discouraged.").

and the time and effort to scramble for substitute performance are not compensable.[22]

To illustrate, in *Lumley*, what would Lumley have received as damages for Wagner's breach of contract? If Wagner were no longer singing, damages for diminished profits (lost ticket sales) would presumably be awarded. As previously discussed, however, Lumley may very well have suffered damages to his business reputation, as he can no longer be trusted to deliver promised artists. This injury to reputation or loss of customer goodwill is likely far too speculative to satisfy the requirement that contract damages must be established with reasonable certainty. As a result, even though the injury is legitimate, it will likely not be compensated. As mentioned, the speculative nature of the reputation/goodwill damages may also make them unrecoverable in tort, but at least the prospect of punitive and/or mental anguish damages in tort provides the possibility of an extra source of recovery for Lumley's injuries. In short, a true efficient breach may only be possible in transactions involving fungible goods with market substitutes that are readily and immediately available. As discussed below, this is not the fact pattern involved in many interference disputes.

(d) Many interference disputes involve personal services (e.g., *Lumley*) or employment arrangements where the parties benefit by maintaining the relationship itself. Such "relational contracts" are typified by long duration, personal involvement by the parties, and the exchange, at least in part, of things difficult to monetize or otherwise measure.[23] In relational contracts, the parties often make contract-specific investments that cannot be adequately recouped if the contract is breached.[24]

---

22 JOSEPH M. PERILLO, CALAMARI & PERILLO ON CONTRACTS § 14.36, at 620 (5th ed. 2003).

23 *See, e.g.*, Lillian R. BeVier, *Reconsidering Inducement*, 76 VA. L. REV. 877, 908–09 (1990) ("Relational contracts 'encompass most generic agency relationships, including distributorships, franchises, joint ventures, and employment contracts.' Such contracts depart from the model of a complete contingent contract upon which the classical bargain theory of contract is based. Whereas parties to complete contingent contracts are assumed to be able to specify and allocate all relevant risks, the contracting environment in relational cases is too dominated by uncertainty and complexity to permit them to do so.").

24 *See, e.g.*, *id.* at 909 ("A noteworthy fact about contracts that fit the relational model is that they, too, inevitably entail contract-specific investments of one form or another. The Promisee will build a physical plant specified to the contract's idiosyncratic requirements, for example, or she will develop a marketing organization specially adapted to the performance of the particular contract, or she will simply tailor patterns of communication with her contracting partner that will not be transferable to her interactions with other business associates. . . . [T]he assurance of a return on contract-specific investments in relational cases requires that the particular contract be performed.").

For example, assume that a small record label spends considerable time, effort, and resources finding local talent, developing the artists (through training with voice coaches, acting coaches, choreographers, etc.), and marketing them. Many of these prospective artists will fail, in which case the above expenditures will never be recouped. The label can only continue if it can retain the few artists who succeed, as the revenue generated from these artists will hopefully offset (and exceed) the costs of the failures.

Assume, however, that after the label incurs expenses to find, develop, and market the artists, its most promising prospects are successfully wooed by a major record company (in breach of the label's contracts with the artists). What would breach of contract damages provide? Future profits from the artist are likely far too speculative to be calculated with reasonable certainty. Compensation for the development and marketing costs associated with the particular artist might be provided, but that certainly will not help offset the costs of the failed artists. If the record label believes that the law will not stop the occurrence of poaching by major record companies, it may no longer find it financially worthwhile to continue in business.[25]

In these relational contract settings, the concept of efficient breach seems out of place, and the goal should be to preserve the relationship. In this setting, the interference tort can be seen as a mechanism that contributes to this goal.[26] A prospective poacher will think twice before approaching the artist who is under contract given that a successful poach could result in an award of punitive and mental anguish damages. This will likely keep the poach from happening,[27] or will encourage the poacher to negotiate with the record label for a release of the artist (for which the record label will

---

[25] *See* David F. Partlett, *From Victorian Opera to Rock and Rap: Inducement to Breach of Contract in the Music Industry*, 66 TUL. L. REV. 771, 818 (1992) ("If the rising young artist may walk away from the first contract on pain of paying contract damages only, the first record company or producer will be disadvantaged. Damages are unlikely to approach the costs of search and development of untried artists. The record company will bear the losses of failing artists it signs without gaining a great deal on the few who are successful but are 'poached.' The incentives for search and development are undermined.").

[26] *See id.* at 774–75 ("In response, I argue that the contracts which are the subject of the tort are not meaningfully elucidated by the efficient-breach analysis. Rather, the contracts are peculiarly relational—they have to do with employment, leases, professional, and long-term business relationships—contracts where the relationship is vital. Such relational contracts lie far afield from the . . . contracts that are the basis of much economic analysis. After an exposition of the scholarship on the tort of inducement to breach of contract, I suggest a justification for its operation . . .—the maintenance of cooperative relationships . . . .").

[27] *See id.* at 803 ("The availability of tort damages, compensatory and punitive, will deter interference with contracts and, thus, operate to maintain the relationship.").

insist on adequate compensation).[28] If the poach occurs anyway, an award of punitive and/or mental anguish damages might deliver more compensation to the injured party than contract remedies would have provided.

(e) While § 774A of the Second Restatement discusses damages for interference with existing contract, the Third Restatement does not have an analogous provision. Nevertheless, comment n to § 17 of the Third Restatement indicates that compensatory damages are recoverable for interference with contract. In addition, comment e suggests that punitive damages are potentially recoverable.

It is important to note that interference liability does not stem merely from an intentional act by the defendant that has the effect of interfering with the plaintiff's contracts. The defendant must interfere by "inducing or otherwise causing" the breach, which requires some sort of active solicitation or encouragement to breach. Consider the decision of *Knight Enterprises v. Beard.*[29] Defendant Mark Beard was the president of defendant M&L Petroleum, Inc.—a corporation in the business of selling gasoline to retail service stations. Plaintiff Knight Enterprises, Inc. was in the same business. Apparently, several service stations that had fuel purchase contracts with Knight contacted M&L and requested to purchase fuel. Beard admitted that he knew that some of the stations had contracts to purchase their fuel from Knight, but he nevertheless sold to them. He argued that he did not contact, induce, solicit, or coerce any of plaintiff's stations to purchase gasoline from M&L; instead, he stated that the station owners contacted him. In response, Knight argued that "if defendants sold gasoline to a station owner cheaper than the stations could buy the product from plaintiff, this was inducement for the station owner to purchase product from defendants instead of plaintiff."

The jury found in favor of the plaintiff, but the trial court granted a directed verdict for defendants. On appeal, the court stated that Knight had to prove that Beard and M&L took affirmative acts to interfere with Knight's contracts. The court discussed the case of *Bahr v. Miller Brothers Creamery*,[30] in which the Michigan Supreme Court held that proof of "active solicitation and instigation of the breach" was required, and that the "mere selling of a product to a person under contract with another is not the active inducement to

---

28 *See id.* at 820 ("The premium extracted will compensate the record company for its search and development costs, allowing it to maintain these activities.").

29 2004 WL 60323 (Mich. Ct. App. 2004).

30 112 N.W.2d 463 (Mich. 1961).

breach a contract required to sustain the tort."[31] The court also cited comment m to § 766 of the Second Restatement, which similarly states the following: "A's freedom to conduct his business in the usual manner, to advertise his goods, to extol their qualities, to fix their prices and to sell them is not restricted by the fact that B has agreed to buy similar goods from C. Even though A knows of B's contract with C, he may nevertheless send his regular advertising to B and may solicit business in the normal course. This conduct does not constitute inducement of the breach of contract." Because the evidence indicated that Beard and M&L simply gave pricing in response to the customers' unsolicited inquiries, the court concluded that Knight "has simply failed to present any evidence whatsoever demonstrating that defendants' conduct induced or otherwise caused the station owners to breach their contracts with plaintiff." The directed verdict for defendants was upheld.

Did M&L have the purpose or desire to interfere with Knight's contracts, or at least did M&L know that interference was substantially certain to result? Yes, because Beard was aware that at least some of the stations that M&L sold to were under contract to purchase their fuel from Knight. (Beard claimed that he did not know about a contract between Knight and some of the stations. With respect to those stations, of course, Beard/M&L did not "intentionally" interfere, as Beard had no idea that those stations were in contractual relationships with Knight.) Did M&L actually interfere with Knight's contracts? Yes, because the customers purchased their fuel from M&L and not from Knight, which resulted in the customers breaching their contracts with Knight. Was Knight injured by the interference? Yes, because it presumably lost profits as a result of its customers' breaches of contract. Did M&L act improperly? Yes (arguably), because knowingly interfering with existing contracts is likely improper in and of itself.

Given that intent, interference, injury, and impropriety all seem to be met, why does Knight lose? Section 766 of the Second Restatement requires the defendant to interfere by "inducing or otherwise causing" a breach of the contract. According to comment m, M&L's conduct—simply conducting its business in the ordinary course and responding to customer inquiries with a better price than a rival—does not constitute the requisite inducement. Some sort of affirmative solicitation of the under-contract customer is required (as discussed in illustration 3 to § 766), rather than the under-contract customer soliciting the defendant. Similarly, as comment n indicates, "[o]ne does not induce another to commit a breach of contract with a

---

31 *Knight Enterprises*, 2004 WL at *6 (citing and quoting *Bahr*, 112 N.W.2d at 468).

third person under the rule stated in this Section when he merely enters into an agreement with the other with knowledge that the other cannot perform both it and his contract with the third person." In short, and as mentioned, interference liability does not stem merely from an intentional act by the defendant that has the effect of interfering with the plaintiff's contracts. The defendant must interfere by "inducing or otherwise causing" the breach, which requires some sort of active solicitation or encouragement to breach.

It can also be argued that M&L prevailed under § 766 because its conduct was not improper. This is simply another way of making the prior point. Merely responding to customer inquiries with a better price than a rival does not constitute the requisite inducement, and it might not be viewed as improper interference.[32]

Section 17 of the Third Restatement does not have comments like comments m and n to § 766. As a consequence, it is harder to explain (in Third Restatement terms) why the defendants prevailed. After all, Knight and his customers had valid contracts (§ 17(1)(a)); M&L/Beard was aware that at least some of the stations that it sold to were under contract to purchase their fuel from Knight (§ 17(1)(b)); M&L/Beard presumably acted for the purpose of appropriating the benefits of Knight's contracts by stepping in as the fuel supplier for Knight's customers (§ 17(1)(c), (2)(a)); M&L/Beard presumably acted for the purpose of causing breaches of the contracts between Knight and some of its customers (§ 17(1)(d)); M&L/Beard's actions did cause some customers to breach their contracts with Knight (§ 17(1)(e)); and Knight suffered economic loss because it presumably lost profits as a result of its customers' breaches of contract. Where in the text of § 17 is it relevant that M&L/Beard did not engage in affirmative solicitation or encouragement to breach?

Perhaps one could argue that affirmative solicitation/ encouragement to breach is a gloss on § 17(2)(a)? That is, perhaps M&L/Beard's desire to appropriate the benefits of Knight's contracts by becoming the new fuel supplier is only problematic if that desire is coupled with efforts to affirmatively solicit or encourage a breach. The text of § 17(2)(a) does not say that, of course, but it is hard to imagine that the Third Restatement meant to reach a different result in this scenario.[33] Without efforts to affirmatively solicit or encourage

---

[32] *See* RESTATEMENT (SECOND) OF TORTS § 767 cmt. c (1979) ("A's active solicitation of B's business is more likely to make his interference improper than his mere response to an inquiry from B.").

[33] *Cf.* RESTATEMENT (THIRD) OF TORTS: LIABILITY FOR ECONOMIC HARM § 17 cmt. a (2020) ("The framework of this Section is meant to promote clarity and predictability. It is not intended to cause substantial changes in the results produced by the tests and privileges in the Restatement Second.").

a breach, the conduct should not be viewed as an act of wrongful interference.

Consider the following hypothetical: Johanna Wagner contacts Gye and states "I would like to sing at your theater from January–March." Gye knows that Wagner is under contract to sing at Lumley's theater from January–March; nevertheless, he makes an offer with better terms than Wagner has with Lumley. Wagner accepts and breaches her contract with Lumley. What result under the Restatement when Lumley sues Gye for interference with the Lumley-Wagner contract? The *Knight* opinion emphasizes whether the defendant actively solicited the breach or simply responded to a customer inquiry. From that standpoint, this hypothetical is very similar to the facts of *Knight*—i.e., Gye, knowing of the Lumley-Wagner contract, merely responded with better terms to an inquiry from Wagner (just like M&L, knowing of at least some of the Knight-customer contracts, merely responded with better terms to an inquiry from those customers).

Why was Gye liable in the actual case? Because he solicited Wagner rather than the other way around. Why should this make a difference? The law is apparently comfortable allowing contracting parties to solicit offers that may result in a breach, but the law does not want outsiders to the contract engaging in similar behavior. Somewhere this gets back to the notion that contracting parties can do what they wish (perform or breach and pay damages), but outsiders to the contract need to respect the contractual relationship and to interact with the contracting parties (if at all) only on a general, passive basis.

What if Gye did more than simply make an offer with better terms in response to Wagner's inquiry? What if he also spent time with Wagner on the phone trying to persuade her to accept the offer by talking up its terms and/or criticizing Lumley? Even though Wagner made the initial contact with Gye, surely the logic of *Knight* does not mean that Gye is now immunized from any liability. The defendant must interfere by "inducing or otherwise causing" a breach. While *merely* responding to a customer inquiry—even with better terms and even to one who is knowingly under contract—is not enough to constitute inducement, surely engaging in active solicitation and persuasion as part of the response is problematic.[34]

---

[34] *Cf.* V. Marangi Carting Corp. v. Judex Enterprises, Inc., 655 N.Y.S.2d 832, 835 (Sup. Ct. 1997) (noting that "an offer of better terms can cross the line into tortious interference with a particular contract by sweetening the deal with something extra in order to induce the customer to breach its contract with its other provider (*see,* Restatement 2d, Torts, § 766, Comment m, Illustration 3)").

As mentioned, the Third Restatement would presumably reach the same result, but one might have to argue that affirmative solicitation/encouragement to breach is a gloss on § 17(2)(a). That is, the defendant's desire to appropriate the benefits of the plaintiff's contract is only problematic if that desire is coupled with efforts to affirmatively solicit or encourage a breach. Under this standard, if Gye did more than simply make an offer with better terms in response to Wagner's inquiry, his efforts would presumably subject him to liability.

## 2. Interfering with the Plaintiff's Performance

*Nesler v. Fisher & Co.*[35] illustrates the difference in the Second Restatement between claims based on interference with the performance owed to the plaintiff (§ 766) and claims based on interference with the plaintiff's performance (§ 766A). Nesler purchased an office building with the intent to refurbish it and to lease it out to commercial and government tenants. Several county agencies committed to relocate to the building, but their relocation had to be approved by the county board of supervisors. Louis Pfohl, president of the defendant corporations who were currently leasing space to the county agencies, dropped his rental price to below what Nesler had offered. Nevertheless, the board of supervisors approved the move.

Pfohl then pressured the city building inspector to take action against Nesler's project and he persuaded one of his tenants to file suit against Nesler regarding disability access. This had the effect of impeding the progress of the refurbishment and making it difficult for Nesler to obtain financing to complete his acquisition of the building.

Ultimately, Nesler's project failed. He sued Pfohl's corporations for interference with his existing contracts: his contract to purchase the building and his lease agreements with the tenants. Although Nesler prevailed at trial (compensatory damages of $576,476 and punitive damages of $100,000), the trial court granted a JNOV because "the court observed that Nesler had introduced no evidence of interference [as] the owners of the building which Nesler was buying on contract, and the potential tenants of the Nesler Centre were still willing to perform, even after the acts of the defendants had occurred."

On appeal, Nesler argued that the trial court confused a § 766A claim (which Nesler brought) with a § 766 claim (which Nesler had not brought). He asserted that, because of the actions of Pfohl and his

[35] 452 N.W.2d 191 (Iowa 1990).

corporations, he (Nesler) was prevented from completing payment on the purchase contract and from finalizing the lessee contracts. He did not contend that the building sellers or his potential lessees were prevented from performance. The court agreed and concluded that the JNOV was in error:

> In this case, there was substantial evidence that the defendants' actions, including the lawsuits, the building department inspections, the publicity, and the resulting loss of investor and bank confidence prevented Nesler's own performance of the contract and lease agreements. This is the gist of an action under section 766A. It is immaterial in a claim under section 766A whether other parties were prevented from performance.

There are two major distinctions between § 766 and § 766A. First, as *Nesler* describes, § 766 addresses claims based on interference with the performance owed to the plaintiff, while § 766A addresses claims based on interference with the plaintiff's own performance. In other words, who is the plaintiff? Is the plaintiff the person to whom contractual performance was promised? If so, it is a § 766 claim. Alternatively, is the plaintiff the person who was prevented or hindered from performing its end of the contract? If so, it is a § 766A claim. For example, assume that Gye kidnapped Wagner, which made her unable to sing for Lumley. When Lumley sues Gye for interference, his claim is a § 766 claim because he is suing for performance owed to him (Lumley). If Wagner chooses to sue Gye as well, her claim is a § 766A claim because she is suing for interference with her own (Wagner's) performance.

The second distinction is that § 766 only covers injury to the plaintiff stemming from nonperformance of the contract. Section 766A covers injury to the plaintiff stemming from (1) nonperformance of the contract or (2) performance of the contract in a more expensive or burdensome manner. What sorts of conduct can make the performance of a contract more "expensive or burdensome"? The Second Restatement gives the following example: "Thus if the plaintiff is under a contract to keep a highway in repair, a defendant who intentionally inflicts additional expense upon him by damaging the highway is subject to liability under this Section."[36] Further examples might include depriving the plaintiff of needed supplies or

---

[36] RESTATEMENT (SECOND) OF TORTS § 766A cmt. g (1979); *see also* RESTATEMENT (THIRD) OF TORTS: LIABILITY FOR ECONOMIC HARM § 17 illus. 18 (2020) ("City hires Builder to install a sewer line under a street. Retailer on the street objects to the project, believing it to be illegal. Retailer unlawfully puts a large obstruction in the road to block Builder's equipment. Removal of the obstruction consumes time and makes the contract between City and Builder more expensive to perform. Retailer is subject to liability to Builder under this Section.").

labor, such that performance can only occur with higher-priced substitutes; causing a delay in the plaintiff's ability to complete a transaction through groundless assertions of contractual or other rights; or making it more difficult for the plaintiff to get to the place of performance.

Why was a § 766A claim available in *Nesler*, but not a § 766 claim? A § 766A claim is based on interference with the plaintiff's own performance. What contractual performance did the plaintiff (Nesler) owe? On the contract to purchase the building, Nesler needed to complete payment for the building. On the lease agreements with tenants, the court indicated that Nesler needed to "complet[e] the contracts with his potential lessees." Because of the defendants' actions, the court concluded that Nesler was prevented from performing these obligations. Thus, a § 766A claim fits the facts. Nesler's claim was based on the defendants preventing him from performing the building contract and the lessee contracts. He was not claiming that his performance occurred (albeit in a more expensive or burdensome fashion); instead, he claimed that he was prevented from performing at all.

A § 766 claim, however, is based on interference with contractual performance that is owed to the plaintiff. What contractual performance was owed to the plaintiff (Nesler)? On the contract to purchase the building, the owners needed to sell it. On the lease agreements with tenants, the tenants needed to fulfill their leases. There was no interference with that performance because, as the court mentioned, "the owners of the building which Nesler was buying on contract, and the potential tenants of the Nesler Centre were still willing to perform, even after the acts of the defendants had occurred." Indeed, Nesler did not even contend that the building sellers or the potential lessees were prevented from performing. Thus, a § 766 claim does not fit the facts.

Would Nesler have prevailed under the Third Restatement? Unlike the Second Restatement, the Third Restatement does not distinguish between claims based on interference with the performance owed to the plaintiff and claims based on interference with the plaintiff's own performance. Instead, § 17 covers both types of claims and subjects the defendant to liability if its wrongful conduct "caused a breach of the contract or disruption of performance." Comment i to § 17 states the following:

> *i. Hindrance of the plaintiff's performance*. In a typical case of liability under this Section, the defendant has convinced another party to breach a contract with the plaintiff and make a contract with the defendant instead. Liability can also result, however, from a defendant's

interference with the plaintiff's own performance of a contract. See Illustration 17. Interference of this kind may cause the plaintiff to commit a breach of the contract, or it may just cause the plaintiff's performance to become more expensive. See Illustration 18. Liability exists in either case so long as the other elements of this Section are satisfied.

Nesler would likely have prevailed under the Third Restatement, as the elements of § 17 would seem to be met: (1) valid contracts existed between (a) Nesler and the building seller and (b) Nesler and the lessees (§ 17(1)(a)); (2) Pfohl knew about these contracts (§ 17(1)(b)); (3) Pfohl's conduct would likely be viewed as wrongful under § 17(2)(a) (he wanted the county agencies to lease from him instead of Nesler) and possibly under § 17(2)(b) (his harassment and encouragement of what might be a frivolous lawsuit, but see the discussion below) (§ 17(1)(c), (2)); (4) Pfohl had the purpose or desire to disrupt Nesler from performing the building contract and the lessee contracts (§ 17(1)(d)); (5) Pfohl's actions did cause a disruption of Nesler's performance (§ 17(1)(e)); and (6) Nesler suffered economic loss as a result of Pfohl's actions.

Not all courts recognize a claim under § 766A of the Second Restatement. In *Price v. Sorrell*,[37] for example, the court declined to adopt § 766A even though it had previously adopted § 766 and § 766B:

> The difference between §§ 766 and 766A is substantial and significant. Where § 766 requires non-performance which includes a breach of the contract for liability to attach, § 766A requires, not a breach or non-performance, but only that performance became more expensive and burdensome. We are convinced that such an element of proof is too speculative and subject to abuse to provide a meaningful basis for a cause of action. The breach or non-performance of a contract, or the loss of a prospective contractual relation, is a reasonably bright line that reduces the potential for abuse of the causes of action defined by §§ 766 and 766B.[38]

---

[37] 784 P.2d 614 (Wyo. 1989).

[38] *See also* St. Louis Convention & Visitors Comm'n v. Nat'l Football League, 154 F.3d 851, 865 (8th Cir. 1998) ("CVC contends, however, that the NFL can be liable for tortious interference even without a breach if it caused the performance of the contract to be more burdensome and expensive, citing Restatement (Second) of Torts, § 766A. CVC points to no Missouri authority which has recognized this theory, and a federal court ruling on a point of state law is obligated to follow the law as announced by that state's highest court. To adopt CVC's theory would be contrary to the Missouri requirement that a plaintiff prove that the defendant induce a breach of contract.").

What does the *Price* court mean when it states that the "more expensive or burdensome" requirement is "too speculative and subject to abuse"? The court does not explain itself, but consider the following observations:

> Interference torts are always formulated broadly, but the rule in § 766A may be broader than many courts will accept. Given that wrongfulness of interference lies in the eye of the beholder and that interference is intentional if the defendant is substantially certain that it will result from his acts, thousands of acts could intentionally interfere with the plaintiff's contract relations by making the contract more difficult to perform. Even the bus driver who sleeps late one morning might be intentionally interfering with his passengers' performance of their employment contracts. No court would hold the driver liable, but that merely shows that liability can not well be based upon the logic of § 766A.[39]

Some courts have criticized § 766A on different grounds. While the threat of a § 766 interference claim may be beneficial because it encourages voluntary bargaining transactions between the third party and the promisee (see the discussion after *Lumley*), that benefit is absent from a § 766A claim:

> However, in the § 766A "hindrance" case, this "bargain-forcing" justification appears absent. Imposition of liability under this theory does not encourage the third party to bargain with the promisee. In cases where a third-party's conduct "burdens" but does not prevent the plaintiff-promisor's performance, plaintiff's performance is rendered more expensive. The question becomes not whether plaintiff will perform but rather at what cost. This dispute does not involve the promisee.[40]

Moreover, because § 766A claims will frequently involve independently tortious conduct against the plaintiff, the need for a distinct interference action has been questioned:

> In cases where plaintiff's performance is prevented, the third party's actions are directed at the plaintiff-promisor. Yet where the defendant prevents plaintiff's performance, plaintiff will presumably not be a willing participant. Generally, such cases will involve force, fraud, or other independently actionable conduct; adverse effects

[39] DAN B. DOBBS, THE LAW OF TORTS § 448, at 1270 (2000).

[40] Windsor Securities, Inc. v. Hartford Life Ins. Co., 986 F.2d 655, 661–62 (3d Cir. 1993).

on contract rights will become an element of damages subject only to the usual limitations of causation, mitigation, and reasonable certainty. As Professor Prosser points out,

> *[t]he bulk of the cases involving interference as distinct from inducement involve . . . physical interference with person or property and also involve the commission of some independent tort,* as where the defendant interferes with the plaintiff's rights by converting goods to which the plaintiff was entitled under the contract, or commits an injurious falsehood of the kind sometimes called slander of title. Methods tortious in themselves are of course unjustified and liability is appropriately imposed where the plaintiff's contract rights are invaded by violence, threats and intimidation, defamation, misrepresentation, unfair competition, bribery and the like. Constitutional violations have been put in the same category. *Thus in many cases interference with contract is not so much a theory of liability in itself as it is an element of damage resulting from the commission of some other tort, or the breach of some other contract.*

W. Page Keeton et al., *Prosser and Keeton on the Law of Torts* § 129, at 992 (5th ed. 1984) (footnotes omitted) (emphasis added).

Thus, in non-inducement cases, expanding the tortious interference principle to recognize a § 766A "hindrance" cause of action may duplicate protection already afforded through tort and contract. But duplication comes at a cost. It risks chilling socially valuable conduct and creates new liability of uncertain dimensions. Some commentators have criticized the amorphous nature of the tortious interference principle, warning that its expansion is ill-conceived, threatening both fairness and efficiency. These concerns counsel some caution in expanding tortious interference liability.[41]

Does this latter criticism apply to the facts of *Nesler*? That is, in *Nesler*, did the § 766A claim "duplicate protection already afforded through tort and contract"? The defendants' conduct consisted of (1) pressuring the building inspector to take action against Nesler's project and (2) persuading a tenant to bring a lawsuit against Nesler over disability access to the building. With respect to the lawsuit, a

[41] *Id.* at 662–63.

malicious prosecution action might have been available to Nesler, but if the lawsuit was reasonably believed to have some merit, a malicious prosecution claim would not be helpful.[42] Although the lawsuit was dismissed on the pleadings, this does not necessarily mean that it was groundless. With respect to the pressuring of the building inspector, what could Nesler have done? Would harassment be recognized as an independent claim? Intentional infliction of emotional distress? (This seems out of place in a commercial dispute.) In short, the facts of *Nesler* suggest a situation where there may have been an independent need for a § 766A claim because there is not a clear alternative to provide protection.[43]

Despite the criticism of § 766A, keep in mind that the Third Restatement still recognizes liability for "a defendant's interference with the plaintiff's own performance of a contract" if the interference "cause[s] the plaintiff's performance to become more expensive."[44]

## B. INTENTIONAL INTERFERENCE WITH PROSPECTIVE CONTRACT

Intentional interference with existing contract and intentional interference with prospective contract are separate torts with distinct elements.[45] In particular, at least with respect to the Second

---

[42] *See generally* RESTATEMENT (SECOND) OF TORTS §§ 674–675 (1979) (discussing the tort of "wrongful use of civil proceedings").

[43] That said, perhaps the lack of other tort or contract remedies suggests that the defendants' conduct should be viewed as permissible and should not give rise to liability at all.

[44] RESTATEMENT (THIRD) OF TORTS: LIABILITY FOR ECONOMIC HARM § 17 cmt. i (2020); *see also id.* § 17(1)(e) (imposing liability if the defendant's wrongful conduct caused a breach of the contract or "disruption of performance").

[45] *Cf.* W. PAGE KEETON ET AL., PROSSER AND KEETON ON TORTS § 129, at 981 (5th ed. 1984) ("Lumley v. Gye and the succeeding cases laid emphasis upon the existence of the contract. . . . The subsequent development of the law has extended the principle to interference with advantageous economic relations even where they have not been cemented by contract, and the liability for inducing breach of contract now is regarded as merely one instance of protection against such unjustified interference.").

Although the interference torts typically address contractual relationships (either existing or prospective), there are cases extending the tortious interference doctrine to other forms of advantageous economic relations. *See, e.g.*, Harmon v. Harmon, 404 A.2d 1020, 1023 (Me. 1979) (involving interference with the plaintiff's expected inheritance under his mother's will: "If the law protects a person from interference with an opportunity to receive a benefit by entering into contractual relations in the future, the same protection should be accorded to a person's opportunity to receive a benefit as a prospective legatee. The uncertainty attendant upon the expectancy is equivalent."); *id.* at 1024 ("We conclude that where a person can prove that, but for the tortious interference of another, he would in all likelihood have received a gift or a specific profit from a transaction, he is entitled to recover for the damages thereby done to him."); Longo v. Reilly, 114 A.2d 302, 305–06 (N.J. Super. Ct. App. Div. 1955) (involving interference with the plaintiff's election bid for union secretary); *see also* RESTATEMENT (SECOND) OF TORTS § 774B (1979) ("One who by fraud, duress or other tortious means intentionally prevents another from receiving from a third person an inheritance or gift that he would otherwise have received is subject to liability to the

Restatement, the torts differ over whether the plaintiff or the defendant has the burden of proof on the element of "improper" interference.

Consider the decision of *Della Penna v. Toyota Motor Sales*.[46] In 1989, Toyota began selling its Lexus automobile in the United States. Fearful that a resale market would develop in Japan that would threaten its fledgling network of American Lexus dealers, Toyota took steps to prevent the exporting of the car to Japan. Toyota inserted a "no export" clause into its dealership agreements preventing dealers from selling Lexus automobiles for resale or use outside of the United States. Toyota also compiled an "offender's list" of those who were believed to be exporting and warned its dealers that doing business with offenders would lead to sanctions.

John Della Penna was an automobile wholesaler doing business as Pacific Motors. In 1989 and 1990, Della Penna ran a profitable business by purchasing Lexus automobiles at near retail price from local dealers and exporting them to Japan for resale. By late 1990, however, Della Penna's Lexus sources began to dry up—largely as a result of the offender's list. Della Penna ultimately sued Toyota Motors, U.S.A., Inc. alleging interference with his economic relationships with Lexus retail dealers. (Notice that Della Penna did not have contracts with retail dealers, but he had the *potential* to enter into contracts with dealers for the purchase of Lexus automobiles, as he had done in the past. Thus, Della Penna's suit is not for interference with existing contract; instead, it is for interference with prospective contract.)

At trial, the jury was instructed that the tort of intentional interference with prospective contract required the plaintiff to establish that the defendant engaged "in wrongful acts or conduct" designed to interfere with the plaintiff's economic relationships. "Wrongful acts" was defined as conduct "outside the realm of legitimate business transactions . . . [which] may lie in the method used or by virtue of an improper motive." The jury returned a verdict in favor of Toyota.

---

other for loss of the inheritance or gift."); RESTATEMENT (THIRD) OF TORTS: LIABILITY FOR ECONOMIC HARM § 19 (2020) (providing a similar action for interference with inheritance or gift, and stating in the Reporter's Note that "[t]he cause of action discussed here has been recognized in courts of about half the states, including most of those that have considered the issue"). Cases have also extended the tortious interference doctrine to familial relationships. *See, e.g.*, Wolf v. Wolf, 690 N.W.2d 887, 892 (Iowa 2005) (involving a claim for "tortious interference with [child] custody"); Padula-Wilson v. Landry, 841 S.E.2d 864, 870 (Va. 2020) (involving the "tort of intentional interference with parental rights").

[46] 902 P.2d 740 (Cal. 1995).

The Court of Appeal reversed the trial court's judgment. It ruled that it was prejudicial error to require the plaintiff to establish "wrongfulness" as an element of its prima facie case. The Supreme Court of California reversed the Court of Appeal and directed that the judgment of the trial court be affirmed. It held that "a plaintiff seeking to recover for an alleged interference with prospective contractual or economic relations must plead and prove as part of its case-in-chief that the defendant not only knowingly interfered with the plaintiff's expectancy, but engaged in conduct that was wrongful by some legal measure other than the fact of interference itself." The court noted that "questions embracing the precise scope of 'wrongfulness' . . . are matters that can await another day and a more appropriate case."

Do the facts of *Della Penna* fall within the scope of the Restatement's provisions? The Second Restatement addresses interference with prospective contract in § 766B. An interference claim under that section still requires intent, interference, impropriety, and injury. Unlike § 766 and § 766A, § 766B covers both interference with prospective performance owed to the plaintiff (§ 766B(a)) and interference with the plaintiff's own prospective performance (§ 766B(b)).

The facts of *Della Penna* clearly fall within the scope of § 766B. By warning its dealers and preparing an offender's list, Toyota acted intentionally, as it had the purpose or desire to interfere with Della Penna's business relationships with Lexus dealers. Interference did occur, as Della Penna's sources dried up as a result of Toyota's actions (thus, the interference consisted of Toyota "inducing or otherwise causing a third person [Lexus of Stevens Creek and other Lexus dealers] not to enter into or continue the prospective relation [with Della Penna]" (§ 766B(a))). Della Penna was presumably injured, as he was running a profitable export business before his sources of supply disappeared. The only question would be whether Toyota acted improperly, which the jury apparently did not find (at least when the burden was placed on the plaintiff). Toyota's conduct could be viewed as proper given that it was simply enforcing its contractual rights as the franchisor, and it could be viewed as competing legitimately with Della Penna in the Japanese market for Lexus automobiles.

The Third Restatement addresses interference with prospective contract in § 18, and the facts of *Della Penna* seem to fall within its scope. First, under § 18(a), Della Penna had a reasonable expectation of economic benefit from his relationships with Lexus dealers. He had apparently bought from the dealers in the past and nothing suggests that the relationships would have changed absent Toyota's warnings and the offender's list. Second, under § 18(c), Toyota intended to interfere with Della Penna's relationships. As mentioned, by warning its dealers and preparing an offender's list, Toyota had the purpose or desire to interfere with Della Penna's business relationships with Lexus dealers. Third, under § 18(d), Toyota's actions did cause Della Penna's sources to dry up. Fourth, under § 18(e), Della Penna presumably suffered economic loss, as he was running a profitable export business before his sources of supply disappeared. Finally, under § 18(b), it is worth noting that Toyota does not seem to have committed an independent and intentional legal wrong. As mentioned, Toyota's conduct could be viewed as proper given that it was simply enforcing its contractual rights as the franchisor, and it could be viewed as competing legitimately with Della Penna in the Japanese market for Lexus automobiles. Further, the jury did not find that Toyota acted wrongfully.

In the *Della Penna* opinion, the court observed that the torts of interference with existing contract and interference with prospective contract were initially treated as having the same elements. The plaintiff was required to establish intent, interference, and injury, and the burden of proof would then switch to the defendant to establish that the interference was "proper" or "privileged."[47] With respect to the tort of interference with prospective contract, however, that construction was criticized:

> Because the plaintiff's initial burden of proof was such a slender one, amounting to no more than showing the defendant's conscious act and plaintiff's economic injury, critics argued that legitimate business competition could lead to time consuming and expensive lawsuits (not to speak of potential liability) by a rival, based on conduct that was regarded by the commercial world as both commonplace and appropriate. The "black letter" rules of the Restatement of Torts surrounding the elements and proof of the tort, some complained, might even suggest to "foreign lawyers reading the Restatement as an original

[47] *See id.* at 744–45 ("One consequence of this superficial kinship was the assimilation to the interference torts of the pleading and burden of proof requirements of the 'true' intentional torts: the requirement that the plaintiff need only allege a so-called 'prima facie tort' by showing the defendant's awareness of the economic relation, a deliberate interference with it, and the plaintiff's resulting injury. By this account of the matter—the traditional view of the torts and the one adopted by the first Restatement of Torts—the burden then passed to the defendant to demonstrate that its conduct was *privileged*, that is, 'justified' by a recognized defense such as the protection of others or, more likely in this context, the defendant's own competitive business interests.").

matter [that] the whole competitive order of American industry is prima facie illegal."[48]

What does this criticism mean? If the plaintiff's prima facie case for the tort of intentional interference with prospective contract consisted merely of the elements of intent, interference, and injury, then competition would be prima facie tortious, and competitors could be dragged into court for conduct that occurs every day in this country. For example, assume that Lexus decides to run a holiday promotion where it decreases the prices of its cars by 5% and offers low-interest financing. As a result of the promotion, several customers who were planning on buying a BMW automobile purchase a Lexus instead.

In running the promotion, does Lexus have the purpose or desire to interfere with the prospective contracts between car buyers and BMW, or at a minimum, does Lexus know that interference with such prospective contracts is substantially certain to occur? Of course. Attracting customers interested in purchasing a luxury automobile away from BMW and other competitors is likely the reason for the promotion. Did interference result? Yes, as customers planning on buying a BMW purchased a Lexus instead. Was BMW injured? Yes, at least to the extent that it lost sales that it would otherwise have made. In short, any competitive act that society views as legitimate (decreasing prices, increasing advertising, providing incentives) is designed to interfere with prospective contracts, and if it is effective, it will in fact interfere and cause injury. If intent, interference, and injury are the only elements that the plaintiff has the burden of proving, competition will be prima facie tortious.

The *Della Penna* court's statement about the plaintiff's "slender" burden of proof conveys the same idea. As mentioned, if all the plaintiff has to prove is intent, interference, and injury, then legitimate acts of competition will be prima facie tortious. Moreover, as the court discussed, even legitimate acts of persuasion will be prima facie tortious. For example, if you persuade your family member—a pack-a-day smoker—to give up the habit, does your family member's regular seller of cigarettes have a tort action against you? After all, you acted with the purpose or desire to interfere with the prospective contracts between your family member and the seller, your effective persuasion did interfere by causing your loved one to quit, and the seller has lost sales revenue.[49]

---

[48] *Id.* at 745.

[49] *See, e.g.*, Top Serv. Body Shop, Inc. v. Allstate Ins. Co., 582 P.2d 1365, 1368 n.3 (Or. 1978) ("In the contemporary context, a broad generalization similarly could make prima facie torts of otherwise lawful activities designed to persuade others to stop smoking cigarettes or eating certain foods, or using certain pesticides, or doing

The *Della Penna* court resolved these concerns by changing the elements of the plaintiff's prima facie case to make the plaintiff's burden of proof harder when asserting a prospective contract claim. The plaintiff must still establish intent, interference, and injury, but the plaintiff must now also establish that the interference is "wrongful by some measure beyond the fact of the interference itself." In other words, *Della Penna* makes clear that, with respect to the tort of intentional interference with prospective contract, the plaintiff has the additional burden of establishing that the defendant's conduct was improper. Thus, even though legitimate competitive conduct may satisfy the intent, interference, and injury elements of the tort, such conduct would not be "prima facie illegal" because the plaintiff could not establish that it was improper/wrongful.[50]

The resolution of the *Della Penna* court is consistent with § 18 of the Third Restatement. The *Della Penna* court required the plaintiff to establish that the defendant's conduct was improper/wrongful as part of the prima facie case. Section 18(b) appears to do that as well—assuming of course that a court interprets the text of § 18 as listing the elements of the plaintiff's prima facie case (for which the plaintiff would have the burden of proof). (See below for a further discussion of whether the text of § 18 lists the elements of the plaintiff's prima facie case.)

Suppose the *Della Penna* court was considering the elements of a tortious interference with *existing* contract claim. Would the court similarly rule that that the plaintiff "has the burden of pleading and proving that the interference was wrongful by some measure beyond the fact of the interference itself"? This is an important question, as it highlights that the elements of the plaintiff's prima facie case for intentional interference with *existing* contract should differ from the elements of the plaintiff's prima facie case for intentional interference with *prospective* contract. In *Quelimane Co. v. Stewart Title Guaranty Co.*,[51] the Supreme Court of California observed:

> Because interference with an existing contract receives greater solicitude than does interference with prospective economic advantage, it is not necessary that the defendant's conduct be wrongful apart from the interference with the contract itself. . . . [I]t is necessary to distinguish the tort of interference with an existing contract because the exchange of promises which cements an economic relationship as a

business in South Africa, or buying grapes or other products, leaving the defense in each case to a showing of privilege.").

50 Section 768 of the Second Restatement "codifies" this notion by making it clear that legitimate competition is not improper when prospective contracts are at issue.

51 960 P.2d 513 (Cal. 1998).

contract is worthy of protection from a stranger to the contract. Intentionally inducing or causing a breach of an existing contract is therefore a wrong in and of itself.[52]

As *Quelimane* makes clear, there would be no need for a court to add to the plaintiff's burden of proof in an existing contract claim in the same way that it might add to the plaintiff's case in a prospective contract claim. Once again, for an existing contract claim, it arguably makes sense to require the plaintiff to prove only intent, interference, and injury. Given the value that society places on existing contracts, impropriety is assumed, in effect, simply by a stranger's intentional efforts to interfere (via inducement or otherwise) with an established contract. Put differently, an outsider's intentional interference with an existing contract is improper in and of itself.[53] This doesn't mean that the plaintiff necessarily wins, of course, as there may be a justification or privilege for the defendant's conduct that outweighs society's interest in the stability of contracts.[54] But it does mean that the plaintiff has satisfied its prima facie case, and liability should result absent proof from the defendant of some compelling justification.

With prospective contract, of course, proof of intent, interference, and injury should be insufficient to establish a prima facie case, as it would ensnare legitimate persuasion and competition. Thus, something more needs to be added to the plaintiff's prima facie case, which is what the *Della Penna* court did by adding an improper/wrongful element.[55]

---

52 *See also id.* ("Because this formal economic relationship does not exist and damages are speculative when remedies are sought for interference in what is only prospective economic advantage, *Della Penna* concluded that some wrongfulness apart from the impact of the defendant's conduct on that prospect should be required. Implicit in the *Della Penna* holding is a conclusion that this additional aspect of wrongfulness is not an element of the tort of intentional interference with an existing contract."); Ixchel Pharma, LLC v. Biogen, Inc., 470 P.3d 571, 576 (Cal. 2020) ("Our decisions since *Della Penna* have reaffirmed the distinction between the two torts. So, while intentionally interfering with an existing contract is generally 'a wrong in and of itself,' intentionally interfering with prospective economic advantage requires pleading that the defendant committed an independently wrongful act."); Korea Supply Co. v. Lockheed Martin Corp., 63 P.3d 937, 953 (Cal. 2003) ("Thus, while intentionally interfering with an existing contract is 'a wrong in and of itself,' intentionally interfering with a plaintiff's prospective economic advantage is not.").

53 *See supra* note 16.

54 *See* Section D.

55 Despite this discussion, some courts nevertheless put the burden of proving impropriety on the plaintiff, even in an interference with existing contract claim. *See, e.g.*, Safeway Ins. Co. v. Guerrero, 106 P.3d 1020, 1025 (Ariz. 2005) ("The tort of intentional interference with contractual relations requires *a plaintiff to prove*: (1) existence of a valid contractual relationship, (2) knowledge of the relationship on the part of the interferor, (3) intentional interference inducing or causing a breach, (4) resultant damage to the party whose relationship has been disrupted, and (5) *that the defendant acted improperly*." (emphasis added)).

Does the Third Restatement draw the same distinction between the interference with existing contract and interference with prospective contract torts? If a court interprets the text of §§ 17–18 as listing the elements of the plaintiff's prima facie case,[56] the plaintiff has the burden of proof in both torts of establishing that the defendant engaged in wrongful conduct.[57] That burden, however, is much easier for the plaintiff to meet in § 17 (interference with existing contract) than in § 18 (interference with prospective contract), which is consistent with the distinction drawn in *Della Penna* and *Quelimane* (the distinction being that it should be easier for the plaintiff to establish interference with existing contract than interference with prospective contract). Under § 17, the plaintiff can establish wrongful conduct in an existing contract claim by proving that (a) the defendant acted for the purpose of appropriating the benefits of the plaintiff's contract, (b) the defendant's conduct constituted an independent and intentional legal wrong, or (c) the defendant engaged in the conduct for the sole purpose of causing harm to the plaintiff. (Most efforts to interfere with an existing contract are likely efforts to appropriate the benefits of the plaintiff's contract; thus, establishing wrongful conduct, in many cases, is unlikely to be much of a burden at all.) Under § 18, the plaintiff can only establish wrongful conduct in a prospective contract claim by proving that the defendant committed an independent and intentional legal wrong.[58]

The jury instruction cited in *Della Penna* stated that interference with a relationship "containing a probable future economic benefit or advantage to plaintiff" was an element of an intentional interference with prospective contract claim. Many articulations of the tort expressly include a similar element, and even

---

[56] Some support for the assertion that the text of §§ 17–18 lists the elements of the plaintiff's prima facie case (such that the plaintiff would have the burden of proof on those elements) can be found in the description of § 20 as the "privileges" that defeat liability for interference with contract. Comment a to § 20 states that "[a] defendant who wishes to invoke the privileges of this Section . . . bears the burden of asserting them and proving that their elements are satisfied." This suggests that §§ 17–18 state elements of the prima facie case (plaintiff's burden) while § 20 states privileges (defendant's burden). *See also* RESTATEMENT (THIRD) OF TORTS: LIABILITY FOR ECONOMIC HARM § 17 cmt. g (2020) ("Some conduct that would have been protected by privileges under the Restatement Second is exempted from *prima facie* liability under this Section." (emphasis added)).

[57] *See* RESTATEMENT (THIRD) OF TORTS: LIABILITY FOR ECONOMIC HARM §§ 17(1)(c), 18(b) (2020).

[58] *Cf. id.* § 18 cmt. a ("Section 17 provides more expansive rules of liability than are found here. Liability for interference with contract may be based on conduct not otherwise regarded as wrongful by the law, such as simple efforts to induce a breach by offering a better deal to one of the parties to a contract. Liability under this Section requires a stronger showing: the defendant must have engaged in conduct that the law regards as wrongful independent of its impact on the plaintiff's expectation.").

if not express, such an element is presumably implied in the definition of a prospective contract. After all, to be a prospective contract that is worthy of protection, surely there must be some showing that the prospective relationship was reasonably likely to become an actual contract.[59]

The Third Restatement explicitly incorporates this element into § 18. Section 18(a) requires the plaintiff to have "a reasonable expectation of economic benefit from a relationship with a third party." Comment d states, in part, the following:

> To be held liable under this Section, a defendant must have interfered with a prospective relationship between the plaintiff and a third party, and that relationship must have had a reasonable probability of resulting in a contract or other economic benefit. A mere hope or possibility of a benefit is not enough to support liability. This requirement helps limit liability to cases in which the plaintiff had a substantial interest at stake and the costs of the defendant's misconduct are not speculative. On the other hand, the plaintiff need not show an expectation that was more likely than not to bear fruit.

Unlike § 766A of the Second Restatement, the language of § 766B does not include liability for making the realization of a prospective contract more expensive or burdensome. Similarly, § 18(d) of the Third Restatement requires that "the defendant's wrongful conduct caused the expectation to fail." If the expectation has to fail, the section does not appear to allow liability for making the realization of a prospective contract more expensive or

---

[59] *See, e.g.*, Nathanson v. Medical College of Pennsylvania, 926 F.2d 1368, 1392 (3d Cir. 1991) ("In order to prove the existence of a prospective contractual relationship, [the plaintiff] must show that there was a 'reasonable probability' that she would have entered into a contract. . . ."); Glenn v. Point Park College, 272 A.2d 895, 898–99 (Pa. 1971) ("But anything that is prospective in nature is necessarily uncertain. We are not here dealing with certainties, but with reasonable likelihood or probability. This must be something more than a mere hope or the innate optimism of the salesman. As the Superior Court of New Jersey has put it, '* * * the rule to be applied * * * is that the broker may recover when the jury is satisfied that but for the wrongful acts of the defendant it is *reasonably probable* that the plaintiff would have effected the sale of the property and received a commission.' This is an objective standard which of course must be supplied by adequate proof."); Suprise v. DeKock, 84 S.W.3d 378, 382 (Tex. App. 2002) ("The law does not require absolute certainty that a prospective contract would have been made were it not for the interference; it must reasonably appear so, in view of all of the circumstances."); *see also* Thompson Coal Co. v. Pike Coal Co., 412 A.2d 466, 471 (Pa. 1979) ("Defining a 'prospective contractual relation' is admittedly problematic. To a certain extent, the term has an evasive quality, eluding precise definition. It is something less than a contractual right, something more than a mere hope.").

burdensome (but ultimately successful). Nevertheless, some courts have extended liability to cover such circumstances.[60]

## C. ESTABLISHING "IMPROPER" INTERFERENCE

How does one establish "improper" interference for purposes of the interference torts? Consider the decision of *Leigh Furniture & Carpet Co. v. Isom*.[61] Leigh Furniture (owned and managed by W.S. "Dub" Leigh) sold its business to T. Richard Isom for $80,000. Isom paid $20,000 up front and was to pay the remaining $60,000 over the next ten years. The purchase contract provided that if Isom defaulted and did not cure, Leigh Furniture could cancel the agreement and repossess the store. The contract also provided Isom with a lease of a portion of the building where the business was located and an option to purchase the entire building once the $60,000 balance had been paid.

One year after the purchase, Leigh began to complain about the contract and his inability to sell the building because of Isom's long-term lease and option to purchase. Leigh began alleging that Isom was in default and he repeatedly interfered with Isom's ability to run the business. He visited Isom in the store and verbally attacked him in front of customers, he wrote Isom letters criticizing various aspects of the business, and he even filed two groundless lawsuits against Isom. The court noted that "[a]ll of this conduct on Leigh's part had the cumulative effect of demoralizing and upsetting Isom and his employees, reducing their productivity, and impairing their ability to deal with the public and to conduct their business."

Leigh ultimately sued Isom seeking to repossess the premises and to terminate Isom's interest under the purchase contract. Isom denied that he was in default under the agreement and alleged that Leigh had refused to accept a tender of the remaining money due under the contract. Isom counterclaimed for interference with prospective contract based on Leigh Furniture's efforts to "intentionally and maliciously force[ ] him out of business and into bankruptcy."

The jury found for Isom and awarded compensatory and punitive damages. On appeal to the Utah Supreme Court, the court began by

---

60 *See, e.g.*, Kelly-Springfield Tire Co. v. D'Ambro, 596 A.2d 867, 871 (Pa. Super. Ct. 1991) ("It also was not fatal to appellant's cause of action [for tortious interference with prospective business relations] that an agreement for the sale of the warehouse property was ultimately reached with National Life Insurance Company. The complaint contains averments that a resale was unnecessarily delayed by the interference . . . and that actual damage was caused thereby. This was sufficient.").

61 657 P.2d 293 (Utah 1982).

explaining that Isom's recovery could not be sustained on interference with existing contract grounds. After all, the only contract at issue was that between Leigh Furniture and Isom, and "[i]t is settled that one party to a contract cannot be liable for the tort of interference with contract for inducing a breach by himself or the other contracting party." The court, however, held that Utah recognized a tort for intentional interference with prospective contract, and it concluded that Isom's award could be sustained on that basis (i.e., Leigh Furniture interfered with Isom's prospective contracts with customers of the store). The elements of the tort were described by the court as follows: "[I]n order to recover damages, the plaintiff must prove (1) that the defendant intentionally interfered with the plaintiff's existing or potential economic relations, (2) for an improper purpose or by improper means, (3) causing injury to the plaintiff."

Why did the *Leigh Furniture* court reject Isom's claim that Leigh Furniture interfered with the existing Isom-Leigh Furniture contract? The interference torts are based on (at least) a three-party relationship—i.e., there are two parties (at least) to a contract or prospective contract, and there is an outsider to that contractual or prospective contractual relationship who interferes with it. Indeed, §§ 766, 766A, and 766B of the Second Restatement all use the same pronouns to make clear that three parties are contemplated—"one," "another," and "third person." Thus, the interference torts are based on interference by someone who is a "stranger" or "outsider" to the contractual or prospective contractual relationship. The Third Restatement uses the pronouns "defendant," "plaintiff," and "third party" to similarly make clear that three parties are contemplated.[62]

Given this structure, a party to a contractual or prospective contractual relationship (i.e., someone who is not a stranger or outsider to it) cannot be sued for interference with that relationship. Were this not the case, every breach of contract by a party would result in an interference claim against that party, as the party's conduct resulting in breach necessarily "interfered" with the performance of the contract. Courts tend to fear legal rules that have the effect of converting every breach of contract claim into a tort claim—presumably because they want to preserve the ability to

---

[62] *See* RESTATEMENT (THIRD) OF TORTS: LIABILITY FOR ECONOMIC HARM §§ 17–18 (2020); *see also id.* § 17 cmt. o ("Liability arises under this Section when the defendant interferes with a contract between the plaintiff and a third party. Liability does not arise when the contractual relationship at issue is between the plaintiff and the defendant. Put differently, a defendant cannot be sued under this Section for interfering with its own contract, whether alone or in a conspiracy with others."); *id.* § 18 cmt. g ("Liability arises under this Section when the defendant interferes with a prospective relationship between the plaintiff and a third party. Liability does not arise when the relationship at issue is between the plaintiff and defendant.").

efficiently breach, they want to avoid undermining the terms of the contract, and they want to maintain the doctrinal distinctions between contract claims and tort claims.

In rejecting Isom's interference with existing contract claim, the *Leigh Furniture* court provided very little explanation, but the court appeared to follow this approach. Isom and Leigh Furniture were parties to a contract, and they cannot be sued for interference with that contractual relationship. Put differently, they are not outsiders to their contractual relationship, and an interference claim can only be brought against someone who is an outsider to the relationship. If Leigh Furniture were being sued by Isom for interference with *another* relationship to which Leigh Furniture was an outsider, that action is permissible, which is why the prospective contract claim was allowed to proceed (Leigh Furniture was a stranger to the prospective contractual relationships between Isom and his customers).[63]

The *Leigh Furniture* court required the plaintiff in an "interference with prospective economic relations" claim to establish that the interference was "for an improper purpose or by improper means." What did the court mean by that language? With respect to "improper purpose," the court was referring to the defendant's improper motive to injure: "[t]he alternative of improper purpose will be satisfied where it can be shown that the actor's predominant purpose was to injure the plaintiff." The court added that "[t]o satisfy the alternative of improper purpose, the defendant's purpose to injure the plaintiff must predominate over all other purposes, including the long-range purpose of achieving some personal economic gain." By "improper means," the court was referring to when "the means used to interfere with a party's economic relations are contrary to law, such as violations of statutes, regulations, or recognized common-law rules." As the court observed:

> . . . . Such acts are illegal or tortious in themselves and hence are clearly "improper" means of interference, unless those means consist of constitutionally protected activity, like the exercise of First Amendment rights. "Commonly included among improper means are violence, threats or other intimidation, deceit or misrepresentation, bribery, unfounded litigation, defamation, or disparaging falsehood." Means may also be improper or wrongful

[63] *Cf.* K&K Mgmt., Inc. v. Lee, 557 A.2d 965, 976 (Md. 1989) ("This is not to say that acts which constitute a breach of contract between P and D can never be the basis of malicious interference by D with business relations between P and T. Unlike appellants' breach of the Agreement, the breach or threatened breach of the P-D contract may be the instrument selected by D for the purpose of interfering with the P-T contract.").

because they violate "an established standard of a trade or profession."

Isom was unable to establish an improper purpose because the court concluded that Leigh Furniture's actions were predominately motivated by its "long-range financial goal of profitably reselling the building free of Isom's interest." According to the court, "[b]ecause that economic interest seems to have been controlling, we must conclude that the evidence in this case would not support a jury finding that the Corporation's predominant purpose was to injure or ruin Isom's business merely for the sake of injury alone."

Isom prevailed, however, because he was able to establish improper means in two ways. First, the court found that Leigh Furniture "force[d] Isom to defend what appear to have been two groundless lawsuits," which was akin to the tort of malicious prosecution. Second, the court concluded that a deliberate breach of contract combined with an immediate motive to injure (it doesn't have to be the predominant motive; just a motive to injure) counted as an improper means. Because Leigh Furniture breached its contract with Isom in various ways (it breached its duties to exercise its rights in good faith, it refused Isom's tender of the balance of the purchase price, and it hindered Isom's exercise of his purchase option by refusing to appoint an appraiser), and because Leigh Furniture acted with an immediate purpose to ruin Isom's business (although it was predominately motivated by its long-term economic goal of reselling the building), the court found that this alternative ground for improper means had been established.

Are there problems with allowing impropriety to be established through improper purpose or motive? Consider the following:

(a) *Motive is difficult to discern*. Because someone's motivation is internal (it's "in one's head"), it is difficult to prove. The problem is compounded when the motivation of a group of people is involved (it's "in the heads" of multiple persons), and it is even harder to ascertain when the motivation of a business organization is at issue. Indeed, how does one determine the motive of a business organization? Ascertain the motivation of the managers? The employees? The owners?

(b) *Motive may not be singular*. Human beings and entities frequently have mixed motives for taking an action. It is hard enough to discern a person's sole motive; ascertaining multiple motives is even more difficult. Even if multiple motives can be determined, questions about which of the motives predominate can add another level of complexity.

(c) *Bad motive is not necessarily correlated with bad conduct.* Action that society views as legitimate and desirable may be performed with a bad motive. If the underlying conduct is desirable, that conduct should be encouraged and the motive for engaging in the conduct should arguably be irrelevant. For example, a competitor may decrease its prices and increase its advertising because the competitor detests a rival and wishes to destroy the rival's business. So long as the actions do not run afoul of antitrust or other concerns, the conduct is beneficial to consumers. Despite the bad motive, the conduct is socially beneficial and is the type of action that should avoid liability.

As another example, a partner leaving a partnership may be required to sign a noncompete agreement in return for severance payments. Assume that the partnership hears that the partner has begun to violate the noncompete, but the partner's violations are causing no measurable harm to the partnership. Nevertheless, because the remaining partners hate the departed partner and wish to do him harm, they sue to enforce the agreement. So long as the noncompete is otherwise legal, why should the partnership have to fear that enforcement of its legal rights might result in liability? If there is a legal right to enforce the agreement, it must be because we think there is a valuable social interest in upholding the bargain that the parties have struck. If that valuable interest is being served, why should the motive of the enforcing party matter?[64]

In light of these concerns, some courts permit impropriety to be established only through improper means and not through improper motive.[65] Even the *Leigh Furniture* majority recognized some of the

---

[64] *See generally* Harvey S. Perlman, *Interference with Contract and Other Economic Expectancies: A Clash of Tort and Contract Doctrine*, 49 U. CHI. L. REV. 61, 95 (1982) (noting that "pure malice is not a perfect predictor of anticompetitive effect, because an actor motivated by pure malice may choose competitive means to accomplish his purpose: if *TP* hates *B* for personal reasons and spitefully searches for a more advantageous opportunity for *A* so as to interfere with *B*'s contract with *A*, he nonetheless may produce a social benefit"); RESTATEMENT (THIRD) OF UNFAIR COMPETITION § 1 cmt. c (1995) (observing that "[t]he public benefits derived from competition are independent of the actor's motivation," and stating that "[l]iability [under this section] is thus determined by an analysis of the business methods employed by the actor and not by the actor's motivation").

[65] *See, e.g.,* Speakers of Sport, Inc. v. ProServ, Inc., 178 F.3d 862, 867 (7th Cir. 1999) ("We agree . . . that the tort of interference with business relationships should be confined to cases in which the defendant employed unlawful means to stiff a competitor. . . ."); Wal-Mart Stores, Inc. v. Sturges, 52 S.W.3d 711, 713 (Tex. 2001) ("[W]e conclude that to establish liability for interference with a prospective contractual or business relation the plaintiff must prove that it was harmed by the defendant's conduct that was either independently tortious or unlawful."); Texas Beef Cattle Co. v. Green, 921 S.W.2d 203, 211 (Tex. 1996) ("Improper motives cannot transform lawful actions into actionable torts. 'Whatever a man has a legal right to do, he may do with impunity, regardless of motive, and if in exercising his legal right in a legal way damage results to another, no cause of action arises against him because of

concerns about using motive to establish impropriety. Indeed, although the court allowed impropriety to be established through evidence of an improper motive, the court observed that "[p]roblems inherent in proving motivation or purpose make it prudent for commercial conduct to be regulated for the most part by the improper means alternative, which typically requires only a showing of particular conduct." In a later decision by the Utah Supreme Court (the same court that decided *Leigh Furniture*), the court rejected the improper purpose prong and held that "a claim for tortious interference may only succeed where the defendant has employed an improper means."[66] Although Utah may have abandoned the improper purpose inquiry, other jurisdictions have not.[67] Moreover, as will be discussed below, improper motive is still a part of the Restatement's inquiry into the impropriety of a defendant's conduct.

Unlike improper motive, improper means focuses on the conduct of the defendant and whether that conduct is permissible or prohibited. If the defendant's conduct violates an objectively determinable standard of conduct (e.g., it is independently tortious or criminal), then interference liability can result. By focusing on objective conduct, improper means is arguably less vague and subjective than predicating the tort on improper motive.

Would unethical conduct be characterized as an improper means of interference? What about conduct that violates a trade or professional standard? If the point of improper means is to focus on objectively determinable standards of conduct, one could argue that unethical behavior and actions violating a trade standard should count. After all, so long as the relevant standard of conduct is clear and established, a failure to meet that standard (whether tortious, criminal, unethical, or otherwise) is what makes the conduct improper.[68] Indeed, the *Leigh Furniture* court described improper

---

a bad motive in exercising the right.' "); Pratt v. Prodata, Inc., 885 P.2d 786, 789 n.3 (Utah 1994) (". . . *Leigh*'s improper-purpose test creates a trap for the wary and unwary alike: business practices that are found to be 'proper means' by a finder of fact and may otherwise be regarded as wholly legitimate under our capitalistic economic system may be recast through a jury's unguided exercise of its moral judgment into examples of spite or malice. For example, the enforcement of a binding, valid contractual noncompete provision can result in liability under *Leigh* merely upon a jury finding of some ill-defined 'improper purpose.' For these reasons, the author of this opinion thinks *Leigh*'s improper-purpose test should be revisited and recast to minimize its potential for misuse.").

66 Eldridge v. Johndrow, 345 P.3d 553, 556 (Utah 2015).

67 *See, e.g.*, Blake v. Levy, 464 A.2d 52, 55 (Conn. 1983); Harsha v. State Sav. Bank, 346 N.W.2d 791, 799 (Iowa 1984); Top Serv. Body Shop, Inc. v. Allstate Ins. Co., 582 P.2d 1365, 1371 (Or. 1978); Crandall Corp. v. Navistar Int'l Transp. Corp., 395 S.E.2d 179, 180 (S.C. 1990).

68 *See also* Reeves v. Hanlon, 95 P.3d 513, 514 (Cal. 2004) (stating that "to recover for a defendant's interference with an at-will employment relation, a plaintiff must plead and prove that the defendant engaged in an independently wrongful act—i.e.,

means broadly as actions "contrary to law, such as violations of statutes, regulations, or recognized common-law rules," or actions that violate "an established standard of a trade or profession."

On the other hand, some courts define improper means as "independently tortious" or "unlawful" conduct. If those phrases are literally understood, unethical behavior and actions violating a trade standard may not count, as such conduct is neither tortious nor a violation of law. In *Speakers of Sport, Inc. v. ProServ, Inc.*,[69] the Seventh Circuit explicitly adopted this position:

> The doctrine's conception of wrongful competition is vague—"wrongful by reason of . . . an established standard of a trade or profession," or "a violation of recognized ethical rules or established customs or practices in the business community," or "improper because they [the challenged competitive tactics] violate an established standard of a trade or profession, or involve unethical conduct, . . . sharp dealing[, or] overreaching." Worse, the established standards of a trade or profession in regard to competition, and its ideas of unethical competitive conduct, are likely to reflect a desire to limit competition for reasons related to the self-interest of the trade or profession rather than to the welfare of its customers or clients. We agree with Professor Perlman that the tort of interference with business relationships should be confined to cases in which the defendant employed unlawful means to stiff a competitor, and we are reassured by the conclusion of his careful analysis that the case law is generally consistent with this position as a matter of outcomes as distinct from articulation.[70]

When discussing improper means, the *Leigh Furniture* court noted that a "deliberate breach of contract . . . is not, by itself, an 'improper means,'" but when a deliberate breach is coupled with a purpose to injure the contracting party, it is an improper means. What is the court's rationale for this distinction? Doesn't such a conclusion interfere with the concept of efficient breach?

According to the *Leigh Furniture* court, a deliberate breach of contract is not an improper means "[b]ecause the law remedies breaches of contract with damages calculated to give the aggrieved

---

an act 'proscribed by some constitutional, statutory, regulatory, common law, *or other determinable legal standard*' " (emphasis added)).

[69] 178 F.3d 862 (7th Cir. 1999).

[70] *See also* Wal-Mart Stores, Inc. v. Sturges, 52 S.W.3d 711, 726 (Tex. 2001) ("Conduct that is merely 'sharp' or unfair is not actionable and cannot be the basis for an action for tortious interference with prospective relations.").

party the benefit of the bargain," and as a result, "there is no need for an additional remedy in tort (unless the defendant's conduct would constitute a tort independent of the contract)." A deliberate breach of contract committed for the purpose of injuring the contracting party is, however, different. As the court stated, "[t]his is so because contract damages provide an insufficient remedy for a breach prompted by an immediate purpose to injure, and that purpose does not enjoy the same legal immunity in the context of contract relations as it does in the competitive marketplace."

What the court seems to have in mind here is that "mean breaches" tend to cause damage (e.g., mental anguish, harm to business reputation, a complete destruction of the business) that contract remedies fail to cover. In the case of mental anguish, a tort claim can provide compensation while a contract claim generally cannot. In the case of reputational loss or business destruction, contract damages may not be awarded because the damages are too speculative to satisfy the requirement that they must be established with "reasonable certainty." As mentioned, the speculative nature of the reputation/destruction damages may make them unrecoverable in tort as well, but at least the prospect of punitive and/or mental anguish damages in tort provides the possibility of an extra source of recovery for the plaintiff's injuries. (See the earlier discussion of these points after *Lumley*.)

In theory, therefore, the court's conclusion that a "mean breach" can serve as the predicate for a tortious interference claim does not interfere with the concept of efficient breach. An efficient breach only takes place if the injured party is made whole through conventional remedies for breach of contract. As explained, however, the *Leigh Furniture* court believed that contract remedies were unable to make the injured party whole when a mean breach had occurred; thus, efficient breaches are not possible in these situations. Nevertheless, as a result of the court's holding, parties who would have otherwise efficiently breached may fear that a jury will assign an improper motive to their breach. Fear of tort liability, therefore, may deter some efficient breaches from occurring.

The court's conclusion that a deliberate breach of contract, by itself, is not an improper means is worthy of further consideration. Assume that X has a contract to sell goods to Y, and that Y has customers who are interested in purchasing those same goods from Y (i.e., prospective contracts). X's deliberate breach of the X-Y contract is likely to interfere with Y's prospective contracts, and X may very well know this. Why shouldn't the breach be viewed as improper conduct giving rise to an interference claim? Presumably it is because of the efficient breach notion that the law does not typically view a breach of contract—even a deliberate one—as a wrongful act. This may explain why *Leigh Furniture* and many other courts (although not all) seem to require a breach of contract "plus" before allowing a breach to serve as the predicate for an interference claim.[71]

At bottom, this discussion boils down to a fundamental question: is a breach of contract "unlawful" or "wrongful" like other improper means of interference? It is to the extent that there are legal consequences when a breach occurs.[72] It is not to the extent that one believes that contract remedies focus on compensation and not punishment because the law is indifferent between (a) performance and (b) breach with full compensation—i.e., both outcomes can be socially beneficial.[73]

How does the Restatement define impropriety? Section 767 of the Second Restatement is effectively a totality of the circumstances inquiry that considers improper means, improper motive, the

---

[71] *See generally* Mark P. Gergen, *Tortious Interference: How it is Engulfing Commercial Law, Why this is Not Entirely Bad, and a Prudential Response*, 38 ARIZ. L. REV. 1175, 1183 (1996) ("The elements of a prima facie interference claim—boiled down these are the defendant's foreknowledge of the interference and actual harm—exist in a case of contract breach if the breach caused consequential damage and the defendant knew at the time of the breach that it would have that effect. . . . The crucial issue in such cases is whether the defendant's conduct in breaching is improper. Courts have struggled with this issue."); *id.* at 1183–84 ("Some cases will hold a breach improper if it was in bad faith, apparently meaning that the defendant must have known that he was not acting within his rights under the contract when he breached. Some cases require that the interference be the intended consequence of the breach. For example, it would be tortious if the defendant breached in order to steal business from the plaintiff. Some cases ground a finding of wrongful interference on actual malice, meaning that the defendant must have acted to harm the plaintiff and not merely to profit himself."); *id.* at 1184 ("The most lenient cases state that any breach of contract is improper, whatever the defendant's motives. This standard would hold a defendant liable even if he did not realize his conduct breached the contract. At the other extreme, some cases hold that a claim that sounds in contract cannot also sound in tort however heinous the defendant's reasons for breaching.").

[72] *Cf.* Buxbom v. Smith, 145 P.2d 305, 311 (Cal. 1944) ("A breach of contract is a wrong and in itself actionable."); Knickerbocker Ice Co. v. Gardiner Dairy Co., 69 A. 405, 408 (Md. 1908) ("It cannot be denied that it is unlawful for a party to a contract to break it, unless, of course, he has sufficient ground for doing so; and therefore, when a third party procures or induces him to do so, he is causing him to do an unlawful act, which is itself unlawful, and the law ought to afford a remedy to the injured party.").

[73] *See, e.g.*, Lillian R. BeVier, *Reconsidering Inducement*, 76 VA. L. REV. 877, 877–78 (1990) ("If Promisor regards herself as worse off performing the contract than she would be paying damages, the law of contract remedies seems to encourage her to breach and pay. The structure of that law has been convincingly interpreted to hold that a fully compensated breach of contract can be socially productive because it can, among other things, cost-effectively move resources from lower to higher valued uses."); *see also* Windsor Securities, Inc. v. Hartford Life Ins. Co., 986 F.2d 655, 663–64 (3d Cir. 1993) ("'Wrongful' conduct requires something more than mere breach of contract. . . . Comment d [to § 767 of the Second Restatement] describes 'independently wrongful' as conduct that is 'illegal' or 'tortious.' But breach of contract rises to neither of these levels.").

defendant's justification or privilege for its action, and other factors. The factors considered under § 767 are the following:

(a) *The nature of the actor's conduct.* This is effectively an inquiry into the means of interference used by the defendant. By including violations of "recognized ethical codes" or "established customs and practices" as examples of improper means, the Second Restatement may go further than some courts.[74]

(b) *The actor's motive. Leigh Furniture* considered improper motive, although the court clearly required a "predominant" improper motive. Section 767 is more vague, as comment d indicates that even a "casual [bad] motive . . . may still be significant in some circumstances."

(c) *The interests of the other with which the actor's conduct interferes.* This factor considers the type of relationship that was interfered with—an existing contract or a prospective contract. Because society has less of an interest in protecting prospective contractual relationships (after all, our competitive system is based on interfering with prospective contractual relationships), there should be more freedom for the defendant to interfere than if existing contracts were at issue.[75]

(d) *The interests sought to be advanced by the actor.*

(e) *The social interests in protecting the freedom of action of the actor and the contractual interests of the other.* These factors ((d) and (e)) examine the defendant's reason for interfering and consider whether that reason is significant enough to outweigh the harm of the interference itself.[76]

(f) *The proximity or remoteness of the actor's conduct to the interference.* This factor considers the "distance" or "degree of attenuation" between the defendant's conduct and the actual interference that serves as the basis for the suit. If A persuades B not to perform its contract with C, and C sues for interference, the Restatement considers that strong evidence of A's impropriety. On the other hand, if A persuades B not to perform its contract with C,

---

[74] RESTATEMENT (SECOND) OF TORTS § 767 cmt. c (1979).

[75] *See id.* § 767 cmt. j ("[G]reater protection is given to the interest in an existing contract than to the interest in acquiring prospective contractual relations, and as a result permissible interference is given a broader scope in the latter instance").

[76] *See, e.g., id.* § 767 cmt. f ("In some cases the actor may be seeking to promote not solely an interest of his own but a public interest. The actor may believe that certain practices used in another's business are prejudicial to the public interest, as, for example, his maintenance of a gambling den in the rear room of his cigar store and in plain sight of his patrons, or his despoiling the environment by polluting a stream or strip-mining an area without restoring the natural conditions, or his racial or sexual discrimination in his employment policy.").

and that has the effect of C not performing its contract with D, D's lawsuit for interference is considered more "remote" to A's actions and is less strong evidence of A's improper conduct.

(g) *The relations between the parties.* This factor seems somewhat redundant with the other factors. Are the parties competitors? Are the parties in a contractual relationship or a prospective contractual relationship?

How does *Leigh Furniture* compare to § 767? *Leigh Furniture,* at least with respect to interference with prospective contract, makes it clear that the plaintiff has the burden to establish intent, interference, injury, and impropriety. Impropriety can be established by improper means or improper motive. If the plaintiff's prima facie case is established, the burden shifts to the defendant to demonstrate the affirmative defense of privilege. For example, if the plaintiff meets his prima facie case by establishing that the defendant acted with a predominant motive to injure, the defendant might still prevail by demonstrating that its conduct was privileged due to First Amendment concerns or some other weighty public interest.

Under § 767, everything related to impropriety and privilege is balanced at once in a totality of the circumstances inquiry, and the Restatement explicitly takes no position on who has the burden of proof on impropriety.[77] Acting with a predominant motive to injure would be good evidence of impropriety (see, e.g., § 767 cmt. d), but First Amendment concerns or some other weighty public interest would also be considered (see *id.* § 767 cmts. f–g). These other interests may outweigh the bad motive.

The Third Restatement moves away from a multi-factor balancing test.[78] Instead, the Third Restatement defines impropriety (i.e., "wrongful conduct") more directly. For interference with existing contract, the defendant's conduct is wrongful under § 17(2) if "(a) the defendant acted for the purpose of appropriating the benefits of the plaintiff's contract; (b) the defendant's conduct constituted an independent and intentional legal wrong; or (c) the defendant engaged in the conduct for the sole purpose of causing harm to the plaintiff." For interference with prospective contract, the defendant

[77] *See id.* (Introductory Note to Chapter 37); *id.* § 767 cmt. k.

[78] *See* RESTATEMENT (THIRD) OF TORTS: LIABILITY FOR ECONOMIC HARM § 18 (2020) (Reporter's Note) ("Liability for interference that is deemed 'improper' proved too vague to provide the clear guidance to which parties are entitled in commercial settings. It invited courts to make open-ended ethical inquiries into a defendant's conduct, and the inquiries did not crystallize into doctrines that allowed for principled and manageable statement—apart from the conclusion that independent wrongs do support liability.").

under § 18(b) has to commit "an independent and intentional legal wrong."

Not surprisingly, given that society values existing contract more than prospective contract, it is harder for a plaintiff to prevail on a prospective contract claim. Whereas the Third Restatement provides only one option to establish wrongful conduct for a prospective contract claim ("independent and intentional legal wrong"), that option exists along with two others for an existing contract claim.[79] In particular, given that many claims for interference with existing contract involve a defendant's successful effort to take the place of the plaintiff in a contractual relationship, § 17 explicitly designates this ground ("the defendant acted for the purpose of appropriating the benefits of the plaintiff's contract") as wrongful.

What does the Third Restatement mean by an "independent and intentional legal wrong"—a ground that is present in § 17 and § 18? Comment b to § 18 observes:

> *Independently wrongful acts.* To support liability under this Section, the defendant's conduct must have been wrongful in some way recognized elsewhere by the law. Liability may be found, for example, if the defendant's act amounted to a tort such as fraud, defamation, or breach of fiduciary duty. Liability may likewise be found if the defendant's act was criminal, or if it otherwise violated a statute or regulation; interference achieved by commission of equitable wrongs, such as duress, may also serve as a basis for recovery. Liability should not be imposed, however, if the defendant's act amounted only to "sharp practice" or unethical behavior. The law does not condone such conduct but does not treat it as a basis for liability in

---

[79] *See id.* § 18 cmt. a ("Section 17 provides more expansive rules of liability than are found here. Liability for interference with contract may be based on conduct not otherwise regarded as wrongful by the law, such as simple efforts to induce a breach by offering a better deal to one of the parties to a contract. Liability under this Section requires a stronger showing: the defendant must have engaged in conduct that the law regards as wrongful independent of its impact on the plaintiff's expectation."); *id.* ("The standard for liability under this Section is more demanding than the standard under § 17, first, because a party with a valid contract holds an interest that the law regards as more important than an expectation of a contract to come. Since a party who merely hopes to make a contract has a weaker interest at stake, recovery for invasion of that interest requires a stronger showing. Second, the countervailing social interest in free competition is greater in cases in which a contract is not yet formed. Business competition usually can be described precisely as rivalrous efforts to win a contract; most claims of interference with economic expectation arise from efforts of that kind that are excessive. Because competition itself is socially beneficial, rules to restrain those excesses are appropriately kept modest and clear.").

tort. Nor will an act of negligence or a breach of contract suffice to support liability under this Section.[80]

The requirement of wrongfulness is supported by two general considerations. First, it helps confine liability under this Section to cases in which liability is best justified. The rationale for such liability is strongest when a defendant commits a wrong that injures the plaintiff, but for which the plaintiff cannot sue directly because the immediate victim of the wrong is someone else. If a defendant commits a fraud against a third party, and as a result the third party cancels a planned transaction with the plaintiff, the plaintiff cannot sue the defendant for fraud. But the fraud may have caused great damage to the plaintiff, and less damage—possibly none—to the third party who was the immediate victim. It is true that a plaintiff ordinarily cannot sue to recover for economic losses that result from a tort committed against someone else. But when the defendant's misconduct is intentional and satisfies the other elements of this Section, the case for recovery is compelling.

Second, the requirement of wrongfulness provides potential defendants with clear guidance about where their exposure to liability starts and stops. In many cases alleging interference with economic expectation, the defendant's conduct is an effort at competition that is alleged to have gone too far. As discussed in Comment a, however, competition is socially valuable, and it should not be discouraged by vague legal standards and outcomes that are hard to predict. Those problems are avoided if the "wrongfulness" required for liability under this Section is defined by reference to rules and standards that exist elsewhere in the law.

This Section does not necessarily require the plaintiff to prove that the independent wrong was completed and that the defendant may be held liable to its immediate victim. For example, a defendant may be held liable under this Section for making fraudulent statements to a third party if those statements interfere with the plaintiff's business expectation, and the claim survives even if the

[80] Does the reference to breach of contract suggest that the Third Restatement would reject the "mean breach" impropriety ground in *Leigh Furniture*? Or should this comment be viewed as solely addressing "ordinary" breaches of contract and not breaches coupled with a motive to injure? *See also* RESTATEMENT (THIRD) OF TORTS: LIABILITY FOR ECONOMIC HARM § 17 (Reporter's Note) (2020) ("One breach of contract can often precipitate others; a breach with that consequence should not easily be turned into a tort claim.").

> third party suffered no damage and so would not be able to sue for fraud. On the other hand, if a defendant can successfully assert a privilege to avoid liability for defamation, a claim under this Section cannot be based on the privileged speech. The court must consider the logic of the legal rules under which the defendant's conduct is wrongful . . . and ask whether the policies behind the rules would be advanced or offended by imposing liability under this Section.
>
> A defendant's violation of a clearly stated code of professional conduct may satisfy this element of the tort in an appropriate case. The existence of such a code supplies a suitably determinate legal standard.[81] But the court should satisfy itself that the rule does not have anticompetitive effects and that its purpose is to protect those in the plaintiff's position. Such cases also must be handled with care because the substance of such codes may vary considerably by jurisdiction.[82]

For the tort of intentional interference with existing contract, improper motive can also serve as wrongful conduct under § 17(2) of the Third Restatement, but only when "the defendant engaged in the conduct for the sole purpose of causing harm to the plaintiff." As comment f to § 17 observes:

> *Purpose to harm.* A final basis for the liability stated in this Section, reflected in Subsection (2)(c), arises when a defendant interferes with the plaintiff's contract solely for the sake of causing the defendant personal or competitive harm. Defendants generally may avoid liability by pursuing their own interests in good faith and by lawful means, so long as they do not attempt to disrupt the contracts of others for the sake of obtaining the benefits of the contracts for themselves. Nor does liability arise from a mere showing

[81] Under the Third Restatement, is unethical conduct an "independent and intentional legal wrong"? The quoted comment states that "[l]iability should not be imposed . . . if the defendant's act amounted only to 'sharp practice' or unethical behavior." It further notes that "[t]he law does not condone such conduct but does not treat it as a basis for liability in tort." Nevertheless, the comment also states the following: "A defendant's violation of a clearly stated code of professional conduct may satisfy this element of the tort in an appropriate case. The existence of such a code supplies a suitably determinate legal standard."

These statements presumably mean that generally unethical behavior—i.e., unethical behavior that is not prohibited by an actual code of professional conduct—is insufficient for liability. If restrictions on such unethical behavior have been "codified," however, the behavior apparently can be characterized as an "independent and intentional legal wrong."

[82] *See also* RESTATEMENT (THIRD) OF TORTS: LIABILITY FOR ECONOMIC HARM § 17 cmt. e (2020) (discussing "independently wrongful acts").

> that a defendant was gratified by the disruption of the plaintiff's contract; even if gratifying, the disruption may have been a byproduct of legitimate efforts at competition or protection of the defendant's own interests. But if a defendant's sole purpose is the infliction of harm on the plaintiff, liability is appropriate. Such cases often involve retaliation against the plaintiff for a perceived wrong. . . .
>
> The requirement that infliction of harm be the defendant's "sole" purpose makes liability under this theory difficult to establish. The standard is kept demanding to protect legitimate commercial activity by rivals who may well dislike each other.

Given this language, any form of mixed motive is insufficient to establish "wrongful conduct" under § 17(2)(c).

For the tort of intentional interference with prospective contract, can an improper motive (by itself) serve as the basis for the tort under the Third Restatement? The text of § 18 would suggest that it cannot, as § 18(b) requires the defendant to have committed "an independent and intentional legal wrong." Nevertheless, comment c notes that the Third Restatement takes no position on the issue:

> *Improper purpose*. This Restatement takes no position on whether liability arises from a lawful act done for an improper purpose, as when a defendant has acted purely out of malice toward the defendant. The behavior at issue in such cases cannot be condoned, but decisions relying on that consideration to support liability in tort are rare. There is also a substantial risk of error in identifying them. Some of these same risks can arise in cases under § 17(2)(c) as well. But the risks are easier to bear, and easier to justify, when the interest under protection is a contract rather than a plaintiff's broader interest in seeking economic gain.
>
> Older cases that have been viewed as basing liability upon malicious intent sometimes may be explained instead as involving independently wrongful acts. More recent cases following the general approach set forth in this Section have declined to recognize liability based on a defendant's bad purpose alone. This Restatement does not commit to a rejection of such liability, however, because the cases taking that view are relatively recent. Assessment of the position they state will benefit from additional testing by experience.

# D. PRIVILEGE OR JUSTIFICATION

Even if a plaintiff has met the prima facie elements of an interference claim, the defendant might still prevail by establishing a privilege or justification for the interference. Indeed, in many jurisdictions, the elements of the plaintiff's prima facie case for tortious interference with *prospective* contract are intent, interference (by inducement or otherwise), impropriety, and injury. (There is also the element that the prospective relationship was reasonably likely to become an actual contract.) If the plaintiff establishes the prima facie case, the burden shifts to the defendant to establish privilege or justification. By contrast, the elements of the plaintiff's prima facie case for tortious interference with *existing* contract are intent, interference (by inducement or otherwise), and injury (impropriety is effectively assumed when the other elements are proven because of the value that society places on existing contracts). If the plaintiff establishes the prima facie case, the burden shifts to the defendant to establish privilege or justification. Because of the value that society places on existing contracts, however, the privileges/justifications should be less expansive than those afforded to defendants in prospective contract claims.[83]

One such privilege or justification involves the defendant's good faith assertion of legal rights. In *Richardson v. La Rancherita*,[84] La Rancherita was leasing restaurant premises to Breg (a corporation). Breg entered into an agreement to sell its assets to Norman Bomze, but the agreement was contingent on La Rancherita agreeing to assign the lease. The lease itself indicated that the lessee could not "sell or assign this lease, either voluntarily or by operation of law, nor allow said property to be occupied by anyone contrary to the terms hereof, without the written consent of the Lessors."

La Rancherita refused to give its consent unless the lease terms were renegotiated to provide it with increased rent and other favorable provisions. Bomze rejected the proposed terms, and he and Breg decided to restructure the transaction to bypass the need for La Rancherita's consent. Instead of a sale of assets from Breg to Bomze, the transaction was restructured as a sale of Breg stock to Bomze. (That way, Breg (the entity) would remain as the tenant under the lease, even though Breg was now controlled by Bomze.) Upon being informed of the new structure, La Rancherita maintained its position that its consent was necessary. The sale of the stock was originally set to close on January 31, 1974, but it was delayed until March 3,

83 *See, e.g.*, RESTATEMENT (SECOND) OF TORTS § 768 & cmt. a (1979).

84 159 Cal. Rptr. 285 (Ct. App. 1979).

1974 because La Rancherita threatened that the lease would be forfeited without its consent.

Breg and its shareholders filed suit against defendants La Rancherita and Louis Martinez. The suit requested (1) a declaration as to whether the transfer of the Breg stock constituted an assignment of the lease, and (2) damages for intentional interference with the contract between the Breg shareholders and Bomze for the sale of stock. The court found that La Rancherita's consent was not required, and after trial, damages of $7,233.06 were awarded for losses sustained by the plaintiffs between January 31 and March 3.

The defendants argued that their actions were justified because they were motivated by a good faith belief, based upon their lawyers' advice, that La Rancherita's consent was necessary before the Breg stock could be sold. After citing § 773 of the Second Restatement, the court ultimately concluded that defendants did not act in good faith. The court found that an earlier precedent, *Ser-Bye Corp. v. C.P. & G. Markets*,[85] held that a corporate lessee's sale of its stock did not constitute an assignment, and that the instant case was not materially different. The core of the court's reasoning, however, was the following:

> . . . . There was ample evidence for the court to find that defendants' concern with the assignment of the lease was only incidental to their predominant motive of terminating the existing lease to obtain a new lease upon more favorable terms to themselves. Defendants made no effort to inquire into the financial condition of the successor stockholders or their intended method of operation. They restricted their negotiations to increasing their financial return and not to preserve their interest as lessor. The record is devoid of any evidence that defendants believed their leasehold interest was threatened by the new owners. The court was justified in finding that "(t)he transaction as ultimately consummated was clearly within the parameters of the *Ser-Bye* case. . . ."
>
> Something other than sincerity and an honest conviction by a party in his position is required before justification for his conduct on the grounds of "good faith" can be established. There must be an objective basis for the belief which requires more than reliance on counsel. It is the opinion of counsel that must be examined, recognizing that creative and conscientious lawyers should be given every opportunity to challenge outmoded precedent to

[85] 179 P.2d 342 (Cal. Dist. Ct. App. 1947).

> permit constructive development of the law. However, to merely equate reliance on an attorney's advice with "good faith" is to shield those parties from liability who seek and obtain counsel. To create such a blanket rule of immunity is unwarranted.

In dissent, Justice Staniforth argued that *Ser-Bye* was inapplicable and that the facts of the case established justification:

> . . . . Here, the lessor is required to respond in damages because he had the temerity to contend and on basis of sound legal advice which sustained him in his contention that the attempted assignment was in violation of express terms of the lease prohibiting assignment or a change in occupancy without written consent. The proposed opinion offers no case, no scholarly authority to indicate that in these conceded factual circumstances the landlord does not have a right, a legally protected interest in making a good faith attempt to enforce the express terms of his lease. . . . We have not yet reached a state in this society where either a landlord or tenant may not advance a position in good faith as regards an interpretation of a document between them. There is a right and a duty upon the part of the landlord or tenant if they in good faith believe that the other party is breaching their lease to maintain that position [and] to defend it stoutly.[86]

The *La Rancherita* court cited § 773 of the Second Restatement in its analysis. That section provides a defense for parties who assert legal rights and interfere with an existing or prospective contract as a result.[87] Section 773 requires, in part, that a defendant "assert[ ] in good faith a legally protected interest of his own," and that the defendant "believe[ ] that his interest may otherwise be impaired or destroyed by the performance of the contract or transaction." Why didn't La Rancherita prevail under this language?

La Rancherita asserted that it had a contractual veto right when the lease was being sold or assigned or when the property was

---

[86] The *La Rancherita* court stated the elements for an intentional interference with existing contract claim. One of the elements required the plaintiff to establish that the defendant engaged in "unjustified and wrongful conduct." As mentioned, most courts would not require the plaintiff to shoulder the burden of proof on this element, as a defendant's intentional, injurious interference with an existing contract is typically wrongful in and of itself. Later California law seems to adopt this position. *See supra* notes 51–52 and accompanying text.

[87] Notice that § 773 provides a defense because it says that the defendant "does not interfere improperly" if the requirements of § 773 are met. Because §§ 766, 766A, and 766B claims under the Second Restatement all require a showing of improper interference, a conclusion that the interference is not improper insulates the defendant from liability.

occupied by others, and it contended that this veto right extended to the sale of its corporate tenant's stock. Was that contractual veto right asserted in good faith? To the extent that good faith means that the defendant honestly believed that it had a legal right in the situation, it is hard to say that La Rancherita was lacking in good faith. After all, La Rancherita sought legal advice on the question and was apparently told that there was at least a credible argument that the stock sale was an improper evasion of the consent requirement and that *Ser-Bye* was distinguishable. (Even the dissent thought that *Ser-Bye* was distinguishable.) Thus, it appears that La Rancherita did hold an honest belief, fueled by the advice of counsel, that it had a contractual veto right in the situation. Moreover, given what its counsel told it, surely La Rancherita believed that its veto right would be impaired by a stock sale that, in substance, resulted in a new lessee, even if not in form.

The court, of course, disagreed with this notion. As mentioned, it concluded that "[s]omething other than sincerity and an honest conviction by a party in his position" is required for good faith. Even more striking, the court stated that "more than reliance on counsel is necessary" and that "[i]t is the opinion of counsel that must be examined." This part of the opinion seems nutty. Why can't La Rancherita rely on what its professional counsel told it? How are clients, particularly non-lawyer clients, supposed to examine the opinion of their professional counsel? Hire more lawyers, and then examine their opinions too? While the court is reluctant to create a "blanket rule of immunity" for parties who seek and obtain counsel, any purported immunity would extend only to those clients who are told that they have a defensible legal position. Ultimately, the dissent would seem to have the better of the argument on this point—to the extent that good faith requires an honest belief that one has a legal right, surely consulting counsel to see if one does have a legal right in the situation should be sufficient.

Perhaps a better explanation for the court's outcome lies in a motive analysis. Does a "good faith" assertion of a legal right also require a proper motive for the assertion of the right? The court certainly thinks so. Directly after noting that "[f]actual issues including elements which bear on 'good faith' were properly before the trial court," the court discussed the defendants' "predominant motive." The court seemed to take the position that a proper motive for the assertion of a legal right must be related to the purpose of the right itself. That is, the purpose of a contractual veto right over the sale or assignment of a lease is to give the lessor control over the identity of the lessee. The lessor does not want to be stuck with a lessee who cannot pay rent or comply with other lease obligations. Thus, the court seemed to believe that a proper motive for the assertion of the veto right would be if La Rancherita was concerned about the fiscal responsibility of Bomze or Bomze's ability to comply with other lease obligations. The defendants, however, did not seem to be concerned about these issues, as they "made no effort to inquire into the financial condition of the successor stockholders [wasn't it just Bomze?] or their intended method of operation," and the court noted that "[t]he record is devoid of any evidence that defendants believed their leasehold interest was threatened by the new owners." (Again, isn't it just one new owner—Bomze?) As a result, the court concluded that the defendants' motive was not proper, as they were simply interested in holding the transaction up as leverage to renegotiate a more lucrative lease for themselves. This, in the court's view, is apparently a bad motive for the assertion of the right.

Perhaps the source of any motive inquiry, however, stems not from the "good faith" provision, but instead from the later language of § 773 indicating that the defendant must "believe[ ] that his interest may otherwise be impaired or destroyed by the performance of the contract or transaction." That language might be construed as requiring a defendant to argue that it acted for a particular purpose—i.e., the defendant believed that its legal rights were threatened. If the defendant acted for a different reason, § 773 arguably provides no protection. Here, one might argue that La Rancherita's legally protected interest was its contractual rights under the lease. Its lack of concern with Bomze's ability to meet the lease obligations, however, suggested that La Rancherita did not believe that its contractual rights under the lease were threatened by the assignment. Instead, La Rancherita had a different motive for acting (i.e., getting more money), which is not protected by § 773.

One might ask why a motive inquiry is even relevant to a defense based on the assertion of a legal right. Defendants negotiated for a contractual veto right when the lease was sold or assigned or when the property was occupied by others. If they honestly believed that such a right was applicable in the situation, why shouldn't they be able to enforce the right without worrying that a jury or court might second-guess their motivations? (Indeed, the dissent rather bluntly stated that "[t]he lessor's motives for asserting his legal rights are totally irrelevant.")

A final explanation for the court's outcome might be the simplest. Section 773 requires a legally protected interest. Defendants thought they had a contractual veto right in the situation, but they were wrong. The court held that *Ser-Bye* governed and that the veto right wasn't triggered by the stock sale. Thus, defendants did not have a legally protected interest in the factual situation at issue. Without a legally protected interest, § 773 does not apply.

This rationale, however, seems unduly harsh. Providing a defense to interference only if the defendant is correct in its belief of an applicable legal right makes it very risky to assert such a defense. If parties are fearful of attempting to enforce their legal rights, the legal rights themselves are weakened. As the dissent suggested, parties who believe in good faith that they have a legal right in the situation should be able to assert that right even if there is uncertainty about how a court might rule.

The Third Restatement (in § 20(b)) recognizes a privilege if the defendant's conduct consists of "lawful and good-faith efforts to protect a legal interest." Comment c to that section states the following:

> *Protection of a legal interest.* A defendant may not be held liable for interference caused by the defendant's good-faith efforts to protect a legal interest. The conduct protected by this privilege can take the form of lawsuits or other legal proceedings. It can also include private measures taken to protect the defendant's legal rights.
>
> The privilege to protect a legal interest is conditional. It does not protect conduct that is wrongful or undertaken in bad faith. It therefore does not protect conduct that results in prima facie liability under § 17(2)(b) or (2)(c).[88] The privilege can, however, protect conduct that would otherwise result in liability under § 17(2)(a): one may assert legal rights in an effort to appropriate the benefits of a contract to which the plaintiff is a party. The conduct is nevertheless privileged if the assertion of rights was made in good faith.
>
> "Good faith" means that the defendant believed the acts taken were appropriate to protect a legitimate interest recognized by law. An incorrect belief can provide a sufficient basis for a privilege if the belief is sincerely held. Good faith is not present if the defendant uses a legitimate interest as a pretext to interfere with the plaintiff's contract out of spite. In a case involving mixed motives, the privilege

---

[88] Section 17(2)(b) is when the defendant's conduct constitutes "an independent and intentional legal wrong." That ground is the only textual basis for interference with prospective contract liability under § 18. Thus, based on the text of § 18, the § 20(b) privilege does not apply to interference with prospective contract liability. If the defendant commits an independent and intentional legal wrong, in other words, the purported protection of a legal interest is not a valid privilege or justification. *See* RESTATEMENT (THIRD) OF TORTS: LIABILITY FOR ECONOMIC HARM § 20 cmt. a (2020).

> prevails if the predominant reason for the interference was legitimate.
>
> A successful lawsuit is conclusively presumed to have been privileged for purposes of this Chapter. A claim under this Section should not be used to relitigate the result of a prior case.[89]

Would the language of the Third Restatement have changed the result in *La Rancherita*? Efforts to protect the legal interest must still be in good faith, which is defined as the defendant's belief that "the acts taken were appropriate to protect a legitimate interest recognized by law." As mentioned, to the extent that La Rancherita did hold an honest belief, fueled by the advice of counsel, that it had a contractual veto right in the situation, it would seem to meet this requirement. The comment does note, however, that motive is relevant to the good faith inquiry and that the predominant reason for the interference must be legitimate. Thus, perhaps the court's motive analysis would have been the same.

With respect to whether the defendant must be correct in its belief of an applicable legal right, the comment does state that "[a]n incorrect belief can provide a sufficient basis for a privilege if the belief is sincerely held." Moreover, illustration 5 to § 20 seems to clearly indicate that the defendant's mistaken belief as to whether it had an enforceable legal right does not defeat the privilege.

Notice that a resort to privileges is only necessary if the plaintiff can establish a prima facie case.[90] Under the Second Restatement, Breg and its shareholders could presumably establish intent (La Rancherita knew of the contract between the Breg shareholders and Bomze and desired to interfere with it), interference, and injury. Impropriety would be effectively assumed because of the value that society places on existing contracts. Thus, it is likely that the prima facie case would be met and a resort to privileges would be necessary for La Rancherita.

Under the Third Restatement, however, it is not clear that Breg and its shareholders would satisfy the prima facie requirements of § 17(1)(c) and (2). After all, La Rancherita was not engaged in an independent and intentional legal wrong (§ 17(2)(b)). Moreover, La

89 *See also id.* § 17 cmt. g ("When a defendant does act for the purpose of appropriating the benefits of the plaintiff's contract, the defendant may nevertheless be able to assert certain privileges stated in § 20. For example, a defendant cannot be held liable for making good-faith efforts to protect a legal interest, even if those efforts cause the defendant to take the plaintiff's place in a contractual relationship. See § 20(b).").

90 *See id.* (noting that conduct "exempted from prima facie liability" is "not a wrongful act under this Section and requires no defense or privilege").

Rancherita appears to have been pursuing financial interests and was not acting for the sole purpose of harming Breg and its shareholders (§ 17(2)(c)). Is it possible to argue that La Rancherita acted for the purpose of appropriating the benefits of the stock sale to Bomze (§ 17(2)(a))? Those benefits were presumably money that would be paid to the Breg shareholders for their stock, and perhaps La Rancherita's objection could be characterized as an attempt to divert some of that money to itself in exchange for its consent to the transaction. Suffice it to say that, under the Third Restatement, there is some question as to whether the plaintiffs could satisfy the prima facie requirements of § 17. If they could not, there would be no need for La Rancherita to resort to the § 20 privileges.

Another privilege or justification for an intentional interference involves the provision of truthful information. Section 772 of the Second Restatement states that "[o]ne who intentionally causes a third person not to perform a contract or not to enter into a prospective contractual relation with another does not interfere improperly with the other's contractual relation, by giving the third person . . . truthful information, or . . . honest advice within the scope of a request for the advice." In *Walnut Street Associates, Inc. v. Brokerage Concepts, Inc.*,[91] the court discussed § 772 and its relationship with the general impropriety provisions of § 767. Walnut Street Associates ("WSA") provided insurance brokerage services and assisted employers in obtaining health insurance coverage. Procacci was one of WSA's clients. Brokerage Concepts, Inc. ("BCI") was a third-party administrator of employee benefit plans, and Procacci retained BCI as administrator of its insurance plans on the recommendation of WSA. BCI paid commissions to WSA based on premiums paid by Procacci.

In 2005, Procacci asked BCI to lower its costs, but BCI rejected Procacci's proposal. As a result, Procacci told BCI that it would be moving its business to another third-party administrator. BCI's employee, Kimberly Macrone, wrote a letter to Procacci asking it to reconsider its decision and revealed the amount of compensation that WSA had been receiving as broker of record. Because that amount was higher than Procacci thought WSA had been earning, Procacci terminated its contract with WSA.

WSA sued BCI and Macrone for tortious interference with the WSA-Procacci contractual relationship because of Macrone's disclosure of WSA's compensation. BCI defended on the ground that the information provided was truthful. At trial, the court denied a § 772 jury instruction and instead submitted an instruction tracking

---

[91] 20 A.3d 468 (Pa. 2011).

§ 766 and § 767 of the Second Restatement. The jury found for the plaintiff and awarded WSA $330,000 in damages.

The Superior Court reversed on § 772 grounds and concluded that truthful statements could not support a tortious interference claim. On appeal to the Supreme Court of Pennsylvania, the court determined that a § 772(a) truthfulness defense supplanted the more general § 767 "improper" analysis. Because Macrone's statement to Procacci was truthful, the court concluded that the statement "was not an improper interference, and cannot, on its own, support a claim for tortious interference with contractual relations."

In *Walnut Street*, BCI prevailed under § 772 because the information that its employee provided was truthful. The jury, however, found that the interference was improper under § 767. What is the relationship between § 767 and § 772 of the Second Restatement, and why did the court effectively conclude that § 772 trumps § 767? Section 767 provides a multi-factor balancing test designed to determine whether a particular act of interference is improper. As comment a to § 767 states, the section "indicates the factors to be taken into consideration in determining whether the interference is improper or not, through an appraisal of the several factors and an evaluation of their comparative weight." Sections 768–773, however, "deal with other special situations in which application of the factors enumerated in [§ 767] have produced more clearly identifiable decisional patterns." Significantly, comment a states that "[t]he specific applications in these Sections therefore supplant the generalization expressed in [§ 767]."

Put differently, there is no reason to go through the general balancing test of § 767 if a more specific privilege has developed that is applicable to the dispute.[92] The court followed this commentary and concluded that the specific § 772 trumped the general § 767. In short, § 767 provides the general rule for whether an interference is improper, but §§ 768–773 provide more specific rules for particular circumstances. When those circumstances are present, the specific rule trumps and displaces the general rule. As the court stated: "This is not an extraordinary proposition; this is the manner in which the

[92] *See* RESTATEMENT (SECOND) OF TORTS § 767 cmt. j (1979) ("In some situations the process of weighing the conflicting factors set forth in this Section has already been performed by the courts, and incipient privileges and rules defining conduct as not improper are developing. When this has been accomplished and the scope of the more or less crystallized rule or privilege has been indicated by the decisions, the responsibility in the particular case is simply to apply it to the facts involved; and there is no need to go through the balancing process afresh. Some of the situations in which this development has occurred are stated in §§ 769–773. When no crystallized pattern is applicable, however, the balancing process must be followed for the individual case.").

law often progresses. As general principles are tested in practice, more specific and accurate paradigms arise."

Why might the jury in *Walnut Street* have concluded that a truthful statement was improper under § 767? Consider the following:

> When BCI refused to meet the reduced cost proposal for the union program, PBS [Procacci] decided to move that plan so it could save $14.65 per person in administrative fees (a saving of over $137,000 per year). Once the client notified BCI that it had terminated BCI as the union plan TPA [third-party administrator] and it was too late to save that relationship, BCI acted intentionally and tortiously to destroy the 25 year business relationship between WSA and PBS. BCI sent a letter to PBS guised as "informative" but clearly intended to anger PBS' human resources manager (George Brack) by placing the blame for BCI's less than competitive rates on the compensation it was paying to WSA for both the union and non-union plans. Knowing PBS' desire to save on administrative fees, BCI disclosed WSA's per person share of the fees. Although correctly stating the share (but omitting other relevant information), its disclosure caused PBS to terminate its relationship with WSA. The letter worked exactly as it was intended. WSA was immediately fired as PBS' Broker of Record for both the union and non-union plans.
>
> As further evidence of BCI's motive and intent, BCI then stopped payment on WSA's commission check containing the payments due to WSA for the PBS account for the previous month (February) and refused to pay WSA commissions earned in March, 2005.[93]

Moreover, consider the following from the trial court decision in the case: "Defendant Macrone testified that at the time she wrote the letter, she knew that her firm had been terminated and that Procacci was bound to another contract with Loomis Company. This knowledge was evident in the letter she had written Procacci. The facts demonstrated that disclosure of [Plaintiff's] compensation was intended to harm Plaintiff rather than to legitimately revive the union account."[94]

---

[93] Plaintiff's Memorandum of Law in Opposition to Defendants' Motion for Summary Judgment and in Support of Cross-Motion for Summary Judgment, 2006 WL 6416321 (Aug. 2, 2006).

[94] Walnut Street Assocs. v. Brokerage Concepts, Inc., No. 2626, 2008 WL 4176752, at *4 (Pa. Ct. of Common Pleas Aug. 6, 2008).

As the quoted passages suggest, a jury may have seized upon BCI's and Macrone's bad motive in finding impropriety under § 767. Indeed, there is some indication that the defendants acted for the purpose of harming WSA. A motive to harm is relevant under § 767(b). The defendants also interfered with an existing contract. This might be viewed as improper in and of itself, even if the means of interference is lawful, because of the value that society places on existing contracts. The fact that an existing contract was interfered with is relevant under § 767(c). In addition, the defendants interfered directly with WSA's contractual relation. According to comment h to § 767, when the interference "is an immediate consequence of the conduct . . . the other factors need not play as important a role in the determination that the actor's interference was improper." This concept of proximity or remoteness of the defendants' conduct to the interference is relevant under § 767(f).

Notice that when § 772(a) is applicable to the dispute, truthful information appears to trump all of these § 767 factors. Truth, in other words, "excuses" a bad motive and an immediate (non-remote) interference with an existing contract.[95]

Under the Third Restatement, § 20(a) provides a privilege for "lawful disclosure of truthful facts to another," even if the defendant's conduct would otherwise subject the defendant to liability under the interference sections (§§ 17–19). Would the plaintiff (WSA) have satisfied the requirements of the prima facie case under § 17? If not, BCI would have prevailed even without establishing the truth privilege in § 20(a).

The only ground that seems plausible under § 17(2) is § 17(2)(c)—"the defendant [BCI] engaged in the conduct for the sole purpose of causing harm to the plaintiff [WSA]." The quoted passages suggest that such a motive to harm was present, but establishing that it was the sole motive would be difficult. Interestingly, if WSA was able to establish a sole motive to harm, the truth privilege in § 20(a) would seem to excuse it.[96]

---

[95] *See* RESTATEMENT (SECOND) OF TORTS § 767 cmt. a (1979) ("The specific applications in these Sections [§§ 769–773] therefore *supplant* the generalization expressed in this Section." (emphasis added)). *But see id.* § 772 cmt. b ("There is of course no liability for interference with a contract or with a prospective contractual relation on the part of one who *merely* gives truthful information to another." (emphasis added)).

[96] *See* RESTATEMENT (THIRD) OF TORTS: LIABILITY FOR ECONOMIC HARM § 20 cmt. b (2020) ("Lawfully disclosing truthful information does not subject a defendant to liability to a plaintiff whose contract is disrupted as a result. This privilege applies even if the information causes a contract to be breached *and was disseminated by the defendant with that hope*. The interest in the free flow of truthful information is generally regarded as sufficiently great to outweigh the other interests protected by § 17." (emphasis added)).

A truth privilege is not universally recognized. In *Pratt v. Prodata, Inc.*,[97] the Utah Department of Transportation terminated Pratt, a computer programmer, based on information provided by Pratt's former employer (Prodata). The jury found that Prodata did not make any false statements. Nevertheless, the jury concluded that tortious interference occurred because Prodata acted with an improper purpose—i.e., its primary motivation was hostility and ill will towards Pratt. In affirming the jury verdict, the Supreme Court of Utah rejected Prodata's § 772(a) argument:

> Finally, we reject defendants' assertion that under *Leigh* a judgment for intentional interference with economic relations cannot be based on the transmission of truthful information. . . .
>
> Defendants' reliance on section 772(a) is misplaced. As our decision in *Leigh* makes clear, this court has rejected the various Restatement formulations of the tort of intentional interference with economic relations. Under *Leigh,* "the alternative of improper purpose (or motive, intent, or objective) will support a cause of action for intentional interference with prospective economic relations *even where the defendant's means were proper.*" Becausc we explicitly rejected the Restatement versions of the tort in *Leigh* and because liability may attach under *Leigh* even where a defendant's means were proper, we reject defendants' call to adopt truthfulness as an absolute defense to the tort of intentional interference with prospective economic relations.

The rationale of the *Pratt* court is that any proper conduct—i.e., truthful statements or other acts—can still be tortious if done with an improper motive. Even though Utah has eliminated the improper purpose inquiry, such a conclusion might still be reached by any jurisdiction that allows an improper motive to serve as the predicate for an interference claim.

Does § 772(a) of the Second Restatement (and § 20(a) of the Third Restatement) change the result in *Lumley v. Gye*? Assume that Gye induced Wagner to breach her contract with Lumley by truthfully telling her "I will pay you twice what Lumley is paying you." Isn't that statement "truthful information," and doesn't it result in no liability for Gye? This is a puzzling issue. The Second Restatement suggests that making an offer of better terms, even if truthful, is impermissible when dealing with an existing contract. Comment m to § 766 provides an illustration of an apparently

---

[97] 885 P.2d 786 (Utah 1994).

truthful offer that results in an inducement, and § 768(2) does not excuse such a truthful offer by a competitor from being improper.[98] How does one distinguish, then, when truthful statements provide a defense under § 772, and when they apparently do not in the "offer of better terms" context?[99]

Perhaps one way to distinguish the situations is to focus on the core set of facts in *Lumley* and other cases involving liability for offers of better terms—the disputes involve the defendant obtaining the performance for itself. When the defendant does not obtain performance for itself, recovery is usually denied, often on privilege grounds such as providing truthful information. As one commentator observed:

> From the disparate, seemingly incoherent set of cases grouped under the interference rubric, however, a core set of facts emerges which serves, in practice, as a reliable predictor of liability. In a long line of cases stretching from *Lumley v. Gye* to *Texaco, Inc. v. Pennzoil Co.*, inducers with notice of the existence of a particular enforceable contract, who induced its breach by offering Promisor better terms and then obtained Promisor's performance for themselves, have consistently been held liable. Their liability has not turned on whether their conduct in inducing the breach and receiving the benefits was otherwise tortious or wrongful
>
> . . . .
>
> This Article considers this core set of facts: Inducer's notice of a prior contract, offer to Promisor of better terms, and receipt of essentially the same performance that was due the Promisee under the original contract. . . . Notice of Promisee's contract rights is not enough by itself, nor is notice combined with persuasion of Promisor by Inducer not to perform. The inducement tort requires the conjunction of

---

98 But maybe § 772(a) does? That is, comment m to § 766 says that an offer of better terms is an inducement, but it does not say that it is improper. Section 768 may not excuse the inducement, but § 772(a) might. If this is permitted, however, § 772(a) would seem to swallow much of § 768(2), as all competitive offers of better terms, if truthful, would be privileged, even when dealing with existing contracts.

99 *Cf.* David A. Anderson, *Torts, Speech, and Contracts*, 75 TEX. L. REV. 1499, 1536 (1997) ("If it were up to me, I would adopt a state law rule that inducement by truthful persuasion, without more, is not improper and therefore is not actionable as a matter of tort law. Authority for this already seems to be in place in section 772 of the Restatement, which says one does not commit an actionable interference by giving truthful information. So far this section seems to have had little effect on the law, probably because of other language in the Restatement saying inducement by an offer of better terms is actionable."); DAN B. DOBBS, THE LAW OF TORTS § 448, at 1269 (2000) ("The Restatement says [that the defendant] can also safely provide truthful information, but presumably does not mean to include the information that the defendant is prepared to offer a better deal.").

> notice, persuasion by the offer of better terms, and receipt of benefits by Inducer. Thus, if Inducer neither seeks nor ultimately receives the benefits of the original contract, then recovery is nearly always denied, despite persuasion not to perform and notice. Often such cases are decided under the rubric of one or another of the defensive privileges.[100]

From a policy standpoint, this distinction might make sense as a way of penalizing the objectionable conduct that, due to the presence of self-interest, has the greatest chance of occurring—i.e., an interference seeking to capture the performance of the contract for the interferor. Allowing a truth defense in this scenario would permit a significant amount of conduct that society might otherwise find objectionable; thus, truth must yield to other interests. An interference that is not designed to capture the benefit of the contract for the interferor is unlikely to occur as often (because people are less likely to act when they have nothing to gain). Carving out space for a truth defense in this scenario is unlikely to cause substantial harm; thus, truth should trump other interests.

Under this rationale, the result in *Lumley* would not change. Because Gye sought to procure Wagner's services for his own theater, his albeit truthful conduct falls into the "offer of better terms" context that is impermissible under § 766 comment m and § 768(2).

The Third Restatement seeks to answer these questions in a comment:

> The privilege stated here does not apply to truthful disclosures that offend applicable law on other grounds—for example, because the disclosure violates a regulation or invades the plaintiff's common-law privacy rights. *The truthful statements protected by this Section also do not include offers to provide a better deal if the recipient of the information will breach a contract with the plaintiff.*[101]

Under the Third Restatement, therefore, the result in *Lumley* would not change. Because Gye sought to procure Wagner's services for his own theater, his truthful offer to provide a better deal would violate § 17(2)(a) and would not be excused by the § 20(a) privilege.

Various other privileges or justifications are recognized by the Restatement. In *J.D. Edwards & Co. v. Podany*,[102] Judge Posner

---

[100] Lillian R. BeVier, *Reconsidering Inducement*, 76 VA. L. REV. 877, 884–85 & n.25 (1990).

[101] RESTATEMENT (THIRD) OF TORTS: LIABILITY FOR ECONOMIC HARM § 20 cmt. b (2020) (emphasis added).

[102] 168 F.3d 1020 (7th Cir. 1999).

discussed the "honest advice" privilege of § 772(b) of the Second Restatement:

> .... The only issue is whether the jury was justified in rejecting, en route to awarding the plaintiff $2.3 million in damages, the defense to inducing breach of contract that is called the "consultant's privilege," or more commonly the privilege of "honest advice." This is the privilege of a consultant, or other advisor, to offer good-faith advice to a client without fear of liability should the client act on that advice to the harm of a third person, in this case the plaintiff.
>
> The privilege resembles the rule in defamation law that where there is a duty to speak, a defamatory utterance, if made in good faith and not disseminated any further than necessary, is privileged. A consultant is hired to give advice. Often the advice is painful, because firms frequently turn to consultants when they are in trouble or when they want to do something that hurts and want to spread the blame a bit. The consultant's advice may lead to downsizing, layoffs, outsourcing, and countless other perturbations, including, as here, contractual terminations. It would cast quite a large, dark cloud over the consulting business if consultants could be hauled into court for having given advice that in hindsight could be characterized as having been ill-advised, ill-informed, or otherwise negligent. The consultant's privilege cuts off this possibility. But it is not absolute. It is a qualified privilege, like qualified immunity as distinct from absolute immunity in the law of public officers' torts.
>
> It is qualified in two ways. First, it is limited to advice given within the scope of the consultant's engagement. *Restatement, supra,* § 772(b) and comment d. If a consultant hired to advise the client, a fast-food chain, on selecting a new telephone system suggested that the client terminate its fast-food franchisee in Oshkosh because the franchisee was serving soggy doughnuts, and the suggestion was adopted, the consultant could not set up the consultant's privilege in defense of the franchisee's suit for interference with contract. Not having been hired to advise on the client's franchise system, the consultant would have no contractual duty to render frank and fearless (or indeed any) advice on the subject.
>
> Second, if the consultant does not give honest advice—if he uses his engagement to hurt other people exclusively for his own benefit (or out of dislike of his victim) rather

> than for the benefit of his client—he forfeits the privilege. If solely to feather his own nest, and without believing that (or caring whether) he is helping his client, he causes the client to break a contract to the detriment of the other party to the contract, he is liable for inducing the breach.

In *Podany*, there was evidence suggesting that a consultant (Podany) recommended that a client (SNE) replace software so that Podany could "land himself a lucrative job with SNE's parent as director of information services." The court observed:

> If Podany was simply a fool, and got SNE to replace [the former] software with [the new software] because he ignorantly believed that the latter really was superior for SNE's needs even though it lacked a configurator, he and his employer would be sheltered from liability by the consultant's privilege. They would be, indeed, securely within the core of the privilege. But if Podany's only object was to enrich himself . . . the privilege is forfeited. . . .
>
> In pointing to Podany's motives, we do not make the mistake of confusing bad faith with greed. A consultant might be in consulting purely for the money, but as long as he made his money by offering honest advice within the scope of his employment, his private motives would be irrelevant. *Restatement, supra,* § 772 comment c. It is when a consultant decides to make money by rendering dishonest advice (or going outside the terms of his engagement) that he loses the protection of privilege and assumes the usual liabilities.
>
> Podany denied any such ulterior motive. But his credibility was impeached, and the jury was not required to believe him. His lack of credibility, like pretext in a discrimination case, combined with circumstantial evidence to justify the jury in finding bad faith.

According to comment c of § 772, the "honest advice" privilege requires "(1) that advice be requested, (2) that the advice given be within the scope of the request and (3) that the advice be honest." As *Podany* suggests, if a defendant gives advice with mixed motives—i.e., partially because he thinks the advice is good for the client, and partially because he wants to harm the third party who will suffer because of the advice—the defense is still available.[103]

---

[103] *See also* RESTATEMENT (SECOND) OF TORTS § 772 cmt. c (1979) ("If these [three] conditions are present, it is immaterial that the actor also profits by the advice or that he dislikes the third person and takes pleasure in the harm caused to him by the advice.").

The Third Restatement has no analogous "black letter" provision to § 772(b). Indeed, there is no honest advice privilege in § 20. Comment g to § 17, however, explains that because prima facie liability is drawn more narrowly in the Third Restatement—i.e., because the plaintiff has to shoulder the burden of establishing wrongful conduct before any privilege would become relevant—there is no need for an honest advice privilege. Stated differently, honest advice would not fall within the wrongful conduct possibilities in § 17(2) and, therefore, the plaintiff's claim against the defendant would fail:

> *The role of privilege.* Some conduct that would have been protected by privileges under the Restatement Second is exempted from prima facie liability under this Section. Liability does not arise, and privileges need not become relevant, when a defendant uses lawful means to protect legitimate interests distinct from competition for the benefits of the contract. Thus a defendant with a stake in another party's business may object to a contract that the party has made with the plaintiff. If the objection is not asserted by wrongful means and is not an effort to secure the benefits of the contract for the defendant (or to injure the plaintiff, as explained in Comment f), it is not a wrongful act under this Section and requires no defense or privilege. . . .
>
> By the same reasoning, no liability arises when a defendant's lawyer, or another party, offers disinterested advice that causes the recipient to breach a contract. See Illustrations 13 and 14. Disinterested advice is advice offered by a party who is neither trying to appropriate the benefits of the contract nor motivated by a desire to injure the plaintiff. It is therefore outside the scope of Subsection (2).[104]

---

[104] *See also* RESTATEMENT (THIRD) OF TORTS: LIABILITY FOR ECONOMIC HARM § 20 cmt. a (2020) ("This Section primarily states privileges that defeat liability for interference with contract under § 17. By its terms, § 17 effectively excludes from liability some forms of conduct that have traditionally been subject to privilege. Thus no privilege is necessary to protect the provider of disinterested advice from liability, because disinterested advice does not satisfy the elements of liability stated in § 17(2). The privileges stated here apply, rather, in cases that otherwise satisfy one or more of the criteria of § 17(2). A defendant who wishes to invoke the privileges of this Section in such a case bears the burden of asserting them and proving that their elements are satisfied."); *id.* § 20 cmt. e ("As noted above and elsewhere in this Chapter, this Section states a modest number of privileges because prima facie liability is defined more narrowly under §§ 17 and 18 than it was under the Restatement Second. If a court continues to use the Restatement Second's framework to define interference with contract or economic expectancy, the privileges stated in the Restatement Second continue to serve as necessary and appropriate limitations on liability.").

Another important privilege or justification is the competition privilege in § 768 of the Second Restatement, which protects persons in certain circumstances from liability for competitive conduct. As one court observed:

> One recognized "just cause for damaging another in his [or her] business is competition." Thus, interference with another's contract or business relations in the name of competition is improper only if the means used are, in themselves, improper. *See Goldman,* 150 Md. at 684, 133 A. at 846, in which we said:
>
> > "Iron sharpeneth iron" is ancient wisdom, and the law is in accord in favoring free competition, since ordinarily it is essential to the general welfare of society, notwithstanding competition is not altruistic but is fundamentally the play of interest against interest, and so involves the interference of the successful competitor in the matter of their common rivalry. Competition is the state in which men live and is not a tort, unless the nature of the method employed is not justified by public policy, and so supplies the condition to constitute a legal wrong.[105]

Does § 768 protect defendants from claims under § 766, § 766A, and § 766B? Section 768(2) indicates that the competition privilege does not apply to interference with existing contract claims (where those existing contracts are not terminable at will). Thus, § 768 does not apply to § 766 and § 766A claims (again, assuming those claims are not dealing with a terminable-at-will contract). Instead, the competition privilege applies to interference with prospective contract claims under § 766B, and to interference with terminable-at-will contract claims (which the Restatement analogizes to prospective contract claims).[106]

---

105 Macklin v. Robert Logan Assocs., 639 A.2d 112, 119 (Md. 1994).

106 *See* RESTATEMENT (SECOND) OF TORTS § 768(1) (1979); *id.* § 768 cmt. a ("This Section differentiates between interference with an existing contract (see §§ 766, 766A) and interference with a prospective contractual relation. (See § 766B). Under the conditions stated in Clauses (a) through (d) of Subsection (1), competition is not an improper basis for interference in the latter situation. . . . But an existing contract, if not terminable at will, involves established interests that are not subject to interference on the basis of competition alone."); *id.* § 768 cmt. h ("The rule that competition is not an improper interference with prospective contractual relations as stated in Subsection (1) does not apply to inducement of breach of contract."); *see also id.* § 766 cmt. g ("One's interest in a contract terminable at will is primarily an interest in future relations between the parties, and he has no legal assurance of them. For this reason, an interference with this interest is closely analogous to interference with prospective contractual relations. If the defendant was a competitor regarding the business involved in the contract, his interference with the contract may be not improper.").

Notice that motive has a role in a § 768 analysis. Section 768(1)(d) requires the defendant's purpose to be "at least in part to advance his interest in competing with the other." If a competitive motive is possessed, the addition of an improper motive to harm is irrelevant.[107]

The Third Restatement has no analogous provision to § 768 of the Second Restatement. Does this mean that lawful competition could result in liability for interference with prospective contract under the Third Restatement? Of course not. As mentioned, because prima facie liability is drawn more narrowly in the Third Restatement, there is less of a need for explicit privileges.[108] In other words, a competition privilege is unnecessary because the plaintiff would be unable to satisfy the prima facie requirements of § 18 (interference with prospective contract) if the defendant simply engaged in lawful competition. Under § 18(b), the plaintiff must establish that the defendant "committed an independent and intentional legal wrong." Lawful competition would not satisfy that requirement.

Under § 17 (interference with existing contract), competition can result in liability for the defendant. Many (if not most) acts of lawful competition are efforts to appropriate the benefits of the rival's contract, which could result in liability under § 17(2)(a).

The Restatement includes a few other privileges or justifications. Section 769 of the Second Restatement provides a defense to an interferor with a financial interest in the business of the induced party. According to comments a and b to § 769, the defense applies only to claims for interference with prospective contract and not to claims for interference with existing contract. Similarly, under the Third Restatement, § 20(c) provides a privilege for "lawful and good-faith efforts to protect an economic interest in the contractual relationship at issue."

Section 770 of the Second Restatement allows one "charged with responsibility for the welfare of a third person" to cause that third person not to perform a contract or enter into a prospective contract.

---

107 *See id.* § 768 cmt. g ("The rule stated in this Section developed to advance the actor's competitive interest and the supposed social benefits arising from it. If his conduct is directed, at least in part, to that end, the fact that he is also motivated by other impulses, as, for example, hatred or a desire for revenge is not alone sufficient to make his interference improper. But if his conduct is directed solely to the satisfaction of his spite or ill will and not at all to the advancement of his competitive interests over the person harmed, his interference is held to be improper.").

108 *See* RESTATEMENT (THIRD) OF TORTS: LIABILITY FOR ECONOMIC HARM § 20 cmt. e (2020) ("As noted above and elsewhere in this Chapter, this Section states a modest number of privileges because prima facie liability is defined more narrowly under §§ 17 and 18 than it was under the Restatement Second.").

Comment b to the section discusses relationships that would meet this standard:

> . . . . The responsibility may exist in such relationships as those of parent, or person standing in loco parentis, and child, of minister and member of his congregation, attorney and client, teacher and pupil or of employer and employee. The rule stated is frequently applicable to those who stand in a fiduciary relation toward another, as in the case of agents acting for the protection of their principals, trustees for their beneficiaries or corporate officers acting for the benefit of the corporation.

The Third Restatement has no analogous provision to § 770. As mentioned, however, fewer privileges are necessary under the Third Restatement because of the stricter requirements for prima facie liability under §§ 17–18.

Section 771 of the Second Restatement allows one "to intentionally cause[ ] a third person not to enter into a prospective contractual relation with another in order to influence the other's policy in the conduct of his business." The Third Restatement has no analogous provision to § 771, but again, fewer privileges are needed because of the stricter requirements for liability under § 18.

## E. THE LIABILITY OF AGENTS

Numerous cases have involved interference claims by one party to a contract against an agent of the other party to the contract. Such cases raise issues about whether the agent is a true "outsider" to the contract to meet the typical three-party interference setting. In *Holloway v. Skinner*,[109] for example, Graham Holloway was the president, director, and largest shareholder of Holligan, Inc. Holligan and Rick Skinner entered into a note and royalty agreement where Holligan was obligated to pay various sums of money to Skinner. The corporation ultimately defaulted on the agreement. Skinner successfully sued Holligan for breach of contract, but the corporation filed for bankruptcy and Skinner's judgment remained unsatisfied. Skinner then filed suit against Holloway claiming "that he tortiously interfered with the note and royalty agreement by inducing the Corporation to default on its obligations."

At trial, the jury found that Holloway was liable for interference and the trial court entered judgment to that effect. The court of appeals affirmed and concluded that Holloway's status as a corporate agent did not bar Skinner's claim. The Supreme Court of Texas reversed. The court began by noting that the interference tort

[109] 898 S.W.2d 793 (Tex. 1995).

required the defendant to be an outsider to the contractual relationship between the plaintiff and the third party. In this case, however, the act of interference was committed by Holloway—"an individual who was also the lawful representative of the contracting party [Holligan]." As the court stated, "[s]uch a case tests the limits of the general rule barring tortious interference claims when the inducing and the breaching party are one and the same."

Where the defendant "serves the dual roles of the corporate agent and the third party who allegedly induces the corporation's breach," the court determined that "the alleged act of interference must be performed in furtherance of the defendant's personal interests so as to preserve the logically necessary rule that a party cannot tortiously interfere with its own contract." As the court stated:

> We hold that to meet this burden in a case of this nature, the plaintiff must show that the defendant acted in a fashion so contrary to the corporation's best interests that his actions could only have been motivated by personal interests. Inasmuch as it is the duty of corporate officers to protect the interests of the corporation, the mere existence of a personal stake in the outcome, especially when any personal benefit is derivative of the improved financial condition of the corporation or consists of the continued entitlement to draw a salary, cannot alone constitute proof that the defendant committed an act of willful or intentional interference. Were this not the rule, virtually every failure to pay a corporate debt would constitute a prima facie case of tortious interference against the corporate officer who decided not to pay the debt.

The evidence at trial indicated that Holloway, in his capacity as president, was required to prioritize between competing claims because Holligan had insufficient cash flow to meet its obligations. As a result, the Skinner note was not paid even though the corporation continued to pay Holloway's salary. As the court concluded: "[T]here is no evidence that the decision to breach the contract was so contrary to the Corporation's best interests that it could only have been motivated by the pursuit of Holloway's personal interests. As we have already noted, a personal benefit limited to the continued entitlement to draw a salary or derivative of the improved financial condition of the corporation does not raise a triable issue of fact in this type of tortious interference case."

*Holloway* involved a suit by one party (Skinner) against another party (Holloway) for interference with an existing contract between Skinner and a third person (Holligan, Inc.). Doesn't this three-party setting fit the typical pattern of an interference claim? What is the conceptual problem that the court is wrestling with?

The typical three-party pattern of an interference claim involves a defendant who interferes with a contractual relationship between the plaintiff and a third party. The defendant is an "outsider" or "stranger" to the plaintiff-third party relationship. This three-party structure prevents interference claims between contractual parties who might claim that the other's breach of contract also resulted in a tortious interference with the contract. As the *Holloway* court explained: "By definition, the person who induces the breach cannot be a contracting party. Were we to recognize the tortious interference claim when this identity of interest exists, any party who breaches a contract could be said to have induced his own breach and would therefore be liable for tortious interference. Such logic would convert every breach of contract claim into a tort claim."

The conceptual problem that the court is wrestling with is that an agent is not typically viewed as an independent actor from the principal; thus, the three-party structure of the interference claim is in question. When the defendant is an agent who allegedly interferes with its principal's contract, the agent is arguably not an outsider or stranger to the principal's contract. As the *Holloway* court observed, this is because "[a]s a general rule, the actions of a corporate agent on behalf of the corporation are deemed the corporation's acts." If the agent's actions are deemed to be the corporation's actions, then the agent should not be viewed as an independent actor. The only parties at issue would be the two contracting parties—i.e., the corporation and the third party. As mentioned, allowing an interference claim in such a two-party setting would convert every breach of contract claim into a tortious interference claim.

The court resolved this conceptual problem by creating a test where the agent will be viewed as an actor separate and distinct from the principal. That test is when the agent "acted in a fashion so contrary to the corporation's best interests that his actions could only have been motivated by personal interests." The idea seems to be that when the agent acts solely for personal interests and not for corporate interests, the agent is functioning independently and should not be viewed as acting for the corporation (the agent's principal). The required three-party structure returns, therefore, as the agent is a distinct actor who can be viewed as an outsider to the principal-third party contract.

It is presumably true that Holloway had a personal interest in preserving sufficient corporate funds to pay his salary. Nevertheless, this interest was insufficient to result in liability. As mentioned, the court concluded that "a personal benefit limited to the continued entitlement to draw a salary or derivative of the improved financial condition of the corporation does not raise a triable issue of fact in this type of tortious interference case." Without this rule, according to the court, "virtually every failure to pay a corporate debt would constitute a prima facie case of tortious interference against the corporate officer who decided not to pay the debt." Moreover, a mixed motive is insufficient to establish liability, as the plaintiff must prove that the defendant's actions "could *only* have been motivated by personal interests" (emphasis added). Thus, even if Holloway had a personal interest in retaining sufficient funds to pay his salary, any motive at all to benefit the company (e.g., ceasing payment on the Skinner contract saved money to meet other corporate obligations) would protect Holloway from liability.

Other courts follow approaches similar to *Holloway.* For example, in *Nordling v. Northern States Power Co.*,[110] the court adopted a "scope of authority" framework, although it held that actions predominantly motivated by ill will would not merit protection:

> . . . . The general rule is that a party cannot interfere with its own contract. If a corporation's officer or agent acting pursuant to his company duties terminates or causes to be terminated an employee, the actions are those of the corporation; the employee's dispute is with the company employer for breach of contract, not the agent individually for a tort. To allow the officer or agent to be sued and to be personally liable would chill corporate personnel from performing their duties and would be contrary to the limited liability accorded incorporation. Nevertheless . . . a corporate officer or agent may be liable for tortious contract interference if he or she acts outside the scope of his or her duties.
>
> It is not always easy to determine when a corporate officer or agent's actions are outside the scope of his company responsibilities, *i.e.,* when he is engaged in a personal vendetta or excursion. Particularly is this true in a job termination case where the officer's duties include the evaluation and supervision of the plaintiff employee's performance or the power to participate in the corporate decision to terminate or otherwise discipline the plaintiff.
>
> . . . .
>
> In this case the contract interfered with is an employment contract and the alleged interferer is employed

[110] 478 N.W.2d 498 (Minn. 1991).

> by the same employer. It becomes important, therefore, to determine first the scope of the defendant officer or agent's duties with respect to the plaintiff employee's employment. Conceivably, there may be instances where the defendant officer or agent's conduct is decidedly outside the scope of his duties. The more common situation, we think, is when the defendant's conduct is subject to conflicting inferences. In this situation, the defendant's motive becomes critical. While motive or malice is only one factor to consider in determining whether a defendant officer or agent is acting outside the scope of his duties in dealing with the plaintiff employee, it can be the critical factor. . . .
>
> . . . .
>
> [W]e conclude that a company officer, agent or employee is privileged to interfere with or cause a breach of another employee's employment contract with the company, if that person acts in good faith, whether competently or not, believing that his actions are in furtherance of the company's business. This privilege may be lost, however, if the defendant's actions are predominantly motivated by malice and bad faith, that is, by personal ill-will, spite, hostility, or a deliberate intent to harm the plaintiff employee.[111]

How would the *Holloway* dispute be resolved under the Restatement? Under the Second Restatement, interference claims against an agent seem to be handled under § 770. Section 770 protects defendants who are "charged with responsibility for the welfare of a third person," and comment b states that the rule "is frequently applicable to those who stand in a fiduciary relation toward another, as in the case of agents acting for the protection of their principals." If the agent does not employ wrongful means and acts to protect the welfare of the principal, the agent's conduct is not considered to be improper. As an example, illustration 3 to § 770 protects an employee (an agent) from liability when the employee urges the principal's management to terminate another employee for the protection of the company.

In *Holloway*, there was evidence suggesting that Holloway was motivated to cease paying Skinner, at least in part, by a desire to

---

[111] *See also* McGanty v. Staudenraus, 901 P.2d 841, 846 (Or. 1995) ("[I]t follows that, when an employee is acting in the scope of the employee's employment, the employee is acting as the employer, and not as an independent entity. Accordingly, when an employee is acting within the scope of the employee's employment, and the employer, as a result, breaches a contract with another party, that employee is not a third party for the tort of intentional interference with economic relations.").

save company funds for other corporate obligations. That would seem to suffice as an action to protect the welfare of the corporation. (If Holloway had a mixed motive, would the presence of *a* motive to protect the corporation's welfare suffice under § 770, or would that protective motive have to be predominant? Section 770 is not entirely clear on this point.)

If § 770 did not exist, would a claim against the agent be viable under § 766? Section 766 contemplates a three-party relationship, but it does not speak to agency law. Agency law, of course, often concludes that the agent's actions are not separate and distinct from the principal's actions. Thus, even if § 770 did not exist, there would still be a question as to whether *Holloway*-like claims against an agent could be brought under § 766.

The Third Restatement has no analogous provision to § 770 of the Second Restatement. Claims against agents would seem to be handled by the stricter requirements for prima facie liability under §§ 17–18 and the same three-party relationship concerns involving when an agent's actions are separate and distinct from the principal's actions.

With respect to the stricter requirements for prima facie liability, Holloway was sued for interference with Skinner's existing contract with the corporation. Under § 17(2)(b), Holloway's conduct does not constitute an independent and intentional legal wrong. He presumably used his management control to cause the corporation to breach the contract, but there is nothing that is independently wrongful about that conduct.[112] Under § 17(2)(c), Holloway did not engage in the disputed conduct for the sole purpose of harming Skinner. As mentioned, there was evidence suggesting that Holloway was at least partially motivated to cease paying Skinner by a desire to save company funds for other corporate obligations. Under § 17(2)(a), is it possible to argue that Holloway acted for the purpose of appropriating the benefits of Skinner's contract? To preserve sufficient corporate funds to pay his salary, Holloway caused the corporation to breach its contract with Skinner—in effect, Holloway diverted the monies to himself that would have gone to Skinner as salary. This seems plausible (indeed, comment d to § 17 mentions the idea of " 'cutting out' the plaintiff" such that "the defendant appropriates benefits to which the plaintiff was contractually entitled"), but it would appear to run afoul of the court's conclusion that "a personal benefit limited to the continued entitlement to draw a salary or derivative of the improved financial condition of the

[112] *See* RESTATEMENT (THIRD) OF TORTS: LIABILITY FOR ECONOMIC HARM § 17 cmt. e (2020) (stating that an independent legal wrong "does not include an act of negligence or breach of contract").

corporation does not raise a triable issue of fact in this type of tortious interference case."

Aside from these arguments under § 17(2), comment o to § 17 addresses the three-party relationship concerns and adopts a *Holloway*-like standard:

> *Third parties*. Liability arises under this Section when the defendant interferes with a contract between the plaintiff and a third party. Liability does not arise when the contractual relationship at issue is between the plaintiff and the defendant. Put differently, a defendant cannot be sued under this Section for interfering with its own contract, whether alone or in a conspiracy with others.
>
> This distinction most often becomes important when the plaintiff had a contract with a corporation and sues one of the corporation's employees for interfering with it. In a case of that kind, the plaintiff can make out a claim of interference only by pointing to acts taken outside the defendant's scope of employment. The plaintiff bears the burden of proof, and it generally must be discharged by proving that the defendant was motivated entirely by personal gain at the corporation's expense. Mixed motives will not suffice. The bar is kept high because corporations can act only through their agents. It should not be easy for a party to turn a contract claim against a corporation into a tort claim by attacking those through whom the corporation carries out its business.
>
> In some cases, a defendant's identity with a corporation is so complete that the plaintiff cannot make out a claim of tortious interference under any circumstances. That is so when the defendant is the sole owner of a corporation; the interests of the defendant and the corporation are then considered identical for purposes of this Section, and the one cannot interfere with contracts of the other as a matter of law.
>
> The principles governing the liability of corporate agents also apply to other agents who are sued for interfering with the relationship between the plaintiff and the agent's principal. To recover from an agent in those circumstances, the plaintiff must show that the acts at issue were outside the agent's scope of authority. An absence of complaint by the principal about the agent's conduct,

> despite knowledge of it, can serve as some evidence that the agent's authority was not exceeded.[113]

Based on this comment, an employee (like Holloway) could not be sued for interfering with an existing contract of its principal (the corporation) unless the employee acted outside of its scope of employment, and that is "generally" established "by proving that the defendant was motivated entirely by personal gain at the corporation's expense." Mixed motives "will not suffice." As mentioned, there was evidence suggesting that Holloway was at least partially motivated to cease paying Skinner by a desire to save company funds for other business obligations. Pursuant to the comment, therefore, Holloway would avoid liability.[114]

---

[113] *See also id.* § 18 cmt. g ("In the eyes of the law, however, employees act on the corporation's behalf so long as they act within the scope of their employment. To establish liability, it therefore is not enough to show that the employee misjudged the corporation's interests or had personal as well as professional motives for his or her conduct. A plaintiff can prevail only by showing that the defendant employee was entirely motivated by personal interest at the expense of the interests of the corporation. The same rule applies to any agent who is sued for interfering with the relationship between the plaintiff and the agent's principal. See § 17, Comment o.").

[114] Under what circumstances would an agent be acting entirely for personal gain at the corporation's expense such that it would be liable for an interference tort (because the agent would be acting outside its scope of authority)? Illustration 34 to § 17 is useful in this regard, as is illustration 19 to § 18.

# Chapter 4

# BREACH OF FIDUCIARY DUTY

Broadly speaking, a fiduciary is a person "who appear[s] to accept, expressly or impliedly, an obligation to act in a position of trust or confidence for the benefit of another or who [has] accepted a status or relationship understood to entail such an obligation, generating the beneficiary's justifiable expectations of loyalty."[1] Courts often speak of two types of fiduciary relationships. First, "formal" fiduciary relationships are those that have categorically been held, as a matter of law, to be fiduciary in nature. Common examples of formal fiduciary relationships include the relationship of an attorney to its client, an agent to its principal, a partner to its fellow partner, and a trustee to its beneficiary.[2] Second, "informal" fiduciary relationships (also referred to as "confidential" relationships) are those that may arise on the facts of particular disputes based on a relationship of trust and confidence between the parties.[3]

Breach of fiduciary duty is a powerful cause of action for plaintiffs because fiduciaries owe very strict obligations to their beneficiaries. In general, because fiduciaries act for the benefit of other persons, they owe duties of care and loyalty to those persons. The duty of care requires the fiduciary to act with the care, competence, and diligence normally exercised by fiduciaries in similar circumstances. The duty of loyalty requires the fiduciary to act solely in the best interests of the beneficiary. This includes (at least traditionally) the fiduciary's obligations to avoid conflicts of interest, to disclose all material information, and to put the

---

1 3 DAN B. DOBBS ET AL., THE LAW OF TORTS § 697, at 749 (2d ed. 2011); *see also* RESTATEMENT (SECOND) OF TORTS § 874 cmt. a (1979) ("A fiduciary relation exists between two persons when one of them is under a duty to act for or to give advice for the benefit of another upon matters within the scope of the relation."); RESTATEMENT (THIRD) OF TORTS: LIABILITY FOR ECONOMIC HARM § 16 cmt. a (2020) (noting that elements of a fiduciary relationship "generally consist of trust and reliance on the fiduciary by another, and often a degree of control by the fiduciary over the other party's person, property, or affairs").

2 These fiduciary relationships are often not reciprocal. For example, an attorney owes a fiduciary duty to its client, but the client does not owe a fiduciary duty to its attorney. Similarly, while an agent owes a fiduciary duty to its principal, the principal does not owe a fiduciary duty to its agent.

3 *See, e.g.*, 3 DAN B. DOBBS ET AL., THE LAW OF TORTS § 697, at 753 (2d ed. 2011) ("Apart from formalized or categorical fiduciary relationships, other fiduciary obligations may arise on the facts of particular cases where the plaintiff reposes special trust and confidence in the defendant and the defendant gives the appearance of tacitly accepting that trust and hence his fiduciary role.").

beneficiary's interests ahead of its own.[4] As an example of the potency of the breach of fiduciary duty action, consider the onerous obligations of a fiduciary as set forth in this Texas pattern jury charge:

> Did [Defendant] comply with his fiduciary duty to [Plaintiff]?
>
> . . . [Defendant] owed [Plaintiff] a fiduciary duty. To prove he complied with his duty, [Defendant] must show:
>
> a. the transaction[s] in question [was/were] fair and equitable to [Plaintiff];
>
> b. [Defendant] made reasonable use of the confidence that [Plaintiff] placed in him;
>
> c. [Defendant] acted in the utmost good faith and exercised the most scrupulous honesty toward [Plaintiff];
>
> d. [Defendant] placed the interests of [Plaintiff] before his own, did not use the advantage of his position to gain any benefit for himself at the expense of [Plaintiff], and did not place himself in any position where his self-interest might conflict with his obligations as a fiduciary; and
>
> e. [Defendant] fully and fairly disclosed all important information to [Plaintiff] concerning the transaction[s].[5]

A breach of fiduciary duty is a tort. As a consequence, a plaintiff may recover compensatory damages and, in egregious cases, punitive damages. Equitable remedies are also available, including

---

[4] *See, e.g.*, Crim Truck & Tractor Co. v. Navistar Int'l Transp. Corp., 823 S.W.2d 591, 594 (Tex. 1992) (noting the "more onerous burden that requires a party to place the interest of the other party before his own, often attributed to a fiduciary duty"); Zastrow v. Journal Communications, Inc., 718 N.W.2d 51, 59 (Wis. 2006) ("A consistent facet of a fiduciary duty is the constraint on the fiduciary's discretion to act in his own self-interest because by accepting the obligation of a fiduciary he consciously sets another's interests before his own."); *see also* 3 DAN B. DOBBS ET AL., THE LAW OF TORTS § 696, at 744–46 (2d ed. 2011) ("On matters within the scope of the fiduciary relationship, fiduciaries owe to their beneficiaries a duty of the 'utmost' good faith and loyalty . . . . Given the duty of good faith and loyalty, fiduciaries must subordinate their own interests to those of their beneficiaries.").

[5] STATE BAR OF TEXAS, TEXAS PATTERN JURY CHARGES PJC 104.2 (2012) (italics omitted).

Persons who aid and abet violations of fiduciary duties are generally subject to liability as well. *See, e.g.*, RESTATEMENT (SECOND) OF TORTS § 874 cmt. c (1979) ("A person who knowingly assists a fiduciary in committing a breach of trust is himself guilty of tortious conduct and is subject to liability for the harm thereby caused." (citing *id.* § 876)); RESTATEMENT (THIRD) OF TORTS: LIABILITY FOR ECONOMIC HARM § 28 & cmt. b (2020) (recognizing aiding and abetting as "a form of secondary liability" and noting that "[a]mong the wrongs discussed in this Restatement, fraud and breach of fiduciary duty are those that most often produce liability for aiding and abetting").

injunctions, rescission, restitution of payments made to the fiduciary, disgorgement of the fiduciary's profits in a particular transaction, or any other equitable remedy deemed appropriate by the court. The Third Restatement captures some of these points in comment b to § 16:

> .... A plaintiff will sometimes be able to choose between multiple theories of recovery. The law of restitution, for example, permits the victim of a breach of fiduciary duty to recover the defendant's gains, and also provides remedial mechanisms unavailable in tort. See Restatement Third, Restitution and Unjust Enrichment § 43. Indeed, a restitution claim is a plaintiff's most common recourse; a breach of fiduciary duty is usually profitable to the fiduciary, so the victim of the breach ordinarily seeks to capture those profits through a constructive trust or other restitutionary remedy. If the breach of fiduciary duty involves a breach of contract, it might be redressed by a claim to recover the plaintiff's contractual expectation.
>
> The cause of action recognized by this Section, in turn, provides recourse to a plaintiff who wishes instead to recover damages that compensate for the loss caused by the fiduciary's breach. A claim in tort may be more attractive than a claim in restitution because the harm caused to the plaintiff by the breach of fiduciary duty was greater than the benefits gained by the defendant. Some breaches of fiduciary duty may also entitle a plaintiff to seek punitive damages, and in many jurisdictions that form of relief may be more readily available in tort than in a suit based on contract or restitution.

As mentioned, fiduciary relationships may be formal (established as a matter of law in a categorical fashion) or informal (established as a matter of fact in a particular case). It is always easier for a plaintiff to assert a formal fiduciary relationship, if available, because no proof is required other than evidence that the parties' relationship falls into one of the established categories. If a formal fiduciary relationship does not exist, however, how can a plaintiff demonstrate an informal fiduciary relationship? What evidence, in other words, will suffice to establish the requisite relationship of trust and confidence between the parties?

Consider the decision of *Crim Truck & Tractor Co. v. Navistar International Transportation Corp.*,[6] which illustrates the difficulties

6 823 S.W.2d 591 (Tex. 1992).

of establishing an informal fiduciary relationship. In 1943, Crim Truck and International Harvester (the predecessor to Navistar) began their business relationship. Crim Truck operated a Navistar dealership as a franchisee and sold Navistar products. In 1958, the parties entered into their first written franchise agreement, which was amended in 1964 and 1979. (Crim Truck, the franchisee, employed Travis Crim and Tim Farley, and the court referred to these parties collectively as "the Crims.")

In 1983, Navistar decided to establish a nationwide dealer communications network to share information between Navistar and its dealers. Navistar called a meeting of all of its franchisees, which the Crims declined to attend. The Crims also refused to sign a contract obligating them to purchase computer equipment needed for the network, even after being notified by Navistar that participation in the network was mandatory. Navistar indicated that it would terminate the Crims' franchise, but it gave the Crims one final opportunity to return the contract. The Crims did not do so, and the franchise was terminated on April 1, 1985.

The Crims sued Navistar for breach of contract, breach of fiduciary duty, and fraud. The jury found for the Crims on all three causes of action. The court of appeals found no evidence of a confidential relationship which would give rise to a breach of fiduciary duty, and it similarly found no evidence of an essential element of the fraud claim. The court did find some evidence of a breach of contract, but it reversed the trial court's judgment because of insufficient evidence to support the damages award. The case was remanded for a new trial on the contract issues. The Supreme Court of Texas also found no evidence of a confidential relationship or an actionable misrepresentation, and it affirmed the judgment of the court of appeals.

It is important to note that the Crims were not asserting a formal fiduciary relationship between themselves and Navistar. In Texas and in many other states, franchisor-franchisee is not a fiduciary relationship as a matter of law.[7] Instead, the Crims were attempting to establish an informal fiduciary relationship between themselves and Navistar based on a relationship of trust and confidence between the parties. As the Supreme Court of Texas observed in *Crim Truck*:

> . . . . Such informal fiduciary relationships have also been termed "confidential relationships" and may arise "where one person trusts in and relies upon another,

[7] *Cf. id.* at 595 n.5 (stating that "[t]he majority of other jurisdictions have rejected the imposition of general fiduciary duties on the franchise relationship").

whether the relation is a moral, social, domestic or merely personal one." *Fitz-Gerald v. Hull,* 150 Tex. 39, 237 S.W.2d 256, 261 (1951). Because not every relationship involving a high degree of trust and confidence rises to the stature of a formal fiduciary relationship, the law recognizes the existence of confidential relationships in those cases "in which influence has been acquired and abused, in which confidence has been reposed and betrayed." *Texas Bank & Trust Co. v. Moore,* 595 S.W.2d 502, 507 (Tex.1980).

What evidence did the Crims introduce to establish this informal fiduciary relationship, and why was it insufficient? Consider the significance of the following evidence and the *Crim Truck* majority's response:

**The beliefs of the plaintiffs:** Travis Crim testified that he believed the relationship with Navistar was one of mutual trust and confidence. According to the dissent, Tim Farley also testified that the termination of the franchise agreement "broke" his "trust" in Navistar.

*Majority's response*: The court observed that "[t]he fact that one businessman trusts another, and relies upon his promise to perform a contract, does not rise to a confidential relationship." Similarly, "mere subjective trust alone is not enough to transform arms-length dealing into a fiduciary relationship."

This is an important point. One person's unilateral trust in another, even if significant, is insufficient to establish an informal fiduciary relationship. As mentioned, a fiduciary is someone "who appear[s] to accept, expressly or impliedly, an obligation to act in a position of trust or confidence for the benefit of another." Thus, an informal fiduciary relationship requires not only the beneficiary to place his trust in the fiduciary, but also the fiduciary to appear to accept the obligation to be trustworthy. An informal fiduciary relationship, therefore, cannot be established unilaterally.[8]

---

[8] *See, e.g.*, Broomfield v. Kosow, 212 N.E.2d 556, 560 (Mass. 1965) ("[T]he plaintiff alone, by reposing trust and confidence in the defendant, cannot thereby transform a business relationship into one which is fiduciary in nature. The catalyst in such a change is the defendant's knowledge of the plaintiff's reliance upon him."); Mabus v. St. James Episcopal Church, 884 So. 2d 747, 758 (Miss. 2004) (discussing an informal fiduciary duty and noting that "there must be evidence that both parties understood that a special trust and confidence was being reposed"); Johnson v. Reiger, 93 P.3d 992, 999 (Wyo. 2004) (stating that fiduciary relationships "are not created by the unilateral decision to repose trust and reliance," and further observing that "[s]uch a relationship exists when one party has gained the confidence of the other and purports to act or advise with the other's interests in mind"); *see also* 3 DAN B. DOBBS ET AL., THE LAW OF TORTS § 697, at 753–54 (2d ed. 2011) ("Apart from formalized or categorical fiduciary relationships, other fiduciary obligations may arise on the facts of particular cases where the plaintiff reposes special trust and confidence in the

**The duration of the parties' relationship:** Both the majority and the dissent in *Crim Truck* referenced the fact that the relationship between the parties was of long duration. It began in 1943 and lasted over 40 years until the termination of the franchise in 1985. Why is that long duration evidence of trust and confidence? As a matter of general human experience, there is some correlation between the length of time that parties are together and the trust between those parties. Trust tends to grow with time and interaction; thus, a newer relationship has had less time to build trust than an older one.

*Majority's response*: The court was very dismissive. It noted that "[n]either is the fact that the relationship has been a cordial one, of long duration, evidence of a confidential relationship."

The duration of the parties' relationship is also significant because of a later Texas case concluding that "[t]o impose an informal fiduciary duty in a business transaction, the special relationship of trust and confidence must exist prior to, and apart from, the agreement made the basis of the suit."[9] That conclusion indicates that the relationship of trust and confidence must predate the agreement that the parties are fighting over. In *Crim Truck*, the 1958 franchise agreement (amended in 1979) was the basis of the Crims' lawsuit, and the dissent noted that there was a fifteen-year business relationship between the parties prior to this written agreement. Whether that fifteen-year period of doing business without a written contract would be sufficient, by itself, to establish a "special relationship of trust and confidence" is questionable. This is particularly so in light of additional language from the same later Texas case indicating that an "arms-length transaction entered into for the parties' mutual benefit" is insufficient to establish a pre-existing relationship of trust and confidence.[10] The franchise relationship between the Crims and Navistar's predecessor from

defendant and the defendant gives the appearance of tacitly accepting that trust and hence his fiduciary role. The defendant's acceptance or his undertaking to act in the plaintiff's interest and not his own can be seen in most cases from the fact that when the plaintiff's trust is demonstrated, the defendant does not disclaim an intent to respect that trust.").

[9] Associated Indem. Corp. v. CAT Contracting, Inc., 964 S.W.2d 276, 288 (Tex. 1998).

[10] *Id.*; *see also* Meyer v. Cathey, 167 S.W.3d 327, 331 (Tex. 2005) ("To impose an informal fiduciary duty in a business transaction, the special relationship of trust and confidence must exist prior to, and apart from, the agreement made the basis of the suit. Here, there is no evidence of such a preexisting relationship between Meyer and Cathey. The court of appeals' reliance on Meyer's and Cathey's work on prior projects is misplaced. These earlier projects were arms-length transactions entered into for the parties' mutual benefit, and thus do not establish a basis for a fiduciary relationship.").

1943–1958 was presumably a series of arm's length transactions entered into for the mutual benefit of both parties.

**Objective indications of trust:** In *Crim Truck*, the franchise agreement between the parties included an anti-assignment clause that explicitly stated that "[t]his is a personal agreement, involving mutual confidence and trust."

*Majority's response*: The court dismissed the language as boilerplate designed merely to prevent the contract from being assignable. In effect, the court did not believe that the language truly reflected the nature of the relationship; instead, the language was used to accomplish a narrow purpose (prohibit assignments) rather than to impose fiduciary obligations. As the court observed: "We are unpersuaded that this language was ever intended to inject an element of personal trust and confidence above and beyond that which is ordinarily contemplated by parties to contracts of this type. . . . Such 'boiler plate' language is designed to give the parties some degree of control over with whom they do business, and nothing more. This language was obviously intended to render the franchise agreement unilaterally unassignable." As the dissent noted, however, if there was no trust and confidence involved, why would Navistar care whether the Crims assigned the contract? Couldn't one say that the mere presence of the anti-assignment clause indicated that Navistar trusted the Crims' solvency and the way the Crims ran the franchise, but didn't trust potential assignees who had not been similarly vetted?

**Objective indications of trust:** The Crims cited examples of requests by Navistar that the Crims complied with: (1) moving the dealership location and constructing a prototype building; and (2) purchasing computer software. How is this evidence of a relationship of trust and confidence? Perhaps because a franchisee would never take such significant action without trusting that the franchisor will be supportive after the changes? Perhaps because it suggested, as did some testimony, that the Crims generally did what Navistar asked, and that would never happen if the Crims did not trust Navistar? The connection of these actions to a relationship of trust and confidence is not entirely clear, and it was obviously not clear to the court as well.

*Majority's response*: "We find nothing extraordinary about these requests in the context of the franchise agreement. But, this is not evidence of a confidential relationship."

**Objective indications of trust:** The dissent observed that "[a]fter the Crims built a prototype building in a new location at Navistar's direction, Navistar placed a newspaper advertisement describing this structure as a symbol of 'good faith and permanency in the progressive community of Henderson, Texas.'" The significance of this observation is not readily apparent. Perhaps the building and the subsequent advertisement created some goodwill between the Crims and Navistar, which engendered some feelings of trust between the parties?

*Majority's response*: "[T]his one occurrence thirty-eight years prior to termination of the franchise agreement is no evidence of a confidential relationship."

**Power dynamics:** It is not clear from the majority opinion if the Crims raised this point, but it is discussed explicitly by the dissent. When one party has most of the power in a relationship, but the relationship continues, it suggests that the weaker party trusts the stronger party not to abuse that power. After all, if such trust didn't exist, the weaker party would be foolish to remain in such an unbalanced (and precarious) situation. As the dissent stated: "If the franchisor has power to control the franchisee, there is an increased likelihood that a fiduciary relationship exists, since trust or confidence necessarily must flow from the controlled or dominated party."

*Majority's response*: The court did not appear to disagree with the premise that a relationship characterized by a power imbalance might be some evidence of trust. Nevertheless, the court seemed to take the position that because the power imbalance in the *general* franchisor-franchisee setting had been mitigated by state and federal statutes, there was no longer a need to impose a fiduciary duty to protect the weaker franchisee (even though in this *specific* franchisor-franchisee relationship, the state statutory protection was unavailable). As the court observed: "We see no good reason to add to the existing regulatory scheme by implication of a common law fiduciary duty."

The above discussion reveals that the Supreme Court of Texas in *Crim Truck* strongly disagreed with the notion that an informal fiduciary relationship existed between the Crims and Navistar. Even if the court had concluded that a fiduciary duty existed, however, would Navistar have breached that duty? After all, the Crims repeatedly refused to sign the dealer communications network contract, even though Navistar had made clear that it was mandatory. Presumably, the franchise agreement gave Navistar the power to terminate franchisees who fail to comply with the franchisor's requirements. While it is true that terminating a franchisee does not seem consistent with a fiduciary franchisor's obligation to put the franchisee's interests ahead of its own, it is also well-accepted that a contract between the parties can define or limit the scope of a fiduciary duty. (In some jurisdictions, a contract can even *eliminate* a fiduciary duty.)[11] Conduct permitted by the franchise agreement, in other words, might be understood as conduct that the parties agreed would not violate any fiduciary duty. Thus, if the contract permitted Navistar to terminate a non-complying franchisee, the termination might not be viewed as a breach of fiduciary duty between the parties.

On the other hand, the dissent noted that other franchisees who failed to sign the dealer communications network contract did not have their franchises terminated. In fact, it did not appear that any franchise was terminated other than the Crims. Even though Navistar may have had the right to terminate non-complying franchisees, its arbitrariness in doing so suggests that the Crims were being singled out. This selective use of the power to terminate when other franchisees had engaged in similar action seems inconsistent with a fiduciary obligation of fairness.

Why was the *Crim Truck* court so hostile to concluding that an informal fiduciary relationship existed between the Crims and Navistar? As mentioned, in a true fiduciary relationship, the fiduciary acts solely in the best interests of the beneficiary and is obligated to put the interests of the beneficiary before its own. This obligation to act selflessly is totally inconsistent with the franchise relationship between the Crims and Navistar. Indeed, both the Crims and Navistar have legitimate selfish interests in making money from their franchise relationship. Navistar granted a franchise to the Crims with the aim of profiting from the grant, and the Crims understood this (as does every franchisee). If a court literally required Navistar to put the Crims' interests ahead of its own, would Navistar have to provide products and services to the Crims for free? After all, charging for the products and services only benefits Navistar. Would Navistar ever be able to terminate the franchise, even if the Crims were stealing or otherwise engaging in clearly objectionable behavior? Terminating the franchise would be in Navistar's interests, but presumably not the Crims. In short, a fiduciary's obligation to place the interests of the beneficiary before its own makes no sense in the relationship between most contracting

---

11 *Cf.* REVISED UNIFORM PARTNERSHIP ACT §§ 103(b)(3), 404(a)–(b) (1997) ("The partnership agreement may not . . . eliminate the [fiduciary] duty of loyalty . . . but . . . the partnership agreement may identify specific types or categories of activities that do not violate the duty of loyalty, if not manifestly unreasonable . . . ."); DEL. CODE tit. 6, § 18–1101(c) ("To the extent that, at law or in equity, a member or manager or other person has duties (including fiduciary duties) to a limited liability company or to another member or manager or to another person that is a party to or is otherwise bound by a limited liability company agreement, the member's or manager's or other person's duties may be expanded or restricted or eliminated by provisions in the limited liability company agreement . . . .").

parties, as each party has legitimate selfish interests in making money from the contractual arrangement.[12]

Thus, part of the court's hostility in *Crim Truck* to concluding that an informal fiduciary relationship existed might be explained by the poor fit between the selflessness obligation of a true fiduciary and the self-interested nature of contractual relationships. No contractual party, including the Crims, believes that the other party should have to subordinate its interests.[13] A finding of fiduciary duty, however, would require just that. Thus, establishing an informal fiduciary relationship is difficult, and should be difficult, because the relationship creates a selflessness obligation that is inconsistent with the expectations of parties in most contractual relationships. The *Crim Truck* court recognized this,[14] and that recognition likely explains why the court made things so difficult for the plaintiffs. In short, *Crim Truck* makes it clear that not every relationship of trust and confidence will suffice to establish an informal fiduciary relationship. An "extraordinary" relationship of trust and confidence, as poorly defined as that is, is necessary.

A few responses might be made here. First, a court could potentially find that a fiduciary relationship exists between contracting parties without the obligation of selflessness. As mentioned, contracts between the parties can define or limit the scope of a fiduciary duty. When parties have entered into a contract for their mutual interests, perhaps the contract could be construed as the parties' agreement that the pursuit of selfish interests (as described in the contract) will not violate any fiduciary duty between the parties.

Second, rather than view the selflessness obligation of a fiduciary as eliminated *by contract*, perhaps the selflessness obligation could be eliminated *as a matter of law* when contracting parties are present. In other words, perhaps a fiduciary duty between contracting parties should not require selflessness as a legal matter; instead, it should

---

[12] *Cf. In re* Express Scripts, Inc., 522 F. Supp. 2d 1132, 1144 (E.D. Mo. 2007) ("Parties entering into contract pursuant to a business relationship do not generally give rise to a fiduciary relationship, absent extraordinary circumstances, because such parties deal with each other at arm's length.").

[13] *Cf.* 2 DAN B. DOBBS, DOBBS LAW OF REMEDIES § 10.4, at 662 (2d ed. 1993) ("Although certain good faith performance of contracts may be required even between those who deal at arms' length, that good faith does not require one party to subordinate her own interests to those of the other.").

[14] *See* Crim Truck & Tractor Co. v. Navistar Int'l Transp. Corp., 823 S.W.2d 591, 594 (Tex. 1992) ("The Crims concede that *not every* franchise agreement creates a fiduciary relationship. But, they argue that the facts here prove a confidential relationship giving rise to an informal fiduciary relationship, imposing the duty on Navistar, not just to seek its own economic interests, but to put the Crims' interests before its own. But, this argument clashes with the rule that a party to a contract is free to pursue its own interests, even if it results in a breach of that contract, without incurring tort liability.").

allow the fiduciary to put the beneficiary's interests on par with its own (rather than ahead of its own) so long as the beneficiary is treated fairly. Such a modification of the legal obligations associated with a traditional fiduciary duty has occurred in the business organizations context, as a fiduciary in some business settings may enter into contracts or other transactions with its beneficiary—even though the fiduciary is obviously self-interested in the transaction—so long as the transaction is fair to the beneficiary.[15]

As mentioned, *Crim Truck* makes it clear that not every relationship involving trust and confidence between the parties rises to the level of an informal fiduciary (or confidential) relationship. Something more is required to create an extraordinary relationship of trust and confidence that warrants fiduciary treatment. Precise rules indicating that such an extraordinary relationship exists are difficult to articulate.[16] In general, a court will find that an informal fiduciary relationship exists only in egregious circumstances where the plaintiff reposes a significant amount of trust and confidence in the defendant and the defendant appears to accept that trust. As one commentator observed:

> . . . . In determining whether a fiduciary relation exists because of special confidence reposed, courts will consider evidence bearing on the plaintiff's reasonable expectations based on the defendant's apparent acceptance of the plaintiff's confidence and his own fiduciary responsibility. Broadly stated, factors include the course of the parties' prior relationship over time, the defendant's evident allegiances, the inability of the putative beneficiary to protect herself and analogies to the recognized categories of fiduciaries. . . . The unequal position of the parties is an important factor—a variation on the idea that the plaintiff is unable to protect herself or her property.[17]

---

15 *See, e.g.*, DEL. CODE tit. 6, § 144(a)(3) (stating that "[n]o contract or transaction between a corporation and 1 or more of its directors or officers [both fiduciaries of the corporation] . . . shall be void or voidable solely for this reason . . . if . . . [t]he contract or transaction is fair as to the corporation as of the time it is authorized, approved or ratified, by the board of directors, a committee or the stockholders").

16 *See, e.g.*, Texas Bank and Trust Co. v. Moore, 595 S.W.2d 502, 508 (Tex. 1980) (noting that "the circumstances out of which a fiduciary relationship will be said to arise are not subject to hard and fast lines"); GEORGE G. BOGERT ET AL., THE LAW OF TRUSTS AND TRUSTEES § 482 (3d ed. 2009) ("Equity has never bound itself by any hard and fast definition of the phrase 'confidential relation' and has not listed the necessary elements for such a relationship to exist but rather has reserved discretion to apply the doctrine whenever it believes that a suitable occasion has arisen.").

17 3 DAN B. DOBBS ET AL., THE LAW OF TORTS § 697, at 754 (2d ed. 2011); *see also* First Nat'l Bank of Meeker v. Theos, 794 P.2d 1055, 1061 (Colo. App. 1990) ("[A] confidential relationship may arise if: (1) one party has taken steps to induce another to believe that it can safely rely on the first party's judgment or advice; (2) one person

Are family ties some evidence of a fiduciary relationship of trust and confidence? In general, courts have not characterized family as a formal fiduciary relationship.[18] With respect to an informal fiduciary relationship, however, a family connection can be evidence of the requisite relationship of trust and confidence between the parties. This is presumably because intimate relationships, such as those between family members, are more associated with trust than other relationships. Indeed, in many situations, the persons we love the most tend to be the persons we trust the most. Nevertheless, the mere existence of family ties is typically insufficient on its own to establish an informal fiduciary relationship.[19]

---

has gained the confidence of the other and purports to act or advise with the other's interest in mind; or (3) the parties' relationship is such that one is induced to relax the care and vigilance one ordinarily would exercise in dealing with a stranger."); Gillespie v. Seymour, 796 P.2d 1060, 1063 (Kan. Ct. App. 1990), *rev'd in part on other grounds*, 823 P.2d 782 (Kan. 1991) ("A fiduciary relationship requires confidence of one in another and a certain inequity or dependence arising from weakness of age, mental strength, business intelligence, knowledge of facts involved, or other conditions which give one an advantage over the other.").

For examples of decisions finding that an informal fiduciary relationship existed, see Nelson v. Dodge, 68 A.2d 51, 55–58 (R.I. 1949) (involving a religious leader who convinced a member of her church that the member needed to sell all of his assets and give the proceeds to her); Dixon v. Dixon, 608 S.E.2d 849, 853–54 (S.C. 2005) (involving an elderly mother who gave her son partial control over her affairs, made her bank accounts available to him, and signed documents that he prepared without reviewing them); Buxcel v. First Fidelity Bank, 601 N.W.2d 593, 595, 597–98 (S.D. 1999) (involving a bank that convinced a customer/borrower to take out a Small Business Administration loan to purchase a failing grocery store).

[18] *See, e.g.*, Francois v. Francois, 599 F.2d 1286, 1292 (3d Cir. 1979) (observing that "[t]he marital relation does not automatically give rise to a confidential relation"); *In re* Kieras, 521 N.E.2d 263, 280 (Ill. App. Ct. 1988) ("However, the relationship between parent and child is not fiduciary as a matter of law."); Simpson v. Dailey, 496 A.2d 126, 128 (R.I. 1985) (stating that "[a] family relationship, of itself, does not create a fiduciary relationship"); Texas Bank and Trust Co. v. Moore, 595 S.W.2d 502, 508 (Tex. 1980) (noting that "the relationship of Mrs. Littell and Moore—that of aunt and nephew—together with Moore's assistance to Mrs. Littell, do not, standing alone, establish a fiduciary relationship").

There are some decisions—often older decisions—to the contrary. *See, e.g.*, Putnam v. Putnam, 150 So. 2d 209, 213 (Ala. 1963) ("The marriage of the complainant and the respondent . . . created between them a relationship of confidence and trust, exacting the utmost good faith in their dealing with each other."). In addition, a statute may change the result. *See, e.g.*, CAL. FAM. CODE § 721(b) (stating that "in transactions between themselves, spouses are subject to the general rules governing fiduciary relationships that control the actions of persons occupying confidential relations with each other").

[19] *See, e.g.*, Francois v. Francois, 599 F.2d 1286, 1292 (3d Cir. 1979) ("The marital relation does not automatically give rise to a confidential relation, but it 'arises when one party places confidence in the other with a resulting superiority and influence on the other side.' Thus, each marriage must be examined on its own facts to determine if a confidential relation exists."); Liapis v. Dist. Ct., 282 P.3d 733, 738 (Nev. 2012) (stating that "although a fiduciary relationship 'is particularly likely to exist when there is a family relationship,' '[a] family relationship, of itself, does not create a fiduciary relationship' unless it is established by additional facts"); Dixon v. Dixon, 608 S.E.2d 849, 853 (S.C. 2005) ("Although this Court has declined to hold that a familial relationship, alone, is sufficient evidence of a confidential relationship, a familial

In contrast to *Crim Truck*, the court in the later Texas decision of *Lee v. Hasson*[20] determined that an informal fiduciary relationship existed between contracting parties. Lou Pai and Lanna Lee married in 1976. In 1993, they met Ted and Terry Hasson and became close friends. The families "spent many vacations and holidays together." Ted Hasson ("Hasson") was a life insurance agent and securities dealer, and he sold several life insurance policies to the Pais from 1995 to 1999. As part of the life insurance process, the Pais shared medical and financial information with Hasson.

In January 1998, Lee discovered that her husband had been having an extra-marital affair. Pai moved out of the family home, and Lee asked Hasson about financial actions that she should take while she was still married. On January 18, 2000, Hasson reached an oral agreement with Lee whereby Hasson agreed to advise Lee through her divorce and property settlement in exchange for, in part, 10% of Lee's share of the marital estate.

In June of 2000, Lee told Hasson that she would not pay him 10% of her share of the marital estate and she requested the return of $4 million that had previously been transferred to Hasson. Lee's divorce was finalized on August 21, 2000. She received 57% of the assets in the marital estate with a corresponding value of $110,536,269, excluding restricted or unissued securities.

In July of 2000, Hasson sued Lee and alleged that her share of the estate totaled approximately $140 million and that Lee owed him 10% of this amount pursuant to their agreement. At trial, Lee denied that she had an agreement with Hasson and argued in the alternative that any agreement with Hasson was unenforceable based, in part, on Hasson's breach of fiduciary duty. She also counterclaimed and alleged that Hasson had converted her funds.

The jury found that Lee had agreed to pay Hasson, that she failed to comply with the agreement, that her failure was not excused, and that she owed Hasson $10 million. (This was presumably because Hasson had already received $4 million; thus, $14 million would be 10% of Lee's alleged $140 million share of the estate.) The jury also found that (a) a relationship of trust and confidence existed between Lee and Hasson at the time they entered into the agreement, and (b) Hasson had complied with his fiduciary

relationship certainly *supports* an argument that a confidential relationship exists."); *cf.* Mendenhall v. Judy, 671 N.W.2d 452, 455 (Iowa 2003) (noting that a confidential relationship "is particularly likely to exist where there is a family relationship"); RESTATEMENT (SECOND) OF TORTS § 551 cmt. f (1977) (noting that "members of the same family normally stand in a fiduciary relation to one another, although it is of course obvious that the fact that two men are brothers does not establish [a] relation of trust and confidence when they have become estranged").

20 286 S.W.3d 1 (Tex. App. 2007).

duty to Lee. The jury failed to find that Hasson or his companies had converted Lee's funds.

Lee and Hasson filed post-trial motions. Lee asked the trial court to disregard the jury's finding that Hasson complied with his fiduciary duty to Lee (Question 17). Conversely, Hasson asked the trial court to disregard the finding that Hasson and Lee shared a confidential relationship (Question 16). As Hasson requested, the trial court entered a final judgment disregarding the jury's answer to Question 16.

On appeal, the court found that there was sufficient evidence of a confidential relationship between Lee and Hasson. The court further concluded that Hasson did not comply with his fiduciary duty to Lee. As a consequence, according to the court, "Hasson has failed to overcome the presumption that his contract with Lee is void." The court ultimately reversed the trial court and rendered judgment that Hasson take nothing.

Are there material differences between *Lee* (Court of Appeals of Texas) and *Crim Truck* (Supreme Court of Texas) that would explain why an informal fiduciary relationship was found in one decision (*Lee*) but not the other (*Crim Truck*)? Consider the following bolded language from the *Lee* decision:

- **"We emphasize that fiduciary relationships are not lightly created. However, the extraordinary facts of this case present a rare example of the type of close personal relationship of trust and confidence that gives rise to a legally cognizable fiduciary duty."**

This language from the conclusion of the *Lee* court sets the appropriate tone. An informal fiduciary relationship is not supposed to be "lightly created." But the court finds one in *Lee* because of the "extraordinary facts of this case." The central issue is whether the court is correct—i.e., are the facts extraordinary enough to warrant the conclusion that an informal fiduciary relationship existed?

- **"The record reveals both legally and factually sufficient evidence that Hasson and Lee shared a long-standing business relationship and a close personal family relationship well beyond casual friendship and that Lee relied on Hasson for moral, financial, and personal guidance or support. Moreover, their relationship began in 1993 and therefore predated their agreements by approximately six years."**

As mentioned, under Texas law, "[t]o impose an informal fiduciary duty in a business transaction, the special relationship of trust and confidence must exist prior to, and apart from, the agreement made the basis of the suit." Moreover, an "arms-length transaction entered into for the parties' mutual benefit" is insufficient to establish this pre-existing relationship of trust and confidence.[21]

In the bolded passage above, the *Lee* court observed that the relationship between Lee and Hasson began in 1993, which was approximately six years before the agreement that was the basis of the lawsuit (January 18, 2000 was the initial oral agreement). The hard question, of course, is whether that 1993–1999 relationship can be characterized as a "special relationship of trust and confidence." As mentioned, the *Crim Truck* court stated the following: "Neither is the fact that the relationship has been a cordial one, of long duration, evidence of a confidential relationship." It is worth noting that the *Lee* court seems less absolute on this point. The court stated that "[t]he length of the relationship is another important factor in determining whether a fiduciary relationship should be recognized," although it acknowledged that "even a longstanding relationship of friendship or cordiality is insufficient, without more, to establish an informal fiduciary relationship." If the length of the parties' association is some evidence of a confidential relationship, six years is not a particularly long time. It is certainly not an extraordinary fact.

- **"Although the friendship between the two families dates back to 1993, the business relationship between Hasson and the Pais began in 1995, when Hasson sold the couple a $6 million life insurance policy. The following year, the couple purchased a second, $15 million policy from Hasson. When the Pais purchased a $50 million policy in 1998, Hasson became the top producing life insurance agent for that insurer in the country, due primarily to the fact that this was the largest life insurance policy written. . . . Before beginning work for Lee in October 1999, Hasson helped Lee apply for yet another life insurance policy in August 1999. Hasson earned commissions on each of these sales."**

It is not entirely clear why the prior insurance relationship is relevant. It would appear to be an "arms-length transaction entered into for the parties' mutual benefit," which is not sufficient to establish a relationship of trust and confidence. (Lee received insurance protection, presumably at market rates, while Hasson received commissions.) It is true that Lee shared personal medical and financial information with Hasson as part of these insurance

[21] *See supra* notes 9–10 and accompanying text.

transactions, and perhaps that is some evidence of an expectation of trust and confidence (i.e., sensitive personal information can be used for identity fraud and other nefarious purposes; one only shares the information with the expectation that it will not be used for anything other than the potential insurance acquisition). That said, sharing personal medical and financial information is part and parcel of any purchase of life insurance—there is nothing unique or extraordinary about that aspect of the transactions.

- **"The evidence is also uncontroverted that the families were unusually close. For example, the Hassons and the Pais vacationed together at Lake Powell, the Cayman Islands, and the Pais' ranches in Texas and Colorado. Not only did the two families vacation together . . . but as Hasson admitted, 'these two families had practically lived together.' "**

In *Crim Truck*, the court stated the following: "Neither is the fact that the relationship has been a cordial one, of long duration, evidence of a confidential relationship." If the *Crim Truck* court is serious about its pronouncement that the "cordial" nature of the relationship is irrelevant, it is hard to understand why the families being "unusually close" and vacationing together is significant. Perhaps the idea is that "unusually close" friendships are similar to family relationships, and family relationships are some evidence of trust and confidence between the parties. Put differently, perhaps *Crim Truck* can be distinguished on the basis that a typical friendly relationship (e.g., dining together occasionally, vacationing together occasionally) is merely "cordial" and no evidence of a confidential relationship, but anything beyond that (e.g., vacationing together frequently/always, "practically liv[ing] together") is more akin to a family relationship and is, consequently, of some evidentiary significance. Indeed, the court noted that Lee and Hasson shared a "close personal family relationship well beyond casual friendship." This may also explain the court's mention of Lee's daughter and her testimony that Hasson had been a "father figure" and that the Hassons "were family." The idea, once again, is that the relationship between Lee and Hasson was more than a mere "cordial" friendship—it was akin to family.

- **"In addition, Lee depended on Hasson for personal and moral support, as evidenced by testimony that Hasson's attorney elicited from both Hasson and Lee . . . ."**

- **"Hasson argues that the evidence at trial showed only that Lee had subjective feelings of trust for him and that her feelings are insufficient to establish an informal fiduciary relationship. However, the record contains repeated examples of objective manifestations of Lee's confidence in**

**and reliance on Hasson. In addition to the 'Be All Lanna Can Be' program described above [an effort by Hasson to provide Lee with emotional and moral support], Lee also shared confidential medical and significant financial information with Hasson, and as Hasson testified, relied on him for financial guidance. For example, Hasson testified that on August 26, 1999—before Lee made any offer of employment—Lee asked Hasson if there were any actions she should take while she remained married. Hasson asked for financial information, and, at Hasson's request, Lee supplied him with more information than Pai ever had shared with Hasson before. On Hasson's advice, Lee began the process of applying for more life insurance. According to Hasson, he also began to teach Lee about diversifying her assets at this time. Eliciting evidence that Lee shared confidential information with Hasson also formed a part of Hasson's trial strategy . . . ."**

- **"Finally, Lee relied on Hasson for personal guidance and support in areas as important to her as achieving reconciliation in her marriage. For example, it is undisputed that Lee initially did not want a divorce. She instead relied on Hasson's advice in joining with him to purchase a boat for Pai in the hope that the gift would help to effect a reconciliation . . . ."**

In *Crim Truck*, the court stated that "mere subjective trust alone is not enough to transform arms-length dealing into a fiduciary relationship." Similarly, the court noted that "[t]he fact that one businessman trusts another, and relies upon his promise to perform a contract, does not rise to a confidential relationship." As mentioned, the plaintiff's unilateral trust in the defendant, even if significant, is insufficient to establish an informal fiduciary relationship. An informal fiduciary relationship requires not only the beneficiary to place its trust in the fiduciary, but also the fiduciary to appear to accept the obligation to be trustworthy.

This seems to be a significant difference from the facts of *Crim Truck*. There was not only evidence that Lee trusted Hasson, but there was also evidence that Hasson understood and accepted that trust. Hasson testified to his understanding that he was uniquely qualified to help Lee and that Lee "relied on him [Hasson] for financial guidance." Hasson also knew that Lee was taking his personal guidance, as she followed Hasson's advice about purchasing a boat for Pai. The court further noted that "establishing the pre-existence of a relationship of trust was an explicit part of Hasson's trial strategy." Even Hasson's wife agreed that there was a relationship of trust and confidence between Lee and Hasson. Admittedly, in *Crim Truck*, the anti-assignment clause appeared to be some evidence that Navistar agreed to a relationship of trust with the Crims, but the court downplayed the language of the clause as boilerplate. In *Lee*, by contrast, Hasson himself (and his wife) provided testimony suggesting that a relationship of trust and confidence was present between Lee and Hasson. It was not merely Lee asserting that such a relationship existed.[22]

What is the significance of the "Be All Lanna Can Be" program? The court seemed to cite it as evidence that Hasson understood that Lee was relying on him for personal support (after all, Hasson apparently came up with the catchy "Be All Lanna Can Be" name). So what? Hasson presumably did know that Lee was relying on him for support, and he tried to keep her spirits up during a difficult time. This seems far from extraordinary and no different from how any friend would act towards another friend going through a rough period. Put differently, it sounds a lot like what one would expect from any "cordial" relationship between friends. According to *Crim Truck*, of course, the fact that the relationship was cordial is irrelevant. It should be noted that the *Lee* court stated that "in order to establish the existence of an informal fiduciary relationship, the record must show that one of the parties relied on the other 'for moral, financial, or personal support or guidance.' " Thus, perhaps the court highlighted the "Be All Lanna Can Be" program simply to show that Lee did rely on Hasson for personal support and not for any further evidence of extraordinary trust and confidence.

The significance of the sharing of medical and financial information has previously been discussed. If the information shared was more than what would typically be given to an insurance agent for the purpose of buying insurance, that would seem to be better evidence of an informal fiduciary relationship (because it suggests an extraordinary level of trust and confidence beyond that associated with any run-of-the-mill insurance acquisition). Although the court mentioned that Lee provided Hasson "with more information than Pai ever had shared with Hasson before," it is not clear whether that information went beyond what is typically provided in a large life insurance transaction.

---

22 Why did Hasson's "trial strategy" (according to the court) include "establishing the pre-existence of a relationship of trust" and "[e]liciting evidence that Lee shared confidential information with Hasson"? Wouldn't Hasson want to defeat the argument that a relationship of trust and confidence existed? Recall that Lee denied that an agreement with Hasson was entered into; thus, perhaps Hasson was trying to establish that a relationship of trust and confidence existed to make it seem plausible that Lee would have entered into an agreement for Hasson's future services. By making these arguments, however, Hasson made it easier for the court to conclude that he owed a fiduciary duty to Lee.

To sum up, although the *Lee* court observed that fiduciary relationships "are not lightly created," it found that the "extraordinary facts of this case present a rare example" of such a relationship. What was so extraordinary about the 1993–1999 relationship between Lee and Hasson? There are only a few notable differences from *Crim Truck*. First, the court appeared to analogize Lee and Hasson to family members, and family connections can be evidence of the requisite relationship of trust and confidence. Second, and perhaps more importantly, Hasson basically agreed (through his testimony, his wife's testimony, and his "trial strategy") that a relationship of trust and confidence existed between Lee and himself.

The disputed agreement seems egregiously unfair to Lee, and that unfairness may have motivated the court to find an informal fiduciary relationship. Upholding the agreement would mean that Hasson was entitled to $14 million (the $10 million jury award plus the $4 million that Hasson had already received) for less than one year of work.[23] Moreover, he would be entitled to that $14 million despite the court mentioning that he gave incorrect advice, and arguably unlicensed legal advice, to Lee. Perhaps the court's decision, in other words, was largely outcome driven. The court wanted to invalidate an unfair agreement, and it stretched to find a fiduciary relationship (and an accompanying breach) to accomplish that goal.[24]

If the case had reached the Supreme Court of Texas, one could imagine a *Crim Truck*-like court reaching a different result. As opposed to *Lee*, *Crim Truck* seems almost hostile to informal fiduciary relationships. Because Lee and Hasson were not actually family members, the court might simply describe their relationship as a "cordial" friendship. Admittedly it was a close relationship, but so are plenty of ordinary friendships. The testimony of Hasson and his wife that a relationship of trust and confidence existed would be harder to overcome, but perhaps it could be downplayed as a layperson admission that the parties trusted each other in the same ordinary way that good friends tend to trust one another. It was not meant to be an admission that the trust was extraordinary and deserving of fiduciary treatment. Finally, courts are not in the business of rewriting or invalidating contracts outside of established contract doctrines (e.g., duress, unconscionability, illegality). The mere fact that Lee may have agreed to a foolish amount of consideration for Hasson's services technically has no relevance to whether an informal fiduciary relationship existed.

---

23 Hasson contended that he began work in October 1999; the agreement was entered into on January 18, 2000; and the divorce was finalized on August 21, 2000.

24 Don't cry too much for Hasson. The case indicated that he apparently kept $4.22 million for his less than one year of work.

As mentioned, breach of fiduciary duty is a powerful cause of action for plaintiffs because fiduciaries owe very strict obligations to their beneficiaries. Moreover, when a fiduciary's compliance with its obligations is challenged, courts in many situations will impose the burden of proof upon the fiduciary itself.[25] For plaintiffs, this potential burden shift is another attractive aspect of the breach of fiduciary duty cause of action.

The *Lee* decision is a nice illustration of these points. After determining that an informal fiduciary relationship existed, the court required Hasson to shoulder the burden of proving that he satisfied *each* of the five fiduciary obligations provided in the jury charge: (i) the transactions were fair to Lee; (ii) Hasson made reasonable use of Lee's confidence; (iii) Hasson exercised utmost good faith and the most scrupulous honesty; (iv) Hasson placed Lee's interests before his own; and (v) Hasson fully and fairly disclosed all important information to Lee concerning the transactions. The court noted that "the existence of such a [fiduciary] relationship not only imposes on Hasson the elevated duty of a fiduciary, but also places the burden on him to prove that he complied with that duty." The court similarly observed that "[t]o find that Hasson complied with his fiduciary duty to Lee, the charge required the jury to find that Hasson proved each of the five specified facts." To be clear, Hasson was required to prove that he met *all five* obligations in the jury charge; if *any one* of those obligations was not met, a breach of fiduciary duty occurred. Ultimately, the court found that Hasson did not meet any of the five obligations, but technically the court could have ended its analysis after concluding that Hasson had not met the first obligation to enter into fair transactions with Lee.

A fiduciary's wrongdoing may not constitute a breach of fiduciary duty if it falls outside the scope of the particular fiduciary obligation. For example, "[a] lawyer, who is a fiduciary to his client, might negligently drive his automobile, causing physical harm to his client, but that would ordinarily not show a breach of fiduciary duty, which relates to loyalty to the client, not to good driving."[26]

---

[25] *See, e.g.*, Cadle Co. v. D'Addario, 844 A.2d 836, 847 (Conn. 2004) ("The superior position of the fiduciary or dominant party affords him great opportunity for abuse of the confidence reposed in him. . . . Once a [fiduciary] relationship is found to exist, the burden of proving fair dealing properly shifts to the fiduciary."); *see also* 3 DAN B. DOBBS ET AL., THE LAW OF TORTS § 696, at 747 (2d ed. 2011) ("Once the beneficiary shows that the fiduciary engaged in a transaction with the beneficiary, or affecting the beneficiary's rights, courts usually impose the burden of proof on fiduciaries to prove they acted in good faith and fairly, with all that implies.").

[26] 3 DAN B. DOBBS ET AL., THE LAW OF TORTS § 699, at 762 n.20 (2d ed. 2011).

# Chapter 5

# THE ECONOMIC LOSS RULE (II)

In Chapter 1, the "stranger" strand of the economic loss rule was discussed. As between parties lacking a contractual relationship, a plaintiff cannot recover for unintentionally caused economic loss in the absence of personal injury to the plaintiff or damage to the plaintiff's property. Business torts usually avoid the application of this strand of the economic loss rule.

This chapter discusses a different fact pattern where the parties to a tort action are also in a contractual relationship. In such "nonstranger" cases, is a tort recovery for pure economic loss permissible? As in the stranger context, do business torts avoid the application of any restrictive doctrine? Consider the decision of *Town of Alma v. AZCO Construction, Inc.*[1] Alma and AZCO entered into a contract for the construction of improvements to Alma's water distribution system. The contract guaranteed AZCO's work for one year after the date of final payment. During the one-year period (apparently), AZCO repaired three leaks at its expense. When further leaks were discovered after the expiration of the one-year period, AZCO refused to repair them, and the individual town residents were forced to bear the expense.

Alma, joined by several individual residents, sued AZCO for breach of contract, breach of the implied warranty of sound workmanship, and negligence. The trial court dismissed the negligence and implied warranty claims, and a jury returned a verdict for AZCO on the breach of contract claim. The court of appeals affirmed. On appeal to the Supreme Court of Colorado, the petitioners argued that their negligence claim should not have been dismissed.

The court began by discussing the origins of the economic loss rule. The rule originated in the products liability context and precluded a negligence or strict liability claim "for damage caused when a product malfunctions and causes purely economic loss through damage to the product itself." The court then set forth an "independent duty" test for determining the availability of a tort action between contracting parties: "We hold that a party suffering only economic loss from the breach of an express or implied

1 10 P.3d 1256 (Colo. 2000).

contractual duty may not assert a tort claim for such breach absent an independent duty of care under tort law."[2]

Applying the test to the facts of the case, the court noted that AZCO breached only a contractual duty of care in the installation of the water system. (There is, in other words, no independent tort duty of care in the performance of a service that only causes economic loss.) Because there was no breach of an independent tort duty, the court concluded that the economic loss rule barred the negligence claim.

As *Town of Alma* illustrates, the economic loss rule has spread beyond its products liability origins. Indeed, the rule now affects any negligence or strict liability claim between contracting parties. According to the court, "[a]lthough originally born from products liability law, the application of the economic loss rule is broader, because it serves to maintain a distinction between contract and tort law."[3]

Alma had entered into a contract with AZCO for the construction of improvements to Alma's water distribution system. What was problematic about allowing Alma to assert a negligence claim against AZCO for AZCO's allegedly deficient work? Alma and AZCO had negotiated a contract that addressed the risk of faulty work. In particular, AZCO had agreed to make repairs or replacements at its own expense, but only for problems that became evident within one year of final payment. If Alma had wanted AZCO to cover problems for a longer period of time, Alma could have attempted to negotiate for that, but presumably AZCO would have charged a higher price for any longer warranty. (Similarly, Alma presumably paid a lower price in exchange for the shorter warranty.) Allowing Alma to bring a negligence action for any faulty work undermines the bargain that the parties struck over pricing, warranties, and other risk adjustments. Moreover, it defeats the purpose of entering into such a bargain in the first place (i.e., it defeats the purpose of allocating risks before the transaction).

---

[2] *See also id.* at 1262 ("A breach of a duty *arising independently* of any contract duties between the parties . . . may support a tort action." (quoting Tommy L. Griffin Plumbing & Heating Co. v. Jordan, Jones & Goulding, Inc., 463 S.E.2d 85, 88 (S.C. 1995)) (emphasis added)).

[3] *See also* RESTATEMENT (THIRD) OF TORTS: LIABILITY FOR ECONOMIC HARM § 3 cmt. a (2020) ("The narrower scope of the rule stated here also ties it more clearly to its origins in cases that involve products liability. A buyer of a product disappointed by its performance cannot sue its maker in tort for negligence. Courts have long recognized that the law of warranty is better suited than the law of tort to address such cases, and that contracts between the parties determine the allocation of economic losses that arise from the transaction. See Restatement Third, Torts: Products Liability § 21. *The rule recognized by this Section generalizes that principle to economic injuries arising from the breach of other sorts of contracts.*" (emphasis added)).

The *Town of Alma* court made these points about undermining the parties' bargain in a number of places. First, the court recited the court of appeals' statement that allowing the negligence claim "would permit the non-breaching party to avoid the contractual limitation of remedy." Second, the court cited passages from a 1986 U.S. Supreme Court decision:

> Contract law, and the law of warranty in particular, is well suited to commercial controversies of the sort involved in this case because the parties may set the terms of their own agreements. The manufacturer can restrict its liability, within limits, by disclaiming warranties or limiting remedies. In exchange, the purchaser pays less for the product. Since a commercial situation generally does not involve large disparities in bargaining power, we see no reason to intrude into the parties' allocation of the risk.[4]

Finally, the court described the purposes of contract law as follows:

> Contract law is intended to enforce the expectancy interests created by the parties' promises so that they can allocate risks and costs during their bargaining. Limiting tort liability when a contract exists between parties is appropriate because a product's potential nonperformance can be adequately addressed by rational economic actors bargaining at arms length to shape the terms of the contract. For example, a buyer may demand additional warranties on a product while agreeing to pay a higher price, or the same buyer may choose to assume a higher level of risk that a product will not perform properly by accepting a more limited warranty in exchange for a lower product price. Limiting the availability of tort remedies in these situations holds parties to the terms of their bargain. In this way, the law serves to encourage parties to confidently allocate risks and costs during their bargaining without fear that unanticipated liability may arise in the future, effectively negating the parties' efforts to build these cost considerations into the contract. The economic loss rule thus serves to ensure predictability in commercial transactions.[5]

---

4 *Town of* Alma, 10 P.3d at 1261 (quoting East River Steamship Corp. v. Transamerica Delaval, Inc., 476 U.S. 858, 872–73 (1986)).

5 *See also* RESTATEMENT (THIRD) OF TORTS: LIABILITY FOR ECONOMIC HARM § 3 cmt. b (2020) ("When a dispute arises, the rule protects the bargain the parties have made against disruption by a tort suit. Seen from an earlier point in the life of a transaction, the rule allows parties to make dependable allocations of financial risk without fear that tort law will be used to undo them later. Viewed in the long run, the

Allowing a tort claim based on the same underlying facts as a breach of contract claim also creates significant confusion for a court. Are the defenses that are applicable to the breach of contract claim equally applicable to the tort claim? Are tort damages available even though the wrongdoing stems from a failure to perform the contract? In addition, arguably duplicative claims increase litigation expenses for the parties.[6]

As mentioned, to alleviate these problems, the *Town of Alma* court adopted the following rule: "[A] party suffering only economic loss from the breach of an express or implied contractual duty may not assert a tort claim for such a breach absent an independent duty of care under tort law." Put differently, the court must determine the source of the duty alleged to have been violated by the defendant. To bring a tort claim in such a context, the plaintiff must establish the existence of a duty *independent* of any contractual obligations. As one court observed:

> If the defendant's conduct—such as negligently burning down a house—would give rise to liability independent of the fact that a contract exists between the parties, the plaintiff's claim may also sound in tort. Conversely, if the defendant's conduct—such as failing to publish an advertisement—would give rise to liability only because it breaches the parties' agreement, the plaintiff's claim ordinarily sounds only in contract.[7]

With respect to protecting the parties' bargain, the rule adopted by the *Town of Alma* court prevents a party from using a negligence claim to circumvent an allocation of risk that the parties contractually agreed upon. Implicit in this rationale is the idea that parties can and do contractually allocate not only the risks of nonperformance, but also the risks of *negligent* nonperformance.[8]

---

rule prevents the erosion of contract doctrines by the use of tort law to work around them.").

[6] *Cf.* RESTATEMENT (THIRD) OF TORTS: LIABILITY FOR ECONOMIC HARM § 3 cmt. b (2020) (noting the "confusion that can result when a party brings suit on the same facts under contract and tort theories that are largely redundant in practical effect").

[7] Southwestern Bell Tel. Co. v. DeLanney, 809 S.W.2d 493, 494 (Tex. 1991).

[8] *See* RESTATEMENT (THIRD) OF TORTS: LIABILITY FOR ECONOMIC HARM § 3 & cmt. b (2020) (stating that "there is no liability in tort for economic loss caused by negligence in the performance or negotiation of a contract between the parties," and noting, as part of the rationale for the rule, that "the rule allows parties to make dependable allocations of financial risk without fear that tort law will be used to undo them later"); *id.* § 3 cmt. b ("[I]f plaintiff and defendant have a valid contract, monetary harm caused by the defendant's negligent performance of it is generally not actionable in tort. Nor does tort law provide a remedy for economic loss caused by negligent statements that parties make during efforts to form a contract. When a party's negligence in performing or negotiating a contract causes economic loss to the counterparty, remedies are determined by other bodies of law: principally the law of

Why do we allow the bargain to be circumvented, however, if some independent tort duty has been violated? Presumably it is for two reasons: (1) parties should not be understood to have allocated the risk of anything beyond negligent nonperformance of the contractual obligations; thus, many independent tort suits (e.g., intentional torts) do not undermine the parties' bargain; and (2) in general, the existence of the independent tort duty reflects the fact that society has deemed that conduct wrongful, and such conduct should be condemned irrespective of the existence of a contract covering the same transaction. (But see the later discussion of negligent misrepresentation and *DSA*.)

With respect to eliminating confusion and expense, the *Town of Alma* rule blocks a negligence claim and limits the plaintiff to a breach of contract action. This prevents duplication and allows the court and the litigants to simply address the breach of contract claim. If there is a tort duty independent of contractual obligations, the tort claim is arguably not duplicative and could be viewed as an appropriate additional claim.[9]

Under the court's rule, Alma's negligence claim failed. As mentioned, there is no general duty of care in the performance of a service that only causes economic loss (and, as discussed below, damage to the water service lines is viewed as economic loss). The only duty of care that supported Alma's claim stemmed from the contract itself. As the court observed: "The contract in the instant case expressly assigned a duty of care to AZCO in the installation of

---

contract, though sometimes also the law of restitution or relevant statutes."); *id.* § 3 cmt. c ("A contract precludes common-law tort claims for financial loss based on negligent conduct that the contract regulates."); *id.* § 3 (Reporter's Note) ("Courts also are reluctant to conclude that a contract allocated to the plaintiff the risk that the defendant was lying. They are more inclined to view fraud as an attack on the integrity of the bargaining process itself. Negligent misrepresentations are not comparable. They are honest mistakes. Allowing defendants to avoid liability for them, where the parties have so agreed, can make good commercial sense."); *cf.* Isler v. Texas Oil & Gas Corp., 749 F.2d 22, 24 (10th Cir. 1984) ("Further, it should not matter whether the breach of a bargained-for duty arises from inattention, a disagreement over the existence of the duty, a dispute over the nature of the duty, an inability to perform the duty, or a simple unwillingness to perform the duty. The parties by contract (or in the absence of an express provision, by implied rules evolved under contract analysis) have themselves defined the consequences of the breach. In the marketplace of contract, a breach is a breach is a breach—unless the parties choose to specify otherwise.").

[9] Keep in mind that a negligence claim is not precluded if the negligence causes the plaintiff personal injury or property damage (other than property damage to the subject of the contract itself, which, as discussed below, is considered economic harm). *See, e.g.*, RESTATEMENT (THIRD) OF TORTS: PHYSICAL AND EMOTIONAL HARM § 7 (2010) ("An actor ordinarily has a duty to exercise reasonable care when the actor's conduct creates a risk of physical harm."); *id.* § 4 ("'Physical harm' means the physical impairment of the human body ('bodily harm') or of real property or tangible personal property ('property damage'). Bodily harm includes physical injury, illness, disease, impairment of bodily function, and death.").

the water system [and] it was this contractual duty that AZCO allegedly breached." Thus, Alma could not establish the existence of a duty independent of any contractual obligations.

The water service lines were Alma's property, and leaks in the lines might be viewed as damage to that property. As a result, why isn't *Town of Alma* a property damage case that avoids the application of the economic loss rule? In other words, didn't Alma suffer more than only economic loss? As the court noted, the economic loss rule originated in the products liability context and evolved into a principle that "there was no cause of action in tort, under either negligence or strict liability, for damage caused when a product malfunctions and causes purely economic loss *through damage to the product itself*" (emphasis added). Stated differently, when the only injury is to the product itself, the harm is characterized as economic loss and not as property damage.

This same concept is sometimes articulated as "when the injury is only the economic loss to the subject of a contract itself, the action sounds in contract alone."[10] The subject of the contract in *Town of Alma* was the water distribution system, and the claimed injury was damage to the system itself (leaks). Under the economic loss rule, that injury is characterized as economic loss and not as property damage. Indeed, the *Town of Alma* court stated the following: "Moreover, the [Petitioners] are only seeking damages for the cost of repair and replacement of the water lines that were the subject of the contract. Damages for the cost of repair and replacement of property that were the subject of the contract constitute economic loss damages that must be supported by an independent duty of care to be recoverable in a negligence action." Despite the damage to the water service lines, therefore, *Town of Alma* is a pure economic loss dispute.

These points are reflected in comment b to § 2 of the Third Restatement:

> Defining economic loss is most challenging when property the plaintiff has bought causes damage to itself. This principle first emerged in earlier cases in which buyers of products sued the sellers when the products did not work. Courts held that a product's failure to operate was a matter best addressed by the law of warranty rather than tort, and the analysis was the same when the product failed because one component damaged another. Liability in tort was recognized only when a product damaged other property besides itself. The reasoning just stated has since been

---

10 Jim Walter Homes v. Reed, 711 S.W.2d 617, 618 (Tex. 1986).

> extended to cases that involve the sale of real property, which typically fall beyond the coverage of the law of products liability as a formal matter. Thus the buyer of a house who discovers that its rafters are rotting may have contractual remedies against the builder; and the claim should not become a matter of tort just because the cause of the rot is found to be a leak in the roof. Though the rot might then be construed as a kind of property damage caused by negligence in building the house, it is more apt to say the house was not properly constructed and disappointed the buyer's economic expectations. Liability in tort does not arise.

Some courts determine whether contractual parties will be permitted to assert tort claims against one another based upon a "nature of the injury" test. For example, in *Jim Walter Homes v. Reed*,[11] the Supreme Court of Texas observed:

> The acts of a party may breach duties in tort or contract alone or simultaneously in both. The nature of the injury most often determines which duty or duties are breached. When the injury is only the economic loss to the subject of a contract itself the action sounds in contract alone. The Reeds' injury was that the house they were promised and paid for was not the house they received. This can only be characterized as a breach of contract. . . .

Under this test, how would the dispute in *Town of Alma* have been resolved? The court noted that Alma was seeking damages only "for the cost of repair and replacement of the water lines that were the subject of the contract," and it stated that "[d]amages for the cost of repair and replacement of property that were the subject of the contract constitute economic loss damages." The nature of Alma's injury, therefore, was purely economic, and according to the *Jim Walter Homes* test, it "sounds in contract alone." Put differently, Alma's injury was that the water lines it was promised and paid for were not the water lines that it received.

As will be discussed below, the problem with a nature of the injury test is that it suggests that pure economic loss can never be the subject of a tort claim. Many business torts (e.g., fraud, negligent misrepresentation, intentional interference with existing and prospective contract, breach of fiduciary duty), however, are primarily designed to remedy economic loss. Consider a seller's contractual representation that a house is free of termites. At the time the representation is made, assume the seller knows that the

11 711 S.W.2d 617 (Tex. 1986).

statement is false. In this example, damages for breach of contract and fraud would presumably be the same—i.e., the diminution in the value of the house because of the termites, or the cost of repairing the termite damage and eradicating the problem. Once again, the house that the buyer was promised and paid for (no termites) was not the house that the buyer received (termites). Why should that mean, however, that the fraud action is precluded? In general, contractual parties are not understood to have allocated the risk of fraudulent conduct; thus, the parties' bargain is not undermined by allowing the fraud claim to proceed. Moreover, fraud is still intentional conduct that society views as wrongful, and the presence of a contract shouldn't change that conclusion. As the *Town of Alma* court observed:

> The phrase "economic loss rule" necessarily implies that the focus of the inquiry under its analysis is on the type of damages suffered by the aggrieved party. However, the relationship between the type of damages suffered and the availability of a tort action is inexact at best. Examining the type of damages suffered may assist in determining the source of the duty underlying the action (e.g., most actions for lost profits are based on breaches of contractual duties while most actions involving physical injuries to persons are based on common law duties of care). However, some torts are expressly designed to remedy pure economic loss (e.g., professional negligence, fraud, and breach of fiduciary duty). It is here that substantial confusion arises from the use of the term "economic loss rule."

In *Formosa Plastics Corp. v. Presidio Engineers & Contractors, Inc.*,[12] the Supreme Court of Texas confronted a dispute over whether a fraud claim could proceed between parties to a contract. The outcome of the dispute seemed to depend upon whether the court emphasized the source of the defendant's duty or the nature of the plaintiff's injury. In 1989, Formosa began an expansion project at its facility in Point Comfort, Texas. Formosa solicited bids for the construction of 300 concrete foundations, and it included a bid package containing certain representations about the job. Presidio won the contract by submitting the lowest bid ($600,000), but it incurred significant unanticipated costs based largely on alleged misrepresentations made by Formosa. After suing for fraud and breach of contract, the jury awarded Presidio $1.5 million in compensatory damages and $10 million in punitive damages. The

[12] 960 S.W.2d 41 (Tex. 1998).

trial judge suggested a remittitur reducing the tort damages to $700,000, which Presidio accepted.

On appeal, Formosa argued that Presidio's fraud claim was barred (and the punitive damages award that went along with it) because "Presidio's losses were purely economic losses related to performance and the subject matter of the contract." The Supreme Court of Texas reviewed its earlier precedents and highlighted the following passage from its opinion in *Southwestern Bell Telephone Co. v. DeLanney*:[13]

> If the defendant's conduct—such as negligently burning down a house—would give rise to liability independent of the fact that a contract exists between the parties, the plaintiff's claim may also sound in tort. Conversely, if the defendant's conduct—such as failing to publish an advertisement—would give rise to liability only because it breaches the parties' agreement, the plaintiff's claim ordinarily sounds only in contract.
>
> In determining whether the plaintiff may recover on a tort theory, it is also instructive to examine the nature of the plaintiff's loss. When the only loss or damage is to the subject matter of the contract, the plaintiff's action is ordinarily on the contract.

The *Formosa* court then noted that several appellate courts had considered the application of *DeLanney* to fraudulent inducement claims. Some of these courts argued that *DeLanney* compelled the conclusion that "tort damages are not recoverable for a fraudulent inducement claim unless the plaintiff suffers an injury that is distinct, separate, and independent from the economic losses recoverable under a breach of contract claim."[14] Other decisions, however, rejected the use of *DeLanney* to preclude the recovery of tort damages for fraudulent inducement actions.

The Supreme Court of Texas agreed with this latter approach and "reject[ed] the application of *DeLanney* to preclude tort damages in fraud cases." The court observed that "[o]ur prior decisions . . . clearly establish that tort damages are not precluded simply because a fraudulent representation causes only an economic loss," and it stated that it "has continued to recognize the propriety of fraud claims sounding in tort despite the fact that the aggrieved party's losses were only economic losses." As the *Formosa* court concluded:

---

13 809 S.W.2d 493 (Tex. 1991).

14 *Formosa*, 960 S.W.2d at 46 (citing cases).

> Accordingly, tort damages are recoverable for a fraudulent inducement claim irrespective of whether the fraudulent representations are later subsumed in a contract or whether the plaintiff only suffers an economic loss related to the subject matter of the contract. Allowing the recovery of fraud damages sounding in tort only when a plaintiff suffers an injury that is distinct from the economic losses recoverable under a breach of contract claim is inconsistent with this well-established law, and also ignores the fact that an independent legal duty, separate from the existence of the contract itself, precludes the use of fraud to induce a binding agreement.

The court also found that legally sufficient evidence supported the jury's fraud findings, as Formosa had fraudulently represented (in the bid package and in the contract) that Presidio would have control over the delivery of concrete.

Notice that the earlier *DeLanney* precedent examined both the source of the defendant's duty and the nature of the plaintiff's injury in attempting to ascertain whether the plaintiff may recover on a tort theory. Under an independent duty test, Presidio's fraud claim would have survived. The tort of fraud is well-entrenched and commonly arises in business or commercial settings. The potential for fraud liability exists independent of the fact that the parties have entered into a contract. On the facts of the case, Formosa made material and knowingly false representations, it intended to induce reliance by the contractors, and Presidio justifiably relied to its detriment on the representations. Such conduct gives rise to fraud liability independent of the fact that a contract later existed between the parties. As the *Formosa* court noted: "[I]t is well established that the legal duty not to fraudulently procure a contract is separate and independent from the duties established by the contract itself."

Under a nature of the injury test, however, Presidio's fraud claim would not have survived. Presidio did not suffer any personal injury or property damage. Presidio simply incurred economic losses when, due to Formosa's misrepresentations, the actual cost of the project exceeded the contract price.

How should the court's conclusion in *Formosa* be understood? Is the court stating that "duty" (focusing on the defendant's conduct) trumps "injury" (focusing on the nature of the plaintiff's loss)? Alternatively, can the conclusion be explained using a *Town of Alma*-like "protection of the bargain" rationale? First, one could understand the Supreme Court of Texas to be saying that the independent duty test trumps the nature of the injury test. That is, so long as there is a defendant's duty that exists independent of the contract, the nature of the injury is irrelevant, as the existence of the independent tort duty reflects the fact that society has deemed that conduct wrongful. Because a duty not to commit fraud exists independent of the parties' contractual relationship, the fact that Presidio suffered only economic damages is unimportant. This is essentially the approach of the *Town of Alma* court—focus on the source of the defendant's duty.

Second, with respect to a "protection of the bargain" rationale, the economic loss rule prevents a party from using a negligence claim to circumvent an allocation of risk that the parties contractually agreed upon. The parties presumably allocated risk, however, on the assumption that they were making representations honestly to one another. A very different risk assessment would likely occur if the parties had to assume the risk of fraud; indeed, the parties might be unwilling to enter into a contract at all. The risk of fraud, in other words, is not one that the parties should be held to have allocated in their contract. Thus, when Presidio sued for fraud, the claim should not be seen as an end-run around the parties' agreed allocation of risk. The court's conclusion, therefore, might be explained on the basis that allowing the fraud claim to proceed did not undermine the bargain struck by the parties.[15]

Third, the court's conclusion in *Formosa* might be explained even more simply as a straightforward application of § 3 of the Third Restatement. Section 3 bars tort claims between contracting parties for economic loss caused by *negligence*. Intentional torts fall outside of that scope[16]—presumably because parties to contracts are not held to have allocated the risk of intentional wrongdoing.

In some jurisdictions, a distinction is drawn between claims for "fraud in the inducement of a contract" and claims for "fraud in the performance of a contract." While claims for fraud in the inducement are not barred by the economic loss rule, claims for fraud in the performance are precluded by the rule. For example, in *Huron Tool*

---

15 *See, e.g.*, RESTATEMENT (THIRD) OF TORTS: LIABILITY FOR ECONOMIC HARM § 3 (2020) (Reporter's Note) ("Courts also are reluctant to conclude that a contract allocated to the plaintiff the risk that the defendant was lying. They are more inclined to view fraud as an attack on the integrity of the bargaining process itself."); *id.* § 9 cmt. a ("The economic-loss rule is meant to protect contractual allocations of risk against interference by the law of tort. Claims for fraud rarely cause such interference because parties to a contract do not usually treat the chance that they are lying to each other as a risk for their contract to allocate. They regard honesty as an assumed backdrop to their negotiations. . . . Liability in tort for fraud thus helps to protect the integrity of the contractual process and sometimes furnishes useful remedies that the law of contract does not as readily provide.").

16 *See, e.g.*, RESTATEMENT (THIRD) OF TORTS: LIABILITY FOR ECONOMIC HARM § 9 cmt. a (2020) ("[T]he economic-loss rule generally forecloses tort liability *for negligence* in the negotiation or performance of a contract, but it does not impair the claims of fraud discussed in this Chapter." (emphasis added)).

*and Engineering Co. v. Precision Consulting Services, Inc.*,[17] the court stated the following:

> ... [W]e decline to adopt defendants' position that the economic loss doctrine precludes *any* fraud claim. Fraud in the inducement presents a special situation where parties to a contract appear to negotiate freely—which normally would constitute grounds for invoking the economic loss doctrine—but where in fact the ability of one party to negotiate fair terms and make an informed decision is undermined by the other party's fraudulent behavior. In contrast, where the only misrepresentation by the dishonest party concerns the quality or character of the goods sold, the other party is still free to negotiate warranty and other terms to account for possible defects in the goods.
>
> The distinction between fraud in the inducement and other kinds of fraud is the same as the distinction drawn by a New Jersey federal district court between fraud extraneous to the contract and fraud interwoven with the breach of contract. *Public Service Enterprise Group, Inc. v. Philadelphia Elec. Co.*, 722 F.Supp. 184, 201 (D.N.J., 1989). With respect to the latter kind of fraud, the misrepresentations relate to the breaching party's performance of the contract and do not give rise to an independent cause of action in tort[:]
>
>> Such fraud is not extraneous to the contractual dispute among the parties, but is instead but another thread in the fabric of [the] plaintiffs' contract claim.... [It] is undergirded by factual allegations identical to those supporting their breach of contract counts.... This fraud did not induce the plaintiffs to enter into the original agreement nor did it induce them to enter into additional undertakings. It did not cause harm to the plaintiffs distinct from those caused by the breach of contract.... [*Id.*]

This excerpt from *Huron Tool* purportedly explains the distinction between claims for fraud in the inducement and fraud in the performance. The idea seems to be that the parties can always contract for the consequences of nonperformance. If nonperformance occurs as a result of the defendant's fraud, negligence, or good-faith "innocent" efforts, it is still nonperformance that the parties have bargained over and whose risks the parties have allocated. A fraud claim related to the contract's performance, therefore, should be

---

[17] 532 N.W.2d 541 (Mich. Ct. App. 1995).

barred as an end-run around the parties' contractual bargain and risk allocation.

By contrast, fraud in the inducement is fraud that causes the plaintiff to enter into the contract in the first place. The harm (entering into a contractual relationship) is not one that the contract itself addresses, as the contract addresses the risks of nonperformance or breach—not the risk that the contractual relationship itself is ill-advised. A fraud in the inducement claim, therefore, is not an end-run around the parties' contractual bargain and risk allocation because that bargain/allocation does not address the risk that the contractual relationship should never have occurred.

This purported distinction, however, can be questioned. First, is it really fair to say that parties bargain over the risk of *fraudulent* nonperformance? As discussed earlier, if a plaintiff had to assume that representations about the quality or character of the goods or services were knowingly false, isn't it more likely that the plaintiff would choose not to enter into the contract in the first place? To say that parties bargain and knowingly allocate the risks of fraudulent nonperformance assumes that parties contemplating the possibility of fraud would choose to mitigate that risk within the contract rather than by avoiding the contract all together. It seems more likely that parties do not use contract to mitigate the risk of fraud; instead, they rely on tort law to mitigate the risk of fraud. If this is true, barring a fraudulent performance of contract claim under the economic loss rule would be contrary to the parties' expectations.[18]

---

18 *See, e.g.*, Stoughton Trailers, Inc. v. Henkel Corp., 965 F. Supp. 1227, 1236 (W.D. Wis. 1997) ("Although it makes sense to allow parties to allocate the risk of mistakes or accidents that lead to economic losses, it does not make sense to extend the doctrine to intentional acts taken by one party to subvert the purposes of a contract. Although theoretically parties could include contractual provisions discussing the allocation of responsibility when one party intentionally lies or misleads the other, it would not be conducive to amicable commercial relations to require parties to include such clauses in contracts. Expressing such a basic lack of trust in the other party would be likely to sour a deal from the start. A party to a contract cannot rationally calculate the possibility that the other party will deliberately misrepresent terms critical to that contract. Public policy is better served by leaving the possibility of an intentional tort suit hanging over the head of a party considering outright fraud."); Budgetel Inns, Inc. v. Micros Systems, Inc., 8 F. Supp. 2d 1137, 1148 (E.D. Wis. 1998) ("The absence of a tort remedy—and thus the absence of possible punitive damages—for the duped party would reward a liar's deceit, yet 'no interest of society is served by promoting the flow of information not genuinely believed by its maker to be true.' "); *cf. id.* ("[C]ontract negotiations that begin with the assumption that the other party is lying will hardly encourage free and open bargaining. The specific duty encompassed by fraud in the inducement is the duty of the parties entering into the contract to speak honestly regarding negotiated terms. How can parties freely allocate risk if they cannot rely on the opposite party to speak truthfully during negotiations regarding the subject matter of the contract—if they cannot tell what is a lie and what is not?"); 3 DAN B. DOBBS ET AL., THE LAW OF TORTS § 686, at 718 (2d ed. 2013) ("[A]ccurate and reliable information about material facts is essential if commercial transactions are to go forward. If information supplied by the seller cannot be relied

Second, why should the law allow a defendant to commit fraud in any context? If a defendant makes knowingly false representations (e.g., lying about the mileage on a car when the odometer has been rolled back, or lying about whether a good or service will be delivered by a particular date), why should that conduct be immunized from a fraud claim simply because those representations are included in a contract? While it is true that the damages may be redundant with breach of contract damages, the conduct is the same sort of objectionable conduct that punitive damages should be available for.[19] Indeed, despite the observation in the *Huron Tool* excerpt, the factual allegations of a fraud action are not identical to the factual allegations of a breach of contract action. Fraud requires scienter, the defendant's intent to induce the plaintiff's reliance, and the plaintiff's justifiable reliance. Breach of contract does not require any of these elements. Moreover, fraud often has heightened pleading and proof standards, while breach of contract does not.

Third, the economic loss rule has historically focused on barring negligence or strict liability claims for pure economic loss. Intentional torts have never been part of the traditional coverage of the rule.[20] As mentioned, even the Third Restatement's articulation of the economic loss rule bars tort claims only for economic loss caused by negligence.

Finally, distinguishing between fraud in the inducement and fraud in the performance can be difficult.[21] The problem lies in what

---

upon, expensive investigations or more intensive and costly contractual negotiations will be required. The prospect of such costs may eliminate some commercial transactions, while it will drive up the costs of others.").

[19] *Cf.* Vincent R. Johnson, *The Boundary-Line Function of the Economic Loss Rule*, 66 WASH. & LEE L. REV. 523, 529 (2009) ("In cases where economic losses are deliberately and tortiously inflicted there is little reason to save the defendant from liability, whether under the economic loss rule or otherwise.").

[20] *See, e.g.*, Ins. Co. of N. Am. v. Am. Aviation, Inc., 891 So. 2d 532, 543 n.3 (Fla. 2004) ("Intentional tort claims such as fraud, conversion, intentional interference, civil theft, abuse of process, and other torts requiring proof of intent generally remain viable either in the products liability context or if the parties are in privity of contract" because "a rule barring recovery for economic loss 'is not an escape hatch from intentional commercial torts' "); *see also* 3 DAN B. DOBBS ET AL., THE LAW OF TORTS § 687, at 723 (2d ed. 2013) ("Scienter fraud is an economic tort primarily invoked in bargaining transactions, and has been recognized for centuries as a ground for recovery. To the extent that the economic loss rule forecloses a tort claim for scienter fraud, it seems to radically change the law as it has been traditionally applied for a very long time.").

[21] *Cf.* Paul J. Schwiep, *Fraudulent Inducement Claims Should Always Be Immune from Economic Loss Rule Attack*, 75 FLA. B.J. 22, 23 (Apr. 2001) (noting that courts have had a difficult time in consistently defining "fraud interwoven with the contract" and "fraud extraneous to the contract"); Christopher J. Faricelli, Note, *Wading into the "Morass": An Inquiry into the Application of New Jersey's Economic Loss Rule to Fraud Claims*, 35 RUTGERS L.J. 717, 746 (2004) (noting that courts have "struggled in maintaining" the distinction between fraud in the inducement and fraud

courts mean by the terms. Does fraud in the inducement simply mean any pre-contract representation that induces a plaintiff to enter into a contract? If so, the claim should be viable even if the representation is repeated in the contract itself—so long as the representation induced the plaintiff to enter into the contract in the first place. (Note that in *Formosa*, the misrepresentations were repeated in the bid package and in the contract.)

Under this definition, however, one might argue that a claim for fraudulent inducement is always available. Indeed, even if there are no pre-contract negotiations between the parties, can't one say that every knowingly false representation stated in a contract induces a party to enter into the contract—at least in the sense that the party reads (or is presumed to have read) the contract before signing, decides that it is comfortable with the terms, and then executes the agreement? In other words, doesn't the mere presence of a material misrepresentation in a contract induce a person to enter into the contract? If so, it would appear that a claim for fraudulent inducement could always be brought if the contractual representation is knowingly false and the other elements of fraud are met.

As an illustration, the *Huron Tool* excerpt suggests that a fraudulent performance claim is when a "misrepresentation[ ] relate[s] to the breaching party's performance of the contract." Assume that a contract is for the delivery of ball bearings. It specifically states that time is of the essence and that the defendant will deliver 5,000 ball bearings to the plaintiff on a certain date. The defendant, when signing the contract, knows that he will not be delivering 5,000 ball bearings on that date. That is clearly fraud.[22] Is it a barred claim because the misrepresentation relates to the defendant's performance of the contract (the defendant represented that he would deliver on the designated date in the contract, and that representation is a lie)? Or is it a fraudulent inducement claim because the plaintiff read that representation before signing and was only willing to execute the contract because of that representation?

Perhaps the label of "fraud in the performance" or "fraud interwoven with the breach of contract" is just shorthand for when a court concludes that the parties' contract addresses the risk of the representation being false. This characterization assumes, however, that contracts allocate the risks of *fraudulently* false

in the performance, and stating that "the practical application of the rule has been unclear at times").

22 *See* RESTATEMENT (SECOND) OF TORTS § 530 (1977); RESTATEMENT (THIRD) OF TORTS: LIABILITY FOR ECONOMIC HARM § 15 (2020); Chapter 2(A)(5)(c) (discussing fraudulent misrepresentations of intention).

representations—a dubious assumption (as previously discussed). Moreover, wouldn't every misrepresentation that is repeated in the terms of a contract be immune from a fraud suit (because a court would conclude that the contract addresses the risk of any of its representations being false)? If so, defendants would seemingly have a strange incentive to repeat their misrepresentations twice—once in pre-contract negotiations, and a second time in the contract itself.[23]

In the Reporter's Note to § 9, the Third Restatement rejects the distinction between fraud in the inducement and fraud in the performance on the ground that the distinction is not clear:

> . . . . The distinction between fraud that is "tangential" to a contract and fraud that is "intertwined" with it is too hard to draw in a satisfactory way. . . .
>
> . . . . "Intertwined" and "tangential" are metaphors, and call for impressionistic judgments that will inevitably produce a loss of clarity. The goals behind these doctrines are understandable; it should not be too easy to turn a contract claim into a tort by raising a cry of fraud. In the view of this Restatement, however, that goal is better advanced by using a high standard of proof on the point that most often separates fraud from breach of contract—scienter—and dismissing cases that do not satisfy it. If the defendant did defraud the plaintiff, even within a contractual relationship, allowing the tort claim is more sensible and manageable than asking whether the tort and contract claims are conceptually extricable or inextricable.

In contrast to *Formosa*, consider the decision of *D.S.A., Inc. v. Hillsboro Independent School District*,[24] also from the Supreme Court of Texas. The Hillsboro Independent School District ("HISD") wanted a new elementary school. DSA, a construction management firm, was hired to oversee construction of the school. Upon completion, the school suffered from severe defects, including a leaky roof and poor drainage. After HISD spent an additional $220,244.33 to repair the defects, it sued DSA for breach of contract, negligent

[23] *Cf.* Allen v. Stephan Co., 784 So. 2d 456, 458–59 (Fla. Dist. Ct. App. 2000) ("More importantly, '[t]he notion that a knowing fraud perpetrated to induce someone to enter a contract can be extinguished by the simple expedience of including the fraudulent representation in the contract makes no sense.' The inclusion of the warranty in the contract that SRP's finances were accurately represented does not eviscerate the fraud."); Formosa Plastics Corp. v. Presidio Engineers & Contractors, Inc., 960 S.W.2d 41, 47 (Tex. 1998) ("Accordingly, tort damages are recoverable for a fraudulent inducement claim irrespective of whether the fraudulent representations are later subsumed in a contract or whether the plaintiff only suffers an economic loss related to the subject matter of the contract.").

[24] 973 S.W.2d 662 (Tex. 1998).

misrepresentation, grossly negligent misrepresentation, and violations of the Texas Deceptive Trade Practices Act ("DTPA").

The jury found for HISD on its claims and awarded $220,661 in actual damages and $170,000 in exemplary damages (plus attorney's fees). On appeal, the DTPA claim was dismissed as barred by limitations, but the court of appeals also held "that during pre-contractual negotiations, DSA negligently misrepresented the functions it would perform and that it was grossly negligent in doing so." The court reduced actual damages by $416.67 but otherwise affirmed based on HISD's grossly negligent misrepresentation claim.

DSA appealed to the Supreme Court of Texas, which reversed the tort finding. The court concluded that the negligent misrepresentation claim failed for "lack of any independent injury," which the court seemed to define as out-of-pocket damages under § 552B of the Second Restatement. It noted that "[t]he *Formosa* opinion's rejection of the independent injury requirement in fraudulent inducement claims does not extend to claims for negligent misrepresentation or negligent inducement." The court further noted that "HISD did not meet its burden of proving the independent injury required under section 552 of the Restatement," as HISD asked only for benefit-of-the-bargain damages.

The *DSA* court also rejected the award of exemplary damages under a theory of gross negligence, "whether evaluated as gross negligence in the breach of contract or gross negligence in the inducement of contract." Because an intentional breach of contract does not result in exemplary damages, the court stated that a grossly negligent breach of contract would also not result in exemplary damages. Further, the court refused to recognize a grossly negligent misrepresentation claim: "Neither HISD nor the court of appeals cites any Texas case recognizing a claim for gross negligence in the inducement of contract. Given the availability of a cause of action for fraudulent inducement, we fail to perceive any rationale for acknowledging a claim for grossly negligent inducement." Finally, although a party may recover for negligent misrepresentation involving physical harm, there was no evidence that "any children were *actually* harmed or that any of the other hypothetical dangers the court of appeals cited actually materialized."

The court did find legally sufficient evidence that DSA neglected its contractual obligation to "endeavor to protect Owner against defects and deficiencies in the work." Thus, the court reversed the judgment of the court of appeals and remanded to the trial court to recalculate damages on HISD's breach of contract claim.

Does the fact pattern in *DSA* fall within the scope of the economic loss rule? In other words, given that HISD suffered property damage (defects to its school), doesn't the dispute fall outside of the pure economic loss focus of the rule? As previously discussed, the products liability origins of the economic loss rule evolved into the concept that damage to property that is the subject of the contract itself is characterized as economic loss. The subject of the contract between DSA and HISD was the school, and the claimed injury was damage to the school itself (construction defects). Thus, the injury would be characterized as economic loss and not as property damage.

While this outcome is fairly clear in cases where the plaintiff is buying property from the defendant and the purchased property is damaged, is it also true where the plaintiff is simply purchasing a service? For example, assume that a plaintiff hires an air conditioning ("AC") repair company to perform a system check on the plaintiff's existing AC equipment. In the course of servicing the AC unit, the defendant technician negligently damages the unit and causes thousands of dollars in damages. Would the plaintiff be permitted to sue the defendant for negligence, or would the economic loss rule limit the plaintiff to a breach of contract action? On the one hand, the plaintiff has only suffered damage to property that is the subject of the contract itself (the AC equipment), which suggests that the damage should be considered pure economic loss. But that result usually follows where the plaintiff has purchased the AC equipment from the defendant, as we assume that the parties' contract would allocate the risks of defects in the purchased property itself. Here, however, the plaintiff is purchasing the technician's services and not property. It does not seem as likely that the parties' services contract would have covered the risk that the service would damage the underlying property, but this is presumably the sort of analysis that a court should engage in.[25] Thus, in a dispute over purchased services, damage to the property that forms the subject of the contract may be characterized as actual property damage in some circumstances, which would remove the dispute from the economic loss rule all together.

Should *DSA* be viewed more as a dispute where HISD was purchasing property (a school), or as a dispute where HISD was purchasing a service (supervision of the construction of a school)? (Note that the case describes DSA as a "construction management firm" who "oversaw" the school construction project.) It may not make

---

[25] *See, e.g.*, RESTATEMENT (THIRD) OF TORTS: LIABILITY FOR ECONOMIC HARM § 3 cmt. c (2020) ("Close cases can arise when an act of negligence occurs at the fringe of a contract's coverage. The important question then is whether allowing the tort claim creates a risk of interference with an allocation of risk made by the parties.").

a difference, as it seems likely that a contract with a construction management firm would allocate the risks of defects in the constructed property. Thus, even if we view *DSA* as a services case, a court may very well treat it like a property case and conclude that damage to the constructed property itself is economic loss that falls within the scope of the rule.

In *Formosa*, there was an independent legal duty not to commit fraud, and the plaintiff only sought economic losses related to the contract. The fraud claim was permitted. In *DSA*, there was an independent legal duty not to make negligent misrepresentations, and the plaintiff only sought economic losses related to the contract. The negligent misrepresentation claim was not permitted. In this sense, the result in *DSA* seems inconsistent with the result in *Formosa*. Stated differently, to the extent that *Formosa* suggested that the "duty" focus on the defendant's conduct trumps the "injury" focus on the nature of the plaintiff's loss, that suggestion was apparently limited to fraud claims. As mentioned, the *DSA* court observed that "[t]he *Formosa* opinion's rejection of the independent injury requirement in fraudulent inducement claims does not extend to claims for negligent misrepresentation or negligent inducement."

Is the result in *DSA* consistent with *Town of Alma*? Under the *Town of Alma* independent duty test, negligent misrepresentation is an independent duty of care under tort law. The *Town of Alma* court even listed a negligent misrepresentation case as an example of an "independent duty of care that supports a tort action even when parties have entered into a contractual relationship." Under the *Town of Alma* test, therefore, the economic loss rule would not bar a negligent misrepresentation claim.[26] To the extent that *DSA* barred a negligent misrepresentation claim on economic loss rule grounds, the results in the two cases are inconsistent.

On the other hand, the principle underlying the test in *Town of Alma* is that the contractual bargain of the parties should be respected. Given the close relationship between breach of contract and negligent misrepresentation (see below), a plaintiff can often bring a negligent misrepresentation action when the plaintiff is dissatisfied with the warranties and other risk allocations that were bargained for in the contract. (Indeed, Alma and AZCO negotiated a contract that addressed the risk of the work failing to meet the requirements of the contract. A negligent misrepresentation claim would have allowed Alma to circumvent the contract and evade the one-year warranty provision.) So long as one assumes that parties

---

[26] *But see* Bermel v. BlueRadios, Inc., 440 P.3d 1150, 1155 (Colo. 2019) ("Notably, however, since adopting the economic loss rule, we have applied it only to bar common law tort claims of negligence *or negligent misrepresentation*." (emphasis added)).

contractually allocate the risk of a breach (including a *negligent* breach), this seems to be the precise end-run around the parties' bargain that the economic loss rule is designed to prevent. To the extent that *DSA* barred a negligent misrepresentation claim on economic loss rule grounds, *DSA* is consistent with the "protect the bargain" principle emphasized in *Town of Alma*. Note, therefore, that the independent duty test—a test that many jurisdictions have adopted—is overinclusive to the extent that it permits a negligent misrepresentation claim to be maintained, even when a contract between the parties has addressed the risk of false (including negligently false) representations.[27]

The *DSA* court referred to "[t]he *Formosa* opinion's rejection of the independent injury requirement in fraudulent inducement claims." What was the "independent injury requirement" in *Formosa*? Is it the same requirement in *DSA*? The independent injury requirement in *Formosa* is presumably a shorthand reference for the requirement in earlier precedents for the plaintiff to suffer some personal injury or property damage (other than to the subject of the contract itself) before a tort claim could be maintained. Indeed, the *Formosa* court quoted from earlier precedents in observing that (a) "[w]hen the injury is only the economic loss to the subject of a contract itself, the action sounds in contract alone"; (b) plaintiffs did not "prove a distinct tortious injury"; and (c) "[w]here the only loss or damage is to the subject matter of the contract, the plaintiff's action is ordinarily on the contract." The *Formosa* court itself made clear in several places that what it was rejecting—and what the *DSA* court must have meant when it mentioned *Formosa*'s "rejection of the independent injury requirement"—is the necessity for the plaintiff to suffer some personal injury or property damage (i.e., something more than pure economic loss) before a fraud claim could be maintained.

In *DSA*, however, the independent injury requirement seems to have morphed into something else. The court referred to the "independent injury requirement of section 552B of the Restatement (Second) of Torts," which is the Restatement section providing for out-of-pocket damages (but not benefit-of-the-bargain damages) for negligent misrepresentation. Of course, *Formosa* never mentioned

---

[27] *See* RESTATEMENT (THIRD) OF TORTS: LIABILITY FOR ECONOMIC HARM § 3 (2020) (Reporter's Note) ("Some courts have suggested that liability in tort exists despite a contract between the parties when a defendant has breached an 'independent duty'—in other words, a duty that exists even without the contract, as distinct from those duties that exist solely because of it. That way of speaking is imprecise because it does not capture the preemptive effect of the economic loss rule. Parties have independent duties—duties that exist in the absence of a contract—not to make negligent misrepresentations or provide negligent services in the circumstances covered by §§ 5 and 6. But, as explained in Comment *h*, those duties are displaced once they become the subject of a contract between the parties.").

§ 552B; as mentioned, *Formosa* and earlier precedents all similarly characterized the independent injury requirement as a requirement for the plaintiff to suffer some personal injury or property damage, as opposed to suffering only economic losses. Thus, the *DSA* court's revisionist description of the independent injury requirement is, to say the least, perplexing.

Perhaps what the *DSA* court meant (but very inartfully stated) is that HISD simply asked for the wrong remedy. HISD apparently asked for benefit-of-the-bargain damages, which are not recoverable in a negligent misrepresentation claim.[28] Thus, the jury's award of benefit-of-the-bargain damages could only be upheld as breach of contract damages. Under this interpretation, *DSA* is simply a remedies case where the plaintiff asked for a remedy that was unavailable in a negligent misrepresentation action. To accept this interpretation, however, one would have to assume that when the *DSA* court used the term "independent injury requirement," it did *not* intend to refer to the requirement that the *Formosa* court rejected (even though it said just the opposite by directly referencing "[t]he *Formosa* opinion's rejection of the independent injury requirement in fraudulent inducement claims"). Instead, the *DSA* court just meant to refer to the out-of-pocket damages limitation in § 552B.

If one plays this interpretation out a little further, it suggests that the *DSA* court would have upheld HISD's negligent misrepresentation action if HISD had simply asked for the correct out-of-pocket measure of damages. After all, a jury award of out-of-pocket damages would meet the "independent injury requirement of section 552B" that the court referenced. If that is the result, then *DSA* is more consistent with *Formosa* than it first appears. A negligent misrepresentation action *seeking the correct remedy* can be maintained between contracting parties, even if it only seeks a recovery for economic losses, presumably because an independent legal duty exists not to make negligent misrepresentations.

To be clear, however, it is likely that most lawyers do not read *DSA* in this manner. Most attorneys presumably view *DSA* as standing for the proposition that a negligent misrepresentation claim for economic loss cannot be maintained between contractual parties,

---

[28] *See* RESTATEMENT (SECOND) OF TORTS § 552B(2) (1977); *see also* RESTATEMENT (THIRD) OF TORTS: LIABILITY FOR ECONOMIC HARM § 5 cmt. 1 (2020) ("Damages under this Section [negligent misrepresentation] aim to restore the plaintiff to the financial position that the plaintiff would have occupied if the defendant had spoken carefully. This is often known as an 'out of pocket' measure of recovery. Damages do not attempt to restore a plaintiff to the position that would have resulted if the false statements the defendant made had in fact been true. That would amount to an expectation or 'loss of bargain' measure of recovery of the kind familiar from contract law and available in some cases of fraud."); Chapter 2(B)(2) (discussing damages for negligent misrepresentation).

even if the plaintiff only seeks out-of-pocket damages, because the Supreme Court of Texas has not rejected the independent injury requirement for negligent misrepresentation (as it has for fraud). Thus, most attorneys likely believe that *DSA* holds that a negligent misrepresentation claim cannot be maintained between contractual parties unless the plaintiff has suffered some personal injury or property damage. Under this interpretation, however, one has to ignore the court's references to the "independent injury requirement of section 552B" and assume instead that the court was using the independent injury requirement in the same way that *Formosa* and earlier precedents used it—i.e., as a requirement for the plaintiff to suffer some personal injury or property damage (other than to the subject of the contract itself) before a tort claim can be maintained.

As part of the rationale for its decision, the *DSA* court noted that "[r]epudiating the independent injury requirement for negligent misrepresentation claims would potentially convert every contract interpretation dispute into a negligent misrepresentation claim." What did the court mean by this statement, and why is there any danger of contract interpretation disputes becoming negligent misrepresentation claims? Breach of contract does not require fault; any misrepresentation, whether innocent or not, can result in breach of contract. Negligent misrepresentation does require fault—i.e., the plaintiff must establish a failure to exercise reasonable care in obtaining or communicating the information. In theory, therefore, a contract interpretation dispute does not necessarily give rise to a negligent misrepresentation claim.

In practice, however, it does not take much to get from breach of contract to negligent misrepresentation. If a contractual representation was not complied with, a good plaintiff's lawyer can almost always find some way to paint the plaintiff's effort to comply as lacking, whether from inattention, incompleteness, or some other reason. In other words, a court might believe that, in practice, there is not enough "distance" between a no-fault breach of contract claim and a negligent misrepresentation claim to dispel the concern that every contract interpretation dispute may become a negligent misrepresentation claim. Fraud is different, as the requirement of scienter is a high standard of fault. There is little concern that every contract interpretation dispute will become a fraud claim because there is sufficient "distance" between a no-fault breach of contract claim and a scienter-based fraud claim.

What is the problem with the potential for every contract interpretation dispute to become a negligent misrepresentation claim? First, the parties' contractual bargain can be evaded. As mentioned, a party might bring a negligent misrepresentation action whenever there is dissatisfaction with the warranties and other risk allocations that were bargained for in the contract. Second, the possibility of bringing a tort claim in every breach of contract dispute may chill efficient breach. Efficient breach can only work if the breaching party can calculate the damages. The possibility of being subject to mental anguish and punitive damages in a tort claim injects a wildcard factor that makes the damages difficult (if not impossible) to calculate in advance. Admittedly, there is little potential for mental anguish and punitive damages in a pure negligent misrepresentation action, but in claims involving a gross negligence finding, there may be some risk.

Why would repudiating the independent injury requirement potentially convert every contract interpretation dispute into a negligent misrepresentation claim? If the independent injury requirement is understood to be a requirement for the plaintiff to suffer some personal injury or property damage (other than to the subject of the contract itself) before a tort claim can be maintained, the court seems to be using the requirement to prohibit all negligent misrepresentation claims between contracting parties that seek recovery for pure economic loss. If that requirement is repudiated, negligent misrepresentation claims between contracting parties that seek recovery for pure economic loss would be permitted, as there is an independent legal duty not to make negligent misrepresentations. Thus, any contract interpretation dispute would have the potential to create a negligent misrepresentation claim as well, which would lead to the above-mentioned problems.

If the independent injury requirement is understood to refer to § 552B's limitation to out-of-pocket damages, repudiating that requirement would result in breach of contract and negligent misrepresentation actions both providing benefit-of-the-bargain damages. Why would that result in any contract interpretation dispute having the potential to become a negligent misrepresentation claim? Presumably because the availability of the same remedy would incentivize a party to bring a negligent misrepresentation action whenever the party is dissatisfied with the contractual bargain. After all, if the party can get the same remedy while avoiding contractual limitations, the party is likely to use tort law to evade the bargain. Why would it make sense, however, to allow a negligent misrepresentation action seeking out-of-pocket damages? The ability to recover out-of-pocket losses for nonperformance may still be better than the parties' bargained-for contractual remedies for nonperformance. If the goal is to protect that bargain, allowing any negligent misrepresentation claim—whether it seeks benefit-of-the-bargain or out-of-pocket damages—seems counterproductive.

How would the disputes in *Town of Alma*, *Formosa*, and *DSA* have been resolved under the Third Restatement? Section 3 of the Third Restatement is referred to (in the section title) as the "Economic Loss Rule." The section states that "[e]xcept as provided elsewhere in this Restatement, there is no liability in tort for economic loss caused by negligence in the performance or negotiation of a contract between the parties." Several points about this section are worth highlighting:

- The rule, according to comment a, is limited to parties who have contracts.

- The purposes of the rule are described in comment b as follows:

> When a dispute arises, the rule protects the bargain the parties have made against disruption by a tort suit. Seen from an earlier point in the life of a transaction, the rule allows parties to make dependable allocations of financial risk without fear that tort law will be used to undo them later. Viewed in the long run, the rule prevents the erosion of contract doctrines by the use of tort law to work around them. The rule also reduces the confusion that can result when a party brings suit on the same facts under contract and tort theories that are largely redundant in practical effect.

- As comment c explains, the rule precludes tort claims for financial loss based on negligent conduct that the contract regulates. It does not foreclose tort claims based on conduct outside of the contract's scope. The question is whether allowing a tort claim creates a risk of interference with an allocation of risk made by the parties.

- The section begins with "[e]xcept as provided elsewhere in this Restatement," so there are exceptions to the rule. As comment g states: "Some well-established exceptions to the rule of this Section are addressed in subsequent parts of this Restatement. The most prominent is the tort liability of professionals to their clients despite (and alongside) any contract between them. See § 4. Fiduciaries likewise have duties recognized in tort notwithstanding the terms of contracts to which they may be subject. See § 16."[29]

Section 3 would have barred the negligence claim in *Town of Alma*. Alma suffered economic loss to the extent that it did not incur any personal injury or property damage other than to the subject of the contract itself (the water distribution system). AZCO and Alma had a contract, and the negligence complained of was regulated by

---

[29] *See also* RESTATEMENT (THIRD) OF TORTS: LIABILITY FOR ECONOMIC HARM § 16 cmt. c (2020) ("In some cases, of course, the same conduct may be both a breach of fiduciary duty and a breach of contract. See Illustration 5.").

the contract. Thus, any claim of negligence in the "performance or negotiation" of the contract is precluded. Illustration 1 to § 3 is based on *Town of Alma,* and the illustration concludes: "Firm is not liable in tort to Town. Town's rights are determined by the contract and the law that governs it."

Section 3 would not have barred the fraud claim in *Formosa.* The section only bars liability in tort for economic loss caused by negligence. Fraud, of course, is an intentional tort.

Section 3 would have barred the negligent misrepresentation claim asserted in *DSA.* HISD suffered economic loss to the extent that it did not incur any personal injury or property damage other than to the subject of the contract itself (the elementary school). The section precludes negligence-based liability in the "performance or negotiation" of a contract between the parties. HISD and DSA had a contract, and the purported misrepresentations were made in pre-contractual negotiations. As comment d to § 3 observes:

> Some courts have used Restatement Second, Torts § 552—the predecessor to § 5 of this Chapter—to hold sellers liable for negligent misrepresentations that cause buyers to enter into contracts with them. The rule of this Section eliminates the tort claim in that circumstance. A seller's negligent misrepresentations are addressed sufficiently by the law of contract and restitution. Such misrepresentations may give the buyer a claim for breach of warranty, for rescission and incidental damages, or for breach of contract accompanied by a claim of estoppel. In other cases, the language of the contract and the parol-evidence rule may foreclose claims based on statements made before a contract was signed. In either event, adding a tort claim to the analysis interferes with the operation of those contract doctrines and creates confusion without offsetting gains. Liability under § 5 of this Chapter is thus limited to negligent misrepresentations that were not made in the performance or negotiation of a contract.[30]

---

[30] *See also id.* § 3 cmt. h ("This Section precludes liability under §§ 5 and 6 [the sections governing negligent misrepresentation and negligent performance of services] when the defendant's negligent conduct occurs in the performance of a contract with the plaintiff. Sections 5 and 6 recognize liability when a defendant acts to provide a basis for reliance by the plaintiff, and the plaintiff in turn relies. The purpose of such liability is usually to provide a substitute for a contract where the parties have not made one and the appropriate allocation of risk between them is clear. Once parties do make a contract, it displaces the obligations of §§ 5 and 6; the contract alone determines the parties' responsibility for economic loss caused by negligence in performing it."); *id.* § 5(5) ("This Section [negligent misrepresentation] does not recognize liability for negligent misrepresentations made in the course of negotiating or performing a contract between the parties."); *id.* § 6(4) (substantially the same).

# Chapter 6

# DECEPTIVE MARKETING

## A. INTRODUCTION

Previous chapters have examined "business torts." In this and subsequent chapters, the field of unfair competition will be examined. Under early common law, unfair competition was a limited concept. The typical case involved one party attempting to sell its goods while claiming the goods were that of another (a practice known as "palming off"). The term has expanded and evolved throughout the twentieth century to now encompass a wide variety of torts. Indeed, in recognition of this fact, the American Law Institute drafted the Restatement (Third) of Unfair Competition, which was published in 1995. This was done by recognizing that unfair competition had become a specialty all of its own.

Today, the term "unfair competition" encompasses a large number of causes of action, including deceptive marketing, intentional interference with contract, fraud, trademark infringement, and misappropriation of trade secrets. Some of these concepts have already been addressed in previous chapters as business torts, and indeed, there is an inevitable amount of overlap between the unfair competition materials and the economic torts materials. This overlap demonstrates how interconnected the subjects are.

The Restatement (Third) of Unfair Competition expressly recognizes three areas for which relief may be sought: deceptive marketing, trademark infringement, and trade secret misappropriation. Commercial disparagement is not listed, but it is nevertheless included here in the unfair competition materials (although it could easily be included in the business torts portion as well). Once again, this demonstrates how unfair competition and business torts topics are related, as they both focus on what actions society will permit in a business context.

This chapter begins with a concept already introduced in the tortious interference with economic relations materials—where do we draw the line between unfair competition and the right to compete? Consider § 1 of the Restatement (Third) of Unfair Competition, which begins with a presumption that pure acts of competition are not actionable unless they fall into a category listed:

**§ 1. General Principles**

One who causes harm to the commercial relations of another by engaging in a business or trade is not subject to liability to the other for such harm unless:

(a) the harm results from acts or practices of the actor actionable by the other under the rules of this Restatement relating to:

(1) deceptive marketing, as specified in Chapter Two;

(2) infringement of trademarks and other indicia of identification, as specified in Chapter Three;

(3) appropriation of intangible trade values including trade secrets and the right of publicity, as specified in Chapter Four;

or from other acts or practices of the actor determined to be actionable as an unfair method of competition, taking into account the nature of the conduct and its likely effect on both the person seeking relief and the public; or

(b) the acts or practices of the actor are actionable by the other under federal or state statutes, international agreements, or general principles of common law apart from those considered in this Restatement.

From the phrasing and comments in this section, it is clear that the burden of proof is upon the one alleging injury. This burden is overcome when there is a violation of state or federal law (such as the Lanham Act) or if one of the Restatement sections dealing with deceptive marketing, infringement of trademarks, or misappropriation of trade secrets is violated. This chapter focuses on deceptive marketing under both state common law and federal law. Discussion of other unfair competition topics is left to later chapters.

The early development of deceptive marketing is covered in Section B. Section C discusses the elements of a deceptive marketing claim in detail. Section D explores two specific types of deceptive marketing—passing-off and reverse passing-off. Section E summarizes the standing requirement for a deceptive marketing claim and the doctrine of contributory liability. Section F then explains the various remedies available to a successful plaintiff. The Chapter finishes with a summary of little FTC acts in Section G.

## B. DECEPTIVE MARKETING AND THE EARLY COMMON LAW

Under the early common law, the tort of unfair competition was severely limited and basically only recognized in instances in which a competitor falsely claimed to have goods from a particular geographic region (Champagne, for example, is meant to come from a particular region in France; otherwise, it is just sparkling wine).

An early case that demonstrates this principle is *American Washboard Co. v. Saginaw Manufacturing Co.*[1]

In *American Washboard*, the plaintiff alleged that it was the only producer of an aluminum rubber-faced washboard. The plaintiff claimed that the defendant advertised that it also produced an aluminum rubber-faced washboard when, in fact, its washboard contained zinc. The court held that unless the defendant was passing off its own washboards as those of the plaintiff's, there was no cause of action. According to the court, if a cause of action were to exist, it was up to the legislature to create it.

Twenty-five years later, Judge Hand sought to escape this harsh rule in *Ely-Norris Safe Co. v. Mosler Safe Co.*[2]

In *Ely-Norris*, the plaintiff manufactured safes with a patented explosion chamber (a feature designed to protect against burglars). Plaintiff sued a competitor who manufactured and sold safes without an explosion chamber. Instead, the competitor placed a metal bank around the door (in the same place where the plaintiff put its chamber) and falsely told its customers that this was an explosion chamber. The defendant never claimed that its safes were manufactured by the plaintiff and so no claim could lie for passing off. Judge Hand acknowledged that under the precedent of *American Washboard*, no action would lie, but he nonetheless held that the defendant's actions should not be permitted:

> We must concede, therefore, that on the cases as they stand, the law is with the defendant and the especially high authority of the court, which decided *American Washboard Co. v. Saginaw Mfg. Co.*, *supra*, makes us hesitate to differ from their conclusion. Yet there is no part of the law which is more plastic than unfair competition, and what was not reckoned an actionable wrong 25 years ago may have become such today. We find it impossible to deny the strength of the plaintiff's case on the allegations of its bill. As we view it, the question is, as it always is in such cases, one of fact. While a competitor may, generally speaking, take away all the customers of another that he can, there are means which he must not use. One of these is deceit. The false use of another's name as maker or source of his own goods is deceit, of which the false use of geographical

1 103 F. 281 (6th Cir. 1900).

2 7 F.2d 603 (2d Cir. 1925), rev'd, 273 U.S. 132 (1927).

> or descriptive terms is only one example. But we conceive that in the end, the questions which arise are always two: Has the plaintiff in fact lost customers? And has he lost them by means which the law forbids? The false use of the plaintiff's name is only an instance in which each element is clearly shown.

The court went on to conclude that because the plaintiff had a monopoly on the explosion chamber safe due to its patent, it was a fair inference that the defendant's customers would have otherwise bought the plaintiff's safes. As the court stated, "If a tradesman falsely foists on a customer a substitute for what the plaintiff alone can supply, it can scarcely be that the plaintiff is without remedy, if he can show that the customer would certainly have come to him, had the truth been told."

The exception crafted by Judge Hand became known as the "single-source" exception. Unfortunately for the plaintiff, the victory was short-lived. On appeal to the U.S. Supreme Court, the case was reversed. However, the basis of the reversal was not necessarily due to the failure to recognize a single-source exception. Writing for the majority, Justice Holmes stated:

> It is consistent with every allegation in the bill and the defendant in argument asserted it to be a fact, that there are other safes with explosion chambers beside that for which the plaintiff has a patent. The defendant is charged only with representing that its safes had 'an explosion chamber, which, so far as appears, it had a perfect right to do if the representation was true. **If on the other hand the representation was false as it is alleged sometimes to have been, there is nothing to show that customers had they known the facts would have gone to the plaintiff rather than to other competitors in the market, or to lay a foundation for the claim for a loss of sales.**

(emphasis added). It appears then that Holmes disagreed only with regard to the fact that Ely-Norris failed to carry its burden that it was the "single-source" as alleged.

In modern times, the single-source exception has largely fallen into disfavor because it is too narrow. (This is reflected in the Restatement (Third) of Unfair Competition (1995), which is discussed below.) In fact, there is a noticeable dearth of cases citing to the doctrine since 2000 (and even in the decades prior). At its heart, the single-source exception was a method of proving damages that may be speculative and difficult to prove when there are multiple competitors. The law now recognizes a cause of action even when the plaintiff is not the single source. For instance, had the facts in *Ely-Norris* occurred today, one way the plaintiff could establish damages would be through the testimony of customers who were actually fooled and who bought the defendant's safes based on the non-existent explosion chamber. Alternatively, if Ely-Norris had established sales prior to the competitor coming into the market and demonstrated a corresponding dip in sales after the competitor's actions, this would be some evidence of harm.

## C. ELEMENTS OF FALSE ADVERTISING

The First Restatement of Torts accepted the single-source exception, but critics and commentators agreed that even with this exception in place, the rule of false advertising was too narrow. The Third Restatement of Unfair Competition recognizes a much broader scope of liability:

> **§ 2. Deceptive Marketing: General Principle**
>
> One who, in connection with the marketing of goods or services, makes a representation relating to the actor's own goods, services, or commercial activities that is likely to deceive or mislead prospective purchasers to the likely commercial detriment of another under the rule stated in § 3 is subject to liability to the other for the relief appropriate under the rules stated in §§ 35–37.

Section 2 is a broad recognition of liability in connection with misrepresentations about one's own goods. (Section 6 also recognizes a limited ability to sue for misrepresentations regarding selling another's goods second-hand and saying they are new.) Section 2 departs, as does federal law under the Lanham Act, from the old common law rule with its narrow single-source exception and now permits a cause of action even when there is no intent to deceive.

Section 2 states that liability is to be determined based upon a finding that the statements are "likely to deceive or mislead prospective purchasers to the likely commercial detriment of another under the rule stated in § 3." Section 3 speaks to the materiality of the harm:

> **§ 3. Commercial Detriment Of Another**
>
> A representation is to the likely commercial detriment of another if:
>
> (a) the representation is material, in that it is likely to affect the conduct of prospective purchasers; and

(b) there is a reasonable basis for believing that the representation has caused or is likely to cause a diversion of trade from the other or harm to the other's reputation or good will.

Section 3 requires only that a prospective purchaser's conduct is likely to be affected, and the comments to §§ 1 and 2 make clear that the burden of proof is on the plaintiff to demonstrate this. This standard differs from the common law approach seen in *Ely-Norris*, as the burden of proof is much lighter than it was under the single-source exception. As opposed to having to prove that it is the single source, a plaintiff under § 3 only needs to show that a representation is "likely to influence prospective purchasers to some substantial degree."[3]

The Restatement does not do away with reliance, however, and it is still a factor in finding liability. Also, the comments note that this is not a subjective test—so "puffing" or "puffery" is still a defense: "This Section does not subject the actor to liability, however, unless a significant number of prospective purchasers have or are likely to rely on the representation. If a reasonably prudent purchaser of the goods or services would not rely on the representation, the actor is not subject to liability in the absence of evidence establishing that the representation is nevertheless likely to be relied upon by a significant number of prospective purchasers."[4]

It has been said that there is no federal law of unfair competition; however, many of the same claims brought under state common law doctrines can be brought in federal court under § 43 of the Lanham Act.[5] Although the Lanham Act is typically associated with trademark infringement, § 43 broadly provides for recovery in a number of false advertising situations regardless of the presence of a trademark or federal registration of a mark:

**15 U.S.C. § 1125 [Lanham Act § 43(a)]. False designations of origin, false descriptions, and dilution forbidden**

(a) Civil action

(1) Any person who, on or in connection with any goods or services, or any container for goods, uses in commerce any word, term, name, symbol, or device, or any combination thereof, or any false designation of origin, false or misleading description of fact, or false or misleading representation of fact, which—

[3] *See* RESTATEMENT (THIRD) OF UNFAIR COMPETITION § 3 cmt. b (1995).

[4] RESTATEMENT (THIRD) OF UNFAIR COMPETITION § 3 cmt. d (1995).

[5] *See* 15 U.S.C. § 1125 (2006).

(A) is likely to cause confusion, or to cause mistake, or to deceive as to the affiliation, connection, or association of such person with another person, or as to the origin, sponsorship, or approval of his or her goods, services, or commercial activities by another person, or

(B) in commercial advertising or promotion, misrepresents the nature, characteristics, qualities, or geographic origin of his or her or another person's goods, services, or commercial activities,

shall be liable in a civil action by any person who believes that he or she is or is likely to be damaged by such act.

As indicated in the statute, § 43(a)(1) is divided into two main subsections. Subsection (A) is sometimes referred to as the "trademark" provision because its scope is broad enough to enforce unregistered trademarks (a concept we discuss in more detail in a later chapter). Subsection (A) also includes deceptive marketing techniques, such as passing off one's own goods as those of another, which we discuss below. Subsection (B) is the false advertising provision. Unlike subsection (A), it requires that the false statements be made as part of commercial advertising.

While § 43 codifies much of the law of unfair competition, especially with regard to deceptive marketing, its language is limited. Section 43 is meant to be supplemental to state unfair competition causes of action and does not preempt state law. Furthermore, due to the limitations of the Commerce Clause, § 43 does not reach purely intrastate activities. Given how much advertising is performed via the internet and television, however, this requirement can be met rather easily in a false advertising claim.

Note that the language of § 43 is broad enough to prohibit not just false advertising, but also advertising and representations that disparage another's products or business. In this regard, § 43 is broader than the Restatement (Third) of Unfair Competition, which does not address this area of law but rather leaves the subject to the Restatement of Torts. We address this area of law in the next chapter, but it is worth noting the overlap that business and product disparagement have with the law of false advertising. Indeed, as you will see, the elements of the causes of action are very similar.

Early courts read § 43 as a codification of the common law and thus imported the single-source exception into the Lanham Act. Amendments to the act now make clear that no such limitation is to be placed on a § 43 claim. In this sense, § 43 is similar to the Restatement (Third) of Unfair Competition. Given its links to the common law, it is perhaps not surprising that the Lanham Act's materiality requirement incorporates a virtually identical rule as the Restatement.

The basic elements of a deceptive marketing claim under the Lanham Act are: (1) the defendant made a false or misleading description of fact or representation of fact in a commercial advertisement about his own or another's product; (2) the misrepresentation is material, in that it is likely to influence the purchasing decision; (3) the misrepresentation actually deceives or has the tendency to deceive a substantial segment of its audience; (4) the defendant placed the false or misleading statement in interstate commerce; and (5) the plaintiff has been or is likely to be injured as a result of the misrepresentation, either by direct diversion of sales or by a lessening of goodwill associated with its products. The elements are identical under the common law (except for the fourth element, as an interstate commerce hook is unnecessary under state common law).

There are two common types of deceptive marketing: false statements concerning product origin and false statements regarding the product's characteristics. Both types can involve alleged violations of § 43 of the Lanham Act as well as the common law. The case of *Black Hills Jewelry Manufacturing Co. v. Gold Rush, Inc.*[6] provides a good illustration of false product origin statements. The plaintiffs in the case were three jewelry manufacturers located in the Black Hills region of South Dakota. These manufacturers only made three-color gold jewelry in a grape and leaf design. They sued a manufacturer, Gold Rush, and two other retailers who were selling Gold Rush's jewelry, which identified the jewelry as "Black Hills Gold Jewelry" even though it was not manufactured in the Black Hills region.

The district court granted the plaintiffs' request for an injunction based upon two alternative grounds: (1) that the plaintiffs had the benefit of the protections of a certification mark, and (2) that the plaintiffs had established a violation of § 43(a) of the Lanham Act regarding false advertising. The appellate court overturned the district court's decision regarding the certification mark[7] but

---

[6] 633 F.2d 746 (8th Cir. 1980).

[7] The court addressed whether the appellees were entitled to the benefits of a certification mark:

> The Lanham Act defines a "certification mark" to be "any word, name, symbol, or device, or combination thereof . . . to certify regional or other origin, material, mode of manufacture, quality, accuracy, or other characteristics of a person's goods or services or that work or labor on the goods or services was performed by a member of a union or other organization." Lanham Act § 45, 15 U.S.C. § 1127 (2006). In effect, a Certification Mark certifies the nature or origin of the goods or services to which it has been applied (it can also certify manufacture or provision of services by members of a union or other organization to certain

affirmed the violation of the Lanham Act. On appeal, the court noted that the Lanham Act brought forward the cause of action from the common law: "Section 43(a) imposes civil liability upon 'any person who shall * * * use in connection with any goods * * * a false designation of origin, or any false description or representation, including words or other symbols tending falsely to describe or represent the same.' " The defendants argued that the term "Black Hills Gold Jewelry" was generic in that it described merely the style of jewelry. If this were true, then the defendants could be no more liable for the use of the term than had they actually described the style as just what it was (three-color gold grape and leaf design jewelry).

Although there was some evidence to support the defendants' claim—for instance, none of the gold used by the plaintiffs was from the Black Hills region—the court rejected this defense. The court noted that the plaintiffs had been diligent in policing the use of the term for jewelry not manufactured in the Black Hills. Moreover, the court observed that the defendants themselves had actively promoted the region in association with the sale of their jewelry, such as by using images of Mount Rushmore, indicating that the defendants had sought to capitalize on the geography rather than on the style. Further, the appellate court noted that the district court found both that there was a likelihood of confusion to consumers and that potential customers would purchase the defendants' jewelry instead

standards). For example, Rochefort is used to certify that cheese bearing the mark "has been manufactured from sheep's milk only, and had been cured in the natural caves of the Community of Roquefort, Department of Aveyron, France, in accordance with the historic methods and usages of production, curing and development which have been in vogue there for a long period of years." Community of Roquefort v. William Faehndrich, Inc., 303 F.2d 494, 496 (2d Cir. 1962). Regional certification marks are frequently challenged as being generic. The general rule is that a regional certification mark will not be deemed to be generic, unless it appears that it has lost its significance as an indication of regional origin for those goods (or the other aspect signifying origin that the Mark was identifying).

To obtain the protections of a certification mark under the Lanham Act, the mark must be registered and the one registering the mark cannot be the one who seeks to use or adopt the mark (for instance, it was the community of Roquefort that registered the mark in the above cited case). As the appellees were the ones who used the mark, they could not have registered it even if they wanted to. There is some question as to whether a common law certification mark can be created without registration. *See* J. THOMAS MCCARTHY, MCCARTHY ON TRADEMARKS AND UNFAIR COMPETITION § 19.90 (4th ed. 2011); Florida v. Real Juices, Inc., 330 F. Supp. 428 (M.D. Fla. 1971) (recognizing an unregistered certification mark that was used to certify Florida citrus products). The Restatement of Unfair Competition takes the position that such certification marks can exist at common law. *See* RESTATEMENT (THIRD) OF UNFAIR COMPETITION § 11 (1995).

of the plaintiffs' due to this confusion—thus meeting the materiality and consumer deception elements.[8]

A case that is illustrative of the second type of deceptive marketing (i.e., false statements about the product's characteristics) is *Cashmere & Camel Hair Manufacturers Institute v. Saks Fifth Avenue*.[9] The plaintiffs were Packard, a producer of cashmere fabric, and the Cashmere & Camel Hair Manufacturers Institute, a trade association of cashmere manufacturers. They sued defendant Harve Benard, Ltd., a manufacturer of women's blazers, which Harve Benard claimed were a cashmere blend of up to 10% cashmere in some instances.

Two statements were at issue, both regarding the qualities of the cashmere blazers. The first had to do with the claim that there was cashmere in the garments when, in fact, there was not. Second was an allegation that use of the word "cashmere" was an indication that any cashmere would be virgin, as opposed to recycled, and the small amount of cashmere that was present in the garments was recycled. The plaintiffs sought different remedies. The Institute only sought an injunction against future mislabeling, but Packard sought monetary damages.

The district court granted partial summary judgment in favor of the defendants, dismissing both plaintiffs' claims for relief. On appeal, the court began by stating the five elements of a Lanham Act false advertising claim: "(1) the defendant made a false or misleading description of fact or representation of fact in a commercial advertisement about his own or another's product; (2) the misrepresentation is material, in that it is likely to influence the purchasing decision; (3) the misrepresentation actually deceives or has the tendency to deceive a substantial segment of its audience; (4) the defendant placed the false or misleading statement in interstate commerce; and (5) the plaintiff has been or is likely to be injured as a result of the misrepresentation, either by direct diversion of sales

[8] The court further noted that the plaintiffs were not guilty of unclean hands. A plaintiff guilty of engaging in inequitable conduct may be subject to a defense of unclean hands. In *Haagen-Dazs, Inc. v. Frusen Gladje Ltd.*, 493 F. Supp. 73 (S.D.N.Y. 1980), the plaintiff sought to enjoin the defendant, claiming that the defendant's trade dress was intended to give consumers the false impression that its ice cream was made in Sweden (when, in fact, it was made in the United States). The only problem was that the plaintiff was itself guilty of attempting to package its ice cream to give the impression that it was of Scandinavian origin when, in fact, it was made domestically. *Id.* at 76. The court denied the relief sought. This defense is only available when the plaintiff's own conduct is both inequitable and involves the same subject matter that the plaintiff is complaining about.

[9] 284 F.3d 302 (1st Cir. 2002).

or by a lessening of goodwill associated with its products."[10] The defendant conceded that it made false statements regarding the cashmere content and that it had placed them in interstate commerce. Among other things, however, the defendant contested (a) that its failure to explicitly state that the little cashmere that was present was not virgin was not a false statement, merely an omission, and (b) that the statements were not material. The appellate court disagreed and reversed the district court's decision.[11]

### 1. False or Misleading Description of Fact or Representation of Fact in a Commercial Advertisement About His Own or Another Product

The first element of falsity can be difficult to establish and involves a two-step process. The court first determines the message being conveyed by the advertisement, and then decides whether the message is false. In the *Cashmere* case, the nature of the falsity was of particular importance, as it affected the plaintiffs' burdens on the element of consumer deception. If a statement is literally false, then consumer deception is presumed. The *Cashmere* court identified three types of false or misleading statements: literally false statements, statements that are literally false by necessary implication, and implied false statements (sometimes referred to as literally true or ambiguous statements that are misleading). Differentiating statements that are literally false by necessary implication from those that are merely impliedly false is no easy matter. In its explanation of the concept of literally false by necessary implication, the *Cashmere* court quoted *Clorox Co. Puerto Rico v. Proctor & Gamble Commercial Co.*,[12] which noted:

> A claim is conveyed by necessary implication when, considering the advertisement in its entirety, the audience would recognize the claim as readily as if it had been explicitly stated. . . . This is not to say, however, that all messages implied by an advertisement will support a finding of literal falsity by a factfinder:
>
> > The greater the degree to which a message relies upon the viewer or consumer to integrate its components

---

10 *Id.* at 310–11 (citing Clorox Co. P.R. v. Proctor & Gamble Com. Co., 228 F.3d 24, 33 n.6 (1st Cir. 2000)).

11 The court further reversed the district court with regard to the plaintiffs' common law claims under state law. The district court had dismissed these claims on the ground that the plaintiffs' failure to satisfy the requirements of the Lanham Act claim resulted in a corresponding failure to establish the state law claims, as the two theories have overlapping requirements.

12 228 F.3d 24 (1st Cir. 2000).

> and draw the apparent conclusion, however, the less likely it is that a finding of literal falsity will be supported. Commercial claims that are implicit, attenuated, or merely suggestive usually cannot fairly be characterized as literally false.

*United Indus. Corp.*, 140 F.3d at 1181. Similarly, a factfinder might conclude that the message conveyed by a particular advertisement remains so balanced between several plausible meanings that the claim made by the advertisement is too uncertain to serve as the basis of a literal falsity claim, though even in that case it could still form the basis for a claim that the advertisement is misleading.[13]

An issue that arose in *Cashmere* was whether an omission could be the basis of a falsity claim. The court in *Cashmere* noted that the failure to disclose the recycled nature of the fabric was a literal falsity. However, a mere failure to disclose does not usually trigger a violation of § 43(a) (but a half-truth, partially incorrect representation, or a statement that is untrue as a result of a failure to disclose a material fact is actionable). Indeed, a number of courts have refused to find that a failure to disclose something that is required under another federal law is actionable under the Lanham Act, particularly when the Food, Drug and Cosmetic Act (FDCA) is involved.[14] For instance, in *IQ Products Co. v. Pennzoil Products Co.*,[15] the plaintiffs alleged a violation of the Federal Hazardous Substances Act (FHSA) when a competitor failed to label its product as "flammable" as required by the act, thus implying that the product was non-flammable. After noting that the FHSA does not provide for a private cause of action, the court refused to recognize a right of action under the Lanham Act. The court held:

> [T]he FHSA vests the [Consumer Product Safety Commission (CPSC)] with the authority to enforce federal labeling requirements. In this case, the CPSC was aware of [defendants'] alleged labeling deficiencies but took no action. As a result, [plaintiff] essentially seeks to enforce the labeling requirements of the FHSA—an action which

---

13 *Id.* at 35.

14 *See* Mylan Labs., Inc. v. Matkari, 7 F.3d 1130, 1139 (4th Cir. 1993); Sandoz Pharmaceuticals Corp. v. Richardson-Vicks, Inc., 902 F.2d 222, 231 (3d Cir. 1990); *see* All One God Faith, Inc. v. Hain Celestial Grp., Inc., No. C 09–03517 JF (HRL), 2009 WL 4907433 (N.D. Cal. 2009) (involving the U.S.D.A. and Organic Food Products Act). *But see* Pom Wonderful LLC v. Coca-Cola Co., 573 U.S. 102 (2014) (holding that the FDCA does not preclude a private party from bringing a Lanham Act claim challenging as misleading a food label that is regulated by the FDCA).

15 305 F.3d 368 (5th Cir. 2002).

> the CPSC, the enforcing agency, declined to do. For these reasons, we conclude that the defendants' failure to label the product in keeping with FHSA regulations, even if true, does not constitute a false or misleading statement that is actionable under the Lanham Act.[16]

Although normally an omission cannot be the basis of a Lanham Act claim, the First Circuit in *Cashmere* held that even where there was not an express misrepresentation, where a "necessary implication" from the advertised message exists, there will be a literal falsity. Looking to the Wool Products Labeling Act, the court held that recycled garments were required to be labeled as such. As the consumer audience at issue were experienced retailers, the court held they would have surely known of the Act's requirements and viewed the failure to label the fabric as recycled as necessarily meaning it was virgin. Other courts that have recognized exceptions for omissions appear to follow similar reasoning as the *Cashmere* court.[17] This reasoning is based upon the nondisclosure being more akin to a half-truth or partial disclosure than a pure omission.

It should also be noted that an affirmative misrepresentation that is prohibited by federal law will still give rise to a Lanham Act claim regardless of a federal act covering the same conduct, unless provided otherwise. This was made clear in the recent U.S. Supreme Court case of *Pom Wonderful LLC v. Coca-Cola Co.*[18] In that case, POM Wonderful LLC, which produces, markets, and sells a pomegranate-blueberry juice blend (among other items), filed a Lanham Act suit against respondent Coca-Cola Company. POM alleged that it lost sales when the name, label, marketing, and advertising of one of Coca-Cola's juice blends misled consumers into believing that the product consisted predominantly of pomegranate and blueberry juice when in fact it consisted predominantly of less expensive apple and grape juices, and that the ensuing confusion caused POM to lose sales. The district court granted partial summary judgment to Coca-Cola, ruling that the FDCA and its regulations precluded Lanham Act challenges to the name and label of Coca-Cola's juice blend. The Ninth Circuit affirmed in relevant part. The Supreme Court, however, reversed, holding that the FDCA does not preclude a private party from bringing a Lanham Act claim challenging a misleading food label that is regulated by the FDCA. The *Pom Wonderful* case also calls into question the validity of cases

---

16 *Id.* at 374.

17 *See* Alto Prods. Corp. v. Ratek Indus. Ltd., 40 U.S.P.Q.2d 1738 (S.D.N.Y. 1996) ("The Court, therefore, holds that the existence of the Tariff Act violation for failing to properly designate national origin establishes 'a likelihood of deception or confusion on the part of the buying public' as to the national origin of the product.").

18 573 U.S. 102 (2014).

holding that "if a Lanham Act false advertising claim is based on a violation of a Food, Drug and Cosmetic Act required form of disclosure for a drug product, a court can dismiss in order to permit the FDA to rule on the legality of the challenged drug labeling."[19]

### 2. Literal Falsity and Puffery

A concept that is related to falsity, as well as to the elements of consumer deception and materiality, is "puffery."[20] The Fifth Circuit, in the oft-cited case of *Pizza Hut, Inc. v. Papa John's International, Inc.*,[21] offered the following summary description of puffery:

> One form of non-actionable statements of general opinion under section 43(a) of the Lanham Act has been referred to as "puffery." Puffery has been discussed at some length by other circuits. The Third Circuit has described "puffing" as "advertising that is not deceptive for no one would rely on its exaggerated claims." *U.S. Healthcare, Inc. v. Blue Cross of Greater Philadelphia*, 898 F.2d 914 (3d Cir.1990). Similarly, the Ninth Circuit has defined "puffing" as "exaggerated advertising, blustering and boasting upon which no reasonable buyer would rely and is not actionable under 43(a)." *Southland Sod Farms v. Stover Seed Co.*, 108 F.3d 1134, 1145 (9th Cir.1997).[22]
>
> . . . A leading authority on unfair competition has defined "puffery" as an "exaggerated advertising, blustering, and boasting upon which no reasonable buyer would rely," or "a general claim of superiority over a comparative product that is so vague, it would be understood as a mere expression of opinion." 4 J. Thomas McCarthy, McCarthy on Trademark and Unfair Competition § 27.38 (4th ed.1996). Similarly, Prosser and Keeton on Torts defines "puffing" as "a seller's privilege to lie his head off, so long as he says nothing specific, on the theory that no reasonable man would believe him, or that no reasonable man would

---

[19] 5 MCCARTHY ON TRADEMARKS § 27:65:50.

[20] *See also* Chapter XX(A)(5)(a) (discussing the role of puffing in the misrepresentation torts).

[21] 227 F.3d 489 (5th Cir. 2000).

[22] In the same vein, the Second Circuit has observed that "statements of opinion are generally not the basis for Lanham Act liability." Groden v. Random House Inc., 61 F.3d 1045, 1051 (2d Cir. 1995). When a statement is "obviously a statement of opinion," it cannot "reasonably be seen as stating or implying provable facts. . . ." *Id.* "The Lanham Act does not prohibit false statements generally. It prohibits only false or misleading descriptions or false or misleading representations of fact made about one's own or another's goods or services." *Id.* at 1052.

> be influenced by such talk." W. Page Keeton, et al., Prosser and Keeton on the Law of Torts § 109, at 757 (5th ed.1984).
>
> Drawing guidance from the writings of our sister circuits and the leading commentators, we think that non-actionable "puffery" comes in at least two possible forms: (1) an exaggerated, blustering, and boasting statement upon which no reasonable buyer would be justified in relying; or (2) a general claim of superiority over comparable products that is so vague that it can be understood as nothing more than a mere expression of opinion.[23]

A claim by a seller that its product is "the best" often is held to be nonactionable puffery. This distinction is sometimes based upon the concept that the statement is one of opinion rather than fact and, therefore, is not false or is not a false statement of fact as required by the Lanham Act. However, even statements of opinion can be transformed into false statements of fact if they imply a factual basis for their assertion.[24] Furthermore, the context in which an assertion is made can affect whether a statement is viewed as one of fact or opinion. The above-quoted case offers a prime example of the role puffery can play in defense of a false advertising claim.

In *Pizza Hut*, a series of advertisements run by Papa John's (a pizza chain) were alleged to have violated the Lanham Act by use of the slogan "Better Ingredients. Better Pizza." Some of the television ads, in addition to promoting the slogan, also compared specific ingredients used by Papa John's in making its pizza sauce and dough to ingredients used by competing chains. Rival pizza vendor Pizza Hut alleged that the slogan, in the context of the ads, was a false statement as there was no scientific evidence that the ingredients used by Papa John's had any discernible effect on the taste of the pizza. Operating under the above definition of puffery, the Fifth Circuit Court of Appeals first examined the slogan itself and found, in isolation, that the slogan "Better Ingredients. Better Pizza" was mere non-actionable puffery that stated an opinion. However, when taken in the context of the sauce and dough comparisons, the court held that there was sufficient evidence to conclude that the ads were misleading:

> We agree that the message communicated by the slogan "Better Ingredients. Better Pizza." is expanded and given additional meaning when it is used as the tag line in the

---

[23] *Pizza Hut*, 227 F.3d at 496–97.

[24] *See* Enigma Software Grp. USA, LLC v. Malwarebytes, Inc., 69 F.4th 665, 668–69 (9th Cir. 2023) (concluding that "when a company in the computer security business describes a competitor's software as 'malicious' and a 'threat' to a customer's computer, that is more a statement of objective fact than a non-actionable opinion.").

> misleading sauce and dough ads. The slogan, when used in combination with the comparison ads, gives consumers two fact-specific reasons why Papa John's ingredients are "better." Consequently, a reasonable consumer would understand the slogan, *when considered in the context of the comparison ads*, as conveying the following message: Papa John's uses "better ingredients," which produces a "better pizza" because Papa John's uses "fresh-pack" tomatoes, fresh dough, and filtered water. In short, Papa John's has given definition to the word "better." Thus, when the slogan is used in this context, it is no longer mere opinion, but rather takes on the characteristics of a statement of fact. When used in the context of the sauce and dough ads, the slogan is misleading for the same reasons we have earlier discussed in connection with the sauce and dough ads.[25]

Despite this finding, the court went on to find that the slogan did not violate the Lanham Act, as there was no showing of either consumer deception or materiality. This serves as a useful reminder that showing that a false or misleading statement of fact has been made is simply one element of a false advertising claim.

The concept of puffery is closely tied to the element of consumer deception. The case of *American Italian Pasta Co. v. New World Pasta Co.*[26] is illustrative of this point. American Italian Pasta Company (AIP) ran advertisements that its brand of pasta was "America's Favorite Pasta." AIP also emphasized its use of 100% Semolina in its pasta in conjunction with its ads and that it had produced "Quality Since 1867." New World sent AIP a letter demanding that AIP cease its claims regarding being America's favorite and AIP responded by seeking a declaratory judgment that the ad did not violate the Lanham Act. New World counterclaimed for violations of § 43(a) of the Lanham Act, alleging that the phrase "America's Favorite Pasta" was false in two ways: (1) it suggested that AIP was a national brand when it was in fact regional and (2) it suggested that AIP's pasta is America's favorite, but when judged by raw sales, Barilla is the most popular.

The court held that even statements that are literally false or false by implication are subject to a puffery defense.[27] The court then noted that puffery exists in two general forms: "(1) exaggerated statements of bluster or boast upon which no reasonable consumer

---

[25] *Pizza Hut*, 227 F.3d at 501–02.

[26] 371 F.3d 387 (8th Cir. 2004).

[27] *See id.* at 390 ("Besides actionable statements, a category of non-actionable statements exists. Many statements fall into this category, popularly known as puffery.").

would rely; and (2) vague or highly subjective claims of product superiority, including bald assertions of superiority."[28]

The court first examined the phrase standing by itself and concluded that it was non-actionable puffery due to its vagueness. The court focused on the term "favorite" and its relation to the vague concepts of "well-liked" and "admired" which provide no empirical benchmark by which to judge the phrase. Similar to the *Pizza Hut* court, the *American Italian* court then looked to the context of the phrase within the advertising to see if a false or misleading message was being conveyed to consumers. Specifically, the court examined the packaging which further asserted that the pasta brand "has existed for 130 years, Mueller's tastes great, cooks to perfect tenderness, and is manufactured from high quality grain."[29] However, even within this context, the court found there was nothing either false (referring to how long the company had existed and what the pasta was made of) or objectively verifiable that was asserted by these additional statements that modified the phrase "America's Favorite Pasta" in such a way as to make it actionable.

New World attempted to introduce evidence that the phrase "America's Favorite Pasta" was misleading by conducting its own consumer survey. Relying upon *Mead Johnson & Co. v. Abbott Laboratories*,[30] the court refused to consider the surveys. The court found that to hold otherwise:

> would subject any advertisement or promotional statement to numerous variables, often unpredictable, and would introduce even more uncertainty into the market place. A manufacturer or advertiser who expended significant resources to substantiate a statement or forge a puffing statement could be blind-sided by a consumer survey that defines the advertising statement differently, subjecting the advertiser or manufacturer to unintended liability for a wholly unanticipated claim the advertisement's plain language would not support.[31]

Although this was not an issue in the *American Italian* case, a frequent method of advertising is to make a claim that a manufacturer's product is more effective or superior in some fashion. Sometimes the bald assertion of superiority is held simply to be puffery. However, it should be noted that this can be a separate inquiry from the puffery defense. If a claim is puffery, then it is non-

28 *Id.* at 391.

29 *Id.* at 392.

30 201 F.3d 883 (7th Cir. 2000), *opinion amended on denial of reh'g*, 209 F.3d 1032 (7th Cir. 2000).

31 *American Italian Pasta Co.*, 371 F.3d at 393–94.

actionable. Superiority claims may still move forward (if not puffery), but the type of claim affects the plaintiff's burden of proof.

These sorts of claims frequently arise in the pain relief industry but are certainly not limited to analgesics. If company A claims that its motor oil provides greater protection from viscosity break-down, and company B brings a claim for false advertising, it is not enough to simply show that the tests performed were flawed, as this does not necessarily demonstrate falsity. But if company A advertises that tests prove its claim, company B may carry its burden by showing that the tests do not support the claim. While it is the burden of the plaintiff to show that the claims are false, it should be noted that this does not preclude the plaintiff from using the defendant's own tests to show that the claims are false. For instance, in *McNeil-P.P.C., Inc. v. Bristol-Myers Squibb Co.*,[32] plaintiff McNeil-PPC successfully used defendant Bristol-Myers own clinical tests to show that Bristol-Myers' product, Excedrin, did not in fact relieve pain better than plaintiff's product, Tylenol, as claimed.

In comparative advertising, however, many courts have distinguished between bald assertions of superiority and claims of superiority that appear to draw upon tests, lowering the burden for establishing falsity in the test-based claims. In *United Industries Corp. v. Clorox Co.*,[33] the Eighth Circuit noted this distinction:

> We have recently distinguished between two types of comparative advertising claims brought under the Lanham Act: (1) "my product is better than yours" and (2) "tests prove that my product is better than yours." When challenging a claim of superiority that does not make express reference to testing, a plaintiff must prove that the defendant's claim of superiority is actually false, not simply unproven or unsubstantiated. Under a "tests prove" claim, in which a defendant has buttressed a claim of superiority by attributing it to the results of scientific testing, a plaintiff must prove only that the tests relied upon were not sufficiently reliable to permit one to conclude with reasonable certainty that they established the proposition for which they were cited. However, to ensure vigorous competition and to protect legitimate commercial speech, courts applying this standard should give advertisers a fair amount of leeway, at least in the absence of a clear intent to deceive or substantial consumer confusion.[34]

---

32 938 F.2d 1544 (2d Cir. 1991).

33 140 F.3d 1175 (8th Cir. 1998).

34 *Id.* at 1181–82 (internal citations and quotations omitted).

As the above passage indicates, it is generally not sufficient to merely show that an advertiser lacked substantiation for its claims; rather, the challenger must affirmatively prove them false. However, if an ad claims its assertion is established through tests or surveys, then these are known as substantiation or "tests prove" ads (also referred to as "establishment claims"). If the challenged advertisement is an establishment claim, a plaintiff need only "prove that these tests did not establish the proposition for which they were cited."[35]

The lower burden for "tests prove" claims appears justified. In a mere claim of superiority, the falsity at issue is whether the product, service, etc. is in fact superior. But in a "tests prove" claim, the falsity at issue is whether a test or survey established the superiority (not the superiority itself). Thus, the focus is different. If a defendant claims that its product has been proven superior through a scientifically conducted test, but it turns out that the results are flawed (or the results don't support the claim), then the message conveyed to the consumer regarding the test is false.[36]

Some advertisers attempt to defend false "tests prove" claims by couching their advertisements as opinions. For instance, in *Osmose, Inc. v. Viance, LLC*,[37] Osmose, a wood preservative manufacturer, brought suit against a competitor, Viance, alleging false advertising. Specifically, Viance had made statements critical of Osmose's wood preservation systems based on studies Viance had conducted. Viance defended that most of the advertising statements at issue were a combination of truthful factual statements and non-actionable statements of opinion, such as "[t]hese findings provide evidence that [Osmose] micronized copper-treated wood is prone to premature decay, and Viance believes that its continued use raises serious consumer safety concerns."[38] The court rejected this defense,

[35] Johnson & Johnson Vision Care, Inc. v. 1-800 Contacts, Inc., 299 F.3d 1242, 1248 (11th Cir. 2002); *see* RESTATEMENT (THIRD) OF UNFAIR COMPETITION § 2 cmt. d (1995).

[36] *See, e.g.*, BASF Corp. v. Old World Trading Co., Inc., 41 F.3d 1081, 1091 (7th Cir. 1994) ("Statements in the form 'tests show x' are literally false if tests do not establish 'x.' But more general comparative claims can only be proven false by affirmative evidence of falsity. Of course, claims of product superiority are a close cousin to claims that 'tests show x,' for 'implicit in most assertions of superiority. . . is that some type of comparison between products has been made.' " (quoting Accu-Sort Systems, Inc. v. Lazerdata Corp., 820 F. Supp. 928, 932 (E.D. Pa. 1993)); Bridal Expo, Inc. v. Van Florestein, 2009 WL 255862, at *7 (S.D. Tex. 2009) ("It is not clear with respect to what metric Defendants claim to be number one, forcing the Court to conclude that this statement is not empirically verifiable. Consequently, Defendants' statement cannot be considered literally false. Furthermore, this statement falls neatly into the category of 'bald assertion of superiority or a general statement of superiority' that the *Pizza Hut* court described as puffery.").

[37] 612 F.3d 1298 (11th Cir. 2010).

[38] *Id.* at 1309–10.

however, noting that the purported opinions were linked to the studies, which suggested that something in the studies justified the opinions. The court concluded "[t]he district court was not clearly erroneous in finding that the claims were 'establishment' claims unambiguously asserting that the tests supported the structural integrity and safety concerns expressed in the advertisements."[39]

### 3. Materiality

Section 3 of the Restatement (Third) of Unfair Competition provides a commonly used standard for establishing materiality: "A representation is to the likely commercial detriment of another if: (a) the representation is material, in that it is likely to affect the conduct of prospective purchasers; and (b) there is a reasonable basis for believing that the representation has caused or is likely to cause a diversion of trade from the other or harm to the other's reputation or good will." Applying the Lanham Act, courts similarly state that the standard used for materiality is that the representation is likely to influence the purchasing decision. Intent to deceive is irrelevant to this inquiry.

One way to show materiality is to demonstrate that the false statement relates to an "inherent quality or characteristic of the product." This "inherent quality or characteristic" test was developed by the Second Circuit and some courts have made this an indispensable prerequisite, or *sine qua non*, of materiality. However, it is not always an easy task to identify what is an inherent quality or characteristic.[40] Courts have found that false claims regarding a product's description of having an "exclusive design" did not meet the "inherent quality or characteristic" test.[41] Furthermore, it does not necessarily follow that every statement regarding an inherent quality of a product is material. For instance, in *Nat'l Basketball Ass'n v. Motorola, Inc.*,[42] the Second Circuit found that although an advertising claim that the defendant's updated basketball game scores were "direct from each arena" was false (the scores in fact came

---

[39] *Id.* at 1312; *see also* Castrol Inc. v. Pennzoil Co., 987 F.2d 939, 946 (3d Cir. 1993) (finding claims actionable when defendant sought "to substantiate its claims of superiority by reference to testing").

[40] *See* Vidal Sassoon, Inc. v. Bristol-Myers Co., 661 F.2d 272, 278 (2d Cir. 1981) ("In a case like this, where many of the qualities of a product (such as 'body') are not susceptible to objective measurement, it is difficult to see how the manufacturer can advertise its product's 'quality' more effectively than through the dissemination of the results of consumer preference studies.").

[41] *See* Sheldon Friedlich Marketing Corp. v. Carol Wright Sales, Inc., No. 82 CIV. 4318, 1983 WL 64848, at *8 (S.D.N.Y. 1983) (determining that although the defendant's use of the phrase "exclusive design" was false, its use did not violate the Lanham Act as this language was mere puffery and did not relate to the quality or characteristics of the defendant's product).

[42] 105 F.3d 841 (2d Cir. 1997).

from broadcasts), the falsity was immaterial because it would not influence consumers.[43]

Although some courts use the "inherent quality or characteristic" test, amendments made to the language of the Lanham Act in 1988 have called into question the continued validity of this approach. In particular, § 43(a)(1)(A) now expressly encompasses misrepresentations relating to the actor's "commercial activities" in addition to misrepresentations relating to "goods" or "services." The reference to "commercial activities" arguably broadens the scope. Indeed, comment c to § 3 of the Restatement cites to this change seemingly in support of a broader view of materiality. Comment c states:

> *c. Subject matter.* Material representations commonly take the form of statements that pertain directly to the quality or characteristics of the actor's goods or services, such as a representation that a piece of jewelry is made of solid gold or that a particular medical preparation will prevent baldness. However, a representation that only indirectly relates to product quality or that in some other manner relates to the desirability of the proposed transaction may also be material. Representations that concern matters that are trivial or of little or no significance to prospective purchasers are not material under the rule of this Section.

The Reporter's Note to § 3 goes on to elaborate on the comment stating:

> Comment c. Several decisions interpreting § 43(a) of the Lanham Act require that the misrepresentation concern an "inherent quality or characteristic" of the actor's goods or services. . . . The "inherent quality or characteristic" standard appears inconsistent with the results of numerous decisions under § 43(a). The boundaries of the limitation are ill-defined, see Illustration 2, and it has been criticized by several commentators. *See, e.g.*, Keller, How Do You Spell Relief? Private Regulation of Advertising Under Section 43(a) of the Lanham Act, 75 Trademark Rep. 227, 237–39 (1985); Bauer, A Federal Law of Unfair Competition: What Should be the Reach of Section 43(a) of the Lanham Act?, 31 U.C.L.A. L.Rev. 671, 742 (1984). The 1988 revision of § 43(a) now expressly encompasses misrepresentations relating to the actor's "commercial

[43] *See id.* at 855 ("Whether the data is taken from broadcasts instead of being observed first-hand, is, therefore, simply irrelevant.").

activities" in addition to misrepresentations relating to the actor's "goods" or "services."

However, McCarthy on Trademarks comments:

> Since the 1989 rewriting of § 43(a), the statute now forbids misrepresentations as to "the nature, characteristics, qualities or geographic origin" of the goods or services. In the author's view, this statutory change neither codifies nor rejects the Second Circuit view, but leaves it an open question of statutory interpretation. The continued viability of the "inherent quality or characteristic" rule has been questioned.[44]

Given the broadening of the language, it would appear that there is room under the Lanham Act for material misrepresentations beyond those that meet the Second Circuit's test, and it is probably best to think of the test as a presumption rather than an absolute test for materiality.[45]

### 4. Consumer Deception

Normally consumer deception is proven by using surveys. This can be a costly proposition and not every competitor is willing or able to conduct them. For small competitors, the cost may be too high to justify moving forward. The survey will also take time. However, there is a presumption of consumer deception when the alleged misrepresentation is literally false. For instance, in the *Cashmere & Camel Hairs Institute* case referenced earlier, the defendant's claim of cashmere when none or negligible amounts were present was a literally false claim which led to a presumption of consumer deception. This presumption can be rebutted, but now the burden has shifted to the defendant to engage in a costly survey.

Consumer deception is also presumed when there is evidence that the defendant intentionally set out to deceive or mislead consumers. Once again, the First Circuit case of *Cashmere & Camel Hairs Institute* is instructive. One of the defenses raised in that case was that the defendants never explicitly claimed that the cashmere was virgin, and therefore any falsity was implied rather than literal (which meant that no consumer deception could be presumed). The First Circuit disagreed on the literal falsity claim, but also held alternatively that consumer deception could be presumed as there was evidence that the defendants knowingly and intentionally

---

[44] 5 McCarthy on Trademarks § 27:64.

[45] *See* Richard J. Leighton, *Materiality and Puffing in Lanham Act False Advertising Cases: The Proofs, Presumptions and Pretexts*, 94 Trademark Rptr. 585, 594 (2004) (asserting that the fact that a representation goes to an inherent quality or characteristic merely creates a presumption of materiality).

withheld the recycled nature of the fabric. Defendants argued that such a presumption was still inappropriate in an implied falsity claim, but the Second Circuit disagreed:

> The justification for applying the presumption whenever there is evidence of intentional deception is perspicuous: "The expenditure by a competitor of substantial funds in an effort to deceive customers and influence their purchasing decisions justifies the existence of a presumption that consumers are, in fact, being deceived." [*U-Haul Int'l, Inc. v. Jartran, Inc.*, 793 F.2d 1034, 1041 (9th Cir. 1986)]. This reasoning holds true regardless of whether the claim that plaintiffs allege involves an implied or literal falsity.[46]

Although the First Circuit is content with mere intent to deceive, not all jurisdictions agree that an "intent to mislead" alone is sufficient to trigger the presumption of customer deception. For instance, the Third Circuit has added that an intent to deceive must be coupled with "deliberate conduct" of an "egregious nature."[47]

A question left open by the consumer deception prong is how many persons need to have been deceived by the advertisement? Courts have required the number to be "statistically significant" or "a substantial portion of the intended audience."[48] This does not mean a majority of consumers and the standard is still a vague one, even with modifiers such as "significant" and "substantial." Percentages of deceived respondents as low as 15% have been found sufficient to meet the burden of proof,[49] but 7.5% has been found insufficient.[50]

Related to establishing that a substantial number of consumers have been deceived (or are likely to be deceived) is the validity of the tests used to establish deception. In evaluating the trustworthiness

---

46 Cashmere & Camel Hair Mfrs. Inst. v. Saks Fifth Ave., 284 F.3d 302, 317 (1st Cir. 2002).

47 *See, e.g.*, Johnson & Johnson-Merck Consumer Pharms Co. v. Rhone-Poulenc Rorer Pharms, Inc., 19 F.3d 125, 131–32 (3d Cir. 1994) (citing to the *Smithkline Beecham* test which has a two-part inquiry that says "where a plaintiff adequately demonstrates that a defendant has intentionally set out to deceive the public," and the defendant's "deliberate conduct" in this regard is of an "egregious nature," a presumption arises 'that consumers are, in fact, being deceived' ") (quoting Johnson & Johnson * Merck Consumer Pharms. Co. v. Smithkline Beecham Corp., 960 F.2d 294, 298–99 (2d Cir. 1992))

48 Johnson & Johnson * Merck Consumer Pharms. Co. v. Smithkline Beecham Corp., 960 F.2d 294, 298 (2d Cir. 1992); Johnson & Johnson-Merck Consumer Pharms. Co. v. Rhone-Poulenc Rorer Pharms., 19 F.3d 125, 134 (3d Cir. 1994).

49 Novartis Consumer Health Inc. v. Johnson & Johnson-Merck Consumer Pharms. Co., 290 F.3d 578, 593–94 (3d Cir. 2002).

50 Johnson & Johnson-Merck Consumer Pharms. Co. v. Rhone-Poulenc Rorer Pharms., 19 F.3d 125, 134 & n.14 (3d Cir. 1994) (noting that 20% would likely be sufficient for other courts).

of consumer surveys, courts have considered a number of criteria such as: (1) was the "universe" (the population the poll aims to measure) properly defined, (2) was a representative sample of that universe selected, (3) were the questions asked of interviewees framed in a clear, precise, and non-leading manner, (4) were sound interview procedures followed by competent interviewers who had no knowledge of the litigation or the purpose for which the survey was conducted, (5) was the data gathered accurately reported, (6) was the data analyzed in accordance with accepted statistical principles, and (7) was the objectivity of the entire process maintained.[51]

### 5. Defendant Placed the False or Misleading Statement into Interstate Commerce

The interstate commerce element is not required in a state common law claim—it is only an element for a claim under the Lanham Act. Even under the Lanham Act, however, the requirement is easily met. What is required is not that the sold goods enter interstate commerce, but that the designation or advertisement is used in interstate commerce. Given the modern ways that advertising takes place, this element is often met. For instance, advertisements placed on the internet have been held to meet this element,[52] as have advertisements via email.[53] Finally, even purely intrastate sales and advertising have met this element if they nonetheless affect plaintiff's interstate sales.[54]

### 6. Plaintiff Likely to Be Injured as a Result of the Misrepresentation

The final element is that plaintiff has been or is likely to be injured as a result of the misrepresentation, either by direct diversion of sales or by a lessening of goodwill associated with its products. (A detailed explanation of the types of remedies available can be found below in Section F.) In order to prove causation under § 1125(a) of the Lanham Act as well as the common law, plaintiff must

---

51 *See* Schering Corp. v. Pfizer Inc., 189 F.3d 218, 225 (2d Cir. 1999), *as amended on reh'g* (Sept. 29, 1999); *see also* Friends of Boundary Waters Wilderness v. Bosworth, 437 F.3d 815, 825 (8th Cir. 2006); Brokerage Concepts, Inc. v. U.S. Healthcare, Inc., 140 F.3d 494, 517 (3d Cir. 1998); Jellibeans, Inc. v. Skating Clubs of Georgia, Inc., 716 F.2d 833, 846 (11th Cir. 1983).

52 *See* TrafficSchool.com, Inc. v. Edriver Inc., 653 F.3d 820, 828 (9th Cir 2011) (involving a web-based for-profit site that assisted consumers with various car-related activities such as license renewal).

53 *See* Grubbs v. Sheakley Grp., Inc., 807 F.3d 785, 802–04 (6th Cir. 2015) (violating the Lanham Act when falsely emailing customers about a business entering into a partnership).

54 *See* Pure Foods v. Minute Maid Corp., 214 F.2d 792, 796 (5th Cir. 1954) (finding that even if a sale of goods is intrastate, it will meet the Lanham Act if it affects the interstate business of the plaintiff).

demonstrate that the false advertisement actually caused harm to its business. One common way that this is demonstrated is through diverted sales from the aggrieved party to the defendant. This means showing not only that consumers were deceived (or establishing a presumption of such), but also that the deception actually negatively affected the plaintiff's business. Although diverted sales are one way to establish causation, plaintiffs can also demonstrate it through customer surveys and direct testimony of customers.

While showing causation and harm is essential to a claim of monetary damages, the same is not true of a claim for purely injunctive relief. A showing that the defendant's activities are likely to cause confusion or to deceive customers is sufficient to warrant injunctive relief. Thus, if a presumption is established regarding consumer deception, such as by showing literal falsity, the plaintiff seeking an injunction has few further obstacles to obtaining relief.

## D. OTHER FORMS OF DECEPTIVE MARKETING: PASSING-OFF AND REVERSE PASSING-OFF

Thus far, false advertising has been discussed in its most straight-forward form: where a competitor makes a false statement about its own products. In *Black Hills*, the statement regarded the origin of the product. In *Cashmere*, the statement regarded the quality of the goods. This Chapter has not yet discussed, however, passing-off claims or reverse passing-off claims. These two additional forms of deceptive marketing[55] warrant separate treatment.

### 1. Passing-Off

Passing-off, simply put, is attempting to convince consumers that your product is actually someone else's. Think of the street vendor selling "Rolex" watches which are undoubtedly knock-offs. This is passing-off. It is easy to see why Rolex would want to prevent such activities, as the potential exists to divert sales of authentic Rolex watches. Moreover, the knock-off watches, which are of inferior quality, may hurt the Rolex image if consumers believe that the shoddy watches are genuine Rolexes.

The language of § 43(a)(1)(A) of the Lanham Act regarding false designations of origin and affiliation encompass passing-off claims. The Restatement of Unfair Competition has similarly addressed the issue in § 4:

---

55 This Chapter refers to these claims as deceptive marketing rather than false advertising because they fall under § 43(a)(1)(A), which, unlike § 43(a)(1)(B), does not require the misrepresentations to be made as part of a commercial advertising or promotion.

### § 4. Misrepresentations Relating To Source: Passing Off

> One is subject to liability to another under the rule stated in § 2 if, in connection with the marketing of goods or services, the actor makes a representation likely to deceive or mislead prospective purchasers by causing the mistaken belief that the actor's business is the business of the other, or that the actor is the agent, affiliate, or associate of the other, or that the goods or services that the actor markets are produced, sponsored, or approved by the other.

From the language of the Lanham Act and § 4, it should be clear that liability is not simply limited to passing-off one's goods as those of another. It can also extend to false association of services or sponsorship. The following illustration from the comments to § 4 helps to demonstrate this point:

> 1. A and B are plumbing firms. A has a contract to provide plumbing services to the University of Nebraska. B falsely represents to prospective customers that it is the firm that does the plumbing work for the University. B is subject to liability to A.

The Restatement takes the view that intent to deceive is irrelevant to imposition of liability, but it can be relevant regarding the level of proof the plaintiff is required to show in consumer deception claims, and it may also be relevant to determining damages:

> Liability for passing off was originally imposed through the common law action for deceit, and thus proof of the actor's fraudulent intent was an essential element of the plaintiff's case. Subsequent developments, however, eroded the emphasis on the actor's subjective state of mind. The requirement of fraud was first discarded in connection with misrepresentations of source accomplished through the infringement of fanciful or arbitrary trademarks. It was later abandoned in cases involving the unauthorized use of other designations that had acquired source significance. See § 9, Comment d. State and federal legislation, ***including § 43(a) of the Lanham Act and the Uniform Deceptive Trade Practices Act***, have also dispensed with the necessity of establishing an intent to deceive in connection with misrepresentations of source or other misrepresentations concerning the actor's goods or services. See § 2, Comment f. Liability under this Section is determined by an evaluation of the probable consequences

> of the actor's conduct and does not depend upon the actor's subjective intent.
>
> Although an intent to deceive is not an element of the cause of action under this Section, evidence that the representation was in fact intended to mislead prospective purchasers with respect to the identity of the actor or the source, sponsorship, or approval of the goods or services may justify an inference that deception is likely. When such evidence is adduced, the burden may properly shift to the actor to demonstrate that deception is unlikely despite the attempt to deceive. The subjective intent of the actor is also relevant to an award of monetary relief under the rules stated in §§ 36 and 37.[56]

The case of *Coca-Cola Company v. Dorris*,[57] one of a series of cases brought in the 1960s and 1970s by Coca-Cola, demonstrates the principle that an intent to deceive is irrelevant to the imposition of liability. Coca-Cola sued Ed. E. Dorris for allegedly serving his own house brand of soda at his two restaurants, Dorris House #1 and Dorris House #2, in response to the requests from patrons for "Coca-Cola" or "Coke." As part of his defense, Dorris stated that he placed signs around his businesses to inform the public that he served his own house brand and did not serve Coca-Cola, and he instructed his staff to tell customers the same. The court held that the signs were insufficient to place the public on notice. With regard to Dorris' other efforts and intent, the court held:

> Defendant undertook in good faith to instruct his waitresses, attendants, and those serving his customers that only Dorris House Cola was being sold. It is well established however that good faith or lack of bad faith is no defense in unfair competition and trade-mark infringement actions. The question is what is the commercial effect of what he is doing? If the effect would be to pass off his goods as those of plaintiff, then his honesty of purpose or the absence of any intention to deceive is no defense.[58]

As the Rolex example suggested, there is a strong tie between passing-off and trademark infringement. Indeed, § 43(a)(1)(A) is often pled in conjunction with a trademark infringement claim brought under § 32 of the Lanham Act (§ 32 covers registered

---

56 RESTATEMENT (THIRD) OF UNFAIR COMPETITION § 4 cmt. d (emphasis added).

57 311 F. Supp. 287 (E.D. Ark. 1970).

58 *Id.* at 290 (internal citations and quotations omitted).

trademarks while § 43 is broad enough to cover unregistered marks). Comment b to § 4 of the Restatement explains this relationship:

> The "passing off" held actionable at common law was frequently accomplished through the use of confusingly similar trade symbols, and during the 19th century this general principle of liability served as the genesis of the technical rules governing the validity and infringement of trademarks and the recognition of secondary meaning. See § 9, Comment d. . . . If a misrepresentation of source or sponsorship arises solely from the unauthorized use of a trademark or other indicia of identification, relief must be sought under the rules stated in [Chapter 3 governing the law of trademarks].

Due to this relationship, a further discussion of passing-off under the Restatement and the Lanham Act will be continued in Chapter 10.

### 2. Reverse Passing-Off

If passing-off is the attempt to convince consumers that your product is actually someone else's, it is not hard to guess what reverse passing-off entails. It is attempting to convince consumers that someone else's product is actually your own. Once again, the language of the Lanham Act under § 43(a)(1)(A) reaches such claims. The Restatement of Unfair Competition has also addressed the claim in § 5:

> **§ 5. Misrepresentations Relating To Source: Reverse Passing Off**
>
> One is subject to liability to another under the rule stated in § 2 if, in marketing goods or services manufactured, produced, or supplied by the other, the actor makes a representation likely to deceive or mislead prospective purchasers by causing the mistaken belief that the actor or a third person is the manufacturer, producer, or supplier of the goods or services if the representation is to the likely commercial detriment of the other under the rule stated in § 3.

Because the product is bought regardless, a reverse passing-off claim requires a showing of likelihood of harm. But, if the product is sold regardless, where is the harm? It becomes problematic when reputation is at stake and a seller plans to use a competitor's goods to imply that the seller's own products are of the same quality. An example of harm caused by reverse passing-off is if an artist, Art, was hired to paint a portrait for a buyer, Bert. Upon completing the work, Bert resells the portrait to an art gallery and claims that it is an original painting, not by Art, but by Bert himself. Based on the strength of the work, the gallery commissions Bert to complete more paintings. Art, understandably upset, feels that if the gallery knew that he was the true artist, he would have received the subsequent commissions. This simplified hypothetical involves another area of law, copyright, and many cases will implicate the Copyright Act rather than the Lanham Act. Illustration 3 to section 5 of the Restatement provides a further example.

> A manufactures jet engine parts sold in domestic and foreign markets. The parts carry a designation indicating that they have been approved for United States military procurement. B, a competitor of A, sells surplus parts manufactured by A, falsely representing that the parts were manufactured by B. The evidence indicates that the misrepresentation is likely to cause prospective purchasers to believe that B has been approved as a source of supply for United States military procurement. The misrepresentation is to the likely commercial detriment of A since it threatens to divert future trade from A to B. B is subject to liability to A.

Recall that the Lanham Act creates a federal remedy against a person who uses in commerce either a "false designation of origin, false or misleading description of fact, or false or misleading representation of fact" in connection with "any goods or services." Often the key to knowing whether the Lanham Act's reverse passing-off cause of action applies centers around the use of the word "origin." The scope of the word "origin" was clarified in the seminal case of *Dastar Corporation v. Twentieth Century Fox Film Corporation.*[59] The facts of the case are somewhat complicated but involved an old TV series called "Crusade in Europe" (which was based on Dwight D. Eisenhower's book recounting the European campaign of World War II). The series was no longer under copyright; therefore, Dastar took old Beta tapes of the original series, edited them, and made them into their own series called "Campaigns" that was marketed at various retail outlets. Fox, who had originally held the rights to "Crusade in Europe," sued and alleged that Dastar's sale of its Campaigns videos without proper credit to the Crusade television series constituted "reverse passing off" in violation of § 43(a) of the Lanham Act and state unfair-competition law. The district court found in favor of Fox and the Ninth Circuit Court of Appeals affirmed.

On appeal, the Supreme Court noted that had Dastar taken the Crusade videotapes and repackaged them as its own, a claim for reverse passing-off would be sustained. But, the Court observed:

---

59 539 U.S. 23 (2003).

> Dastar's alleged wrongdoing, however, is vastly different: It took a creative work in the public domain—the Crusade television series—copied it, made modifications (arguably minor), and produced its very own series of videotapes. If "origin" refers only to the manufacturer or producer of the physical "goods" that are made available to the public (in this case the videotapes), Dastar was the origin. If, however, "origin" includes the creator of the underlying work that Dastar copied, then someone else (perhaps Fox) was the origin of Dastar's product. At bottom, we must decide what § 43(a)(1)(A) of the Lanham Act means by the "origin" of "goods."[60]

Relying in part on dictionary definitions, the Court held that origin refers to the physical origin of the goods in question and not "the person or entity that originated the ideas or communications that 'goods' embody or contain."[61]

The Court identified at least two policy-based reasons and two practical reasons for its decision. From a policy perspective, the Court noted that to allow "origin" to extend also to the authors of communicative works would conflict with the provisions of the Copyright Act. If works have fallen out of copyright, then they should be in the public domain and free to copy. To hold that a cause of action will remain under the Lanham Act "would create a species of mutant copyright law that limits the public's federal right to copy and to use expired copyrights."[62] In a related line of reasoning, the Court held that to extend the word "origin" in such a way would conflict with previous case law interpreting the Lanham Act in light of trade dress and patent claims. To allow a Lanham Act claim to succeed when patent or trade dress would fail creates an end-run around the carefully crafted limits on such claims:

> In sum, reading the phrase "origin of goods" in the Lanham Act in accordance with the Act's common-law foundations (which were not designed to protect originality or creativity), and in light of the copyright and patent laws (which were), we conclude that the phrase refers to the producer of the tangible goods that are offered for sale, and not to the author of any idea, concept, or communication embodied in those goods. To hold otherwise would be akin

60 *Id.* at 31.

61 *Id.* at 32.

62 *Id.* at 35–37.

> to finding that § 43(a) created a species of perpetual patent and copyright, which Congress may not do.[63]

It seems clear from this language that the Court was leery of creating liability in authorship cases where the Copyright Act would have found none.

From a practical standpoint, the Court articulated two concerns. First, to require attribution to the true originator entails a fair bit of research and, as the case before the Court demonstrated, no clear answer as to who or what party needs to be attributed. Is it just Fox or does it go all the way back to the original cameraman? Does every party even remotely connected to the production need to be given credit? Second, even if Dastar could identify the origin, doing so opens them up to potential litigation under § 43(a)(1)(A). How? Through falsely implying the creator's "sponsorship or approval" of the copy. Although the original plaintiffs apparently denied that they would have brought such a suit, the Court was not convinced. Thus, such a reading of the word "origin" would place defendants between a rock and a hard place.

Despite finding no liability under § 43(a)(1)(A), in the penultimate paragraph of the case the court noted that, had the factual circumstances been slightly different than alleged, the plaintiffs may have had a case under § 43(a)(1)(B):

> If, moreover, the producer of a video that substantially copied the Crusade series were, in advertising or promotion, to give purchasers the impression that the video was quite different from that series, then one or more of the respondents might have a cause of action—not for reverse passing off under the "confusion . . . as to the origin" provision of § 43(a)(1)(A), but for misrepresentation under the "misrepresents the nature, characteristics [or] qualities" provision of § 43(a)(1)(B).[64]

Under the changed facts, Dastar would be making a false statement about the qualities of the product as part of its commercial advertising. Assuming this is literally false, consumer deception is presumed, leaving the plaintiffs to just prove that it was material to qualify for an injunction (i.e., it would likely affect the purchasing decision of a consumer).

Although the Court indicated that the facts would need to be different than as presented, it is interesting to consider whether the plaintiffs could bring such a claim under the facts that they actually

---

[63] *Id.* at 37.

[64] *Id.* at 38.

alleged. In other words, if the defendant Dastar advertised on the packages (either impliedly or explicitly) that it was the creator of the Campaigns videos when in fact they were substantially lifted from another source (and indeed a competitor), would this not meet the standard for false advertising under § 43(a)(1)(B)? If placing Dastar's name on the videos is sufficient to qualify as commercial advertising, could this not qualify as a false misrepresentation of the "nature, characteristics, [or] qualities" of the goods? In other words, does the Court's reasoning regarding limiting the language of "origin" under subsection (A) apply equally to subsection (B)? Or does Congress' inclusion of the language "nature, characteristics, [or] qualities" demonstrate an intent to extend liability even beyond the life of a copyright when it comes to advertising?

The scope of the *Dastar* opinion and whether its limits on authorship claims apply to § 43(a)(1)(B) is somewhat of an open question. A number of courts hold that the words "nature, characteristics, [or] qualities" in § 43(a)(1)(B) cannot be read to refer to authorship.[65] For instance, *Lapine v. Seinfeld,*[66] Missy Chase Lapine sued Jessica Seinfeld (wife of comedian Jerry Seinfeld) and her publishers for copyright and trademark infringement as well as for a violation of § 43(a)(1)(B). Lapine had authored a book entitled *The Sneaky Chef: Simple Strategies for Hiding Healthy Food in Kids' Favorite Meals,* which, as the title indicates, is a book on sneaking healthy foods, such as vegetables, into children's meals. Lapine's book came out, and in the same year, Seinfeld released her thematically similar book, *Deceptively Delicious: Simple Secrets to Get Your Kids Eating Good Food.* After reviewing and comparing the two books, the court dismissed the copyright claims, finding that the books were not substantially similar (as is required for a copyright infringement claim), and also dismissed the trademark claims. The court then turned to the § 43(a)(1)(B) claim that Seinfeld had taken Lapine's ideas and used them in her book without permission or attribution to the source of the ideas and work. Relying upon the *Dastar* limitation on the word "origin," the court held that § 43(a)(1)(B) did not apply to claims of failure to attribute

---

65 *See* Antidite Intern. Films, Inc. v. Bloomsbury Pub., PLC, 467 F. Supp. 2d 394, 400 (S.D.N.Y. 2006) ("If authorship were a 'characteristic[ ]' or 'qualit[y]' of a work, then the very claim *Dastar* rejected under § 43(a)(1)(A) would have been available under § 43(a)(1)(B)."); Baden Sports, Inc. v. Molten USA, Inc., 556 F.3d 1300, 1307 (Fed. Cir. 2009) (concluding that authorship is not a "nature, characteristic, [or] quality" as those terms are used in § 43(a)(1)(B)); *cf.* Sybersound Records, Inc. v. UAV Corp., 517 F.3d 1137, 1144 (9th Cir. 2008) (holding that the "nature, characteristics, and qualities" language of § 43(a)(1)(B) does not refer to the licensing status of a copyrighted good because to hold otherwise would create overlap between the Copyright Act and the Lanham Act).

66 No. 08 Civ. 128 (LTS) (RLE), 2009 WL 2902584 (S.D.N.Y. 2010).

authorship.[67] In reaching that conclusion, the court relied upon other courts which had held that, under *Dastar*, authorship is not a characteristic or quality.

At first blush, this limitation seems to make sense. After all, if a copyright claim doesn't exist under the Copyright Act, why should the Lanham Act provide one? But does *Dastar* really exclude all false claims of authorship under § 43(a)(1)(B)? Is a holding that authorship is not a "nature, characteristic, [or] quality" consistent with the reasoning in *Dastar* in all circumstances? This broad reading of *Dastar* is not universally accepted. Consider the following excerpt and hypothetical from an article by Professor David Nimmer:

> The broad reading is that the opinion negates any regulation by the Lanham Act that is geared at works of authorship, rather than being limited to the domain under review of reverse passing off. Under this interpretation, the tort of authorial passing off . . . as well as reverse passing off is no longer cognizable under federal law. The result would be that a publisher could hire a hack to write a potboiler and proceed to emblazon the resulting cover with the false legend "By John Grisham and Stephen King, in an unprecedented collaboration."[68]

Under the broad view in which authorship claims are outside the scope of § 43(a)(1)(B), no cause of action would exist. But in doing so, we allow a series of misrepresentations that would otherwise be actionable. In Nimmer's example, we have a marketing technique that is false and it is easy to assume that such claims would both deceive consumers and be material. Unlike the *Dastar* facts, however, there is no concern with creating a cause of action in conflict with the Copyright Act, nor would allowing the cause of action conflict with the precedents cited by the Court. Further, none of the practical concerns from *Dastar* are present. There is no need to worry about tracking down the true origin and the defendants will not be placed in the position of facing liability if they fail to falsely attribute King and Grisham (it is doubtful they would go around demanding that their name be placed on books that they had nothing to do with). Nonetheless, a number of cases articulate a sweeping view that authorship claims are also outside the scope of § 43(a)(1)(B).

Thus far the discussion has been limited to reverse passing-off claims under the Lanham Act. As for the common law, under § 5 of the Restatement (Third) of Unfair Competition, the language is much

---

67 *Id.* at *15.

68 David Nimmer, *The Moral Imperative Against Academic Plagiarism (Without a Moral Right Against Reverse Passing Off)*, 54 DEPAUL L. REV. 1, 43 (2004).

more restrictive in that it only applies to misrepresentations concerning who is the "manufacturer, producer, or supplier." The language of the comments seems to indicate that § 5 only applies by its terms to the physical source of goods or services.[69] Therefore, it seems that *Dastar* is consistent with the Restatement's view of reverse passing-off.

## E. STANDING FOR FALSE ADVERTISING CLAIMS AND CONTRIBUTORY LIABILITY

### 1. Prudential Standing

An important concern for plaintiffs under both the Lanham Act and in states that follow the Restatement is who can sue, i.e., who has standing? A quick review of the language in § 43(a) of the Lanham Act reveals few limitations on who can sue for a violation of its provisions. By its terms, "any person who believes that he or she is or is likely to be damaged" is capable of suing. Thus, it appears that a consumer on the street who believes a false advertisement and makes a purchase could sue for a violation of the Lanham Act. However, this is not the case. Courts have read into the Lanham Act a limit on who can sue under the concept of prudential standing. This is a judicially created limit on who can sue under an act based upon what conduct the act is aimed at and which parties the act seeks to protect. In the false advertising area, courts have determined that § 43 of the Lanham Act is meant to protect commercial interests. Thus, consumers cannot sue for violations of the Lanham Act (although, as Section G. discusses below, there are a number of state statutes prohibiting deceptive practices that do convey standing upon consumers).

Although the federal courts agree that consumers cannot sue for violations of the Lanham Act, for many years there was disagreement over what limits should be placed on parties with a commercial interest. Consider the following example. Brock's Menswear is the exclusive distributor of Venture Brand watches (manufactured by Venture Industries). Brock's competitor, Black Heart's Apparel, begins falsely advertising that it also sells Venture Brand watches, but the watches are actually cheap knock-offs. Brock's is the main competitor of Black Heart's, but is there any doubt that this false advertising will also harm Venture Industries? Should the Lanham Act apply only to direct competitors, or can it also apply to those farther up (or down) the supply chain who are also injured by a false or misleading advertisement?

---

69 *See* RESTATEMENT (THIRD) OF UNFAIR COMPETITION § 5 cmt. c (1995).

Until 2014, the federal circuit courts were split over how to approach this problem. One approach, known as the "categorical" test, limited standing only to those persons in actual competition with each other. A second approach, known as the "reasonable interest" test, looked to whether the plaintiff had a reasonable interest to be protected. Finally, other courts adopted the "Conte Brothers" test, which was taken from the Third Circuit decision of *Conte Brothers Automotive, Inc. v. Quaker State-Slick 50, Inc.*[70] That test considered five factors in weighing whether a plaintiff had standing. In 2014, the U.S. Supreme Court finally resolved the split in *Lexmark International, Inc. v. Static Control Components, Inc.*[71] That case involved Lexmark International, Inc., a manufacturer and seller of laser printers and toner cartridges. These toner cartridges were the only type that Lexmark printers were designed to accept. However, other businesses refurbished used Lexmark toner cartridges and sold them in competition with Lexmark.

To prevent the remanufacturing market from eating into its own market, Lexmark introduced a "Prebate" program through which customers received a discount on new toner cartridges in exchange for agreeing to return used cartridges directly to Lexmark. The terms of the Prebate program were communicated to consumers through notices printed on the toner-cartridge boxes ("shrinkwrap licensing") and enforced by embedding a microchip that disabled an empty cartridge until Lexmark replaced it. Component supplier Static Control Components, Inc. was the leading supplier of components "necessary to remanufacture Lexmark cartridges" including toner, replacement parts, and most importantly, a microchip that mimicked Lexmark's microchip. Without such a chip, the refurbished toner cartridges would not work in the Lexmark printers.

Lexmark sued Static Control, alleging that Static Control's microchips violated the Copyright Act of 1976 and the Digital Millennium Copyright Act. Static Control counterclaimed, alleging, among other things, violations of the Lanham Act's prohibition on false advertising. Static Control's Lanham Act claim alleged two types of objectionable conduct by Lexmark. First, it asserted that Lexmark misled consumers to believe that they were legally bound by the Prebate terms. Second, it claimed that Lexmark sent letters to most of the toner cartridge manufacturers, falsely advising them that it was illegal to sell refurbished Prebate cartridges and to use Static Control's products to refurbish those cartridges. According to Static Control, this misrepresented "the nature, characteristics, and qualities" of both Lexmark's and Static Control's products. Static

[70] 165 F.3d 221 (3d Cir. 1998).

[71] 572 U.S. 118 (2014).

Control also argued that these misrepresentations had "proximately caused and [we]re likely to cause injury" to Static Control by "diverting sales from [Static Control] to Lexmark" and had "substantially injured [its] business reputation" by leading consumers and others to believe that Static Control was engaged in illegal conduct.

The district court granted Lexmark's motion to dismiss the Lanham Act claim, holding that Static Control lacked "prudential standing" under a multifactor balancing test based on the *Conte Brothers* case. The Sixth Circuit reversed the Lanham Act dismissal. It identified the three competing approaches for determining whether a plaintiff had standing to sue under the Lanham Act and ultimately adopted the Second Circuit's "reasonable interest" approach, under which a plaintiff has standing "if the claimant can demonstrate '(1) a reasonable interest to be protected against the alleged false advertising and (2) a reasonable basis for believing that the interest is likely to be damaged by the alleged false advertising.' "[72] The Sixth Circuit concluded that Static Control had standing because it "alleged a cognizable interest in its business reputation and sales to remanufacturers and sufficiently alleged that th[ose] interests were harmed by Lexmark's statements."[73]

On appeal, the Supreme Court rejected and replaced the existing prudential standing tests with its own two-part inquiry. First, are the claimed injuries within the "zone of interests" the Lanham Act was passed to address? Second, were the injuries proximately caused by the defendant's violation(s) of the Lanham Act? The Court held that the first inquiry was met, noting that it was made easy due to the Lanham Act's clear statement of purpose. The Court then noted that "[m]ost of the enumerated purposes are relevant to false-association cases; a typical false-advertising case will implicate only the Act's goal of 'protect[ing] persons engaged in [commerce within the control of Congress] against unfair competition.' "[74] The Court agreed that under the zone of interests inquiry, only commercial interests are protected, and thus consumers cannot sue under the Act. The Court then concluded that to satisfy this test, a plaintiff must "allege an injury to a commercial interest in reputation or sales."[75] Static's claim met the zone of interests part of the test because it alleged a loss of sales and damage to its business reputation.

---

[72] *Id.* at 124 (quoting Famous Horse, Inc. v. 5th Avenue Photo Inc., 624 F.3d 106, 113 (2d Cir. 2010)).

[73] *Id.*

[74] *Id.* at 131.

[75] *Id.* at 119.

The proximate cause requirement is more difficult to define—which the Court itself noted. However, the Court found "that courts have a great deal of experience applying it [proximate cause], and there is a wealth of precedent for them to draw upon in doing so."[76] About the most guidance the Court provided on this analysis is that proximate cause prevents suits for damages that are "too remote" from the defendant's unlawful conduct, but this does not mean that only direct competitors can bring suit. The Court concluded:

> We thus hold that a plaintiff suing under § 1125(a) [of the Lanham Act] ordinarily must show economic or reputational injury flowing directly from the deception wrought by the defendant's advertising; and that that occurs when deception of consumers causes them to withhold trade from the plaintiff. That showing is generally not made when the deception produces injuries to a fellow commercial actor that in turn affect the plaintiff.[77]

Static's claim met the "proximate cause" part of the test even though it was not a competitor of Lexmark because it alleged both reputational injury and loss of sales flowing from Lexmark's false statements. The allegedly false statements were that Static's microchips were illegal infringements. The Court noted that "when a party claims reputational injury from disparagement, competition is not required for proximate cause; and that is true even if the defendant's aim was to harm its immediate competitors, and the plaintiff merely suffered collateral damage."[78] As for the loss of sales, although Static Control was not a direct competitor of Lexmark, the Court nonetheless held that proximate cause was shown:

> In addition, Static Control adequately alleged proximate causation by alleging that it designed, manufactured, and sold microchips that both (1) were necessary for, and (2) had no other use than, refurbishing Lexmark toner cartridges. It follows from that allegation that any false advertising that reduced the remanufacturers' business necessarily injured Static Control as well. Taking Static Control's assertions at face value, there is likely to be something very close to a 1:1 relationship between the number of refurbished Prebate cartridges sold (or not sold) by the remanufacturers and the number of Prebate microchips sold (or not sold) by Static Control.[79]

---

76 *Id.* at 133.

77 *Id.* at 133–34.

78 *Id.* at 138.

79 *Id.* at 139.

One of the more striking aspects of *Lexmark* is Justice Scalia's treatment of the prudential standing doctrine in general. Scalia begins by noting that Article III standing is clearly present (and was not contested by Lexmark). Lexmark, however, wished to have the case dismissed upon the premise that certain prudential concerns mitigated against Static Control's ability to bring suit. The Court described prudential standing as generally encompassing "at least three broad principles: 'the general prohibition on a litigant's raising another person's legal rights, the rule barring adjudication of generalized grievances more appropriately addressed in the representative branches, and the requirement that a plaintiff's complaint fall within the zone of interests protected by the law invoked.' "[80] Scalia then reframed the case relied upon by the Sixth Circuit as one that was based not on prudential concerns but on statutory considerations.

As part of his analysis, Scalia noted that the Court had moved away from prudential standing concepts as being in "tension with our recent reaffirmation of the principle that 'a federal court's 'obligation' to hear and decide' cases within its jurisdiction 'is 'virtually unflagging.''"[81] Scalia stated that the prudential standing label was inappropriate as only Article III standing and a statutory basis to bring suit was required. Thus, the Supreme Court has essentially demolished prudential standing in the deceptive marketing context and replaced it with the concept of statutory standing (which Scalia noted in a footnote was an improved label, although also not entirely accurate).

### 2. Contributory Liability of Manufacturers and Publishers

Once a plaintiff has standing, a broader class of defendants may be sued for contributory liability. For instance, the Restatement of Unfair Competition allows for liability to attach to those who are not necessarily in direct competition with the plaintiff. This should have been apparent from the above discussion on standing—if a plaintiff does not have to be a direct competitor to bring suit, then the defendant does not have to be a direct competitor. Section 3 speaks only in terms of the materiality of the representation and a reasonable basis for believing that the representation will cause the plaintiff harm; thus, it does not limit the class of defendants to direct competitors. Liability can also extend to those who assist defendants in making false or misleading advertisements under a theory of contributory liability. This is provided for in §§ 7–8 of the

---

80 *Id.* at 126.

81 *Id.*

Restatement, which extends contributory liability to the publishers of false or misleading advertising and to those who market goods to retailers who in turn engage in false advertising.

The Restatement recognizes two forms of contributory liability: (1) the publisher of the false statements (such as the newspaper that runs a false ad); and (2) the manufacturer or supplier who induces or knows (or should know) that the retailer is committing a violation and does nothing. Importantly, § 7 limits the remedy to injunctive relief for the innocent publisher (which mirrors § 2 of the Lanham Act):

> **§ 7. Contributory Liability Of Printers, Publishers, And Other Suppliers**
>
> (1) One who, by supplying materials or rendering services to a third person, directly and substantially assists the third person in making a representation that subjects the third person to liability to another for deceptive marketing under the rules stated in §§ 2–6 is subject to liability to that other for contributory deceptive marketing.
>
> (2) If an actor subject to contributory liability under the rule stated in Subsection (1) acted without knowledge that the actor was assisting the third person in making a representation likely to deceive or mislead, the actor is subject only to appropriate injunctive relief.

Thus, if a newspaper runs advertisements for a retailer that turn out to be false or deceptive, the newspaper would be liable under § 7(1) for rendering services that substantially assist the retailer in making its false ads. Under § 7(1), the newspaper's intent or knowledge of the false misrepresentations is irrelevant. However, under § 7(2), if the newspaper acts without knowledge, then the only remedy available is injunctive relief.

Intent also plays a role in the liability of manufacturers and distributors, as articulated in § 8:

> **§ 8. Contributory Liability Of Manufacturers And Distributors**
>
> One who markets goods or services to a third person who further markets the goods or services in a manner that subjects the third person to liability to another for deceptive marketing under the rules stated in §§ 2–6 is subject to liability to that other for contributory deceptive marketing if:
>
> (a) the actor intentionally induces the third person to engage in such conduct; or

> (b) the actor fails to take reasonable precautions against the occurrence of the third person's conduct in circumstances in which that conduct can be reasonably anticipated.

Notice that liability is assigned both for inducement under § 8(a) and turning a blind eye to the misrepresentations under § 8(b). Thus, once the conduct is reasonably anticipated, there will be liability if the contributor failed to take reasonable precautions against the occurrence of the false advertising. The Reporter's Note makes clear that "reasonable anticipation" by itself is not enough:

> This Section rejects the stated rationale although not necessarily the results of those decisions that impose liability on the basis of the actor's "reasonable anticipation" alone. Under the rule stated in Subsection (b), an actor is not subject to liability if it has taken precautions against the other person's misrepresentations that are reasonable under the circumstances; liability may be imposed only upon a showing of both reasonable anticipation and a failure to take reasonable precautions.

*Sealy, Inc. v. Easy Living, Inc.*[82] demonstrates how such liability might attach. In that case, Danco, which advertised and sold a variety of bedding products, began to offer genuine Sealy mattresses together with non-Sealy Pacifica foundations made by Pacifica with identical fabric covering or "ticking." The foundations bore no identifying labels and therefore the mattress and foundation combination gave the impression of being a matched set. Indeed, at Danco's suggestion, the set was advertised by some retailers as a "Sealy Back-Saver and matching foundation." Sealy, Inc. brought suit against Danco seeking an injunction against sale of the mixed Sealy-Pacifica bed sets and also joined Pacifica as a defendant for contributory liability. The district court found for Sealy despite the fact that Pacifica took remedial measures, such as attaching labels to the top of each non-Sealy matching foundation identifying it as a "Quality Foundation Manufactured by Pacifica Mattress Co." The Seventh Circuit affirmed the district court's finding that the defendants foresaw and intended that Pacifica foundations would be passed off as Sealy products. Further, it affirmed the district court's conclusion that defendants' remedial measures were inadequate:

> The labels attached to the foundations could not easily be seen. Even if they were noticed, neither they nor the signs belatedly distributed to retailers explicitly denied that the Pacifica foundation was a Sealy product. Even a relatively

[82] 743 F.2d 1378 (7th Cir. 1984).

> sophisticated consumer might suppose that the "matching" Pacifica foundation was made under license from Sealy, Inc. Plaintiff's witnesses testified at trial that retail salesmen made no attempt to correct their misunderstanding that the Sealy mattress and Pacifica foundation were both made by Sealy. Defendants' measures did not overcome the misleading impression conveyed by the matching fabric ticking.[83]

Although § 43(a)(1) of the Lanham Act does not address contributory liability, § 32 of the Lanham Act provides for a similar standard as § 7 of the Restatement. Further, the U.S. Supreme Court has long recognized contributory liability for trademark violations,[84] and it has been extended to § 43.[85] Under § 43 of the Lanham Act, however, these claims are usually in relation to subsection (a)(1)(A) rather than (a)(1)(B). It is important to note that although publishers can be liable for contributory liability, innocent publishers are only subject to injunctive relief.[86]

## F. REMEDIES FOR FALSE ADVERTISING

The primary remedy sought in a deceptive marketing case is injunctive relief. Both the Restatement of Unfair Competition and the Lanham Act refer to the remedies available for trademark infringement for guidance on the issue of remedies. Injunctive relief is not the sole remedy. As noted above, however, seeking monetary damages rather than injunctive relief will affect the plaintiff's burden of proof on its common-law or § 43(a) false advertising claim. This was noted by the *Cashmere* court (recall that the two plaintiffs sought different forms of relief) which stated, "unlike a plaintiff seeking injunctive relief who only has to show that the misrepresentation had the tendency to deceive, a plaintiff seeking monetary damages must show that consumers were actually deceived by the misrepresentation, unless he can avail himself of a presumption to that effect."[87]

Along with affecting the consumer deception element, a party asking for monetary relief also bears a higher burden on causation. Once again, this was discussed in the *Cashmere* decision, in which the court stated that a plaintiff seeking monetary damages must

---

83 *Id.* at 1382.

84 *See* Inwood Labs., Inc. v. Ives Labs., Inc., 456 U.S. 844, 854 (1982).

85 *See* Procter & Gamble Co. v. Haugen, 317 F.3d 1121, 1128–30 (10th Cir. 2003) (recognizing a possible § 43 claim but ultimately rejecting the contributory liability claim on the merits).

86 *See* RESTATEMENT (THIRD) OF UNFAIR COMPETITION § 7(2) (1995); Lanham Act § 32, 15 U.S.C. § 1125 (2012).

87 Cashmere & Camel Hair Mfrs. Inst., 284 F.3d 302, 311 n.9 (1st Cir. 2002).

show *actual harm* to its business and a causal link between the defendant's actions and the damages. A plaintiff seeking only an injunction, on the other hand, has sufficiently met its burden once it has shown that there is a likelihood of harm (rather than having to show actual harm or damages). As comment a to § 35 of the Restatement (Third) of Unfair Competition notes, "[f]requently, the harm is not reparable by an award of monetary relief because of the difficulty of proving the amount of loss and a causal connection with the defendant's wrongful conduct."

Section 34 of the Lanham Act provides the courts with the power to issue injunctive relief "according to the principles of equity and upon such terms as the court may deem reasonable . . . to prevent a violation under [§ 43]." When injunctive relief is sought, the primary goal is to protect both the plaintiff and the public from future harm. Fashioning an appropriate remedy can be a difficult task and is highly fact specific, as demonstrated by § 35(2) of the Restatement:

> **§ 35. Injunctions: Trademark Infringement and Deceptive Marketing**
>
> . . . .
>
> (2) The appropriateness and scope of injunctive relief depend upon a comparative appraisal of all the factors of the case, including the following primary factors:
>
> (a) the nature of the interest to be protected;
>
> (b) the nature and extent of the wrongful conduct;
>
> (c) the relative adequacy to the plaintiff of an injunction and of other remedies;
>
> (d) the relative harm likely to result to the legitimate interests of the defendant if an injunction is granted and to the legitimate interests of the plaintiff if an injunction is denied;
>
> (e) the interests of third persons and of the public;
>
> (f) any unreasonable delay by the plaintiff in bringing suit or otherwise asserting its rights;
>
> (g) any related misconduct on the part of the plaintiff; and
>
> (h) the practicality of framing and enforcing the injunction.

Obviously, a number of factors are considered by the court when issuing an injunction. The Restatement in § 35(2) has attempted to capture the various factors, but there is no mechanical way to predict how a court will weigh the factors or what injunction it will ultimately issue.

Under §§ 32 and 35 of the Lanham Act, a violation of § 43 makes a defendant liable for damages. The Restatement in § 36(2) lists four possible sources for determining damages:

> (2) The pecuniary loss for which damages may be recovered under this Section includes:
>
> (a) loss resulting to the plaintiff from sales or other revenues lost because of the actor's conduct;
>
> (b) loss resulting from sales made by the plaintiff at prices that have been reasonably reduced because of the actor's conduct;
>
> (c) harm to the market reputation of the plaintiff's goods, services, business, or trademark; and
>
> (d) reasonable expenditures made by the plaintiff in order to prevent, correct, or mitigate the confusion or deception of prospective purchasers resulting from the actor's conduct.

Additionally, § 35 of the Lanham Act permits a court, in appropriate circumstances, to increase the award of actual damages by as much as three times the amount. Generally, under both the Lanham Act and the Restatement, the burden of proof is upon the plaintiff to show that it is entitled to damages and to establish the amount. However, once the fact of damages has been proven, a court may be more forgiving of the degree of certainty that it requires from the plaintiff in showing the exact amount. Relevant to this inquiry is the intent of the defendant and the clean hands of the plaintiff. Section 36(3) of the Restatement then lists a number of factors to be considered in awarding damages, including the intent of the parties.

Two additional remedies that may be sought are worthy of special mention. First, in certain circumstances, a plaintiff may be awarded the defendant's net profits instead of its own actual damages. Both § 35 of the Lanham Act and § 37 of the Restatement provide for this option. The Restatement § 37 mentions two important limitations upon this remedy: "(a) the actor engaged in the conduct with the intention of causing confusion or deception; and (b) the award of profits is not prohibited by statute and is otherwise appropriate under the rule stated in Subsection (2)." Subsection (2) takes into account such factors as the degree of certainty that the actor benefitted from the unlawful conduct, the relative adequacy to the plaintiff of other remedies, including an award of damages, and the interests of the public in depriving the actor of unjust gains and discouraging unlawful conduct.

Second, the Lanham Act specifically provides that the prevailing party may be awarded reasonable attorney's fees. However, such fees are only to be awarded in "exceptional cases." This "exceptional cases" language has been interpreted to mean only in cases of deliberate infringement or when the prosecution of the claim is in bad faith. The Restatement does not provide for attorney's fees as "[m]ost states do not provide for the recovery of attorney's fees in actions at common law."[88]

The case of *ALPO Petfoods, Inc. v. Ralston Purina Co.*[89] demonstrates some of the obstacles inherent in awarding lost profits, attorney's fees, and injunctive relief. In *ALPO*, Ralston changed the formula for its food and began running ads (both print and television) stating that its new food could lessen the severity of Canine Hip Dysplasia (CHD). Ralston directed this advertising at veterinarians, breeders, dog enthusiasts, and others interested in dog nutrition. Ralston's claims, however, had a weak empirical basis. The hypothesis was based on the "anion gap theory" of Dr. Richard Kealy, a Ralston nutritionist. Dr. Kealy conducted a series of studies (4 were conducted) exploring this theory. He then briefed Ralston's marketing executives leading to the product reformulation and advertising campaigns. When Dr. Kealy began a fifth trial to study the long-term effects of his theory, he found that the results undermined Ralston's CHD claims. Over roughly the same period as Ralston's CHD claims, ALPO claimed that veterinarians preferred the formula of ALPO's food over that of the leading puppy food two to one.

Ralston and ALPO sued each other for false advertising related to each party's claims about its puppy food brand. The district court found that each was liable and imposed injunctions on both parties. The district court also awarded ALPO $10.4 million in damages (which was deemed to be based upon Ralston's profits) and granted costs and attorney's fees to both sides.

On appeal, the D.C. Circuit overturned the award of damages. The court subscribed to the theory, held by many other courts, that awarding damages to a plaintiff based upon the defendant's profits (i.e., a disgorgement of profits) required a showing of willfulness or bad faith, which was lacking. Similarly, the court overturned the award of attorney's fees because the Lanham Act only permits such an award in "exceptional circumstances." As mentioned, although the

---

88 RESTATEMENT (THIRD) OF UNFAIR COMPETITION § 36 cmt. o (1995).

89 913 F.2d 958 (D.C. Cir. 1990).

term is not defined in the Lanham Act, exceptional circumstances have been found when there is a finding of willfulness or "bad faith"—findings which were absent in this case. Finally, with regard to the injunction, the court upheld it as to both parties but limited the scope as it applied to Ralston. The injunction issued by the district court was so broad as to require non-Ralston scientists to obtain court approval before publishing articles on CHD (studies of which were at issue in the case). In addressing the scope of the injunction, the court stated:

> The law requires that courts closely tailor injunctions to the harm that they address. In enjoining Ralston, the district court identified the harm redressed by the injunctions as deception of puppy food buyers and erosion of ALPO's business. Yet the prohibitory injunction, both as entered and, particularly, as implemented, suppresses more speech than protecting these interests requires. ALPO's false-advertising claim against Ralston involves a dispute over whether Ralston may commercially claim that Puppy Chow confers certain unproved health benefits [related to CHD]. Redressing the harm that these claims have caused in the puppy food market does not require that a court supervise all future debate on [a CHD-related theory].[90]

In remanding the case, the court did not leave the parties without guidance on damages that could still be available to them. In particular, the court noted that the parties could seek actual damages, including "profits lost by the plaintiff on sales actually diverted to the false advertiser," "profits lost by the plaintiff on sales made at prices reduced as a demonstrated result of the false advertising," "the costs of any completed advertising that actually and reasonably responds to the defendant's offending ads," and "quantifiable harm to the plaintiff's good will, to the extent that completed corrective advertising has not repaired that harm."[91]

The parties took the court's advice and the district court awarded damages to both sides for their costs in producing responsive marketing. Generally, this is advertising that is meant to correct a competitor's false advertising, be it through correcting a misimpression about a competitor's own product, correcting misstatements made about the plaintiff's product, or perhaps just increasing a marketing budget to counter the effect of the false advertising. Specifically, the district court awarded $12 million to ALPO for the cost of responsive ads, the delay Ralston caused ALPO in achieving national distribution of ALPO Puppy Food, and a 50%

---

90 *Id.* at 972.

91 *Id.* at 969.

enhancement to compensate ALPO for profits lost on sales diverted to Ralston, as well as the permanent distortion of the puppy food market caused by the false advertising, interest, and inflation. The district court also awarded Ralston $53,434 for the cost of its advertising responsive to ALPO's false claims.

Responsive advertising is the fourth source of damages listed in § 36(2) of the Restatement. An interesting advantage to claiming this as a source of damages has to do with the burden of proof. Recall that a plaintiff seeking monetary damages usually must show actual consumer confusion, but only a likelihood of confusion if the plaintiff is seeking an injunction. However, many courts only require a showing of a likelihood of confusion for a recovery of money spent on responsive advertising.[92] The reasoning often employed is that it is unfair to require a plaintiff to wait until it has suffered injury to start corrective advertising. In addition, it would be unfair to punish a plaintiff who may have successfully avoided injury through expenditures on such corrective advertising.

The decision of *Balance Dynamics Corp. v. Schmitt Indus.*[93] offers useful insight into the practical considerations of having a lower burden of proof:

> [A] rule that predicated recovery of damage control expenses on a showing of marketplace damages would penalize successful efforts at mitigating damages. That is, under such a rule, a plaintiff who is successful in preventing marketplace damages would not be able to recover under the Lanham Act, but a plaintiff who is unsuccessful would be permitted to recover. That would be an anomaly.
>
> We also note that the practical realities of business litigation favor a rule that damage control costs should be recoverable even where plaintiffs do not demonstrate actual confusion or marketplace injury. For one, marketplace damages and actual confusion are notoriously difficult and expensive to prove. *See PPX Enterprises, Inc. v. Audiofidelity Enterprises, Inc.*, 818 F.2d at 272–73; *U-Haul Int'l, Inc. v. Jartran, Inc.*, 793 F.2d at 1041. More importantly, however, even where marketplace damages or actual confusion are provable in theory, such proof often

---

[92] *See* Balance Dynamics Corp. v. Schmitt Indus., 204 F.3d 683, 692–93 (6th Cir. 2000) (stating that to recover damage control expenses, plaintiffs must show that a violation of the Lanham Act occurred and that (1) there was a likelihood of confusion or damages to sales, profits, or goodwill; (2) its damage control expenses were attributable to the violation (i.e., caused by the violation); and (3) its damage control efforts were reasonable under the circumstances and proportionate to the damage that was likely to occur).

[93] 204 F.3d 683 (6th Cir. 2000).

> requires that a plaintiff solicit its own customers for affidavits, which puts the customers at risk of being subpoenaed by the defendant. Plaintiffs are justifiably hesitant to alienate or upset their customers in this way. In addition, plaintiffs may hesitate to put marketplace damages at issue because that would entitle a defendant to discover information about plaintiff's business. As may have been the case here, oftentimes the rational business decision is for a plaintiff to embark on a campaign of damage control and forego a demonstration of injury in the marketplace or actual confusion of their customers. Such a plaintiff should not be required to give up compensation for its damage control expenses when the defendant's wrongful action necessitated those expenses in the first place.[94]

In other words, the remedy is analogous to injunctive relief in that a court could force a defendant to run corrective ads itself; therefore, if the plaintiff undertakes the task, it is only fair to have the defendant reimburse such expenses.

Although the second award in *ALPO* included responsive marketing, this was also appealed as issues remained. In *ALPO Petfoods, Inc. v. Ralston Purina Co.* (*ALPO II*),[95] the court recognized the right to recover damages for responsive marketing, but it remanded to the district court to account for the fact that some of the responsive marketing was itself deceptive. This is based upon an unclean hands concept. While plaintiffs are entitled to issue corrective ads, they cannot engage in false advertising themselves while doing so. However, unclean hands is not necessarily an all-or-nothing proposition.[96] Sometimes a plaintiff can have unclean hands and still recover if it is in the best interests of the public:

> [I]t appears in the light of the clear purpose of Section 43(a) that to permit a suitor with unclean hands to obtain injunctive relief would run afoul of the legislative goals. Accordingly, we conclude that the equitable maxim of clean hands is clearly applicable and may be raised in actions seeking injunctive relief under Section 43(a). While unarticulated in the Act itself, an underlying purpose of Section 43(a) appears to be protection of the consuming public from false representations and descriptions in connection with the advertising of goods and services. See

---

94 *Id.* at 692.

95 997 F.2d 949 (D.C. Cir. 1993).

96 *See* Ames Pub. Co. v. Walker-Davis Publications, Inc., 372 F. Supp. 1, 13–15 (E.D. Pa. 1974) (permitting a plaintiff to recover, despite unclean hands, in part because of the harm to the public that would result if recovery were denied).

> J. T. McCarthy, Trademarks and Unfair Competition, § 27:3 at 246–47. Thus, in balancing the equity between the parties, it is appropriate that the Court also weigh the interest of the consuming public.
>
> . . . .
>
> In summary, the equitable doctrine of clean hands is not a rigid formula, but requires the free and just exercise of discretion. In exercising our discretion we must strike an equitable balance not only between the interests of the parties, but also the interests of the consuming public. Since the advertisers, with whom we are concerned in this action, lack standing to bring suit on their own behalf, they must rely on a 'vicarious avenger' of their interest, who has emerged from this case somewhat tarnished. To deny an injunction on the basis that plaintiffs are also blameworthy would leave two wrongs unremedied and thereby increase the injury to the public. Thus, considering the facts (1) that the vindication of the wrong committed against the public interest mandates a remedy; (2) that plaintiffs' conduct occurred prior to the formation of defendants' enterprise and was not directed at defendants and did not injure them in any way, and (3) that some of the individual defendants participated in the conduct of which they now complain, we conclude that the doctrine of unclean hands does not apply in this case to bar injunctive relief.[97]

A final remedy that is not available under the common law but is available under the Lanham Act is a damages enhancement. Section 35(a) of the Lanham Act authorizes the court to award up to three times a plaintiff's actual and proven damages so long as it is compensatory and not punitive. This was an issue in *ALPO II*, as the district court enhanced the award to ALPO by 50% in order to cover its lost profits, compensate ALPO for a permanent distortion in the market for puppy food, and provide for interest and inflation. The court of appeals noted that an enhancement is appropriate to compensate a Lanham Act plaintiff "only for such adverse effects as can neither be dismissed as speculative nor precisely calculated." As interest and inflation were not difficult to calculate, the court remanded for a precise computation. But the court noted that "[l]ost profits and market distortion are, however, appropriate bases for the catch-all enhancement contemplated by § 35(a)." Moreover, the court observed that the enhancement could be appropriate if solely to "compensate ALPO for its lost profits on sales diverted to Ralston and

---

97 *Id.*

the continuing distortion of the market owing to Ralston's false advertising."[98]

## G. THE ROLE OF THE FTC AND "LITTLE FTC ACTS"

As noted above, consumers have no standing to sue under the Lanham Act and the Restatement. Nevertheless, two important avenues exist for protecting consumer interests in the absence of a suit by competitors: actions brought by the Federal Trade Commission ("FTC") under § 5 of the Federal Trade Commission Act ("FTCA"), and suits brought by consumers themselves under what have become known as "Little FTC Acts." Although a thorough coverage of each is beyond the scope of this text, they are mentioned here to give a sense of other causes of action that may be asserted against a business engaged in deceptive marketing.

Congress first enacted the FTCA in 1914. Of particular importance, § 5 of the Act made "[u]nfair methods of competition" unlawful. The Act also created a new federal agency, the FTC, whose responsibilities would include investigating and prosecuting violations of the Act. Due to the "competition" language used in the original act, some courts construed the FTC's authority as limited to those cases involving injury to competitors. Thus, in 1938, Congress amended § 5 of the FTCA keeping the "[u]nfair methods of competition" language and adding that "unfair or deceptive acts or practices" were also unlawful.[99] As § 5 reads today, it prohibits not just activities "in commerce," but also activities "affecting commerce."

The FTC is a quasi-judicial body that administers the FTCA. It issues complaints and conducts hearings before administrative law judges. These decisions are reviewable by the full Commission (there are five commissioners), and further appeals may be heard by any federal circuit court of appeals. Typically, the FTC seeks injunctive relief in the form of "cease and desist" letters, but it may seek other corrective actions, such as assessing civil penalties or having violators issue refunds.

The FTC's powers under the FTCA are great because the definition of "unfair methods of competition" has been construed broadly. The FTC has sought to challenge various types of conduct, including false and misleading use of trademarks, trade names, unsubstantiated product claims, testimonials, and even unfair credit practices and product disparagement claims. Furthermore, the FTC's

[98] *ALPO Petfoods, Inc.*, 997 F.2d at 955.

[99] That same year, Congress added a new § 12, which defined the terms "unlawful" and "unfair or deceptive act or practice" with a particular focus on false advertising.

grant of power authorizes it to bring federal antitrust actions. In short, § 5 grants the FTC the ability to challenge conduct which would often be actionable under the Lanham Act, as well as conduct that would fall outside of the Lanham Act's scope.

Although the FTC acts for the benefit of the public, there is no private right of action under the FTCA. If the FTC chooses not to pursue or challenge a particular practice, private parties or state attorneys general may still move forward under what have been dubbed "Little FTC Acts." These acts are state consumer protection statutes that typically prohibit a broad range of unfair or deceptive trade and business practices. Many are based upon the recommendations of the FTC, as found in its Unfair Trade Practices and Consumer Protection Act.

Although these Little FTC Acts come from a common origin, it would be a mistake to assume that they offer little variation. For instance, some statutes provide a laundry list of specifically prohibited conduct while others do not. Some statutes provide that only consumers may sue, others also permit business consumers to sue, while still others permit business competitors to sue. Some statutes place a greater emphasis on the role of intent, while others indicate that an intent to deceive is unnecessary for an action to lie. Some statutes even permit the imposition of punitive damages in certain cases. Despite these variations, common elements shared by many of these Little FTC Acts include the ability of plaintiffs to obtain damages in excess of their actual damages (typically treble damages in an appropriate case), the authorization of injunctive relief, and the recovery of attorney's fees.

# Chapter 7

# COMMERCIAL DISPARAGEMENT

## A. INTRODUCTION

In the prior chapter, the law of deceptive marketing was reviewed, which, in essence, involves making false statements about one's own products or services. A closely related legal theory, and one that is often intertwined with deceptive marketing, is commercial disparagement, i.e., making or publishing disparaging statements about another's goods or services. Indeed, in the last chapter there were instances where the deceptive marketing also included disparaging remarks about a competitor. In this chapter, commercial disparagement is examined under both the common law and the Lanham Act (which is broadly worded to include disparagement claims). The similar but distinct concept of business defamation is also discussed.

Section B gives a background on common law commercial disparagement and also distinguishes disparagement from defamation. Section C discusses the elements of a commercial disparagement claim in detail as well as the privileges that may exist. Section D briefly touches on actions for false statements in the sale of another's goods. Finally, Section E discusses commercial disparagement under the Lanham Act with a particular focus on what qualifies as "commercial advertising or promotion" and on First Amendment free speech concerns that can arise in such an action.

## B. DISPARAGEMENT UNDER THE COMMON LAW GENERALLY

A cause of action for slander of title—i.e., for falsely claiming an ownership interest in property—has long been a part of the common law. The law eventually broadened to include liability for false statements concerning a plaintiff's products, and today, it includes any false statement that harms a plaintiff's pecuniary interest.[1] Unfortunately, courts have tended to use a variety of names for this cause of action, including "commercial disparagement," "product disparagement," "disparagement of property," "trade libel," and "injurious falsehood." For simplicity's sake, this chapter refers to the cause of action as commercial disparagement, but one should be aware of these variants.

---

1 *See* RESTATEMENT (SECOND) OF TORTS § 623A (1977).

### 1. Business Disparagement Under the Restatement (Second) of Torts

The Restatement (Second) of Torts provides that a defendant may be liable to a plaintiff for publishing a false statement that is harmful to the plaintiff's pecuniary interest:

> **§ 623A. Liability For Publication Of Injurious Falsehood—General Principle**
>
> One who publishes a false statement harmful to the interests of another is subject to liability for pecuniary loss resulting to the other if
>
> (a) he intends for publication of the statement to result in harm to interests of the other having a pecuniary value, or either recognizes or should recognize that it is likely to do so, and
>
> (b) he knows that the statement is false or acts in reckless disregard of its truth or falsity.

Sections 624 and 626 specifically provide that a defendant may be liable for slander of title (calling into question the ownership rights of the plaintiff in land or other property) as well as for trade libel (disparaging the quality of the plaintiff's land or other property). Liability under § 623A is not limited to these two instances, however, and extends to any pecuniary harm resulting from disparaging the "interests" of the plaintiff. The following illustrations from § 623A are instructive on this point:

> 3. A, knowing his statement to be false, tells C that B has died. As a result C, who had intended to purchase goods from B, buys them elsewhere. A is subject to liability to B.
>
> 4. A, knowing his statement to be false, tells C that B, an importer of wood, does not deal in mahogany. As a result C, who had intended to buy mahogany from B, buys it elsewhere. A is subject to liability to B.[2]

Note how in each of the above illustrations, neither the title nor quality of property owned by the plaintiff is called into question, yet § 623A is broad enough to encompass both. This standard is also broad enough to cover services and other pecuniary interests as demonstrated by these illustrations.

A question may arise as to why the statements in Illustrations 3 and 4 are not actionable as fraud. Unlike fraud, there is no requirement that the defendant intend to induce reliance by the

---

[2] RESTATEMENT (SECOND) TORTS § 623A cmt. a (1977).

plaintiff under the Restatement standard. This is articulated in the definition of disparagement in Restatement § 629(b):

> A statement is disparaging if it is understood to cast doubt upon the quality of another's land, chattels or intangible things, or upon the existence or extent of his property in them, and
>
> (a) the publisher intends the statement to cast the doubt, or
>
> (b) the recipient's understanding of it as casting the doubt was reasonable.

While (a) involves intent, (b) does not require it. Furthermore, under fraud, it is the plaintiff who must be induced to act by the misrepresentation, while here, the plaintiff is not the one that acted in reliance—it was a third party (such as a consumer) who chooses not to buy the plaintiff's wares. Of course, this could also give rise to a tortious interference with prospective contract claim, and it is not uncommon to see both causes of action raised from the same set of facts.

As a result of this overlap, some courts have been unwilling to recognize the injurious falsehood cause of action. For instance, in *Kenney v. Hangar Prosthetics & Orthotics, Inc.*,[3] the court was faced with a plaintiff claiming a number of causes of action against his former employer, including breach of contract, defamation, and tortious interference with prospective business advantage. The plaintiff attempted to amend his complaint to include an injurious falsehood claim, but he was denied by the trial court. In affirming the trial court's denial, the *Kenney* court noted that an injurious falsehood claim was not recognized in Kentucky, as it was really just a form of intentional interference with economic relations.[4] Similarly, some courts have failed to recognize injurious falsehood as a separate tort on the ground that it is nothing more than a defamation claim.[5]

## 2. Disparagement Distinct from Defamation

Given the nature of disparagement, it is tempting to lump it together with the common law tort of defamation. After all, both causes of action involve the publication of false statements that affect the plaintiff. However, the two causes of action are, in fact, separate

---

3 269 S.W.3d 866 (Ky. Ct. App. 2007).

4 *Id.* at 873 (citing W. PAGE KEETON ET AL., PROSSER AND KEETON ON THE LAW OF TORTS § 128, at 964 (5th ed. 1984)).

5 *See* DAN B. DOBBS ET AL., THE LAW OF TORTS § 656 (2d ed. 2012) (citing Davita Inc. v. Nephrology Assocs., P.C., 253 F. Supp. 2d 1370, 1374–75 (S.D. Ga. 2003) (applying Georgia law)).

and they evolved from completely different origins. This distinction is important as the causes of action protect different interests and carry different burdens of proof on key elements. Section 558 of the Restatement (Second) of Torts covers the defamation cause of action:

> **§ 558. Elements Stated**
>
> To create liability for defamation there must be:
>
> (a) a false and defamatory statement concerning another;
>
> (b) an unprivileged publication to a third party;
>
> (c) fault amounting at least to negligence on the part of the publisher; and
>
> (d) either actionability of the statement irrespective of special harm or the existence of special harm caused by the publication.

The primary distinction between a defamation action and a disparagement claim is not apparent from the text of this section unless we focus on the word "defamatory." A defamatory statement impugns the character or reputation of the plaintiff, whereas the sections on disparagement speak to harming the interests of the plaintiff, such as by calling into question the title or quality of the plaintiff's property. Some false statements, of course, may harm both the plaintiff's reputation and the interests of the plaintiff. For instance, a false allegation that a grocer has been selling non-organic fruits as "organic" harms both the reputation of the grocer in the community and the pecuniary interest of the grocer (assuming that the grocer can show a drop-off in sales). While it is possible that a false statement could be actionable as both defamation and disparagement, such cases are few and far between. Courts, in general, are reluctant to characterize a commercial disparagement cause of action as a defamation claim. The Eighth Circuit has utilized the following oft-cited test for when a commercial disparagement action can also be recognized as a defamation claim:

> [W]here the publication on its face is directed against the goods or product of a corporate vendor or manufacturer, it will not be held libelous per se as to the corporation, unless by fair construction and without the aid of extrinsic evidence it imputes to the corporation, fraud, deceit, dishonesty, or reprehensible conduct in its business in relation to said goods or product.[6]

However, sometimes a case seems more properly characterized as defamation rather than disparagement. If a case can be made for

[6] National Refining Co. v. Benzo Gas Motor Fuel Co., 20 F.2d 763, 771 (8th Cir. 1927).

defamation, there are advantages to doing so that stem from three differences in the treatment of a defamation claim. The first is with regard to the burden of proof on falsity. The common law presumes the defamatory statement to be false and truth is a defensive matter. The plaintiff in a business disparagement claim, however, must plead and prove the falsity of the statement as part of his cause of action.

The second difference has to do with fault. The defendant in a defamation action is held strictly liable for its false statement, whereas the defendant in an action for business disparagement or injurious falsehood is subject to liability "only if he knew of the falsity or acted with reckless disregard concerning it, or if he acted with ill will or intended to interfere in the economic interest of the plaintiff in an unprivileged fashion."[7]

The final difference is with regard to damages. The common law requires the plaintiff in a defamation action to prove special damages in only a limited number of situations. But for a business disparagement claim, pecuniary loss to the plaintiff must always be proven for the plaintiff to prevail.

What justification is there for requiring that a plaintiff prove more in a business disparagement claim than a defamation claim? The distinction stems from the interest each cause of action seeks to protect. Defamation seeks to protect personal reputation, which by its nature is difficult to measure. Disparagement is meant to protect an economic interest. This difference alone justifies the different standards with regard to the proof of special damages. As for the various burdens for falsity and degree of fault, the common law development of defamation placed the importance of a person's reputation at such an elevated level that to require the plaintiff to prove the falsity of a statement that potentially caused irreparable harm in the community was seen as improper. Thus, the plaintiff simply has the burden to plead falsity and the defendant must show that it was not false. Similarly, defamation has been held to be akin to a strict liability tort in that it is no excuse that the speaker bore no ill-will or actual malice (although Constitutional implications may require it). When the concern is only a pecuniary interest, the relative harm is less and the burden is greater upon the plaintiff. Mulling around in the background of both of these causes of action and their different burdens is the concern over chilling free speech. When personal reputation is at stake, the law is less concerned about the chilling effect litigation may have (with the caveat of matters of public concern or public figures as reflected in the U.S. Supreme Court's jurisprudence discussed at the end of this chapter).

---

7 RESTATEMENT (SECOND) OF TORTS § 623A cmt. g (1977).

## C. ELEMENTS OF A COMMERCIAL DISPARAGEMENT CLAIM

The elements of a commercial disparagement claim are (1) publication by the defendant of the disparaging words, (2) falsity, (3) malice, and (4) special damages. Although courts vary in how they articulate these elements, this listing is generally accurate. Some courts add lack of privilege as an element, but this is more accurately described as an affirmative defense.

### 1. Publication by the Defendant of Disparaging Words

The first element, publication by the defendant of disparaging words, has two parts: disparagement and publication. Recall that § 629 of the Restatement (Second) of Torts defines a disparaging statement as one that "is understood to cast doubt upon the quality of another's land, chattels or intangible things, or upon the existence or extent of his property in them," and also requires either intent by the publisher to cast doubt or that "the recipient's understanding of it as casting the doubt was reasonable." Note, therefore, that it is not enough to merely cast doubt; the defendant must also speak with *the intent* to cast doubt, *or* it must be reasonable for the recipient to have understood the statement as casting doubt.

A simple hypothetical demonstrates how these two alternatives can be met. Savannah and George are neighbors with oceanfront property. George is selling his house. Savannah, who has designs to buy George's house herself, falsely tells people who look at the house that there is a public easement allowing people to cross the property to gain beach access. Savannah makes these statements in the hopes of deterring buyers and driving the price down so that she can swoop in and purchase the property. Under this hypothetical, Savannah has clearly met the standard under § 629. Her words cast doubt on George's property, and it was her intent to do so.

But assume instead that Savannah has no interest in buying George's house. One day, a prospective buyer comes to view George's house and sees Savannah outside gardening. The potential buyer tells Savannah that he is interested in purchasing the house and asks if there are any easements on the property. Savannah replies that there is a public easement allowing beach access (Savannah assumes this is true because she frequently sees people cut through the property to get to the beach). Based on this information, the potential buyer does not pursue the purchase of the house. Under this changed fact pattern, § 629 would still be met. Once again, the words cast doubt on George's property. Although Savannah did not intend to cast doubt, so long as a reasonable construction of the words by the recipient (here the potential buyer) would cast doubt, § 529(b) is met. Comment f to § 629 notes that the publisher's intent is immaterial so long as the doubt cast is a reasonable construction of the language used.

With respect to publication, the law of disparagement is very broad, as it permits liability for either intentional or negligent publications.[8] Furthermore, disparagement makes actionable any publication, be it spoken, written, or communicated in some other manner, and the form taken does not necessarily affect the other elements of the claim (unlike defamation which makes some distinction between slander and libel).[9] The standard is broad enough to include more modern forms of publication such as online or via social media.

### 2. Falsity

Another element of a disparagement claim is that the disparaging comment is, in fact, false. The phrase "truth is always a defense" is misleading in the commercial disparagement area, as it misstates the burden. Recall that, unlike a defamation claim, in a commercial disparagement claim the burden is upon the plaintiff to show falsity. Thus, while a truthful statement is not actionable, it is inaccurate to call truth a "defense."[10]

The burden upon the plaintiff is not to show that its goods or services are perfect in every way, but merely to show that the specific statement at issue is false.[11] Thus, if a car dealership accuses a competitor of rolling back the odometers on its used cars, the plaintiff dealership need only prove that it does not roll back the odometers (although the cars may have many other serious problems) to establish falsity.

---

8 *See* RESTATEMENT (SECOND) OF TORTS § 630 (1977). *But see id.* cmt. a ("[I]f a communication is purely accidental, as when it is overheard without any reason to expect eavesdropping, it is not a publication . . . and it therefore does not subject the speaker to liability. . . ."). Not only does section 630 permit publication in a number of ways, but it also includes publications that are negligently communicated. But comment a. states: "if a communication is purely accidental, as when it is overheard without any reason to expect eavesdropping, it is not a publication . . . and it therefore does not subject the speaker to liability. . . ." *Id.* at comment a.

9 Libel, which generally refers to printed defamatory words, requires no showing of special damages for recovery. Slander, which generally refers to spoken defamatory words, requires a showing of special damages and excuses such a showing only in a limited number of circumstances. *Compare* RESTATEMENT (SECOND) OF TORTS § 569 (1977), *with id.* § 570.

10 *See id.* § 651(1)(c).

11 *See id.* § 634 cmt. b.

Two concepts closely related to the element of falsity are the actionability of opinions and puffery. These concepts were addressed in the chapters on misrepresentation and deceptive marketing. In the commercial disparagement area, liability for opinions has come into question due to First Amendment concerns (which are covered more fully at the end of this chapter). At one time, pure expressions of opinion were actionable under both defamation and disparagement law. The defamation rule has changed, and an expression of mere opinion is no longer actionable unless it also implies the existence of defamatory facts. A similar rule presumably applies to injurious falsehood, although it is unclear.

As for puffery, it is difficult to tell if this concept has its basis in the falsity of the statement, or in the relation of the statement to causation and injury. The Restatement (Second) of Torts has explicitly provided for a conditional privilege between competitors that speaks directly to the puffery concept:

> **§ 649. Conditional Privilege Of Competitors**
>
> A competitor is conditionally privileged to make an unduly favorable comparison of the quality of his own land, chattels or other things, with the quality of the competing land, chattels or other things of a rival competitor, although he does not believe that his own things are superior to those of the rival competitor, if the comparison does not contain false assertions of specific unfavorable facts regarding the rival competitor's things.

The link to puffing is noted in comment c to § 649, which states:

> .... These statements have a strong analogy to the 'sales talk' or 'puffing' that a vendor is permitted to indulge in without liability to a purchaser who alleges that he was thereby misled. In both cases the practice of vendors to make consciously exaggerated claims for their goods is so well known that little or no importance is attached to the statements.... If, however, [the defendant] goes further and makes a direct attack upon the quality of his competitor's things by stating specific unfavorable facts even though he does so to supply a reason for his claim that his own things are superior, he cannot successfully claim a privilege under the rule stated in this Section.

Thus, this section is consistent with the concepts of puffery previously discussed—the vaguer the statement, the less actionable it is. The competitor's privilege is a recognition that competitors engage in puffery when selling goods, and puffery specifically permits "better than" claims with an important caveat—the privilege only applies "if the comparison does not contain false assertions of specific unfavorable facts regarding the rival competitor's things." Thus, "tests prove" or substantiation types of claims would still be subject to attack. It is worth noting that this conditional privilege applies to the common law, but puffery is still an affirmative defense. Under the Lanham Act, additional privileges available to a commercial disparagement defendant are discussed in more detail below.

### 3. Malice

The malice element of a disparagement cause of action does not mean malice in the sense that many would think. Usually, the term "malice" invokes a sense of evil or ill will regarding motive. Such is not the case (or at least not necessarily under the Restatement's view) when speaking of malice in a disparagement action. Section 623A(a) of the Restatement requires that the maker of the false statement intends "for publication of the statement to result in harm to interests of the other having a pecuniary value, or either recognizes or should recognize that it is likely to do so," and "knows that the statement is false or acts in reckless disregard of its truth or falsity." This is a two-step inquiry.

First, the publication must be made either with intent to harm (which is consistent with the ill-will association) or recognition that the statement will or is likely going to cause harm. Note that this second way of meeting the first inquiry does not require evil motive, but simply recognition that the likely result is harm.

Similarly, the second inquiry asks if the statement is known to be false or is made with reckless disregard for the truth. Typically, this second inquiry is what is being referred to when courts mention the malice requirement, and it is often referred to as "actual malice." Thus, the Restatement does not necessarily care about the motive or ill will of the defendant with regard to malice. However, not all courts or jurisdictions limit the scope of this second inquiry so narrowly. Some jurisdictions permit this second inquiry to be met through "common law" malice, meaning spite, ill will, or an intent to interfere in an unprivileged manner. This alternative way of showing the malice element is not universally followed. It is recognized by a caveat in § 623A of the Restatement, but that is only to say that the Institute did not take a position on the appropriateness of the approach. The majority of courts appear to follow the Restatement's actual malice approach and not the caveat.

*Fashion Boutique of Short Hills, Inc. v. Fendi USA, Inc.*[12] demonstrates the common law malice standard in action. Fashion Boutique operated a retail store in New Jersey from 1983–1991. In

12 No. 91 Civ. 4544(MGC), 1998 WL 259942 (S.D.N.Y. 1998).

1988, Fashion Boutique entered into a franchise agreement with Fendi to sell Fendi products. One year later, Fendi opened a store on Fifth Avenue in New York City. Fashion Boutique alleged that Fendi, through its agents, began to disparage Fashion Boutique's business by telling customers that the Fashion Boutique store sold different and inferior products to those sold at the New York store.

In analyzing the malice standard, the court noted that it could be met either by proof of common law malice or by proof of actual malice. Some of the disparaging comments met the actual malice standard under the Restatement as there was evidence that the speakers knew that the alleged statements were false. However, for other statements, there was a lack of evidence as to the knowledge possessed by the speakers. Nonetheless, the court concluded that a rational juror could conclude that the "alleged statements were gratuitous, unsolicited comments published with the intent to injure plaintiff, and, hence, that these statements were malicious."[13] Under an actual malice standard, these statements would have failed. Thus, courts that adopt this alternative approach to satisfying the malice requirement allow for a wider array of claims.

### 4. Special Damages

Under the law of defamation, an allegedly false and defamatory statement, negligently made and without privilege, is enough to incur damages regardless of whether special damages are proven. This is not true for a commercial disparagement claim. The first line of § 623A states that the publisher of the false statement is only subject to liability for "pecuniary loss resulting to the other." This is not an issue of just showing the amount of damages.[14] To succeed on a commercial disparagement claim, a plaintiff must prove a direct and causal connection between an identifiable pecuniary loss and the disparaging publication. The Restatement sets forth the types of loss a publisher is liable for and how a plaintiff may establish loss in § 633:

> **§ 633. Pecuniary Loss**
>
> (1) The pecuniary loss for which a publisher of injurious falsehood is subject to liability is restricted to
>
> > (a) the pecuniary loss that results directly and immediately from the effect of the conduct of third persons,

---

[13] *Id.* at *4.

[14] The terms "special damages" and "pecuniary loss" are often used interchangeably by the courts. Black's defines "special damages" as "[d]amages that are alleged to have been sustained in the circumstances of a particular wrong. To be awardable, special damages must be specifically claimed and proved." BLACK'S LAW DICTIONARY, Damages-special damages (10th ed. 2014).

including impairment of vendibility or value caused by disparagement, and

(b) the expense of measures reasonably necessary to counteract the publication, including litigation to remove the doubt cast upon vendibility or value by disparagement.

(2) This pecuniary loss may be established by

(a) proof of the conduct of specific persons, or

(b) proof that the loss has resulted from the conduct of a number of persons whom it is impossible to identify.

Courts vary with regard to the level of particularity by which damages must be shown. Some require a showing of loss of a particular sale or customer. This is demonstrated in *Hurlbut v. Gulf Atlantic Life Insurance Co.*[15] In that case, at the urging of Gulf Atlantic Life Insurance Company (Gulf), C. Danial Hurlbut and A.C. Hovater formed a partnership, Agency Associates (AA), to sell insurance policies underwritten by Gulf. Hurlbut and Hovater began selling the policies. Although they never had a copy of the master policy, Gulf sent them a copy of a different master policy which Gulf's officer, Kenneth Thompson, told them was virtually identical to the one they were selling.

Unfortunately for Hurlbut, Hovater, and AA, it turned out that Gulf had failed to get approval of the policy from the State Board of Insurance. When a potential client of AA called Gulf to confirm that a master policy was in place, the president of Gulf denied that Gulf was underwriting AA. Despite assurances from other Gulf officers (and the Vice-President of Gulf's parent, Nationwide) that Gulf was underwriting AA, an investigation was launched at the behest of Gulf's president, which ultimately led to Hurlbut and Hovater's arrest, civil and criminal charges, and imprisonment.

The denial of coverage turned out to be part of a plan by Gulf. Gulf had difficulty obtaining approval of the master policy for West Texas Pipe Trades Health Insurance Trust, the same policy previously provided to Hurlbut and Hovater with the explanation that theirs would be the same. Gulf authorized the sale of group health insurance prior to the approval of this master policy, and rather than acknowledge additional misconduct and complicity in the sales that Hurlbut and Hovater had made prior to the issuance of a master policy, Hurlbut and Hovater asserted that Gulf decided to conceal its role. They alleged that Gulf denied that it had ever agreed to underwrite the program or obtain the state's approval of the master policy in an effort to shift the entire responsibility to Hurlbut

---

15 749 S.W.2d 762 (Tex. 1987).

and Hovater. Hurlbut and Hovater sued alleging fraud, business disparagement, and tortious interference with contract rights.

In analyzing the disparagement claim, the Texas Supreme Court concluded that there was evidence that the elements of falsity and malice were met, but that special damages had not been shown. The court denied relief because no evidence was offered of "damages resulting from loss of business expected from any particular customer or prospective customer."[16] This requirement that loss be shown through a specific customer is not universally accepted and is not necessarily consistent with the Restatement's view.[17]

One common way to demonstrate loss is through a decrease in sales. Although this would not be acceptable in a court such as *Hurlbut* that requires the loss of specific customers, comment h to § 633 states that "[w]hen this [loss] can be shown with reasonable certainty, the rule requiring the identification of specific purchasers is relaxed and recovery is permitted for the loss of the market." Note that this requires a dip in sales to be shown with reasonable certainty. Therefore, to meet the burden under the Restatement, the plaintiff will need to show more than just lost sales; it will likely also have to negate other possible explanations for the lost sales, such as a declining market. However, the plaintiff does not have to show that the disparagement is the sole source of the lost business—just that it is a substantial factor.[18]

It is worth noting that the Restatement does not contemplate the recovery of all damages. If a loss is classified as a consequential damage rather than a direct loss sale, it is not recoverable under the Restatement. Comment i to § 633 states:

> The damages recoverable under the rule stated in Clause (1)(a) of this Section are restricted to the pecuniary loss that results directly and immediately from the effect of the injurious falsehood in influencing the conduct of third persons. They do not include any loss resulting from the plaintiff's failure to make an advantageous use of money that he would have made if a prospective sale had been consummated, since this is not the direct and immediate consequence of the injurious falsehood but depends upon the situation of the disappointed vendor and the particular

---

16 *Id.* at 767 (citing Gulf Atl. Life Ins. Co. v. Hurlburt, 696 S.W.2d 83, 98–99 (Tex. Ct. App. 1985)).

17 *See* RESTATEMENT (SECOND) OF TORTS § 633 cmt. h (1977).

18 *See* RESTATEMENT (SECOND) TORTS § 632 & cmt. c (1977) ("In order for the false statement to be a substantial factor in determining the conduct of an intending or potential purchaser or lessee, it is not necessary that the conduct should be determined exclusively or even predominantly by the publication of the statement.").

purposes for which it would have been necessary or advantageous for him to apply the purchase money.

Despite this limitation, the Restatement does allow the recovery of increased finance charges. Comment i to § 633 (along with § 632) indicates that increased finance charges should be recoverable so long as the disparagement was a substantial factor causing the increase: "Similarly, an owner of land who is refused a mortgage loan by his bank because of disparagement of his title cannot recover for the loss of his intended use of the money he was seeking to borrow. *On the other hand, if it can be proved with reasonable certainty that he could obtain another loan only at a higher rate of interest, the loss of the favorable interest rate is a result directly and immediately caused by the disparagement and is recoverable*" (emphasis added).

Perhaps the more interesting question is why shouldn't the failure to get financing also be recoverable? It is doubtful that any court would allow such a claim, either because it is a consequential damage (but if this is so, then shouldn't it be true of the increased finance rate) or it is too speculative. It may be that it is too hard to show anything but speculative damages at this point, but if this is the rule from the Restatement, it would appear to punish those who don't have the ability to move forward at a higher rate of interest—a rather arbitrary line.

Given that special damages (or pecuniary loss to use the phrasing from the Restatement) is an element of the commercial disparagement cause of action, it should come as no surprise that damages are the most frequent remedy sought. Although injunctive relief is also a possibility, courts are generally reluctant to order such a remedy. This is due in part to First Amendment concerns and the frequent overlap that occurs between defamation and disparagement. Nonetheless, in an appropriate case, injunctive relief may be issued.

### 5. Lack of Privilege

Although some courts adopt lack of privilege as an element of a disparagement cause of action, privilege is an affirmative defense. The Restatement (Second) of Torts recognizes both absolute and conditional privileges, utilizing the same privileges available to a defendant in a defamation cause of action.[19] Absolute privileges cover instances such as when the defendant was granted consent by the plaintiff to publish the materials (§ 583), statements made to a spouse (§ 592), and various statements that relate to judicial and legislative proceedings (§§ 585–590A). The conditional privileges

---

19 *See* RESTATEMENT (SECOND) OF TORTS §§ 635, 646A (1977).

include situations in which the publisher of the disparaging information has done so to protect a sufficiently important interest of its own, a recipient or third party, or the public (§§ 594–598). These privileges are labeled conditional because they can be lost if abused, such as when publication occurs with knowledge of the falsity of the statements or with reckless disregard for their truth.[20] The law of disparagement contains two conditional privileges, however, that are not subject to this abuse qualification. The first is the privilege found in § 649 pertaining to the right of a competitor to make an unduly favorable comparison of its own goods, which has already been discussed above in Section C.2. Because this privilege extends to statements of superiority not made with an honest belief, it is obviously not abused by the lack of honest belief in the superiority claim. The second privilege is found in § 647, which permits a publisher to assert that the publisher, rather than the plaintiff, has a legal right to property. Such claims are privileged despite being incorrect or unreasonable so long as the claim is asserted in good faith (as judged subjectively).[21]

Recall, however, that malice is a required element of a common law commercial disparagement claim. Given that malice is an element of such an action, what function do the conditional privileges serve (other than those found in §§ 647 and 649)?[22] The presence of the conditional privileges is somewhat confounding when one considers that malice, which can be used to defeat a conditional privilege, is an element of a plaintiff's prima facie case. This phenomenon was noted by the Texas Supreme Court in *Hurlbut*:

> A conditional privilege is defeated when the privilege is abused. Abuse may be found when the person making the defamatory statement knows the matter to be false or does not act for the purpose of protecting the interest for which the privilege exists. The distinction between absolute and conditional privileges significant to our present case is that an absolute privilege confers immunity regardless of motive whereas a conditional privilege may be lost if the actions of the defendant are motivated by malice.
>
> In the context of a tort such as business disparagement or injurious falsehood, only absolute privileges have relevance to the defendant. This is because the tort itself incorporates malice as an element of recovery; hence, if the plaintiff

---

20 *See id.* §§ 599–601, 650A.

21 *See id.* § 647 cmts. b, d.

22 *Compare id.* § 623A, *with id.* §§ 599–601, 650A.

carries his burden, he likewise defeats any conditional privilege.[23]

## D. FALSE STATEMENTS IN THE SALE OF ANOTHER'S GOODS

A claim that is related to commercial disparagement involves false statements in marketing another's goods. This claim encompasses, for example, a seller who makes misrepresentations about another's goods that he is selling. At first this may seem like an odd claim—after all, why would the original manufacturer or producer of the goods care about false statements that presumably help to sell its product (other than to worry about contributory liability)? To answer this, consider the example of a beer manufacturer who sends products to distributors with the understanding that beer that sits idle beyond its expiration date will not be sold. The manufacturer's reasoning is that beer sold past this expiration date can become stale and the taste may be altered. If distributors continue to sell the product to retailers as unexpired beer, the consuming public may receive stale beer and associate the resulting poor taste with the manufacturer's brand. Although a sale of the manufacturer's beer has occurred, the manufacturer would prefer not to have the sale than to lose goodwill and future sales due to an association with stale, poor-tasting beer. The Third Restatement of Unfair Competition addresses this issue:

> **§ 6. Misrepresentations In Marketing The Goods Or Services Of Another**
>
> One is subject to liability to another under the rule stated in § 2 if, in marketing goods or services of which the other is truthfully identified as the manufacturer, producer, or supplier, the actor makes a representation relating to those goods or services that is likely to deceive or mislead prospective purchasers to the likely commercial detriment of the other under the rule stated in § 3.

The text and the comments note that this provision covers representations that are likely to deceive or mislead prospective purchasers with respect to a matter that relates to the goods or services, although the goods are truthfully identified as originating from another. The comments also provide examples that would encompass our beer manufacturer scenario and other similar situations. As one comment states: "The misrepresentations described in this Section are typically made in an attempt to sell goods that the actor has on hand and are thus generally laudatory

---

[23] Hurlbut v. Gulf Atlantic Life Insurance Co., 749 S.W.2d 762, 768 (Tex. 1987).

rather than derogatory. A seller may assert, for example, that the goods are fresh when in fact they are stale or deteriorated, that they are the manufacturer's latest style or highest quality when in fact they are outdated or seconds, or that they are warranted by the manufacturer in respects that exceed the manufacturer's actual undertaking."[24] The language of § 43(a) of the Lanham Act is also broad enough to encompass such claims, as it prohibits a person from falsely misrepresenting the "nature, characteristics [or] quality" of another's goods, services, or commercial activities.

The above beer hypothetical bears some similarities to the case of *Adolph Coors Co. v. A. Genderson & Sons, Inc.*,[25] where the plaintiff, Coors, complained that the defendant was selling Coors' beer but did not maintain the quality control standards required by Coors, such as proper refrigeration, resulting in beer of an inferior quality. Although the actual claims were based on both trademark and unfair competition law, the case would just as easily fit into § 6's formulation of the tort. "Defendant's acts constitute unfair competition. As has already been mentioned, the beer sold by defendant was of inferior quality. Also, as pointed out by plaintiff, defendant has acted in total disregard of the distribution and quality maintenance standards of Coors. Furthermore, customers are likely to be confused and will hold Coors responsible for any loss of high quality resulting from defendant's acts."[26]

Unlike a typical disparagement case, § 6 violations do not require malice or intent.[27] In addition, proof of actual harm is not required (unlike disparagement), but the original manufacturer, producer, or supplier of the goods or services bears the burden of proving that the misrepresentation is likely to its commercial detriment.

## E. COMMERCIAL DISPARAGEMENT UNDER THE LANHAM ACT

While false advertising under the Lanham Act focused upon false claims made about a party's own goods or services, disparagement focuses on false claims made about another's goods or services. Despite this difference, the elements of a false advertisement claim under the Lanham Act are identical to the elements of a disparagement claim under the Act. Recall that the elements of a false advertising claim under the Act are the following:

---

24 RESTATEMENT (THIRD) OF UNFAIR COMPETITION § 6 cmt. b (1995).

25 486 F. Supp. 131 (D. Colo. 1980).

26 *Id.* at 136.

27 *See* RESTATEMENT (THIRD) OF UNFAIR COMPETITION § 6 cmt. b (1995).

(1) A false statement of fact by the defendant in a commercial advertisement about its own product;

(2) The statement actually deceives or has a tendency to deceive a substantial segment of its audience;

(3) The deception is material, in that it is likely to influence the purchasing decision;

(4) The defendant placed the false or misleading statement in interstate commerce; and

(5) The plaintiff has been or is likely to be injured as a result of the false statement.

For a disparagement claim, the term "its own" is simply replaced by "another's" in the first element. Thus, much of the discussion of these elements from the previous chapter on deceptive marketing under the Lanham Act is applicable in this area as well.

One part of the first element that was not developed earlier is the requirement that the statement be made in a commercial advertisement. Although this is a requirement for both false advertising and disparagement claims under the Lanham Act (but not for their common law analogs), it tends to be more of an issue in the disparagement context.

After briefly exploring the development of the Lanham Act disparagement cause of action below, the text discusses how to determine whether the "in commercial advertising or promotion" element has been met. First Amendment concerns that may arise in connection with a commercial disparagement claim are also explored. It should be noted that although First Amendment concerns are also relevant to false advertising claims, they are implicated more frequently in disparagement actions.

### 1. Development of Liability Under § 43(a) of the Lanham Act

For many years after the enactment of the Lanham Act, the tort of commercial disparagement was left exclusively to the common law. Prior to 1989, § 43 of the Lanham Act was interpreted purely as a false advertising statute and not as a prohibition on commercial disparagement. In fact, prior to the 1989 amendments, § 43(a) did not specifically contain language referring to "another person's" goods, services, or commercial activities. This change was a deliberate decision by Congress to prohibit commercial disparagement as part of a national policy of promoting fair competition. However, this expansion also brought First Amendment concerns over the chilling of free speech. Thus, the language of § 43(a)(1)(B) was limited to instances of commercial advertising or promotion.[28]

The federalization of commercial disparagement calls into question the extent to which the common law development of the tort should carry over to Lanham Act claims. This is particularly relevant to the issue of malice. Recall that the common law tort requires a showing of malice for recovery, but this element is absent from a § 43(a) claim. Indeed, malice is only relevant to the issue of damages (although it can also help excuse the burden of proof for a plaintiff on the issue of consumer deception). Absent a showing of malice, First Amendment concerns over the chilling effect of a lawsuit on free speech raise serious questions about the validity of the Lanham Act's disparagement action. As will be discussed, this issue is related to the commercial nature of the speech.

## 2. Commercial Advertising or Promotion

An essential element of a § 43(a)(1)(B) Lanham Act claim is that the false statement be made "in [a] commercial advertising or promotion." Where the claim is made in a television or newspaper commercial, this element is easily met. However, issues can arise when the statements are made orally to select customers. This raises the question of what qualifies as commercial advertising or promotion. *Fashion Boutique of Short Hills, Inc. v. Fendi USA, Inc.*[29] demonstrates the limits this phrase can place on a plaintiff's ability to bring suit under the Lanham Act.

The case flows from the same facts as the *Fashion Boutique* decision described earlier in this chapter, but the issue in this later opinion involved Fashion Boutique's Lanham Act claims. Fashion Boutique noticed a sharp decline in its sales after the opening of the defendants' New York store and was ultimately forced to close its retail operations. Fashion Boutique alleged that the precipitous fall in its sales was caused by a corporate policy carried out by Fendi to misrepresent the quality and authenticity of the products sold at Fashion Boutique. However, Fashion Boutique could not show that many of its customers heard disparaging statements first-hand at the defendants' Fifth Avenue store. Rather, it alleged that Fendi employees made misrepresentations to some customers at the Fifth Avenue store, these customers relayed the comments to others, and

---

[28] It was also limited to misrepresentations of fact (so as to exclude opinions that do not imply false facts). For an in-depth history of the development of the 1989 Amendments and their impact, see 5 McCARTHY ON TRADEMARKS §§ 27:91–27:97 (4th ed. 2015).

[29] 314 F.3d 48 (2d Cir. 2002).

the false rumors were thus spread throughout Fashion Boutique's customer base of over 8,000 buyers.[30]

In challenging the district court's grant of partial summary judgment, Fashion Boutique relied primarily on (a) reported conversations between Fendi personnel and nine undercover investigators hired to pose as shoppers and (b) declarations by forty Fashion Boutique customers. In none of the proffered interactions did employees at the Fifth Avenue store initiate conversations about Fashion Boutique. They commented on Fashion Boutique only after the customers mentioned the plaintiff. For example, several customers who reported their conversations with Fendi employees went to the Fifth Avenue store seeking to repair or exchange products or, alternatively, were wearing Fendi products as they shopped at that store. After the customer informed Fendi personnel that the item had been bought at Fashion Boutique, the employee reacted by making critical comments about the quality of Fashion Boutique's merchandise and, on several occasions, refused to exchange or repair the product. Fashion Boutique produced evidence that Fendi salespersons followed a practice of disparaging the customer service at Fashion Boutique.[31]

On appeal, the court noted that although the statute left the term "commercial advertising or promotion" undefined, most courts have adopted the test set forth in *Gordon & Breach Sci. Publishers S.A. v. Am. Inst. of Physics*.[32] Under that test, the representations must meet four elements to qualify as "commercial advertising or promotion":

> (1) commercial speech; (2) by a defendant who is in commercial competition with plaintiff; (3) for the purpose of influencing consumers to buy defendant's goods or services; and, (4) although representations less formal than those made as part of a classic advertising campaign may suffice, they must be disseminated sufficiently to the relevant purchasing public.[33]

The court assumed that the speech at issue was commercial and then focused its inquiry on the definition of "advertising or promotion." The court cited to the Seventh Circuit's definition: "advertising defined as 'a form of promotion to anonymous recipients, as distinguished from face-to-face communication . . . [and] a subset of persuasion [that relies on] dissemination of prefabricated

30 *Id.* at 53.

31 *See id.*

32 859 F. Supp. 1521, 1535–36 (S.D.N.Y. 1994).

33 *Fashion Boutique,* 314 F.3d at 56 (internal quotations omitted).

promotional material.' "[34] However, although the *Fashion Boutique* court did not disagree with the definition of advertising, it criticized the lack of guidance given to whether speech qualifies as a promotion. It noted that the key to both "advertising" and "promotion" is "activity designed to disseminate information to the public" and held that, to qualify, the complained-of representations must be part of "an organized campaign to penetrate the relevant market."[35] Perhaps ironically, given its criticism of the Seventh Circuit, the *Fashion Boutique* court gave little additional guidance on when something will qualify as a promotion. But the decision does demonstrate that face-to-face communications could count if they were part of a campaign "designed to disseminate information to the public." Although the district court had made a distinction between proactive statements and reactive ones, the court of appeals found this merely "instructive, but not necessarily dispositive."[36] Despite this, the court of appeals affirmed the district court on the basis that the statements at issue did not rise to the level of advertising or promotion: "Fashion Boutique has presented a total of twenty-seven oral statements regarding plaintiff's products in a marketplace of thousands of customers. Such evidence is insufficient to satisfy the requirement that representations be disseminated widely in order to constitute 'commercial advertising or promotion' under the Lanham Act."[37]

This raises an interesting question: what level of dissemination is required to qualify as "commercial advertising or promotion"? Should dissemination be to a majority of the consuming public? Who gets to decide the appropriate level? It should be noted that not all courts adopting the *Gordon & Breach* standard are equally demanding.[38] It may be that a lower level of dissemination would

---

[34] *Id.* at 57 (quoting First Health Group Corp. v. BCE Emergis Corp., 269 F.3d 800, 803 (7th Cir. 2001)).

[35] *Id.*

[36] *Id.* at 58.

[37] *Id.*

[38] *See, e.g.*, Seven-Up Co. v. Coca-Cola Co., 86 F.3d 1379, 1386 (5th Cir. 1996) (holding that a sales presentation made by Coca-Cola to eleven soft drink bottlers was a "commercial advertising or promotion" because the potential purchasers in the market were relatively limited such that "even a single promotional presentation to an individual purchaser may be enough to trigger the protection[ ]"); Mobius Mgmt. Sys., Inc. v. Fourth Dimension Software, Inc., 880 F. Supp. 1005, 1019 (S.D.N.Y. 1994) (finding, under the fourth prong of the *Gordon & Breach* test, that a letter to a single customer was an "advertising or promotion"); Nat'l Artists Mgmt. Co., Inc. v. Weaving, 769 F. Supp. 1224, 1235 (S.D.N.Y. 1991) (holding that a former employee's denigration of the plaintiff in telephone calls to persons who were both friends and professional contacts was actionable in the "theatre-booking industry," although the calls were not advertising or promotion in the usual sense of those words). *But see* Am. Needle & Novelty, Inc. v. Drew Pearson Mktg., Inc., 820 F. Supp. 1072, 1077–78 (N.D. Ill. 1993) (relying upon dictionary definitions and finding that both "advertising" and "promotion" included connotations of public dissemination of information; thus, a

have sufficed in *Fashion Boutique* if there was stronger evidence of an effort to engage customers aggressively in a smear campaign. Indeed, the court says as much: "we leave open the possibility that a cause of action might exist where a defendant maintains a well-enforced policy to disparage its competitor each time it is mentioned by a customer, if such a policy of reactive disparagement successfully reaches a substantial number of the competitor's potential customers."[39] Nevertheless, this "substantial number" language does not give much guidance.

Moreover, although the raw number of recipients may be small in some cases, the percentage of customers may be large. This has been noted as a distinguishing characteristic:

> Plaintiff points to cases in which courts have found sufficient statements made to a small number of customers; these cases are easily distinguished as they involved a significantly larger percentage of affected customers. *See, e.g., National Artists Mgmt. v. Weaving*, 769 F. Supp. 1224 (S.D.N.Y.1991) (ten out of thirty customers); *Coastal Abstract Serv., Inc. v. First Am. Title Ins. Co.*, 173 F.3d 725 (9th Cir.1999) (one out of three customers). In this case, the potential customer base ranges from 36 to more than one hundred people. Evidence of one customer having heard the disparaging statement certainly does not suggest "an organized campaign to penetrate the relevant market." *Fashion Boutique*, 314 F.3d at 57. Therefore, plaintiff fails to support an essential element of its Lanham Act claim for product disparagement, and defendants' motion for summary judgment on this claim is granted.[40]

One final note on *Fashion Boutique* should be made. Despite listing four elements, the court did not address the second element requiring commercial competition.[41] Perhaps this is because the court did not want to limit itself to competitors only. Recall from the prudential standing section in the previous chapter that many courts believe that indirect competition is sufficient for standing (and this view was adopted by the U.S. Supreme Court in *Lexmark*). The second element does not necessarily limit competition to direct

single copy of a letter "addressed to a non-consuming licensor" did not fall under § 43(a)).

39 *Fashion Boutique,* 314 F.3d at 58 (emphasis added).

40 Pro. Sound Servs., Inc. v. Guzzi, 349 F. Supp. 2d 722, 729 (S.D.N.Y. 2004).

41 *See Fashion Boutique,* 314 F.3d at 58 ("In sum, we adopt the first, third and fourth elements of the *Gordon & Breach* test. To decide this appeal, we need not decide whether [to adopt] the second element—that defendant and plaintiff be competitors. We note that the requirement is not set forth in the text of Section 43(a) and express no view on its soundness.").

competitors, but it could certainly be read this way. It would hardly make sense to extend standing to an indirect competitor to bring suit under the Lanham Act only to pour the plaintiff out for the same indirect competitor status under the "commercial advertising or promotion" prong. This relationship to standing was recognized in an article by authors Michael A. Albert and Robert L. Bocchino Jr.: "The competition requirement appearing in *Gordon & Breach* and in some Section 43(a) false advertising cases seems to be a misleading label for a set of judicially-created standing rules limiting the application of Section 43(a), which, on its face, requires only likely injury caused by false advertising or disparagement."[42]

### 3. First Amendment Concerns and Disparagement

The above section set forth the test for determining whether a representation qualifies as "commercial advertising or promotion," but it did not define the first requirement, i.e., that the representation involve "commercial speech." It would be tempting to assume that if speech qualifies as "advertising or promotion," it should automatically constitute commercial speech. However, a communication is not necessarily commercial speech for First Amendment purposes merely because it is contained in an advertisement. In addition, recall that malice is not an element of a Lanham Act § 43(a) claim. This has important implications with regard to First Amendment concerns.

The distinction between commercial and noncommercial speech is critical to determining what level of protection the speech receives under U.S. Supreme Court precedent. Noncommercial speech, even if false, generally receives full First Amendment protection. This is qualified by the famous case of *New York Times Co. v. Sullivan*,[43] which added a scienter element to a defamation claimant's burden of proof in circumstances involving public figures. Specifically, the Supreme Court required a plaintiff to prove that the false statement at issue was made either with knowledge of its falsity, or with reckless disregard for the truth.[44] (As mentioned, this scienter element is known as the "actual malice" requirement.) Although *New York Times* involved a defamation action rather than a disparagement claim, the Supreme Court has left open the possibility that the same actual malice requirement would apply to a commercial disparagement claim (as will be discussed below).

---

[42] Michael A. Albert & Robert L. Bocchino Jr., *Trade Libel: Theory and Practice Under the Common Law, the Lanham Act, and the First Amendment*, 89 TRADEMARK REP. 826, 859–60 (1999).

[43] 376 U.S. 254 (1964).

[44] *Id.* at 280.

As opposed to noncommercial speech, commercial speech generally receives a lesser level of protection. It is protected only if truthful and, even then, is subject to some governmental regulation. In short, false commercial speech receives the least amount of First Amendment protection.

The Supreme Court has not yet determined whether the *New York Times* actual malice requirement applies to commercial disparagement claims. In the 1984 case of *Bose Corp. v. Consumers Union of United States, Inc.*,[45] the Court applied the actual malice standard to deny Bose's (a manufacturer of speakers) recovery based on an allegedly disparaging article reviewing one of its products that was published in the defendant's "Consumer Reports" magazine. However, the Court was not squarely faced with the issue of whether actual malice applied to disparagement claims. As the Court stated: "The Court of Appeals entertained some doubt concerning the ruling that the *New York Times* rule should be applied to a claim of product disparagement. . . . We express no view on that ruling. . . ."[46] The Court also did not have to decide the issue of whether a company offering goods for sale to the public qualifies as a public figure, as Bose did not contest such status.

At the time of the *Bose* decision, the Lanham Act was not worded to include commercial disparagement claims. In 1989, amendments were added to § 43 that expanded the scope of the section's coverage to include commercial disparagement actions. Congress was concerned about the chilling effect that such an expansion could have on free speech, and it thus restricted the scope of the expansion to "commercial advertising or promotion." The remarks made by Representative Robert Kastenmeier of Wisconsin at the time are enlightening on this issue:

> To avoid legitimate constitutional challenge, it was necessary to carefully limit the reach of the subsection. Because section 43(a) will now provide a kind of commercial defamation action, the reach of the section specifically extends only to false and misleading speech that is encompassed within the "commercial speech" doctrine by the United States Supreme Court. . . . Thus . . . innocent dissemination and communication of false and misleading advertising, including promotional material, by the media are excluded from the reach of section 43(a). For a defendant who is a member of the media to be found liable under section 43(a), the plaintiff must show that the defendant was not "innocent" under section 32(2) and, as

45 466 U.S. 485 (1984).

46 *Id.* at 513.

> noted, that state of mind must encompass the *New York Times v. Sullivan* standard.
>
> S. 1883 is limited in another important sense. It uses the word "commercial" to describe advertising or promotion for business purposes, whether conducted by for-profit or nonprofit organizations or individuals. Political advertising and promotion is political speech, and therefore not encompassed by the term "commercial."[47]

Although the intent of inserting the "commercial advertising or promotion" language seems clear, there is still no direct guidance from the Supreme Court on whether this will avert the Constitutional issue or what impact the status of the plaintiff will have (i.e., whether a public figure plaintiff is still held to the *New York Times* actual malice standard). Recall that, by the terms of § 43(a), a competitor may attack misleading commercial speech under § 43(a)(1)(B) without showing malice. If the Congressional intent is upheld, this means that a court's decision to classify speech as commercial may be pivotal.

*U.S. Healthcare, Inc. v. Blue Cross of Greater Philadelphia*[48] demonstrates the complex analysis that courts often must go through in deciding what level of scrutiny to give to a commercial disparagement case under the Lanham Act. This case stemmed out of a competitive advertising campaign in which Blue Cross/Blue Shield made efforts to regain some of its lost market share from U.S. Healthcare and its HMO product. Blue Cross started to offer its own product, the Personal Choice PPO, and began to run a series of television, print, and radio ads to try and not only market its PPO, but to aggressively take customers away from U.S. Healthcare by highlighting what it claimed were the negative aspects of the HMO. In response, U.S. Healthcare ran its own ads, similarly promoting its product and pointing out the shortcomings of the Personal Choice plan. The ads tended to be quite outrageous in their imagery—in one ad, a woman was sobbing over her decision to use an HMO, while another ad involved a deathbed scene and implied that a PPO was used.

U.S. Healthcare filed suit alleging commercial disparagement, defamation, and tortious interference with contractual relations. Blue Cross brought counterclaims alleging the same. After a jury trial, Blue Cross's counterclaims were dismissed but the jury was deadlocked on the remaining issues and U.S. Healthcare's claims

---

47 Remarks of Rep. Kastenmeier on S. 1883, 134 Cong. Rec. 31850–52 (Oct. 19, 1988).

48 898 F.2d 914 (3d Cir. 1990).

were set for a new trial. However, prior to trial, Blue Cross moved to dismiss the case as the alleged acts were afforded protection under the First Amendment and the *New York Times* actual malice standard based upon the fact that the object of the ads, U.S. Healthcare, was a public figure. The court agreed that both parties were public figures, and thus neither party had carried its burden of proving, through clear and convincing evidence, that the statements at issue were made with actual malice. As a result, both sides' claims were dismissed.

On appeal, the court had to address whether, in the context of a competitive advertisement campaign, the advertisements should be subject to the *New York Times* actual malice standard. The court began its analysis by reviewing the level of protection afforded to speech and how it is affected by the plaintiff's status. The court articulated three "black letter" rules with regard to the types of plaintiffs:

> 1) When the plaintiff is a public official or a "public figure" and the speech is of public concern, the plaintiff must prove by clear and convincing evidence that the defamatory falsehood was made with "actual malice" by a media defendant. In such situations, the plaintiff must prove the falsity of the statements to prevail.
>
> 2) When the plaintiff is a private figure, but the speech involves a matter of "public concern," the states may define for themselves the appropriate standard of liability; however, they may not impose liability without fault, nor allow presumed or punitive damages without a showing of actual malice. In such instances, the plaintiff must prove the falsity of the speech to recover damages from a media defendant.
>
> 3) When the plaintiff is a private figure and the speech regards matters of "purely private concern," the plaintiff may prove presumed and punitive damages without a showing of "actual malice."[49]

Thus, public figure plaintiffs and private figure plaintiffs complaining about speech of "public concern" are subject to the heightened burdens of the *New York Times* standard, but private plaintiffs complaining of matters of private concern are not.

The court offered two reasons justifying this disparate treatment:

---

[49] *Id.* at 929–30.

> [1] First, because public officials and public figures enjoy "greater access to the channels of effective communication and hence have a more realistic opportunity to counteract false statements than private individuals," the states have a greater interest in protecting private persons whose relative lack of "self-help" remedies render them "more vulnerable to injury."
>
> [2] Second, the state has a stronger interest in protecting the reputations of private individuals because, unlike public persons, they have not voluntarily placed themselves in the public eye.[50]

Ultimately, the court concluded that commercial speech does get First Amendment protection, but it is limited. As the court noted: "In the area of protected speech, the most prominent example of reduced protection for certain kinds of speech concerns commercial speech. Such speech, we have noted, occupies a 'subordinate position in the scale of First Amendment values.' "[51]

The court then resolved whether the speech at issue was in fact "commercial speech." The court cited to three factors as indicating whether speech is commercial or not, although it should be mentioned that the factors are not determinative but merely offer "strong support" for the conclusion that speech is commercial. The three factors are: "1) Is the speech an advertisement; 2) Does the speech refer to a specific product or service; and 3) Does the speaker have an economic motivation for the speech."[52]

All three factors were easily met here, but the court nonetheless continued to examine why the speech at issue also satisfied the policy concerns expressed by the Supreme Court regarding why commercial speech should receive less protection. The court identified four such rationales: 1) "[C]ommercial speech generally makes a different contribution to the exposition of ideas" as such speech relates to the economic interests of the speaker and its audience; 2) "[C]ommercial speech tends to be more durable and chill-resistant due to the economic self-interest that drives the speech."; 3) "[C]ommercial speakers have extensive knowledge of both their market and their own products and are thus uniquely situated to evaluate the truthfulness of their speech."; and 4) Giving equal protection to

---

50 *Id.* at 930.

51 *Id.* at 932.

52 *Id.* at 933 (citing Bolger v. Youngs Drug Prods. Corp., 463 U.S. 60, 66–67 (1983)).

commercial and non-commercial speech would dilute the value of the First Amendment protections afforded non-commercial speech.[53]

The first rationale appears to be speaking to how society values speech. Free speech allows us to develop new ideas and to criticize positions, ideas, government actions, etc. without fear of reprisal (economic or otherwise). Commercial speech generally serves an informational function, which, although valuable, must be viewed through the lens of the economic interests behind the information being provided. In other words, commercial speech is, perhaps, less "pure" than non-commercial speech in that it is tainted by the economic interests that drive it.

The second rationale certainly seems to be true, although one could envision scenarios where even commercial speech could be chilled by a litigious competitor.[54] The third rationale seems a little odd. Why would we seemingly punish the holder of more knowledge with less protection? This would seem to be based on a sort of "they should know better" rationale. If they are speaking falsely about their own or a competitor's products or services, they likely know or should know that the statements are false. Thus, a heightened burden of proof requiring actual malice is unnecessary.

The fourth rationale is the most elusive to pin down. It is arguably fair to question if free speech is really devalued by giving more protection to commercial speech.[55] The *U.S. Healthcare* court did not really address this rationale as it applied to the facts at issue.

The *U.S. Healthcare* court found that the case easily involved all of the characteristics important in a First Amendment analysis. The speech was certainly motivated by money and was geared toward convincing customers to pick one product over another. Although the speech discussed costs and some of the aspects offered by each plan,

---

53 *Id.* at 933–34.

54 For arguments that commercial speech should receive stronger First Amendment protection, see Adam Thierer, *Advertising, Commercial Speech, and First Amendment Parity*, 5 CHARLESTON L. REV. 503, 506 (2011) (proposing symmetrical protection under the First Amendment for both commercial and non-commercial speech based upon blurring boundaries due to media convergence and user-generated content); Nicole B. Casarez, *Don't Tell Me What to Say: Compelled Commercial Speech and the First Amendment*, 63 MO. L. REV. 929, 932 (1998) (arguing for intermediate-level scrutiny by the courts for restrictions on commercial speech imposed by a state in the name of consumer protection); Alex Kozinski, *Who's Afraid of Commercial Speech?*, 76 VA. L. REV. 627, 628 (1990) (offering the proposition that the commercial/noncommercial distinction makes no sense); Mary B. Nutt, *Trends in First Amendment Protection of Commercial Speech*, 41 VAND. L. REV. 173, 175–76 (1988) (stressing the applicability of intermediate-level scrutiny instead of a deferential review to non-deceptive commercial speech).

55 *See, e.g.*, Alex Kozinski, *Who's Afraid of Commercial Speech?*, 76 VA. L. REV. 627, 648 (1990) (criticizing the justification that protecting commercial speech devalues the protections under the First Amendment).

the court held that the advertisements "add[ed] little information and even fewer ideas to the marketplace of health care thought."[56] Further, given the money at stake, the court noted that the speech was certainly chill-resistant, stating: "[I]t would have to be a cold day before these corporations would be chilled from speaking about the comparative merits of their products."[57] Finally, the court noted that the speakers had the type of superior information that justified affording commercial speech less protection:

> [T]hese are advertisements for products and services in markets in which U.S. Healthcare and Blue Cross/Blue Shield deal—and, presumably, know more about than anyone else. The facts upon which the advertisements are based—comparative price, procedures, and services offered—are readily objectifiable. These advertisements were precisely calculated, developed over time and published only when the corporate speakers were ready. Consequently, the advertisements were unusually verifiable.[58]

Ultimately the *U.S. Healthcare* decision is useful in that it provides a three-part test for identifying commercial speech. The opinion also demonstrates, however, that the rationales underlying the lesser protection for commercial speech must be examined.

As part of its opinion, the *U.S. Healthcare* court observed:

> At the outset, we note that it is of no consequence that the defendants (and counterclaim defendants) here are not members of the broadcast and print media. Although the Supreme Court has not finally settled whether "non-media" defendants should receive protections identical to those afforded "media" defendants, this court has so far declined to limit the protections of the *New York Times* standard to media defendants only.[59]

What if, instead of suing over statements made as part of a competitive advertising campaign, Blue Cross/Blue Shield was suing a consulting firm hired by the state to make a recommendation about which plan to adopt for state employees? What if the recommendation revealed severe deficiencies in the hospital coverage of the "Personal Choice" plan? Such cases would be difficult to bring under the Lanham Act, as they would likely fail the "commercial advertising

---

56 *U.S. Healthcare, Inc.*, 898 F.2d at 935.

57 *Id.*

58 *Id.*

59 *Id.* at 930–31.

and promotion" prong.[60] Furthermore, there could be standing issues. A common law disparagement claim could get around the standing issue, but most states' common law follows the Restatement approach requiring a showing of actual malice, which would heighten the burden of Blue Cross/Blue Shield.

A defamation claim would be more interesting. This would bring the issue of whether the consultants' speech was commercial speech back into the *U.S. Healthcare* analysis. Going through the three factors is somewhat inconclusive. The speech is not an advertisement; it does refer to a specific product or service; and the speaker does have an economic motivation for the speech. As the court demonstrated in *U.S. Healthcare*, however, the rationales underlying the lesser protection for commercial speech must also be examined.

First, commercial speech makes a different contribution to the exposition of ideas, as such speech relates to the economic interests of the speaker and its audience. This seems to lean toward the report being commercial speech. Second, commercial speech tends to be more durable and chill-resistant due to the economic self-interest that drives the speech. Once again, this could lean toward a finding of commercial speech. Third, commercial speakers have extensive knowledge of both their market and their own products and are thus uniquely situated to evaluate the truthfulness of their speech. This could go either way and could depend on the expertise of the consulting firm. Fourth, giving equal protection to commercial and non-commercial speech would dilute the value of the First Amendment protections afforded to non-commercial speech. It is difficult to see how protecting a consultant's work would dilute the value of non-commercial speech.

If this is commercial speech, then Blue Cross/Blue Shield would presumably get the lower burden under our hypothetical, but perhaps this would be an instance in which the "public figure" analysis would come into play. The court in *U.S. Healthcare* limited its holding to the context of a comparative advertising war. With regard to a consultant's report, a court may impose a higher burden based upon the "public figure" status of the claimant. But this assumes that the report would qualify as commercial speech. In

[60] *See, e.g.*, Kansas Bankers Sur. Co. v. Bahr Consultants, Inc., 69 F. Supp. 2d 1004, 1011–12 (E.D. Tenn. 1999) (holding that a consulting firm that did independent comparative analyses of insurance policies for the benefit of insurance buyers was not liable under the Lanham Act, as the statements did not qualify under the "commercial advertising or promotion" language).

general, media about products and services that appear in editorial content or trade journals will not qualify as "commercial speech."[61]

Note, however, that this analysis has focused on the type of speech at issue and the claimant's status, not on the status of the defendant (although the defendant's status may implicate the commercial speech analysis). Generally, media defendants and others independently and objectively evaluating a plaintiff's products and services get the benefit of the actual malice standard. Competitor defendants who are primarily interested in taking sales away from a plaintiff typically do not. There may exist defendants in between these two types—i.e., a defendant who is not a disinterested member of the press or product evaluator, but who is also not a competitor. In such cases, if the speech is a matter of public concern, the actual malice requirement would seem to be justified. For instance, in the area of scientific inquiry and debate, it has been held that scientific articles allegedly containing incorrect factual statements are outside of the Lanham Act.[62]

The parties in *U.S. Healthcare* also brought state common law actions for commercial disparagement. As has been discussed, a common law disparagement claim, at least in a jurisdiction that follows the Restatement, must still meet the actual malice standard.[63] Thus, the nature of the speech as commercial becomes irrelevant, unless the state at issue varies from the Restatement standard by eliminating the actual malice requirement.

In the 2010 decision of *Citizens United v. Fed. Election Comm'n*,[64] the U.S. Supreme Court sustained a challenge to a federal law that prohibited political speech during elections based upon the speaker's corporate identity. The Court held that First Amendment protection extended to corporations for political speech. In its analysis, the Court used the rationale that the press is made up of media companies which fall into the definition of corporations, and thus prohibitions on the political speech of corporations would result in a possible chilling effect on desirable political speech. The Court did not discuss the lesser protections afforded by the First Amendment to commercial speech. Nevertheless, some commentators have argued that the natural trajectory of the decision is for the Court to do away with the "commercial speech doctrine" in

---

[61] *See* 4 MCCARTHY ON TRADEMARKS AND UNFAIR COMPETITION § 27:71 (5th ed. 2024).

[62] *See, e.g.*, ONY, Inc. v. Cornerstone Therapeutics, Inc., 720 F.3d 490, 492 (2d Cir. 2013) ("[S]tatements of scientific conclusions about unsettled matters of scientific debate cannot give rise to liability" under the Lanham Act).

[63] RESTATEMENT (SECOND) OF TORTS § 623A cmt. d (1977).

[64] 558 U.S. 310 (2010).

the near future.[65] The argument seems based, in part, on the attitudes reflected by the Supreme Court in its opinion. It may be true that the decision has changed the focus of commercial speech from the status of the speaker to the nature of the speech. However, even if that is true, it seems that *Citizens United* could easily be confined to a corporation's ability to speak on political matters and should have no impact on commercial speech (such as the speech at issue in *U.S. Healthcare*).

Assuming these commentators are correct, what then of the Lanham Act and its regulation of commercial speech? It may not be dead—as Darrel C. Menthe notes in his article:

> I propose that the longevity of [the] commercial speech doctrine is because it supports—albeit crudely—a set of popular policy goals concerning the restriction of commercial advertising, in particular constraints on false advertising and the location of billboards. Part of the task of abolishing [the] commercial speech doctrine will be locating a new constitutional framework for these policy goals without tacking footnotes onto the First Amendment.[66]

Menthe goes on to conclude that such regulations should be more closely tied to fraud protection, although he would limit plaintiffs to those who relied upon the misstatements.[67]

---

65 *See* Tamara R. Piety, Commentary, *Citizens United and the Threat to the Regulatory State*, 109 MICH. L. REV. FIRST IMPRESSIONS 16, 16–17 (2010) (suggesting that the *Citizens United* decision is a sign that the Supreme Court may do away with the commercial speech doctrine in the near future, which would leave commercial and non-commercial speech with equivalent First Amendment protection); Darrel C. Menthe, *The Marketplace Metaphor and Commercial Speech Doctrine: Or How I Learned to Stop Worrying About and Love Citizens United*, 38 HASTINGS CONST. L.Q. 131, 135 (2010) (theorizing that the protection of the "marketplace of ideas" in *Citizens United* must necessarily lead to the end of the commercial speech doctrine).

66 Darrel C. Menthe, *The Marketplace Metaphor and Commercial Speech Doctrine: Or How I Learned to Stop Worrying About and Love Citizens United*, 38 HASTINGS CONST. L.Q. 131, 134–35 (2010).

67 *Id.* at 166–67.

# Chapter 8

# MISAPPROPRIATION

## A. INTRODUCTION TO THE COMMON LAW TORT OF MISAPPROPRIATION

The common law tort of misappropriation is neither well defined nor widely accepted. Section 38 of the Restatement of Unfair Competition limits its use to misappropriation of trade values, with specific reference to trade secrets, misappropriation of another's identity, and violations of copyright. The tort's origins, however, are much broader. Perhaps the best way to summarize the tort is with reference to a quote from the *International News Service v. Associated Press*[1] case summarized below, in which Justice Pitney condemned attempts by competitors to "reap where [they had] not sown." But taken to its logical extension, this would prohibit all types of activities without regard to what has been misappropriated. For instance, shouldn't a bar located near a sports arena be permitted to benefit from the increased patronage that comes with game days (and a successful team), even though the bar has, in a sense, misappropriated the team's goodwill? Moreover, the tort runs afoul of many federally preempted areas of law, such as copyright and patent law. Due to these concerns, the courts that have been willing to recognize misappropriation as a general cause of action have done so cautiously. Section B of this chapter sets out the origins of the general tort of misappropriation. Section C then summarizes modern-day misappropriation and "Hot News" claims.

## B. THE ORIGINS OF THE TORT OF MISAPPROPRIATION

The seminal case on the tort of misappropriation is the above-cited U.S. Supreme Court decision in *INS v. Associated Press*. Copyright law at the time of the decision was not as developed as it is today, but the basic premise underlying the perceived need for a misappropriation tort is that information alone is not copyrightable. Rather, it is the original expression, selection, or arrangement of facts or ideas that is the subject of copyright protection. International News Service (INS) and Associated Press (AP) were two competitors in the news business. They both gathered and distributed news that they later published in their respective papers and sold to their

1 248 U.S. 215 (1918).

respective customers. At the heart of the case was information that AP had collected. This information involved World War I updates from Europe that AP apparently could access, but INS could not due to foreign government prohibitions. Thus, if INS was to report the news, it had to copy it from AP. INS did just that and then published the copied news in its West Coast papers. Due to the time difference between the East and West Coast, this erased any advantage that AP gained by being the first to have the news.

INS obtained the news in one of three ways. First, by bribing employees of newspapers published by AP's members to furnish the news to it before publication. Second, by inducing AP members to violate AP's bylaws to permit INS to obtain news before publication. Finally, INS would copy news from bulletin boards and from early editions of AP's newspapers and sell the stories to its own customers.

AP sued and the district court granted a preliminary injunction prohibiting INS from getting the news by bribing employees or inducing AP members to violate AP's bylaws. The court did not grant a preliminary injunction, however, with regard to INS simply copying the news from the bulletin boards and early editions. The appeals court remanded and ordered the district court to expand the injunction to include a prohibition on copying. An appeal to the Supreme Court followed.

The Supreme Court began by noting that there is no copyright protection in the news per se. However, with regard to whether there is some other property right, the Court found that the case was not about AP's right to the news, but instead about AP's right to be the first to report the news. As the Court stated: "The peculiar value of news is in the spreading of it while it is fresh . . . What we are concerned with is the business of making it known to the world, in which both parties to the present suit are engaged."[2] In this sense, it appears that the misappropriation claim was based upon general concepts of unfair competition. As the Court noted:

> The parties are competitors in this field; and, on fundamental principles, applicable here as elsewhere, when the rights or privileges of the one are liable to conflict with those of the other, each party is under a duty so to conduct its own business as not unnecessarily or unfairly to injure that of the other.[3]

INS argued that once the information was made available to the public, AP no longer had a right to complain if others (whether a member of the public or a competitor) passed that information along.

---

[2] *Id.* at 235.

[3] *Id.* at 235–36.

In response, the Court distinguished between rights AP might have against the public versus rights it would have against a competitor:

> The right of the purchaser of a single newspaper to spread knowledge of its contents gratuitously, for any legitimate purpose not unreasonably interfering with complainant's right to make merchandise of it, may be admitted; but to transmit that news for commercial use, in competition with complainant—which is what defendant has done and seeks to justify—is a very different matter.[4]

The Court felt that AP, as a competitor, did retain some right to limit INS's ability to copy and distribute the news in a way that took away the competitive advantage that AP sought by being the first to report the news. Put another way, the majority's view was that although AP did not retain a right in the information conveyed, it did retain a right to be the first to report it. This right was not abandoned when AP first published the material.

The Court noted that "irrespective of time differentials, irregularities in telegraphic transmission on different lines, and the normal consumption of time in printing and distributing the newspaper, result in permitting pirated news to be placed in the hands of defendant's readers sometimes simultaneously with the service of competing Associated Press papers, occasionally even earlier."[5] Thus, the speed with which information travels appears to be the problem—a problem that is probably more relevant today. But why is this such a problem?

Two justifications could be offered based on the language of the opinion. First, the opinion may be a broad recognition that others should not be allowed to "reap where they have not sown"—that is, they should not be allowed to profit off another's labor. This broad view would create a sort of "sweat equity" right in the news. Second, a more nuanced view would be that it isn't so much the reaping that is the problem, but the disincentive it creates and the harm this would do to the public. If INS's conduct is not enjoined, AP loses a valuable incentive to expend resources to get the news. If this incentive is removed, AP may not expend the money to gather news and the public suffers.

At first glance, the *INS* decision seems consistent with the Restatement of Unfair Competition. Comment g to § 1 of the Restatement states in part:

---

4 *Id.* at 239.

5 *Id.* at 238–39.

> A primary purpose of the law of unfair competition is the identification and redress of business practices that hinder rather than promote the efficient operation of the market. Certain recurring patterns of objectionable practices form the basis of the traditional categories of liability specifically enumerated in Subsection (a)(1)–(3). However, these specific forms of unfair competition do not fully exhaust the scope of statutory or common law liability for unfair methods of competition, and Subsection (a) therefore includes a residual category encompassing other business practices determined to be unfair.

This comment seems to be consistent with the language of *INS*. However, as comment b to § 38 makes clear, the drafters of the Restatement do not seem to think much of the *INS* decision. The last paragraph of comment b states:

> Although courts have occasionally invoked the *INS* decision on an ad hoc basis to grant relief against other commercial appropriations, they have not articulated coherent principles for its application. It is clear that no general rule of law prohibits the appropriation of a competitor's ideas, innovations, or other intangible assets once they become publicly known. In addition, the federal patent and copyright statutes now preempt a considerable portion of the domain in which the common law tort might otherwise apply. *See* Comment e. The better approach, and the one most likely to achieve an appropriate balance between the competing interests, does not recognize a residual common law tort of misappropriation.

Thus, the *INS* decision may be limited to the unique set of facts involved in the case. Comment c to § 38 goes on to note:

> Although the decision appears to rest on a rationale of unjust enrichment potentially applicable to a wide range of competitive conduct, subsequent decisions have recognized that broad application of the unjust enrichment rationale in a competitive marketplace would unreasonably restrain competition and undermine the public interest in access to valuable information. The facts of the *INS* decision are unusual and may serve, in part, to limit its rationale. The originator of valuable information or other intangible assets normally has an opportunity to exploit the advantage of a lead time in the market. This can provide the originator with an opportunity to recover the costs of development and in many cases is sufficient to encourage continued investment. However, the appropriation in *INS* deprived

Associated Press of any lead-time advantage, at least on the West Coast. Associated Press thus faced a direct threat to its primary market by a competitor who had incurred none of the development costs associated with collecting the news. Such circumstances present the most compelling case for protection against appropriation, although even on these facts Justice Brandeis argued persuasively in dissent that the proper balance between protection and access could be drawn only through legislation.

In his dissent, Justice Brandeis admitted that what INS had done resulted in an injustice, but he still refused to recognize a right to enjoin INS's actions. His dissent highlights the fragile nature of the misappropriation theory in light of countervailing public policies and federal law. As Brandeis stated:

> The general rule of law is, that the noblest of human productions—knowledge, truths ascertained, conceptions, and ideas—become, after voluntary communication to others, free as the air to common use. Upon these incorporeal productions the attribute of property is continued after such communication only in certain classes of cases where public policy has seemed to demand it. These exceptions are confined to productions which, in some degree, involve creation, invention, or discovery. But by no means all such are endowed with this attribute of property. The creations which are recognized as property by the common law are literary, dramatic, musical, and other artistic creations; and these have also protection under the copyright statutes. The inventions and discoveries upon which this attribute of property is conferred only by statute, are the few comprised within the patent law.[6]

This passage hints at a recurring problem that a general misappropriation theory faces—to what degree should the misappropriation theory be preempted by federal laws such as the Copyright Act? Brandeis believes that when it comes to the long-standing policy of only limiting the free flow of information in certain recognized areas, the Court should not step in and carve out a new area of protection.

Justice Holmes also dissented from the majority opinion in *INS*, stating that "[w]hen an uncopyrighted combination of words is published there is no general right to forbid other people [from] repeating them—in other words there is no property in the

6 *Id.* at 250.

combination or in the thoughts or facts that the words express."[7] However, he posited that the claim of Associated Press was better suited for another cause of action:

> If a given person is to be prohibited from making the use of words that his neighbors are free to make some other ground must be found. One such ground is vaguely expressed in the phrase unfair trade. . . . The ordinary case, I say, is palming off the defendant's product as the plaintiff's but the same evil may follow from the opposite falsehood—from saying whether in words or by implication that the plaintiff's product is the defendant's, and that, it seems to me, is what has happened here.[8]

Holmes believed that there may be a route to recovery without recognizing a new cause of action, and his quote seems to hint at a reverse passing-off claim. However, as we learned from the *Dastar* case in a previous chapter, protection from reverse passing-off only applies if the plaintiff is the actual manufacturer of the product or service at issue. It would be a hard sell for AP to argue that it was the manufacturer of the information at issue because the information already existed—AP just reported it. However, perhaps a false advertising claim could be made if INS was, by omitting AP's name, impliedly and falsely stating that INS had gathered the news. It seems that this is what Holmes was actually describing.

Although the *INS* decision is over 100 years old, the issues of misappropriation of news still persist—and by the same plaintiff. Associated Press brought a claim similar to the one asserted in *INS* as recently as 2009. In *Associated Press v. All Headline News Corp.*,[9] Associated Press sued All Headline News Corp. (AHN) for misappropriation. AHN did not engage in any original reporting, but instead hired individuals to find news stories on the internet, rewrite the text, or copy the stories in full for publication on the AHN website. Although many of the stories were based on the work of Associated Press, AHN marketed itself as the original provider. The district court denied AHN's motion to dismiss based on the continued recognition of misappropriation as a valid cause of action under New York law.

---

[7] *Id.* at 246.

[8] *Id.* at 246–47.

[9] 608 F. Supp. 2d 454 (S.D.N.Y. 2009).

## C. MODERN DAY MISAPPROPRIATION: "HOT NEWS" CLAIMS

The continued validity of the misappropriation action under *INS* came into question after the U.S. Supreme Court's decision in *Erie Railroad v. Tompkins*,[10] which abolished claims based upon any sort of federal common law in diversity cases. Furthermore, courts and commentators questioned whether such an action could survive the preemptive effect of federal copyright and patent laws, which are often implicated in such cases. For example, absent a patent, ideas and innovations are generally unprotected from exploitation by others. In *Bonito Boats, Inc. v. Thunder Craft Boats, Inc.*,[11] the U.S. Supreme Court stated with regard to patent protection that "[a] state law that substantially interferes with the enjoyment of an unpatented utilitarian or design conception which has been freely disclosed by its author to the public at large impermissibly contravenes the ultimate goal of public disclosure and use which is the centerpiece of federal patent policy."[12] Similarly, § 301 of the 1976 Copyright Act precludes recognition of a state law cause of action which protects rights "equivalent" to any of the exclusive rights of copyright recognized by the Act.[13] Nevertheless, a number of states have continued to recognize misappropriation as a state common law theory of recovery. In such states, however, courts have often limited the misappropriation doctrine to so-called "hot news" cases, which mirror the facts of *INS*. But even in such cases, preemption may remain an issue.

The hot news misappropriation theory and its interaction with federal preemption is demonstrated in *The National Basketball Association v. Motorola, Inc.*[14] decision. The case involved a handheld pager sold by Motorola and marketed under the name "SportsTrax." The pager displayed updated information of professional basketball games in progress. The operation relied on a "data feed" supplied by reporters who watched the games on television or listened to them on radio. The NBA sought to enjoin Motorola from transmitting scores or other data about NBA games in progress via the pagers. In addition to the pagers, Motorola had a website that similarly updated scores, but the court treated the pagers and the website the same for the purposes of analysis.

---

10 304 U.S. 64 (1938).

11 489 U.S. 141 (1989).

12 *Id.* at 156–57.

13 *See* 17 U.S.C. § 301.

14 105 F.3d 841 (2d Cir. 1997).

One of the initial issues faced by the court was whether the NBA's claim was preempted by the Copyright Act. The district court found for the NBA, concluding that the NBA's misappropriation claim was only partially preempted. On appeal, the court noted that although game broadcasts are copyrightable while the underlying games are not, the Copyright Act does not distinguish between the two when analyzing the preemption of a misappropriation claim based on copying or taking from the copyrightable work. The court of appeals went on to state that copyrightable material often contains non-copyrightable elements within it, but preemption bars state law misappropriation claims with respect to non-copyrightable as well as copyrightable elements. Indeed, most books, magazines, articles, etc. convey some information and this would limit perhaps only pure fiction and poetry as wholly within the scope of preemption (and maybe not even then). The court found that adoption of a partial preemption doctrine would expand the reach of state law claims and render the preemption intended by Congress unworkable. As such, for purposes of preemption, the court rejected using a separate analysis for broadcasts and the underlying facts that were the basis of the broadcasts.

Nevertheless, the court held that the misappropriation claim at issue could survive preemption. The court found that, despite being within the scope of the Copyright Act, state law claims can move forward if there exists an "extra element" in addition to (or instead of) the normal elements associated with copyright infringement. The court enunciated 5 elements for an *INS*-type hot news claim:

(1) a plaintiff generates or gathers information at a cost;

(2) the information is time-sensitive;

(3) a defendant's use of the information constitutes free riding on the plaintiff's efforts;

(4) the defendant is in direct competition with a product or service offered by the plaintiffs; and

(5) the ability of other parties to free-ride on the efforts of the plaintiff or others would so reduce the incentive to produce the product or service that its existence or quality would be substantially threatened.

After enunciating these elements, the court found that the "extra" elements were numbers 2, 3, and 5. However, not all courts agree with these elements, particularly the element of competition (number 4), which is not necessarily required.

Despite recognizing that a hot news claim could survive preemption, the court concluded that Motorola did not engage in the unlawful misappropriation of hot news. The court recognized that although the information was time-sensitive, there were elements missing, as the NBA was actually engaged in three different activities: "The first product is generating the information by playing the games; the second product is transmitting live, full descriptions of those games; and the third product is collecting and retransmitting strictly factual information about the games."[15] The court noted that the primary business of the NBA was to produce basketball games for live attendance and broadcast. However, the collection of strictly factual material was a different product. As such, the NBA failed to show any competitive effect on its first two products (a pager was not really a substitute for watching the game live). Additionally, the NBA failed to show free-riding on the factual information. Motorola expended its own resources to collect the purely factual information to transmit. In this sense, it was easy to distinguish Motorola's conduct from INS's conduct in the original *INS* case.

In *Barclays Capital Inc. v. Theflyonthewall.com, Inc.*,[16] the Second Circuit re-examined its analysis in *NBA v. Motorola*. Barclays Capital, Merrill Lynch, and Morgan Stanley (the Firms) brought suit against Theflyonthewall.com (Fly) for hot news misappropriation under New York law. Each Firm would develop market research about major publicly traded equity securities. Once compiled, the Firms would sell this research (along with trading recommendations) to clients who would act on the information. In producing this research, the Firms limited their disclosure and attempted to protect the information in a variety of ways—e.g., safeguarding passwords, forbidding clients from redistributing, etc. Despite their efforts, much of the Firms' research would leak and would be posted by online aggregators or reported as financial news. The Firms identified Fly as one of the more systematic unauthorized publishers. Evidence introduced at trial was compelling and demonstrated that the unauthorized redistribution was a major contributor to the decline in resources that each Firm devoted to market research.

The district court applied the five-element test from *NBA* and found that Fly was liable for misappropriation. On appeal, the court engaged in a somewhat convoluted explanation of the rationale of *NBA*. The court stated that the five-part test in *NBA* articulated the elements of a hot news misappropriation claim, but a later three-part test in the opinion articulated the "extra elements" needed to avoid preemption. However, the court went on to question the rationale of

---

15 *Id.* at 853.

16 650 F.3d 876 (2d Cir. 2011).

*NBA*: "The *NBA* panel decided the case before it, and we think that the law it thus made regarding 'hot news' preemption is, as we have tried to explain, determinative here. But the Court's various explanations of its five-part approach are not."[17] The Second Circuit then reversed the district court based on what it viewed as a lack of free-riding:

> . . . the Firms' claim is not a so-called *INS*-type non-preempted claim because Fly is not, under *NBA*'s analysis, "free-riding." It is collecting, collating and disseminating factual information—the facts that Firms and others in the securities business have made recommendations with respect to the value of and the wisdom of purchasing or selling securities—and attributing the information to its source. The Firms are making the news; Fly, despite the Firms' understandable desire to protect their business model, is breaking it.[18]

The *Barclays* decision is a bit dizzying, but the court engaged in a rather detailed discussion of *NBA* and noted that there were actually three iterations of the hot news test. The court summarized the three iterations as follows:

> The first is a general introduction, by way of summary, of what the decision concludes. The second may be described as "stating the elements of the tort." *ConFold Pac., Inc. v. Polaris Indus.*, 433 F.3d 952, 960 (7th Cir.2006) (Posner, *J.*). And the third focuses on what "extra elements" are necessary to avoid preemption despite the conclusion that the "general scope requirement" and the "subject matter requirement," *NBA*, 105 F.3d at 848, have been met.[19]

Given the inconsistencies between the different iterations, however, the court concluded that the hot news test from *NBA* could not be controlling: "In our view, the several *NBA* statements were sophisticated observations in aid of the Court's analysis of the difficult preemption issues presented to it. Inconsistent as they were, they could not all be equivalent to a statutory command to which we or the district court are expected to adhere."[20] This conclusion would seem to call into question the applicability of the 5-element test to any fact scenario that isn't strongly analogous to the facts of *NBA*. It should be noted, however, that the court still resolved the issue under one of the principles addressed in *NBA*—namely free-riding.

---

[17] *Id.* at 899.

[18] *Id.* at 902.

[19] *Id.* at 900–01.

[20] *Id.* at 901.

Direct competition played a role in the misappropriation analysis in *NBA*. The *NBA* court noted in a footnote that direct competition in a primary market is typically a requirement of a misappropriation claim. Similarly, in *U.S. Golf Association v. St. Andrews Systems, Data-Max, Inc.*,[21] the U.S. Golf Association (USGA) developed a mathematical formula for amateur golf players to determine their handicap. Data-Max developed and marketed small computers that were programmed to calculate a golfer's handicap based on USGA's equation. USGA brought a misappropriation claim under New Jersey law seeking to enjoin Data-Max's use of its handicapping formula. The court looked at whether there was direct competition and concluded that there was not. The USGA was not involved in marketing the formula; it was simply promoting discussion. Data-Max, on the other hand, was involved in providing "instant handicaps." Because the two parties were not in direct competition, the court rejected the misappropriation claim.

Under very similar facts, however, an injunction barring the use of USGA's handicap formula was upheld in *U.S. Golf Association v. Arroyo Software Corp.*[22] Arroyo argued that USGA's claims should be collaterally estopped due to the Third Circuit's opinion in *St. Andrews*. The California Court of Appeal in *Arroyo* rejected this argument: "Collateral estoppel does not apply where there are changed conditions or new facts which did not exist at the time of the prior judgment, or where the previous decision was based on different substantive law."[23] The court held that the factual circumstances were different, as USGA's formula was new and much more complex, involved the expenditure of millions of dollars, and was developed after the *St. Andrews* decision. The court also held that California substantive law regarding the misappropriation claim was different from the corresponding New Jersey law at issue in *St. Andrews*:

> The elements of a claim for misappropriation under California law consist of the following: (a) the plaintiff invested substantial time, skill or money in developing its property; (b) the defendant appropriated and used the plaintiff's property at little or no cost to the defendant; (c) the defendant's appropriation and use of the plaintiff's property was without the authorization or consent of the plaintiff; and (d) the plaintiff can establish that it has been injured by the defendant's conduct. The principal basis for the decision of the Third Circuit in *St. Andrews* was the fact

[21] 749 F.2d 1028 (3d Cir. 1984).

[22] 69 Cal. App. 4th 607 (Ct. App. 1999).

[23] *Id.* at 616.

> that New Jersey law required proof of direct competition between the plaintiff and the defendant as an essential element of any misappropriation claim. Under the California law applicable here, on the other hand, the essential elements of a misappropriation claim simply do not include any such requirement of proof of direct competition between the plaintiff and the defendant. Because California law does not require a showing of direct competition between the parties before conduct otherwise constituting misappropriation can be prohibited, the trial court was correct in holding both that the issues decided under New Jersey law in *St. Andrews* were not identical to those arising under California law in this case, and that collateral estoppel does not preclude USGA's claims in this case.[24]

The *USGA* cases demonstrate how the direct competition element is not consistent between jurisdictions. It is also worth noting that although the California elements of a misappropriation claim differ from the five elements listed in *NBA*, direct competition was not one of the three "extra elements" necessary to avoid federal preemption.

As noted in the introduction to this chapter, misappropriation is far from a uniformly accepted cause of action. The states of California, Connecticut, Colorado, Delaware, Hawaii, Illinois, Maryland, Missouri, New York, New Jersey, Texas, Pennsylvania, Washington, and Wisconsin recognize a general common law misappropriation claim. However, the Third Restatement of Unfair Competition rejects a general cause of action for misappropriation.[25]

Given that many jurisdictions do not recognize a misappropriation claim, and considering the difficulties involved in prevailing on such a claim when it is recognized, how is a party to protect the fruits of its labor from free-riders? One solution, discussed in a later chapter, is through the law of trade secrets. However, a trade secret claim requires the information to not be publicly disseminated, which can pose problems for parties like Associated Press. A better solution, therefore, may be through contract law.

In *ProCD, Inc. v. Zeidenberg*,[26] an opinion known more for its discussion of what have been termed "rolling contracts," Judge Easterbrook found that a breach of contract claim was not preempted

---

[24] *Id.* at 618–19.

[25] *See* RESTATEMENT (THIRD) OF UNFAIR COMPETITION § 38 cmt. b (1995) ("The better approach ... does not recognize a residual common law tort of misappropriation.").

[26] 86 F.3d 1447 (7th Cir. 1996).

by federal copyright law. Matthew Zeidenberg entered a local retail store and bought ProCD's product, "Select Phone," which was a CD-ROM disk containing over 95,000,000 telephone listings compiled by ProCD. Inside the package was a user guide containing a "Single User License Agreement," which prohibited the purchaser from copying the software for non-personal use (the license would appear on most computer screens before the listings could be accessed). The license stated the following: "By using the discs and the listings licensed to you, you agree to be bound by the terms of this License. If you do not agree to the terms of this License, promptly return all copies of the software . . . to the place where you obtained it."

Zeidenberg soon realized that he could copy the information and make it available to the public himself. He subsequently incorporated under the name Silken Mountain Web Services, Inc. and purchased an updated version of Select Phone. ProCD sued to enjoin Zeidenberg and the district court denied relief. The court concluded that the terms of the license were not part of the contract between Zeidenberg and ProCD. Alternatively, the court found that any breach of contract claim was preempted by the Copyright Act.

On appeal, the Seventh Circuit reversed and remanded. The court held that the contract was not formed in the store but was instead consummated when Zeidenberg reviewed the terms of the license and proceeded to use the software. (This method of contract formation is often referred to as a "rolling" or "layered" contract.) In addition, the court held that contract claims were not preempted by the Copyright Act:

> But are rights created by contract "equivalent to any of the exclusive rights within the general scope of copyright"? Three courts of appeals have answered "no." *National Car Rental System, Inc. v. Computer Associates International, Inc.*, 991 F.2d 426, 433 (8th Cir.1993); *Taquino v. Teledyne Monarch Rubber*, 893 F.2d 1488, 1501 (5th Cir.1990); *Acorn Structures, Inc. v. Swantz*, 846 F.2d 923, 926 (4th Cir.1988). The district court disagreed with these decisions, 908 F.Supp. at 658, but we think them sound. Rights "equivalent to any of the exclusive rights within the general scope of copyright" are rights established *by law*—rights that restrict the options of persons who are strangers to the author. Copyright law forbids duplication, public performance, and so on, unless the person wishing to copy or perform the work gets permission; silence means a ban on copying. A copyright is a right against the world. Contracts, by contrast, generally affect only their parties;

> strangers may do as they please, so contracts do not create "exclusive rights."[27]

Judge Easterbrook's position on contract preemption appears to have prevailed across jurisdictions.[28]

*ProCD* also presents a possible solution for the NBAs of the world who wish to prevent similar behavior. If the NBA can somehow get patrons of the games to agree not to report live, then perhaps the NBA could enjoin such behavior. But how do you propose such terms? The obvious place where such a term could be placed is on the ticket itself.[29] However, such clauses would still face scrutiny under contract law for conspicuousness, unconscionability, and maybe even formation issues.

In the *NBA* decision, it was noted that a misappropriation claim may be preempted by copyright law. In the landmark case of *Feist Publications, Inc. v. Rural Telephone Service Co.*,[30] the U.S. Supreme Court rejected "sweat of the brow" as a valid basis for a cause of action for copyright infringement. Rural was a local telephone company that was required by Kansas state law to publish annually a telephone directory for its service area. Feist was a publisher in the business of publishing directories covering larger geographical areas. The companies were in competition for the advertising revenue from the directories. Unable to procure a license from Rural for its subscriber information, Feist decided to misappropriate the information from Rural's directory. Feist included the material in its own directory after sorting and verifying the information. Rural brought a copyright infringement action against Feist claiming that Feist had reproduced Rural's copyrighted material without authorization—material that Rural had invested substantial resources in creating.

The Supreme Court held that Rural's material was not original enough to be covered by copyright law. In so doing, the Court rejected "sweat of the brow" (substantial investments made by Rural in creating its directory) as a basis for a copyright infringement claim. The Court held that names, towns, and telephone numbers of Rural's subscribers were uncopyrightable facts, and these bits of information were not selected, coordinated, or arranged in an original way in Rural's directory. As a result, Rural's claim did not meet

---

27 *Id.* at 1454.

28 *See* Richard A. Epstein, *ProCD v. Zeidenberg: Do Doctrine and Function Mix?*, in CONTRACTS STORIES 122 (Foundation Press, 2007 Douglas G. Baird editor).

29 *See* Carnival Cruise Lines, Inc. v. Shute, 499 U.S. 585 (1991) (upholding a forum selection clause that was found on pages attached to tickets for a cruise).

30 499 U.S. 340 (1991).

constitutional or statutory requirements for copyright protection. (It is worth noting that Rural did not raise a misappropriation claim.)

A misappropriation action is generally filed in conjunction with other unfair competition claims. In *eBay, Inc. v. Bidder's Edge, Inc.*,[31] eBay filed for injunctive relief against Bidder's Edge for misappropriating its auction data. Along with a misappropriation claim, eBay brought eight other causes of action: trespass, false advertising, federal and state trademark dilution, computer fraud and abuse, unfair competition, interference with prospective economic advantage, and unjust enrichment. In an attempt to create its own "one-stop shop" auction website, Bidder's Edge was using robotic software to crawl the eBay site for the purpose of aggregating eBay data with data from other auction sites. Not surprisingly, this action was without eBay's consent and violated eBay's user agreement. The court preliminarily enjoined Bidder's Edge from accessing eBay's computer systems without eBay's written authorization, and it based its decision on a trespass to chattels theory. As is evident from the various claims listed above, a single infringing act may give rise to multiple causes of action depending upon the nature of the misappropriation.

---

[31] 100 F. Supp. 2d 1058 (N.D. Cal. 2000).

# Chapter 9

# TRADE SECRETS

## A. INTRODUCTION TO THE LAW OF TRADE SECRETS: FROM COMMON LAW TO STATUTE

Trade secret law builds upon a theme developed in the previous chapter that it is unfair in some instances for a competitor to reap where he has not sown. The law has protected trade secrets since the time of ancient Rome, and the legal principles have developed and evolved over the years. A business may create many different forms of intellectual property that could qualify under the term "trade secret." A new, more efficient process for manufacturing a product, for instance, may qualify as a trade secret, but so may a customer list, pricing information, market research, and marketing strategies. The choice to protect one's intellectual property via trade secret law may be due to a lack of alternative means of protection or may be a reasoned decision, weighing the benefits and detriments of seeking protection through federal copyright or patent law.

For example, assume that a business has developed a machine that makes door hinges twice as fast and at a greatly reduced cost. The business now faces a choice: it can seek to patent the machine under federal law or resort to trade secret protection. In order to qualify for a patent, the business would have to overcome a number of hurdles, such as showing that the machine is novel and not obvious.[1] Furthermore, even if granted, the protection offered by patent law only lasts for twenty years from the date of application. After that date, the machine's design is open for anyone to use. On the other hand, trade secret protection is governed by state common law and requires no registration. Such protection has no time limit and the subject matter of what qualifies for protection may be broader than what is available under patent law. Given such a choice, a business may very well decide to forgo the cost of registering a patent and simply rely upon the common law's protection of trade secrets.

---

1 *See* 35 U.S.C. §§ 102–103 ("A patent for a claimed invention may not be obtained, notwithstanding that the claimed invention is not identically disclosed as set forth in section 102, if the differences between the claimed invention and the prior art are such that the claimed invention as a whole would have been obvious before the effective filing date of the claimed invention to a person having ordinary skill in the art to which the claimed invention pertains.").

While the above example demonstrates a reasoned choice by a business, sometimes the choice is made simply due to the subject matter. Take, for instance, a customer list. Such a collection of information will not qualify for protection under the Copyright Act (as discussed in the previous chapter). Of course, it is unlikely that the business would want to make this information public anyway, as a customer list is no longer valuable if competitors have access to it. As such, the list is a perfect candidate for trade secret protection.

Trade secret is a field of growing importance in the United States and internationally. A 2009–2010 study of trade secret law found that trade secret litigation in federal courts is growing exponentially, doubling in the seven years from 1988 to 1995, and doubling again in the nine years from 1995 to 2004.[2] This same study noted that trade secret misappropriation costs businesses an estimated $300 billion per year. "When the Defend Trade Secrets Act was passed in 2016, trade secret litigation skyrocketed, increasing more than 25 percent in a single year."[3] And while the number of trade secret cases filed in federal court fell during COVID, that number was back on the rise by 2024.

Taking advantage of trade secret law is not necessarily as easy as it sounds. Not everything that a business keeps confidential qualifies as a trade secret, although secrecy is an important element. Furthermore, even when something qualifies as a trade secret, another's subsequent use of the secret may not qualify as a misappropriation. Before delving into the nuances of a trade secret claim, a brief discussion of the relevant sources of law is in order.

Trade secret law draws largely from state common law.[4] Section 757 of the First Restatement of Torts sets forth some early principles of trade secret protection. In 1979, the National Conference of Commissioners on Uniform State Laws approved the Uniform Trade Secrets Act (UTSA), which was amended in 1985. Since its approval, 48 states, the District of Columbia, Puerto Rico, and the U.S. Virgin Islands have adopted it, although uniformity has been weakened somewhat by state legislatures that have "tweaked" the UTSA's standards. Only two states have not adopted the UTSA, New York and North Carolina. North Carolina has its own trade secret act that

---

[2] *See* David S. Almeling et al., *A Statistical Analysis of Trade Secret Litigation in Federal Courts*, 45 GONZ. L. REV. 291, 292–93 (2010).

[3] Steven Hollman, Hannah Wigger & Tifenn Drouaud, TRADE SECRETS LAW BLOG, *The Rise of Trade Secret Litigation*, Sept. 23, 2024 *available at* https://www.tradesecretslawblog.com/2024/09/the-rise-of-trade-secret-litigation/.

[4] The term "largely" is used because certain federal laws address trade secrets in some areas, such as in the international misappropriation of trade secrets and in certain criminal statutes. The federal Defense of Trade Secrets Act, however, is derived from the Uniform Trade Secret Act.

appears to borrow from the UTSA, whereas New York continues to rely upon the First Restatement. Even in states that have adopted the UTSA, however, courts may look to the First Restatement for guidance. The Third Restatement of Unfair Competition has also chosen to address trade secrets, although not as a substitute for the UTSA: "Except as otherwise noted, the principles of trade secret law described in this Restatement are applicable to actions under the [UTSA] as well as to actions at common law. The concept of trade secret as defined in this Section is intended to be consistent with the definition of 'trade secret' in § 1(4) of the [UTSA]."[5]

Although there are three sources to draw upon, a vast majority of the jurisdictions have adopted the UTSA. But even in these jurisdictions, there are variations. Furthermore, even where the language is the same, there are differences in interpretation. For example, consider the California decision of *Abba Rubber Co. v. Seaquist*[6] and the Illinois decision of *Hamer Holding Group, Inc. v. Elmore*.[7] In both cases, the state legislatures had deleted the phrase "and not being readily ascertained by proper means by" from the definition of "trade secrets," which under UTSA § 1(4) reads: "information, including a formula, pattern, compilation, program device, method, technique, or process that: (i) derives independent economic value, actual or potential, from not being generally known to, and not being readily ascertained by proper means by, other persons who can obtain economic value from its disclosure or use, and (ii) is the subject of efforts that are reasonable under the circumstances to maintain its secrecy." The *Abba* court took this to mean that the fact that a secret was ascertainable was not enough to destroy trade secret protection so long as the secret had not actually been ascertained. However, the *Hamer* court reached the opposite result, despite the exclusion of the language from the statute, reasoning that "the key to 'secrecy' is the ease with which information can be developed through other proper means: if the information can be readily duplicated without involving considerable time, effort or expense, then it is not secret."[8]

With a variety of approaches to trade secret law, federal legislation was enacted in 2016 under the Defense of Trade Secrets Act (DTSA) to add a uniform law.[9] The DTSA does not replace or preempt state trade secret law, but it does do away with the need to meet the diversity requirements to bring a federal trade secret case.

---

5 RESTATEMENT (THIRD) OF UNFAIR COMPETITION § 39 cmt. b (1995).

6 286 Cal. Rptr. 518 (Ct. App. 1991).

7 560 N.E.2d 907 (Ill. Ct. App. 1990).

8 *Id.* at 918.

9 *See* 18 U.S.C. § 1836 *et seq.*

The DTSA was itself modeled on the UTSA, with the elements of a trade secret claim and many definitions mirroring the UTSA. Remedies also track the UTSA but with one added remedy under the DTSA—the availability of an *ex parte* seizure.[10] As noted above, many states tweak the UTSA. The presence of a uniform federal law now presents plaintiffs with the ability to choose a federal cause of action if the DTSA is more favorable than the state law, and vice versa.

With so many sources, it may be tempting to conclude that there is no uniformity in state trade secret principles. As will be explored, however, there are a number of generalities that can be made regarding trade secret law. The various sources of law are described to convey that courts have a number of resources to draw upon in making decisions. These various sources will be discussed throughout the chapter.

## B. ELEMENTS OF A TRADE SECRET CLAIM

There are two basic elements to a trade secret claim: (1) the subject of the suit must qualify as a trade secret; and (2) the secret must be misappropriated. This standard is deceptively simple. In fact, each element involves a detailed inquiry into several matters, including the nature of the secret, what steps were taken to protect it, and how it fell into the hands of the alleged misappropriator.

### 1. Qualification as a Trade Secret

Comment b to § 757 of the First Restatement of Torts defines a trade secret as "any formula, pattern, device or compilation of information which is used in one's business, and which gives him an opportunity to obtain an advantage over competitors who do not know or use it." It goes on to list six factors which may be used to determine whether something qualifies as a trade secret:

> (1) the extent to which the information is known outside of his business;
>
> (2) the extent to which it is known by employees and others involved in his business;
>
> (3) the extent of measures taken by him to guard the secrecy of the information;
>
> (4) the value of the information to him and to his competitors;
>
> (5) the amount of effort or money expended by him in developing the information;

---

10 *See* 18 U.S.C. § 1836(b)(2)(A)(i).

(6) the ease or difficulty with which the information could be properly acquired or duplicated by others.

The UTSA, DTSA, and the Third Restatement of Unfair Competition all provide similar definitions of a trade secret. As mentioned, the UTSA provides that a trade secret is "information, including a formula, pattern, compilation, program device, method, technique, or process that: (i) derives independent economic value, actual or potential, from not being generally known to, and not being readily ascertained by proper means by, other persons who can obtain economic value from its disclosure or use, and (ii) is the subject of efforts that are reasonable under the circumstances to maintain its secrecy."[11] The DTSA varies only slightly from this definition, but the import is the same.[12] The Third Restatement provides perhaps the most succinct definition of all: "A trade secret is any information that can be used in the operation of a business or other enterprise and that is sufficiently valuable and secret to afford an actual or potential economic advantage over others."[13]

Although neither the UTSA nor the Third Restatement of Unfair Competition explicitly utilizes the six-factor test of the First Restatement of Torts, the comments to both reference the First Restatement's elements, and courts in jurisdictions that have adopted the UTSA still look to those elements for guidance. The Third Restatement of Unfair Competition, however, rejects the notion of any set test to establish a trade secret: "It is not possible to state precise criteria for determining the existence of a trade secret. The status of information claimed as a trade secret must be ascertained through a comparative evaluation of all the relevant factors, including the value, secrecy, and definiteness of the information as well as the nature of the defendant's misconduct."[14]

---

11 UNIFORM TRADE SECRETS ACT § 1(4) (1985).

12 The DTSA defines a trade secret to mean:

> [A]ll forms and types of financial, business, scientific, technical, economic, or engineering information, including patterns, plans, compilations, program devices, formulas, designs, prototypes, methods, techniques, processes, procedures, programs, or codes, whether tangible or intangible, and whether or how stored, compiled, or memorialized physically, electronically, graphically, photographically, or in writing if—
>
> (A) the owner thereof has taken reasonable measures to keep such information secret; and
>
> (B) the information derives independent economic value, actual or potential, from not being generally known to, and not being readily ascertainable through proper means by, another person who can obtain economic value from the disclosure or use of the information.

18 U.S.C. § 1839(3).

13 RESTATEMENT (THIRD) OF UNFAIR COMPETITION § 39 (1995).

14 *Id.* § 39 cmt. d.

The various definitions of trade secret might tempt one to conclude that there is no uniformity in this area, but an examination of the six-factor test and definitions laid out by both Restatements and the UTSA reveals that they have much in common. The first and second factors of the six-factor test both speak to the degree that the secret is not known by others, which is also articulated in the UTSA (the Third Restatement of Unfair Competition simply refers to "sufficiently" secret and elaborates on this in comment f to § 39). The fourth and fifth factors speak to the value of the secret, also referenced by the UTSA, which refers to the secret deriving "independent economic value."[15] Finally, the third and sixth factors both speak to the efforts taken to maintain secrecy, which is found in the UTSA where it states that the trade secret must be "the subject of efforts that are reasonable under the circumstances to maintain its secrecy." The Third Restatement of Unfair Competition elaborates on this as well in comment g to § 39: "Precautions taken to maintain the secrecy of information are relevant in determining whether the information qualifies for protection as a trade secret." Despite the lack of agreement on a single applicable test for the existence of a trade secret, all of the standards tend to include three common elements: (1) the trade secret must not be known by others; (2) the trade secret must be valuable; and (3) the plaintiff must have taken reasonable steps to maintain the secrecy. However, as will be explored, these are not hard-and-fast elements, and often the discussions of one factor will overlap with another.

### *a. Not Known by Others*

Benjamin Franklin is widely credited as having said that "three can keep a secret, if two of them are dead." Luckily for trade secret plaintiffs, the law is not nearly as demanding. It may seem unnecessary to state that a trade secret, by its very nature, must not be known by others. The degree of secrecy required, however, can be quite confusing. As comment f to § 39 of the Third Restatement of Unfair Competition notes: "The secrecy, however, need not be absolute. The rule stated in this Section requires only secrecy sufficient to confer an actual or potential economic advantage on one who possesses the information." Revealing information to employees (who are agents of the business) usually does not destroy trade secret protection, but what about revealing the same information to potential customers who may wish to license a process? What about independent contractors who must have access to the trade secret to complete work? To what degree can a secret be divulged and still maintain its status as a secret? The case of *Metallurgical Industries,*

---

15 *See also id.* § 39 cmt. e.

*Inc. v. Fourtek, Inc.*[16] demonstrates that trade secret protection is not destroyed simply because the secret comprises techniques that are commonly known. In addition, the case illustrates that protection is not necessarily lost when the secret is divulged in limited circumstances.

Metallurgical was in the business of reclaiming tungsten carbide and it ordered two zinc recovery furnaces from a company called Therm-O-Vac. Metallurgical made a number of improvements on the first furnace received from Therm-O-Vac to increase its effectiveness (installing chill plates, replacing the large crucible, replacing the heating elements, and installing vacuum pumps). None of these modifications, in and of themselves, were novel or unknown. A year later, Metallurgical attempted to get a different manufacturer (Consarc) to make a second furnace with the modifications, but it ultimately went back to Therm-O-Vac.

Subsequently, Therm-O-Vac filed for bankruptcy and four of its former employees formed Fourtek, Inc. Fourtek contracted to make a furnace with the same modifications that Metallurgical had made for a competitor of Metallurgical, Smith International, Inc. Metallurgical brought a diversity action against Smith and the four former employees of Therm-O-Vac alleging misappropriation of trade secrets. The case went to trial and the district court granted the defendants' motion for a directed verdict. The court concluded that no trade secret was involved, as it found that the modifications involved information that was "too general to be legally protected."

On appeal, the Fifth Circuit began by discussing the characteristics of a trade secret. The defendants argued that the modifications made were all well-known and should therefore not qualify as trade secrets. Metallurgical admitted that there was nothing secret about the changes it made to the furnace. All of its techniques, such as using chill plates, were generally known.[17] Nevertheless, the court found that the modifications qualified as trade secrets. The court noted that the mere fact that the secret was discoverable does not destroy the secrecy element, especially when extensive and expensive trial-and-error was involved. Moreover, the court observed that a high degree of novelty was not required. Citing

16 790 F.2d 1195 (5th Cir. 1986).

17 The Restatement recognizes that self-evident modifications may lack secrecy. *See* RESTATEMENT (THIRD) OF UNFAIR COMPETITION § 39 cmt. f (1995) ("Self-evident variations or modifications of known processes, procedures, or methods . . . lack the secrecy necessary for protection as a trade secret."). *But see* Penalty Kick Mgmt. Ltd. v. Coca Cola Co., 318 F.3d 1284, 1291 (11th Cir. 2003) ("[E]ven if all of the information is publicly available, a unique combination of that information, which adds value to the information, also may qualify as a trade secret.").

the Supreme Court decision of *Kewanee Oil Co. v. Bicron Corp.*,[18] the court explained novelty in the trade secret setting: "Novelty, in the patent law sense, is not required for a trade secret . . . However, some novelty will be required if merely because that which does not possess novelty is usually known; secrecy, in the context of trade secrets, thus implies at least minimal novelty."[19] Similarly, although comment f to § 39 of the Restatement (Third) of Unfair Competition speaks of self-evident improvements, it also notes the following: "[I]t is the secrecy of the claimed trade secret as a whole that is determinative. *The fact that some or all of the components of the trade secret are well-known does not preclude protection for a secret combination, compilation, or integration of the individual elements*" (emphasis added). Thus, the *Metallurgical* decision seems consistent with the Restatement's view. The combination of the processes was sufficient to qualify as a trade secret.

The defendants also alleged that Metallurgical revealed its modifications to two parties, Consarc and La Floridienne (a licensee), prior to the alleged misappropriation. The defendants argued that Metallurgical had disclosed the secret by revealing the modifications and that protection should no longer be available. The court noted, however, that absolute secrecy is not required. When analyzing the degree of disclosure that is permitted, the court looked to the economic interests of the secret's holder. To profit from the secret, Metallurgical had to reveal its modifications to those charged with building the furnace (Consarc). La Floridienne stood in a different posture, as it was licensing the information in exchange for royalty payments, but again, revealing the modifications would be part and parcel of Metallurgical's ability to make money from the innovations.

The Restatement (Third) of Unfair Competition is consistent with this aspect of the *Metallurgical* decision. As comment f to § 39 states:

> Information known by persons in addition to the trade secret owner can retain its status as a trade secret if it remains secret from others to whom it has potential economic value. Independent discovery by another who maintains the secrecy of the information, for example, will not preclude relief against an appropriation by a third person. Similarly, confidential disclosures to employees, licensees, or others will not destroy the information's status as a trade secret. Even limited non-confidential disclosure

---

18 416 U.S. 470 (1974).

19 *Id.* at 475 (internal citations and quotations omitted).

will not necessarily terminate protection if the recipients of the disclosure maintain the secrecy of the information.

Although Metallurgical failed to get a confidentiality agreement from the parties, the court noted that this was not dispositive (That said, the court mentioned that Metallurgical's case would have been stronger had it shown that a confidential relationship existed). The court found that the disclosures to Consarc and La Floridienne were meant to be limited, which is consistent with the Restatement comment above.

Metallurgical only revealed its modifications to two parties, but other disputes might involve disclosure to a larger group.[20] This raises issues regarding the scope of the disclosure and the purpose for which the disclosure is made. So long as those to whom the information is revealed are bound to confidentiality, the number of "disclosees" should not matter. However, revealing the information to a wide swath of parties without obtaining confidentiality agreements could lead a court to question more seriously whether the disclosing party really expected the information to remain confidential. Indeed, as will be discussed later, without such explicit agreements, the trade secret holders run the risk of a court finding that they did not take reasonable steps to maintain secrecy, or that there was no misappropriation.

The plaintiff in a trade secret case bears the burden of establishing the existence of a trade secret.[21] As a policy matter, this rule makes sense as trade secret litigation should not be used as a tool to discourage legitimate competition in an area. After all, some lawsuits may simply be veiled fishing expeditions to see the information that a competitor possesses. Recall that § 1 of the Third Restatement of Unfair Competition rejected placing the burden on the defendant. Comment a to § 1 states:

> [I]n the case of harm resulting from competition in the marketplace, the privilege rationale appears inconsistent

---

20 *See* INEOS Group Ltd. v. Chevron Phillips Chem. Co. LP, 312 S.W.3d 843, 852–54 (Tex. App.—Houston [1st Dist.] 2009) (upholding the grant of a preliminary injunction despite evidence of disclosure to numerous licensees, some of whom were no longer bound by the terms of a written confidentiality agreement, and concluding that the plaintiff had established that the information was entitled to trade secret protection pending a trial on the merits); Data General Corp. v. Digital Computer Controls, Inc., 297 A.2d 433, 436 (Del. Ch. 1971) (finding that giving design drawings of a computer to requesting customers, subject to an agreement not to disclose, did not defeat a trade secret claim).

21 *See* RESTATEMENT (THIRD) OF UNFAIR COMPETITION § 39 cmt. d (1995) ("A person claiming rights in a trade secret bears the burden of defining the information for which protection is sought with sufficient definiteness to permit a court to apply the criteria for protection described in this Section and to determine the fact of an appropriation.").

> with the basic premise of our free enterprise system. Rather than adopting the view that such harm is prima facie tortious subject to a competitive privilege, this Restatement rejects the privilege rationale in favor of a general principle of non-liability. A person alleging injury through competition must therefore establish facts sufficient to subject the actor to liability under one or more of the rules enumerated in this Section.

Along with discouraging fishing expeditions, imposing the burden of proof on the plaintiff assists courts in determining what discovery is relevant, aids in assessing the outer permissible bounds of discovery, and prevents needless exposure of the defendant's trade secrets.[22] The plaintiff's burden also provides the defendant with the information needed to mount a defense[23] and ensures that the plaintiff will not "mold its cause of action around the discovery it receives."[24]

Given that the plaintiff must describe the secret with some particularity, practical reasons exist that may make a plaintiff reluctant to bring a claim for trade secret misappropriation. To bring the claim inevitably means that some level of disclosure of the secret will be required. Judge Easterbrook addressed this concern in *IDX Systems Corp. v. Epic Systems Corp.*:[25]

> Thus to show that particular information is a trade secret, a firm such as IDX must demonstrate that it is valuable, not known to others who might profit by its use, and has been handled by means reasonably designed to maintain secrecy. Like the district judge, we think that IDX failed to do this. It has been both too vague and too inclusive, effectively asserting that all information in or about its software is a trade secret. That's not plausible—and, more to the point, such a broad assertion does not match up to the statutory definition. Reluctance to be specific is understandable; the more precise the claim, the more a party does to tip off a business rival to where the real secrets lie and where the rival's own development efforts should be focused. Still, tools such as protective orders are available to make this process less risky, and unless the

---

22 *See* DeRubeis v. Witten Technologies, Inc., 244 F.R.D. 676, 680 (N.D. Ga. 2007).

23 *See id.* ("[I]t is difficult, if not impossible, for the defendant to mount a defense until it has some indication of the trade secrets allegedly misappropriated.").

24 *Id.*

25 285 F.3d 581 (7th Cir. 2002).

> plaintiff engages in a serious effort to pin down the secrets a court cannot do its job.[26]

A potential trade secret plaintiff has to balance these concerns before moving forward with a lawsuit. As in *Metallurgical*, it may be that the plaintiff has little to worry about because the secret is already out. In other cases, however, such as where a former employee helps a competitor to develop a similar product, the disclosure needed to bring the claim may provide the competitor with more information about the trade secret than the plaintiff wishes.

With regard to the secrecy element, not all states follow the UTSA verbatim. The UTSA provides that a trade secret is "information, including a formula, pattern, compilation, program device, method, technique, or process that: (i) derives independent economic value, actual or potential, from not being generally known to, **and not being readily ascertained by proper means by**, other persons who can obtain economic value from its disclosure or use . . . ." (emphasis added). As mentioned, not all states include the bolded language. For instance, the Illinois version of the UTSA omits this language, but some Illinois courts have nonetheless struck down claims of trade secret when the information was publicly available. In *Office Mates 5, North Shore, Inc. v. Hazen*,[27] for example, a personnel placement agency maintained that it had a protectable interest in its client information, which included, among other things, the client's name, address, key contact person, the client's benefit package, the type of word-processing equipment the client used, its products and services, the number of its employees, the fee the client was willing to pay for placement, and the history of placements. The court held that this information was not protectable because the information was "readily available to anyone in the business capable of canvassing or finding a directory, whether it be the Yellow Pages or a specialized directory, placing a cold call to that business, and asking specific questions designed to elicit the information above."[28]

Similarly, in *System Development Serv., Inc. v. Haarmann*,[29] a provider of computer network services sued former employees for misappropriating its customer lists and information about its customers' computer systems. Although the plaintiff won at trial, the Illinois court of appeals reversed:

---

[26] *Id.* at 583.

[27] 599 N.E.2d 1072 (Ill. App. Ct. 1992).

[28] *Id.* at 1084.

[29] 389 Ill.App.3d 561 (2009).

> In the present case, the evidence at the trial was insufficient to establish that the identity and contact information of potential customers of computer network services was sufficiently secret to qualify for trade secret status. In today's modern world, computers and computer networks are common business tools, and all businesses are potential customers of computer network services. Locating potential customers is merely a matter of identifying businesses in a particular town, county, or area and looking up their contact information. This information is easily obtained from telephone directories, chamber of commerce directories, the Internet, and a variety of other sources.[30]

California has similarly omitted the "not being readily ascertained" language but appears to take the omission more seriously than Illinois. In *Abba Rubber Co. v. Seaquist*,[31] a case often cited by California courts, the court held that a defense based on the fact that a consumer list was available via other sources failed due to California's definition of "trade secret":

> The defendants argue that the identity of the consumers of rubber rollers nevertheless fails to meet the definition of a trade secret because those identities are "readily ascertainable," and thus not secret. Specifically, they claim that the identity of those consumers is revealed in trade directories, telephone books, and other sources which list the names of "several types of businesses which commonly use rubber rollers . . ."
>
> This contention must fail, because whether a fact is "readily ascertainable" is not part of the definition of a trade secret in California. Section 1, subdivision (4)(i), of the Uniform Trade Secrets Act, as proposed by the National Conference of Commissioners on Uniform State Laws, refers to information which "derives independent economic value, actual or potential, from not being generally known to, and not being readily ascertainable by proper means by, other persons who can obtain economic value from its disclosure or use . . ." However, when the Legislature adopted that provision as Civil Code section 3426.1, subdivision (d)(1), it deleted the highlighted phrase. That deletion apparently resulted from arguments that conditioning the scope of a trade secret on the extent to which the information was not readily ascertainable would " 'mudd[y] the meaning of the term trade secret' " and

30 *Id.* at 574–75.

31 286 Cal. Rptr. 518 (Ct. App. 1991).

> " 'invite[ ] the various parties to speculate on the time needed to discover a secret.' " (Comment, supra, 20 LOYOLA L.A. L. REV. at p. 1214, fn. 231, quoting from Senate Com. on Judiciary, Selected Bill Analyses (1984) Assem. Bill No. 501, pp. 5–6.)
>
> In short, our Legislature chose to exclude from the definition only that information which the industry already knows, as opposed to that which the industry could easily discover. Therefore, under California law, information can be a trade secret even though it is readily ascertainable, so long as it has not yet been ascertained by others in the industry.[32]

The DTSA uses language very similar to the UTSA and retains the "not being readily ascertained" language. As mentioned, the presence of the DTSA presents the opportunity for a bit of forum shopping. A trade secret plaintiff in California may very well prefer to sue in state court if it believes that the definition is more favorable.

### *b. The Value of the Secret*

As noted above, trade secret standards require the secret to be valuable. The fourth and fifth factors of the First Restatement of Torts address the value of the secret. Comment e to § 39 of the Restatement (Third) of Unfair Competition similarly observes: "A trade secret must be of sufficient value in the operation of a business or other enterprise to provide an actual or potential economic advantage over others who do not possess the information. The advantage, however, need not be great. It is sufficient if the secret provides an advantage that is more than trivial." The UTSA also states that a trade secret "derives independent economic value, actual or potential, from not being generally known to, and not being readily ascertained by proper means by, other persons who can obtain economic value from its disclosure or use." The DTSA uses nearly identical language.

While each of these sources speaks to the value of the secret, none require the value to be significant. (Indeed, the comment to the Third Restatement requires only that the value be more than "trivial.") Furthermore, the UTSA speaks of value as it relates to "not being generally known" or "readily ascertained." This suggests that it is not enough for a secret to be valuable—its value must also derive from its secrecy.

The *Metallurgical* court discussed the role that the value of the secret played. The court described value as a necessary criterion, one

---

32 *Id.* at 528–29.

which was easily met in the case as demonstrated by testimony that described the competitive advantages the process gave Metallurgical. The court also discussed the related concept of cost of development, which the court found influential. This factor, however, is not dispositive. The court described the underpinnings of this factor:

> It seems only fair that one should be able to keep and enjoy the fruits of his labor. If a businessman has worked hard, has used his imagination, and has taken bold steps to gain an advantage over his competitors, he should be able to profit from his efforts. Because a commercial advantage can vanish once the competition learns of it, the law should protect the businessman's efforts to keep his achievements secret. As is discussed below, this is an area of law in which simple fairness still plays a large role.[33]

There is, therefore, a common theme from the general misappropriation materials in the previous chapter—a competitor should not be able to reap what he has not sown.

The value inquiry overlaps with the other two elements of secrecy and reasonable steps to maintain secrecy. For instance, in *Metallurgical*, the court commented on the disclosures to third parties as being necessary to take economic advantage of the secret, which surely involves the value of the secret. In other cases, courts have looked to the steps taken to maintain confidentiality as some evidence of the value of the secret. Thus, the three inquiries—secrecy, value, and efforts to maintain confidentiality—frequently overlap.

A very basic inquiry in a trade secret case is how do we know if something is valuable? Influential factors may include the amount of money and time that went into discovering or developing the secret, as well as the amount of money the holder of the secret can make from using it. But what if there was little effort or time expended to develop a trade secret? Under the UTSA and the Restatement (Third) of Unfair Competition, a trade secret may still be valuable in such circumstances. Comment e to § 39 of the Third Restatement notes that considerations such as money expended to discover the secret are relevant. It further notes that "the willingness of others to pay for access to the information" is also relevant to the value inquiry. Finally, the comment observes that although the secret must be of sufficient value to provide an actual or potential economic advantage over others, "[t]he advantage . . . need not be great."

It is not necessary that the trade secret claimant use the trade secret itself. Both the Uniform Act and the Third Restatement reject

---

[33] Metallurgical Industries, Inc. v. Fourtek, Inc., 790 F.2d 1195, 1201 (5th Cir. 1986).

such a requirement.[34] However, in a jurisdiction that is following the Restatement (First) of Torts, there may be a different result. Comment b to § 757 of the First Restatement states that "[a] trade secret is a process or device for continuous use in the operation of the business." Despite this distinction, even in jurisdictions that purport to follow the First Restatement, there is some confusion over whether failure to use the secret is a bar to recovery.[35] Furthermore, as pointed out in comment d to § 39 of the Restatement (Third) of Unfair Competition, case law and § 759 of the First Restatement often permitted an alternative avenue for recovery. Section 759, entitled "Procuring Information by Improper Means," states that "[o]ne who, for the purpose of advancing a rival business interest, procures by improper means information about another's business is liable to the other for the harm caused by his possession, disclosure or use of the information." Comment b to that section makes clear that the information need not qualify as a trade secret under the rule. Thus, it would seem that recovery is still possible so long as the acquisition of the information was improper.

### c. *Reasonable Steps to Maintain Secrecy*

Trade secret standards also consider the plaintiff's efforts to maintain the secrecy of the information. Think of effort as a continuum and use a fast-food chain's chicken-frying recipe as an example. On one end, the plaintiff makes absolutely no effort to protect the recipe. It is emailed and shared frequently with employees and customers with no language, contractual or otherwise, that attempts to limit its dissemination. On the other end, the plaintiff takes significant steps to protect the recipe. It is kept in a lockbox at a remote location, and only high-level employees, bound by strict non-disclosure provisions in their employment contracts, can access it. Moreover, any accessing employee must first provide a retinal scan and thumbprint to enter the facility.

Obviously, neither of these extreme positions is likely for something that the company values but still uses regularly. The first position leaves the secret open to so many people that it probably is

---

[34] *See* RESTATEMENT (THIRD) OF UNFAIR COMPETITION § 39 cmt. e. (1995) ("Such a 'use' requirement, however, imposes unjustified limitations on the scope of trade secret protection."); UTSA § 1 cmt. ("The definition of 'trade secret' contains a reasonable departure from the Restatement of Torts (First) definition which required that a trade secret be 'continuously used in one's business.' ").

[35] *Compare* Astro Tech., Inc. v. Alliant Techsystems, Inc., No. H-03-0745, 2005 WL 6061803 (S.D. Tex. 2005) (finding that "undeveloped ideas or plans do not rise to the level of a trade secret") *with* Elcor Chem. Corp. v. Agri-Sul, Inc., 494 S.W.2d 204, 213 (Tex. Civ. App.—Dallas 1973, writ ref'd n.r.e.) (citing Harris Manufacturing Co. v. Williams, 157 F. Supp. 779 (W.D.Ark.1957), in support of the assertion that information not being presently utilized by the owner may still constitute a trade secret).

no longer a secret. The second position is so strict that the company might not be able to efficiently utilize the recipe. Thus, a reasonable effort to maintain secrecy likely falls in between these two extremes, and courts must consider the issue based upon the facts of each case. Consider the following excerpt which describes the steps Coca-Cola takes to protect its secret formula for Coke, known as "Merchandise 7X":

> The written version of the secret formula is kept in a security vault at the Trust Company Bank in Atlanta, and that vault can only be opened by a resolution from the Company's Board of Directors. It is the Company's policy that only two persons in the Company shall know the formula at any one time, and that only those persons may oversee the actual preparation of Merchandise 7X. The Company refuses to allow the identity of those persons to be disclosed or to allow those persons to fly on the same airplane at the same time. The same precautions are taken regarding the secret formulae of the Company's other cola drinks—diet Coke, caffeine free diet Coke, TAB, caffeine free TAB, and caffeine free Coca-Cola. The secret formula for each drink is only known to three or four persons in the Company.[36]

An oft-cited decision in this area is *Rockwell Graphic Systems, Inc. v. DEV Industries, Inc.*[37] Rockwell was a printing press manufacturer who brought a trade secret misappropriation claim against DEV, a competing printing press manufacturer who had hired former employees of Rockwell. Rockwell alleged that DEV stole secret piece-part drawings which were used to create individual parts for the printing press. Rockwell subcontracted the production of replacement parts for its printing presses to various machine shops, called vendors, and supplied the vendors with the necessary piece-part drawings. DEV argued that the drawings did not qualify as trade secrets, in part because Rockwell did not take steps to maintain their confidentiality.

The district court granted DEV's motion for summary judgment, but the Seventh Circuit reversed. The court explained that Rockwell kept all of its engineering drawings in a vault. Moreover, access to the vault and the building containing the vault was limited to authorized employees who displayed identification (mainly engineers, of whom Rockwell employed two hundred). Rockwell also required employees to sign agreements promising not to disseminate

---

36 Coca-Cola Bottling Co. of Shreveport, Inc. v. The Coca-Cola Co., 107 F.R.D. 288, 294 (D. Del. 1985).

37 925 F.2d 174 (7th Cir. 1991).

the drawings or disclose their contents, except as authorized by the company. Although some outsiders were permitted to have copies of the drawings (such as vendors), they too were required to sign confidentiality agreements. Finally, each drawing was stamped with a legend stating that it contained proprietary material. According to the court, the issue of reasonable efforts was more appropriate for a factfinder:

> [O]nly in an extreme case can what is a "reasonable" precaution be determined on a motion for summary judgment, because the answer depends on a balancing of costs and benefits that will vary from case to case and so require estimation and measurement by persons knowledgeable in the particular field of endeavor involved. On the one hand, the more the owner of the trade secret spends on preventing the secret from leaking out, the more he demonstrates that the secret has real value deserving of legal protection, that he really was hurt as a result of the misappropriation of it, and that there really was misappropriation. On the other hand, the more he spends, the higher his costs. The costs can be indirect as well as direct. The more Rockwell restricts access to its drawings, either by its engineers or by the vendors, the harder it will be for either group to do the work expected of it. . . .
>
> There are contested factual issues here, bearing in mind that what is reasonable is itself a fact for purposes of Rule 56 of the civil rules. Obviously Rockwell took some precautions, both physical . . . and contractual, to maintain the confidentiality of its piece part drawings. Obviously it could have taken more precautions. But at a cost, and the question is whether the additional benefit in security would have exceeded that cost.[38]

The Restatement (Third) of Unfair Competition and the UTSA also emphasize the need to examine what is "reasonable under the circumstances to maintain secrecy."[39] Furthermore, the precautions taken may inform whether the secret is known by others and whether

---

[38] *Id.* at 179–80.

[39] UTSA § 1(4)(ii); *see* RESTATEMENT (THIRD) OF UNFAIR COMPETITION § 39 cmt. f (1995).

The DTSA does not refer to surrounding circumstances. Instead, it simply states that "the owner thereof has taken reasonable measures to keep such information secret." 18 U.S.C. § 1836(3)(A). The word "reasonable" by itself, however, would seem to suggest the need to examine surrounding circumstances.

the secret is valuable.[40] The more valuable a secret is, the more likely it is that additional steps are taken to maintain secrecy.

The efforts taken to maintain secrecy require a factual inquiry into the circumstances. In perhaps a rather extreme example of what is reasonable under the circumstances, the Federal Circuit Court of Appeals held that a prisoner's invention (a device used to cut Kevlar), which he built in his cell, was protected as a trade secret.[41] The prisoner, Earl Lariscey, was part of a federal prisoner work program working for UNICOR, a military manufacturer. Lariscey became aware of his employer's failed attempts to come up with an affordable method of cutting Kevlar. Lariscey revealed his device to his employers but also expressed his intent to patent the device and his desire to profit from his invention. UNICOR subsequently replicated and used his invention without compensating him, and Lariscey brought suit. UNICOR defended by arguing that Lariscey's invention was no longer a trade secret because he revealed the device to others and could have made greater efforts to protect the secret, such as by only reducing the device to writing rather than building it. The court of appeals rejected these arguments:

> The construction in the prison environment and the demonstration of a working model by Lariscey to his employer and potential customer, under the circumstances that here prevailed, was not a dedication or waiver of property rights. It was not a dedication of the information and an abandonment of ownership. Even without giving weight to the exigencies of the prison environment insofar as it affected Lariscey's negotiating posture, the precautions to protect this information from public disclosure were reasonable under the circumstances that prevailed. When property rights are at issue, the common law weighs heavily against forfeiture by implication.[42]

Protection measures can generally be divided into two categories, physical protection measures and notice measures. Physical protection measures include efforts to physically prevent others from viewing the secret, such as the efforts made by Coca-Cola described above. Under the notice category, trade secret holders can require those that are exposed to the secret to sign confidentiality agreements or non-disclosure agreements. Another form of notice would be to post signs and stamp warnings such as "confidential" on the subject of the trade secret. Viewed from a cost-benefit analysis,

---

[40] *See* RESTATEMENT (THIRD) OF UNFAIR COMPETITION § 39 cmt. f (1995).

[41] Lariscey v. United States, 949 F.2d 1137, 1142–45 (Fed. Cir. 1991), *on reh'g*, 981 F.2d 1244 (Fed. Cir. 1993) (affirming by an equally divided court).

[42] *Id.* at 1143.

the notice provisions are usually the easiest and most feasible measures to implement. As mentioned, the steps that are reasonable under the circumstances are often a function of the value of the secret. One would assume that the higher the value of the secret (such as Coke's secret formula), the more effort that will be put into protecting it.

That is not to say that all feasible protective measures must be taken for a trade secret plaintiff to prevail. *Learning Curve Toys, Inc. v. PlayWood Toys, Inc.*[43] provides a colorful example of just such a case. Robert Clausi and his brother-in-law, Scott Moore, began creating prototypes of wooden toys under the name PlayWood Toys, Inc. ("PlayWood"). PlayWood did not own a facility in which it could produce toys, but instead, worked with Mario Borsato, who owned a wood-working facility. Subject to a written confidentiality agreement, Borsato manufactured prototypes for PlayWood. PlayWood met with representatives from Learning Curve at Borsato's facility to discuss the possibility of obtaining a manufacturing contract with Learning Curve. During the meeting, both sides orally agreed that the information discussed would be confidential. Learning Curve showed some designs for its Thomas the Tank Engine toys that had not been released yet. PlayWood then suggested a way that Learning Curve could distinguish its train tracks from Learning Curve's main competitor, Brio. PlayWood suggested that Learning Curve should cut grooves in its tracks to make the tracks sound and feel more realistic. PlayWood created a prototype, on the spot, which Learning Curve's representatives took with them. The two sides suggested calling the product the "clickety clack track," based on the sound the train made on the tracks. Despite multiple attempts by PlayWood to get Learning Curve to agree to a licensing agreement, no contract was ever agreed to. Almost two years after revealing the clickety clack track to Learning Curve, PlayWood discovered that Learning Curve was producing the clickety clack track on its own (and had patented the concept).

PlayWood sued Learning Curve for misappropriation of a trade secret and received a jury verdict awarding it 8% of Learning Curve's royalties from the clickety clack track. The district judge ignored the verdict, however, and ruled as a matter of law in favor of Learning Curve. The court held that PlayWood did not have a protectable trade secret and cited, among other grounds, that PlayWood failed to guard the secrecy of its concept and that the concept had no economic value. PlayWood appealed.

---

43 342 F.3d 714 (7th Cir. 2003).

With regard to the efforts to maintain secrecy, Learning Curve raised the fact that no written confidentiality statements had been entered into and that PlayWood actually allowed the prototype to be removed from its facility. Looking to the overall circumstances, the court of appeals found that PlayWood took sufficient steps for a jury to find in its favor. The court noted that Borsato, who may have been nothing more than an independent contractor, manufactured the prototypes for PlayWood subject to a confidentiality agreement. Furthermore, after the meeting with Learning Curve's reps, Clausi amended PlayWood's confidentiality agreement with Borsato to ensure that materials discussed during the meeting would remain confidential. Thus, the efforts to maintain secrecy, with regard to Borsato, appeared to be adequate, even if more could have been done.

With regard to Learning Curve's representatives, the steps taken by Clausi and Moore were quite minimal, yet the court found the steps taken sufficient to uphold a jury verdict. Clausi and Moore were asked to keep the information they received confidential and apparently asked the Learning Curve representatives to do the same. Apparently, Clausi also stamped many of the documents received from Learning Curve at the meeting as confidential, which supported the notion that Clausi and Moore believed that the meeting was to be kept confidential.

Ultimately, the context of the transaction may have swayed the court. Reasonableness of steps must take into consideration the surrounding circumstances. For instance, it appeared that Learning Curve suggested the oral agreement of confidentiality. If it was satisfied with a mere oral agreement, it seems insincere for Learning Curve to then say that PlayWood should have required more. The context of the meeting was also to do business with Learning Curve, which necessarily meant disclosing PlayWood's ideas. If such disclosures were not confidential, then each party could use or disclose what was learned with impunity. Thus, it made sense that each party felt bound by the oral agreement. In addition, there was evidence that such oral agreements were common in the industry (or at least were common for Learning Curve). Finally, the court noted the relative sophistication of the parties and that a more informal way of doing business was likely given the nature and smaller size of the companies.

The court also considered the value of the trade secret. The most direct evidence presented was the sales figures, which skyrocketed after introduction of the clickety clack track. Furthermore, there was evidence that the track helped differentiate Learning Curve's product from its competitors, which was something the company had been trying to do for some time. The court further noted that under the modern conception of trade secret law, actual use of the secret is not required (a break from the approach of the First Restatement of Torts).

Recall that to be afforded protection, the trade secret must give an "economic advantage over others who do not possess the information." Thus, the value must derive from the secrecy. Put another way, a secret that is easily discovered does not have sufficient value. In the opinion, the court of appeals noted that the clickety clack track allowed Learning Curve to differentiate itself from its competitors (which had value). The value of the idea was further evidenced by the fact that Learning Curve sought and obtained a patent on the track (because once produced, the track would no longer be secret). The value, therefore, must have derived from its secrecy.

Although PlayWood prevailed on appeal, its failure to do more to protect its trade secret could have proved fatal to its claim. For instance, in *Niemi v. Am. Axle Mfg. & Holding, Inc.*,[44] plaintiffs had contracted with defendants to prepare designs and drawings for machines in accordance with the plaintiffs' specifications. The plaintiffs did not mark the documents as confidential or otherwise agree in writing that the designs were confidential; instead, the plaintiffs relied upon implied agreements of confidentiality. The court concluded that the plaintiffs' efforts were inadequate:

> Plaintiffs argue that the trial court erred in determining that they failed to demonstrate reasonable efforts to maintain the secrecy of their technological information. Plaintiffs maintain that the parties implicitly understood, based on a 30-year relationship, that the technological information was meant to remain confidential, and that confidentiality was in the interests of all of the parties. Plaintiffs aver that both Springfield and AAM required their employees to keep the information confidential, and that AAM emphasized the need for confidentiality in its internal memoranda. Plaintiffs contend that these efforts were reasonable under the circumstances, pursuant to MCL 445.1902(d)(ii).
>
> Viewing the evidence in a light most favorable to plaintiffs, the only "effort" plaintiffs made to maintain confidentiality was their reliance on an implied agreement that Springfield and AAM would not release the information because they understood the proprietary value of it. Plaintiffs acknowledge that they did not enter into written

---

[44] 2007 WL 29383 (Mich. Ct. App. 2007).

> confidentiality agreements, or label the documents confidential. They do not identify any express oral agreement regarding confidentiality. Plaintiffs emphasize that there were internal confidentiality agreements within defendants' companies, but these do not reflect any effort by plaintiffs to impose confidentiality. Under these circumstances, there is no genuine issue of material fact that plaintiffs failed to make reasonable efforts to safeguard the confidentiality of their designs. Consequently, the designs and technological information at issue were not "trade secrets" within the meaning of the MUTSA.[45]

The court did distinguish *Learning Curve*, however, on the ground that there was evidence of an express oral agreement in *Learning Curve* that was not present in the case before it. The court also noted that plaintiffs were not a fledgling or inexperienced company. The main point is that a plaintiff does not want protection of its purported trade secret coming down to a close call of whether the steps taken to protect the secret were reasonable.

Interestingly, the definition of trade secret provided in § 39 of the Third Restatement of Unfair Competition does not explicitly require reasonable efforts to maintain secrecy, in contrast to the definitions found in comment b to § 757 of the First Restatement of Torts, § 1(4) of the UTSA, and 18 U.S.C. § 1839(3) of the DTSA. Section 39 explains that "[p]recautions taken to maintain the secrecy of information are relevant in determining whether the information qualifies for protection as a trade secret," but it also states the following:

> Whether viewed as an independent requirement or as an element to be considered with other factors relevant to the existence of a trade secret, the owner's precautions should be evaluated in light of the other available evidence relating to the value and secrecy of the information. Thus, if the value and secrecy of the information are clear, evidence of specific precautions taken by the trade secret owner may be unnecessary.[46]

As this passage suggests, the Restatement (Third) of Unfair Competition treats the inquiry as informing other issues, such as value and secrecy. The more efforts that are expended in keeping

---

[45] *Id.* at *2.

[46] RESTATEMENT (THIRD) OF UNFAIR COMPETITION § 39 cmt. g (1995); *see also id.* (noting that "[t]he precautions taken by the trade secret owner are also relevant to other potential issues in an action for the appropriation of a trade secret").

something secret, the more valuable the secret presumably is (which has already been addressed).

Comment f to § 39 of the Third Restatement also notes that the efforts taken to protect the secret may, among other things, inform the secrecy inquiry as well:

> Circumstantial evidence is admissible to establish that information is not readily ascertainable through proper means and hence is eligible for protection as a trade secret. **Precautions taken by the claimant to preserve the secrecy of the information** (see Comment g), the willingness of licensees to pay for disclosure of the secret, unsuccessful attempts by the defendant or others to duplicate the information by proper means, and resort by a defendant to improper means of acquisition are all probative of the relative accessibility of the information (emphasis added).

In the earlier-discussed decision of *Rockwell Graphic Systems, Inc. v. DEV Industries, Inc.*,[47] Judge Posner gave some other possible purposes for the requirement that reasonable efforts be taken. Judge Posner noted that such protective efforts could have both evidentiary and remedial significance. The evidentiary significance is that efforts to maintain secrecy would help to distinguish improper misappropriation from proper conduct. Thus, the efforts to maintain confidentiality would help to inform the misappropriation analysis, which is separate from the analysis of whether a trade secret exists. As the court observed: "The greater the precautions that Rockwell took to maintain the secrecy of the piece part drawings, the lower the probability that DEV obtained them properly and the higher the probability that it obtained them through a wrongful act; the owner had taken pains to prevent them from being obtained otherwise."[48] Comment g to § 39 of the Restatement (Third) of Unfair Competition also indicates that the protective efforts taken inform the misappropriation analysis:

> The precautions taken by the trade secret owner are also relevant to other potential issues in an action for the appropriation of a trade secret. They can signal to employees and other recipients that a disclosure of the information by the trade secret owner is intended to be in confidence. See § 41. They can also be relevant in determining whether a defendant possessed the knowledge necessary for the imposition of liability under the rules

[47] 925 F.2d 174 (7th Cir. 1991).

[48] *Id.* at 179.

> stated in § 40 (see § 40, Comment d), whether particular means of acquisition are improper under the rule stated in § 43 (see § 43, Comment c), and whether an accidental disclosure results in the loss of trade secret rights (see § 40, Comment e).

As mentioned, in *Rockwell*, Judge Posner also explained the remedial significance of the reasonable efforts requirement, which goes to the value of the trade secret:

> Under the second theory of trade secret protection [the remedial significance], the owner's precautions still have evidentiary significance, but now primarily as evidence that the secret has real value. For the precise means by which the defendant acquired it is less important under the second theory, though not completely unimportant; remember that even the second theory allows the unmasking of a trade secret by some means, such as reverse engineering. If Rockwell expended only paltry resources on preventing its piece part drawings from falling into the hands of competitors such as DEV, why should the law, whose machinery is far from costless, bother to provide Rockwell with a remedy? The information contained in the drawings cannot have been worth much if Rockwell did not think it worthwhile to make serious efforts to keep the information secret.
>
> The remedial significance of such efforts lies in the fact that if the plaintiff has allowed his trade secret to fall into the public domain, he would enjoy a windfall if permitted to recover damages merely because the defendant took the secret from him, rather than from the public domain as it could have done with impunity.[49]

As these passages illustrate, efforts to maintain secrecy primarily helps to inform other inquiries. In analyzing whether a trade secret exists, the efforts taken factor assists in determining value and in judging whether the trade secret is known by others. The efforts may also help to put others on notice that the property being acquired is meant to be secret, thus informing the misappropriation inquiry. Perhaps the closest one can get to an independent basis for having such a requirement is that the law should not help those who take no steps to help themselves. Judge Posner mentioned this, although he did so in terms of value, as he opined that a trade secret that the holder takes no effort to protect must not be very valuable.

---

49 *Id.*

Returning to the discussion of *Learning Curve*, it is interesting to note that by the time PlayWood discovered the misappropriation, a patent had been issued. The acquisition of a patent for the clickety clack track would defeat the secrecy requirement, as the patent application must describe the invention in some detail, and issued patents are available to the public. Does this notion of public disclosure suggest a defense for a trade secret misappropriator—i.e., publicly disclose the misappropriated secret and then defend on the ground that the secret is now known by others? Not surprisingly, courts are not very sympathetic to this argument. In *Syntex Ophthalmics, Inc. v. Tsuetaki*,[50] a Syntex employee, Novicky, went to work for a competitor, Fused Kontacts of Chicago, Inc. Four days after leaving Syntex, Novicky prepared a patent disclosure statement that revealed Syntex trade secrets. Syntex sued Novicky and his new employer for trade secret misappropriation. On appeal, the defendants argued that the disclosure statement defeated the secrecy element of the claim. The court rejected the argument:

> Appellants' second argument is that Novicky's wrongful patent application of Syntex's trade secrets deprives Syntex of its trade secret protection and permits appellants to use those secrets. In support of their argument, they cite *Sears, Roebuck & Co. v. Stiffel Co.*, 376 U.S. 225 (1964), and *Compco Corp. v. Day-Brite Lighting, Inc.*, 376 U.S. 234 (1964), which stand for the proposition that an owner of a trade secret who voluntarily discloses his trade secret makes an election to seek federal patent protection. That situation, though, is not present in the instant case. Here the holder of the trade secret did not make an election to obtain a patent, but instead it was appellants who had misappropriated the trade secrets and secured the patent. In 1936 we held in *Shellmar Products Co. v. Allen-Qualley Co.*, 87 F.2d 104 (7th Cir. 1936), that a wrongdoer who has made an unlawful disclosure of another's trade secrets cannot assert that publication to escape the protection of trade secret law. We believe that principle to be equally vital today. To hold otherwise in the instant case would be to permit appellants to profit from their own wrong.[51]

---

50 701 F.2d 677 (7th Cir. 1983).

51 *Id.* at 683; *see also* Rhone-Poulenc Agro, S.A. v. DeKalb Genetics Corp., 272 F.3d 1335, 1359–60 (Fed. Cir. 2001) ("Therefore, assuming arguendo that DeKalb's PCT application did disclose the RD-125 trade secret, we hold that DeKalb in this case cannot use its own wrongful disclosure of RPA's trade secrets in order to overcome a claim of trade secret misappropriation.").

## 2. Misappropriation

As mentioned, a trade secret claim has two basic elements: (1) the subject of the suit must qualify as a trade secret, and (2) the trade secret must be misappropriated. A plaintiff can establish misappropriation by showing that the secret was acquired by improper means, or by showing that the secret was disclosed or used in an unauthorized manner.[52] The First Restatement of Torts did not make the acquisition of a trade secret through improper means actionable without an accompanying use or disclosure; however, courts still granted relief if use or disclosure was likely.

### *a. Acquisition by Improper Means*

Section 40 of the Third Restatement of Unfair Competition makes actionable the acquisition of a trade secret by "means that are improper." What exactly are improper means? Section 43 provides some guidance:

> "Improper" means of acquiring another's trade secret under the rule stated in § 40 include theft, fraud, unauthorized interception of communications, inducement of or knowing participation in a breach of confidence, and other means either wrongful in themselves or wrongful under the circumstances of the case. Independent discovery and analysis of publicly available products or information are not improper means of acquisition.

The UTSA, DTSA, and comments to § 757 of the First Restatement of Torts also list similar activities as improper (adding espionage, wiretapping, and eavesdropping). Criminal or independently tortious conduct will likely fall into the improper definition as well. The acquisition of a trade secret can be improper, however, even if the means of acquisition are not independently wrongful. *E.I. duPont deNemours & Co. v. Christopher*[53] provides a colorful example of this point.

The defendants, the Christophers, flew an airplane over the top of a Dupont factory under construction to take photographs. They took 16 photographs of a new method for producing methanol and sold the pictures to an unknown third party. Dupont insisted that a skilled person would be able to deduce their method, which was a trade secret, from the pictures. Dupont argued, and the court agreed, that it had taken reasonable precautions to protect its trade secret. However, the Christophers defended by arguing that that they were

---

[52] *See* RESTATEMENT (THIRD) OF UNFAIR COMPETITION § 40 (1995); UTSA § 1(2); DTSA, 18 U.S.C. § 1839(5).

[53] 431 F.2d 1012 (5th Cir. 1970).

in public airspace and broke no laws in obtaining the photographs; therefore, the acquisition was not improper. The court was faced with the issue of whether legal aerial photography of plant construction is an improper means of obtaining another's trade secret.

At the time, the relevant jurisdiction (Texas) followed the First Restatement of Torts, which provided the following in § 757:

> One who discloses or uses another's trade secret, without a privilege to do so, is liable to the other if (a) he discovered the secret by improper means, or (b) his disclosure or use constitutes a breach of confidence reposed in him by the other in disclosing the secret to him.

The court focused on subsection (a) and defined improper means as any means which is not in accordance with accepted standards of commercial morality. The court held that unless the owner of the trade secret voluntarily disclosed the idea or failed to maintain the secrecy of the idea through reasonable precautions, the means are improper. Here, Dupont took reasonable means to safeguard its facility, and the trade secret could only have been seen by flying directly over the unfinished building. Although the facility would not have been vulnerable to aerial photography if the roof were finished, the court held that it was unreasonable to expect Dupont to safeguard against what others should not be doing.

The court further pointed to comment f to § 757 of the First Restatement of Torts, which points out that eavesdropping, wiretapping, and other forms of espionage are all improper means of acquiring a trade secret. The court emphasized that a company is still expected to exercise reasonable means to protect its trade secrets; however, it is not reasonable to expect a company to guard against extreme means that are unanticipated.

In its decision, the court emphasized that DuPont had taken reasonable steps and that the Christophers' shenanigans were intentional efforts to circumvent DuPont's efforts. The court noted that the Christophers deliberately flew over the DuPont plant to get pictures of a process which DuPont had attempted to keep secret and handed the photos over to a third party. It is interesting to consider whether the result would have differed if the Christophers just happened to be flying over the plant and took pictures because they thought the photos were interesting. If the Christophers were simply engaged in a sort of accidental espionage, it is unlikely that liability would have been imposed. It should be noted that the same conclusion could be reached under the Restatement (Third) of Unfair Competition, as § 40 requires knowledge or a reason to know that what is being appropriated is a trade secret.

The justifications for a rule that prohibits misappropriation by improper means are both economic and practical. The *DuPont* court noted that "[o]ur tolerance of the espionage game must cease when the protections required to prevent another's spying cost so much that the spirit of inventiveness is dampened." This hints at the costs that are associated with maintaining the secret. As one commentator has noted, the effect of the rule is to prevent a corporate espionage arms race, which is ultimately inefficient:

> On this general theme of how legal rules can be used to lure parties away from more costly forms of self-help, one special category merits particular attention: the arms race. . . The [*DuPont*] court noted that DuPont could have protected itself by covering the construction zone with a tarp, but nevertheless sustained the trade secret claim. Explained the court, "To require DuPont to put a roof over the unfinished plant to guard its secret would impose an enormous expense to prevent nothing more than a school boy's trick." Thus trade secret law was used to avoid an arms race, with DuPont investing in guards and a fence, competitors procuring airplanes and cameras, DuPont responding with a tarp and perhaps radar detection, competitors returning with (say) satellite images and heat-sensitive camera technology, and so on and so on.[54]

Put another way, trade secret owners develop their processes at some expense. If misappropriators can easily obtain the value of owners' work by engaging in relatively low-cost conduct, they will do so. The trade secret owner is then faced with a choice: spend more money to prevent discovery or simply allow the misappropriation. At some point, spending additional sums will not be worthwhile; indeed, innovators will be deterred from spending money on a new process unless the law affords some protection. The law's solution is to only require *reasonable* steps to maintain secrecy.

The U.S. Supreme Court has offered some insight into the justifications behind state laws that prohibit the misappropriation of trade secrets:

> Another problem that would arise if state trade secret protection were precluded is in the area of licensing others to exploit secret processes. The holder of a trade secret would not likely share his secret with a manufacturer who cannot be placed under binding legal obligation to pay a license fee or to protect the secret. The result would be to

---

[54] Douglas Lichtman, *How the Law Responds to Self-Help*, 1 J. L. ECON. & POL'Y 215, 232 (2005).

> hoard rather than disseminate knowledge. Instead, then, of licensing others to use his invention and making the most efficient use of existing manufacturing and marketing structures within the industry, the trade secret holder would tend either to limit his utilization of the invention, thereby depriving the public of the maximum benefit of its use, or engage in the time-consuming and economically wasteful enterprise of constructing duplicative manufacturing and marketing mechanisms for the exploitation of the invention. The detrimental misallocation of resources and economic waste that would thus take place if trade secret protection were abolished with respect to employees or licensees cannot be justified by reference to any policy that the federal patent law seeks to advance.
>
> Nothing in the patent law requires that States refrain from action to prevent industrial espionage. In addition to the increased costs for protection from burglary, wire-tapping, bribery, and the other means used to misappropriate trade secrets, there is the inevitable cost to the basic decency of society when one firm steals from another. A most fundamental human right, that of privacy, is threatened when industrial espionage is condoned or is made profitable; the state interest in denying profit to such illegal ventures is unchallengeable.[55]

This passage adds a moral justification for preventing misappropriation of trade secrets, as the Court notes that "basic decency" requires prohibition of such activities. The Court appears to be taking a property view of trade secrets, describing the misappropriation as stealing. If one analogized a trade secret to a car in a neighbor's garage, the taking of the car would undoubtedly be amoral. Interestingly, the Court followed up this observation with a comment about privacy, which does not necessarily implicate the conversion of property. The privacy concern is based more upon the morality of the act itself.

The *DuPont* court seemed to believe that DuPont made reasonable efforts to maintain secrecy under the circumstances. The opinion, however, predated the widespread use and availability of satellite photography. Nevertheless, the outcome may not be different today.[56] The *DuPont* court noted that " '[i]mproper' will always be a word of many nuances, determined by time, place, and circumstances." With that in mind, is flying overhead to take pictures

---

55 Kewanee Oil Co. v. Bicron Corp., 416 U.S. 470, 486–87 (1974).

56 *See* RESTATEMENT (THIRD) OF UNFAIR COMPETITION §§ 39 cmt. f, 43 cmt. c (1995).

still improper in a world where the same information may be easily obtained on the internet? If the layout is publicly available, trade secret law may not protect it. This is not because of a lack of misappropriation, however, but because of a lack of secrecy. The scenario would implicate the analysis of whether a trade secret even exists, as discussed in comment f to § 39 of the Third Restatement of Unfair Competition. However, rather confusingly, comment f brings back the "improper" inquiry, stating that "[i]nformation that is generally known or readily ascertainable through proper means (see § 43) by others to whom it has potential economic value is not protectable as a trade secret." It is doubtful that a court would find the use of Google Earth to be improper given its general availability and widespread use. But the mere fact that satellite images are available does not settle the issue. The satellite imagery on Google Earth can be 1–3 years old. If the current information is not otherwise available, the flyover could still be an improper means. Along these lines, it may be worth noting that the illustrations to § 39 still list the flyover example as an improper means (although the section was written in 1995, perhaps too soon to contemplate Google Earth and similar technology). It may also be worth noting the *DuPont* court's observation that "[p]erhaps ordinary fences and roofs must be built to shut out incursive eyes, but we need not require the discoverer of a trade secret to guard against the unanticipated, the undetectable, **or the unpreventable methods of espionage** now available" (emphasis added).

### *b. Unauthorized Disclosure or Use*

Along with improper means, § 40 of the Third Restatement of Unfair Competition provides that misappropriation can be established by showing that the secret was disclosed or used in an unauthorized manner:

> **§ 40 Appropriation of Trade Secrets**
>
> One is subject to liability for the appropriation of another's trade secret if:
>
> . . .
>
> (b) the actor uses or discloses the other's trade secret without the other's consent and, at the time of the use or disclosure,
>
> > (1) the actor knows or has reason to know that the information is a trade secret that the actor acquired under circumstances creating a duty of confidence owed by the actor to the other under the rule stated in § 41; or

(2) the actor knows or has reason to know that the information is a trade secret that the actor acquired by means that are improper under the rule stated in § 43; or

(3) the actor knows or has reason to know that the information is a trade secret that the actor acquired from or through a person who acquired it by means that are improper under the rule stated in § 43 or whose disclosure of the trade secret constituted a breach of a duty of confidence owed to the other under the rule stated in § 41; or

(4) the actor knows or has reason to know that the information is a trade secret that the actor acquired through an accident or mistake, unless the acquisition was the result of the other's failure to take reasonable precautions to maintain the secrecy of the information.

Similar language is present in § 757 of the First Restatement of Torts, § 1(2) of the UTSA, and 18 U.S.C. § 1839(5) of the DTSA.

Notice that § 40 requires the actor to use or disclose the information. Mere possession, unless the possession is the equivalent of use, is not enough. Comment c to § 40 provides further guidance:

> There are no technical limitations on the nature of the conduct that constitutes "use" of a trade secret for purposes of the rules stated in Subsection (b). As a general matter, any exploitation of the trade secret that is likely to result in injury to the trade secret owner or enrichment to the defendant is a "use" under this Section. Thus, marketing goods that embody the trade secret, employing the trade secret in manufacturing or production, relying on the trade secret to assist or accelerate research or development, or soliciting customers through the use of information that is a trade secret (see § 42, Comment f) all constitute "use."

Can the use of negative knowledge—i.e., knowing what not to do—be actionable under § 40? Comment c is sufficiently broad to include the use of negative knowledge if it is employed in the manufacturing process or used to accelerate research. The comments to § 39 of the Third Restatement and to § 1 of the UTSA provide further support.[57]

---

57 *See* RESTATEMENT (THIRD) OF UNFAIR COMPETITION § 39 cmt. e (1995) ("Some early cases elevated use by the trade secret owner to independent significance by establishing such use as an element of the cause of action for the appropriation of a trade secret. Such a 'use' requirement, however, imposes unjustified limitations on the scope of trade secret protection . . . The requirement . . . places in doubt protection for so-called 'negative' information that teaches conduct to be avoided, such as knowledge

Section 40 of the Restatement (Third) of Unfair Competition also requires the defendant to know or have reason to know that the information is a trade secret. How might an actor have possession of a trade secret and yet not have knowledge of that fact? To illustrate, assume that Company X, a manufacturer of cogs, hires Z as a consultant on its manufacturing process. During the course of the engagement, Z learns of X's secret process for manufacturing cogs in a manner that is twice as efficient as any other manufacturer. As part of Z's engagement, he signs a confidentiality agreement that he will not reveal or disclose this information to anyone. Z finishes his consulting job and goes to work for Company Y over a year later. Z reveals the secret process to Y but claims that he developed the process himself. So long as Y has no reason to know that the process is actually X's trade secret, Y will not be liable to X for implementing and using the process (although Z will surely be liable for his disclosure).[58]

The case of *Vantage Point, Inc. v. Parker Brothers, Inc.*[59] offers a good illustration of the role that knowledge can play. Vantage developed a board game based on oil exploration called "Wildcat." In July of 1972, Vantage sent the concept (photographs, rules, etc.) to Milton Bradley's ("MB") president for review. MB had a formal policy of not considering unsolicited submissions, and it returned the materials unexamined. Subsequently, Vantage sent letters to other companies urging them to review the game. Parker Brothers ("Parker") showed interest, and Vantage sent a working version of the game so that Parker could further evaluate it. Ultimately, Parker decided that the cost of manufacturing the game was too high and returned the game to Vantage.

One of the Parker employees who had access to Wildcat during its evaluation was Robert Baron. Baron soon left Parker and joined two other men in a venture to create and sell toy ideas to game

---

that a particular process or technique is unsuitable for commercial use. Cases in many jurisdictions expressly renounce any requirement of use by the trade secret owner . . . Use by the person asserting rights in the information is not a prerequisite to protection under the rule stated in this Section."); UTSA § 1 cmt. ("The definition includes information that has commercial value from a negative viewpoint, for example, the results of lengthy and expensive research which proves that a certain process will **not** work could be of great value to a competitor."); *see also* On-Line Technologies, Inc. v. Perkin-Elmer Corp., 253 F. Supp. 2d 313, 323 (D. Conn. 2003) (stating that "[n]egative knowledge is one form of 'using' trade secrets that is proscribed by [Connecticut's version of the UTSA] because one may 'use' a trade secret in ways other than direct manufacture and marketing").

[58] This does not necessarily mean that Y will be able to continue using the process in the future. Nevertheless, the relief available to X may be limited because of Y's good faith employment of Z, and because of subsequent expenses incurred by Y in implementing the process. *See* RESTATEMENT (THIRD) OF UNFAIR COMPETITION §§ 44 cmt. b, 45 cmt. b (1995). Remedies are discussed more fully in Section D.

[59] 529 F. Supp. 1204 (S.D.N.Y. 1981).

companies. The three men developed an oil exploration game called "Oil Baron," which they successfully marketed to MB. MB developed the game and renamed it "King Oil." In February of 1974, MB published the game at a toy fair and Vantage subsequently learned of the product, which was similar to Wildcat.

Vantage brought suit claiming that MB had misappropriated the Wildcat game concept by either (1) using the materials Vantage had sent MB in July of 1972, or (2) using the concept when it knew or should have known that the idea was being disclosed to it in breach of a confidential relationship (i.e., Baron breached a duty when he divulged the game idea). As for the first claim, the court found that there was insufficient evidence demonstrating that MB had reviewed the materials in question. As for the second ground, the court held that MB's lack of knowledge of the trade secret precluded liability:

> Even if Baron misappropriated plaintiff's submission, no liability attaches because Milton Bradley did not have notice of any misconduct by Baron. . . . Furthermore, by the time defendant arguably was put on notice [of the possible misappropriation], it had changed its position by investing time and money in making Oil Baron into the marketable game King Oil. Under the theory plaintiff has used to support its second claim for relief, this change in position precludes liability.[60]

As mentioned, MB had a formal policy of returning unsolicited game concepts without reviewing them. The purpose of this policy was in part to help avoid claims such as the one at issue:

> Milton Bradley's ostensible reasons for limiting its review of unsolicited submissions to those of professional designers were, first, that such persons possessed the combined creative and business sense to know whether an idea could be successfully developed. The policy also would protect the company from litigation resulting from examination of the unsolicited submissions of countless "non-professionals," and minimize conflicts with its own development department.[61]

It should be noted that although the policy did not prevent MB from being sued, it certainly helped MB to get the case dismissed. In the decision itself, the policy and the affidavits in support of MB's contention that no one ever reviewed the concept were discussed at

---

60 *Id.* at 1214.

61 *Id.* at 1211.

length, and ultimately the court concluded that there was insufficient evidence to raise an issue of fact.

Sometimes a misappropriator of a trade secret attempts to defend by arguing that the product it has developed is different from the product protected by the trade secret.[62] The number of modifications and how much the concept changed will play a role. In one case, the defendant changed a non-essential ingredient in a mold release agent (used by rubber and plastic manufacturers). However, the defendant still used the same essential secret ingredient, and thus the court found that it was using the trade secret despite the alterations to the overall formula.[63] In short, liability does not require the misappropriator to use the secret in the exact same way as the owner. As comment c to § 40 notes, "any exploitation of the trade secret that is likely to result in injury to the trade secret owner or enrichment to the defendant is a 'use' under this Section."

*i. Breach of Duty of Confidence*

Section 40(b)(1) and (3) of the Third Restatement of Unfair Competition speaks of use or disclosure that breaches a duty of confidence. Similarly, § (1)(1) and (1)(2)(ii)(B)(II)–(III) of the UTSA and § 1839(5)(B)(ii)(I)–(III) and 6(A) of the DTSA speak of a duty to maintain secrecy. Who owes such a duty? Certainly current employees, as will soon be explored, but what about third parties who are privy to trade secrets as part of a negotiation or licensing agreement? Recall that in the *Learning Curve* decision, the parties had entered into an oral agreement to keep the information confidential. Such an express agreement is one of the two ways to establish a duty of confidence under the Third Restatement:

**§ 41 Duty of Confidence**

A person to whom a trade secret has been disclosed owes a duty of confidence to the owner of the trade secret for purposes of the rule stated in § 40 if:

(a) the person made an express promise of confidentiality prior to the disclosure of the trade secret; or

(b) the trade secret was disclosed to the person under circumstances in which the relationship between the parties to

---

62 *See* Mangren Rsch. & Dev. Corp. v. Nat'l Chem. Co., 87 F.3d 937, 944 (7th Cir. 1996) ("We have observed before, in fact, that if trade secret law were not flexible enough to encompass modified or even new products that are substantially derived from the trade secret of another, the protections that law provides would be hollow indeed."); RESTATEMENT (THIRD) OF UNFAIR COMPETITION § 40 cmt. c (1995).

63 *See Mangren Rsch.*, 87 F.3d at 944.

the disclosure or the other facts surrounding the disclosure justify the conclusions that, at the time of the disclosure,

(1) the person knew or had reason to know that the disclosure was intended to be in confidence, and

(2) the other party to the disclosure was reasonable in inferring that the person consented to an obligation of confidentiality.

Express agreements are covered under subsection (a). As subsection (b) makes clear, however, in the right circumstances a duty of confidence can arise even absent an express agreement.

The case of *Phillips v. Frey*[64] demonstrates how a duty of confidence can arise absent an express agreement. Phillips owned Ambusher, Inc., which manufactured, among other things, single-pole deer stands. Phillips had started development of the stands in 1967 and apparently had refined the process over the years to develop the V-Lok tree stand and manufacture it efficiently. Three men, Collins, Frey, and Arnold, expressed some interest in buying Ambusher in 1990 for $140,000. To help evaluate the business, Phillips sent the men a package with a financial statement, an inventory of his equipment, and tools by make and model. He also included a video tape of the component manufacturing process from the previous year. He subsequently sent another tape demonstrating the manufacturing process for tree stands and accessories. Soon after that, Phillips took Collins, Frey, and Arnold on a tour of the manufacturing shop and showed them how to manufacture the V-Lok stand (this was followed up by a second visit).

After the visits, Collins tried to negotiate down the price (he lied by saying that his group had problems securing financing). After these attempts failed, Collins told Phillips that they couldn't buy the business and returned some of the materials that Phillips had sent them. Less than a year later, Frey and Arnold were manufacturing V-Lok stands (they called their stands "BP91") under the name Buck-Pro, Inc.

Phillips filed suit against Buck-Pro alleging misappropriation of both the V-Lok design and the manufacturing process. A jury awarded Phillips $56,500 in actual damages, $75,000 in punitive damages, and $7,000 in attorney's fees. The judge also signed a permanent injunction enjoining Buck-Pro from manufacturing, selling, or marketing deer stands and assorted accessories. Buck-Pro appealed and contended, among other things, that no confidential

64 20 F.3d 623 (5th Cir. 1994).

relationship existed preventing its subsequent use of the secret manufacturing process.[65]

As part of its defense, Buck-Pro claimed that the alleged trade secret was voluntarily disclosed and was no longer protected. Buck-Pro further noted that no express agreement of confidentiality was entered into; therefore, any subsequent use was not improper. The court disagreed on both points, noting that an express agreement was not necessary where "the actions of the parties and the nature of their relationship, taken as a whole, established the existence of a confidential relationship."[66] The following excerpt from comment b to § 41 of the Third Restatement of Unfair Competition is also instructive on this point:

> A duty of confidence may also be inferred from the relationship between the parties and the circumstances surrounding the disclosure. However, no duty of confidence will be inferred unless the recipient has notice of the confidential nature of the disclosure. Although no specific form of notice is required, the circumstances must indicate that the recipient knew or had reason to know that the disclosure was intended as confidential. In addition, the circumstances must justify the other party's belief that the recipient has consented to the duty of confidence. . . . Solicitation of the disclosure by the recipient can also contribute to an inference of confidentiality, particularly if the disclosure is prompted by a misrepresentation or other improper conduct on the part of the recipient.

In *Phillips*, the defendants were interested in purchasing the business, and Phillips made the disclosures to facilitate the deal. There was also evidence that the defendants made misrepresentations regarding their financing, which may have helped convince Phillips that the defendants were legitimately interested in purchasing his business. The court noted the fact that all parties came to the negotiating table and that the disclosure was made within the course of the negotiations.

As *Phillips* demonstrates, a confidential relationship does not have to involve an express agreement. A number of other cases have found that, under the right circumstances, the absence of an express

---

[65] Buck-Pro also asserted that no trade secret existed as it had properly reverse engineered the stand, and it argued that Phillips did not take reasonable steps to maintain secrecy. The court found that a trade secret existed not as to the stand, which could have been reverse engineered, but as to the manufacturing process. In addition, the court found that Phillips did take reasonable steps because the process was not revealed until negotiations had begun. *See id.* at 628–629.

[66] *Id.* at 631.

confidentiality agreement does not defeat a trade secret claim.[67] In some instances, the relationship itself indicates the existence of a confidential relationship, such as with fiduciaries or other close, personal relationships.[68] In business relationships, the question of whether a confidential relationship exists can be much closer, and the absence of an express agreement may be fatal to the claim.[69] The unifying theme of all of these cases seems to be that courts will find a confidential relationship when a trade secret is revealed to facilitate a specific relationship and the receiving party knew, or should have known, that the information was secret.

*ii. Breach of a Duty by Current and Former Employees*

The Third Restatement of Unfair Competition provides that current and former employees who disclose or use a trade secret in violation of a duty of confidence are liable for misappropriation. Employees are typically agents of their employers; thus, current employees generally owe a duty of confidence under basic principles of agency law. Section 387 of the Second Restatement of Agency provides that "[u]nless otherwise agreed, an agent is subject to a duty to his principal to act solely for the benefit of the principal in all matters connected with his agency."[70] This duty to act solely for the benefit of the principal includes a duty of confidentiality. Indeed, with regard to trade secrets, § 395 of the Second Restatement of Agency is particularly relevant:

> **§ 395 Using or Disclosing Confidential Information**
>
> Unless otherwise agreed, an agent is subject to a duty to the principal not to use or to communicate information

[67] *See* Hicklin Eng., L.C. v. Bartell, 439 F.3d 346, 350 (7th Cir. 2006) (holding that an express agreement was unnecessary because the defendant understood that the information should have been kept confidential); Speedry Chem. Prods., Inc. v. Carter's Ink Co., 306 F.2d 328, 332 (2d Cir. 1962) ("It is true, as plaintiffs contend, that it is not necessary to show an express agreement to hold in confidence and not to use trade secrets obtained as the result of a confidential relationship."); *cf.* Burten v. Milton Bradley Co., 763 F.2d 461, 463 (1st Cir. 1995) (finding that general and somewhat ambiguous language disclaiming a relationship between the parties was insufficient to defeat a confidential relationship).

[68] *See* Elm City Cheese Co. v. Federico, 752 A.2d 1037 (Conn. 1999) (finding that a confidential relationship existed between an accountant and his client without a written agreement of confidentiality due partly to the nature of the relationship).

[69] *See* Hoffman-La Roche Inc. v. Yoder, 950 F. Supp. 1348, 1354 (S.D. Ohio 1997) (rejecting a trade secret claim due to a lack of evidence indicating that the defendant was informed of the confidential nature of the information, including the absence of an express written or oral agreement to keep the information confidential); Aerospace Am., Inc. v. Abatement Tech., Inc., 738 F. Supp. 1061, 1071 (E.D. Mich. 1990) (finding that without an express agreement of confidentiality, a confidential relationship did not exist because there is no implied confidential relationship between a manufacturer and a distributor).

[70] The Third Restatement of Agency similarly provides that an agent owes a fiduciary duty to the principal. *See* RESTATEMENT (THIRD) OF AGENCY § 8.01 (2006).

> confidentially given him by the principal or acquired by him during the course of or on account of his agency or in violation of his duties as agent, in competition with or to the injury of the principal, on his own account or on behalf of another, although such information does not relate to the transaction in which he is then employed, unless the information is a matter of general knowledge.[71]

With respect to current employees,[72] therefore, establishing a duty of confidence is rarely an issue. Such cases frequently turn more on whether what was disclosed qualified as a trade secret or whether the owner of the trade secret sufficiently conveyed the confidential nature of the information to the current employee.[73]

Former employees are also subject to duties of confidence. Section 42 of the Third Restatement of Unfair Competition provides that former employees are to be treated the same as current employees. In addition, the Second Restatement of Agency imposes a duty upon former employees not to use or disclose trade secrets:

> **§ 396 Using Confidential Information after Termination of Agency**
>
> Unless otherwise agreed, after the termination of the agency, the agent:
>
> (a) has no duty not to compete with the principal;
>
> (b) has a duty to the principal not to use or to disclose to third persons, on his own account or on account of others, in competition with the principal or to his injury, trade secrets, written lists of names, or other similar confidential matters given to him only for the principal's use or acquired by the agent

---

71 Section 8.05 of the Third Restatement of Agency is more succinct, but it has the same meaning:

> § 8.05 Use of Principal's Property; Use of Confidential Information
>
> An agent has a duty
>
> (1) not to use property of the principal for the agent's own purposes or those of a third party; and
>
> (2) not to use or communicate confidential information of the principal for the agent's own purposes or those of a third party.

72 Independent contractors can pose a problem with regard to a duty of confidence because not all independent contractors qualify as agents. *See* RESTATEMENT (SECOND) OF AGENCY §§ 2(3), 220 (1958). If an independent contractor is not an agent, then a different basis for a duty of confidence must be found under § 41 of the Third Restatement of Unfair Competition.

73 *See, e.g.*, Omega Optical, Inc. v. Chroma Tech. Corp., 800 A.2d 1064, 1066 (Vt. 2002) (holding that the failure to put employees on explicit or implicit notice that the information being conveyed to them was confidential meant that the employees did not breach a duty of confidence and were therefore not liable for misappropriating a trade secret).

in violation of duty. The agent is entitled to use general information concerning the method of business of the principal and the names of the customers retained in his memory, if not acquired in violation of his duty as agent;

(c) has a duty to account for profits made by the sale or use of trade secrets and other confidential information, whether or not in competition with the principal;

(d) has a duty to the principal not to take advantage of a still subsisting confidential relation created during the prior agency relation.

Comment c to § 8.05 of the Third Restatement of Agency also provides that former employees are not free to use confidential information learned during their employment, but it makes an important clarification. While § 396(b) above suggests a possible defense for an employee who commits certain trade secrets to memory, the Third Restatement eliminates this possibility:

> An agent is not free to use or disclose a principal's trade secrets or other confidential information whether the agent retains a physical record of them or retains them in the agent's memory. If information is otherwise a trade secret or confidential, the means by which an agent appropriates it for later use or disclosure should be irrelevant. Feats of human memory, however commendable and intriguing in many respects, should not be privileged as instruments of disloyal conduct.

While the rules governing former employees may seem rather straightforward, they are complicated by the tendency of former employees to go work for competitors. The rules stated above specifically provide that former employees do not owe a duty to avoid competing with their former principals (absent an agreement to the contrary), but many employers are understandably uncomfortable with the prospect of former employees, who have intimate knowledge of their former employers' inner workings and trade secrets, going to work for a competitor (or becoming competitors themselves). The employer may believe that the former employee will use a skill set against the employer—a skill set that the employee only gained after considerable investment by the employer. Moreover, the employer may be fearful that the employee will take clients when he leaves or will try to convince other key employees to leave with him. Finally, the employer may simply not trust the former employee to keep the employer's trade secrets confidential.

To combat these fears, employers have developed a number of contractual provisions aimed at limiting a former employee's ability to compete with the employer. Listed below are a number of such provisions, which are collectively referred to as "restrictive covenants," and which are typically found in an employment agreement.

*Covenant not to compete*—A promise not to engage in the same type of business for a stated time in the same market as the buyer, partner, or employer.[74]

*Confidentiality agreement*—A promise not to disclose trade secrets or other proprietary information learned in the course of the parties' relationship.

*Nonsolicitation agreement*—A promise to refrain from trying to lure customers away from the employer for a specified period of time.

*"No-hire" or employee nonsolicitation agreement*—A promise to refrain from enticing employees to leave the company for a specified period of time.

Another type of clause frequently found in employment agreements is a "trailer clause." As will be discussed, not all trade secrets developed during the employment relationship belong to the employer. Thus, many employers insert trailer clauses which require employees to assign their rights to inventions developed during the employment relationship to the employer. These clauses also frequently require the employees to assign their rights to inventions developed post-employment for a specified period of time. Trailer clauses are subject to the same limitations as the above restrictive covenants.

Restrictive covenants are creatures of contract law rather than trade secret law. In most jurisdictions, such covenants are subject to scrutiny because of their effect on commerce. While employers may well have a right to protect their legitimate business interests, former employees also have a right to work and engage in their trades. Furthermore, such covenants may injure the public at large by denying the public access to the full range of skills that former employees have to offer. For these reasons, restrictive covenants are typically subject to a reasonableness analysis by the courts that weighs the interests of the employee and the former employer. Although such covenants can reach a broad range of conduct, the existence and possible use of trade secrets is often an issue in

---

[74] In April of 2024, the FTC announced a new rule banning noncompete agreements. *See FTC Announces Rule Banning Noncompetes*, FEDERAL TRADE COMMISSION (Apr. 23, 2024), https://www.ftc.gov/news-events/news/press-releases/2024/04/ftc-announces-rule-banning-noncompetes. *See also* https://www.ftc.gov/system/files/ftc_gov/pdf/noncompete-rule.pdf. The rule has been challenged on the ground that it is beyond the FTC's authority, and as of this writing, it is uncertain if it will survive.

restrictive covenant disputes. *Sigma Chemical Co. v. Harris*[75] demonstrates how a court might approach geographic and temporal limitations in a restrictive covenant when a trade secret is at issue. Harris was a former employee and purchasing agent of Sigma, a seller of esoteric chemicals. While employed at Sigma, Harris signed an agreement with a restrictive covenant that prevented Harris from working for one of Sigma's competitors within two years of his termination from Sigma. The covenant also prohibited Harris from using or disclosing Sigma's trade secrets within two years of his termination from Sigma. The agreement further provided that "[f]ollowing expiration of said two-year period, [Harris] shall continue to be obligated under the 'Confidential Information' section of this Agreement not to use or to disclose Confidential Information so long as it shall remain proprietary or protectible as confidential or trade secret information." Harris allegedly violated the terms of this agreement by going to work for ICN Pharmaceuticals, Inc. (ICN), one of Sigma's top competitors.

Sigma sought to enjoin Harris from working at ICN for the two-year period provided in the agreement. It also sought to enjoin Harris from revealing Sigma's trade secrets. The district court granted Sigma's requested relief. On appeal, Harris argued that under Missouri law, the geographic and temporal scope of the restrictions must be reasonable. Despite the restrictions having no limitations on geography, the district court found them to be reasonable, as Sigma competed on a worldwide basis. The court of appeals also concluded that, under the facts of the dispute, the restrictions that Sigma sought to enforce were reasonable. ICN was close enough in proximity to Sigma for the court to consider the restrictions reasonable as applied to the facts, regardless of whether the worldwide ban was reasonable on its face.

As to the temporal scope of the restrictions, the district court held that former employees are under a "temporally unlimited" duty not to disclose trade secret information. The court of appeals disagreed with this approach and decided to remand for a determination of how long it would take to develop the information independently. Implicitly, one could argue that the court of appeals was of the opinion that the unlimited time in the agreement was unreasonable. Given that the information, such as who supplied suitable salt to Sigma, was discoverable, perhaps the nature of the secret made the court of appeals' resolution more suitable.[76]

---

[75] 794 F.2d 371 (8th Cir. 1986).

[76] *See* RESTATEMENT (THIRD) OF UNFAIR COMPETITION § 44 cmt. f. (1995) ("An injunction also should not ordinarily extend beyond the time when the defendant could have properly acquired and implemented the information through reverse engineering

Restrictive covenants may also be useful to address and protect information that does not quite rise to the level of a trade secret. *Bernier v. Merrill Air Engineers*[77] demonstrates the utility of such a covenant as well as the scrutiny that it may receive. Bernier, an engineer, worked at Merrill for 8 years. Bernier's employment was subject to restrictive covenants regarding the disclosure of confidential information. During the time of his employment, he worked on developing a product dryer for Henry Molded Products (Henry). Indeed, the description of Bernier's responsibilities suggested that he was an integral part of the project. The district court found that Henry made a preliminary agreement to purchase the dryer that had been developed, but after hiring Bernier from Merrill, Henry cancelled the order. Bernier subsequently helped Henry to develop its own product dryer. It appeared that Bernier's ability to produce the product dryer played a significant role in his employment by Henry. Indeed, Bernier was informed that Henry's objectives included obtaining dryers at the lowest price, and Bernier told a Henry employee that he had his own dryer design. Further, the offer of employment that Bernier accepted included bonuses for dryers built while he was at Henry.

Merrill brought suit and alleged breach of contract and misappropriation of trade secrets. The district court held that Bernier did not violate the UTSA by revealing trade secrets, but he did breach his contract. Merrill was awarded damages in the amount of Merrill's expected net profit from the construction and design of the dryer for Henry. Bernier appealed claiming that the restrictive covenant was unreasonable and that there was a lack of evidence that he used the confidential information. The court of appeals affirmed, finding that the nondisclosure clause in the Bernier-Merrill employment contract was reasonable. The court noted that the nondisclosure clause did not prohibit Bernier from using the general skills and knowledge that he acquired during his employment with Merrill, but it did protect the use of confidential information—even if that information did not rise to the level of a trade secret.

Bernier also argued that the nondisclosure clause was unreasonable as it did not place a time limit on the nondisclosure obligation. Unlike the *Sigma* court, the *Bernier* court had no problem concluding that a nondisclosure clause was reasonable even though it was unlimited in duration. The court distinguished the lack of limits in noncompete obligations from the lack of limits in

---

or independent discovery. . . . The most efficient procedure depends on the ease and certainty with which the appropriate duration of relief can be determined in advance.").

[77] 770 A.2d 97 (Me. 2001).

nondisclosure obligations, holding that the "imposition of geographic or durational limitations 'would defeat the entire purpose of restricting disclosure, since confidentiality knows no temporal or geographical boundaries.' "[78]

While information not rising to the level of a trade secret is entitled to protection under a restrictive covenant, the reasonableness of a covenant may be judged in part by whether the information qualifies as a trade secret.[79] As the reasonableness of such a covenant is judged by the legitimate business interest that the employer seeks to protect, a finding that the information is less than a trade secret should probably trigger a higher degree of scrutiny. Comment d to § 41 of the Restatement (Third) of Unfair Competition offers the following guidance:

> The reasonableness of an agreement that merely prohibits the use or disclosure of particular information depends primarily upon whether the information protected by the agreement qualifies as a trade secret. If the information qualifies for protection [as a trade secret], a contract prohibiting its use or disclosure is generally enforceable according to its terms. . . . However, a nondisclosure agreement that encompasses information that is generally known or in which the promisee has no protectable interest, such as a former employee's promise not to use information that is part of the employee's general skill and training (see § 42, Comment d), may be unenforceable as an unreasonable restraint of trade.

Most states subject restrictive covenants to some form of reasonableness review. Although the states vary in their approaches, the Guide to Protecting and Litigating Trade Secrets notes that most states share the following queries:

1. Does the restriction protect a legitimate business interest?

---

78 *Id.* at 104 (quoting Revere Transducers, Inc. v. Deere & Co., 595 N.W. 2d 751, 761 (Iowa 1999) (citing 2 RUDOLF CALLMANN, THE LAW OF UNFAIR COMPETITION, TRADEMARKS & MONOPOLIES § 14.04, at 222–23 (Supp. 1998))).

79 *See* RESTATEMENT (THIRD) OF UNFAIR COMPETITION § 41 cmt. d (1995). *But see* Empire Farm Credit ACA v. Bailey, 657 N.Y.S.2d 211, 212 (App. Div. 1997) (holding that restrictive covenants "will be enforced to the extent necessary to prevent the use of trade secrets *or confidential customer information*, but only so long as they are reasonable in time and area, not harmful to the general public and not unreasonably burdensome to the employee" (emphasis added)); Lifetec, Inc. v. Edwards, 880 N.E. 2d 188, 192 (Ill. App. Ct. 2007) ("In determining whether a restrictive covenant is enforceable, courts must determine whether the terms of the agreement are reasonable and necessary to protect a legitimate business interest of the plaintiff." (internal quotations omitted)).

2. Are geographic and temporal restrictions reasonable?
3. Is the covenant supported by adequate consideration?
4. Does the covenant impose an undue burden on the party bound?
5. Is the restriction in the public interest?

New York, for example, adopts a "prevailing standard of reasonableness."[80] Similarly, Illinois examines the totality of the circumstances to determine if an employer's protectable interest is being advanced without unreasonably limiting competition.[81] Texas has adopted a statutory regime which focuses upon reasonableness.[82] Florida has also codified its law of restrictive covenants. Rather than rely purely on a general reasonableness analysis, Florida's statute provides a number of "safe harbors" where reasonableness is presumed.[83]

California has notably broken from the traditional reasonableness analysis by viewing restrictive covenants as unlawful restraints of trade.[84] This creates some conflict with trade secret law, however, as California has adopted the UTSA. To mitigate this conflict, California courts have created a "trade secret exception," which allows an employer to restrain a former employee who has knowledge of trade secrets from accepting work with a competitor.[85] The scope of this exception has been called into doubt by recent decisions, but the ability to prevent disclosure of confidential information under the exception appears to be intact.[86]

---

[80] *See* BDO Seidman v. Hirshberg, 712 N.E.2d 1220, 1223 (N.Y. 1999) (explaining that a non-compete agreement is reasonable if it: "(1) is *no greater* than is required for the protection of the *legitimate interest* of the employer, (2) does not impose undue hardship on the employee, and (3) is not injurious to the public").

[81] *See* Lifetec, Inc. v. Edwards, 880 N.E.2d 188, 192 (Ill. App. Ct. 2007) ("Because restrictive covenants in employment agreements are a form of restraint of trade, they are scrutinized carefully to ensure their intended effect is not to prevent competition *per se*.").

[82] *See* Marsh USA, Inc. v. Cook, 354 S.W.3d 764, 777 (Tex. 2011) ("Rather, the statute's core inquiry is whether the covenant contains limitations as to time, geographical area, and scope of activity to be restrained that are reasonable and do not impose a greater restraint than is necessary to protect the goodwill or other business interest of the promisee." (internal quotations omitted)).

[83] *See* FLA. STAT. § 542.335.

[84] *See* CAL. BUS. & PROF. CODE § 16600 ("[E]very contract by which anyone is restrained from engaging in a lawful profession, trade, or business of any kind is to that extent void.").

[85] *See* Whyte v. Schlage Lock Co., 125 Cal. Rptr. 2d 277, 293 (Ct. App. 2002) ("Nearly 40 years ago, the California Supreme Court recognized [that] covenants not to compete are enforceable notwithstanding Business and Professions Code section 16600 if 'necessary to protect the employer's trade secrets.' ").

[86] *Compare* Edwards v. Arthur Andersen LLP, 189 P.3d 285, 288 (Cal. 2008) (stating that "[w]e conclude that section 16600 prohibits employee noncompetition

California's hostility towards restrictive covenants is notable, particularly given the innovation that has taken place in Silicon Valley. Some commentators have gone so far as to attribute the success in Silicon Valley to the absence of enforceable restrictive covenants.[87]

## C. DEFENSES

### 1. Reverse Engineering and Independent Discovery

Section 1(2) of the UTSA provides that misappropriation occurs when a trade secret is "acquired by improper means." The comments to § 1 clarify that proper means include reverse engineering and independent discovery. The DTSA provides an identical definition of misappropriation and improper means and also codifies that reverse engineering and independent derivation are not improper.[88] Section 43 of the Third Restatement of Unfair Competition similarly notes that "[i]ndependent discovery and analysis of publicly available products or information are not improper means of acquisition."

Under the comments to § 1 of the UTSA, reverse engineering is defined as discovery "by starting with the known product and working backward to find the method by which it was developed." Thus, if a product is on the open market and a competitor purchases the item, takes it apart, and discovers how to manufacture it, the competitor is free to do so (absent protection under another theory, such as patent law). Of course, this assumes that the acquisition of

---

agreements unless the agreement falls within a statutory exception"), *with id.* at 289 n.4 ("We do not here address the applicability of the so-called trade secret exception to section 16600, as Edwards does not dispute that portion of his agreement or contend that the provision of the noncompetition agreement prohibiting him from recruiting Andersen's employees violated section 16600."), *and* Bank of America, N.A. v. Lee, No. CV 08–5546, 2008 WL 4351348, at *6 (C.D. Cal. Sept. 22, 2008) ("The Court concludes that [the] trade secret exception to § 16600 still applies. Nothing in *Edwards* is to the contrary."). *But see* Robinson v. U-Haul Co. of Calif., Nos. A124070, A124097, A124096, 2010 WL 4113578, at *10–11 (Cal. Ct. App. Oct. 20, 2010) (noting that "the so-called 'trade secrets' exception to Business and Professions Code section 16600 . . . rests on shaky legal grounds," and observing that "[e]ven assuming the continued viability of this exception, it has no application here").

[87] *See* Ronald J. Gilson, *The Legal Infrastructure of High Technology Industrial Districts: Silicon Valley, Route 128, and Covenants Not to Compete*, 74 N.Y.U. L. REV. 575, 603 (1999) (comparing the state laws governing non-compete covenants in Massachusetts and California, and finding that California's laws promote the growth of a second-stage agglomeration economy); *see also* AnnaLee Saxenian, REGIONAL ADVANTAGE: CULTURE AND COMPETITION IN SILICON VALLEY AND ROUTE 128, at 161 (1994) (concluding that Silicon Valley's success is derived from a culture where individual firms "learn collectively and adjust to one another's needs through shifting patterns of competition and collaboration").

[88] *See* 18 U.S.C. § 1839(6)(B).

the product itself was lawful. If a prototype was stolen from a competitor, for example, reverse engineering would not be a defense.

Independent discovery is arguably further removed from the trade secret than reverse engineering, as it does not rely on copying or taking apart a competitor's process or product. For instance, assume that two competitors, X and Y, are both trying to develop a new method of hydraulic fracturing (or "fracking" as it is often called) that conserves water.[89] X develops a method and begins to use it, but soon after, Y discovers the same method and begins to use it. Assuming that none of X's employees had left to work for Y, and absent a claim that Y committed some form of corporate espionage, a suit by X would likely fail due to Y's defense of independent discovery. In claiming independent discovery, the defendant is essentially saying that there was no misappropriation.

The claims of reverse engineering and independent discovery are strongest when the defendant has not had any prior exposure to the trade secret. However, the defenses are much more questionable when the two parties have shared information. Assume that Y had approached X to develop a new method of hydraulic fracturing. The two shared some initial thoughts on the matter, but eventually Y ended the negotiations. X and Y subsequently develop very similar methods. Given that Y has been exposed to X's ideas, can Y successfully raise an independent discovery defense?

At this point, it may be worth reviewing the difference between the burdens of proof, persuasion, and production. The burden of proof is a party's duty to prove a disputed assertion or charge. It includes both the burden of persuasion and the burden of production. The burden of persuasion is a party's duty to convince the factfinder to view the facts in a way that favors that party. The burden of production is a party's duty to introduce enough evidence on an issue to have the issue decided by the factfinder instead of decided against the party in a peremptory ruling such as a summary judgment or a directed verdict.

Initially, X will have the burden of both persuasion and production, i.e., X must produce enough evidence to survive a summary judgment motion and must also convince the jury that there has been a misappropriation. Once X does this, what burden (if any) does Y have? This depends on whether independent development (and reverse engineering) are viewed as affirmative defenses. An affirmative defense is a defendant's assertion of facts and arguments that, if true, will defeat the plaintiff's claim, even if

---

[89] Hydraulic fracturing is a method of oil and gas production whereby rock is fractured by a pressurized water compound.

all of the allegations in the complaint are true. However, the defendant bears the burden of proving an affirmative defense. The prevalent view is that independent development and reverse engineering are not affirmative defenses, but rather they negate an element of the plaintiff's prima facie case. The burden of persuasion, therefore, remains with the plaintiff.

Although the prevalent view is to treat the burden of persuasion as remaining with the plaintiff, there is some confusion on this point. The Third Circuit Court of Appeals described this confusion:

> While some other federal courts appear to have held that independent development is not an affirmative defense under Pennsylvania law, many of them do not clarify whether they are referring to the burden of production or the burden of persuasion, so it is sometimes difficult to determine the holding. *See e.g. Greenberg v. Croydon Plastics Co., Inc.*, 378 F.Supp. 806, 815–16 (E.D.Pa.1974) ("This inference [that defendants used the plaintiff's trade secret] may be overcome by a showing by defendants that they arrived at the flavoring method independently . . . we conclude that plaintiffs have proved by a fair preponderance of the evidence that the defendants did not arrive at the . . . method through independent investigation."); *but see Henry Hope X-Ray Prod., Inc. v. Marron Carrel, Inc.*, 674 F.2d 1336, 1341 (9th Cir.1982) (interpreting Pennsylvania law and concluding that "[w]here the plaintiff shows . . . manufacture of a closely similar device by the defendants, the burden shifts to the defendant to show that, at the time, it could have arrived at the process by independent invention, inspection, or reverse engineering").
>
> Courts interpreting independent development under the trade secret misappropriation laws of other states have come to differing results. *Bolt Associates, Inc. v. Alpine Geophysical Associates, Inc.*, 365 F.2d 742, 749–750 (3d Cir.1966) (interpreting New Jersey law, which is also based upon the Restatement (First) of Torts § 757, and finding that "a heavy burden of persuasion rests upon one so charged to show that the production was the result of independent development and not from the use of information confidentially reposed"); *but see Pioneer Hi-Bred Int'l v. Holden Foundation Seeds, Inc.*, 35 F.3d 1226, 1241 (8th Cir.1994) (noting in a case brought under Iowa trade secret misappropriation law that "[t]he court's . . . discussion of 'burden shifting' merely ex-presses its appreciation of the fact that once [the plaintiff] produced

> convincing evidence of misappropriation, [the defendant] was obligated to provide persuasive evidence of lawful derivation . . . The court's procedure can simply be read as an allocation of the burdens of going forward with the evidence").[90]

The effect of these burdens was a central issue in *Penalty Kick Management LTD. v. Coca Cola Co.*[91] In early November of 1995, Penalty Kick Management (PKM) representatives met with Coca-Cola representatives to demonstrate PKM's "Magic Windows" concept, which consisted of a scrambled message on the inside of a beverage container label which could be decoded and read only after the beverage container was emptied. Before divulging the information, PKM orally expressed the confidential nature of the meeting and the information to be conveyed. PKM proposed that Coca-Cola could have the exclusive ability to use Magic Windows under a license agreement. As it so happened, Coca-Cola was simultaneously meeting with BrightHouse, an Atlanta-based ideation company, to create a promotion for the upcoming 1996 NFL season. One of the ideas presented was the creation of a bottle label with a scrambled message on the back side of the label and a red decoder filter printed on the front side of the label.

In subsequent meetings between PKM and Coca-Cola, the parties entered into a non-disclosure agreement, but the agreement provided a number of exceptions, such as if the information was to become public or if Coca-Cola were to independently develop the concept. Thereafter, the parties began licensing negotiations, but some investigation by Coca-Cola revealed prior art in the form of a patent application by a company called Virtual Image. In light of this prior art, Coca-Cola did not believe that PKM could grant an exclusive license, and negotiations broke down in November of 1996.

In September of 1996, while still in negotiations with PKM, Coca-Cola approached ITW to develop a label promotion for its Argentinean markets similar to the Magic Windows concept. ITW's graphic arts manager, Jeffrey Albaugh, developed the concept to fruition during a three-week time span, and Coca-Cola used it in promotions. PKM learned of the Argentinean promotion in February of 1997 and brought suit against Coca-Cola.

PKM's lawsuit alleged conversion, misappropriation of trade secrets (based on Coca-Cola divulging the disclosed information to ITW, who in turn, used that information to develop its label), breach of the non-disclosure agreement, breach of a confidential relationship

---

[90] Moore v. Kulicke & Soffa Indus., 318 F.3d 561, 568 n.6 (3d Cir. 2003).

[91] 318 F.3d 1284 (11th Cir. 2003).

and duty of good faith, unjust enrichment, and failure to compensate PKM for the services and property provided to Coca-Cola. The district court granted Coca-Cola's motion for summary judgment on all counts, finding that although there was a trade secret, Coca-Cola did not misappropriate it. The court concluded that Coca-Cola and ITW had independently developed their version of the concept and that any remaining causes of action were preempted under the Georgia Trade Secret Act. PKM appealed.

The manner in which Magic Windows was produced was found by the court of appeals to be a trade secret. The concept of having a scrambled message on the inside of the label that was only viewable through a colored opening on the other side of the label once the liquid in the container was gone, however, was not a trade secret, as it was publicly available. PKM claimed that the trade secret was either disclosed to ITW in violation of a duty of confidence and/or was used by Coca-Cola and ITW to develop its version of the concept.

To support its claim, PKM pointed to a number of suspicious facts. First, PKM initially contacted Coca-Cola in November of 1995, revealing its Magic Windows concept. Second, Coca-Cola continued to negotiate until November of 1996. Soon after negotiations broke down, Coca-Cola was marketing a very similar product as the Magic Windows concept. Third, it was learned that in September of 1996, while still in negotiations with PKM, the same Coca-Cola representatives who had been dealing with PKM approached ITW to develop a label. Fourth, a sample label provided to Coca-Cola had been shared with ITW, but the actual label that was shared was lost (and the court refused to find that any adverse inference should be made of this). Finally, PKM pointed to notes and a voice mail from Coca-Cola representatives that indicated that a label was shared as evidence of disclosure.

Coca-Cola did not offer much in the way of counter evidence, but the court of appeals noted that the fact that the same representatives were involved was not extraordinary, as it was their job to approach multiple parties. As for the disclosure of the label, the court found that the testimony offered by multiple witnesses all indicated that the label was different from the one provided by PKM. Ultimately, PKM had the burden of proof as to both initial production and persuasion. Although the surrounding facts were somewhat suspicious, this is not the same as producing evidence of disclosure. The court of appeals held that PKM had failed to provide evidence that Coca-Cola had actually disclosed its trade secrets to ITW.[92]

---

[92] Circumstantial evidence is not always insufficient. *See, e.g.*, Greenberg v. Croydon Plastics Co., 378 F. Supp. 806, 814 (E.D. Pa. 1974) ("Misappropriation and misuse can rarely be proved by convincing direct evidence."); Stratienko v. Cordis

Reverse engineering is also a proper means of discovery under the law. Just because one person has discovered a trade secret through reverse engineering, however, does not mean that the secret has lost all legal protection.[93] Although reverse engineering is a proper means, some courts have focused upon the "readily ascertainable" language to distinguish between secrets that can simply be figured out upon observation and those that take effort. As one court noted:

> Defendants next argue the COMPU-RIP software was not a trade secret since defendant Browning rediscovered the COMPU-RIP source code by means of reverse engineering. A party asserting the existence of a trade secret does not have to establish the impossibility of reverse engineering. Plaintiff must merely show the alleged trade secret was not "readily ascertainable through . . . reverse engineering." G.S. 66–152(3) (emphasis added).[94]

Furthermore, reverse engineering only protects the reverse engineer.[95]

Once a product is on the market, it is susceptible to reverse engineering. If the trade secret owner has not patented the device, this susceptibility is problematic, as competitors will be free to discover the trade secret and to market the device themselves. To counteract this, a trade secret owner could turn to contract law for help. For instance, the owner could require the purchaser to agree not to reverse engineer the device as a condition to a sale or license.[96]

---

Corp., 429 F.3d 592, 601–02 (6th Cir. 2005) ("[R]equiring direct evidence would foreclose most trade-secret claims from reaching the jury because corporations rarely keep direct evidence of their use ready for another party to discover."); USA Power, LLC v. PacifiCorp, 235 P.3d 749, 761 (Utah 2010) (holding that circumstantial evidence is enough to defeat a motion for summary judgment on the issue of misappropriation).

93 *See, e.g.*, Reingold v. Swiftships, 126 F.3d 645, 652 (5th Cir. 1997) (rejecting defendant's argument that it could have reverse engineered chattel because "protection will be accorded to a trade secret holder against disclosure or unauthorized use gained by improper means, even if others might have discovered the trade secret by legitimate means"); *cf.* Barr-Mullin, Inc. v. Browning, 424 S.E.2d 226, 230 (N.C. Ct. App. 1993) ("A party asserting the existence of a trade secret does not have to establish the *impossibility* of reverse engineering. Plaintiff must merely show the alleged trade secret was not *readily ascertainable* through . . . reverse engineering.").

94 Barr-Mullin, Inc. v. Browning, 424 S.E.2d 226, 230 (N.C. Ct. App. 1993).

95 *See* Reingold v. Swiftships, 126 F.3d 645, 652 (5th Cir. 1997).

96 *See* Bowers v. Baystate Tech., Inc., 320 F.3d 1317, 1325 (Fed. Cir. 2003) (upholding a breach of contract determination that was based on a provision in a licensing agreement that prohibited reverse engineering). *But see* Vault Corp. v. Quaid Software Ltd., 847 F.2d 255, 270 (5th Cir. 1988) (striking down a contract provision that banned reverse engineering and copying because the Copyright Act preempted the relevant sections of the Louisiana License Act, which explicitly permitted such a provision).

## 2. Shop Rights

In general, when an employee is hired specifically to develop an invention, the invention is owned solely by the employer, regardless of whether the employee has agreed to assign trade secrets to the employer. Under the doctrine of "shop rights," when an employee not hired to specifically develop an invention does invent something during the hours of employment and using the employer's facilities, the employee retains ultimate ownership of the invention, but the employer is deemed to have a perpetual, non-exclusive license to use it.[97] Although these concepts usually relate to patents, they have been applied to trade secrets as well.[98]

However, when an employee develops a trade secret on his or her own time—outside the scope of employment and without using the employer's facilities or information—the employee owns the trade secret, and the employer acquires no license. Thus, employers may wish to have invention disclosure and assignment agreements with their employees (in addition to confidentiality and nondisclosure agreements). These agreements were referred to above as "trailer clauses" and they are subject to the same limitations as other restrictive covenants.

Even with a trailer clause, issues can arise as to whether an innovation happened within the protected time frame. For example, what should an employer do when a former employee has seemingly "gamed" the clause by claiming that she developed a process shortly after the clause expired? This factual scenario occurred in *General Signal Corp. v. Primary Flow Signal, Inc.*[99] In that case, Dezsoe Halmi, a 25-year employee of General Signal Corporation (GSC), left and formed his own company, Primary Flow Signal, Inc. Halmi was bound by a trailer clause which provided that Halmi would assign his interest in any inventions and ideas relating to his employment at GSC and for a six-month period after leaving. Five days after the trailer clause expired, Halmi alleged that he conceived of a modified universal flow meter that was similar to one developed by GSC, and he subsequently received a patent on the flow meter. GSC sued, as it did not believe that Halmi conceived of the new flow meter after the expiration of the trailer clause.

---

97 *See* RESTATEMENT (SECOND) OF AGENCY § 397 cmts. a, c (1958). There is not an analogous provision in the Third Restatement of Agency.

98 *See* Avtec Sys., Inc. v. Peiffer, 805 F. Supp. 1312, 1319–20 (E.D. Va. 1992) (concluding that an employer may acquire a trade secret in a "program's use for demonstration and marketing purposes in a similar manner as an employer may possess 'shop rights' to an employee's patented invention").

99 1987 WL 147798 (D.R.I. 1987).

Halmi defended by arguing that the trailer clause lacked consideration. The court rejected the argument, as it adopted the position of many courts that continued employment is sufficient consideration to support an assignment. Halmi also repeated his assertion that he conceived of the new flow meter after expiration of the trailer clause. The court was not convinced:

> Defendants assert that Mr. Halmi did not violate the agreement, as he developed the NTV after leaving GSC. The trial as to the infringement claim in this case made clear that the industry involved is not only competitive but highly complex. The perfection of a flow meter proved to be a painstakingly intricate process involving extensive testing. It is therefore difficult to believe that after a long and distinguished career with Plaintiff, Mr. Halmi in his musing five days after the trailer clause expired for the first time came up with the idea for the NTV. Although the word "Eureka!" has allegedly been uttered by more than one inventor over the years, the concept at issue does not lend itself to such sudden discovery. The Court finds that the concept of the '434 patent must have existed in Mr. Halmi's mind before his employment with GSC ended. Mr. Halmi therefore violated his agreement with GSC.[100]

### 3. Preemption of Other Common Law Claims

Preemption is not so much a defense to trade secret misappropriation as it is a defense to other related causes of action that may arise. Section 7 of the UTSA preempts other civil remedies for trade secret misappropriation:

> **SECTION 7. EFFECT ON OTHER LAW.**
>
> (a) Except as provided in subsection (b), this [Act] displaces conflicting tort, restitutionary, and other law of this State providing civil remedies for misappropriation of a trade secret.
>
> (b) This [Act] does not affect:
>
> (1) contractual remedies, whether or not based upon misappropriation of a trade secret;
>
> (2) other civil remedies that are not based upon misappropriation of a trade secret; or
>
> (3) criminal remedies, whether or not based upon misappropriation of a trade secret.

100 *Id.* at *4.

Although this preemptive language is broad, notice that civil remedies not based upon misappropriation of a trade secret are still available.[101] Section 40 of the Restatement (Third) of Unfair Competition similarly provides that "[t]his section does not govern the imposition of liability for conduct that infringes other protected interests such as interference with contractual relations (see Restatement, Second, Torts §§ 766–774A (1979)), breach of the duty of loyalty owed by an employee or other agent (see Restatement, Second, Agency §§ 387–398 (1958)), or a breach of confidence not involving a trade secret (see § 41, Comment c)." In addition, contract-based claims are not preempted. Thus, the restrictive covenants discussed earlier are still governed by normal contract principles.

The preemption provisions are meant to displace inconsistent and conflicting state law. Despite the uniform language of the UTSA, there is some degree of variance in what qualifies as a preempted claim:

> Like other tort plaintiffs, plaintiffs suing to protect a secret often take a "shotgun" approach to litigation, asserting all potentially-applicable legal claims for relief. And because of the proliferation of business torts over the years, dozens of courts have had occasion to consider whether the UTSA displaces these various state laws. On an initial reading, these cases can be quite confusing, as the courts cite widely-varying factors when deciding whether a particular claim is displaced. In some cases, the court focuses on whether the information in question qualifies as a UTSA Trade Secret, while other opinions place no significance on that fact. Similarly, while some courts carefully consider the elements of the state law in question, others will find a state law claim displaced without regard to how similar its elements are to a UTSA claim. Therefore, not only are the results in these cases impossible to reconcile, but there also seems to be little rhyme or reason to the methodology.[102]

Recall that in the *Penalty Kick* decision discussed above, PKM had brought additional tort claims for conversion, breach of confidential relationship and duty of good faith, unjust enrichment, and quantum meruit. PKM argued that such claims were not dependent on the existence of a trade secret, were not "based" upon the misappropriation of a trade secret and were therefore not

---

101 The DTSA explicitly provides that it does not preempt or displace state law remedies for misappropriation of a trade secret. Any ancillary state law claims (e.g., tortious interference with contract) brought in federal court under the DTSA, however, would be subject to the state's UTSA provisions, including § 7.

102 John T. Cross, *USTA Displacement of Other State Law Claims*, 33 HAMLINE L. REV. 445,450–51 (2010).

preempted. The court noted, however, that while it was true that the claims did not require the existence of a trade secret, the subject of the claims was a trade secret. The court's preemption analysis, therefore, focused on the subject of the claim; if the subject is a trade secret, the other claims are preempted. In a footnote, the court observed that some courts have "indicated that blanket preemption applies to all claims involving information that the plaintiff claims is a trade secret."[103] Other courts "have held that claims are only preempted to the extent that they contain the same factual allegations as the claim for use or misappropriation of trade secrets."[104]

These divergent approaches raise questions regarding whether claims involving information that does not rise to the level of a trade secret can be preempted. For instance, should a plaintiff be able to sue in tort for the misappropriation of confidential information that does not qualify as a trade secret? If so, how would that claim differ from a trade secret claim? Black's Law Dictionary defines "confidential information" as "[k]nowledge or facts not in the public domain but known to some, esp. to those having a fiduciary duty not to misuse the knowledge or facts for their own advantage." This seems very close to the definition of a trade secret under the UTSA, but without the need to show value or steps to maintain secrecy. As discussed, these two elements are important parts of trade secret law. To allow a claim to move forward under the guise of "confidential information" without meeting these two elements would seem to undermine the purpose of the UTSA. Nevertheless, the issue has caused confusion in the courts.

Courts appear to be of two views regarding whether UTSA § 7 covers such confidential (but not trade secret) information. A majority seem to adopt the "All Confidential Information" view, which applies to all causes of action where a party invokes state law to protect a secret, regardless of whether the secret qualifies as a trade secret under the UTSA.[105] Other courts adopt a "Trade Secrets

---

103 *Penalty Kick Management Ltd.*, 318 F.3d at 1297, n.11.

104 *Id.*

105 *See, e.g.*, Embarcadero Tech., Inc. v. Redgate Software, Inc., No. 1:17–cv–444–RP, 2018 WL 315753, at *3 (W.D. Tex. Jan. 5, 2019) (noting that it joined the majority of courts in holding that the preemption provisions encompass "all claims based on the alleged improper taking of confidential business information"); BlueEarth Biofuels, LLC v. Hawaiian Elec. Co., 235 P.3d 310, 323 (Haw. 2010) ("[T]he [Hawaii UTSA] preempts non-contract, civil claims based on the improper acquisition, disclosure or use of confidential and/or commercially valuable information that does not rise to the level of a . . . trade secret."); *see also* Charles Tait Graves & Elizabeth Tippett, *UTSA Preemption and the Public Domain: How Courts Have Overlooked Patent Preemption of State Law Claims Alleging Employee Wrongdoing*, 65 RUTGERS L. REV. 59, 72–77 (2012) ("It appears that the majority of courts that have considered UTSA preemption—and certainly a substantial majority of state supreme courts to have

Only" view.[106] Under this approach, if the information qualifies as a trade secret under the UTSA, the UTSA preempts other claims. If the information does not qualify as a trade secret, the plaintiff is free to seek a recovery under any cause of action.[107]

Why should the UTSA preempt claims based on information that does not rise to the level of trade secret? The courts following the majority view see the adoption of the UTSA as the exclusive remedy for misappropriating information. In other words, in enacting the UTSA, the states wanted this statute to be the only method of recovery. The California Court of Appeals offered the following rationale in declining to adopt the minority "Trade Secrets Only" approach:

> We emphatically reject the *Cenveo* court's suggestion that the uniform act was not intended to preempt "common law conversion claims based on the taking of information that, though not a trade secret, was nonetheless of value to the claimant." On the contrary, a prime purpose of the law was to sweep away the adopting states' bewildering web of rules and rationales and replace it with a uniform set of principles for determining when one is—and is not—liable for acquiring, disclosing, or using "information . . . of value." Central to the effort was the act's definition of a trade secret. Information that does not fit this definition, and is not otherwise made property by some provision of positive law, belongs to no one, and cannot be converted or stolen. By permitting the conversion claim to proceed on a contrary rationale, the *Cenveo* court impliedly created a new category of intellectual property far beyond the contemplation of the Act, subsuming its definition of "trade secret" and effectively obliterating the uniform system it seeks to generate.[108]

Courts that adopt the minority approach appear to focus on the language of the UTSA itself. Consider the following observations:

---

addressed the question—have ruled that the UTSA displaces alternative state law tort claims that seek to hold the defendant liable for misusing the plaintiff's information."); John T. Cross, *UTSA Displacement of Other State Law Claims*, 33 HAMLINE L. REV. 445, 452–54 (2010) ("Based upon those cases in which the court's view is clear or can be gleaned from the context, it appears a significant majority follows the All Confidential Information view.").

106 *See* AMID, Inc. v. Medic Alert Found. U.S., Inc., 241 F. Supp. 3d 788, 826–27 (S.D. Tex. 2017) (concluding that an unfair competition claim based on confidential information was not preempted by the Texas UTSA).

107 *See* Graves & Tippett, *supra* note 105, at 77–78; Cross, *supra* note 102, at 452.

108 Silvaco Data Sys. v. Intel Corp., 184 Cal. App. 4th 210, 239 n.22 (Ct. App. 2010).

> Courts taking the minority position do so in different ways, though they reach the same result. One common line of reasoning focuses on the wording in the UTSA's preemption clause, which states that civil remedies not based on "misappropriation of a trade secret" are not preempted by the statute. Because the preemption language makes no reference to claims that use the words "confidential" or "proprietary" information, these courts reason that the UTSA only preempts state law tort claims that use the word "trade secret."[109]

The majority and minority approaches discussed above are the most commonly cited by the courts, but within the minority approach there appears to be quite a bit of variance. Furthermore, a number of courts fail to address whether they are adopting one of the above two approaches.

## D. REMEDIES

Remedies for misappropriation of trade secrets are available under the UTSA and the common law. Specifically, the UTSA provides for injunctive relief, monetary damages (including, in appropriate circumstances, exemplary damages), attorney's fees, or any combination of these remedies. Other remedies, such as for breach of contract or for common law torts that are not preempted, may also be available.

### 1. Injunctive Relief

#### *a. Preliminary and Permanent Injunctions*

An injunction is a court order that generally prevents a person from engaging in specific conduct or commands a person to take certain actions (such as removing trade secrets from a publicly available website). UTSA § 2 specifically provides for injunctive relief:

> **SECTION 2. INJUNCTIVE RELIEF.**
>
> (a) Actual or threatened misappropriation may be enjoined. Upon application to the court, an injunction shall be terminated when the trade secret has ceased to exist, but the injunction may be continued for an additional reasonable period of time in order to eliminate commercial advantage that otherwise would be derived from the misappropriation.[110]

---

109 Graves & Tippett, *supra* note 105, at 77.

110 *See also* RESTATEMENT (THIRD) OF UNFAIR COMPETITION § 44 (1995) (providing for injunctive relief).

Injunctive relief is an important remedy to the victim of trade secret misappropriation and can take many forms. It may prohibit a misappropriator from contacting a victim's clients, using a confidential manufacturing process, or even working for a competitor. It may also compel affirmative acts, such as destroying documents or giving back a prototype. Notice that relief under the UTSA is available for "[a]ctual or threatened misappropriation." This means that former employees may be enjoined prospectively, even if they have not yet used or disclosed a trade secret.

Injunctive relief comes in two forms: preliminary and permanent. A preliminary injunction issues prior to a final determination on the merits. To obtain a preliminary injunction, a plaintiff must file a complaint which is usually accompanied by an ex parte application for a temporary restraining order (which will last until the preliminary injunction can be considered). The court will then hold a hearing on whether to order a preliminary injunction based upon four equitable criteria: (1) the likelihood of success on the merits; (2) the threat that the plaintiff will suffer irreparable harm if the injunction is denied; (3) a balance of the threat to the plaintiff with the harm to the nonmoving party; and (4) whether the public interest favors such relief. The moving party bears the burden of proof on each of these factors.

The issuance or denial of a preliminary injunction is a key component of subsequent settlement negotiations, as the granting of such an injunction suggests to the defendant that its position is not going to prevail. Conversely, the denial of such relief means that the plaintiff must try the case, involving money and time, before relief will be granted. If a preliminary injunction is granted, it stays in place while a trial is held on the merits.

Upon the completion of the trial, a permanent injunction may be entered. The word "permanent," however, does not mean that the injunction will last forever. The length and type of injunctive relief will vary from case to case. With respect to length, the Third Restatement and the UTSA both indicate that an injunction should be long enough to eliminate the commercial advantage gained by the misappropriator, but should not be longer than necessary.[111] With respect to type, although the UTSA does not identify the factors that should be considered in determining the type of injunctive relief, § 44 of the Third Restatement of Unfair Competition provides a useful list:

---

111 *See, e.g.*, UTSA § 2 cmt.

(2) The appropriateness and scope of injunctive relief depend upon a comparative appraisal of all the factors of the case, including the following primary factors:

(a) the nature of the interest to be protected;

(b) the nature and extent of the appropriation;

(c) the relative adequacy to the plaintiff of an injunction and of other remedies;

(d) the relative harm likely to result to the legitimate interests of the defendant if an injunction is granted and to the legitimate interests of the plaintiff if an injunction is denied;

(e) the interests of third persons and of the public;

(f) any unreasonable delay by the plaintiff in bringing suit or otherwise asserting its rights;

(g) any related misconduct on the part of the plaintiff; and

(h) the practicality of framing and enforcing the injunction.

While the DTSA is largely duplicative of the UTSA, including in its remedies provisions, it does provide for one new remedy: civil seizure. Under the DTSA, a court may issue an ex parte order "but only in extraordinary circumstances . . . providing for the seizure of property necessary to prevent the propagation or dissemination of the trade secret that is the subject of the action."[112] The eight requirements for issuing such an order, however, are demanding:

1. an order pursuant to FED. R. CIV. P. 65 (addressing injunctive relief) or other equitable relief would be inadequate;
2. an immediate and irreparable injury will occur if seizure is not ordered;
3. harm to the applicant from denial of a seizure order: (1) outweighs the harm to the person against whom seizure is ordered; and (2) substantially outweighs the harm to any third parties by such seizure;
4. the applicant is likely to succeed in showing that the person against whom the order is issued misappropriated the trade secret through improper means or conspired to do so;

[112] 18 U.S.C. § 1836(2)(A)(i).

5. the person against whom the order will be issued has possession of the trade secret and any property to be seized;
6. the application describes with reasonable particularity the property to be seized and, to the extent reasonable under the circumstances, the property's location;
7. the person against whom seizure is ordered, or persons acting in concert with such person, would destroy, move, hide, or otherwise make such property inaccessible to the court if put on notice; and
8. the applicant has not publicized the requested seizure.[113]

To demonstrate how these remedies might be applied, consider the following hypothetical: Rich owns a company that provides janitorial services to business customers in Houston, Texas. The company is new and spends a good portion of its first year contacting various companies in town to see what their cleaning needs might be, including types of cleaning, size of the businesses, and frequency. Rich does this by cold-calling companies in the phone book and asking them basic questions about their janitorial needs. From these efforts, Rich has compiled a customer list (both actual and potential) which he uses to send out special promotions and offers.

Ed is a mid-level employee who works for Rich. He leaves to start up his own competing company. Prior to leaving, Ed downloads a copy of the customer list to assist him in his new venture. Rich learns of Ed's actions and sues to enjoin Ed from using the list.

Turning to the Restatement's factors, one must ask about the interest being harmed by this misappropriation. Here, it is the potential use of Rich's client list, which took a year to compile. If Ed is not enjoined, he will be at a commercial advantage, as his start-up will be able to use the list immediately rather than having to go through the long process of developing one himself. Based upon these considerations, Rich would seem to have a strong case, but there are other interests that must also be considered.

First, assuming that the injunction prevents Ed from using the list, what harm might there be to the public? Companies needing Ed's services may not become aware of Ed's business, and Ed may offer a better or cheaper service than Rich. Of course, nothing is preventing Ed from simply going to the phone book and calling potential customers himself, but there may be a delay in Ed's ability to put together a list. Looking at § 44(2)(h) of the Third Restatement of

---

113 18 U.S.C. § 1836(2)(A)(ii).

Unfair Competition, a practical problem also exists—assuming that Ed has made copies on his computer, how is the court going to ensure that Ed does not use some version of the list in the future? A court could simply prohibit Ed from contacting anyone on the list for a set period of time, but this would effectively deny Ed the ability to make a living (which should be considered under factor (2)(d)).

Based on these concerns, if a court decides that enjoining the use of the list is inappropriate, other possible types of injunctive relief may still be available. This is where UTSA § 2(b) may have some relevance. If exceptional circumstances exist, a court could order that a reasonable royalty payment be made.[114] What sort of exceptional circumstances might help Ed? If he had the honest belief that the list could be used when he left Rich's company (perhaps he thought incorrectly that it was readily accessible) and materially changed his position (such as by taking out a loan for his new venture or leasing facilities for it), then perhaps the equities of the case would favor this remedy. In such a case, a court will have to determine what the value of the list would be to a licensee.

Assuming that an injunction is deemed appropriate, there is still the matter of what length of time to place on the injunction. Some courts conclude that the time it would take a "legitimate competitor" to independently reproduce the information is the appropriate time frame.[115] The comments to § 44 of the Third Restatement similarly speak of limiting the injunction to a time period under which a competitor could have discovered the secret itself through proper means. In addition, the comment to § 2 of the UTSA speaks of eliminating a "lead time" commercial advantage. Under these guiding principles, it would seem that an appropriate length will account for how long it would take a competitor to recreate the list. Assuming that the one-year period it took Rich is reasonable, a one-year injunction would seem sufficient.

As for the DTSA and a civil seizure, the very first requirement is that injunctive relief is inadequate. Given the above discussion, this may not be the case. However, if there is evidence that Ed is immediately using the list to poach away customers, perhaps a seizure is warranted. A practical problem mentioned above is that the list could be stored on his computer and in several other places—how would the trade secret be seized? Perhaps the order would permit seizure of any physical copies of the list as well as Ed's computers, but this would add to the burden on Ed and may be

---

[114] Note that this is still injunctive relief rather than monetary damages. This is an order to pay a sum to compensate for future conduct rather than an amount for past conduct. *See* UTSA § 3 cmt.

[115] *See, e.g.*, Sigma Chem. Co. v. Harris, 794 F.2d 371 (8th Cir. 1986).

harder to justify. Moreover, Rich would need to know where to find these copies—the DTSA requires Rich to identify the property and the location with a reasonable degree of certainty. Furthermore, is there any evidence that Ed will try to move or hide the list? Given the requirements, it seems possible to use the DTSA's civil seizure provisions, but more facts would be needed to establish the propriety of such an action.

The comments to the UTSA and the Restatement both indicate that an injunction should cease once a secret becomes publicly available. However, just because another competitor has developed a list does not mean that it is now publicly available. This is not to say that the competitor's development is not worth considering. If the competitor developed the list in a much shorter period, this could be offered as evidence of how long an injunction should last.

### *b. Inevitable Disclosure*

Perhaps one of the most powerful uses of injunctive relief is the ability to prohibit a former employee from working for a competitor under the "inevitable disclosure" doctrine. Recall that an injunction can issue under the UTSA for actual or threatened misappropriation. Based upon a threatened misappropriation, some courts will enjoin a departing employee who has possession of trade secrets from working for a competitor. This is to avoid the inevitable disclosure of those trade secrets to the new employer. The doctrine can be invoked even if the former employee is not in possession of confidential documents, and even in the absence of a non-compete agreement.

An oft-cited decision discussing the inevitable disclosure doctrine is *PepsiCo, Inc. v. Redmond.*[116] In *PepsiCo,* William Redmond, a former high-ranking employee of PepsiCo, attempted to work in an executive capacity for Quaker Oats, a direct competitor in the beverage industry.[117] PepsiCo sought to enjoin Redmond from working for Quaker by claiming that Redmond had knowledge of PepsiCo's trade secrets, such as strategic plans for specific markets. Although Redmond had signed a confidentiality agreement and had not yet disclosed any secrets, the court found that "a plaintiff may prove a claim of trade secret misappropriation by demonstrating that defendant's new employment will inevitably lead him to rely on the plaintiff's trade secrets."[118]

---

[116] 54 F.3d 1262 (7th Cir. 1995).

[117] Quaker Oats makes Gatorade and Snapple.

[118] *PepsiCo,* 54 F.3d at 1269.

The court discussed three factors for successfully invoking the inevitable disclosure doctrine.[119] First, the employee must have "extensive and intimate knowledge"; in other words, the employee must possess knowledge of a trade secret. Second, the old and new positions must be so similar that the former employee would have to rely on the trade secrets to adequately perform in the new position. Third, the plaintiff must demonstrate proof of the employee's willingness to exploit the secrets, such as through a lack of candor by the former employee or the new employer. Under the circumstances of the *PepsiCo* case, the court found that an injunction was appropriate. The case is often cited as the modern origin of the inevitable disclosure doctrine (although its roots can be traced much earlier). The label "doctrine" is somewhat confusing, as the doctrine may be nothing more than a description of when relief may be appropriate due to irreparable harm. Nevertheless, courts use the term.

*Bimbo Bakeries, U.S.A., Inc. v. Botticella*[120] illustrates the contours of the doctrine and its application. Botticella was a high-level executive at Bimbo and had been at the company for approximately nine years before accepting a job at rival baked goods company Hostess. At Bimbo, Botticella had signed a "Confidentiality, Non-Solicitation and Invention Assignment Agreement," in which he agreed, among other things, not to use or disclose any of Bimbo's confidential or proprietary information during or after the term of his employment. The agreement, however, did not include a covenant restricting where Botticella could work after the termination of his employment with Bimbo. While working at Bimbo, Botticella was privy to a number of trade secrets, including Bimbo's products and its business strategy.

Although Botticella accepted employment with Hostess, he continued to work for Bimbo for several months before it was revealed (not by him) that he had accepted the new position. Not surprisingly, Bimbo immediately let Botticella go. Prior to leaving, there was evidence that Botticella had been exposed to trade secret information in meetings[121] and email, and he had also accessed and possibly downloaded trade secret information (including accessing the system minutes after being let go). Of particular concern to Bimbo

---

[119] Although the court did not describe the three factors discussed as elements, a number of courts and commentators have cited to these factors when describing the decision.

[120] 613 F.3d 102 (3d Cir. 2010).

[121] Botticella claimed that he mentally "blocked out" the information from his head—a claim the court was understandably dubious of.

was the secret behind its Thomas' English Muffins unique "nooks and crannies" texture.

Bimbo sued to protect its trade secrets and specifically sought a preliminary injunction preventing Botticella from commencing work at Hostess. The district court granted Bimbo's motion and preliminarily enjoined Botticella from commencing employment with Hostess and from divulging to Hostess any confidential or proprietary information belonging to Bimbo. The court further ordered Botticella to return to Bimbo any of the company's confidential or proprietary information in his possession. Botticella appealed.

On appeal, the court considered four factors: "(1) a likelihood of success on the merits; (2) he or she will suffer irreparable harm if the injunction is denied; (3) granting relief will not result in even greater harm to the nonmoving party; and (4) the public interest favors such relief."[122] In discussing the likelihood of success, the court reviewed the status of the inevitable disclosure doctrine under Pennsylvania law. According to the court, the standard is not so high as to actually require that disclosure be inevitable; instead, "Pennsylvania law permits the issuance of an injunction where a defendant's new employment is *likely* to result in the disclosure of a former employer's trade secrets."[123]

Reviewing Botticella's behavior, the court found that there was ample evidence to suggest that Botticella intended to disclose Bimbo's trade secrets. First, the positions at the two companies were very similar and seemed to entail similar duties. Thus, it was likely that Botticella would put his knowledge of a competitor's trade secrets to use. Second, there was circumstantial evidence, such as Botticella accessing Bimbo computer files, that suggested a high probability that he was planning on taking these secrets with him. If he did not plan on using them, what was the purpose of accessing the files so close to (and even after) his termination? Botticella's decision to not inform Bimbo that he had accepted the Hostess position was also highly suspect. Taken together, the appeals court upheld the district court's ruling and concluded that the lower court was justified in finding there to be a likelihood of success.

Interestingly, although the *Bimbo Bakeries* court cited to the *PepsiCo* decision, it did not apply the three-factor test from that case. Nevertheless, its analysis follows the test very closely. Did Botticella have "extensive and intimate knowledge" of Bimbo's business? Yes,

---

122 *Bimbo Bakeries*, 613 F.3d at 109.

123 Air Prods. & Chems., Inc. v. Johnson, 442 A.2d 1114, 1120 (Pa. Super. Ct. 1982).

Botticella had been exposed to business strategies as well as products. Were the old and new positions so similar that Botticella would have to rely on the trade secrets to adequately perform in the new position? It appears so—the court described the title and salary paid at both positions and agreed with the conclusion that "in his new position at Hostess, Botticella would have broad oversight over bakery operations, just as he had at Bimbo."[124] Finally, did Bimbo demonstrate a willingness on the part of Botticella to exploit the secrets, such as by a lack of candor by the former employee (or the new employer)? Yes, as Botticella was less than forthcoming with his acceptance of the new position. When he finally did tell Bimbo, he only revealed that he was leaving, not that he had accepted a position (three months earlier) at competitor Hostess. Beyond this, the suspicious timing of his access to computer files also supported the finding of a willingness to exploit the secrets.

A question that has arisen with regard to the inevitable disclosure doctrine is if an employee has trade secret information and is planning to work for a competitor in the same or similar capacity, is that enough to show a likelihood of disclosure? Courts appear to be split on this question. On the one hand, the *PepsiCo* standard requires some showing of the employee's willingness to exploit secrets.[125] On the other hand, some courts have granted relief without a showing of a willingness to exploit secrets when the defendant has intimate knowledge of the plaintiff's business.[126]

These latter cases appear to apply a slightly different standard than *PepsiCo*. They will consider granting relief even in the absence of a demonstration by the plaintiff of a willingness by the former employee to disclose, such as by lying to the former employer. Interestingly, these courts often seem to rely on strong language requiring a substantial threat or probability of disclosure, but they

---

124 *Bimbo Bakeries*, 613 F.3d at 117.

125 *See also* Les Concierges, Inc. v. Robeson, No. C–09–1510, 2009 WL 1138561, at *2 (N.D. Cal. 2009) ("At the outset, the Court finds [that] a threat of misappropriation cannot, as a matter of California law, be inferred from the fact [that] Robeson, upon voluntarily terminating his employment with LC US, immediately began working for a direct competitor and appears to be performing for his new employer the same or similar job duties he performed while employed by LC US."); Bayer Corp. v. Roche Molecular Sys., Inc., 72 F. Supp. 2d 1111, 1120 (N.D. Cal. 1999) ("A trade-secrets plaintiff must show an actual use or an actual threat."); FLIR Sys., Inc. v. Parrish, 95 Cal. Rptr. 3d 307, 316 (Ct. App. 2009) (stating that California law requires a plaintiff to show "a threat by a defendant to misuse trade secrets, manifested by words or conduct, where the evidence indicates imminent use").

126 *See, e.g.*, Proctor & Gamble Co. v. Stoneham, 747 N.E.2d 268, 279–80 (Ohio Ct. App. 2000) (finding a threat of inevitable disclosure when "an employee with detailed and comprehensive knowledge of an employer's trade secrets and confidential information has begun employment with a competitor of the former employer in a position that is substantially similar to the position held during the former employment").

then find the substantial threat to be met without a showing of misconduct when there is intimate knowledge of the plaintiff's business.[127]

California is an interesting jurisdiction with regards to the inevitable disclosure doctrine because it seems to contradict the California law forbidding covenants not to compete (except in limited statutory circumstances). Thus, it makes sense that California would choose to adopt a narrow construction of the UTSA's provision that actual or threatened misappropriation may be enjoined. Essentially, California will not equate intimate knowledge plus going to work in the same capacity for a competitor with "threatened."

This brings up an interesting point—if all that can be enjoined is "actual or threatened" misappropriation, why do any jurisdictions allow something less? An employee could certainly leave with trade secret knowledge to work for a competitor without ever doing or saying anything that could be construed as a threat. But if the employee eventually does use the knowledge, an injunction could be issued. The problem for the former employer is that the damage is done by this time.

Perhaps the best way of making sense of these various standards is to simply consider them as different ways of showing the appropriateness of an injunction under the factors set forth in § 44 of the Restatement (Third) of Unfair Competition. Viewed in this manner, the inevitable disclosure doctrine is really nothing more than a particular application of the factors.

### 2. Monetary Damages

Both the UTSA and the Third Restatement of Unfair Competition provide for the possibility of monetary damages regardless of whether an injunction is also ordered. In relevant part, § 3 of the UTSA states the following:

> Damages can include both the actual loss caused by misappropriation and the unjust enrichment caused by misappropriation that is not taken into account in computing actual loss. In lieu of damages measured by any other methods, the damages caused by misappropriation may be measured by imposition of liability for a reasonable royalty for a misappropriator's unauthorized disclosure or use of a trade secret.

---

[127] *But see* Lexis-Nexis v. Beer, 41 F. Supp. 2d 950, 959 (D. Minn. 1999) (denying injunctive relief, despite evidence that the employee lied about his new position, because the employee did not have intimate familiarity with corporate policies and strategies).

In essence, this statutory language provides for three categories of damages. The first is for compensatory damages based upon the owner's actual loss of the trade secret. The second is for unjust enrichment, which seeks to measure the advantage enjoyed by the defendant as a result of the misappropriation. The third is a provision for a reasonable royalty based upon the presumed market value of a license at the time of the misappropriation. The comments to UTSA § 3 provide that both compensatory and unjust enrichment damages may be available in the same case so long as there is no "double counting." Section 3 does not provide much guidance, however, as to when to award any particular category of damages.

Comment d to § 45 of the Third Restatement of Unfair Competition similarly recognizes the ability to recover compensatory damages and a reasonable royalty. It also identifies two other categories of damages, which may simply be different ways of measuring the unjust enrichment of the defendant. First, it provides for a measure of damages that awards the plaintiff the profits derived by the defendant from the misappropriation. Second, it allows the plaintiff to recover the savings enjoyed by the defendant that are attributable to the misappropriation.

The case of *University Computing Co. v. Lykes-Youngstown Corp.*[128] provides a very useful discussion of the types of available damages and when they may be appropriate. University Computing Company (UCC) entered into an agreement to form a joint corporation with Lykes-Youngstown Corporation (LYC) for the purpose of offering computer services. After taking some initial steps toward forming the new company, the relationship between the parties broke down. LYC formed a wholly owned subsidiary, LYCSC, and transferred property from the UCC/LYC venture to LYCSC without UCC's consent. Among the property transferred by LYC was a computer system called AIMES III. LYCSC then competed with UCC and unsuccessfully tried to market the system. The court found that LYC had misappropriated the AIMES III system, which qualified as a protected trade secret. The court then discussed possible measures of damages and their applicability.[129]

*Compensatory*—The court noted that awarding the actual damages suffered is one way to measure damages, but this is often hard to prove. In most cases, the defendant has utilized the secret to his advantage with no obvious effect on the plaintiff. A plaintiff might show actual damages through lost sales, but there can be causation

---

128 504 F.2d 518 (5th Cir. 1974).

129 The court's opinion pre-dates the UTSA but is nonetheless a very useful discussion of when to apply the various remedy measures and the problems associated with each one.

issues. Comment e to § 45 of the Third Restatement of Unfair Competition discusses some of these difficulties:

> The plaintiff may prove lost profits by identifying specific customers diverted to the defendant. The plaintiff may also prove lost profits through proof of a general decline in sales or a disruption of business growth following the commencement of use by the defendant, although the presence of other market factors that may affect the plaintiff's sales bears on the sufficiency of the plaintiff's proof. If the evidence justifies the conclusion that the sales made by the defendant would have instead been made by the plaintiff in the absence of the appropriation, the plaintiff may establish its lost profits by applying its own profit margin to the defendant's sales. Upon sufficient proof, the plaintiff may also recover lost profits on sales of spare parts, service, supplies, or other items normally purchased from the original seller.

The *University* court concluded that the actual damages remedy is most useful when the trade secret has been destroyed, such as by publication. However, this situation can also be problematic, as comment e to § 45 further discusses:

> Damages resulting from the unauthorized disclosure of a trade secret are frequently more difficult to measure than damages caused by unauthorized use. For example, in some cases a defendant's unauthorized disclosure to one competitor of the plaintiff may cause the trade secret to become known to other competitors or to enter the public domain, thus destroying the value of the secret. The appropriate measure of relief may then be the fair market value of the trade secret at the time of the appropriation. This measure can depend upon a variety of factors, including the likelihood that the trade secret would have become known in the absence of the defendant's appropriation. See Comment h. If the destroyed trade secret is a central asset of the plaintiff's business, the plaintiff can in some cases measure damages by the reduction in the capital value of the business caused by the appropriation.

*Value to the defendant (unjust enrichment)*—The court next discussed measuring damages based upon the trade secret's value to the defendant. The court stated that this measure is best used when the secret is still maintained but the plaintiff is having a difficult time demonstrating direct damages. The court then listed two ways that this measure could be calculated.

### *Defendant's Profits*

One way is to simply look at the profits the defendant reaped from the misappropriation. In the dispute before the *University* court, the problem with this approach was that there were no profits to measure. Although the court did not go any further with its analysis, it is worth considering how such profits should be measured. Should any accounting be made for the defendant's efforts in contributing to the profits? What if the misappropriated trade secret only makes up a small portion of a larger product or sale? Comment f to § 45 of the Third Restatement addresses these issues:

> The plaintiff is entitled to recover the defendant's net profits. The plaintiff has the burden of establishing the defendant's sales; the defendant has the burden of establishing any portion of the sales not attributable to the trade secret and any expenses to be deducted in determining net profits . . . . The defendant must account not only for profits earned on sales of products incorporating the trade secret, but also on other sales dependent on the appropriation. For example, profits on the sale of consumable supplies used in a machine embodying the trade secret or profits on spare parts and service may be included in the accounting to the extent that such profits were made possible by the defendant's sale of the original product.
>
> If the trade secret accounts for only a portion of the profits earned on the defendant's sales, such as when the trade secret relates to a single component of a product marketable without the secret, an award to the plaintiff of defendant's entire profit may be unjust. The royalty that the plaintiff and defendant would have agreed to for the use of the trade secret made by the defendant may be one measure of the approximate portion of the defendant's profits attributable to the use.

The *University* court determined that although the defendant did not profit, it should not escape liability. The court explained that to allow the defendant to misappropriate without paying damages would amount to letting the plaintiff bear the risk of the defendant's failure.

### *Defendant's Savings ("Standard of Comparison")*

Another way to measure value to the defendant is through the "standard of comparison" method. This method looks at how much the defendant saved in development costs, typically by looking at how much the plaintiff spent on the same endeavor. Comment f to § 45 of the Third Restatement explains:

> If the benefit derived by the defendant consists primarily of cost savings, such as when the trade secret is a more efficient method of production, the "standard of comparison" measure that determines relief based on the savings achieved through the use of the trade secret may be the most appropriate measure of relief. The standard of comparison measure determines the defendant's gain by comparing the defendant's actual costs with the costs that the defendant would have incurred to achieve the same result without the use of the appropriated trade secret. When it would have been possible for the defendant to acquire the trade secret by proper means such as reverse engineering or independent development, the appropriate comparison may be between the costs of such acquisition and the cost of using the appropriated information. In determining the costs of proper acquisition, the court may consider the actual development costs of the plaintiff and, if available, the development or reverse engineering costs of third persons. When acquisition of the trade secret by proper means is unlikely, the appropriate comparison may be between the costs of using the trade secret and the costs of alternative methods available to the defendant to achieve the same result.

The *University* court noted that this measure can often be inadequate because it fails to "take into account the commercial context in which the misappropriation occurred."[130] The court seems to mean that the standard of comparison measure does a poor job of compensating the plaintiff for difficult to prove (but real) damages caused by the defendant's competition in the same market. The court concluded that this measure is most appropriate when the use of the trade secret is limited and the two parties are not in direct competition.

*Reasonable royalty*—The *University* court appeared to think that this was the most appropriate measure of damages for the situation before it. According to the court, this method is most useful when the defendant has not profited from the misappropriation (or profits are difficult to apportion) and direct losses to the plaintiff are difficult to prove. Consider the following observations from comment g to § 45 of the Third Restatement:

> There are at least three situations in which the reasonable royalty measure of relief has been applied. First, when the defendant has made a substantial good faith investment in

130 *University Computing Co.*, 504 F.2d at 538.

> the trade secret prior to receiving notice of the plaintiff's claim, it may be inequitable to require the relinquishment of all profits earned by the defendant after notice. An award of damages measured by a reasonable royalty for use subsequent to the notice and an injunction conditioning future use on the payment of a reasonable royalty gives the plaintiff the market value of the trade secret but protects the defendant's good faith reliance. Second, when the plaintiff's loss, although difficult to measure, is apparently greater than any gain acquired by the defendant, a reasonable royalty may be the most appropriate measure of relief. For example, if the defendant's inefficiency results in little or no profit from the exploitation of the trade secret and the loss to the plaintiff cannot otherwise be established, a reasonable royalty may be the best available approximation of the plaintiff's loss. Third, in cases in which the defendant's gain from the trade secret is difficult to measure but apparently exceeds the plaintiff's loss, a reasonable royalty may be the best means of approximating the defendant's unjust enrichment.

Notice that the observations of the *University* court are consistent with the second situation mentioned in the above passage.

The reasonable royalty standard measures relief to the plaintiff by the price that would have been agreed upon between a willing buyer and a willing seller for use of the trade secret by the defendant. Although the *University* court did not discuss the weaknesses of this approach, the Third Restatement does mention the following: "Since the imposition of a reasonable royalty requires the defendant to pay only the amount it would have paid had it fairly bargained for use of the plaintiff's secret, it may not adequately discourage the appropriation of trade secrets."[131]

1. The *University* court considered five factors in its determination of a reasonable royalty: the resulting and foreseeable changes in the parties' competitive posture";

[131] The reasonable royalty standard as applied here is not the same as under UTSA § 3. The comments to the UTSA explain that § 3 is to address past misconduct while § 2 is for future use. UTSA § 3 Comment ("The reasonable royalty alternative measure of damages for a misappropriator's past conduct under Section 3(a) is readily distinguishable from a Section 2(b) royalty order injunction, which conditions a misappropriator's future ability to use a trade secret upon payment of a reasonable royalty. A Section 2(b) royalty order injunction is appropriate only in exceptional circumstances; whereas a reasonable royalty measure of damages is a general option. Because Section 3(a) damages are awarded for a misappropriator's past conduct and a Section 2(b) royalty order injunction regulates a misappropriator's future conduct, both remedies cannot be awarded for the same conduct.")

2. the prices past purchasers or licensees may have paid;
3. the total value of the secret to the plaintiff, including the plaintiff's development costs and the importance of the secret to the plaintiff's business
4. the nature and extent of the use the defendant intended for the secret";
5. and whatever other unique factors in the particular case which might have affected the parties' agreement, such as the ready availability of alternative processes.

Section 3 of the UTSA also has a provision for exemplary damages. The decision to award exemplary damages is left to the court (rather than the jury), and the amount of such damages is limited to twice the amount of any compensatory award. Exemplary damages under the UTSA require a showing of "willful and malicious misappropriation" by clear and convincing evidence. The DTSA has similar provisions.[132] In New York, which has not adopted the UTSA, punitive damages are permitted in similar circumstances.[133]

Finally, § 4 of the UTSA provides for attorney's fees under limited circumstances. It states that a court may award reasonable attorney's fees to the prevailing party if: "(i) a claim of misappropriation is made in bad faith; (ii) a motion to terminate an injunction is made or resisted in bad faith; or (iii) willful and malicious misappropriation exists." In jurisdictions that have not adopted the UTSA, a plaintiff wishing to recover attorney's fees would need to prevail on another cause of action that provides such fees (and avoids preemption).

## E. FEDERAL LAW AFFECTING TRADE SECRETS

Although trade secret law is primarily left to the states, there are a number of federal laws in the area. Two noteworthy federal statutes are the Computer Fraud and Abuse Act (CFAA) and the Economic Espionage Act of 1996 (EEA).

The CFAA was passed in 1984 and was intended to protect classified financial and credit information on government and financial institution computers. Although it was a criminal statute

---

[132] *See* 18 U.S.C. § 1836(3)(c).

[133] *See, e.g.*, Huschle v. Battelle, 308 N.Y.S.2d 235, 236 (App. Div. 1970) (permitting punitive damages where the misconduct is accompanied by "malice, insult, reckless and willful disregard of the plaintiff's rights, or other proof showing the aggravated nature of the act"); RESTATEMENT (SECOND) OF TORTS § 908 (1977) ("Punitive damages may be awarded for conduct that is outrageous, because of the defendant's evil motive or his reckless indifference to the rights of others.").

initially, it was amended in 1994 to include civil remedies. The three most relevant provisions of the CFAA with respect to trade secret misappropriation are 18 U.S.C. § 1030(a)(2)(C), (a)(4), and (a)(5)(C).

Under § 1030(a)(2)(C), "[w]hoever . . . intentionally accesses a computer without authorization or exceeds authorized access, and thereby obtains . . . information from any protected computer if the conduct involved an interstate or foreign communication . . . shall be punished" as provided in the statute. In addition, § 1030(g) provides that "[a]ny person who suffers damage or loss by reason of a violation of this section may maintain a civil action against the violator to obtain compensatory damages and injunctive relief or other equitable relief." A "protected computer" means a computer "which is used in interstate or foreign commerce or communication."[134] The term "exceeds authorized access" means "to access a computer with authorization and to use such access to obtain or alter information in the computer that the accesser is not entitled so to obtain or alter."[135]

A person violates § 1030(a)(4) if he or she:

> knowingly and with intent to defraud, accesses a protected computer without authorization, or exceeds authorized access, and by means of such conduct furthers the intended fraud and obtains anything of value, unless the object of the fraud and the thing obtained consists only of the use of the computer and the value of such use is not more than $5,000 in any 1-year period . . . .

The primary difference between this section and § 1030(a)(2)(C) is that § 1030(a)(4) requires an intent to defraud. Moreover, courts have indicated that the use of "fraud" in § 1030(a)(4) "simply means wrongdoing and not proof of the common law elements of fraud."[136]

Under § 1030(a)(5)(C), "[w]hoever . . . intentionally accesses a protected computer without authorization, and as a result of such conduct, causes damage" violates the CFAA. This provision requires the plaintiff to allege that "damage" occurred. Section 1030(e)(8) indicates that damage "means any impairment to the integrity or availability of data, a program, a system, or information." Allegations that the defendant infiltrated the plaintiff's computer network and collected and disseminated confidential information have been held to be enough to constitute damage under the statute.[137]

---

134 18 U.S.C. § 1030(e)(2)(B).

135 *Id.* § 1030(e)(6).

136 Shurgard Storage Centers, Inc. v. Safeguard Self Storage, Inc., 119 F. Supp. 2d 1121, 1126 (W.D. Wash. 2000).

137 *See id.* at 1126–27.

Taken together, these CFAA provisions can serve as powerful weapons for employers to use against former employees who access computers without authorization. Importantly, CFAA claims do not require proof of a trade secret, but they do require proof of computer access. Given the amount of work that is done on computers, this requirement is typically not difficult to satisfy.

The EEA criminalizes trade secret misappropriation to combat espionage against private entities and threats to corporate security. The relevant portions of the Act make it a crime to knowingly convert a trade secret placed in interstate commerce. At one time, the statute was limited to trade secrets that related to (or were included in) tangible products, but this limitation has been removed by the Theft of Trade Secrets Clarification Act of 2012. The EEA's definition of trade secrets mirrors the UTSA's, but its definition of misappropriation does not:

> **§ 1832. Theft of trade secrets**
>
> (a) Whoever, with intent to convert a trade secret, that is related to a product or service used in or intended for use in interstate or foreign commerce, to the economic benefit of anyone other than the owner thereof, and intending or knowing that the offense will, injure any owner of that trade secret, knowingly—
>
> > (1) steals, or without authorization appropriates, takes, carries away, or conceals, or by fraud, artifice, or deception obtains such information;
> >
> > (2) without authorization copies, duplicates, sketches, draws, photographs, downloads, uploads, alters, destroys, photocopies, replicates, transmits, delivers, sends, mails, communicates, or conveys such information;
> >
> > (3) receives, buys, or possesses such information, knowing the same to have been stolen or appropriated, obtained, or converted without authorization. . . .

The EEA is striking in that its definition of misappropriation, particularly under (2), is much broader than the UTSA's definition. Subsection (2) appears to prohibit reverse engineering given that such processes frequently involve copying, duplicating, or sketching the information.[138] This is especially troubling when the potential penalties are considered. Although the EEA provides no civil remedy, an individual convicted of theft of a trade secret faces a maximum sentence of up to fifteen years in prison and a fine of up to $5,000,000

138 *See* James H.A. Pooley et al., *Understanding the Economic Espionage Act of 1996*, 5 TEX. INTELLECTUAL PROP. L.J. 177, 195 (1997).

for foreign espionage. For domestic theft, the penalty is up to ten years' imprisonment and a fine.[139] Corporations are subject to fines of up to $10,000,000 or three times the value of the stolen trade secret to the organization (whichever is greater) for foreign theft, and up to $5,000,000 for domestic theft.[140]

139 *See* 18 U.S.C. §§ 1831(a), 1832(a).

140 *Id.* §§ 1831(b), 1832(b).

# Chapter 10

# TRADEMARK INFRINGEMENT

## A. INTRODUCTION TO TRADEMARK LAW

Trademark law is concerned with the protection of goodwill established by a provider of goods or services. In this regard, trademark continues the theme developed in the previous two chapters—namely, it is not fair to let others reap where they have not sown. Trademark law also serves another purpose that relates to a theme discussed in the deceptive marketing chapter—preventing consumer confusion or deception. In that chapter, one of the concepts discussed was the deceptive practice of "passing off," such as by substituting a seller's product for the requested item. If a customer asks for Coca-Cola and the restaurant instead serves its own house brand of soda without telling the consumer, it has passed-off its soda as Coca-Cola. This not only harms Coca-Cola, in that the restaurant is profiting from Coca-Cola's good name, but it also deceives the consumer. As previously explored, this conduct is prohibited under state unfair competition law as well as the Lanham Act. The dual purposes of trademark and its relation to unfair competition law were aptly summarized as follows: "The law of unfair competition has traditionally been a battleground for competing policies. The interest of the public in not being deceived has been called the basic policy. Moreover, the plaintiff's interest in not having the fruit of his labor misappropriated should not be disregarded. But there is also the policy of encouraging competition from which the public benefits."[1]

In this chapter, these concepts will be further discussed as they relate to a business's trademarks. First, the requirements for trademark protection are explored, both under the Lanham Act and at common law (it should come as no surprise that not every word or symbol used by a business is protected). Second, the various types of marks, how marks are infringed, and the commonly raised defenses for trademark infringement are examined. Finally, the chapter concludes with a discussion of remedies.

## B. REQUIREMENTS FOR PROTECTION

Trademark protection was recognized under state common law long before the federal government stepped in. In the late 1800s, however, the first federal act governing trademark protection was

---

1 Zippo Mfg. Co. v. Rogers Imports, Inc., 216 F. Supp. 670, 694 (S.D.N.Y. 1963).

passed, and federal law in this area has expanded ever since. Today, the Lanham Act is the primary source of federal trademark law, but it has not displaced state common law; indeed, trademark rights can exist under both federal and state law.

The Lanham Act defines a trademark as:

> any word, name, symbol, or device, or any combination thereof
>
> (1) used by a person, or
>
> (2) which a person has a bona fide intention to use in commerce and applies to register on the principal register established by this chapter,
>
> to identify and distinguish his or her goods, including a unique product, from those manufactured or sold by others and to indicate the source of the goods, even if that source is unknown.[2]

To put this more succinctly, a trademark is a word or symbol used to identify a particular manufacturer's or seller's products and to distinguish them from the products of others. From this definition, two primary elements have been developed: (1) the mark must be either used in commerce (or there is a bona fide intention to do so); and (2) the mark must be distinctive. At one time, it was a prerequisite that the mark be used in commerce before protection could be obtained. The Lanham Act was amended, however, to provide that "intention to use" was sufficient to allow a party to obtain temporary preemptive rights to a mark that it intended in good faith to use in commerce.[3] Such a party must file a statement of use of the mark within six months of the issuance of a notice of allowance by the U.S. Patent and Trademark Office (PTO).

While the use requirement can raise issues, particularly for unregistered trademarks, the distinctiveness requirement has received much more attention from the courts. The famous Second Circuit case of *Abercrombie & Fitch Co. v. Hunting World, Inc.*,[4] established a spectrum of classifications for distinctiveness. Citing to *Abercrombie & Fitch*, many courts divide the distinctiveness requirement into one of four categories: (1) generic, (2) descriptive, (3) suggestive, or (4) arbitrary or fanciful. The court in *Zatarains, Inc.*

---

[2] 15 U.S.C. § 1127. The Restatement uses a similar definition: "A trademark is a word, name, symbol, device, or other designation, or a combination of such designations, that is distinctive of a person's goods or services and that is used in a manner that identifies those goods or services and distinguishes them from the goods or services of others." RESTATEMENT (THIRD) OF UNFAIR COMPETITION § 9 (1995).

[3] *See* 15 U.S.C. § 1051(b).

[4] 537 F.2d 4 (2d Cir. 1976).

*v. Oak Grove Smokehouse, Inc.*[5] aptly summarized each classification:

> A generic term is "the name of a particular genus or class of which an individual article or service is but a member." A generic term connotes the "basic nature of articles or services" rather than the more individualized characteristics of a particular product. Generic terms can never attain trademark protection. Furthermore, if at any time a registered trademark becomes generic as to a particular product or service, the mark's registration is subject to cancellation. Such terms as aspirin and cellophane have been held generic and therefore unprotectable as trademarks.
>
> A descriptive term identifies a characteristic or quality of an article or service, such as its color, odor, function, dimensions, or ingredients. Descriptive terms ordinarily are not protectable as trademarks; they may become valid marks, however, by acquiring a secondary meaning in the minds of the consuming public. Examples of descriptive marks would include "Alo" with reference to products containing gel of the aloe vera plant, and "Vision Center" in reference to a business offering optical goods and services. As this court has often noted, the distinction between descriptive and generic terms is one of degree. The distinction has important practical consequences, however; while a descriptive term may be elevated to trademark status with proof of secondary meaning, a generic term may never achieve trademark protection.
>
> A suggestive term suggests, rather than describes, some particular characteristic of the goods or services to which it applies and requires the consumer to exercise the imagination in order to draw a conclusion as to the nature of the goods and services. A suggestive mark is protected without the necessity for proof of secondary meaning. The term "Coppertone" has been held suggestive in regard to sun tanning products.
>
> Arbitrary or fanciful terms bear no relationship to the products or services to which they are applied. Like suggestive terms, arbitrary and fanciful marks are protectable without proof of secondary meaning. The term "Kodak" is properly classified as a fanciful term for

---

5 698 F.2d 786 (5th Cir. 1983).

> photographic supplies; "Ivory" is an arbitrary term as applied to soap.[6]

These designations can also be found in the Restatement (Third) of Unfair Competition. Section 15 of the Restatement addresses the generic category:

> A designation that is understood by prospective purchasers to denominate the general category, type, or class of the goods, services, or business with which it is used is a generic designation. A user cannot acquire rights in a generic designation as a trademark, trade name, collective mark, or certification mark.

Section 13(a) and (b) of the Restatement state:

> A word, name, symbol, device, or other designation, or a combination of such designations, is "distinctive" under the rules stated in §§ 9–12 if:
>
> (a) the designation is "inherently distinctive," in that, because of the nature of the designation and the context in which it is used, prospective purchasers are likely to perceive it as a designation that, in the case of a trademark, identifies goods or services produced or sponsored by a particular person, whether known or anonymous, or in the case of a trade name, identifies the business or other enterprise of a particular person, whether known or anonymous, or in the case of a collective mark, identifies members of the collective group or goods or services produced or sponsored by members, or in the case of a certification mark, identifies the certified goods or services; or
>
> (b) the designation, although not "inherently distinctive," has become distinctive, in that, as a result of its use, prospective purchasers have come to perceive it as a designation that identifies goods, services, businesses, or members in the manner described in Subsection (a). Such acquired distinctiveness is commonly referred to as "secondary meaning."

Although the terms descriptive, suggestive, arbitrary and fanciful don't appear in the Restatement, the concepts are part of the inherently distinctive language. Comments b and c specifically refer to fanciful, arbitrary, and suggestive terms, noting that they are inherently distinctive. Comment e then goes on to address "descriptive" marks and the role that secondary meaning plays in

---

6 *Id.* at 790–91 (internal citations omitted).

establishing protection. Section 14 of the Restatement also defines the descriptive category:

> A designation that is likely to be perceived by prospective purchasers as merely descriptive of the nature, qualities, or other characteristics of the goods, services, or business with which it is used, or as merely geographically descriptive of their origin or location, or as the personal name of a person connected with the goods, services, or business, is not inherently distinctive under the rule stated in § 13(a). Such a designation is distinctive only if it has acquired secondary meaning under the rule stated in § 13(b).

In *Abercrombie & Fitch*, Abercrombie attempted to trademark the use of "Safari Hat" and "Safari Boots" and enforce those marks against Hunter's World. After laying out the distinctiveness spectrum, the court engaged in the task of determining whether "Safari" was generic or descriptive. Turning to the definition of the word, the court concluded that the term was generic with regard to hats (as well as jackets and suits). The court also pointed to the wide use of the term by the general public and trade in association with such items. However, the court concluded that with regard to boots, there was a dearth of use of the term "safari" outside of the use by Abercrombie and Hunter's World. The court therefore concluded that the term was descriptive and could be protected if there existed secondary meaning.[7]

Often it is difficult to discern between generic and descriptive terms and descriptive and suggestive terms. Although the court in *Abercrombie & Fitch* looked to the definition of the word, this is but one test to help resolve the issue. In *Zatarains*, the court identified four tests to help resolve the issue before it. Zatarains was the manufacturer and distributor of a line of food products including "Fish-Fri" and "Chick-Fri," which are batter mixes used to fry foods. "Fish-Fri" was packaged as "Wonderful FISH-FRI ®" (Chick-Fri was similarly packaged with "Wonderful CHICK-FRI" displayed on the front panel). Both had been federally registered as trademarks.

Defendants Oak Grove and Visko marketed batter mixes for fried foods that are denominated "fish fry" or "chicken fry." Zatarains' original complaint alleged trademark infringement and unfair competition under the Lanham Act and Louisiana state law. With respect to the alleged infringement of the term "Fish-Fri," the trial court classified it as a descriptive term which identified a function of the product being sold, while also acquiring a secondary meaning in the New Orleans geographical area. Thus, it was entitled to

---

7 *See Abercrombie*, 537 F.2d at 5, 11–13.

trademark protection. With respect to the alleged term "Chick-Fri," the trial court classified it as a descriptive term that had not acquired a secondary meaning. Consequently, Zatarains' claim for infringement of its trademark "Chick-Fri" failed and the court further ordered that Zatarains' trademark registration be cancelled.

On appeal, the court had to decide whether Zatarains' trademarks "Fish-Fri" and "Chick-Fri" were descriptive marks that had acquired secondary meaning rather than suggestive marks (and therefore not subject to the "fair use" defense). The court noted that often the lines delineating the categories are fuzzy, but it identified four commonly used tests to assist courts. Under each test, the court found that both terms were descriptive.

- **The dictionary definition of the word:** This is an appropriate and relevant indication of the ordinary significance and meaning of words to the public. In the case before it, the court noted that the term referred to the preparation and consumption of fried fish. This was at least preliminary evidence that the term "Fish-Fri" was descriptive of Zatarain's product in the sense that the words naturally direct attention to the purpose or function of the product.
- **The "imagination test":** This test seeks to measure the relationship between the actual words of the mark and the product to which they are applied. If a term requires imagination, thought, and perception to reach a conclusion as to the nature of the goods, it is considered a suggestive term. The court determined that a product labeled "Fish-Fri" compels the conclusion that the mix is to be applied to fish prior to cooking. Even a consumer unfamiliar with the product would have an idea of its purpose or function. It does not require an exercise of the imagination to deduce that "Fish-Fri" is used to fry fish. Thus, under this test, "Fish-Fri" was a descriptive term.
- **Whether competitors would likely need the terms used in the trademark to describe their products:** A descriptive term generally relates so closely and directly to a product or service that other merchants marketing similar goods would find the term useful in identifying their own goods. The court found that merchants other than Zatarains might find the term "fish-fry" to be useful in describing their own particular batter mixes.

- **The extent to which a descriptive term has been used by others marketing a similar service or product:** The court noted that a number of companies other than Zatarains had chosen the term "fish fry" to identify their batter mixes.

The court therefore affirmed the trial court and found that both terms were descriptive and capable of protection if secondary meaning was established.[8]

It is important to note that courts use these tests not just to help designate the marks as descriptive, but also to eliminate the marks from the categories of generic or suggestive. The definition test (and perhaps also the competitor need test) is particularly useful in helping to determine if a term is generic. Comment a to § 15 of the Restatement states that a generic term is one "that denominates a general type or class of goods, services, or business." It goes on to list terms like "bank" and "diet" (with regard to soda) as generic terms. In *Zatarains*, a decent argument could be made that the marks at issue were generic, but it seems that because the definition referred to what the product did, the court was willing to lift it above the generic label. Perhaps this elevation is based on no more than describing an act rather than a product, i.e., what a product does versus what it is. One commentator echoes this approach:

> Making the distinction between descriptive terms and generic names has proven to be a challenge for the courts. Results are hard to reconcile. The generic-descriptive line is too often smudged by the courts and the USPTO. Conceptually, a descriptive term is usually an adjective that describes a thing, while a generic term names the thing. But in applying this to actual words, one quickly realizes that at the margin, there is sometimes only a fine line between a highly descriptive designation and a generic name.
>
> Some courts and the USPTO have even said that some highly descriptive adjectives can be characterized as "generic adjectives" and put into the "generic" category. This kind of classification seems to be the result of a policy choice to ensure that a highly descriptive term can never achieve trademark status.[9]

The second test (the imagination test) is particularly relevant to seeing if the term is going to qualify as suggestive rather than just descriptive. Comment c to § 13 of the Restatement appears to refer

---

8 *See Zatarains*, 698 F.2d at 792–93.

9 2 McCarthy on Trademarks and Unfair Competition § 12:20 (5th ed. 2024).

to this as does comment b to § 14. The last two tests (competitor need and use by others) similarly help to determine whether the term at issue is descriptive rather than suggestive. If a term is needed by others to describe their own products, then this is not merely a suggestive term and protection might inhibit competition. This last test similarly helps to determine the necessity of others to use the term and how the public perceives the term.

As mentioned, the designation of a mark as descriptive does not end the analysis because the party holding the mark must also establish that the mark has acquired secondary meaning for the consuming public.[10] In *Zatarains*, the court noted that secondary meaning recognizes that words with an ordinary and primary meaning of their own may, by long use with a particular product, come to be known by the public as specifically designating that product. To establish a secondary meaning for a term, a plaintiff must show that the primary significance of the term in the minds of consumers is not the product itself, but is instead the producer. This is commonly established through surveys and expert testimony. Indeed, this was how Zatarain's established secondary meaning, but only with regard to Fish-Fri.[11] The Restatement of Unfair Competition supports the use of surveys, as it notes that secondary meaning can be established by direct or indirect evidence. Surveys, however, must be "properly formulated and conducted." Further, the Restatement indicates that testimony from consumers is relevant but only if a representative sample is used.[12]

## C. COMMON LAW MARKS AND FEDERAL REGISTRATION

To register a mark, an application must first be made to the PTO.[13] The bases for filing can be on the actual use of the mark in commerce, intent-to-use, or on foreign registration. After the mark has been registered, the applicant negotiates with an examiner at the PTO. Although it is not an adversarial proceeding, the examiner may have questions about the mark that need to be resolved prior to moving on to the next step. If an applicant obtains registration through fraud, the registration may later be subject to cancellation. If the PTO determines that the mark is entitled to registration, it is

---

10 As will be discussed below, even when secondary meaning is established, the mark may be subject to a "fair use" defense.

11 The court found that the survey evidence presented with regard to Chick-Fri was not properly designed to test the secondary meaning of the term. *See Zatarains*, 698 F.2d at 797.

12 *See* RESTATEMENT (THIRD) OF UNFAIR COMPETITION § 13 cmt. e (1995).

13 The PTO explains the process for registering a mark at https://www.uspto.gov/trademarks/basics/trademark-process#step2.

published in the Official Gazette of the PTO and interested parties may file an opposition within thirty days of the publication. An interested party is one who believes that it would be damaged by the registration. Opposition proceedings are held before the Trademark Trial and Appeal Board (TTAB). Once the thirty-day window has passed (or oppositions have been resolved), the mark is registered in the Principal Register and is entitled to use the ® ("R-in-circle") trademark notice in connection with the registered mark.

Registration lasts ten years and may be renewed by the registrant filing a renewal application and an affidavit attesting to the continued use of the mark in connection with the goods or services.

### 1. Advantages of Registration

Once a mark has been used in interstate commerce and is distinctive, it is eligible for trademark protection under both the Lanham Act and the common law.[14] Under the Lanham Act, trademark holders may also register trademarks in the Principal Register[15] with the PTO. As mentioned, unless a trademark is used in interstate commerce, it is ineligible to be registered.[16]

Given that protection exists regardless of registration, why bother registering a trademark? In short, registration offers a number of advantages, including the giving of constructive notice to other parties that the trademark is owned by the registrant. This is important as it eliminates a defense that a subsequent user might raise—namely, that the user had adopted a mark in its geographic area in good faith and with lack of knowledge of the mark. By eliminating this defense of good faith and lack of knowledge, registration provides nationwide protection for marks regardless of the geographic area in which the registrant actually uses the mark.

Other advantages of registration include:

- The Trademark Revision Act of 1988 changed the system from one based on use in commerce to a dual

[14] *See* Lanham Act § 43(a) (15 U.S.C. § 1125(a)); RESTATEMENT (THIRD) OF UNFAIR COMPETITION § 9 (1995).

[15] A Supplemental Register also exists for marks that are not yet eligible for protection but that are capable of distinguishing the applicant's goods or services. This is sometimes used as an interim form of registration for marks that may eventually develop secondary meaning. Registration in the Supplemental Register does not confer the benefits of registration in the Principal Register, but it does allow U.S. applicants to satisfy certain home registration requirements that are necessary to obtain protection in some foreign trademark systems.

[16] Even if ineligible to register under the Lanham Act, every state has enacted legislation providing for the registration and protection of trademarks. Many of these state registration systems are based upon the Model State Trademark Bill. *See* RESTATEMENT (THIRD) OF UNFAIR COMPETITION § 9 (1995) (Statutory Note).

system based on use or bona fide "intent-to-use." This allows one to register before the mark is actually used in commerce, which provides the advantage of an earlier priority date.

- After a registered mark has been in continuous use for 5 consecutive years, the registrant's right to use the mark in commerce shall be uncontestable subject to certain exceptions, such as abandonment, fraudulent registration, or where the mark becomes the common generic name of the good or service.
- The certificate of registration constitutes prima facie evidence of the validity of the registration, the registrant's ownership of the mark, and the registrant's exclusive right to use the registered mark in commerce with respect to the goods or services described in the certificate.
- Registration confers the ability to bring an action concerning the mark in federal court.
- A federal registration in the United States facilitates registration in some foreign countries.
- Registration may deter others from adopting the mark when they discover it in conducting a "right to use" search. This will avoid confrontation and legal expense at a later time.

## 2. Marks Precluded from Registration

Not all marks are eligible for registration. The PTO or a private party may raise substantive challenges to the registration of a mark under § 2(a)–(f) of the Lanham Act.[17] Some of these subsections simply incorporate common law concepts such as distinctiveness and likelihood of confusion. Others represent public policy restrictions, such as § 2(b), which forbids the use of a mark that "comprises the flag or coat of arms or other insignia of the United States, or of any State or municipality, or of any foreign nation, or any simulation thereof." Section 2(c) forbids the use of a person's name or likeness without the person's written consent.

One of the more interesting restrictions is found in § 2(a), which allows the PTO to deny registration for a mark that "[c]onsists of or comprises immoral, deceptive, or scandalous matter; or matter which may disparage or falsely suggest a connection with persons, living or dead, institutions, beliefs, or national symbols, or bring them into

[17] *See* 15 U.S.C. § 1052.

contempt, or disrepute." This provision can be broken down into at least three different types of restrictions—a deceptive restriction, a scandalous restriction, and a disparaging restriction.

With respect to the deceptive restriction, the Federal Circuit in *In re Budge Manufacturing Co.*[18] has articulated a three-part test for analyzing whether a mark is deceptive:

> (1) Is the term misdescriptive of the character, quality, function, composition or use of the goods?
>
> (2) If so, are prospective purchasers likely to believe that the misdescription actually describes the goods?
>
> (3) If so, is the misdescription likely to affect the decision to purchase?[19]

(Note that, much like the materials covered in the deceptive marketing chapter, the focus of this test is the effect upon consumers. Scienter is not required.) In *Budge*, the court upheld the rejection of the mark LOVEE LAMB for automotive seat covers, as the covers were made wholly from synthetic materials. Under the three-part test, the court found that LAMB was misdescriptive and that "purchasers [were] likely to believe automobile seat covers denominated by the term LAMB or SHEEP [were] actually made from natural sheep or lamb skins."[20]

The scandalous and disparaging restrictions have long been associated with inconsistent decisions by the PTO. Many times, these decisions reflect the ever-changing attitudes about what is considered scandalous and disparaging. The PTO's ability to bar such trademarks had long-been assumed to be within its power until the U.S. Supreme Court case of *Matal v. Tam*.[21] *Tam* involved the attempted registration of a band named "the Slants"—an Asian-American dance-rock band that wished to "reclaim" the derogatory term and thus remove its denigrating force. The PTO declined the application based on the disparagement clause. On appeal, the Federal Circuit overturned the PTO and the case went to the Supreme Court. Although the rationale of the Justices differed somewhat,[22] all members of the Supreme Court agreed that the PTO's actions denying the registration amounted to unconstitutional viewpoint discrimination.

---

[18] 857 F.2d 773 (Fed. Cir. 1988).

[19] *Id.* at 775.

[20] *Id.* at 776.

[21] 582 U.S. 218 (2017).

[22] The Justices split on whether a Lanham Act bar is a condition on a government benefit or a simple restriction on speech.

The invalidation of the disparagement clause left open the question of whether the scandalous clause would meet a similar fate. Two years later, the Supreme Court addressed the issue in *Iancu v. Brunetti*.[23] Erik Brunetti founded a clothing line that used the trademark FUCT. According to Brunetti, the mark (which functions as the clothing's brand name) is pronounced as four letters, one after the other: F-U-C-T. Obviously this could phonetically be pronounced as a common curse word and so the trademark triggered extra scrutiny. The trademark specifically ran afoul of § 1052(a) of the Lanham Act, which prohibits registration for marks that "[c]onsist[ ] of or comprise[ ] immoral[ ] or scandalous matter." The PTO views these not as separate grounds but as a unitary provision. To determine whether a mark fits in the category, the PTO asks whether a "substantial composite of the general public" would find the mark "shocking to the sense of truth, decency, or propriety"; "giving offense to the conscience or moral feelings"; "calling out for condemnation"; "disgraceful"; "offensive"; "disreputable"; or "vulgar."[24] Under this standard, both a PTO examining attorney and the PTO's Trademark Trial and Appeal Board decided that Brunetti's mark flunked the test. On appeal, as in *Tam,* the Federal Circuit found the prohibition to violate the First Amendment and the case was taken to the Supreme Court.

The Supreme Court began it analysis by summarizing the *Tam* case. The Court noted that although there was a 4–4 split in the *Tam* decision, all of the Justices "found common ground in a core postulate of free speech law: The government may not discriminate against speech based on the ideas or opinions it conveys."[25] In reviewing the immoral and scandalous bar, the Court first adopted the same unitary approach as the PTO, reading immoral or scandalous together. It then turned to a number of dictionary definitions of "immoral" and "scandalous" and concluded that the Lanham Act allowed registration of marks when their messages accorded with (but not when their messages defied) society's sense of decency or propriety. The provision therefore was viewpoint discriminatory in its application and was therefore unconstitutional. To demonstrate its point, the Court recounted a number of examples in which the bar amounted to viewpoint discrimination.

The government appeared to acknowledge that it could be viewed as such, but claimed that the examples given by the Court in which the PTO denied applications due to viewpoint discrimination were mistakes, and it urged that "the statute is 'susceptible of' a

23 588 U.S. 388 (2019).

24 *Id.* at 391.

25 *Id.* at 393.

limiting construction that would remove this viewpoint bias." Essentially, the government asked the Court to narrow the statutory bar to "marks that are offensive [or] shocking to a substantial segment of the public because of their mode of expression, independent of any views that they may express." The government urged that this reinterpretation would mostly restrict the PTO to "refusing marks that are 'vulgar'—meaning 'lewd,' 'sexually explicit or profane,' " and therefore would not turn on viewpoint.[26]

The majority of the Court rejected the government's interpretation and found it to be at odds with the language of the statute itself:

> The "immoral or scandalous" bar stretches far beyond the Government's proposed construction. The statute as written does not draw the line at lewd, sexually explicit, or profane marks. Nor does it refer only to marks whose "mode of expression," independent of viewpoint, is particularly offensive. It covers the universe of immoral or scandalous—or (to use some PTO synonyms) offensive or disreputable—material. Whether or not lewd or profane. Whether the scandal and immorality comes from mode or instead from viewpoint. To cut the statute off where the Government urges is not to interpret the statute Congress enacted, but to fashion a new one.[27]

Writing for the dissent, Justice Sotomayor argued that the term scandalous is capable of a more limited interpretation. Sotomayor found that the term could be read broadly to include the majority's interpretation, or more narrowly to include only obscene, vulgar, or profane marks—which would be a viewpoint-neutral interpretation. Given this ambiguity, Sotomayor found it more appropriate to apply a narrow interpretation to avoid invalidating the clause. In a footnote, she further articulated the impact that the majority holding would have:

> There is at least one particularly egregious racial epithet that would fit this description as well. While *Matal v. Tam*, 582 U. S. ___, 137 S.Ct. 1744, 198 L.Ed.2d 366 (2017), removed a statutory basis to deny the registration of racial epithets in general, the Government represented at oral argument that it is holding in abeyance trademark applications that use that particular epithet. As a result of today's ruling, the Government will now presumably be compelled to register marks containing that epithet as well

---

[26] *Id.* at 397.

[27] *Id.*

> rather than treating it as a "scandalous" form of profanity under § 1052(a).[28]

Of course, Sotomayor's concerns are not just about that particular epithet, but about opening the door to a wide range of similarly repulsive language that may have minimal (if any) value beyond to shock or offend.

In the aftermath of *Tam* and *Brunetti*, scholars have also expressed concerns that these decisions have opened the door to racist and misogynist marks.[29] Others have offered interpretive solutions to address the problem. For instance, Professor R. Randall Kelso has advocated that tolerance of differing viewpoints should not include tolerance of intolerant viewpoints. He concludes that "[v]iewpoint discrimination law should take this insight into account when resolving the problematic reasoning of the viewpoint discrimination cases of the last four decades."[30] Professor Yvette Joy Liebesman has argued that although registration may trigger First Amendment protections for mark owners, the same should not hold true for government enforcement of infringement of the mark.[31] She notes that *Tam* and *Brunetti* did not address enforcement rights of a mark, arguing that "[t]hrough enforcement, the government is actively condoning this speech beyond the amorphous and challenging constitutional gray area of being government-sponsored or government-subsidized speech; instead, it can be characterized as government speech. . . . The upshot is that offensive, vulgar, and scandalous marks could be denied enforcement because enforcing them through these government actions would constitute government speech, and any First Amendment protections on which these marks received registration would not be applicable."[32]

## D. TYPES OF MARKS

Thus far, the chapter has primarily discussed marks that are written words associated with products. However, marks can also be verbal or image-based (the Nike "swoosh," for example, or the use of the color orange by Home Depot), and they can describe entire

---

[28] *Id.* at 415 n.5 (Sotomayor, J., concurring in part and dissenting in part).

[29] *See* Ilhyung Lee, Tam *Through the Lens of* Brunetti*: The Slants, Fuct*, 69 EMORY L.J. ONLINE 2001, *2001–05 (2019) (questioning whether "there is now a constitutional right to register a racial epithet as a trademark"); Ann Bartow, *Are you There, Trademark Law? It's Me, Misogyny*, 41 COLUM. J. GENDER & L. 11, 11–12, 23–26 (2021) ("But one consequence of these holdings is that unambiguous hate speech can now become a federally registered trademark . . .").

[30] R. Randall Kelso, *Substantive Toleration and Viewpoint Discrimination*, 61 S. TEX. L. REV. 97, 101 (2021).

[31] Yvette Joy Liebesman, *Offensive Mark Owners Have an Enforcement Problem*, 59 HOUS. L. REV. 57, 65–69 (2021).

[32] *Id.* at 65–67.

businesses or services. Although the distinctiveness spectrum may apply to such marks, the spectrum is a poor fit in some instances. As a result, courts have developed alternative means for determining which marks are entitled to protection. The various types of marks are discussed below.

### 1. Service Marks and Trade Names

A service mark is simply a trademark that is used in connection with services rather than goods. It qualifies for protection in the same way as a trademark for goods. As the Restatement of Unfair Competition explains:

> The Lanham Act . . . limit[s] the term "trademark" to marks used to identify the source of goods. A mark used to identify the source of services is denominated a "service mark." The substantive rules applicable to both types of marks are fundamentally identical, however, and the term "trademark" is generally understood to include marks used in the marketing of either goods or services. The definitions in this Section adopt this convenient usage. The term "service mark" as defined here thus denotes a specific type of trademark.[33]

A trade name, on the other hand, can sometimes cause confusion with a trademark. A trade name is simply a name used by a business that is not its legal name. A business may have a trade name and may register that name (called a "doing business as" (d/b/a) designation). However, this trade name registration is not the same as a trademark registration. While the same word or phrase may be used as a trade name and a trademark, the word or phrase only qualifies for trademark protection if it qualifies under the trademark standards (i.e., it must meet the use and distinctiveness requirements).

### 2. Trade Dress

Marks can be more than just words. Many marks take the form of the shape or appearance of the product or may even reflect the way the product is designed. Such marks are designated as "trade dress." Trade dress is an important protection that is consistent with the overall purpose of trademark law to protect symbols that are used to associate goods and services with particular merchants. Historically, trade dress occupied a separate sphere from trademark, being protected under the general common law action of unfair competition. However, both the common law and the Lanham Act now recognize trade dress as protectable if distinctive and non-functional. Comment

---

[33] RESTATEMENT (THIRD) OF UNFAIR COMPETITION § 9 cmt. f (1995).

a to § 16 of the Restatement of Unfair Competition defines the concept:

> The term "trade dress" is often used to describe the overall appearance or image of goods or services as offered for sale in the marketplace. "Trade dress" traditionally includes the appearance of labels, wrappers, and containers used in packaging a product as well as displays and other materials used in presenting the product to prospective purchasers.

Section 16 provides that trade dress qualifies for protection if it is distinctive and non-functional. Both of these requirements present special issues for the party seeking protection.

The distinctiveness requirement for trade dress raises questions of how to apply the distinctiveness spectrum, such as whether trade dress can be inherently distinctive and whether secondary meaning must be established before the mark is entitled to protection. The U.S. Supreme Court addressed these questions in part in *Two Pesos, Inc. v. Taco Cabana, Inc.*[34] Taco Cabana, a Mexican restaurant chain located in Texas, brought suit against Two Pesos, another Mexican restaurant chain located in Texas, for infringing the unregistered trade dress of Taco Cabana. The trade dress was described as follows:

> [A] festive eating atmosphere having interior dining and patio areas decorated with artifacts, bright colors, paintings and murals. The patio includes interior and exterior areas with the interior patio capable of being sealed off from the outside patio by overhead garage doors. The stepped exterior of the building is a festive and vivid color scheme using top border paint and neon stripes. Bright awnings and umbrellas continue the theme.[35]

A jury found that the trade dress was inherently distinctive and nonfunctional, but also found that it had not acquired secondary meaning. On appeal, the Fifth Circuit affirmed, holding that because the trade dress was inherently distinctive, there was no need to establish secondary meaning. This ruling conflicted with a Second Circuit opinion concluding that an unregistered trade dress required a showing of secondary meaning before protection would be granted. The Supreme Court accepted the case to resolve the split.

The Court ultimately agreed with the Fifth Circuit and held that inherently distinctive trade dress is protected without a showing that it has acquired secondary meaning. As the Court noted: "There is no persuasive reason to apply to trade dress a general requirement of

---

34 505 U.S. 763 (1992).

35 *Id.* at 765.

secondary meaning that is at odds with the principles generally applicable to infringement suits under § 43(a)."[36] In *Two Pesos*, however, a jury had already found that the overall appearance was inherently distinctive and that the dress itself did not involve a product design. In 2000, in *Wal-Mart Stores, Inc. v. Samara Brothers, Inc.*,[37] the Court made clear that not all trade dress cases are to be treated the same.

Samara Brothers brought suit against Wal-Mart alleging infringement of an unregistered trade dress under section 43(a) of the Lanham Act (15 U.S.C. § 1125(a)). Samara Brothers was a designer and manufacturer of children's clothing. It had copyrighted its unique articles of clothing and had only contracted to sell the clothes to a few stores. Samara Brothers discovered that Wal-Mart and several other major retailers were selling knockoffs of major Samara Brothers' garments. After the major retailers refused to cease and desist, Samara Brothers brought a suit in the Southern District of New York. A jury found in favor of Samara Brothers on all of its claims and the Second Circuit affirmed.

On appeal, the Supreme Court began by noting the development of trade dress protection and distinguishing two types of trade dress—product packaging and product design. Both types of trade dress require distinctiveness either by being inherently distinctive, such as in the *Two Pesos* case, or by achieving secondary meaning. Analogizing to the *Abercrombie* distinctiveness spectrum, the Court held that product packaging could be inherently distinctive just as arbitrary, fanciful, or suggestive words can. However, the Court held that product design was more akin to descriptive words or colors, in that it serves a purpose other than source identification:

> . . . In the case of product design, as in the case of color, we think consumer predisposition to equate the feature with the source does not exist. Consumers are aware of the reality that, almost invariably, even the most unusual of product designs—such as a cocktail shaker shaped like a penguin—is intended not to identify the source, but to render the product itself more useful or more appealing.
>
> The fact that product design almost invariably serves purposes other than source identification not only renders inherent distinctiveness problematic; it also renders application of an inherent-distinctiveness principle more harmful to other consumer interests. Consumers should not be deprived of the benefits of competition with regard to the

---

[36] *Id.* at 770.

[37] 529 U.S. 205 (2000).

> utilitarian and esthetic purposes that product design ordinarily serves by a rule of law that facilitates plausible threats of suit against new entrants based upon alleged inherent distinctiveness. How easy it is to mount a plausible suit depends, of course, upon the clarity of the test for inherent distinctiveness, and where product design is concerned we have little confidence that a reasonably clear test can be devised.[38]

The Court went on to distinguish *Two Pesos* by observing that the trade dress at issue in that case was either product packaging or something akin to product packaging. Although the Court noted that the distinction between whether something is product packaging or product design may be a close call, it believed the issue to be less troublesome than trying to develop a test for inherently distinctive product design. Some general observations can be made, however, about whether trade dress is product design or packaging. For instance, if the trade dress being claimed is a part of the good itself rather than the package it comes in, that would seem to indicate product design. Indeed, many of the cases decided thus far seem to follow this distinction.[39] Further, trade dress for services, such as in *Two Pesos*, would seem to favor non-product design.[40] This need not be limited to restaurants, however. In *In re Chippendales USA, Inc.*,[41] the Federal Circuit classified the wrist cuffs and bowtie collar costume of the "Chippendales" male dancers as "part of the packaging" of the adult entertainment services rendered by the performers.[42] As per the Supreme Court's ruling in *Wal-Mart*, the courts should err on the side of product design rather than packaging in close cases.

The *Wal-Mart* Court based its reasoning on a practical concern that product designs will invariably serve purposes other than source identification, and on the ground that permitting product designs to be inherently distinctive would hurt consumers. As the Court noted:

> Consumers should not be deprived of the benefits of competition with regard to the utilitarian and esthetic purposes that product design ordinarily serves by a rule of law that facilitates plausible threats of suit against new entrants based upon alleged inherent distinctiveness. How

---

38 *Id.* at 213.

39 *See* 1 MCCARTHY ON TRADEMARKS AND UNFAIR COMPETITION § 8:12.50 (4th ed.) (listing examples).

40 *See id.*

41 622 F.3d 1346 (Fed. Cir. 2010).

42 *Id.* at 1351. The court nevertheless held that the packaging was not inherently distinctive under the *Seabrook* test described below.

> easy it is to mount a plausible suit depends, of course, upon the clarity of the test for inherent distinctiveness, and where product design is concerned we have little confidence that a reasonably clear test can be devised. . . . It is true, of course, that the person seeking to exclude new entrants would have to establish the nonfunctionality of the design feature, see § 43(a)(3), 15 U.S.C. § 1125(a)(3) (1994 ed., Supp. V)—a showing that may involve consideration of its esthetic appeal. Competition is deterred, however, not merely by successful suit but by the plausible threat of successful suit, and given the unlikelihood of inherently source-identifying design, the game of allowing suit based upon alleged inherent distinctiveness seems to us not worth the candle.[43]

The *Wal-Mart* decision established the rule that product design trade dress can never be inherently distinctive; thus, it requires a showing of secondary meaning. But product packaging trade dress *may* be inherently distinctive. The question then is how does one determine whether such trade dress is in fact inherently distinctive? In its opinion, the *Wal-Mart* Court noted that the test formulated by the Court of Customs and Patent Appeals for product packaging in *Seabrook Foods, Inc. v. Bar-Well Foods, Ltd.*[44] is often applied. The *Wal-Mart* Court neither accepted nor rejected the *Seabrook* test for inherent distinctiveness; it simply stated that the test was an ill-fit for product design. Nevertheless, the *Seabrook* test is used by a majority of courts to determine inherent distinctiveness. Under the test, three questions are asked: (1) whether the design or shape is a common, basic shape or design?; (2) whether it is unique or unusual in a particular field?; and (3) whether it is a mere refinement of a commonly-adopted and well-known form of ornamentation for a particular class of goods which consumers would view as mere ornamentation? While the Restatement doesn't lay out the test explicitly, comment b to § 16 is consistent with the *Seabrook* test: "Trade dress that is unique and prominent can thus be inherently distinctive. If the trade dress is descriptive (see § 14) or inconspicuous, or not sufficiently different from that used by others to justify a conclusion of inherent distinctiveness, trademark rights will depend upon proof of distinctiveness through evidence of secondary meaning." At its heart, the *Seabrook* test's questions are aimed at determining whether the consuming public will automatically associate the packaging with the producer.

---

[43] *Wal-Mart Stores, Inc.*, 529 U.S. at 213.

[44] 568 F.2d 1342 (C.C.P.A. 1977).

Under the *Abercrombie* distinctiveness spectrum (and under the Restatement), the category that is never protected is generic marks. Some courts have similarly found that trade dress can be generic.[45] For instance, courts have held that the general use of a color-coding system for language manuals,[46] the use of a grape-leaf on wine bottles,[47] and the shape of a guitar are all generic.[48]

As noted above, for trade dress to qualify for protection, it must be distinctive as well as non-functional. Section 17 of the Restatement elaborates on when a design is functional:

> A design is "functional" for purposes of the rule stated in § 16 if the design affords benefits in the manufacturing, marketing, or use of the goods or services with which the design is used, apart from any benefits attributable to the design's significance as an indication of source, that are important to effective competition by others and that are not practically available through the use of alternative designs.[49]

If a product's design is functional, it is more appropriate to seek the limited protection offered by the patent system. The U.S. Supreme Court addressed functionality in *TrafFix Devices, Inc. v. Marketing Displays, Inc.*[50] Marketing Displays, Inc. (MDI) created a "dual-spring design" mechanism that kept temporary road and other outdoor signs upright in adverse wind conditions. The designs were patented, but eventually the utility patents expired. However, MDI claimed that its sign stands were recognizable to buyers because the patented design was visible near the base of the sign stand. After the utility patent expiration, TrafFix Devices, Inc., began marketing sign stands with a dual-spring mechanism copied from MDI's design.

---

[45] *See, e.g.*, Jeffrey Milstein, Inc. v. Greger, Lawlor, Roth, Inc., 58 F.3d 27 (2d Cir. 1995) ("Just as the first company to depict a heart and arrow on Valentine's cards or to produce cards depicting tabby cats could not seek protection for those designs because they are concepts, defined abstractly, so [plaintiff] cannot obtain protection for its general idea of creating cards out of die-cut photographs."); Landscape Forms, Inc. v. Columbia Cascade Co., 113 F.3d 373 (2d Cir. 1997) ("While trademarking a generic term would create a monopoly in a necessary word or phrase, granting trade dress protection to an ordinary product shape would create a monopoly in the goods themselves.").

[46] *See* Casa Editrice Bonechi, S.R.L. v. Irving Weisdorf & Co., 45 U.S.P.Q.2d 1360 (S.D.N.Y. 1997).

[47] *See* Kendall-Jackson Winery, Ltd. v. E. & J. Gallo Winery, 150 F.3d 1042, 1048 (9th Cir. 1998).

[48] *See* Stuart Spector Designs, Ltd. v. Fender Musical Instruments Corporation, 94 U.S.P.Q.2d 1549, 1555, 1567 (T.T.A.B. 2009) ("In the context of product design, genericness may be found where the design is, at a minimum, so common in the industry that it cannot be said to identify a particular source.")

[49] RESTATEMENT (THIRD) OF UNFAIR COMPETITION § 17 (1995).

[50] 532 U.S. 23 (2001).

MDI brought suit under the Trademark Act of 1946 for trade dress infringement. The district court found against MDI on two grounds. First, it found that MDI had failed to establish secondary meaning. Second, and alternatively, the district court found that the trade dress at issue—dual-spring design—was functional. As a consequence, secondary meaning was irrelevant because there can be no trade dress protection if the trade dress is functional. On appeal, the Sixth Circuit reversed on both grounds. With regard to the dual-spring design, the court found that an alternate design could be used to avoid infringement even if the design at issue was functional. In its criticism of the district court's ruling on the trade dress question, the court of appeals noted that there was a split among other circuits on the issue of whether the existence of an expired utility patent forecloses the possibility of trade dress protection in the product's design for the patentee. The Supreme Court accepted the appeal to resolve the split, but the opinion also illuminates some of the nuances of functionality as a bar.

The *TrafFix* Court began by providing a framework for determining functionality: " '[I]n general terms, a product feature is functional, and cannot serve as a trademark, if it is essential to the use or purpose of the article or if it affects the cost or quality of the article.' Expanding upon the meaning of this phrase, we have observed that a functional feature is one the 'exclusive use of [which] would put competitors at a significant non-reputation-related disadvantage.' "[51] The Fifth Circuit has interpreted the above framework as providing two tests:

> The Supreme Court has recognized two tests for determining functionality. "[T]he primary test for determining whether a product feature is functional is whether the feature is essential to the use or purpose of the product or whether it affects the cost or quality of the product." This is the "traditional" test. "Under this traditional definition, if a product feature is 'the reason the device works,' then the feature is functional." Under a secondary test for functionality "a functional feature is one the exclusive use of which would put competitors at a significant non-reputation-related disadvantage." This is the "competitive necessity" test.[52]

Judge Easterbrook has given an even more concise interpretation of the framework: "So if a design enables a product to operate, or improves on a substitute design in some way (such as by making the

[51] *Id.* at 32.

[52] Board of Supervisors for Louisiana State University Agricultural and Mechanical College v. Smack Apparel Co., 550 F.3d 465, 485–86 (5th Cir. 2008).

product cheaper, faster, lighter, or stronger), then the design cannot be trademarked . . ."[53] A noted treatise is even briefer, stating that "something is 'functional' if it works better in this shape."[54]

This last quote may overstate the functionality doctrine. If a competitor can easily reap the design advantages through an alternate design, protection may still be available. This nuance appears to have tripped-up the court of appeals in *TrafFix*. As the Supreme Court noted: "The Court of Appeals in the instant case seemed to interpret this language to mean that a necessary test for functionality is 'whether the particular product configuration is a competitive necessity.' "[55] In other words, the court of appeals seemed to believe that even after a design is held to be functional, it may still be saved if the design is not a competitive necessity. As the Supreme Court clarified, however, if a design is functional, that is the end of the matter. Another way to view this is that a functionality analysis already accounts for whether competitors will be placed at a non-reputational disadvantage.

In the case before it, the Supreme Court in *TrafFix* had no trouble classifying the dual-spring design as functional. The design was necessary to the operation of the device, permitting temporary outdoor signs to withstand adverse wind conditions. This was undoubtedly a functional advantage. MDI's only real arguments to the contrary involved hiding the dual springs or possibly the use of additional springs. As mentioned, however, the Court noted that once a design is functional, that is the end of the matter. The Court articulated a few reasons why a different design would not work as a viable alternative. For one, hiding the springs would probably cost more money, placing competitors at a disadvantage. For this same reason, the use of additional springs would not be acceptable, as there was evidence that the dual springs were the most efficient means of making the signs wind resistant. Furthermore, the Court noted that it was not just the presence of the dual springs, but also that they could be seen that offered the competitive advantage, as seeing the springs assured buyers that the product served its purpose.

The fact that the dual-spring design was claimed in a patent also played a role in the Court's decision. The Court noted that the burden is heavy on the party trying to claim that the elements of its now-expired utility patent are non-functional:

> A prior patent, we conclude, has vital significance in resolving the trade dress claim. A utility patent is strong

[53] Jay Franco & Sons, Inc. v. Franek, 615 F.3d 855, 857 (7th Cir. 2010).

[54] 1 MCCARTHY ON TRADEMARKS AND UNFAIR COMPETITION § 7:63 (4th ed.).

[55] *TrafFix Devices, Inc.*, 532 U.S. at 32.

> evidence that the features therein claimed are functional. If trade dress protection is sought for those features the strong evidence of functionality based on the previous patent adds great weight to the statutory presumption that features are deemed functional until proved otherwise by the party seeking trade dress protection. Where the expired patent claimed the features in question, one who seeks to establish trade dress protection must carry the heavy burden of showing that the feature is not functional, for instance by showing that it is merely an ornamental, incidental, or arbitrary aspect of the device.[56]

Despite the heavy burden imposed on the claimant, the Court noted that trade dress protection could still be obtained for purely ornamental elements of the patent. Once again, however, the burden would be on the claimant. As the Court explained:

> In a case where a manufacturer seeks to protect arbitrary, incidental, or ornamental aspects of features of a product found in the patent claims, such as arbitrary curves in the legs or an ornamental pattern painted on the springs, a different result might obtain. There the manufacturer could perhaps prove that those aspects do not serve a purpose within the terms of the utility patent. The inquiry into whether such features, asserted to be trade dress, are functional by reason of their inclusion in the claims of an expired utility patent could be aided by going beyond the claims and examining the patent and its prosecution history to see if the feature in question is shown as a useful part of the invention. No such claim is made here, however. MDI in essence seeks protection for the dual-spring design alone. The asserted trade dress consists simply of the dual-spring design, four legs, a base, an upright, and a sign. MDI has pointed to nothing arbitrary about the components of its device or the way they are assembled. The Lanham Act does not exist to reward manufacturers for their innovation in creating a particular device; that is the purpose of the patent law and its period of exclusivity.[57]

The *TrafFix* case dealt with the functional utility of a physical design. Some courts have also extended the functionality concept to hold that some trade dress is aesthetically functional. Comment c to § 17 of the Restatement of Unfair Competition explicitly accepts aesthetic functionality:

56 *Id.* at 29.

57 *Id.* at 34.

> When aesthetic considerations play an important role in the purchasing decisions of prospective consumers, a design feature that substantially contributes to the aesthetic appeal of a product may qualify as "functional." As with utilitarian design features, however, the fact that the design performs a function by contributing to the aesthetic value of the product does not in itself render the design ineligible for protection as a trademark. A manufacturer thus does not forfeit trademark rights simply because prospective purchasers find the design aesthetically pleasing. A design is functional because of its aesthetic value only if it confers a significant benefit that cannot practically be duplicated by the use of alternative designs. Because of the difficulties inherent in evaluating the aesthetic superiority of a particular design, a finding of aesthetic functionality ordinarily will be made only when objective evidence indicates a lack of adequate alternative designs. Such evidence typically is available only when the range of alternative designs is limited either by the nature of the design feature or by the basis of its aesthetic appeal. The ultimate test of aesthetic functionality, as with utilitarian functionality, is whether the recognition of trademark rights would significantly hinder competition.

As an example of aesthetic functionality, the Restatement provides an illustration of a manufacturer of chocolates claiming trade dress protection in a heart-shaped box that it uses to sell its products around Valentine's Day.[58] Doesn't recognition of such aesthetic functionality have the potential to encompass a number of otherwise valid trade dresses? Indeed, despite its acceptance in the Restatement, aesthetic functionality has been criticized as undermining the very purpose of trademark. For instance, the Fifth Circuit has rejected the concept:

> Smack urges, however, that the Universities' colors on the t-shirts serve several functional purposes. It contends that the shirts allow groups of people to bond and show support for a philosophy or goal; facilitate the expression of loyalty to the school and a determination of the loyalties of others; and identify the wearer as a fan and indicate the team the fan is supporting. These claimed functional uses are nothing more than the kind of aesthetic uses at issue in *Boston Hockey*. Our circuit has consistently rejected the

[58] *See* RESTATEMENT (THIRD) OF UNFAIR COMPETITION § 17 illus. 8 (1995); *see also* E.R.B.E. Elektromedizin GmbH v. Canady Tech., LLC, 629 F.3d 1278, 1288–89 (Fed. Cir. 2010) (holding that the color blue was functional for purposes of use on certain medical devices).

> concept of aesthetic functionality. . . . [N]either *Qualitex* nor *TrafFix* addressed aesthetic functionality as the dispositive issue, let alone the purported aesthetic functionality of a color-scheme that acts to identify and create a desired association with the particular source. . . . We agree with the Ninth Circuit that "the fact that a trademark is desirable does not, and should not, render it unprotectable."[59]

It may be that that such aesthetic functionality claims are better addressed on the distinctiveness prong. After all, if consumers do not associate the claimed aesthetic with a particular source, then no protection is necessary. For instance, the heart-shaped box illustration would appear to fail the distinctiveness prong as to any one producer or source. As a result, it could be struck down as being akin to a generic mark.[60]

### 3. Colors and Non-Visual Marks

As previously suggested, trademarks can come in a number of media, including color. In both the *Wal-Mart* and *TrafFix* opinions, the U.S. Supreme Court referenced the previous case of *Qualitex Co. v. Jacobson Products Co.*,[61] in which the court held that color alone could not qualify for trademark protection without a showing of secondary meaning. *Qualitex* involved an alleged trademark in green-gold laundry press pads. The manufacturer of the press pads, Qualitex, obtained a registered trademark in the color and then sued a competitor for using a similarly colored press pad. Although Qualitex won at trial, the Ninth Circuit held that color alone could not be the subject of a trademark. The Supreme Court disagreed:

> The Lanham Act gives a seller or producer the exclusive right to "register" a trademark, 15 U.S.C. § 1052 (1988 ed. and Supp. V), and to prevent his or her competitors from using that trademark, § 1114(1). Both the language of the Act and the basic underlying principles of trademark law would seem to include color within the universe of things

59 Board of Supervisors for Louisiana State University Agricultural and Mechanical College v. Smack Apparel Co., 550 F.3d 465, 487–88 (5th Cir. 2008) (internal citations omitted); *see also* Allison Midei, *Getting to Functional: Limiting the Applicability of the Trademark Aesthetic Functionality Doctrine*, 41 AIPLA Q.J. 467, 510 (2013) (criticizing aesthetic functionality jurisprudence and the Supreme Court for providing too little guidance on the matter, which has resulted in "some courts [that] apply the doctrine too liberally and inappropriately abrogate the right of a producer to provide identification of its mark, while other courts do not apply the doctrine at all and impinge on the competitors right to imitate useful product features").

60 *See* 1 MCCARTHY ON TRADEMARKS AND UNFAIR COMPETITION § 7:81 (4th ed.).

61 514 U.S. 159 (1995).

> that can qualify as a trademark. The language of the Lanham Act describes that universe in the broadest of terms. It says that trademarks "includ[e] any word, name, symbol, or device, or any combination thereof." § 1127. Since human beings might use as a "symbol" or "device" almost anything at all that is capable of carrying meaning, this language, read literally, is not restrictive. The courts and the Patent and Trademark Office have authorized for use as a mark a particular shape (of a Coca-Cola bottle), a particular sound (of NBC's three chimes), and even a particular scent (of plumeria blossoms on sewing thread). If a shape, a sound, and a fragrance can act as symbols why, one might ask, can a color not do the same?[62]

The *Qualitex* Court went on to qualify its views by analogizing to the descriptive category of the distinctiveness spectrum:

> True, a product's color is unlike "fanciful," "arbitrary," or "suggestive" words or designs, which almost automatically tell a customer that they refer to a brand. The imaginary word "Suntost," or the words "Suntost Marmalade," on a jar of orange jam immediately would signal a brand or a product "source"; the jam's orange color does not do so. But, over time, customers may come to treat a particular color on a product or its packaging (say, a color that in context seems unusual, such as pink on a firm's insulating material or red on the head of a large industrial bolt) as signifying a brand. And, if so, that color would have come to identify and distinguish the goods—i.e., "to indicate" their "source"—much in the way that descriptive words on a product (say, "Trim" on nail clippers or "Car-Freshener" on deodorizer) can come to indicate a product's origin. In this circumstance, trademark law says that the word (e.g., "Trim"), although not inherently distinctive, has developed "secondary meaning." Again, one might ask, if trademark law permits a descriptive word with secondary meaning to act as a mark, why would it not permit a color, under similar circumstances, to do the same?
>
> We cannot find in the basic objectives of trademark law any obvious theoretical objection to the use of color alone as a trademark, where that color has attained "secondary meaning" and therefore identifies and distinguishes a particular brand (and thus indicates its "source"). In principle, trademark law, by preventing others from

---

[62] *Id.* at 162 (internal citations omitted).

> copying a source-identifying mark, "reduce[s] the customer's costs of shopping and making purchasing decisions," 1 J. MCCARTHY, MCCARTHY ON TRADEMARKS AND UNFAIR COMPETITION § 2.01[2], p. 2–3 (3d ed. 1994) (hereinafter McCarthy), for it quickly and easily assures a potential customer that this item—the item with this mark—is made by the same producer as other similarly marked items that he or she liked (or disliked) in the past. At the same time, the law helps assure a producer that it (and not an imitating competitor) will reap the financial, reputation-related rewards associated with a desirable product. The law thereby "encourage[s] the production of quality products," *ibid.*, and simultaneously discourages those who hope to sell inferior products by capitalizing on a consumer's inability quickly to evaluate the quality of an item offered for sale. It is the source-distinguishing ability of a mark—not its ontological status as color, shape, fragrance, word, or sign—that permits it to serve these basic purposes. And, for that reason, it is difficult to find, in basic trademark objectives, a reason to disqualify absolutely the use of a color as a mark.[63]

Along with requiring secondary meaning, the Court later stated in the opinion that color would be subject to the functionality doctrine.

Based upon the *Qualitex* Court's reasoning, it would appear that any media—visual, audio, or even scent-based—could qualify for trademark protection so long as the claimed mark has inherent or acquired distinctiveness, is capable of distinguishing the source, and is not functional. Indeed, as mentioned in the *Qualitex* excerpt, scents and sounds have been granted trademark registrations.[64] The big takeaway here is that a trademark can exist in just about any type of media subject to the three previously mentioned qualifiers: (1) the mark must be distinctive (which may require a showing of secondary meaning if the mark is product design or color); (2) the mark must distinguish the source; and (3) the mark must not be functional. A fourth qualifier could also be listed—the mark cannot be confused with another enforceable mark. This last qualifier is explored in the discussion of infringement below.

### 4. Collective Marks and Certification Marks

The Restatement of Unfair Competition describes two other types of marks—collective marks and certification marks—which are

---

63 *Id.* at 162–64 (internal citations omitted).

64 *See also* Registration No. 75807526 (April 10, 2001) (involving the yodeling sound trademarked by Yahoo, Inc.).

often confused. A collective mark is a mark used by members of a cooperative, association, or other collective group to identify the goods or services of such members or to indicate membership in the group.[65] A collective mark indicates that goods or services originate from a member of the group, but not necessarily from a particular person within the group. (If the organization itself uses a mark to identify its own goods or services, this is not a collective mark but may simply be a trademark in its own right.) Examples of collective marks include the Professional Golfers Association, whose members use the "PGA" mark in providing services such as golf lessons, and the National Association of Realtors, whose members use the "REALTOR" mark in providing real estate services.[66]

Certification marks are defined in the Lanham Act as "any word, name, symbol, or device, or any combination thereof . . . used by a person other than its owner . . . to certify regional or other origin, material, mode of manufacture, quality, accuracy, or other characteristics of such person's goods or services or that the work or labor on the goods or services was performed by members of a union or other organization."[67] Unlike collective marks, which indicate an association with a group, certification marks speak to an aspect of the good or service itself. An example of a certification mark is the "Good Housekeeping Seal of Approval." The Good Housekeeping Institute awards the Good Housekeeping Seal, which represents Good Housekeeping Magazine's limited warranty that if any product carrying the seal is found to be defective within two years from the date of purchase, Good Housekeeping will either replace the product or refund the purchase price up to $2,000.[68]

Distinguishing between a collective mark and a certification mark can be tricky, but it is useful to ask whether the mark is indicating that the seller is a member of a group (or that the product came from a seller who is a member of a group), or whether the mark speaks to a specific aspect of the good. The former indicates that it is a collective mark, whereas the latter indicates that it is a certification

---

[65] *See* Lanham Act § 45, 15 U.S.C.A. § 1127; RESTATEMENT (THIRD) OF UNFAIR COMPETITION § 10 (1995). The Restatement actually distinguishes between marks used to indicate that the goods or services originate from a member of a group, and marks used to indicate that a person or entity is a member of a group. The former are "collective marks" and the latter are "collective membership marks." RESTATEMENT (THIRD) OF UNFAIR COMPETITION § 10 cmt. a (1995).

[66] For a discussion of collective marks, see 3 MCCARTHY ON TRADEMARKS AND UNFAIR COMPETITION § 19:99 (4th ed. 2015). McCarthy also cites an agricultural cooperative of sellers of farm produce as an example of a group that may use a collective mark.

[67] Lanham Act § 45, 15 U.S.C.A. § 1127; *see also* RESTATEMENT (THIRD) OF UNFAIR COMPETITION § 11 (1995) (providing a similar definition).

[68] *See* http://www.goodhousekeeping.com/institute/about-the-institute/a22148/about-good-housekeeping-seal/ (last visited Dec. 31, 2024).

mark. This distinction can be meaningful, as certification marks are seen as more burdensome to register.[69] One thing that both collective marks and certification marks have in common, however, is that someone other than the holder of the mark is using it (the group holds the mark and the member uses it).

## E. INFRINGEMENT

The previous sections have primarily discussed how to establish trademark rights. If the holder of a mark wishes to bring suit, however, it is not enough to simply establish a protected trademark. The holder must also establish the most basic prerequisite to a trademark suit—i.e., prove that the infringing defendant's use is likely to confuse a purchaser as to the source. The infringer, of course, may attack the holder's right to the trademark (such as by alleging lack of secondary meaning or invoking the functionality doctrine), and may have a number of additional defenses available. All of these issues will be explored below.

### 1. Likelihood of Confusion

Once a mark has been established, the holder can enjoin others from using it. This right, however, does not necessarily extend to every use of the mark. For instance, should Nike be able to prevent the use of a checkmark symbol, even for scholastic supplies that have nothing to do with sportswear, just because its "swoosh" symbol resembles a checkmark (or vice versa)? The answer is "no," as trademark law is only meant to protect the holder of a mark to the extent that a consumer would be confused as to the source. Determining when a consumer would be confused, however, is not always a simple inquiry.

The oft-cited case of *Polaroid Corp. v. Polarad Electronics Corp.*[70] provides a framework for evaluating whether a likelihood of confusion exists. In that case, Polaroid Corporation, owner of the Polaroid trademark, brought an action for an injunction in the Eastern District of New York. Polaroid alleged that the defendant's use of the name Polarad as a trademark and part of its corporate name infringed Polaroid's federal and state trademarks and constituted unfair competition. Polaroid was a known name in optics and photography, but in the mid-1940s, it had been involved in electro-optical devices employing electronic circuitry in combination with optical apparatuses. Polarad was started in 1944 and was

---

69 *See* 3 McCarthy on Trademarks and Unfair Competition § 19:99 (4th ed. 2015) (citing the stricter requirements for registration of certification marks under the Lanham Act § 14(e) as a reason why some holders may opt to form groups with standards and to register collective marks instead).

70 287 F.2d 492 (2d Cir. 1961).

involved in the sale of microwave generating, receiving, and measuring devices and of television studio equipment. Polaroid knew of Polarad for years, but Polaroid did nothing to prevent Polarad from using Polaroid's allegedly distinctive mark.

In 1956, a suit was finally brought when a trademark was given to Polarad for radio and television units and other electronic devices. Conceding that the bulk of its business was in optics and photography (lines not pursued by Polarad), Polaroid nevertheless claimed to be entitled to protection of its distinctive mark in at least certain portions of the large field of electronics. Polaroid relied in part on certain instances of confusion, predominantly communications intended for Polarad but directed to Polaroid. In response, Polarad asserted that its business was the sale of complex electronics equipment to relatively few customers, that Polaroid's excursions into electronics were insignificant in light of the size of the field, that the instances of confusion were minimal, and that there was no evidence that Polaroid had suffered either loss of customers or injury to reputation. Polarad also countersued and sought an injunction against Polaroid's use of its mark in the television and electronics fields (as well as other relief). The district court dismissed the claim and the counterclaim, concluding that neither party had made an adequate showing of confusion and that both parties had been guilty of laches.

Although the Second Circuit ultimately agreed with the district court based on laches, the decision is widely cited for its listing of relevant factors to consider when determining whether there has been a likelihood of confusion. The *Polaroid* factors include the following: (1) the strength of the mark, (2) the degree of similarity between the two marks, (3) the marketplace proximity of the products, (4) the likelihood that the prior owner will bridge the gap, (5) actual confusion, (6) the alleged infringer's good faith in adopting its own mark, (7) the quality of defendant's product, and (8) the sophistication of the buyers. (It should be noted that this is not a comprehensive list.) These factors, or a variation of them, have been used by a number of courts. For instance, in *AMF Inc. v. Sleekcraft Boats*,[71] the Ninth Circuit articulated the following factors: strength of mark, relatedness of goods, similarity between marks, actual confusion, marketing channels used, the degree of purchaser care, the alleged infringer's intent, and the likelihood of expansion of product lines. Most other circuits have similar tests.[72]

---

[71] 599 F.2d 341 (9th Cir. 1979).

[72] *See, e.g.*, Scott Paper Co. v. Scott's Liquid Gold, Inc., 589 F.2d 1225, 1229 (3d Cir. 1978); Pizzeria Uno Corp. v. Temple, 747 F.2d 1522, 1527 (4th Cir. 1984); Frisch's

One of the most important factors is similarity between marks. To determine if marks are similar, most courts generally consider three types of similarity: sight, sound, and meaning.[73] It should be noted that similarity as to one aspect of the sight, sound, and meaning trilogy will not automatically result in a finding of a likelihood of confusion, but such a similarity on one factor *may* be sufficient to support a finding of likelihood of confusion under the right circumstances. In addition, some courts will refer to the overall "commercial impression" when a mark is similar across all three.

Many of the *Polaroid* factors appear in the Restatement's standard for likelihood of confusion.[74] Strength of mark is similar to § 21(d), similarity is covered by § 21(a) and (b), the marketplace factor is covered by § 21(f), the bridging the gap factor is § 21(e), and the sophistication of the buyers is covered in § 21(c). Actual confusion, the alleged infringer's good faith in adopting its own mark, and the quality of defendant's product factors, however, are harder to find analogs for in § 21. The actual confusion can probably be inferred from § 21(a) and (c). Although quality of the goods is not explicitly listed as a factor, the comments make clear that it is relevant:

> The quality of the actor's goods or services may be relevant in assessing the likelihood of confusion. For purposes of determining whether confusion is likely, the relevant factor is the extent of the difference in quality between the goods or services of the subsequent user and those of the trademark owner. Markedly different quality may suggest that the goods are sold to different purchasers or in different market channels, or that the products are unlikely to be associated with a common source. On the other hand, if the subsequent user's goods are inferior to those of the prior user and confusion does occur, the threat to the reputation of the prior user is particularly acute. Although courts sometimes require less evidence of confusion when the subsequent use is on inferior goods, evidence of inferior quality is more properly relevant to fashioning appropriate relief if a likelihood of confusion is otherwise established.[75]

---

Restaurants, Inc. v. Elby's Big Boy of Steubenville, Inc., 670 F.2d 642, 648 (6th Cir. 1982); SquirtCo v. Seven-Up Co., 628 F.2d 1086, 1091 (8th Cir. 1980).

[73] *See* J. THOMAS MCCARTHY, 4 MCCARTHY ON TRADEMARKS AND UNFAIR COMPETITION § 23:21 (4th ed. 2015); *see* also RESTATEMENT (THIRD) OF UNFAIR COMPETITION §§ 20–22 (1995).

[74] *See* RESTATEMENT (THIRD) OF UNFAIR COMPETITION §§ 20–22 (1995).

[75] *Id.* § 21 cmt. k.

Finally, the actor's good faith (or intent) is a relevant consideration, but it is found in § 22, which states:

> (1) A likelihood of confusion may be inferred from proof that the actor used a designation resembling another's trademark, trade name, collective mark, or certification mark with the intent to cause confusion or to deceive.
>
> (2) A likelihood of confusion should not be inferred from proof that the actor intentionally copied the other's designation if the actor acted in good faith under circumstances that do not otherwise indicate an intent to cause confusion or to deceive.

It may be worth asking why good faith/intent is a relevant factor—after all, there can be trademark infringement even without intent. Moreover, what does intent have to do with the consumer, who the law is ultimately trying to protect? The comments to the Restatement offer some explanation, as they note that intent is not necessary to prove confusion but that it may create a presumption of confusion. The comments also make clear, however, that not all attempts to copy a trademark indicate that there is an intent to create confusion. For instance, if the actor believed that the mark was functional, then the copying may not justify an inference of confusion.

Although the *Polaroid* court ultimately ruled on the laches issue, it is interesting to speculate how the court would have evaluated the factors absent laches, and there are some indications from the court as to how it might have ruled. The court appeared to side with Polaroid on the first and second factors, but it stated that the fifth factor, actual confusion, was weak given that there was only one product that overlapped (and even that product was not very significant).[76] The court did note that Polarad's excursion into television equipment overlapped with Polaroid's and that this could have provided some form of relief, but the court did not justify this conclusion with regard to the factors. Nevertheless, given that the court already found for Polaroid on the first two factors, the use of a similar product would likely have swayed the court on the fifth factor. Marketplace proximity seemed to favor Polaroid as the company presumably had a nationwide market. The fourth factor is probably a close call—Polaroid certainly seemed to indicate that it had already bridged the gap between products in some instances, although the court minimized the impact of this overlap. The good faith factor could, likewise, go either way. Polarad gave a plausible explanation

---

[76] *See Polaroid Corp.*, 287 F.2d at 495 ("The filter seems to be the only case where defendant has sold, but not manufactured, a product serving a function similar to any of plaintiff's, and plaintiff's sales of this item have been highly irregular, varying, e.g., from $2,300 in 1953 to $303,000 in 1955, and $48,000 in 1956.").

of how it came upon its name, borrowing the first letters of the founders' names and adding -rad to indicate radio, although a finder of fact could certainly determine this to be a flimsy explanation. However, Polarad appeared to have been up front with Polaroid about its use, even going so far as to forward a communication that had been erroneously sent to Polorad instead of Polaroid (although this would seem to help support Polaroid's confusion argument). There was little indication of the quality of the products, but the last factor would seem to favor Polarad, as it appeared to be marketing not to general consumers but to manufacturers and television studios. Thus, factors 4–8 could all have come down in favor of Polarad, except with regard to products that Polaroid also sold, in which the confusion factor weighed in favor of Polaroid. Perhaps this would be enough to tip the factors in Polaroid's favor.

In *Polaroid*, the court noted that the defendant's use of the mark was mostly in conjunction with different products. As case law has developed, the same factors have been used regardless of whether the trademark has been used for a different or similar product. However, the likelihood of confusion seems to increase when the same or similar product is at issue. Use of the mark in relation to the same product would carry weight in factors 3–5 and possibly in factor 6 (good faith). Comment c to § 21 of the Restatement of Unfair Competition seems to agree, as it states that "[t]he use of an identical designation on goods similar to those of the prior user is strong evidence of a likelihood of confusion."

As for whether certain factors should carry more weight than others, at least one empirical study has suggested that for a plaintiff to prevail, it must win on the similarity factor. The study examined preliminary injunctions issued on trademark disputes and found that in every case where the court ruled against the plaintiff on the similarity factor (65 out of 192 cases), the plaintiff was also denied a preliminary injunction. The study also found that intent was a strong indicator. Of the 67 cases in which the court found for the plaintiff on the intent factor, in 65 of those cases the court found in favor of the plaintiff on the overall test (the two outliers were instances in which the similarity factor favored the defendant).[77]

Recall that the *Polaroid* court ultimately found for Polarad on the equitable defense of laches. Federal courts are vested with the power to grant injunctions and to award profits and damages subject to the "principles of equity." Laches is included as a power granted to the courts under these principles. This is an additional defense that can arise in a trademark infringement claim. There is technically no

[77] *See* Barton Beebe, *An Empirical Study of the Multifactor Tests for Trademark Infringement*, 94 CAL. L. REV. 1581, 1608, 1613–14 (2006).

statute of limitations under the Lanham Act. Arguably, the federal "catch-all" statute of limitations enacted in 1990 could apply. It provides: "Except as otherwise provided by law, a civil action arising under an Act of Congress enacted after the date of enactment of this section may not be commenced later than 4 years after the cause of action accrues."[78] This has been held to apply only to post-enactment acts of Congress, however, and so it should not apply to trademark causes of action.[79] Without a federal statute of limitations, many courts simply look to the state statute of limitations to aid in determining whether the time period is sufficient to claim laches.

Even if a statute of limitations existed, would it be effective? The *Polaroid* opinion explained that a statute of limitations would not help, as it noted that every sale was a separate wrong. While the court did not delve much deeper into this concept, it is true that every instance of using another's trademark constitutes a new wrong. A statute of limitations, therefore, would have little effect, except perhaps to limit how far back damages may be claimed.

With no statute of limitations in place, why should claims be limited with doctrines such as laches? Simply put, it would be inequitable to allow a plaintiff to sit on its trademark rights while another entity spends money and time developing its own products under the similar mark. The *Polaroid* case provides a good illustration. Polaroid knew about Polarad for a number of years and allowed Polarad to develop products under the mark. With the passage of time and so little overlap in the products, it is not surprising that the court found for Polarad. Note, however, that a mere delay in bringing suit is insufficient to support laches, especially if the plaintiff is unaware of the defendant's conduct or if the defendant is not harmed by the delay.

## 2. Dilution

As previously discussed, trademark infringement requires there to be a likelihood of confusion. Without proof of such likelihood, a mark holder may have no cause of action for a person's use of a similar mark to sell a totally different product. Does this make sense? After all, although an ordinary consumer may not be confused when a completely different product is at issue, isn't there some damage to

[78] 28 U.S.C.A. § 1658.

[79] *See* J. THOMAS MCCARTHY, 6 MCCARTHY ON TRADEMARKS AND UNFAIR COMPETITION § 31.23 (4th ed. 2015) (internal citations omitted) ("In the author's view, traditional trademark claims for infringement of registered marks under Lanham Act § 32(1) and of unregistered marks under Lanham Act § 43(a) are probably not covered by this federal four year statute because their operative elements were in place before 1990. However, newer claims such as those under the Trademark Dilution Revision Act of 2006 and the Anti-Cybersquatting Consumer Protection Act of 1999 probably will be covered by the federal four-year statute.").

the distinctive quality of the mark holder's brand name? This concern has led some holders to sue for mark dilution, which is the weakening in the ability of a mark to clearly distinguish only one source.

Dilution was first recognized by various state statutes, and federal legislation addressing dilution was passed in 1995 (and revised in 2006).[80] In general, dilution occurs through blurring or tarnishment. Blurring "is association arising from the similarity between a mark or trade name and a famous mark that impairs the distinctiveness of the famous mark."[81] Tarnishment "is association arising from the similarity between a mark or trade name and a famous mark that harms the reputation of the famous mark."[82]

*Mead Data Central, Inc. v. Toyota Motor Sales, U.S.A., Inc.*[83] provides a rather famous example of a dilution "blurring" analysis—and one familiar to lawyers, as it involved the LEXIS legal research database. Toyota announced a new line of luxury automobiles to be called LEXUS in 1987. In marketing its new cars, Toyota believed that there was no clash or confusion between its LEXUS car mark and Mead's LEXIS computer research mark. Mead disagreed and sued claiming dilution. The district court enjoined Toyota from using LEXUS as the name of its new luxury line. The court determined that under New York's antidilution statute, Toyota's use of LEXUS was likely to dilute the distinctive quality of the LEXIS mark. Toyota appealed.

The court of appeals first reviewed whether the two names LEXUS and LEXIS were in fact similar. The court rejected Mead's argument that it had coined the word "lexis," holding that "lexis" was a fairly common word. The court also found that other companies had adopted "Lexis" in identifying their business or product, e.g., Lexis Ltd., and Lexis Computer Systems Ltd. The court agreed, however, that Mead had made LEXIS a strong mark in the field of computer research. Nevertheless, the court found that the similarity had to be substantial before the doctrine of dilution could be applied. The court believed that television and radio announcers would be more careful and precise in their diction than the man on the street, and the court also observed that television commercials had a visual reference to the mark and product. Therefore, in the field of commercial advertising, which was the field subject to regulation, there was no substantial similarity between the marks.

---

[80] *See* 15 U.S.C. § 1125(c).

[81] *Id.* § 1125(c)(2)(B).

[82] *Id.* § 1125(c)(2)(C).

[83] 875 F.2d 1026 (2d Cir. 1989).

Despite this finding, the court continued to analyze the dilution claim. The court articulated a now well-known standard for such claims: "Such a [dilution] finding must be based on two elements. First, plaintiff's mark must possess a distinctive quality capable of dilution. Second, plaintiff must show a likelihood of dilution. As section 368–d expressly states, a plaintiff need not show either competition between its product or service and that of the defendant or a likelihood of confusion as to the source of the goods or services." The concurrence also noted these two elements: "It has become talismanic in the New York courts and in this Circuit that a cause of action under section 368–d involves two elements: 1) an extremely strong mark—either because of the mark's distinctive quality or because it has acquired secondary meaning—and 2) a likelihood of dilution. No showing of competition between the parties or confusion about the source of products is required."

These two factors have been characterized as the "famous and distinct" element and the "likelihood of dilution" element. The court found that Mead failed to establish both. As to the famous and distinct element, the court found that the LEXIS mark for a computerized legal database did not possess the required degree of fame and strength among the relevant potential market for the LEXUS automobile. Although the court noted that LEXIS was a strong mark in the field of attorneys and accountants, only 1% of the general public recognized LEXIS as a mark. "For the general public, LEXIS has no distinctive quality that LEXUS will dilute." The court also found that blurring was unlikely in the minds of the general public, as the LEXIS mark was not known to them. Blurring was unlikely in the minds of attorneys for their "recognized sophistication" would prevent "any significant amount of blurring."[84]

In a concurrence in *Mead*, Judge Sweet disagreed with the majority on two points. First, he did not believe that the failure of the mark to have reached a more general audience should be dispositive of the distinctiveness element. "Its lack of selling power among the general public—i.e., the nonconsuming public—should not deprive the company of [the dilution statute's] protection against dilution."[85] Sweet believed that this element was met by Mead due to the distinctiveness of the mark in its relevant market. That is not to say that the mark's failure to reach a larger audience isn't relevant—Sweet would just consider it as part of the second element: "The

---

[84] While the two aspects of a dilution claim are the famous and distinct element and the likelihood of dilution element, a third element could be articulated. The marks must be substantially similar as a condition precedent to a dilution claim. As noted, the court of appeals found that LEXIS and LEXUS were not substantially similar.

[85] *Mead Data Central,* 875 F.2d at 1033 (Sweet, J., concurring).

renown of a senior mark is a factor a court should assess when evaluating the likelihood of dilution, not the strength of the mark."[86]

Sweet's second disagreement was with the way the majority reached its conclusion as to likelihood of dilution. Although he agreed with the ultimate conclusion, he believed that the majority failed to adequately define the likelihood of dilution concept. He then articulated relevant factors drawn from existing case law (factors which bear some similarity to the *Polaroid* factors): (1) similarity of the marks; (2) similarity of the products covered by the marks; (3) sophistication of consumers; (4) predatory intent; (5) renown of the senior mark; (6) renown of the junior mark.

Notice that confusion is missing as a factor from the likelihood of dilution standard. Simply put, confusion is not required in a dilution claim. This marks a break from traditional trademark law which normally has consumer protection as one of its primary concerns. Such is not the case with dilution. In this sense, dilution laws can be viewed more as providing protection of marks as a property right.

At the time the *Mead* case was decided, the Lanham Act did not include an anti-dilution provision. In 1995, Congress enacted the federal Trademark Dilution Act, which made dilution a matter of federal trademark law. For many years, however, the federal statute was interpreted to require actual dilution—not just a likelihood of dilution (the standard from the *Mead* decision). In 2006, Congress enacted the Trademark Dilution Revision Act (Revision Act), which replaced the actual dilution standard with a likelihood of dilution standard. The Revision Act also explicitly recognized dilution by tarnishment claims.[87]

The Revision Act altered Lanham Act § 43(c) in a number of ways, including: (1) making clear that the standard to be applied is a likelihood of dilution (akin to *Mead*) and not actual dilution; (2) expressly recognizing tarnishment claims; (3) more precisely defining what constitutes a famous mark (it must be famous to general consumer audiences in the U.S.); and (4) setting forth factors to determine whether a mark is famous and if blurring has occurred. Section 1125(c) states:

(c) Dilution by blurring; dilution by tarnishment

. . . .

---

86 *Id.*

87 *See* 15 U.S.C. § 1125(c)(1).

(2) Definitions

(A) For purposes of paragraph (1), a mark is famous if it is widely recognized by the general consuming public of the United States as a designation of source of the goods or services of the mark's owner. In determining whether a mark possesses the requisite degree of recognition, the court may consider all relevant factors, including the following:

(i) The duration, extent, and geographic reach of advertising and publicity of the mark, whether advertised or publicized by the owner or third parties.

(ii) The amount, volume, and geographic extent of sales of goods or services offered under the mark.

(iii) The extent of actual recognition of the mark.

(iv) Whether the mark was registered under the Act of March 3, 1881, or the Act of February 20, 1905, or on the principal register.

(B) For purposes of paragraph (1), "dilution by blurring" is association arising from the similarity between a mark or trade name and a famous mark that impairs the distinctiveness of the famous mark. In determining whether a mark or trade name is likely to cause dilution by blurring, the court may consider all relevant factors, including the following:

(i) The degree of similarity between the mark or trade name and the famous mark.

(ii) The degree of inherent or acquired distinctiveness of the famous mark.

(iii) The extent to which the owner of the famous mark is engaging in substantially exclusive use of the mark.

(iv) The degree of recognition of the famous mark.

(v) Whether the user of the mark or trade name intended to create an association with the famous mark.

(vi) Any actual association between the mark or trade name and the famous mark.

A review of the statute compared to the *Mead* majority and concurring opinions suggests that Congress borrowed a little from both opinions. Judge Sweet's view that a mark can be famous/distinct under the first element without being generally recognized is explicitly rejected; however, the factors to consider in a blurring analysis are similar to the factors articulated by Sweet for likelihood of dilution.

As an aside, § 1125(c)(2) gives little direction on tarnishment claims, stating simply: "(C) For purposes of paragraph (1), 'dilution by tarnishment' is association arising from the similarity between a mark or trade name and a famous mark that harms the reputation of the famous mark." The Restatement provides the following distinction between blurring and tarnishment:

> The antidilution statutes have been invoked against two distinct threats to the interests of a trademark owner. First, a mark may be so highly distinctive and so well advertised that it acts as a powerful selling tool. Such a mark may evoke among prospective purchasers a positive response that is associated exclusively with the goods or services of the trademark owner. To the extent that others use the trademark to identify different goods, services, or businesses, a dissonance occurs that blurs this stimulant effect of the mark. The antidilution statutes protect against this dilution of the distinctiveness and selling power of the mark.
>
> The selling power of a trademark also can be undermined by a use of the mark with goods or services such as illicit drugs or pornography that "tarnish" the mark's image through inherently negative or unsavory associations, or with goods or services that produce a negative response when linked in the minds of prospective purchasers with the goods or services of the prior user, such as the use on insecticide of a trademark similar to one previously used by another on food products.[88]

A memorable tarnishment case involving the famous Coca-Cola trademark is *Coca Cola Co. v. Gemini Rising, Inc.*[89] In that case, Coca-Cola sued the maker of a poster that had used the Coca-Cola font and color scheme with the words "Enjoy Cocaine" instead of "Enjoy Coca-Cola." The district court agreed to issue a preliminary injunction on the grounds that the association tarnished Coca-Cola's mark.[90]

---

88 RESTATEMENT (THIRD) OF UNFAIR COMPETITION § 25 cmt. c (1995).

89 346 F. Supp. 1183 (E.D.N.Y. 1972).

90 *See id.* at 1186–87; *see also id.* at 1189 ("To associate such a noxious substance as cocaine with plaintiff's wholesome beverage as symbolized by its 'Coca-Cola' trademark and format would clearly have a tendency to impugn that product and injure plaintiff's business reputation, as plaintiff contends.").

### 3. Genericide

Under the distinctiveness spectrum, generic terms are not entitled to trademark protection. Once a company registers a trademark under an arbitrary or fanciful name and uses it for some time, any concern over genericness typically dissipates. However, sometimes a company is the victim of its own success. *King-Seeley Thermos Co. v. Aladdin Industries, Inc.*[91] demonstrates how a successful brand can become generic despite a company's efforts to police its mark.

King-Seeley brought an appeal to the Second Circuit, alleging that the district court had abused its discretion in stating that Aladdin Industries had not infringed King-Seeley's trademark of "Thermos." The district court reviewed King-Seeley's corporate history and its use of the Thermos trademark, noting that between 1907 and 1923, King-Seeley's own advertising and educational campaigns alluded to thermos as a generic term descriptive of the product rather than of its origin. The district court held that the advertisements failed to include any of the other generic terms then used, such as "Thermos vacuum-insulated bottle." However, after 1923, King-Seeley attempted to bring awareness to the public that Thermos reflected the source and was a trademark, and King-Seeley prevented some companies from using the mark generically. By 1957, King-Seeley had intensified its policing activities of trade and non-trade publications. However, despite the company's extraordinary efforts, it was too late to keep thermos from falling into the public domain. However, the district court also held that King-Seeley's trademarks were valid. Because there was an appreciable (although a minority) segment of the consuming public which knew and recognized King-Seeley's trademarks, the court imposed certain restrictions and limitations on the use of the word thermos by the defendant.

On appeal, King-Seeley argued that the district court had misapplied holdings from similar cases involving Aspirin and Cellophane. In those cases, King-Seeley argued that there was no generic name, such as vacuum bottle, that was suitable for use by the general public. Thus, it was understandable that the court found that Aspirin and Cellophane had become generic terms that described any similar product. The court of appeals disagreed, holding that in the Aspirin case, the test was not what was available as an alternative to the public, but what was the public's understanding of the word. The court explained that the public had become accustomed to calling vacuum bottles by the word thermos. According to the court, if a

---

[91] 321 F.2d 577 (2d Cir. 1963).

buyer walked into a retail store asking for a thermos bottle—meaning any vacuum bottle and not specifically plaintiff's product—the fact that the appellation "vacuum bottle" was available to him was of no significance, as the two terms had become synonymous. In other words, although the court agreed that the Aspirin and Cellophane cases involved products without easy generic descriptions, it did not follow that the availability of a generic term such as vacuum bottle prevented thermos from becoming generic. Simply put, genericness focuses on how the consuming public associates the term. If the consuming public equates thermos with the product rather than the source, then the term has become generic.

King-Seeley also argued that the courts in a number of cases had allowed the continued exclusive use of a dual-functioning trademark—i.e., a trademark that identified the class of product as well as its source. The court disagreed that such a case was present and stressed that for a trademark to become generic, the principal significance of the mark must have changed from an indication of the origin to an indication of the nature or class of an article. Furthermore, survey evidence showed that only a small percentage of consumers actually knew that thermos was a mark, while the vast majority (75%) associated the term with a container for keeping a package hot or cold. Thus, while some marks can act with a dual function, thermos was not such a mark. There was no dual understanding, as the consuming public did not see the trademark as showing the source. As a result, thermos was clearly generic.

It is worth highlighting the early steps that King-Seeley took that led to its mark being used generically. First, it appears that King-Seeley itself was somewhat responsible for the genericness of the term. In its advertising campaigns, it sought to make thermos a generic term descriptive of the product rather than of its origin. As the court noted, in its early ads King-Seeley did not use the generic term vacuum bottle along with the word thermos, thus associating thermos with the product itself. Although King-Seeley did take steps to rectify the situation, it still did not police the use of the word sufficiently in non-trade circles until much later, which contributed to the genericness.

King-Seeley did subsequently police the trade for uses of its mark and notified those using thermos in a descriptive sense that it was a trademark. But as the court noted: "[King-Seeley] failed, however, to take affirmative action to seek out generic uses by non-trade publications and protested only those which happened to come to its attention."[92] Even if it had policed non-trade publications earlier, the court seemed doubtful that King-Seeley could undo the harm caused by its successful advertising campaigns:

> We are not convinced that the trademark's loss of distinctiveness was the result of some failure on plaintiff's part. Substantial efforts to preserve the trademark significance of the word were made by plaintiff, especially with respect to members of the trade. However, there was little they could do to prevent the public from using 'thermos' in a generic rather than a trademark sense. And whether the appropriation by the public was due to highly successful educational and advertising campaigns or to lack of diligence in policing or not is of no consequence; the fact is that the word 'thermos' had entered the public domain beyond recall. Even as early as 1910 plaintiff itself asserted that 'Thermos had become a household word.'[93]

It is not so clear that the result was as inevitable as this passage suggests. King-Seeley could have launched a massive ad campaign geared toward educating the public on the term and its proper use. But the effectiveness would be speculative and the result could be the same. This is the irony of genericide—a company that is too successful in branding its name could find that the public has made the company's once arbitrary name into a generic one. This is not to say that all successful branding efforts will end-up like thermos—the key is to associate the mark with a source rather than just the product.

In determining whether a mark has become generic, courts may turn to a number of sources. One source mentioned in *King-Seeley* was the plaintiff's own use of the mark as a generic descriptor. Another source mentioned by the decision was surveys of the consuming public. Dictionary definitions may also be useful as they usually reflect the public's perception, although courts have cautioned that dictionaries alone are not conclusive. Other sources may include competitors' generic use of the mark, generic use in media, and testimony from people within the trade.[94]

Trade dress is also susceptible to genericide. For instance, in *Sunrise Jewelry Manufacturing Corp. v. Fred S.A.*,[95] the Federal Circuit reviewed Fred's registration of a mark described as a " 'metallic nautical rope design as an integral feature of the goods,'

---

[92] *Id.* at 579.

[93] *Id.*

[94] 2 MCCARTHY ON TRADEMARKS AND UNFAIR COMPETITION § 12:13 (4th ed. 2015).

[95] 175 F.3d 1322 (Fed. Cir. 1999).

which include[d] clocks, watches, and jewelry made of precious metal." Fred contended that a mark could only be cancelled for becoming generic if it was a name. The court disagreed and held that, despite the federal registration and the use of the phrase "mark name" in the Lanham Act, the mark could be challenged as having become generic:

> Our review of the Lanham Act and relevant case law persuades us that the term "generic name" as used in 15 U.S.C. § 1064(3), must be read expansively to encompass anything that has the potential but fails to serve as an indicator of source, such as names, words, symbols, devices, or trade dress. Any narrower interpretation of "generic name" would allow incontestable trademarks other than names that become generic to retain incontestable status despite their inability to serve as source designators. This would directly contravene the purpose of the Lanham Act.[96]

### 4. Fair Use Defense

Recall from the *Zatarains* discussion at the beginning of this chapter that although "Fish-Fri" was held to be a descriptive term that had acquired secondary meaning, the court still found for the defendants under the "fair use" doctrine. As the court observed:

> Even when a descriptive term has acquired a secondary meaning sufficient to warrant trademark protection, others may be entitled to use the mark without incurring liability for trademark infringement. When the allegedly infringing term is "used fairly and in good faith only to describe to users the goods or services of [a] party, or their geographic origin," Lanham Act § 33(b)(4), 15 U.S.C. § 1115(b)(4) (1976), a defendant in a trademark infringement action may assert the "fair use" defense. The defense is available only in actions involving descriptive terms and only when the term is used in its descriptive sense rather than its trademark sense. In essence, the fair use defense prevents a trademark registrant from appropriating a descriptive term for its own use to the exclusion of others, who may be prevented thereby from accurately describing their own goods. The holder of a protectable descriptive mark has no legal claim to an exclusive right in the primary, descriptive meaning of the term; consequently, anyone is free to use the term in its primary, descriptive sense so long as such use does not lead

---

96 *Id.* at 1325–26.

> to customer confusion as to the source of the goods or services.[97]

As noted by the above passage, the fair use defense applies only to marks which are descriptive and have acquired secondary meaning. The defense does not apply to suggestive marks or to other marks which are inherently distinctive. The fair use defense is recognized in both the Restatement of Unfair Competition and the Lanham Act. Section 28 of the Restatement provides:

> In an action for infringement of a trademark, trade name, collective mark, or certification mark, it is a defense that the term used by the actor is descriptive or geographically descriptive of the actor's goods, services, or business, or is the personal name of the actor or a person connected with the actor, and the actor has used the term fairly and in good faith solely to describe the actor's goods, services, or business or to indicate a connection with the named person.

Similarly, the Lanham Act in 15 U.S.C. § 1115(b)(4) states that it is a defense to trademark infringement if the defendant can establish:

> That the use of the name, term, or device charged to be an infringement is a use, otherwise than as a mark, of the party's individual name in his own business, or of the individual name of anyone in privity with such party, or of a term or device which is descriptive of and used fairly and in good faith only to describe the goods or services of such party, or their geographic origin.

Essentially, these standards establish three elements that must be met for a trademark defendant to successfully claim fair use. First, the defendant must use the term other than as a mark. Second, the defendant must use the term fairly and in good faith. Finally, the defendant must use the term descriptively.[98]

Comment a to § 28 of the Restatement of Unfair Competition describes the justification for the fair use defense in similar terms as the *Zatarains* court:

> Section 14 recognizes trademark rights in descriptive and geographically descriptive terms upon proof that the designation has acquired secondary meaning as a symbol of identification. Trademark rights, however, extend only to the source significance that has been acquired by such

[97] Zatarains, Inc. v. Oak Grove Smokehouse, Inc., 698 F.2d 786, 791 (5th Cir. 1983).

[98] The federal Trademark Dilution Revision Act expressly permits a fair use defense for claims of dilution. *See* 15 U.S.C. § 1125(c)(3).

> terms, not to their original descriptive meanings. The owner of a trademark thus cannot deprive others of the use of the term in its original descriptive sense. Reasonable use of a descriptive term by another solely to describe the nature or characteristics of its own goods or services will not subject the user to liability for infringement. An analogous rule is applicable to personal name designations. A subsequent user is not subject to liability if the name is used solely to indicate truthfully the named person's connection with the goods, services, or business.

If a descriptive term can still be used by other market participants, what is the value of a descriptive mark? The mark still has value because even those using the mark can only do so in a descriptive sense. This will likely require using lowercase letters and may also require placement of the term in such a way to emphasize its descriptive nature. For instance, in *Sands, Taylor & Wood Co. v. The Quaker Oats Co.*,[99] the defendant failed to establish fair use of the mark "Thirst Aid" when it adopted a campaign "Gatorade is Thirst Aid" because it was found that the Thirst Aid portion was emphasized and used in a non-descriptive manner.

An important advantage of the fair use defense is that the defendant need not disprove the element of likelihood of confusion. In *KP Permanent Make-Up, Inc. v. Lasting Impression I, Inc.*,[100] the U.S. Supreme Court stated that "defendant has no independent burden to negate the likelihood of any confusion in raising the affirmative defense that a term is used descriptively, not as a mark, fairly, and in good faith." The Court further noted that some likelihood of confusion will exist in many instances, but such likelihood is not relevant once the elements of the defense are established.

The disregard for the likelihood of confusion element is described in comment b to § 28 of the Restatement of Unfair Competition:

> The fair use defense recognized in this Section can be applicable even if the trademark owner presents evidence sufficient to prove a likelihood of confusion. If the manner of use by the defendant is reasonable in light of the commercial justification for the use, the possibility or even certainty that some prospective purchasers will perceive the term as an indication of source despite the reasonableness of the defendant's use is not sufficient to

[99] 978 F.2d 947 (7th Cir. 1992).

[100] 543 U.S. 124 (2004).

> deprive the defendant of the right to employ the term in its descriptive sense. Thus, a defendant who uses a descriptive term fairly and in good faith to describe its goods or services is not liable for infringement even if some residual confusion is likely. However, the strength of the plaintiff's mark and the extent of likely or actual confusion are important factors in determining whether a use is fair. Surveys and other evidence relating to the perceptions of prospective purchasers are thus relevant to the application of the defense, and a use that is likely to create substantial confusion will not ordinarily be considered a fair use. The defendant bears the burden of establishing the defense of fair use under this Section.

This comment is consistent with the Supreme Court's *KP Permanent* ruling—once the elements of fair use are established, a likelihood of confusion is irrelevant. But the strength of a mark may play a role in deciding if the elements of fair use have been met.

Another type of fair use is "nominative fair use," in which a defendant uses the protected mark solely to describe or identify the product or service. For instance, in *New Kids on the Block v. New America Publishing, Inc.*,[101] New Kids on the Block, a popular "boy band" from the late 1980s, sued two newspapers of national circulation who "conducted separate polls of their readers seeking an answer to a pressing question: Which one of the New Kids is the most popular?" The lawsuit asserted trademark infringement because the newspapers were using the trademarked name.[102] In rejecting the claim, the court described why such nominative use is not actionable under trademark law:

> Cases like these are best understood as involving a non-trademark use of a mark—a use to which the infringement laws simply do not apply, just as videotaping television shows for private home use does not implicate the copyright holder's exclusive right to reproduction. *See Sony Corp. v. Universal City Studios, Inc.*, 464 U.S. 417, 447–51 (1984). Indeed, we may generalize a class of cases where the use of the trademark does not attempt to capitalize on consumer confusion or to appropriate the cachet of one product for a different one. Such nominative use of a mark—where the only word reasonably available to describe a particular thing is pressed into service—lies outside the strictures of trademark law: Because it does not implicate the source-identification function that is the purpose of trademark, it

---

[101] 971 F.2d 302 (9th Cir. 1992).

[102] *See id.* at 304–05.

> does not constitute unfair competition; such use is fair because it does not imply sponsorship or endorsement by the trademark holder.[103]

Not all circuits agree with the Ninth Circuit's approach in *New Kids*, which appears to be a way of analyzing whether there is a likelihood of confusion.[104] The Third Circuit, for example, has changed the Ninth Circuit's nominative fair use analysis into an affirmative defense to infringement:

> . . . . Once plaintiff has met its burden of proving that confusion is likely, the burden then shifts to defendant to show that its nominative use of plaintiff's mark is nonetheless fair. To demonstrate fairness, the defendant must satisfy a three-pronged nominative fair use test, derived to a great extent from the one articulated by the Court of Appeals for the Ninth Circuit. Under our fairness test, a defendant must show: (1) that the use of plaintiff's mark is necessary to describe both the plaintiff's product or service and the defendant's product or service; (2) that the defendant uses only so much of the plaintiff's mark as is necessary to describe plaintiff's product; and (3) that the defendant's conduct or language reflect the true and accurate relationship between plaintiff and defendant's products or services.[105]

It should be noted that the Third Circuit decision draws upon factors similar to those articulated in the *New Kids* case. The main difference between the two approaches appears to be that the Third Circuit recognizes nominative fair use as an affirmative defense.

## F. REMEDIES

The remedies for deceptive marketing and trademark violations are the same.[106] Both the Restatement and the Lanham Act provide for injunctive relief and monetary damages in appropriate cases, but the primary remedy for trademark infringement (or dilution) is injunctive relief. Section 34 of the Lanham Act, 15 U.S.C. § 1116, grants courts the power to issue injunctive relief "according to the principle of equity and upon such terms as the court may deem reasonable, to prevent the violation of any right [of a mark holder]."

---

[103] *Id.* at 307–08.

[104] *See* 4 McCarthy on Trademarks and Unfair Competition § 23:11 (4th ed. 2015).

[105] Century 21 Real Estate Corp. v. Lendingtree, Inc., 425 F.3d 211, 222 (3d Cir. 2005).

[106] *See generally* Chapter 7(D) (discussing remedies in deceptive marketing disputes).

As discussed in Chapter 7(D), fashioning an injunctive remedy can be a difficult task, and courts may consider a number of factors. (Many of the primary considerations are listed in § 35 of the Restatement of Unfair Competition.) As with deceptive marketing claims, courts can also order corrective advertising in appropriate disputes.

Section 35 of the Lanham Act provides for monetary damages in appropriate cases.[107] It states, in part, the following:

> (a) Profits; damages and costs; attorney fees
>
> When a violation of any right of [a mark holder] shall have been established in any civil action arising under this chapter, the plaintiff shall be entitled, . . . subject to the principles of equity, to recover (1) defendant's profits, (2) any damages sustained by the plaintiff, and (3) the costs of the action. The court shall assess such profits and damages or cause the same to be assessed under its direction. In assessing profits the plaintiff shall be required to prove defendant's sales only; defendant must prove all elements of cost or deduction claimed. In assessing damages the court may enter judgment, according to the circumstances of the case, for any sum above the amount found as actual damages, not exceeding three times such amount. If the court shall find that the amount of the recovery based on profits is either inadequate or excessive the court may in its discretion enter judgment for such sum as the court shall find to be just, according to the circumstances of the case. Such sum in either of the above circumstances shall constitute compensation and not a penalty. The court in

---

[107] The courts are far from uniform on when it is appropriate to award monetary damages, in part due to the lack of guidance provided in the statute. The Restatement lists the following as relevant factors:

> (3) Whether an award of damages for pecuniary loss is appropriate depends upon a comparative appraisal of all the factors of the case, including the following primary factors:
>
> (a) the degree of certainty with which the plaintiff has established the fact and extent of the pecuniary loss caused by the actor's conduct;
>
> (b) the relative adequacy to the plaintiff of other remedies, including an accounting of the actor's profits;
>
> (c) the intent of the actor and the extent to which the actor knew or should have known that the conduct was unlawful;
>
> (d) the role of the actor in bringing about the infringement or deceptive marketing;
>
> (e) any unreasonable delay by the plaintiff in bringing suit or otherwise asserting its rights; and
>
> (f) any related misconduct on the part of the plaintiff.

RESTATEMENT (THIRD) OF UNFAIR COMPETITION § 36(3) (1995).

exceptional cases may award reasonable attorney fees to the prevailing party.[108]

Notice that § 35 provides three particular monetary remedies: (1) an award of the defendant's profits, (2) actual damages sustained by the plaintiff, and (3) costs of the action, which may include attorney's fees.

Before delving further into monetary damages, it should be noted that such awards are discretionary and subject to "principles of equity." This means that if a court deems an injunction adequate to protect the plaintiff's interests, it may decline to award damages. Although intent or willfulness is not required under the statute as a condition precedent to recovery, many courts find such intent to be a relevant factor in determining whether to award damages. The same is true for "actual confusion"—the statute does not require actual consumer confusion (recall that only a likelihood of confusion is necessary), but courts often look for actual confusion before awarding damages.[109]

The first monetary remedy under § 35—an award of the defendant's profits—involves a two-step process. First, the plaintiff must establish the defendant's gross revenues. The burden then shifts to the defendant to demonstrate deductions (if any), such as by introducing evidence of expenses related to sales or proving that certain profits are not attributable to the infringing acts. The award of profits does not require the plaintiff to show its own actual damages (indeed, if the plaintiff's actual damages are shown, the court may decide that such actual damages are a more appropriate remedy).

An award of the defendant's profits is a rather extraordinary remedy. Courts do not automatically grant it, and both courts and commentators have noted that it is a "rough" measure of damages. Courts will refuse to make the award (or limit it to only a percentage of the defendant's profits) if there is concern that the award will result in a windfall. In addition, most courts require the infringer's actions to be intentional or willful before making such an award.

The second monetary remedy under § 35 is the plaintiff's actual damages. As mentioned, the court has discretion to "enter judgment, according to the circumstances of the case, for any sum above the amount found as actual damages, not exceeding three times such

---

[108] 15 U.S.C. § 1117; *see also* RESTATEMENT (THIRD) OF UNFAIR COMPETITION §§ 36–37 (1995) (allowing plaintiff to recover its actual damages or the defendant's profits).

[109] *See* RESTATEMENT (THIRD) OF UNFAIR COMPETITION § 37(3) (1995) (listing relevant factors).

amount." While an increased award is possible, courts generally grant it only in disputes involving intentional or willful conduct. Such an enhanced award is not meant as a penalty; indeed, plaintiffs are not entitled to punitive damages under the Lanham Act. Depending upon the jurisdiction, however, punitive damages may be recoverable under a state common law action.[110]

Recovering the plaintiff's actual damages is subject to the usual requirements for damages—i.e., the plaintiff must prove both causation of harm and the amount of the damages (although courts are generally less demanding on the sufficiency of the evidence of amount once the fact of damages has been proven). Plaintiff's damages can be measured in a number of ways, such as by its own lost profits, injury to its goodwill and reputation, and costs incurred by the plaintiff when engaging in corrective advertising.[111] Generally speaking, a plaintiff cannot recover both the defendant's profits and the plaintiff's actual damages, as this would result in a double recovery. In some instances, however, courts have awarded both when the harm does not stem from the same lost sales. The comments to the Restatement clarify:

> In some cases courts have permitted the recovery of both damages under the rule stated in this Section and an accounting of the defendant's profits . . . , with the caveat that the plaintiff may not recover twice for the same loss. The prohibition against double recovery most clearly applies when the goods of the parties directly compete and the plaintiff seeks to recover both damages for losses attributable to diverted sales and the profits earned on sales made by the defendant. Although the two sums are not necessarily identical since the parties may have different profit margins and not all of the defendant's sales may represent sales diverted from the plaintiff, in the absence of contrary evidence the court may conclude that the defendant's profits adequately reflect the sales lost by the plaintiff. In such cases an award of both profits and damages is therefore prohibited under the rule precluding double recovery for the same loss. Recovery of both profits and damages is most clearly appropriate when the profits of the defendant are used as a measure of the loss attributable to sales diverted from the plaintiff, and the

---

[110] *See* J. THOMAS MCCARTHY, 5 MCCARTHY ON TRADEMARKS AND UNFAIR COMPETITION § 30:96 (4th ed. 2015) ("In jurisdictions where punitive damages are allowable in tort cases, they are equally allowable in cases of trademark infringement and unfair competition.").

[111] *See* RESTATEMENT (THIRD) OF UNFAIR COMPETITION § 36(2) (1995).

plaintiff in addition proves other losses such as harm to reputation.[112]

The final remedy under § 35 of the Lanham Act is the "costs of the action," which may include an award of "reasonable attorney fees to the prevailing party" in exceptional cases. As with a recovery of the defendant's profits and an enhanced damages award, courts tend to reserve this remedy for instances of intentional or willful conduct.

[112] *Id.* § 36 cmt. c.

# Table of Cases